T0212648

Lecture Notes in Computer Science   9137

Commenced Publication in 1973
Founding and Former Series Editors:
Gerhard Goos, Juris Hartmanis, and Jan van Leeuwen

More information about this series at http://www.springer.com/series/7407

Julian M. Kunkel · Thomas Ludwig (Eds.)

High Performance Computing

30th International Conference,
ISC High Performance 2015
Frankfurt, Germany, July 12–16, 2015
Proceedings

 Springer

Editors
Julian M. Kunkel
Deutsches Klimarechenzentrum (DKRZ)
Hamburg
Germany

Thomas Ludwig
Deutsches Klimarechenzentrum (DKRZ)
Hamburg
Germany

ISSN 0302-9743   ISSN 1611-3349 (electronic)
Lecture Notes in Computer Science
ISBN 978-3-319-20118-4   ISBN 978-3-319-20119-1 (eBook)
DOI 10.1007/978-3-319-20119-1

Library of Congress Control Number: 2015940735

LNCS Sublibrary: SL1 – Theoretical Computer Science and General Issues

Springer International Publishing AG Switzerland is part of Springer Science+Business Media
(www.springer.com)

Preface

ISC High Performance, formerly known as the International Supercomputing Conference, was founded in 1986 as the Supercomputer Seminar. Originally organized by Professor Hans Meuer, Professor of Computer Science at the University of Mannheim and former director of the computer center, the seminar brought together a group of 81 scientists and industrial partners who all shared an interest in high-performance computing. Since then the annual conference has become a major international event within the HPC community, and accompanying its growth in size over the years, the conference has moved from Mannheim via Heidelberg, Dresden, Hamburg and Leipzig to Frankfurt. With 2,405 attendees and 156 exhibitors from over 51 countries in 2014, we were happy to see that this steady growth of interest also turned ISC High Performance 2015 into a powerful and memorable event.

In 2007, we decided to strengthen the scientific part of the conference by presenting selected talks on relevant research results within the HPC field. These research paper sessions began as a separate day preceding the conference, where slides and accompanying papers were made available via the conference website. The research paper sessions have since evolved into an integral part of the conference, and this year the scientific presentations took place over a period of three days.

This year, the organizers of the ISC High Performance conference reintroduced an ISC-sponsored award to encourage outstanding research in high-performance computing and to honor the overall best research paper submitted to the conference. This annual award is now called the Hans Meuer Award in memory of the late Dr. Hans Meuer, general chair of the ISC conference from 1986 through 2014, and co-founder of the TOP500 project. From all research papers submitted, the Research Paper Committee consider the three papers with the highest review scores for the award and elect the winner among them.

The call for participation was issued in fall 2014, inviting researchers and developers to submit the latest results of their work to the Program Committee. As in the year before, we invited the submission of full papers and technical short papers. In all, 67 papers were submitted from authors all over the world. In a peer-review process, an international committee selected 27 full papers and 10 short papers for publication and for presentation in the research paper sessions.

We are pleased to announce that many fascinating topics in HPC are covered by the proceedings. The papers address the following issues in regards to the development of an environment for exascale supercomputers:

- Cost-efficient data centers
- Scalable applications
- Advancements in algorithms
- Scientific libraries
- Programming models
- Architectures

- Performance models and analysis
- Automatic performance optimization
- Parallel I/O
- Energy efficiency

We believe that this selection is highly appealing across a number of specializations and that the presentations will foster inspiring discussions with the audience.

Three award committees selected papers considered to be of exceptional quality and worthy of special recognition.

- The Hans Meuer Award honors the overall best research paper submitted to the conference. The award went to:
  "Accelerating LBM and LQCD Application Kernels by In-Memory Processing" by Paul F. Baumeister, Hans Boettiger, José R. Brunheroto, Thorsten Hater, Thilo Mauer, Andrea Nobile and Dirk Pleiter

- PRACE, the Partnership for Advanced Computing in Europe, awards a prize to the best scientific paper by a European student or scientist. This year's award was granted to:
  "Lattice-CSC: Optimizing and building an efficient supercomputer for Lattice-QCD and to achieve first place in Green500" by David Rohr, Matthias Bach, Gvozden Neskovic, Volker Lindenstruth, Christopher Pinke and Owe Philipsen

- The Gauss Centre for Supercomputing sponsors the Gauss Award. This award is assigned to the most outstanding paper in the field of scalable supercomputing and went to:
  "Updating the Energy Model for Future Exascale Systems" by Peter M. Kogge.

We would like to express our gratitude to all our colleagues for submitting papers to the ISC scientific sessions, as well as to the members of the Program Committee for organizing this year's attractive program.

June 2015   Julian M. Kunkel
                                                                             Thomas Ludwig

Organization

Program Committee

Balaji, Pavan	Argonne National Laboratory, USA
Bohlouli, Mahdi	University of Siegen, Germany
Bönisch, Thomas	HLRS, Germany
Brown, Jed	Argonne National Laboratory, USA
Burrows, Eva	University of Bergen, Norway
Cai, Xing	Simula Research Laboratory, Norway
Flouri, Tomas	HITS, Germany
Fröning, Holger	University of Heidelberg, Germany
Gross, Lutz	School of Earth Sciences, The University of Queensland, Australia
Hackenberg, Daniel	TU Dresden, Germany
Ham, David	Imperial College London, UK
Hannig, Frank	Friedrich-Alexander University Erlangen-Nürnberg, Germany
Haveraaen, Magne	University of Bergen, Norway
Herhut, Stephan	Intel Labs, Santa Clara, USA
Huang, Weicheng	National Center for High-Performance Computing, Taiwan
Huynh, Huynh Phung	A*Star, Singapore
Kindratenko, Volodymyr	National Center for Supercomputing Applications, USA
Koshulko, Oleksiy	Glushkov Institute of Cybernetics NAS, Ukraine
Kunkel, Julian	University of Hamburg, Germany
Li, Dong	Oak Ridge National Laboratory, USA
Lin, Fang-Pang	National Center for High-Performance Computing, Taiwan
Liu, Qing	Oak Ridge National Laboratory, USA
Ludwig, Thomas	DKRZ, Germany
Manjunathaiah, Manjunathaiah	University of Reading, UK
McIntosh-Smith, Simon	University of Bristol, UK
Membarth, Richard	Intel Visual Computing Institute, Saarland University, Germany
Mohr, Bernd	Jülich Supercomputing Centre, Germany
Moskovsky, Alexander	RSC SKIF, Russia
Müller, Matthias	RWTH Aachen University, Germany
Nakajima, Kengo	University of Tokyo, Japan
Nou, Ramon	Barcelona Supercomputing Center, Spain
Olbrich, Stephan	University of Hamburg, Germany

Ortega, Julio	University of Granada, Spain
Poulet, Thomas	CSIRO, Australia
Qian, Ying	KAUST, Saudi Arabia
Resch, Michael M.	HLRS, Germany
Duro, Francisco Rodrigo	Universidad Carlos III de Madrid, Spain
Rouson, Damian	Center for Computational Earth and Environmental Sciences at Stanford University, USA
Scholz, Sven-Bodo	Heriot-Watt University, UK
Solnushkin, Konstantin S.	Saint Petersburg State Polytechnic University, Russia
Stamatakis, Alexandros	TU München, Germany
Tatebe, Osamu	University of Tsukuba, Japan
Thiyagalingam, Jeyarajan	University of Liverpool, UK
Tolentino, Matthew E.	Intel, USA
Tsujita, Yuichi	RIKEN AICS, Japan
Vigouroux, Xavier	Bull, France
Wang, Zhonglei	Intel Mobile Communications, Germany
Wild, Thomas	TU München, Germany
Ziegenhein, Peter	The Institute of Cancer Research, UK

Program Committee for the Research Poster Session

Aguilera, Alvaro
Blas, Javier Garcia
Bohlouli, Mahdi
Bönisch, Thomas
Cai, Xing
Ham, David
Hannig, Frank
Huang, Weicheng
Kunkel, Julian
Li, Dong

Membarth, Richard
Moskovsky, Alexander
Nakajima, Kengo
Ortega, Julio
McIntosh-Smith, Simon
Solnushkin, Konstantin S.
Tatebe, Osamu
Thiyagalingam, Jeyarajan
Tsujita, Yuichi
Ziegenhein, Peter

Additional Reviewers

Armour, Wes
Chasapis, Konstantinos
Czech, Lucas
Dao, David
Darriba, Diego
Fenwick, Joel
Gao, Jinfang
Geyer, Robin
Gong, Zhenhuan
Hu, Qi

Kozlov, Alexey
Langguth, Johannes
Lu, Mian
Miller, Felix
Miranda, Alberto
Mu, Kimmy
Ong, Zhong Liang
Osprey, Annette
Parayil, Preethi
Reiche, Oliver

Riley, Graham
Schmid, Moritz
Schmitt, Christian
Schuchart, Joseph
Shaw, Simon
Tang, Wai Teng
Witterauf, Michael
Zou, Hongbo

Contents

Asynchronous Iterative Algorithm for Computing Incomplete Factorizations on GPUs

Edmond Chow[1], Hartwig Anzt[2(✉)], and Jack Dongarra[2]

[1] Georgia Institute of Technology, Atlanta, GA, USA
[2] University of Tennessee, Knoxville, TN, USA
hanzt@icl.utk.edu

Abstract. This paper presents a GPU implementation of an asynchronous iterative algorithm for computing incomplete factorizations. Asynchronous algorithms, with their ability to tolerate memory latency, form an important class of algorithms for modern computer architectures. Our GPU implementation considers several non-traditional techniques that can be important for asynchronous algorithms to optimize convergence and data locality. These techniques include controlling the order in which variables are updated by controlling the order of execution of thread blocks, taking advantage of cache reuse between thread blocks, and managing the amount of parallelism to control the convergence of the algorithm.

1 Introduction

Asynchronous algorithms, with their ability to tolerate memory latency, form an important class of algorithms for modern computer architectures. In this paper, we develop a GPU implementation for a recently proposed asynchronous iterative incomplete factorization algorithm [4]. In particular, we consider the following techniques to enhance data locality and convergence that may be considered non-traditional as they are not strictly allowed in standard GPU implementations.

- In an asynchronous iterative method, variables are updated using values of other variables that are currently available, rather than waiting for the most updated values of these other variables (this will be made more precise later). The rate of convergence of the method may depend on the order in which variables are updated. In traditional GPU computations, there is no defined ordering in which thread blocks are executed, making it impossible to control the update order. For the NVIDIA K40c GPU, however, we were able to determine the order in which thread blocks are executed, thereby allowing us to control the order of the updates of the variables.
- Efficient GPU performance requires that GPU thread blocks reuse data brought into shared memory. Shared memory must be configured as cache when the working set is large, otherwise few thread blocks can run in parallel.

J.M. Kunkel and T. Ludwig (Eds.): ISC High Performance 2015, LNCS 9137, pp. 1–16, 2015.
DOI: 10.1007/978-3-319-20119-1_1

However, without control over the order in which thread blocks are executed, *temporal locality* cannot be properly exploited. Since we are able to control the execution order of thread blocks on the K40c GPU, we can assure that data in cache is efficiently used. As mentioned, traditionally this order is not known.

- In GPU computing, the amount of parallelism is typically not controlled; work is scheduled onto all multiprocessors. Using less parallelism and updating fewer variables simultaneously in order to use more recently updated variables may lead to faster convergence than using more parallelism. We investigate this tradeoff by using the unconventional approach of controlling the occupancy, or the fraction of the maximum number of threads executing simultaneously per multiprocessor.

There has been some past work on asynchronous algorithms on GPUs for linear iteration methods. See [1] for a comprehensive study on block-asynchronous Jacobi iterations. Venkatasubramanian et al. [18] solve a 2D Poisson equation on a structured grid using asynchronous stencil operations on a hybrid CPU/GPU system. Contassot-Vivier et al. [5] investigated the impact of asynchronism when solving an advection-diffusion problem with a GPU-accelerated PDE solver. The work in this paper on investigating data locality and update order for asynchronous algorithms on GPUs is new.

This paper is organized as follows. In Sect. 2, we provide background on incomplete factorizations and the recently proposed iterative ILU algorithm. Then in Sect. 3, we discuss the implementation of the algorithm on GPUs and consider how convergence and data locality are impacted by the order in which computations are performed. Experimental tests with this implementation are reported in Sect. 4, and we conclude in Sect. 5.

2   Iterative ILU Algorithm

Preconditioners are a critical part of solving large sparse linear systems via iterative methods. A popular class of preconditioners is incomplete LU (ILU) factorizations. These preconditioners are generally computed using a Gaussian elimination process where small non-diagonal elements are dropped in some way. The problem-independence of ILU preconditioners makes this class attractive for a wide range of problems, particularly for optimization problems.

An ILU factorization is the approximate factorization of a nonsingular sparse matrix A into the product of a sparse lower triangular matrix L and a sparse upper triangular matrix U ($A \approx LU$), where nonzeros or fill-in are only permitted in specified locations, (i, j) of L and U. Define the sparsity pattern S to be the set of matrix locations where nonzeros are allowed, i.e., $(i, j) \in S$ implies that entry l_{ij} in matrix L is permitted to be nonzero ($i \geq j$), or that entry u_{ij} in matrix U is permitted to be nonzero ($i \leq j$). The set S always includes the diagonal of the L and U factors so that these factors are nonsingular. The basic algorithm, called ILU(0), approximates the LU factorization by allowing only nonzero elements in L and U that are nonzero in A. To enhance the accuracy of the preconditioner, one can allow for additional fill-in in the incomplete factors. The choice of S can be made either before the factorization, or may be made dynamically, during elimination. The classical factorization algorithm, based on Gaussian elimination, is inherently sequential, but some parallelism does exist, as it is usually possible to find multiple rows that can be eliminated in parallel, i.e., those that only depend on rows that already have been eliminated; see [17] for an overview. Parallelism is usually reduced when more fill-in is allowed. Multicoloring and domain decomposition reordering can be used to enhance the available parallelism [2,7,11,16]. However, these approaches generally have limited scalability, as they are unable to exploit the computing performance of thousands of light-weight cores that we expect in future HPC architectures [3].

For large amounts of parallelism, a new algorithm for computing ILU factorizations was recently proposed [4], and is the focus of this paper. This algorithm uses the property of ILU factorizations that

$$(LU)_{ij} = a_{ij}, \quad (i,j) \in S \tag{1}$$

where $(LU)_{ij}$ denotes the (i,j) entry of the product of the computed factors L and U, and a_{ij} is the corresponding entry in matrix A. For $(i,j) \in S$, the iterative ILU algorithm computes the unknowns l_{ij} (for $i > j$) and u_{ij} (for $i \leq j$) using the bilinear constraints

$$\sum_{k=1}^{\min(i,j)} l_{ik}u_{kj} = a_{ij}, \quad (i,j) \in S \tag{2}$$

which corresponds to enforcing the property (1). We use the normalization that the diagonal of the lower triangular L is fixed to one. Thus we need to solve a system of $|S|$ equations in $|S|$ unknowns.

To solve this system, Ref. [4] proposed writing

$$l_{ij} = \frac{1}{u_{jj}} \left(a_{ij} - \sum_{k=1}^{j-1} l_{ik}u_{kj} \right), \ i > j \qquad u_{ij} = a_{ij} - \sum_{k=1}^{i-1} l_{ik}u_{kj}, \ i \leq j \tag{3}$$

which has the form $x = G(x)$, where x is a vector containing the unknowns l_{ij} and u_{ij} for $(i,j) \in S$. The equations are then solved by using the fixed-point iteration $x^{(p+1)} = G(x^{(p)})$, for $p = 0, 1, \ldots$, starting with some initial $x^{(0)}$. See [4] for details on the convergence of this method. In brief, it can be proven that the iteration is locally convergent for standard (synchronous) and asynchronous iterations [9].

The iterative ILU algorithm, which solves the Eq. (2), is given in Algorithm 1. The actual implementation that served as the basis for this study can be found in the MAGMA open-source software library [10]. Each fixed-point iteration updating all the unknowns is called a "sweep." In this algorithm, an important question is how to choose the initial values of the l_{ij} and u_{ij} variables (line 1). In many applications, a natural initial guess is available; for example, in time-dependent problems, the L and U computed at the previous time step may be an excellent initial guess for the current time step. In other cases, there may be no natural initial guess. In [4], the matrix A is symmetrically scaled to have a unit diagonal, and the initial guess for L and U are then chosen to be the lower and upper parts of A, respectively. We also use this initial guess for the experiments in this paper.

Algorithm 1. Fine-Grained Parallel Incomplete Factorization

---

1 Set unknowns l_{ij} and u_{ij} to initial values
2 **for** $sweep = 1, 2, \ldots \ until \ convergence$ **do**
3   **parallel for** $(i, j) \in S$ **do**
4   **if** $i > j$ **then**
5              $l_{ij} = \left(a_{ij} - \sum_{k=1}^{j-1} l_{ik} u_{kj} \right) / u_{jj}$
6   **else**
7              $u_{ij} = a_{ij} - \sum_{k=1}^{i-1} l_{ik} u_{kj}$
8   **end**
9   **end**
10 **end**

We conclude this section by pointing out several features of this algorithm that make it different than existing methods, and relevant to parallel computing on emerging architectures:

- The algorithm is fine-grained, allowing for scaling to very large core counts, limited only by the number of nonzero elements in the factorization.
- The algorithm does not need to use reordering to enhance parallelism, and thus reorderings that enhance the accuracy of the incomplete factorization can be used.
- The algorithm can utilize an initial guess for the ILU factorization, which cannot be exploited by conventional ILU factorization algorithms.
- The bilinear equations do not need to be solved very accurately since the ILU factorization itself is only an approximation.

3   GPU Implementation

3.1   General Parallelization Strategy

When multiple processors are available, an iteration based on $x^{(p+1)} = G(x^{(p)})$ may be parallelized by assigning each processor to compute a subset of the components of $x^{(p+1)}$ using values of $x^{(p)}$, such that each component is updated by exactly one processor. This is called a synchronous iteration, as all values of $x^{(p)}$ must generally be computed before the computation of $x^{(p+1)}$ may start. In contrast, an asynchronous iteration is one where the computation of components of x may use the latest components of x that are available. Convergence may

be faster than the synchronous iteration because more updated values are used
(e.g., Gauss-Seidel type of iteration compared to Jacobi type) or may be slower
than synchronous iteration in the case that some components are rarely updated.
In general, there may be a tradeoff between parallelism and convergence: with
less parallel resources, the asynchronous iterations tend to use "fresher" data
when computing updates; with more parallel resources, the iterations tend to
use older data and thus converge more slowly.

For GPU computing, subsets of the components of x are assigned to GPU
thread blocks. Each thread block updates the components of x assigned to it.
The thread blocks are scheduled onto GPU multiprocessors. Within each thread
block, the components of x are updated simultaneously (in Jacobi-like fashion).
As there are generally more thread blocks than multiprocessors, some thread
blocks are processed before others, and thus update their components of x before
others. Thus some thread blocks within one fixed-point sweep may use newer
data than others (in Gauss-Seidel-like fashion). However, there is no guarantee
of the order in which thread blocks are scheduled onto multiprocessors. Overall,
the iteration may be considered to be "block-asynchronous" [1].

3.2   Component Update Order

The convergence rate of an asynchronous fixed-point iteration for the system of
equations $x = G(x)$ may depend on the order in which the components of x are
updated, particularly if some equations have more dependencies on components
of x than others. Specifically, for the computations (3) that are performed in
the new ILU formulation, there is a tree of dependencies between the variables
(components) being updated. Thus convergence will be faster if the asynchronous
updates of the variables are ordered roughly following these dependencies. Such
orderings are called "Gaussian elimination orderings" in [4].

On GPUs, each thread block is responsible for updating a given set of variables. Unfortunately, there is no guarantee of thread block execution order for
current generation GPU programs. Using a simple kernel that records the order
in which thread blocks are executed, we observed on the NVIDIA K40c GPU that
block indices are always assigned in order of execution of the thread blocks. (On
some earlier GPU models, we observed that the order of execution appears random.) Using this result, we can explicitly set a component update order that will
be approximately followed by the asynchronous iterations (approximate because
the iterations are asynchronous). In Sect. 4, we will test the effect of component
update order on convergence rate.

3.3   Data Locality and Cache Reuse

GPU access of data in global memory (off-chip DRAM) is expensive, and the
performance of any GPU code depends on how efficiently memory is reused after
it has been brought into cache or shared memory. In this section, we consider
how to partition the computational work into thread blocks in order to maximize

data reuse. We note that such partitionings also affect component update order and thus convergence.

Each thread is associated with an element $(i, j) \in S$. Each thread thus computes either l_{ij} or u_{ij} in Eq. (3). This computation requires reading row i of L and column j of U. This row and column may be reused to compute other elements in S. Thus we have the problem of partitioning the $(i, j) \in S$ among a given number of thread blocks such that threads in the thread block require, in aggregate, as few rows of L or columns of U as possible. (In the above, only part of the row or column is needed by each thread, due to the upper limit on the summations in (3), but this will only affect our analysis by a constant factor.)

Another way to view this problem is to maximize the number of times each row of L and each column of U is reused by a thread block. We define the reuse factor of thread block l as

$$f_{\text{reuse}}(l) := \frac{1}{2} \left(\frac{|S_l|}{m_l} + \frac{|S_l|}{n_l} \right)$$

where $|S_l|$ is the number of elements of S assigned to thread block l, and where m_l and n_l are the number of rows of L and columns of U, respectively, required by thread block l. The first term in the brackets is the average number of times that the rows are reused, while the second is the average number of times that the columns are reused. If the elements of S are assigned arbitrarily to the thread blocks, then the reuse factor is 1 in the worst case. For simplicity, we assume below that $m_l = n_l$, since m_l and n_l approximately equal will give higher reuse factors than m_l and n_l being very different.

We first consider a matrix corresponding to a 2D mesh problem using a 5-point stencil. Figure 1 (middle) shows the sparsity pattern of the matrix corresponding to a 6×6 mesh (left). The mesh has been partitioned into 9 subdomains of size 2×2, and the rows and columns of the matrix are ordered such that the rows and columns corresponding to the same subdomain are ordered together. Horizontal and vertical lines are used to separate the rows and columns corresponding to subdomains.

Now, assuming the ILU(0) case, each nonzero in the matrix corresponds to an element of S to assigned to a thread block. If we use the partitioning of the mesh into subdomains just described, then thread block l is assigned the nonzeros a_{ij} corresponding to edges (i, j) in the mesh within and emanating from subdomain l. For one subdomain, these correspond to the nonzeros marked as red squares in Fig. 1 (middle). For a partitioning of the mesh into subdomains of size $b \times b$, each thread block is assigned $5b^2$ edges (b^2 nodes in the subdomain and 5 edges per node). A typical thread block (corresponding to an interior subdomain) also requires $(b + 1)^2 - 1$ rows of L and the same number of columns of U to be read. Thus the reuse factor is $f_{\text{reuse}}(l) := \frac{5b^2}{(b+1)^2-1}$ in this case. The limit of the maximum size of the reuse factor is 5, for large values of b. Note that $b \times b$ is a blocking of the mesh, while $m_l \times m_l$ used above is a blocking of the matrix.

In general, if a regular mesh is partitioned into subdomains of size $b \times b$ and an s-point stencil is used, then there are $s \cdot b^2$ matrix entries corresponding to the

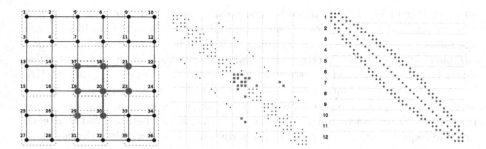

Fig. 1. A 6×6 mesh using a 5-point stencil partitioned into 9 subdomains of size 2×2 (left). The corresponding matrix (middle) orders rows and columns subdomain by subdomain. The bold edges in the mesh correspond to the nonzeros in the matrix marked with squares, and identify the elements assigned to one of the thread blocks. The right side shows the partitioning of the matrix after applying reverse Cuthill-McKee (RCM) and using 12 partitions.

subdomain, and the number of rows needed by the subdomain is b^2 (highest order term). The reuse factor therefore approaches s for large block sizes, showing that a larger stencil gives rise to a larger reuse factor.

In the 3D case, if a regular mesh is partitioned into subdomains of size $b \times b \times b$ and an s-point stencil is used, then there are $s \cdot b^3$ matrix entries corresponding to the subdomain, and the number of rows needed by the subdomain is b^3 (highest order term). The reuse factor again approaches s for large block sizes. As apparent from this analysis, 3D problems do not inherently have a larger reuse factor than 2D problems, except for generally using larger stencils. We note that in the sparse case, the maximum reuse factors are bounded independent of the partitioning, whereas for the dense case, the reuse factors increase with the size of the partitioning, may however be limited by the size of the shared memory.

3.4 Cache Reuse Between Thread Blocks

The working set of rows of L and columns of U needed by each thread block can be large, especially for large values of the blocking parameter b. However, if this working set can be shared between thread blocks by using the shared L2 cache [13], the communication volume from global memory can be reduced, compared to the case where each thread block uses its own scratchpad memory. To this end, in this section, we explore the idea of sharing the cache between thread blocks, i.e., one thread block using data brought into the L2 cache by another thread block. This idea is non-traditional because GPU programs generally assume that thread blocks that are not communicating through global memory are completely independent. This is because there is no guarantee of the order in which thread blocks are executed.

By using our previous observation in Sect. 3.2 that thread blocks are assigned indices in order of execution, we were able to verify through a simple performance test that thread blocks can indeed reuse data brought into the multiprocessor cache by an earlier thread block. Thus we can assign work to thread blocks such that reuse of cache between thread blocks is high. The right side of Fig. 1 shows a simple example for the matrix corresponding to the 6×6 mesh on the left. The matrix has been reordered to reduce its bandwidth using reverse Cuthill-McKee (RCM) ordering. Horizontal lines show a partitioning of the elements of S, and assume that the partitions are assigned to thread blocks such that the partitions are executed from top to bottom. From the figure, it can be observed that each partition requires different rows of L; these rows are reused within a thread block but not across thread blocks. We also observe that partitions numbered nearby use a very similar set of columns of U. These columns of U may be shared across thread blocks using cache. Experiments are reported in Sect. 4 to test the cache behavior of this partitioning of S and this ordering of the thread blocks.

3.5   Parallelism Vs Convergence

The convergence rate of an asynchronous iteration depends on the amount of parallelism used in the iteration, with more parallelism usually resulting in a reduced convergence rate. We aim to control the amount of parallelism in order to investigate the tradeoff between parallelism and convergence. NVIDIA provides no interface for direct manipulation of parallelism; thus we will control the amount of parallelism indirectly.

To quantify the parallelism of a code running on GPUs, we may use the concept of "occupancy." While occupancy is defined as the ratio between the number of threads (grouped in thread blocks) that are scheduled in parallel and the hardware-imposed thread limit (threads per streaming multiprocessor, tpsm), certain algorithms may benefit from using less than the maximum occupancy [19]. A metric for quantifying the *actual* parallelism is the number of executed instructions per cycle (IPC), which reflects not only the number of active threads, but also stalls due to communication bottlenecks.

To indirectly control the number of thread blocks that are simultaneously scheduled onto a multiprocessor, note that the available shared memory, registers, the number of individual threads and thread blocks are limited for each streaming multiprocessor, which bounds the total number of thread blocks being executed in parallel. Thus we can artificially reduce parallelism by explicitly allocating scratchpad memory that we do not use in the kernel execution.

The multiprocessor's local memory is partitioned between scratchpad memory and L1 cache. We have configured shared memory to maximize cache and minimize scratchpad memory. The minimum amount of shared memory that can be configured is 16,384 bytes per multiprocessor on the K40X architecture [13]. In compute capability 3.5, the value of tpsm is 2048. Therefore, requesting 1,024 bytes or less of scratchpad memory for each thread block consisting of 128 threads results in 16 thread blocks running in parallel and 100 % multiprocessor occupancy, while doubling the allocated scratchpad memory reduces the number of active blocks to 8, and decreases the occupancy to 50 %. In Sect. 4.6, we use this technique to control parallelism and observe its affect on the convergence rate and performance of the asynchronous iterations.

3.6   Implementation Issues

Our CUDA kernel is designed to perform one sweep of the iterative ILU algorithm (Algorithm 1) for computing the factorization $A \approx LU$. Additional sweeps are performed by launching this kernel multiple times. The input to the kernel are arrays corresponding to matrices A, L, and U. The arrays for L and U, stored in CSR and CSC format, respectively, contain an initial guess on input and the approximate factorizations on output.

The matrix A, stored in coordinate (COO) format, can be regarded as a "task list." The thread with global thread index `tid` is assigned to update the variable corresponding to element `tid` in the COO array. Effectively, thread block 0 is assigned the first `blockDim` elements in the COO array, thread block 1 is assigned the next `blockDim` elements, etc., (where `blockDim` is the number of threads in a thread block). By changing the order in which the elements are stored in the COO array, the order of the updates can be controlled. Note that changing this order does not change the ordering of the rows and columns of the matrix A.

Reads of the arrays corresponding to matrix A are coalesced. However, each thread in general reads different rows of L and columns of U that are not coalesced, so that we rely on this data being read into cache and reused as much as possible, as described above.

Significant thread divergence will occur if the partial sum (lines 5 and 7 of Algorithm 1) computed by a thread contains a different number of addends than for other threads in the same warp. Thus, to minimize the cost of divergence, the partial sums for the updates handled by threads in the same warp should be of similar length. This, however, conflicts with optimizing component assignment for cache reuse, and we experimentally identified that data locality is more important.

To end this section, we summarize the parameters that affect the convergence behavior and data locality of the kernel.

- Task list ordering: the ordering of the elements of S in the task list. Except when specified otherwise, the *default task list ordering* is as follows: the elements of S are ordered such that if the elements were placed in a matrix, the elements are ordered row by row, from left to right within a row. This is a Gaussian elimination ordering. The order in which variables are updated can be changed by changing the task list ordering.
- Thread block order: the order of execution of the thread blocks. Except when specified otherwise, the thread blocks are ordered by increasing thread block index, i.e., the first thread block is assigned the first chunk of the task list, etc. We can also order the thread blocks in reverse order or in a random, arbitrary order.
- Matrix ordering: the ordering of the rows and columns of the matrix. Changing the matrix ordering changes the problem. We use the symmetric RCM ordering of the matrix, except for the finite difference discretizations of the Laplace problem L2D and L3D, for which the natural ordering can be used.

The RCM and natural orderings are good choices for computing accurate incomplete factorization preconditioners [8].

4   Experimental Results

4.1   Experimental Setup

Our experimental setup is an NVIDIA Tesla K40c GPU (Rpeak 1,682 GFLOP/s) with a two socket Intel Xeon E5-2670 (Sandy Bridge) host. The iterative incomplete factorization GPU kernels were implemented in CUDA version 6.0 [15] and use a default thread block size of 128. The conjugate gradient linear solver and the iterative incomplete factorization routine are taken from the MAGMA opensource software library [10]. The sparse triangular solve routines are from the NVIDIA cuSPARSE library [14]. The results below used double precision computations for the iterative ILU code; timings were 20–40 percent slower than for single precision computations.

The test matrices were selected from Tim Davis's sparse matrix collection [6] and include the problems used by NVIDIA for testing the ILU factorization code in cuSPARSE [12]. We have reordered these test matrices using RCM reordering. Additionally, we use test matrices arising from a finite difference discretization of the Laplace operator in 2D and 3D with Dirichlet boundary conditions. For the 2D case, a 5-point stencil was used on a 1024×1024 mesh, and for the 3D case, a 27-point stencil was used on a $64 \times 64 \times 64$ mesh. All test matrices (Table 1) are symmetric positive definite and we used the symmetric, or incomplete Cholesky (IC) version of the iterative ILU algorithm [4]. However, we still refer to the algorithm as the *iterative ILU algorithm* for generality.

Table 1. Test matrices.

Name	Abbrev.	Nonzeros n_z	Size n	Name	Abbrev.	Nonzeros n_z	Size n
APACHE2	APA	4,817,870	715,176	PARABOLIC_FEM	PAR	3,674,625	525,825
ECOLOGY2	ECO	4,995,991	999,999	THERMAL2	THM	8,580,313	1,228,045
G3_CIRCUIT	G3	7,660,826	1,585,478	LAPLACE2D	L2D	5,238,784	1,048,576
OFFSHORE	OFF	4,242,673	259,789	LAPLACE3D	L3D	6,859,000	262,144

4.2   Convergence Metrics

For an incomplete Cholesky factorization, $A \approx LL^T$, we measure how well the factorization works as a preconditioner for the preconditioned conjugate gradient (PCG) method for solving linear systems. Thus we will report PCG solver iteration counts. Linear systems were constructed using a right-hand side of all ones. The iterations start with a zero initial guess, and the iterations are stopped when the residual norm relative to the initial residual norm has been reduced beyond 10^{-6}.

We also measure the *nonlinear residual norm* $\|(A - LL^T)_S\|_F$, where the Frobenius norm is taken only over the elements in S. The expression $(A - LL^T)_S = 0$ corresponds to the nonlinear equations being solved by the fixed-point sweeps of the asynchronous iterative algorithm. Finally, we can also measure the *ILU residual norm* $\|A - LL^T\|_F$, which has been shown to correlate well with the number of PCG iterations in the SPD case [8]. This quantity is relatively expensive to compute since all elements of LL^T are required, but it can be useful for diagnostic purposes. Note that this quantity is not zero for an incomplete factorization.

We show how the above quantities change for matrices L computed using different numbers of asynchronous fixed-point sweeps, beginning with an initial guess for L (corresponding to sweep 0). In this paper, the level 0 factorizations are computed, although any sparsity pattern S can be used in the GPU kernel. We use the notation "IC" to indicate results for an incomplete factorization computed "exactly" using the conventional Gaussian elimination process.

4.3   Preconditioner Quality and Timings

We begin by demonstrating the convergence and performance of the iterative ILU algorithm using our GPU implementation. Figure 2 shows the convergence of the nonlinear residual norm (left) and ILU residual norm (right) as a function of the number of nonlinear sweeps, for several test matrices. The results show that the nonlinear residual norm converges very steadily. Also, the ILU residual norm converges very rapidly, i.e., after a small number of steps, to the ILU residual norm of the conventional ILU factorization (which is necessarily nonzero because the factorization is approximate). This suggests that the factorization computed by the new algorithm after a small number of steps may be comparable to the factorization computed by the conventional algorithm.

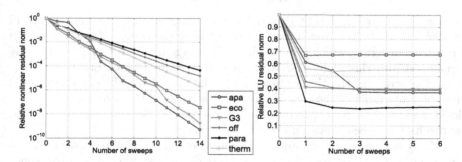

Fig. 2. Relative nonlinear residual norm (left) and relative ILU residual norm (right) for different numbers of sweeps.

This is indeed the case, as shown on the left side in Table 2, which shows the PCG solver iteration counts when the incomplete factors are used as a preconditioner. The iteration counts indicate that only a few sweeps are usually sufficient to generate a preconditioner similar in quality to the preconditioner computed conventionally. This is consistent with the ILU residual norm typically having converged after the first 5 iterations. It is thus not necessary to fully converge the nonlinear residual.

The right side of Table 2 shows the timings for IC computed using the NVIDIA cuSPARSE library, and for the 5 sweeps of the new algorithm. Significant speedups are seen over the cuSPARSE implementation, which uses level scheduling to exploit parallelism.

Table 2. PCG solver iteration counts using preconditioners constructed with up to 5 sweeps, and timings for 5 sweeps. IC denotes the exact factorization computed using the NVIDIA cuSPARSE library. Speedup shown is that of 5 sweeps relative to IC.

	Solver iteration counts for given number of sweeps						Timings [ms]		
	IC	0	1	2	3	4	5	IC	5 swps	speedup
APA	958	1430	1363	1038	965	960	958	61.	8.8	6.9
ECO	1705	2014	1765	1719	1708	1707	1706	107.	6.7	16.0
G3	997	1254	961	968	993	997	997	110.	12.1	9.1
OFF	330	428	556	373	396	357	332	219.	25.1	8.7
PAR	393	763	636	541	494	454	435	131.	6.1	21.6
THM	1398	1913	1613	1483	1341	1411	1403	454.	15.7	28.9
L2D	550	653	703	664	621	554	551	112.	7.4	15.2
L3D	35	43	37	35	35	35	35	94.	47.5	2.0

4.4   Thread Block Ordering and Convergence

We now show the effect that thread block ordering has on the convergence of the iterative ILU algorithm. First, the ordering of the tasks follows a Gaussian elimination ordering, which is beneficial for convergence. This task list is linearly partitioned into thread blocks. We tested three thread block orderings: (1) a forward ordering of the thread blocks, i.e., the first thread block is associated with the first chunk of the task list, etc., (2) a backward ordering of the thread blocks, and (3) a random ordering of the thread blocks. For the random ordering, the results have been averaged over several trials.

Table 3 reports the time and the relative nonlinear residual norm after 5 sweeps for various problems. The forward ordering leads to the best convergence rate and the backward ordering leads to the worst convergence rate. The random ordering, corresponding to the convergence behavior of an unpredictable GPU thread block scheduling gives results in between these two. Note that there is no significant difference between the timings using the three different orderings.

Table 3. Comparison of different thread block orderings, showing time and relative nonlinear residual norm after 5 sweeps of the iterative ILU algorithm. Forward ordering gives the fastest convergence rate, and timings are not impacted.

	Order	Time [s]	Res. norm			Order	Time [s]	Res. norm
APA	Forward	9.04e-03	2.23e-04		PAR	Forward	5.90e-03	1.54e-02
	Backward	8.84e-03	1.03e-02			Backward	5.97e-03	2.83e-02
	Random	8.68e-03	4.46e-03			Random	6.06e-03	2.32e-02
ECO	Forward	6.62e-03	9.36e-04		THM	Forward	1.54e-02	7.25e-03
	Backward	6.61e-03	6.23e-03			Backward	1.53e-02	1.44e-02
	Random	6.77e-03	3.82e-03			Random	1.64e-02	1.04e-02
G3	Forward	1.20e-02	6.31e-04		L2D	Forward	7.38e-03	1.58e-04
	Backward	1.19e-02	6.98e-03			Backward	7.36e-03	2.30e-03
	Random	1.30e-02	5.09e-03			Random	7.35e-03	1.27e-03
OFF	Forward	2.49e-02	1.16e-02		L3D	Forward	4.73e-02	1.35e-03
	Backward	2.46e-02	7.21e-02			Backward	4.71e-02	7.17e-03
	Random	2.50e-02	5.93e-01			Random	4.73e-02	3.25e-03

4.5   Data Locality

In this section we show the effect of the ordering of the task list, which affects data locality. In Sect. 3.3, orderings of the task list were proposed for problems that are discretized on regular meshes. These are based on partitioning the graph corresponding to the matrix (using $b \times b$ blockings of the 2D regular mesh was the prototypical example). In Sect. 3.4, it was proposed to enhance cache reuse *between thread blocks* by using a RCM reordering of the matrix combined with the default task list ordering.

Results are shown along with metrics from NVIDIA's NVPROF profiler in Table 4 for the L3D problem. We used a randomly permuted task list as an extreme case of disordered memory access and $b \times b \times b$ blockings of the mesh.

The results show that large block sizes give better performance. RCM ordering also gives good performance. The random case is the slowest, due to low L2 hit rate and low global load throughput, resulting in low executed instructions per cycle. For the blockings, the high L2 hit rate indicates that most data is already present in local memory, and only small amounts must be reloaded from DRAM. Luckily, we also find that orderings that have better memory access locality also lead to better convergence rates.

4.6   Parallelism Vs Convergence

Increased parallelism may result in slower convergence because variables being updated at the same time use "older" rather than "refreshed" values in their update formulas. As described in Sect. 3.6, the amount of parallelism can be controlled explicitly by allocating different amounts of scratchpad memory (that will not be used) in the kernel code. Table 5 shows several kernel configurations, for different amounts of requested scratchpad memory, and the result of running these configurations for the L3D problem. As can be observed, the theoretical

Table 4. Comparison of strategies for enhancing data locality for the L3D problem. The time and relative nonlinear residual norm are for 5 nonlinear sweeps. RCM and orderings for large block sizes $m \times m \times m$ give best results in terms of both timing and convergence.

Task list ordering	Random	2	4	8	16	32	64	RCM
Time $\times 10^{-2}$ [s]	20.0	5.54	5.37	5.15	4.96	4.89	4.78	4.92
Rel. nonlin. res. norm $\times 10^{-3}$	2.66	3.08	4.35	4.86	4.63	1.87	1.35	1.58
Global load throughput [GB/s]	83.35	237.34	247.71	249.45	251.38	253.00	258.00	252.97
DRAM read throughput [GB/s]	119.00	16.70	15.93	16.43	17.13	16.62	22.10	20.02
L2 read throughput [GB/s]	83.35	237.34	247.71	249.45	251.38	253.00	258.00	252.97
L2 hit rate (L1 reads) [%]	19.02	96.68	96.97	96.91	96.79	96.93	95.88	96.02
Global store throughput [GB/s]	1.08	3.70	3.79	3.88	3.98	4.05	3.86	3.74
Ex. instructions per cycle (IPC)	0.21	0.75	0.78	0.81	0.85	0.85	0.87	0.86

and observed occupancy decreases with increasing requested memory. For our algorithm, the IPC also generally decreases with increasing requested memory, but the relation is not exact. For example, config_1 has the highest occupancy but not the highest IPC. As expected, reducing the parallelism slightly improves the convergence rate, but at the same time, the time scales almost linearly with the inverse of parallelism quantified by IPC. Figure 3 graphs the relative nonlinear residual norm as a function of time, for different configurations. The results show that the degradation in convergence due to additional parallelism is small, and the penalty is more than compensated by the additional parallelism.

Table 5. Several configurations of the kernel code to control parallelism, and the corresponding runtime and relative nonlinear residual norm for 5 sweeps. Results are for the L3D problem.

		config_1	config_2	config_3	config_4	config_5	config_6
Requested scratchpad mem. [B]		1024	2048	3072	4096	6144	9216
Active thread blocks		16	8	5	4	2	1
Active threads		2048	1024	640	512	256	128
Theoretical occupancy [%]		100.0	50.0	31.3	25.0	12.5	6.3
Reported occupancy [%]		98.7	49.6	31.0	24.8	12.4	6.2
Global load throughput [GB/s]		258.00	269.34	209.70	175.00	92.32	46.34
DRAM read throughput [GB/s]		22.10	23.23	18.06	15.07	7.98	4.01
L2 read throughput [GB/s]		258.00	269.34	209.70	175.00	92.32	46.34
Global store throughput [GB/s]		3.86	4.04	3.15	2.62	1.38	0.69
IPC		0.8572	0.91184	0.7120	0.5941	0.3134	0.1598
5 sweeps	Time:	4.88e-02	4.57e-02	5.89e-02	7.01e-02	1.33e-01	2.62e-01
	Rel. nonlin. res. norm:	1.35e-03	1.22e-03	1.16e-03	1.14e-03	9.84e-04	8.00e-04

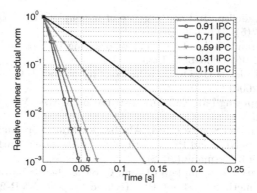

Fig. 3. Relationship between runtime and nonlinear residual norm for different amounts of parallelism, for the L3D problem.

5   Conclusions

A GPU implementation of an asynchronous iterative algorithm for computing incomplete factorizations has been presented. Significant speedups over the level scheduling implementation of the cuSPARSE library were reported. Several techniques were discussed for controlling the order of the asynchronous computations to enhance convergence and data locality. These techniques may be applied in general to other asynchronous iterative algorithms.

Acknowledgments. This material is based upon work supported by the U.S. Department of Energy Office of Science, Office of Advanced Scientific Computing Research, Applied Mathematics program under Award Numbers DE-SC-0012538 and DE-SC-0010042. Support from NVIDIA is also acknowledged.

References

1. Anzt, H., Tomov, S., Dongarra, J., Heuveline, V.: A block-asynchronous relaxation method for graphics processing units. J. Parallel Distrib. Comput. **73**(12), 1613–1626 (2013)
2. Benzi, M., Joubert, W., Mateescu, G.: Numerical experiments with parallel orderings for ILU preconditioners. Electron. Trans. Numer. Anal. **8**, 88–114 (1999)
3. Bergman, K. et al.: ExaScale computing study: technology challenges in achieving exascale systems peter kogge, editor & study lead (2008)
4. Chow, E., Patel, A.: Fine-grained parallel incomplete LU factorization. SIAM J. Sci. Comput. **37**, C169–C193 (2015)
5. Contassot-Vivier, S., Jost, T., Vialle, S.: Impact of asynchronism on gpu accelerated parallel iterative computations. In: Jónasson, K. (ed.) PARA 2010, Part I. LNCS, vol. 7133, pp. 43–53. Springer, Heidelberg (2012)
6. Davis, T.A.: The University of Florida Sparse Matrix Collection. NA DIGEST 92 (1994). http://www.netlib.org/na-digesthtml/

7. Doi, S.: On parallelism and convergence of incomplete LU factorizations. Appl. Numer. Math. **7**(5), 417–436 (1991)
8. Duff, I.S., Meurant, G.A.: The effect of ordering on preconditioned conjugate gradients. BIT **29**(4), 635–657 (1989)
9. Frommer, A., Szyld, D.B.: On asynchronous iterations. J. Comput. Appl. Math. **123**, 201–216 (2000)
10. Innovative Computing Lab: Software distribution of MAGMA, July 2015. http://icl.cs.utk.edu/magma/
11. Lukarski, D.: Parallel Sparse Linear Algebra for Multi-core and Many-core Platforms - Parallel Solvers and Preconditioners. Ph.D. thesis, Karlsruhe Institute of Technology (KIT), Germany (2012)
12. Naumov, M.: Parallel incomplete-LU and Cholesky factorization in the preconditioned iterative methods on the GPU. Technical report. NVR-2012-003, NVIDIA (2012)
13. NVIDIA Corporation: NVIDIA's Next Generation CUDA Compute Architecture: Kepler GK110. Whitepaper (2012)
14. NVIDIA Corporation: CUSPARSE LIBRARY, July 2013
15. NVIDIA Corporation: NVIDIA CUDA TOOLKIT V6.0, July 2013
16. Poole, E.L., Ortega, J.M.: Multicolor ICCG methods for vector computers. SIAM J. Numer. Anal. **24**, 1394–1417 (1987)
17. Saad, Y.: Iterative Methods for Sparse Linear Systems. Society for Industrial and Applied Mathematics, Philadelphia (2003)
18. Venkatasubramanian, S., Vuduc, R.W.: Tuned and wildly asynchronous stencil kernels for hybrid CPU/GPU systems. In: Proceedings of the 23rd International Conference on Supercomputing, ICS 2009, pp. 244–255. ACM, New York (2009)
19. Volkov, V.: Better performance at lower occupancy. In: GPU Technology Conference (2010)

Matrix Multiplication on High-Density Multi-GPU Architectures: Theoretical and Experimental Investigations

Peng Zhang[1(✉)] and Yuxiang Gao[2]

[1] Biomedical Engineering Department,
Stony Brook University, Stony Brook, NY 11794, USA
peng.zhang@stonybrook.edu
[2] Cluster Solution Department, Cray Inc., San Jose, CA 95112, USA

Abstract. Matrix multiplication (MM) is one of the core problems in the high performance computing domain and its efficiency impacts performances of almost all matrix problems. The high-density multi-GPU architecture escalates the complexities of such classical problem, though it greatly exceeds the capacities of previous homogeneous multicore architectures. In order to fully exploit the potential of such multi-accelerator architectures for multiplying matrices, we systematically evaluate the performances of two prevailing tile-based MM algorithms, standard and Strassen. We use a high-density multi-GPU server, CS-Storm which can support up to eight NVIDIA GPU cards and we test three generations of GPU cards which are K20Xm, K40m and K80. Our results show that (1) Strassen is often faster than standard method on multicore architecture but it is not beneficial for small enough matrices. (2) Strassen is more efficient than standard algorithm on low-density GPU solutions but it quickly loses its superior on high-density GPU solutions. This is a result of more additions needed in Strassen than in standard algorithm. Experimental results indicate that: though Strassen needs less arithmetic operations than standard algorithm, the heterogeneity of computing resources is a key factor of determining the best-practice algorithm.

Keywords: Matrix multiplication · Performance evaluation · Heterogeneous architectures · High-density multi-GPU architectures

1 Introduction

Since ENIAC was announced in 1946, researchers never stop to seek a faster approach for multiplying matrices. Not only one of the kernels in numerical linear algebra, the problem of matrix multiplication (MM) is also a bottleneck for almost all matrix problems such as least square problem and eigenvalue problem [1–5]. The key problem has widely been studied in computing theory and in practical implementation. Mathematicians have been looking for the possible lowest bound for multiplying matrices. The standard method for multiplying two $n \times n$ matrices is $O(n^3)$. In 1969, Strassen reduced the computing complexity to $O(n^{2.807})$ [6]. In 1987, a big breakthrough of this problem is the Coppersmith-Winograd algorithm which can do MM in $O(n^{2.376})$

© Springer International Publishing Switzerland 2015
J.M. Kunkel and T. Ludwig (Eds.): ISC High Performance 2015, LNCS 9137, pp. 17–30, 2015.
DOI: 10.1007/978-3-319-20119-1_2

operations [7]. More new algorithms are proposed for beating the records and approaching the true lowest bound [8].

Practical implementation is essential to exploit the proposed algorithms on the novel parallel computing facilities [5, 9–20]. Different from theoretical studies, the complex characteristics of computing facilities need to be taken into the design of parallel programs. In distributed computing, communication needs to be minimized [12, 19, 21]. Particularly the task mapping problem for the Strassen algorithm is addressed for balancing multiplications [9, 18]. In the latest heterogeneous architectures, MM needs to be optimized on special-purposed processors and accelerators, such as CELL processor [5] and graphics processing units (GPUs) [11]. Besides, many high-performance implementations of MM are developed such as in GotoBLAS [22, 23], ATLAS [10], LAPACK [24] and CUBLAS [23]. To accommodate the ever-changing computing architectures, new algorithms have been designed and developed with the birth of new technologies. Recently, high-density multi-GPU technologies are available to the community of supercomputing. For example, a 2U server node can be configurated with 8 NVIDIA GPU cards in CS-Storm [25, 26], featuring up a high-density space-efficient design for integrating multiple GPUs. This design has significantly escalated computing complexities, though it greatly improves computing performance. There is a need to investigate MM algorithms on this novel architecture.

This motivated the work to investigate the performance of the standard and Strassen tile-based algorithms on the high-density multi-GPU architecture. Our contributions in the work are: (i) to systematically compare the performances of the standard and Strassen algorithms on the high-density multi-GPU platforms; (ii) to find out the optimal algorithms through extensive experiments for a wide range of problem sizes under different system configurations; (iii) to present the performance characteristics to the researchers and the engineers for better algorithmic and engineering designs.

The paper is organized as follows: standard and Strassen algorithms are reviewed in Sect. 2. Theoretical evaluation is presented in terms of floating-point operations and execution time in Sect. 3. High-density multi-GPU architecture is described in terms of hardware specifications and software stacks in Sect. 4. Experimental results are presented and analyzed in Sect. 5. Conclusion is drawn in Sect. 7.

2   Matrix Multiplication Algorithms

We consider the tiled matrix multiplication (MM) algorithms on shared-memory multicore and multi-accelerator systems. The first method is the standard tiled MM algorithm and it is also referred to as the *Naïve* method thereafter. Naïve method partitions each input matrix into a block matrix whose tiles are submatrices of identical sizes. Based on the given partition, the computing products of submatrices are performed concurrently. The other method is the *Strassen* algorithm, which is often faster than Naïve on the multicore systems for large size matrices. Figure 1 gives the examples to show the data partition and computing flows for both methods. In the examples, the input matrices A and B are partitioned into 2 × 2 block matrices. Each tile (namely, submatrix) is referred to as atomic data module. Intermediate data modules are needed to buffer intermediate results. Finally, the resultant matrix C is computed and stored in the same manner. This case of multiplying two 2 × 2 matrices shows that Strassen saves one multiplication at the expense of 14 more additions. The cost of multiplying matrices is often highlighted; however, the cost of adding matrices is somewhat ignored in the analysis of most algorithms. This could result in the problems in practical implementations. For example, clearly the benefit of Strassen would be marginal for small enough matrices. It is observed that in practice on the multicore systems, there is a performance crosspoint between Strassen and Naïve [10, 27]. However, in this work, we'd ask one question: is there a performance crosspoint for large matrices on heterogeneous architectures?

For convenience of description, we assume that: input matrix is a square matrix of size $N \times N$; the tiled partition is $(2p) \times (2p)$; and, each tile is a square submatrix of size $n \times n$. Thus, $N = 2p \times n$. N, p and n are positive integers. p is called as partition factor. In the example (Fig. 1), the titled partition is 2 × 2 and $p = 1$.

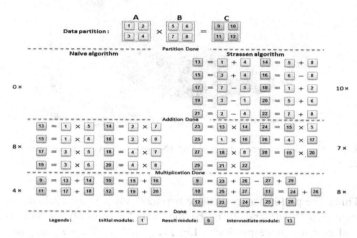

Fig. 1. Data partitions and computing procedures for Naïve and Strassen algorithms

3 Theoretical Evaluation

We conduct the theoretical evaluation for two methods in terms of floating-point operations (FLOP) and execution time.

Floating-point operations (FLOP): Let $F_{mm}(p, n)$ and $F_{st}(p, n)$ be the number of floating-point operations (FLOP) that is required by Naïve and Strassen, respectively. The formulas are written as:

$$F_{mm}(p,n) = 8p^3 \cdot f_m(n) + p^2(8p - 4) \cdot f_a(n) \tag{1}$$

$$F_{st}(p,n) = 7p^3 \cdot f_m(n) + p^2(22p - 4) \cdot f_a(n) \tag{2}$$

Here $f_m(n) = n^2(2n - 1)$ and $f_a(n) = n^2$ are the FLOP for multiplying and adding $n \times n$ matrices.

Let the ratio of $F_{st}(p,n)$ over $F_{mm}(p,n)$ be $\gamma(p,n)$ written as:

$$\gamma(p,n) = \frac{F_{st}(p,n)}{F_{mm}(p,n)} = \frac{7p(2n-1) + 22p - 4}{8p(2n-1) + 8p - 4} \sim 0.875 - \frac{15}{n} \tag{3}$$

The partition factor p is often small in tiled algorithms. Then, we see: $\gamma(p,n) \to 0.875$ as $n \to \infty$. Figure 2 illustrates the evolution of ratio $\gamma(p,n)$ under certain conditions. This reaffirmed the asymptotic complexities for Naïve and Strassen and it also indicated the performances on multicore architectures [6].

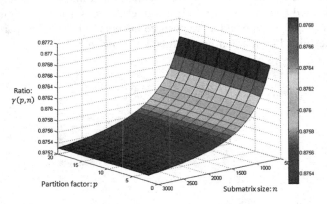

Fig. 2. Ratio of FLOP (Strassen) over FLOP (Naïve) with varied partition factor p and submatrix size n

Execution Time: The performances of these two methods are then evaluated in terms of execution time. Let $T_m(n)$ and $T_a(n)$ be the time for multiplying and adding two submatrices of size $n \times n$, respectively. Let $T_{mn}(p,n)$ and $T_{st}(p,n)$ are the total time needed for Naïve and Strassen and written as:

$$T_{mm}(p,n) = 8p^3 \cdot T_m(n) + p^2(8p - 4) \cdot T_a(n) \tag{4}$$

$$T_{st}(p,n) = 7p^3 \cdot T_m(n) + p^2(22p - 4) \cdot T_a(n) \tag{5}$$

On homogeneous multicore architectures, multiplication is often more time-consuming than addition for large enough matrices so we assume: $T_m(n) \gg T_a(n)$ for large n. Let n_p be the number of processor cores that process concurrently. Thus, we have the facts on homogenous multicore systems that:

- Strassen is more efficient than Naïve and its improvement is $\sim 12.5\ \%$.
- Parallel efficiency is nearly perfect when the number $7p^3$ is a multiple of n_p. Naturally, it is because $7p^3$ multiplication instances could be distributed evenly on the n_p processor cores, thus leading to perfect balanced multiplying operations [9].

However, the situation may be different on the heterogeneous multi-GPU architecture. The difference is due to the disparity of GPU and CPU performances (Table 1). We calculate the ratio of $T_{st}(p,n)$ over $T_{mm}(p,n)$ as:

Table 1. Performance comparison between GPUs and CPUs

	Peak floating point performances (TFlops)	
	Double-precision	Single-precision
Tesla K20	1.17	3.52
Tesla K40	1.43	4.29
Tesla K80	1.87	5.60
Xeon E5-2670	0.166	0.333

$$\beta(p,n) = \frac{T_{st}(p,n)}{T_{mm}(p,n)} = \frac{p(7 \cdot \kappa(n) + 22) - 4}{p(8 \cdot \kappa(n) + 8) - 4} \sim \frac{7 \cdot \kappa(n) + 22}{8 \cdot \kappa(n) + 8} \qquad (6)$$

Here $\kappa(n) = T_m(n)/T_a(n)$ is the ratio of multiplication time over addition time for submatrices of size $n \times n$. Smaller $\beta(p,n)$ means that Strassen is more efficient than Naïve. Writing $\kappa(n)$ as a function of $\beta(p,n)$ yields:

$$\kappa(n) \sim -\frac{8 \cdot \beta(p,n) - 22}{8 \cdot \beta(p,n) - 7} \qquad (7)$$

This helps find out the asymptotic trend:

$$\lim_{\beta(p,n) \to 1} \kappa(n) = 14 \qquad (8)$$

Secondly, we have:

$$\frac{\partial \beta(p,n)}{\partial \kappa(n)} \sim \frac{-15}{8(\kappa(n) + 1)^2} < 0 \qquad (9)$$

From Eqs. (8) and (9), we find out that:

- If $\kappa(n) > 14$, Strassen could be faster than Naïve. On the other hand, if $\kappa(n) < 14$, Naïve could outperform Strassen, though it required more FLOP.
- Thus, when multiplication is much faster than addition, Strassen is greatly beneficial, compared to Naïve. However, when multiplication becomes as fast as addition, Naïve may in turn surpass Strassen.

Figure 3 shows the changes of $\beta(p,n)$ under varied p and $\kappa(n)$. Therefore, this made a possible: when/if the multiplication could be as fast as addition, Naïve could outperform Strassen. This assumption is hardly achievable in today's processors but it maybe holds on the hybrid multi-GPU architectures.

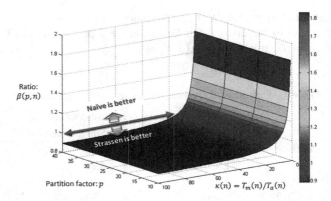

Fig. 3. Ratio of $T_{st}(p, n)$ (Strassen) over $T_{mm}(p, n)$ (naïve) with varied partition factor p and $\kappa(n)$

4   High-Density Multi-GPU Architecture

4.1   Hardware

CS-Storm [25] is used for performing all experiments and it is a 2U sever that can be equipped with up to 8 NVIDIA Tesla GPU cards and 2 Intel Xeon processors. In this work, we test three multi-GPU systems. Table 2 lists the hardware specifications. On the board, four PCIe switches are enclosed; each hooking up to 2 GPUs with the host.

Table 2. Hardware specification for multi-K20/K40/K80 server nodes

Systems	GPU hardware				CPU hardware			
	Model	# of GPUS	Total CUDA Cores	GDDR5 / GPU (GB)	Model	# of CPUS	Total CPU Cores	Total Host Memory (GB)
K20	K20Xm (1x Kepler GK110)	4	10,752	5.76	Intel Xeon E5-2670 v2	2	20	165
K40	K40m (1x Kepler GK110B)	8	23,040	11.52	Intel Xeon E5-2670 v2	2	20	165
K80	K80 (2x Kepler GK210)	16	39,936	11.52	Intel Xeon E5-2680 v3	2	24	165

4.2   Software

System software includes RHEL 6.5 and NVIDIA driver 340.32. For best performances of subprograms on CPUs and GPUs, we select two BLAS (basic linear algebra subprograms) libraries: Intel Math Kernel Library (MKL v11.2) for CPUs and CU-BLAS (CUDA 6.5) for GPUs. Complier package is Intel Parallel Studio 2015.

A data-oriented mapping paradigm (DMP) is extended to distribute tasks among CPUs and GPUs [28]. Following the work [28], we describe the scheduler work. In the tiled algorithms, the tiles are treated as data modules. All the tiles associated with input matrices are treated as initial data modules. All the tiles that belong to the resultant matrix are referred to as resultant data modules. Intermediate tiles are treated as intermediate data modules. All of data modules are given by an identifier. In the method, when a function is defined as $d_s = f(d_1, d_2)$, we say d_s depends on d_1 and d_2. Here, d_s, d_1 and d_2 are the identifiers of data modules and the function f is either the multiplication or the addition. In this manner, the data dependency is defined. A function in the method is referred to as a task in the computing. In the computing, initial data modules are first loaded and ready to use. Then a dedicated scheduler checks the availability of new tasks until all tasks are done. A task is available as long as the input data modules it requires are ready to use. The scheduler sends a new task to the next available CPU core or GPU card, as long as the task is available. We further add an arbitrator layer in the scheduler, which allows the scheduler to distribute specified tasks to preferred platforms. For example, the scheduler could distribute the addition tasks only on CPUs and the multiplication tasks only on GPUs.

5   Experimental Evaluation

5.1   Performance Metrics

Wallclock time (in seconds) is used for timing. $T(A)/T(B)$ denotes the wallclock time for method A and B. $S(A, B) = T(B)/T(A)$ is the speedup for A over B. Performance improvement for A over B is defined as $P(A, B)$ and calculated as:

$$P(A, B) = \frac{T(B) - T(A)}{T(B)} = 1 - S(A, B)^{-1} \tag{10}$$

As this equation suggests, a positive $P(A, B)$ implies A is faster than B; otherwise, B is faster than A. In addition, for the clarity of showing schedulability, parallel activities trace (PAT) is proposed to illustrate the activities of concurrent computations. PAT is the 2D graphic scheme, in which the horizontal axis shows wallclock time and the vertical axis implies the device type (CPU/GPU) and thread identifiers (IDs). Different colors refer to different types of tasks (functions). Naturally, two ends of a color bar indicate starting and ending time points of data processing of a particular task so the length means the amount of time the task takes. PAT graphically helps illustrate the complexities of parallel activities of parallel programs. 64-bit and 32-bit precision floating-point formats are tested. Input matrices are partitioned as 4×4 tiles.

5.2   Homogeneous Multicore Architectures

Parallel efficiency is nearly perfect when the number of concurrent processes is a multiple of 7 thanks to the nature of Strassen [9, 29]. Thus, we benchmark both methods using 7 and 14 processor cores for a range of varied problem sizes. Figures 6 and 7 present the performances for Strassen and Naïve using the 64-bit (double) and 32-bit (single) precisions, respectively. Performance improvements of Strassen over

Naïve are accordingly calculated. From these results, we can find out: (i) Strassen lost its superiority for small enough sizes. With the increase of problem sizes, Strassen gains more benefits and it becomes consistently more efficient than Naïve. On seven cores, Strassen improved the performance by a factor of $13 \sim 14\%$, compared with Naïve. On 14 cores, performance improvements of Strassen over Naïve increase to $16 \sim 17\%$. This reaffirms: Strassen is more beneficial for large enough sizes. The precision of floating-point numbers has a dominating impact on absolute performances but it has a relatively small impact on performance improvements of Strassen over Naïve.

5.3   Heterogeneous Multi-GPU Architectures

5.3.1   Heterogeneity of Performances

When migrating from homogeneous multicore to heterogeneous multi-GPU architectures, we need to exam the performances of two key operations, multiplication and addition, on processors and accelerators. Figure 4 presents the performances for varied problem sizes. The results show that: (i) GPU multiplication (CUBLAS_DGEMM/ CUBLAS_SGEMM) is dominantly faster than CPU multiplication (MKL_DGEMM/ MKL_SGEMM). (ii) CPU addition (MKL_DOMATADD/MKL_SOMATADD) is even faster than GPU addition (CUBLAS_DAXPY/CUBLAS_SAXPY), due to data transfer overhead between the host and the GPU devices. Thus, CPU is still the optimal platform to perform the matrix addition but GPU becomes the best choice for the matrix multiplication for large enough size. (iii) Lastly, CPU multiplication is typically $2 \sim 3$ orders of magnitude slower than CPU addition; however, GPU multiplication is merely one order of magnitude slower than CPU addition. Figure 5 shows the ratios. This trend made a possible that Naïve may outperform Strassen on multi-GPU architectures, on which multiplication is not that slower than addition.

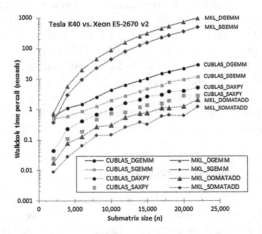

Fig. 4. Multiplication and addition performances on CPU/GPU

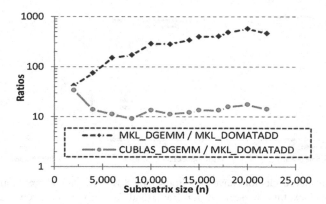

Fig. 5. Ratios of CPU-/GPU multiplication time over CPU addition time

5.3.2   Strassen vs. Naïve on 8x K40m

Figures 6 and 7 present the absolute performances of two methods in (a) and (b), and then the performance improvements for Strassen over Naïve in (c), for 64-bit (double) and 32-bit (single) precision, respectively. From the results, we can find out that: (i) The GPU-solutions are often superior to the CPU-only solutions for large enough matrices. (ii) High-density GPU-solutions are always better than low-density GPU-solutions. (iii) In the single-GPU solution (i.e., 1-GPU), Strassen still retains its superiority over Naïve. This could be because single GPU per node cannot give enough competitive performance for multiplying matrices, compared with the performance for adding matrices given by the many processor cores. Under this condition, Strassen could be still more efficient than Naïve since it needs fewer multiplications than Naïve. (iv) However, with the increase of GPU cards in one system, the efficiency of Naïve is greatly improved and in turn, Naïve outperforms Strassen. For examples, in the 4-GPU and 8-GPU solutions, Naïve appears much more efficient than Strassen. The results from the high-density multi-GPU tests verified the assumption that: Naïve may surpass Strassen under the condition that the time of multiplying two matrices is approx. one order of magnitude slower than the time of adding matrices of same sizes. Currently, this condition is hardly satisfied on low-density multi-GPU configurations since the processor cores are relatively more powerful than single GPU card. However, with the capability of densely integrating accelerators, the performance gap between multiplying and adding matrices is further reduced, thus directly affecting the best practice for MM on these novel architectures. (v) Naïve is more efficient than Strassen on 4-/8-GPU solutions regardless of floating-point precision (32-bit/64-bit). Figure 8 shows the parallel activities traces (PAT) of the case for multiplying two matrices of size 48,000, partitioned as 4 × 4 tiles, on the 8-K40 m system. PAT illustrates that (i) multiplication tasks are evenly distributed on GPU cards; and (ii) Strassen needs significantly more addition tasks than Naïve. Particularly, Fig. 8 shows that, at the beginning of program, all of cores are busy with these substantial additions for Strassen. Similarly, at the finishing of program, Strassen needs more addition tasks than Naïve (Fig. 1). In the middle of program, multiple GPU cards could be more efficient for multiplication tasks, compared with traditional processor cores. In this, the results show that Naïve becomes more efficient than Strassen.

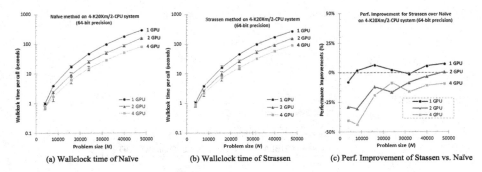

(a) Wallclock time of Naïve   (b) Wallclock time of Strassen   (c) Perf. Improvement of Stassen vs. Naïve

Fig. 6. Experimental results for Naïve and Strassen on 8-K40 m (double precision): (a) and (b) present the wallclock time in seconds for Naïve and Strassen, respectively. (c) shows the performance improvements for Strassen over Naïve. In the legend, 7 CORE (14 CORE) means a CPU-only solution using 7 (14) processor cores. The rest of tests are GPU solutions where 16 CPU cores used. Figures 7, 9, 10, 11 and 12 use the same legends.

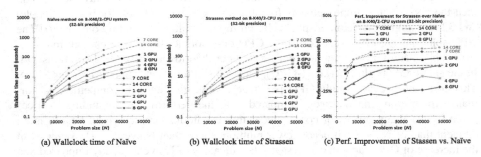

(a) Wallclock time of Naïve   (b) Wallclock time of Strassen   (c) Perf. Improvement of Stassen vs. Naïve

Fig. 7. Experimental investigation for Naïve and Strassen on 8-K40 m (single precision).

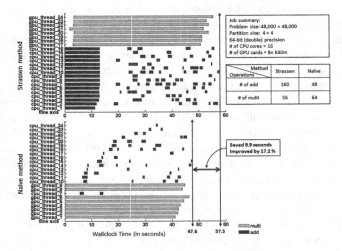

Fig. 8. Parallel activities traces for Naïve and Strassen for problem size 48,000 on 8x K40 m

5.3.3   Strassen vs. Naïve on 4x K20Xm and 16x K80

In the literature of NVIDA GPU cards, K20Xm and K80 are the predecessor and successor of K40m. Figures 9 and 10 show the absolute performances and performance comparisons between Strassen and Naïve on 4-K20Xm, using double and single precisions, respectively. Similarly, Figs. 11 and 12 show the results on 16-K80 system. Furthermore, Fig. 13 presents the best performances of three multi-GPU platforms, which undoubtedly shows that 16-K80 is the optimal. The results on 4-K20Xm system reaffirm previous discoveries: on 1-GPU configuration, Strassen is the optimal algorithm while on 2-/4-GPU configurations, Naïve appears more efficient than Strassen. The same results appear in the 16-K80 tests.

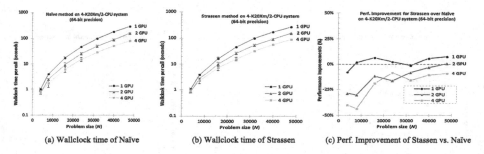

(a) Wallclock time of Naïve   (b) Wallclock time of Strassen   (c) Perf. Improvement of Stassen vs. Naïve

Fig. 9. Experimental investigation for Naïve and Strassen on 4-K20Xm (double precision)

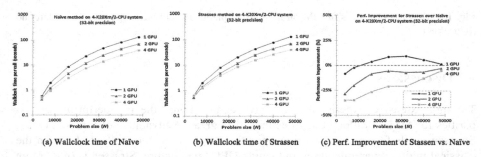

(a) Wallclock time of Naïve   (b) Wallclock time of Strassen   (c) Perf. Improvement of Stassen vs. Naïve

Fig. 10. Experimental investigation for Naïve and Strassen on 4-K20Xm (single precision).

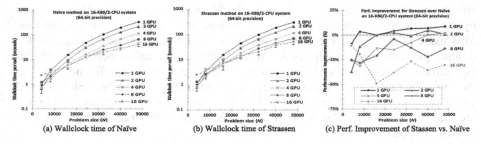

(a) Wallclock time of Naïve   (b) Wallclock time of Strassen   (c) Perf. Improvement of Stassen vs. Naïve

Fig. 11. Experimental investigation for Naïve and Strassen on 16-K80 (double precision)

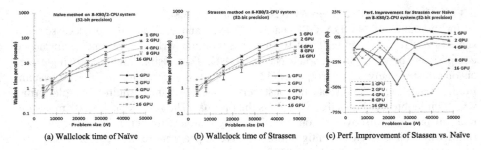

(a) Wallclock time of Naïve   (b) Wallclock time of Strassen   (c) Perf. Improvement of Stassen vs. Naïve

Fig. 12. Experimental investigation for Naïve and Strassen on 16-K80 (single precision)

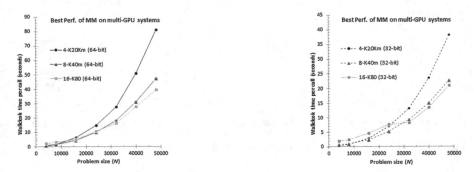

Fig. 13. Best performances of MM on multi-GPU platforms (double/single precisions: left and right plots)

6 Discussions

Through extensive experiments, we have demonstrated the big performance disparities for MM on different architectures. The greatest advantage of Strassen is that Strassen needs fewer multiplication operations than the naïve method. Thus on the classical multicore architectures and single-GPU architecture, Strassen is often more efficient than the naïve method for large enough problem size. However, on the novel high-density multi-GPU architectures, the efficiency of multiplying two matrices is significantly improved but the efficiency of adding two matrices is still constrained by the overhead of data transfer between the host and multiple accelerator devices. This made processors as the optimal platform for additions and accelerators as the optimal platform for multiplications. In this scenario, the naïve method could outperform the Strassen method. This indicates that the performance difference between the multiplication and addition operations would finally determine which method would be the best-practice solution. In this regard, the high-density multi-GPU architecture is widely different from the homogenous multi-core systems and low-density systems.

7 Conclusion

In this work, we test the standard (Naïve) and Strassen tile-based MM methods on novel high-density multi-GPU systems. Three generations of NVIDIA GPU cards, K20Xm, K40m and K80 are benchmarked on the systems. Both 64-bit double and 32-bit single precisions are tested. The results show that multi-GPU solutions can significantly improve the performances, in comparison with CPU-only solutions. The Strassen method is often beneficial on the multicore and the low-density GPU solutions; however it is beaten by the Naïve method on the high-density multi-GPU solutions. The reason is that the Strassen needs more additions than the Naïve method but GPU is not efficient enough for these additions thanks to the host-device overhead. The results in the work give a handy guide for the practitioners to use the methods for multiplying matrices on heterogeneous systems.

With the birth of new technologies, it is undoubted that the intra-chip and the inter-chip communication capability could and should be improved. By then, performance comparisons between different MM methods should be re-evaluated to find out the best-practice algorithm on novel architectures.

References

1. Robinson, S.: Toward an optimal algorithm for matrix multiplication. SIAM News **38**, 1–3 (2005)
2. Lancaster, P., Tismenetsky, M.: The Theory of Matrices: with Applications. Academic Press, Waltham (1985)
3. Dorn, F.: Dynamic programming and fast matrix multiplication. In: Azar, Y., Erlebach, T. (eds.) ESA 2006. LNCS, vol. 4168, pp. 280–291. Springer, Heidelberg (2006)
4. Gunnels, J.A., Henry, G.M., Van De Geijn, R.A.: A Family of high-performance matrix multiplication algorithms. In: Alexandrov, V.N., Dongarra, J.J., Juliano, B.A., Renner, R.S., Kenneth Tan, C.J. (eds.) ICCS 2001. LNCS, vol. 2073, pp. 51–60. Springer, Heidelberg (2001)
5. Kurzak, J., Alvaro, W., Dongarra, J.: Optimizing matrix multiplication for a short-vector SIMD architecture–CELL processor. Parallel Comput. **35**, 138–150 (2009)
6. Strassen, V.: Gaussian elimination is not optimal. Numer. Math. **13**, 354–356 (1969)
7. Coppersmith, D., Winograd, S.: Matrix multiplication via arithmetic progressions. In: Proceedings of the Nineteenth Annual ACM Symposium on Theory of Computing, pp. 1–6 (2004)
8. Williams, V.V.: Multiplying matrices faster than Coppersmith-Winograd. In: Proceedings of the Forty-Fourth Annual ACM Symposium on Theory of Computing, pp. 887–898 (2012)
9. Chou, C.C., Deng, Y.F., Li, G., Wang, Y.: Parallelizing strassens method for matrix multiplication on distributed-memory mimd architectures. Comput. Math. Appl. **30**, 49–69 (1995)
10. D'Alberto, P., Nicolau, A.: Using recursion to boost ATLAS's performance. In: Labarta, J., Joe, K., Sato, T. (eds.) ISHPC 2006 and ALPS 2006. LNCS, vol. 4759, pp. 142–151. Springer, Heidelberg (2008)

11. Ohshima, S., Kise, K., Katagiri, T., Yuba, T.: Parallel processing of matrix multiplication in a CPU and GPU heterogeneous environment. In: Daydé, M., Palma, J.M.L.M., Coutinho, A. L.G.A., Pacitti, E., Lopes, J.C. (eds.) VECPAR 2006. LNCS, vol. 4395, pp. 305–318. Springer, Heidelberg (2007)
12. Irony, D., Toledo, S., Tiskin, A.: Communication lower bounds for distributed-memory matrix multiplication. J. Parallel Distrib. Comput. **64**, 1017–1026 (2004)
13. Fatahalian, K., Sugerman, J., Hanrahan, P.: Understanding the efficiency of GPU algorithms for matrix-matrix multiplication. In: Proceedings of the ACM SIGGRAPH/EUROGRAPHICS Conference on Graphics Hardware, pp. 133–137 (2004)
14. Beaumont, O., Boudet, V., Rastello, F., Robert, Y.: Matrix multiplication on heterogeneous platforms. IEEE Trans. Parallel Distrib. Syst. **12**, 1033–1051 (2001)
15. Thottethodi, M., Chatterjee, S., Lebeck, A.R.: Tuning Strassen's matrix multiplication for memory efficiency. In: Proceedings of the 1998 ACM/IEEE Conference on Supercomputing (CDROM), pp. 1–14 (1998)
16. Luo, Q., Drake, J.B.: A scalable parallel Strassen's matrix multiplication algorithm for distributed-memory computers. In: Proceedings of the 1995 ACM Symposium on Applied Computing, pp. 221–226 (1995)
17. Choi, J., Walker, D.W., Dongarra, J.J.: PUMMA: parallel universal matrix multiplication algorithms on distributed memory concurrent computers. Concurrency: Pract. Experience **6**, 543–570 (1994)
18. Zhang, P., Gao, Y., Fierson, J., Deng, Y.: Eigenanalysis-based task mapping on parallel computers with cellular networks. Math. Comput. **83**, 1727–1756 (2014)
19. Zhang, P., Powell, R., Deng, Y.: Interlacing bypass rings to torus networks for more efficient networks. IEEE Trans. Parallel Distrib. Syst. **22**, 287–295 (2011)
20. Zhang, P., Deng, Y., Feng, R., Luo, X., Wu, J.: Evaluation of various networks configurated by adding bypass or torus links. IEEE Trans. Parallel Distrib. Syst. **26**, 984–996 (2015)
21. Ballard, G., Demmel, J., Holtz, O., Lipshitz, B., Schwartz, O.: Communication-optimal parallel algorithm for strassen's matrix multiplication. In: Proceedings of the 24th ACM Symposium on Parallelism in Algorithms and Architectures, pp. 193–204 (2012)
22. Goto, K., Geijn, R.A.: Anatomy of high-performance matrix multiplication. ACM Trans. Math. Softw. (TOMS) **34**, 12 (2008)
23. Barrachina, S., Castillo, M., Igual, F.D., Mayo, R., Quintana-Orti, E.S.: Evaluation and tuning of the level 3 CUBLAS for graphics processors. In: IEEE International Symposium on Parallel and Distributed Processing, IPDPS 2008, pp. 1–8 (2008)
24. Demmel, J.: LAPACK: a portable linear algebra library for supercomputers. In: IEEE Control Systems Society Workshop on Computer-Aided Control System Design, pp. 1–7 (1989)
25. CS-Storm specification. (2014). http://www.cray.com/sites/default/files/CrayCS-Storm.pdf
26. Fang, Y.-C., Gao, Y., Stap, C.: Future enterprise computing looking into 2020. In: Park, J.J., Zomaya, A., Jeong, H.-Y., Obaidat, M. (eds.) Frontier and Innovation in Future Computing and Communications. LNEE, vol. 301, pp. 127–134. Springer, Heidelberg (2014)
27. Skiena, S.S.: The Algorithm Design Manual, vol. 1. Springer, Heidelberg (1998)
28. Zhang, P., Ling, L., Deng, Y.: A data-driven paradigm for mapping problems. Parallel Comput. (2015). doi: 10.1016/j.parco.2015.05.002 (In press)
29. Huss-Lederman, S., Jacobson, E.M., Johnson, J.R., Tsao, A., Turnbull, T.: Implementation of Strassen's algorithm for matrix multiplication. In: Proceedings of the 1996 ACM/IEEE Conference on Supercomputing, pp. 32–32 (1996)

A Framework for Batched and GPU-Resident Factorization Algorithms Applied to Block Householder Transformations

Azzam Haidar[1]($\boxtimes$), Tingxing Tim Dong[1], Stanimire Tomov[1], Piotr Luszczek[1], and Jack Dongarra[1,2,3]

[1] University of Tennessee, Knoxville, USA
haidar@icl.utk.edu
[2] Oak Ridge National Laboratory, Oak Ridge, USA
[3] University of Manchester, Manchester, UK

Abstract. As modern hardware keeps evolving, an increasingly effective approach to developing energy efficient and high-performance solvers is to design them to work on many small size and independent problems. Many applications already need this functionality, especially for GPUs, which are currently known to be about four to five times more energy efficient than multicore CPUs. We describe the development of one-sided factorizations that work for a set of small dense matrices in parallel, and we illustrate our techniques on the QR factorization based on Householder transformations. We refer to this mode of operation as a *batched factorization*. Our approach is based on representing the algorithms as a sequence of batched BLAS routines for GPU-only execution. This is in contrast to the hybrid CPU-GPU algorithms that rely heavily on using the multicore CPU for specific parts of the workload. But for a system to benefit fully from the GPU's significantly higher energy efficiency, avoiding the use of the multicore CPU must be a primary design goal, so the system can rely more heavily on the more efficient GPU. Additionally, this will result in the removal of the costly CPU-to-GPU communication. Furthermore, we do not use a single symmetric multiprocessor (on the GPU) to factorize a single problem at a time. We illustrate how our performance analysis, and the use of profiling and tracing tools, guided the development and optimization of our batched factorization to achieve up to a 2-fold speedup and a 3-fold energy efficiency improvement compared to our highly optimized batched CPU implementations based on the MKL library (when using two sockets of Intel Sandy Bridge CPUs). Compared to a batched QR factorization featured in the CUBLAS library for GPUs, we achieved up to 5× speedup on the K40 GPU.

1 Introduction

Accelerators and coprocessors have enjoyed widespread adoption in computational science, consistently producing many-fold speedups across a wide range of scientific disciplines and important applications [13]. The typical method of

© Springer International Publishing Switzerland 2015
J.M. Kunkel and T. Ludwig (Eds.): ISC High Performance 2015, LNCS 9137, pp. 31–47, 2015.
DOI: 10.1007/978-3-319-20119-1_3

utilizing the GPU accelerators is to increase the scale and resolution of an application, which in turn increases its computational intensity; this tends to be a good match for the steady growth in performance and memory capacity of this type of hardware. Unfortunately, there are many important application types for which the standard approach turns out to be a poor strategy for improving hardware utilization[1]. Numerous modern applications tend to be cast in terms of a solution of *many small matrix operations*, e.g., computations that require tensor contraction (such as quantum Hall effect), astrophysics [28], metabolic networks [26], CFD and the resulting PDEs through direct and multifrontal solvers [45], high-order FEM schemes for hydrodynamics [10], direct-iterative preconditioned solvers [20], and some image [29] and signal processing [5]. That is, at some point in their execution, such programs must perform a computation that is cumulatively very large, but whose individual parts are very small; these parts cannot be efficiently mapped as separate individuals on to the modern accelerator hardware. Under these circumstances, the only way to achieve good performance is to find a way to group these small inputs together and run them in large "batches."

The emergence of large-scale, heterogeneous systems with GPU accelerators and coprocessors has made the *near total absence of linear algebra software for such small matrix operations* especially noticeable. Due to the high levels of parallelism they support, accelerators or coprocessors, like GPUs, efficiently achieve very high performance on large data parallel computations, so they have often been used in combination with CPUs, where the CPU handles the small and difficult to parallelize tasks. Moreover, by using efficient GPU-only codes, linear algebra problems can be solved on GPUs with four to five times more energy efficiency than one can get from multicore CPUs alone citebatchedCholesky. For both of these reasons, and given the fundamental importance of numerical libraries to science and engineering applications of all types [25], the need for software that can perform batched operations on small matrices is acute. The concepts in this paper work towards filling this critical gap, both by providing a library that addresses a significant range of small matrix problems, and by driving progress toward a standard interface that would allow the entire linear algebra (LA) community to attack the issues together.

To better understand the problem, consider Fig. 1, which shows a simple batched computation that factorizes a sequence of small matrices A_i. The word *small* is used in relative terms as the beneficial size of A_i will depend on the circumstances. A straightforward guideline to determine this size is the

> **for** $A_i \in A_1, A_2, \ldots, A_k$ **do**
>   GenerateSmallLinearSystem(A_i)
> **for** $A_i \in A_1, A_2, \ldots, A_k$ **do**
>   Factorize(A_i)

Fig. 1. Batched computation example.

ability of processing the matrices in parallel rather then sequentially. To achieve this goal it is necessary to co-locate a *batch* of A_i in a fast GPU store – a cache

---

[1] Historically, similar issues were associated with strong scaling [14] and were attributed to a fixed problem size.

or shared memory – and process it there with a better use of parallel execution units.

This kind of optimization cannot be made by the compiler alone for two primary reasons: the lack of standardized interfaces and the opaque implementation of the factorization routine. The former derives from the fact that, until recently, batched computations were not the primary bottleneck for scientific codes because it was the larger problems that posed a performance challenge. Once appreciable increases in the processing power and memory capacity of GPUs removed this bottleneck, the small size problems became prominent in the execution profile because they significantly increased the total execution time. The latter is a simple consequence of separation of concerns in the software engineering process, whereby the computational kernels are packaged as standalone modules that are highly optimized and cannot be inlined into the batched loop in Fig. 1. What we propose is to define the appropriate interfaces so that our implementation can work seamlessly with the compiler and use the *code replacement* technique so that the user has an option of expressing the computation as the loop shown in the figure or a single call to a routine from the new standard batch library.

Against this background, the goal of this work is two-fold: first, to deliver a high-performance numerical library for batched linear algebra subroutines tuned for the modern processor architectures and system designs. The library must include LAPACK routine equivalents for many small dense problems as well as routines for many small sparse matrix solvers, which should be constructed, as much as possible, out of calls to batched BLAS routines and their look-alikes required in the context of sparse computations. Second, and just as importantly, it must define modular interfaces so that our implementation can seamlessly work with the compiler and use *code replacement* techniques. This will provide the developers of applications, compilers, and runtime systems with the option of expressing computation as a loop (as shown in the figure), or a single call to a routine from the new batch operation standard.

As might be expected, a batched BLAS forms the foundation of the framework for the batched algorithms proposed, with other tasks building up in layers above. The goal of this approach is to achieve portability across various architectures, sustainability and ease of maintenance, as well as modularity in building up the framework's software stack. In particular, on top of the batched BLAS (by algorithmic design), we illustrate the building of a batched LAPACK. The new batched algorithms are implemented and currently released through the MAGMA 1.6.1 library [21]. The framework will allow for future work extension to batched sparse linear algebra, and application-specific batched linear algebra. Finally, all the components are wrapped up in a performance and energy autotuning framework.

In terms of the framework's sustainability, it is important to note that batched operations represent the next generation of software that will be required to efficiently execute scientific compute kernels on self-hosted accelerators that do not have accompanying CPUs, such as the next generation of Intel Xeon Phi processors, and on accelerators with a very weak host CPU, e.g., various AMD APU models and NVIDIA Tegra platforms. For such hardware, performing any non-trivial work on the host CPU would slow down the accelerator dramatically, making it essential to develop new batched routines as a basis for optimized routines for accelerator-only execution.

2   Related Work

There is a lack of numerical libraries that cover the functionalities of batched computation for GPU accelerators and coprocessors. NVIDIA started to add certain batch functions in their math libraries; NVIDIA's CUBLAS 6.5 [36] includes batched Level 3 BLAS for gemm and trsm (triangular matrix solver), the higher-level (LAPACK) LU and QR factorizations, matrix inversion, and a least squares solver. All of these routines are for uniform size matrices. AMD and Intel's MKL do not provide batched operations yet. For higher-level routines, NVIDIA provides four highly-optimized LAPACK-based routines, but they do not address the variable sizes, extended functionality, portability and device-specific redesigns of the LAPACK algorithms. Our work shows the potential of addressing these issues, e.g., as illustrated in this paper by a 3× speedup compared to the batch-optimized QR in CUBLAS.

Batched LA ideas can be applied to multicore CPUs as well. Indeed, small problems can be solved efficiently on a single core, e.g., using vendor supplied libraries such as MKL [23] or ACML [4], because the CPU's memory hierarchy would back a "natural" data reuse (small enough problems can fit into small fast memory). To further speedup the computation, beyond memory reuse, vectorization can be added to use SIMD supplementary processor instructions—either explicitly as in the Intel Small Matrix Library [22], or implicitly through the vectorization in BLAS. Batched factorizations can then be efficiently computed for multicore CPUs by having a single core factorize a single problem at a time. However, as we will show in this paper, the energy consumption is higher than the GPU-based factorizations, and our GPU-based routine is about 2 times faster than the multicore implementation.

Despite the lack of support for batched operations, application developers implemented particular routines for certain cases, trying various approaches. For example, when targeting very small problems (matrix sizes up to 128), Villa et al. [37,38] obtained good results for batched LU developed entirely for GPU execution, where a single CUDA thread, or a single thread block, was used to solve one system at a time. Similar techniques, including the use of a single CUDA thread warp for single factorization, were investigated by Wainwright [43] for LU with full pivoting on matrix sizes up to 32. Although the problems considered were often small enough to fit in the GPU's shared memory, e.g., 48 KB on a K40 GPU, and thus able to benefit from data reuse, the results showed that the performance in these approaches, up to about 20 Gflop/s in double precision, did not exceed the performance of memory bound kernels like gemv (which achieves up to 46 Gflop/s on a K40 GPU). Batched-specific algorithmic improvements were introduced for the Cholesky factorization [9] and the LU factorization [8,17], that exceed the memory bound limitations mentioned above in terms of performance. Here we further develop and conceptualize an approach, based on batched BLAS plus a number of batched-specific algorithmic innovations to significantly improve in performance the previously published results on batched linear algebra.

3 Methodology and Algorithmic Design

In a number of research papers [8,9,19], we have shown that high-performance batched algorithms can be designed so that the computation is performed by calls to batched BLAS kernels, to the extent possible by the current BLAS API. This is important since the use of BLAS has been crucial for the high-performance sustainability of major numerical libraries for decades, and therefore we can also leverage the lessons learned from that success. To enable the effective use of a batched BLAS based approach, there is a need to develop highly efficient and optimized batched BLAS routines that are needed by many high-level linear algebra algorithms such as Cholesky, LU, and QR, either in batched or classical fashion.

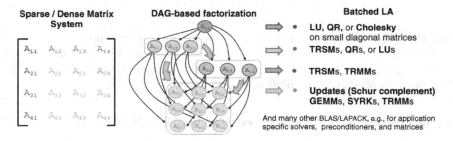

Fig. 2. Direct sparse or dense factorizations—a DAG approach that needs efficient computation of many small linear algebra tasks. Thin DAG edges represent data dependencies among individual small tasks and if small data-parallel tasks are grouped together in batches, the thick edges represent dependencies among the resulting batched tasks.

To put the proposed methodology in context, Fig. 2 illustrates our work on direct linear system solvers, be it sparse or dense, for many-core heterogeneous architectures. To provide parallelism in these solvers, the computation can be expressed as a Directed Acyclic Graph (DAG) of small tasks with labeled edges designating data dependencies, which naturally leads to the need to handle many small LA problems in parallel. Our work with vendors (through vendor recognition centers), collaborators (from the HPC community), and application developers has resulted in the accumulation of expertise, technologies, and numerical software [1,3,6,7,12,15,27,30–32,40–42,42] that can be directly leveraged in the development of state-of-the-art, portable, cross-platform batched BLAS. The objective of our methodology is to minimize the development effort and have a parametrized kernels that can be used for tuning on different architectures without the need to re-implement the kernel.

3.1 Algorithmic Baseline

The QR factorization of an m-by-n matrix A is of the form $A = QR$, where Q is an m-by-m orthonormal matrix, and R is an m-by-n upper-triangular matrix. The LAPACK routine GEQRF implements a right-looking QR factorization algorithm, whose first step consists of the following two phases:

1) **Panel factorization:** The first panel $A_{:,1}$ is transformed into an upper-triangular matrix.
   1. GEQR2 computes an m-by-m Householder matrix H_1 such that $H_1^T A_{:,1} = \begin{pmatrix} R_{1,1} \\ 0 \end{pmatrix}$, and $R_{1,1}$ is an n_b-by-n_b upper-triangular matrix.
   2. LARFT computes a block representation of the transformation H_1, i.e., $H_1 = I - V_1 T_1 V_1^H$, where V_1 is an m-by-n_b matrix and T_1 is an n_b-by-n_b upper-triangular matrix.
2) **Trailing submatrix update:** LARFB applies the transformation computed by GEQR2 and LARFT to the submatrix $A_{:,2:n_t}$:

$$\begin{pmatrix} R_{1,2:n_t} \\ \widehat{A} \end{pmatrix} := (I - V_1 T_1 V_1^H) \begin{pmatrix} A_{1,2:n_t} \\ A_{2:m_t,2:n_t} \end{pmatrix}.$$

Then, the QR factorization of A is computed by recursively applying the same transformation to the submatrix $\widehat{A}$. The transformations V_j are stored in the lower-triangular part of A, while R is stored in the upper-triangular part. Additional m-by-n_b storage is required to store T_j.

3.2 Optimized and Parametrized Batched BLAS Kernels

We developed the most needed and performance-critical Level 3 and Level 2 batched BLAS routines. Namely, we developed the batched gemm (general matrix-matrix multiplication), trsm (triangular matrix solver), and gemv (general matrix-vector product) routines, as well as a number of Level 1 BLAS such as the dot product, the norm functionality, and the scal scaling routine. There are a number of feasible design choices for batched BLAS, each best suited for a particular case. Therefore, to capture as many of them as possible, we designed a space for batched BLAS that includes parametrized algorithms enabling an ease of tuning for modern and future hardware and take into account the matrix size. Thus, a parametrized-tuned approach can find the optimal implementation within the confines of the said design space.

We developed a parametrized basic kernel, that uses multiple levels of blocking, including shared memory and register blocking, as well as double buffering techniques to hide the data communication with the computation. This kernel allowed us to optimize and tune the MAGMA gemm routine for large matrix sizes — originally for Fermi GPUs [32], and later for the Kepler GPUs. Recently, we extended it to a batched gemm [18,19], and it is now available through MAGMA 1.6.1 [21]. The extension was done by autotuning the basic kernel and adding one more thread dimension to account for the batch count. Our goal is to develop optimized components that can be used easily as a plug-in device routine to provide many of the Level 3 and Level 2 BLAS routines. Following the techniques for batched gemm for example, we developed a batched trsm kernel. It consists of a sequence of calls to invert a 16×16 diagonal block followed by a call to the gemm components which are already optimized and tuned.

Moreover, we developed the batched equivalent of LAPACK's geqr2 routine to perform the Householder panel factorizations. For a panel of nb columns, it consists of nb steps where each step calls a sequence of the larfg and the larf routines. At every step (to compute one column), the larfg involves a norm computation followed by a scal that uses the results of the norm computation in addition to some underflow/overflow checking. These Level 1 BLAS kernels have been developed as device component routines to all for easy plug-in when needed. The norm computation is a sum reduce and thus a synchronization step. To accelerate it, we implemented a two-layer tree reduction where, for sizes larger than 32, all 32 threads of a warp progress to do a tree reduction similar to the MPI_REDUCE operation, and the last 32 elements are reduced by a single thread. Our parametrized technique lets us run our autotuner and tune these kernels. As a result, custom batched implementations of both larfg and the larf have been developed. When the panel size is small enough, we use the shared memory to load the whole panel and to perform its computation in fast memory. For larger panel sizes, we load only the vector that is annihilated at each step, meaning that the norm, scal, and thus the larfg computation operate on data in shared memory; the larf reads data from shared memory, but writes data in main memory since it cannot fit into the shared memory. When the panel is very large, the BLAS kernel operates using many thread-blocks and an atomic synchronization.

3.3 Development of Batched LAPACK Algorithms

The development of batched LAPACK algorithms and implementations is our main example of how to use the batched BLAS for higher-level algorithms. We show an approach based on batched BLAS and batched-specific algorithmic improvements that overcomes the memory bound limitations that previous developers had on small problems. Moreover, we exceed the performance of even state-of-the-art vendor implementations by up to $3\times$. Similarly to the batched BLAS, we build a design space for batched LAPACK that includes parametrized algorithms that are architecture and matrix size aware. An autotuning approach is used to find the best implementation within the provisioned design space.

We developed the performance-critical LAPACK routines to solve small dense linear systems or least squares problems. Namely, we developed the LU and Cholesky factorizations previously in [8,9,19], and we present our progress and development for the QR decomposition in this paper.

We developed technologies for deriving high-performance from GPU-only implementations to solve sets of small linear algebra problems (as in LAPACK) in parallel. Note that GPU-only implementations have been avoided up until recently in numerical libraries, especially for small and difficult to parallelize tasks like the ones targeted by the batched factorization. Indeed, hybridization approaches were at the forefront of developing large scale solvers as they were successfully resolving the problem by using CPUs for the memory bound tasks [2,11,16,40,44]. For large problems, the panel factorizations (the source of memory bound, not easy to parallelize tasks) are always performed on the CPU. For small problems, however, this is not possible, and our experience has shown that hybrid algorithms would not be as efficient as they are for large problems. Therefore, we developed an approach based on a combination of 1) batched BLAS, 2) batched-specific, and 3) architecture-aware algorithmic improvements. Batched-specific algorithms that were different from LAPACK were needed since we could not outperform the NVIDIA-optimized LAPACK-based implementation by only using our own aggressive optimizations on top of the standard LAPACK algorithm. In particular, for our QR decomposition, besides high-performance batched BLAS, we also used batch-specific and architecture-aware algorithmic advances described below.

Recursive Multilevel Nested Blocking. The panel factorizations (geqr2) described above factorize the nb columns one after another, similarly to the LAPACK algorithm. At each of the nb steps, a rank-1 update is required to update the vectors to the right of the factorized column i. This operation is done by the larf kernel. Since we cannot load the entire panel into the shared memory of the GPU, the columns to the right are loaded back and forth from the main memory at every step except for the very small size cases (e.g., size less than 32×8). Thus, one can expect that this is the most time consuming part of the panel factorization.

Our analysis using the NVIDIA Visual Profiler [33] shows that a large fraction of even a highly optimized batched factorization is spent in the panels, e.g., 40 % of the time for the QR decomposition. The profiler reveals that the larf kernel requires more than 75% of the panel time by itself. The inefficient behavior of these routines is also due to the memory access. To resolve this challenge, we propose to improve the efficiency of the panel and to reduce the memory access by using a two-level nested blocking technique as depicted in Fig. 3. First, we recursively split the panel to an acceptable block size nb as described in Fig. 3. In principle, the panel can be blocked recursively until a single element remains. Yet, in practice, 2-3 blocked levels (an $nb = 32$ for double precision was the best) are sufficient to achieve high performance. Then, the routine that performs the panel factorization (geqr2) must be optimized, which complicates the implementation. This optimization can bring between 30 % to 40 % improvement depending on the panel and the matrix size. In order to reach our optimization goal, we also blocked the panel routine using the classical blocking fashion to small blocks of size ib ($ib = 8$ was the optimized choice for double precision) as described in Fig. 3b. More than a 25% boost in performance is obtained with this optimization.

Block Recursive dlarft Algorithm. The larft is used to compute the upper triangular matrix T that is needed by the QR factorization in order to update either the trailing matrix or the right hand side of the recursive portion of the

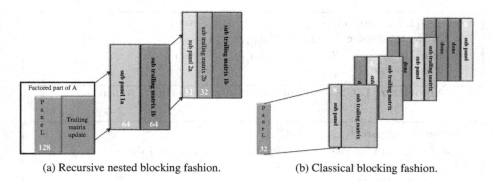

(a) Recursive nested blocking fashion.   (b) Classical blocking fashion.

Fig. 3. The recursive two-level nested blocking fashion is used in our implementation to achieve high-performance batched kernels.

QR panel. The classical LAPACK computes T column by column in a loop over the nb columns as described in Algorithm 1. Such an implementation takes up to 50% of the total QR factorization time. This is due to the fact that the kernels needed – gemv and trmv – require implementations where threads go through the matrix in different directions (horizontal vs. vertical, respectively). An analysis of the mathematical formula of computing T allowed us to redesign the algorithm to use Level 3 BLAS and to increase the data reuse by putting the column of T in shared memory. One can observe that the loop can be split into two loops – one for gemv and one for trmv. The gemv loop that computes each column of $\widehat{T}$ (see the notation in Algorithm 1 can be replaced by one gemm to compute all the columns of $\widehat{T}$ if the triangular upper portion of A is zero and the diagonal is made of ones. For our implementation, replacing a gemv loop with one gemm is already done for the trailing matrix update in the larfb routine, and thus can be exploited here as well. For the trmv phase, we load the T matrix into shared memory as this allows all threads to read/write from/into shared memory during the nb steps of the loop. The redesign of this routine is depicted in Algorithm 2. Since we developed a recursive blocking algorithm, we must compute the T matrix for every level of the recursion. Nevertheless, the analysis of Algorithm 2 leads us to conclude that the portion of the T's computed in the lower recursion level are the same as the diagonal blocks of the T of the upper level (yellow diagonal blocks in Fig. 4), and thus we can avoid their (re-)computation. For that we modified Algorithm 2 in order to compute either the whole T or the upper rectangular portion that is missed (red/yellow portions in Fig. 4). Redesigning the algorithm to block the computation using Level 3 BLAS accelerated the overall algorithm on average by about $20 - 30\,\%$ (depending on various parameters).

Trading Extra Computation for Higher Performance. The goal here is to replace the use of low performance kernels with higher performance ones— often for the cost of more flops, e.g., trmm used by the larfb can be replaced by

---

for $j \in \{1, 2, \ldots, nb\}$ **do**

    dgemv to compute $\widehat{T}_{1:j-1,j} = A^H_{j:m,1:j-1} \times A_{j:m,j}$

    dtrmv to compute $T_{1:j-1,j} = T_{1:j-1,1:j-1} \times \widehat{T}_{1:j-1,j}$

    $T(j,j) = tau(j)$

Algorithm 1. Classical implementation of the dlarft routine.

---

dgemm to compute $\widehat{T}_{1:nb,1:nb} = A^H_{1:m,1:nb} \times A_{1:m,1:nb}$

load $\widehat{T}_{1:nb,1:nb}$ to the shared memory. **for** $j \in \{1, 2, \ldots, nb\}$ **do**

    dtrmv to compute $T_{1:j-1,j} = T_{1:j-1,1:j-1} \times \widehat{T}_{1:j-1,j}$

    $T(j,j) = tau(j)$

write back T to the main memory.

Algorithm 2. Block recursive dlarft routine.

gemm. The QR trailing matrix update uses the larfb routine to perform $A = (I - VT^HV^H)A$. The upper triangle of V is zero with ones on the diagonal, and also the matrix T is upper triangular. The classical larfb uses trmm to perform the multiplication with T and with the upper portion of V. If one can guarantee that the lower portion of T is filled with zeroes and the upper portion of V is filled with zeros and ones on the diagonal, then the trmm can be replaced by gemm. Thus we implemented a batched larfb that uses three gemm kernels by initializing the lower portion of T with zeros, and filling up the upper portion of V with zeroes and ones on the diagonal. Note that this brings $3nb^3$ extra operations. The benefits again depend on various parameters, but on current architectures we observe an average of 10 % improvement, and see a trend where its effect on the acceleration grows from older to newer systems.

4 Performance Results

4.1 Hardware Description and Setup

We conducted our experiments on a two-socket multicore system with two 8-core Intel Xeon E5-2670 (Sandy Bridge) processors, each running at 2.6 GHz. Each socket has 20 MiB of shared Level 3 cache, and each core has a private 256 KiB Level 2 and 64 KiB Level 1 cache. The system is equipped with the total of 52 GiB of main memory and a theoretical peak, in double precision, of 20.8 Gflop/s per core, i.e., 332.8 Glop/s in total for the two sockets. It is also equipped with three NVIDIA K40c cards with 11.6 GiB of GDDR memory per card running at 825 MHz. The theoretical peak in double precision is 1,689.6 Gflop/s per GPU. The cards are connected to the host via two PCIe I/O hubs with 6 GB/s bandwidth. A number of software packages were used for the experiments. On the CPU side, we used MKL (Math Kernel Library) [23] with the icc compiler (version 2013.sp1.2.144) and on the GPU accelerator we used CUDA version 6.5.14.

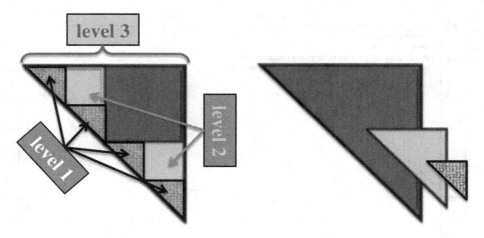

Fig. 4. The shape of the matrix T for different level of the recursion during the QR decomposition.

Regarding energy use, we note that in this particular setup the CPU and the GPU have about the same theoretical power draw. In particular, the Thermal Design Power (TDP) of the Intel Sandy Bridge is 115 W per socket, or 230 W in total, while the TDP of the K40c GPU is 235 W. Therefore, we expect that a GPU would have a power consumption advantage if it outperforms (in terms of time to solution) the 16 Sandy Bridge cores. Note that, based on the theoretical peaks, the GPU's advantage should be about 4 to 5×. This is observed in practice as well, especially for regular workloads on large data-parallel problems that can be efficiently implemented for GPUs.

4.2 Performance Results

Getting high performance across accelerators remains a challenging problem that we address with the algorithmic and programming techniques described in this paper. These efficient strategies are used to exploit parallelism and increase the use of Level 3 BLAS operations across the GPU. We highlighted this through a set of experiments that we performed on our system. We compare our batched implementations with the dgeqrfBatched routine from the CUBLAS [35] library. Our experiments were performed on batches of 1,000 matrices of different sizes ranging from 32 × 32 to 1024 × 1024.

We also compare our batched QR to two CPU implementations. First is the simple CPU implementation which operates in a loop style to factorize matrix after matrix, where each factorization is using the multi-thread version of the MKL Library. This implementation is limited in terms of performance and does not achieve more than 90 Gflop/s. The main reason for this low performance is the fact that the matrix is small – it does not exhibit parallelism and so the multithreaded code is not able to feed work to all 16 threads used. For that we

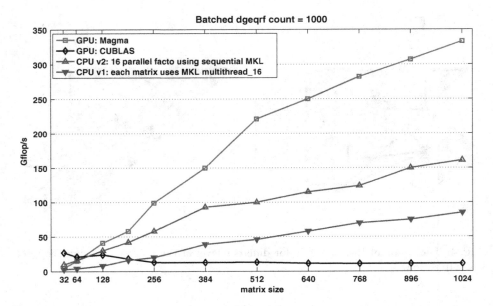

Fig. 5. Performance in Gflops/s of the GPU *vs.* the CPU versions of our batched QR decomposition for different matrix sizes, where $m = n$.

proposed another version of the CPU implementation. Since the matrices are small (< 1024) and at least 16 of them fit in the Level 3 cache, one of the best techniques is to use each thread to independently factorize a matrix. This way 16 factorizations are conducted independently, in parallel. We believe that this implementation is one of the best optimized implementations for the CPU. This later implementation is 2× faster than the simple implementation. It reaches around 160 Gflop/s in factorizing 1,000 matrices of size 1024×1024.

The progress of our batched QR implementation over the various optimizations shows promise. For a 1000 matrix of size 512×512 each, the classical block implementation does not attain more than 55 Gflop/s. The inner panel blocking allows for performance of around 70 Gflop/s; and the recursive blocking alone improves performance up to 108 Gflop/s; combined, the two-level blocking brings performance up to around 136 Gflop/s. The optimized computation of T draws it up to 195 Gflop/s. The other optimizations (replacing dtrmm with dgemm in both dlarft and dlarfb), combined with the streamed/batched dgemm calls, bring the performance of the GPU implementation to around 221 Gflop/s. Despite the CPU's hierarchical memory advantage, our experiments show that our GPU batched QR factorization is able to achieve a speedup of 2× *vs.* the best CPU implementation using 16 Sandy Bridge cores, and 4× *vs.* the simple one. Moreover, our algorithm — which reaches around 334 Gflop/s for matrices of size 1024×1024 — is between 5× to 20× faster than the CUBLAS implementation for matrices in the range of 512 to 1024. We should mention that the CUBLAS implementation is well suited for very small matrices such as matrices of size less than 64×64. The performance of CUBLAS for these sizes outperforms our proposed algorithm as well as both of the CPU implementations Fig. 5.

4.3   Energy Efficiency

For our energy efficiency measurements, we use power and energy estimators built into the modern hardware platforms. In particular, on the tested CPU, the Intel Xeon E5-2690, we use RAPL (Runtime Average Power Limiting) hardware counters [24,39]. By the vendor's own admission, the reported power/energy numbers are based on a model which is tuned to match the actual measurements for various workloads. Given this caveat, we can report that the idle power of the tested Sandy Bridge CPU, running at a fixed frequency of 2600 MHz, consumes about 20 W of power per socket. Batched operations raise the consumption from 125 to 140 W per socket, and the large dense matrix operations, which reach the highest fraction of the peak performance, raise the power draw to about 160 W per socket. We should mention that the CPU measurements do not include the power cost of the memory access, while the GPU measurements include it. In order to include the power for the CPU, we had to change in the BIOS and we were not allowed to do it on our testing machine. However, results on other systems showed that the power of the CPU memory access can be estimated to be 40 W on average. On some systems, energy consumption numbers do not include the power consumed by the main memory as the memory modules do not report their voltage levels to the CPU's memory controller on those systems, which renders RAPL ineffective for the purpose of estimating temporal power draw. However, based on estimates from similarly configured systems, we estimate that the power consumption for the main memory under load is between 30 W and 40 W, depending on the memory size and configuration.

For the GPU measurements we use NVIDIA's NVML (NVIDIA Management Library) library [34]. NVML provides a C-based programmatic interface for monitoring and managing various states within NVIDIA Tesla GPUs. On Fermi and Kepler GPUs (like the K40c used) the readings are reported to be accurate to within +/-5% of current power draw. The idle state of the K40c GPU consumes about 20 W. Batched factorizations raise the consumption from 150 to 180 W, while large dense matrix operations raise the power draw to about 200 W. For reference, it is worth noting that the active idle state draws 62 W.

In Fig. 6 we depict the comparison of the power consumption required by the three implementations of the batched QR decomposition: the best GPU and the two CPU implementations. The problem solved here is about 1,000 matrices of size 1024 × 1024 each. The green curve shows the power required by the simple CPU implementation. In this case the batched QR proceeds as a loop over the 1,000 matrices where each matrix is factorized using the multithreaded dgeqrf routine from the Intel MKL library on the 16 Sandy Bridge CPU cores. The blue curve shows the power required by the optimized CPU implementation. Here, the code proceeds with sweeps of 16 parallel factorizations each using the sequential dgeqrf routine form the Intel MKL library. The red curve shows the power consumption of our GPU implementation of the batched QR decomposition. One can observe that the GPU implementation is attractive because it is around 2× faster than the optimized CPU implementation, and moreover, because it consumes 3× less energy.

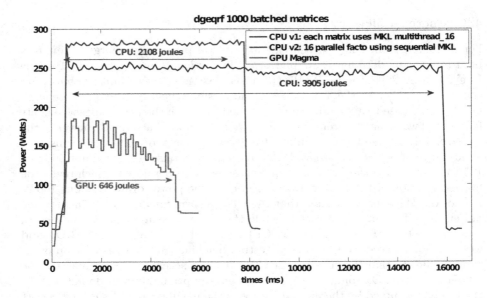

Fig. 6. Comparison of the power consumption for the QR decomposition of 1,000 matrices of size 1024 × 1024.

According to the experiments we conducted to measure the power, we found that the GPU implementations of all of the batched one-sided factorizations reach around 2× speedup over their best CPU counterpart and are 3× less expensive in terms of energy consumption.

5   Conclusions an Future Work

Designing algorithms to work on small problems is a concept that can deliver higher performance through improved data reuse. Many applications have relied on this design concept to get higher hardware efficiency, and users have requested it as a supported functionality in linear algebra libraries. Besides having the potential to improve the overall performance of applications with computational patterns ranging from dense to sparse linear algebra, developing these algorithms for the new low-powered and power-efficient architectures can bring significant savings in energy consumption as well, as we showed. Therefore, by solving the technical issues and providing the needed batched LA tools, the future development on the framework presented will also address the following long term goals: 1) define a new standard for the use of small matrix computations in applications; 2) provide a methodology to solve many small size LA problems and an initial implementation that is portable at all levels of the platform pyramid, from embedded devices to supercomputers; and 3) establish grounds for the next generation of innovations in HPC applications and sustainability of high-performance numerical libraries. The algorithms described are already available in the open-source MAGMA library. The proposed framework and the algorithms to be developed for batched linear algebra will be open for input and contributions from the community, similar to LAPACK, and will be incorporated into the MAGMA Batched library.

Future work extensions include building batched sparse, and application-specific batched linear algebra capabilities. Of specific interest will be the effect of the batched framework on high-performance numerical libraries and run-time systems. Current approaches, e.g., in dense tiled algorithms, are based on splitting algorithms into small tasks that get inserted into, and scheduled for execution by, a run-time system. This often amounts to splitting large gemms into many small gemms, which is known to encounter overheads for scheduling and saving parameters (although most are the same). The batched approach, besides providing high performance for small tasks, will be a natural fit to extend these and similar libraries, as well as provide a new hierarchical scheduling model for queuing jobs, organizing run-time systems, and interacting with accelerators/co-processors.

Acknowledgments. This material is based upon work supported by the National Science Foundation under Grant No. ACI-1339822, the Department of Energy, and Intel. The results were obtained in part with the financial support of the Russian Scientific Fund, Agreement N14-11-00190.

References

1. Agullo, E., Demmel, J., Dongarra, J., Hadri, B., Kurzak, J., Langou, J., Ltaief, H., Luszczek, P., Tomov, S.: Numerical linear algebra on emerging architectures: the PLASMA and MAGMA projects. J. Phys.: Conf. Ser. **180**(1), 012037 (2009)
2. Agullo, E., Augonnet, C., Dongarra, J., Ltaief, H., Namyst, R., Thibault, S., Tomov, S.: Faster, cheaper, better - a hybridization methodology to develop linear algebra software for GPUS. In: Hwu, W.W. (ed.) GPU Computing Gems. Morgan Kaufmann, California (2010)
3. Agullo, E., Dongarra, J., Nath, R.,Tomov, S.: Fully empirical autotuned qr factorization for multicore architectures (2011). CoRR, abs/1102.5328
4. ACML - AMD Core Math Library (2014). http://developer.amd.com/tools-and-sdks/cpu-development/amd-core-math-library-acml
5. Anderson, M.J., Sheffield, D., Keutzer. K.: A predictive model for solving small linear algebra problems in gpu registers. In: IEEE 26th International Parallel Distributed Processing Symposium (IPDPS) (2012)
6. Buttari, A., Dongarra, J., Kurzak, J., Langou, J., Luszczek, P., Tomov, S.: The impact of multicore on math software. In: Kågström, B., Elmroth, E., Dongarra, J., Waśniewski, J. (eds.) PARA 2006. LNCS, vol. 4699, pp. 1–10. Springer, Heidelberg (2007)
7. Cao, C., Dongarra, J., Du, P., Gates, M., Luszczek, P., Tomov, S.: clMAGMA: high performance dense linear algebra with OpenCL. In: The ACM International Conference Series, Atlanta, May 13–14 (2013). (submitted)
8. Dong, T., Haidar, A., Luszczek, P., Harris, A., Tomov, S., Dongarra, J.: LU factorization of small matrices: accelerating batched DGETRF on the GPU. In: Proceedings of 16th IEEE International Conference on High Performance and Communications (HPCC 2014), August 2014

9. Dong, T., Haidar, A., Tomov, S., Dongarra, J.: A fast batched cholesky factorization on a GPU. In: Proceedings of 2014 International Conference on Parallel Processing (ICPP-2014), September 2014
10. Dong, T., Dobrev, V., Kolev, T., Rieben, R., Tomov, S., Dongarra, J.: A step towards energy efficient computing: redesigning a hydrodynamic application on CPU-GPU. In: IEEE 28th International Parallel Distributed Processing Symposium (IPDPS) (2014)
11. Dongarra, J., Haidar, A., Kurzak, J., Luszczek, P., Tomov, S., YarKhan, A.: Model-driven one-sided factorizations on multicore accelerated systems. Int. J.Supercomputing Frontiers Innovations 1(1), 85 (2014)
12. Peng, D., Weber, R., Luszczek, P., Tomov, S., Peterson, G., Dongarra, J.: From CUDA to OpenCL: towards a performance-portable solution for multi-platform GPU programming. Parallel Comput. 38(8), 391–407 (2012)
13. Oak Ridge Leadership Computing Facility. Annual report 2013–2014 (2014). https://www.olcf.ornl.gov/wp-content/uploads/2015/01/AR_2014_Small.pdf
14. Gustafson, J.L.: Reevaluating Amdahl's law. Commun. ACM 31(5), 532–533 (1988)
15. Haidar, A., Tomov, S., Dongarra, J., Solca, R., Schulthess, T.: A novel hybrid CPU-GPU generalized eigensolver for electronic structure calculations based on fine grained memory aware tasks. Int. J. High Perform. Comput. Appl. 28(2), 196–209 (2012)
16. Haidar, A., Cao, C., Yarkhan, A., Luszczek, P., Tomov, S., Kabir, K., Dongarra, J.: Unified development for mixed multi-gpu and multi-coprocessor environments using a lightweight runtime environment. In: IPDPS 2014 Proceedings of the 2014 IEEE 28th International Parallel and Distributed Processing Symposium, pp. 491–500. IEEE Computer Society, Washington, (2014)
17. Haidar, A., Dong, T., Luszczek, P., Tomov, S., Dongarra, J.: Batched matrix computations on hardware accelerators based on GPUs. Int. J. High Performance Comput. Appl. 18(1), 135–158 (2015). doi:10.1177/1094342014567546
18. Haidar, A., Luszczek, P., Tomov, S., Dongarra, J.: Optimization for performance and energy for batched matrix computations on GPUs. In: PPoPP 2015 8th Workshop on General Purpose Processing Using GPUs (GPGPU 8) co-located with PPOPP 2015, ACM, San Francisco, February 2015
19. Haidar, A., Luszczek, P., Tomov, S., Dongarra, J.: Towards batched linear solvers on accelerated hardware platforms. In: PPoPP 2015 Proceedings of the 20th ACM SIGPLAN Symposium on Principles and Practice of Parallel Programming, ACM, San Francisco, February 2015
20. Im, E.-J., Yelick, K., Vuduc, R.: Sparsity: optimization framework for sparse matrix kernels. Int. J. High Perform. Comput. Appl. 18(1), 135–158 (2004)
21. Matrix algebra on GPU and multicore architectures (MAGMA), MAGMA Release 1.6.1 (2015). http://icl.cs.utk.edu/magma/
22. Intel Pentium III Processor - Small Matrix Library (1999). http://www.intel.com/design/pentiumiii/sml/
23. Intel Math Kernel Library (2014). http://software.intel.com/intel-mkl/
24. Intel 64 and IA-32 architectures software developer's manual, July 20 (2014). http://download.intel.com/products/processor/manual/
25. Keyes, D., Taylor, V.: NSF-ACCI task force on software for science and engineering, December 2010
26. Liao, J.C., Khodayari, A., Zomorrodi, A.R., Maranas, C.D.: A kinetic model of escherichia coli core metabolism satisfying multiple sets of mutant flux data. Metab. Eng. 25C, 50–62 (2014)

27. Li, Y., Dongarra, J., Tomov, S.: A note on auto-tuning GEMM for GPUs. In: Allen, G., Nabrzyski, J., Seidel, E., van Albada, G.D., Dongarra, J., Sloot, P.M.A. (eds.) ICCS 2009, Part I. LNCS, vol. 5544, pp. 884–892. Springer, Heidelberg (2009)
28. Messer, O.E.B., Harris, J.A., Parete-Koon, S., Chertkow, M.A.: Multicore and accelerator development for a leadership-class stellar astrophysics code. In: Manninen, P., Öster, P. (eds.) PARA. LNCS, vol. 7782, pp. 92–106. Springer, Heidelberg (2013)
29. Molero, J.M., Garzón, E.M., García, I., Quintana-Ortí, E.S, Plaza, A.: Poster: a batched Cholesky solver for local RX anomaly detection on GPUs. In: PUMPS (2013)
30. Nath, R., Tomov,S., Dong, T., Dongarra, T.: Optimizing symmetric dense matrix-vectormultiplication on GPUs. In: Proceedings of 2011 International Conference for High PerformanceComputing, Networking, Storage and Analysis, November 2011
31. Nath, R., Tomov, S., Dongarra, T.: Accelerating GPU kernels for dense linear algebra. In: VECPAR 2010 Proceedings of the 2009 International Meeting on High Performance Computing for Computational Science, pp. 22–25. Springer, Berkeley, June 2010
32. Nath, R., Tomov, S., Dongarra, J.: An improved magma gemm for fermi graphics processing units. Int. J. High Perform. Comput. Appl. **24**(4), 511–515 (2010)
33. Nvidia visual profiler
34. https://developer.nvidia.com/nvidia-management-library-nvml (2014)
35. CUBLAS (2014). http://docs.nvidia.com/cuda/cublas/
36. CUBLAS 6.5, January 2015. http://docs.nvidia.com/cuda/cublas/
37. Villa, O., Fatica, M., Gawande, N., Tumeo, A.: Power/performance trade-offs of small batched LU based solvers on GPUs. In: Wolf, F., Mohr, B., an Mey, D. (eds.) Euro-Par 2013. LNCS, vol. 8097, pp. 813–825. Springer, Heidelberg (2013)
38. Nitin, V.O., Gawande, A., Tumeo, A.: Accelerating subsurface transport simulation on heterogeneous clusters. In: IEEE International Conference on Cluster Computing (CLUSTER 2013), pp. 23–27, Indiana, September 2013
39. Rotem, E., Naveh, A., Rajwan, D., Ananthakrishnan, A., Weissmann, E.: Power-management architecture of the intel microarchitecture code-named sandy bridge. IEEE Micro. **32**(2), 20–27 (2012). doi:10.1109/MM.2012.12. ISSN: 0272-1732
40. Tomov, S., Dongarra, J., Baboulin, M.: Towards dense linear algebra for hybrid gpu accelerated manycore systems. Parellel Comput. Syst. Appl. **36**(5–6), 232–240 (2010). doi:10.1016/j.parco.2009.12.005
41. Tomov, S., Nath, R., Ltaief, H., Dongarra, J.: Dense linear algebra solvers for multicore with GPU accelerators. In: Proceedings of the IEEE IPDPS 2010, pp. 1–8. IEEE Computer Society, Atlanta, 19–23 April 2010. doi:10.1109/IPDPSW.2010.5470941
42. Tomov, S., Dongarra, J.: Dense linear algebra for hybrid gpu-based systems. In: Kurzak, J., Bader, D.A., Dongarra, J. (eds.) Scientific Computing with Multicore and Accelerators. Chapman and Hall/CRC, UK (2010)
43. Wainwright, I .: Optimized LU-decomposition with full pivot for small batched matrices, GTC 2013 - ID S3069. April 2013
44. Yamazaki, I., Tomov, S., Dongarra, J.: One-sided dense matrix factorizations on a multicore with multiple GPU accelerators. In: Proceedings of the International Conference on Computational Science, ICCS 2012, pp. 37–46. Procedia Computer Science, 9(0):37 (2012)
45. Yeralan, S.N., Davis, T.A., Ranka, S.: Sparse mulitfrontal QR on the GPU. Technical report, University of Florida Technical report (2013)

Parallel Efficient Sparse Matrix-Matrix Multiplication on Multicore Platforms

Md. Mostofa Ali Patwary[1]([✉]), Nadathur Rajagopalan Satish[1],
Narayanan Sundaram[1], Jongsoo Park[1], Michael J. Anderson[1],
Satya Gautam Vadlamudi[1], Dipankar Das[1], Sergey G. Pudov[2],
Vadim O. Pirogov[2], and Pradeep Dubey[1]

[1] Parallel Computing Lab, Intel Corporation, Santa Clara, USA
mostofa.ali.patwary@intel.com
[2] Software and Services Group, Intel Corporation, Santa Clara, USA

Abstract. Sparse matrix-matrix multiplication (SpGEMM) is a key kernel in many applications in High Performance Computing such as algebraic multigrid solvers and graph analytics. Optimizing SpGEMM on modern processors is challenging due to random data accesses, poor data locality and load imbalance during computation. In this work, we investigate different partitioning techniques, cache optimizations (using dense arrays instead of hash tables), and dynamic load balancing on SpGEMM using a diverse set of real-world and synthetic datasets. We demonstrate that our implementation outperforms the state-of-the-art using Intel® Xeon® processors. We are up to 3.8X faster than Intel® Math Kernel Library (MKL) and up to 257X faster than CombBLAS. We also outperform the best published GPU implementation of SpGEMM on nVidia GTX Titan and on AMD Radeon HD 7970 by up to 7.3X and 4.5X, respectively on their published datasets. We demonstrate good multi-core scalability (geomean speedup of 18.2X using 28 threads) as compared to MKL which gets 7.5X scaling on 28 threads.

1 Introduction

Sparse Matrix-Matrix Multiplication (SpGEMM) is an important kernel used in many applications in High Performance Computing such as algebraic multigrid solvers [4] and graph analytic kernels [7,10,12,17]. Compared to the efficiency of the corresponding dense GEMM routines, SpGEMM suffers from poor performance on most parallel hardware. The difficulty in optimizing SpGEMM lies in the irregular memory access patterns, unknown pattern of non-zeros in the output matrix, poor data locality and load imbalance during computation. For sparse matrices that have non-zero patterns following power law distributions (e.g. graphs from social network and recommendation system domains), this leads to poor efficiency as some portions of the output are very dense while others are very sparse.

This paper presents an optimized implementation of SpGEMM on two matrices A and B that efficiently utilizes current multicore hardware. We have parallelized SpGEMM through row and column based blocking of A and B respectively.

J.M. Kunkel and T. Ludwig (Eds.): ISC High Performance 2015, LNCS 9137, pp. 48–57, 2015.
DOI: 10.1007/978-3-319-20119-1_4

By using a dense array to accumulate partial (sparse vector) results, we get superior performance compared to previous implementations. We also maintain a CSR input and output format and include data structure transformation and memory allocation costs in our runtime.

Our main contributions are as follows:

- We present the fastest SpGEMM results on a single node on a variety of different sparse matrices drawn from various domains. Our implementation running on Intel® Xeon® E5-2697 v3 processor based system is faster than Intel® MKL by up to 3.8X and CombBLAS by up to 257X. Our implementation also outperforms previously published GPU implementations [13] on nVidia GTX Titan and on AMD Radeon HD 7970 by up to 7.3X and 4.5X, respectively.
- We have explored different partitioning schemes for SpGEMM. We provide intelligent heuristics that combine row-wise partitioning of one matrix and column-wise partitioning of the second matrix to get the best performance (up to 1.4X improvement) on a single node.
- We divide the matrices into small partitions and perform dynamic load balancing over the partitions, resulting in speedups of up to 1.49X and 1.24X respectively.
- We demonstrate good multi-core scalability (geomean speedup of 18.2X using 28 threads) as compared to MKL, which gets 7.5X scaling on 28 threads.

2 SpGEMM Algorithm and Optimizations

2.1 Overview

Sparse Matrix-Matrix Multiply (SpGEMM) involves the multiplication of two sparse matrices A of dimension $m \times k$ and B of dimension $k \times n$ to yield a resultant matrix C of dimension $m \times n$. In this paper, for presentation simplicity, we assume we deal with square matrices where $m = n = k$ (represented as n hereafter). However, our techniques are general and applicable to other matrices as well.

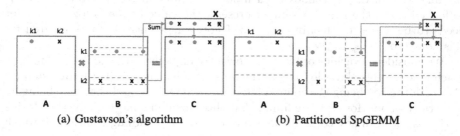

(a) Gustavson's algorithm   (b) Partitioned SpGEMM

Fig. 1. Data access pattern of Gustavson [11] and Partitioned SpGEMM algorithms.

Consider the following notations. $A_{i,j}$ denotes a single entry of matrix A. $A_{i,:}$ denotes the ith row of matrix A, and $A_{:,i}$ represents the ith column of A. Then the computation of the entire row i of C can be seen to be $C_{i,:} = \sum_k A_{i,k} * B_{k,:}$. This computation is shown in Fig. 1(a). The figure shows the situation for a sparse matrix A, where $A_{i,k}$ is non-zero only for some values of k, and computations only occur on the corresponding rows of B. The product of the scalar $A_{i,k}$ with the non-zeros in $B_{k,:}$ basically scales the elements of the row $B_{k,:}$ and has the same sparsity structure as $B_{k,:}$. This product then needs to be summed into $C_{i,:}$. Note that $C_{i,:}$ is the sum of various sparse vectors obtained from the products above, and is in general sparse, although its non-zero structure and density may be quite different from that of A and B.

Gustavson [11] proposed a single-threaded algorithm for SpGEMM based on the Compressed Sparse Row (CSR) format. This is a straightforward implementation of the computations described in Fig. 1(a). This algorithm can be parallelized over rows of A to run on multi-core processors. However, as we show below, this basic algorithm does not take full advantage of architectural features such as caches present on modern hardware and makes inefficient

```
1 part = Partition(A, B)
2 #pragma omp parallel for
  schedule(dynamic)
3 forall the p in part do
4     for all rows A_{i,:} in p do
5         Reset X to 0
6         for each nonzero A_{i,j} in A_{i,:} do
7             Load partition B_{j,cols(p)} in p
8             X += A_{i,j} · B_{j,cols(p)}
9         Sparsify X to C_{i,cols(p)}
```

Algorithm 1. Psuedocode for partitioned SpGEMM

use of the limited bandwidth available at various levels of the memory hierarchy. We now show the optimizations that we perform to overcome these bottlenecks.

2.2   Performance Optimizations

We make a number of improvements to the algorithm described previously.

Adding Sparse Vectors. Whenever a new sparse vector is to be added to the running sum for $C_{i,:}$, the index of each non-zero value in the sparse vector needs to looked up in the running sum. If present, the value of the non-zero element needs to be added to that in $C_{i,:}$, and if not, a new entry is to be created for this non-zero.

We considered various options to efficiently implement this lookup. One approach is to use a hash table to store the non-zero elements of the running sum for $C_{i,:}$, with the key being the column index of the non-zero, and the value being its numerical value. However, we found that this technique had high overheads due to (i) cost of hash key computations and (ii) cost of handling collisions through chaining.

Since the range of elements is known apriori (equal to the matrix dimension n), it is much more efficient to use a dense array to store the running sum. We initialize this array X to zero. When we need to add a new sparse vector, we take each non-zero entry and simply add its value to $X[c]$, where c is the column index of the non-zero. Finally, once all additions are complete, we need to convert this dense array back to a sparse CSR representation when writing back to C. While the additions themselves have very low overhead with this data structure, it is very inefficient to have to scan the entire dense X array (most of whose elements are zero) and write back only the few non-zero elements into a sparse format. Indeed, our experiments indicate that this scan takes more than 20X the time required for the additions themselves. Hence, in addition to X, we keep a index array that stores the non-zero indices of X. This can be cheaply maintained during the addition process by simply appending a column index c when it is first written to, i.e. when the existing array value $X[c]$ is zero. We then iterate only over this sparse index array when writing to C and reset the corresponding value in X.

Partitioning Schemes. The computation of individual rows of C can be done independently, and hence rows of C (and the computation on the corresponding rows of A) can be trivially partitioned among the threads.

However, we need to pay careful attention to cache behavior during the sparse addition. Depending on the number of distinct cache lines of the dense array X that are touched during the update of a row of C, the X data structure may not completely reside in a close enough level of the cache hierarchy. Since this update is in the inner loop of the code, this can significantly affect performance. Specifically, for the datasets we describe in the evaluation section, we see a number of potential misses to the private second level (L2) cache. These misses are usually captured in the shared last level (LLC) cache, however we do find a significant performance impact due to L2 misses. In general for larger data sets, one could see misses to LLC as well. Hence we need a general scheme to localize accesses to the X array through blocking.

Blocking accesses to X in an efficient manner is non-trivial. Without any modifications, blocking along a row of B is difficult to achieve (as there are only few non-zeros per row on average). We hence propose to change the data structure of matrix B, and store it in a partitioned manner. We store individual CSRs for each partition of B. The number of partitions required for B depends on the L2 cache size. Figure 1(b) shows this scheme, where accesses to X get blocked. There are, of course, overheads in creating this blocked CSR data structure from the original CSR, and it may not be worthwhile to perform this transformation. We discuss this shortly.

Algorithm 1 shows the overall pseudocode for our algorithm. We use a hybrid scheme where we partition both the rows of A and the columns of B. Each partition updates a 2D block of matrix C. Each block of C is computed independently as an SpGEMM of the corresponding row partition of A and column partition of B.

As mentioned before, there is overhead in creating the blocked CSR representations of B. Further, each block of B is much sparser than the full row of B, and accesses to row pointers are not well amortized. This can lead to some bandwidth overhead when reading B as well. Consequently it only makes sense to perform the transformation when we know that the benefits when accessing X are large. If we know that, for a significant fraction of rows, the number of non-zeros of the final X after all updates is greater than the L2 cache size (usually 256 KB, or 64 K single-precision numbers), then blocking accesses to X makes sense. Since we do not apriori know the density of the output rows, we need to estimate it. We use a simple upper-bound estimate described in [13], where we merely count the number of multiplications involved in computing each row of C. This can be done cheaply without any actual floating point operations by merely looking at the non-zero structure of A and the row pointer array of B. This usually takes just 1-2 % of overall runtime to compute. We use these estimates $e\_nnz(i)$ for each row i to define an overall metric : $e\_nnz = \frac{\sum_{i:e\_nnz(i)>64K} e\_nnz(i)}{\sum_i e\_nnz(i)}$. If this is sufficiently large (greater than 30 %), our results show that we should partition B.

Dynamic Scheduling. Different partitions in the computations described in Algorithm 1 have differing amounts of computation and store different numbers of non-zeros. This leads to severe load imbalance. We have found that reducing the size of each partition so that the total number of partitions is 6–10 times the number of threads leads to significantly better load balance.

3   Experimental Results

3.1   Experimental Setup

We used an Intel® Xeon®[1] E5-2697 v3 processor based system for the experiments. The system consists of two processors, each with 14-cores running at 2.6 GHz (a total of 28 cores) with 36 MB L3 cache and 64 GB memory. The system is based on the Haswell microarchitecture and runs Redhat Linux (version 6.5). All our code is developed using C/C++ and is compiled using the Intel® C++ compiler[2] (version: 15.0.1) using the -O3 flag. We pins threads to cores for efficient NUMA behavior by setting KMP_AFFINITY to *granularity=fine,compact,1* in our experiments [2].

---

[1] Intel, Xeon, and Intel Xeon Phi are trademarks of Intel Corporation in the U.S. and/or other countries.

[2] Intel's compilers may or may not optimize to the same degree for non-Intel microprocessors for optimizations that are not unique to Intel microprocessors. These optimizations include SSE2, SSE3, and SSE3 instruction sets and other optimizations. Intel does not guarantee the availability, functionality, or effectiveness of any optimization on microprocessors not manufactured by Intel. Microprocessor-dependent optimizations in this product are intended for use with Intel microprocessors. Certain optimizations not specific to Intel micro-architecture are reserved for Intel microprocessors. Please refer to the applicable product User and Reference Guides for more information regarding the specific instruction sets covered by this notice. Notice revision #20110804.

Table 1. Structural properties of the datasets. C denotes the resultant matrix.

Name	Rows	nnz	Avg Degree	Max Degree	nnz (C)	Time (sec)	Type
harbor	46,835	4,701,167	100	289	7,900,918	0.0681	Symmetric
hood	220,542	10,768,436	49	77	34,242,181	0.0802	Symmetric
qcd	49,152	1,916,928	39	39	10,911,745	0.0373	Asymmetric
consph	83,334	6,010,480	72	81	26,539,737	0.0675	Symmetric
pwtk	217,918	11,634,424	53	180	32,772,237	0.0821	Symmetric
PR02R	161,070	8,185,136	51	92	30,969,454	0.0756	Asymmetric
mono	169,410	5,036,288	30	719	41,377,965	0.0965	Asymmetric
webbase	1,000,005	3,105,536	3	4,700	51,111,997	0.1597	Asymmetric
audikw	943,695	39,297,771	42	346	164,772,225	0.2053	Asymmetric
mou.gene	45,101	14,506,196	322	8033	190,430,984	0.9016	Asymmetric
cage14	1,505,785	27,130,349	18	82	236,999,813	0.2469	Asymmetric
dielFilt	1,102,824	45,204,422	41	271	270,082,366	0.2687	Asymmetric
rmat_er	262,144	16,777,150	64	181	704,303,135	0.7538	Asymmetric
rmat_g	262,144	16,749,883	64	3283	1,283,506,475	1.1721	Asymmetric
rmat_b	262,144	16,749,883	64	54250	1,648,990,052	2.4519	Asymmetric

We used both real-world and synthetic matrices for performance analysis. Table 1 shows the structural properties of the datasets. Our real-world matrices consist of 12 datasets collected from the Florida Matrix collection [8] covering many applications including structural engineering, web connectivity, electromagnetics, and medical science. Six of these datasets (*harbor, hood, qcd, pwtk, mono*, and *webbase*) are the same as those used in [13]. We specifically picked datasets where the authors' implementation shows the best performance and augmented this set with the largest datasets considered in that work. To increase the diversity of use cases considered, we additionally included 6 more datasets, which are up to an order of magnitude larger (in terms of nonzeros) than those previously experimented.

We also generated 3 types of synthetic datasets using the Graph500 RMAT data generator [14] by varying the RMAT parameters (similar to previous work [6]). These are (i) *rmat_b* (parameters 0.55, 0.15, 0.15, 0.15), (ii) *rmat_g* (parameters 0.45, 0.15, 0.15, 0.25), and (iii) *rmat_er* (0.25, 0.25, 0.25, 0.25). These matrices vary mainly in terms of degree distributions (e.g. *rmat_b* is highly skewed) to cover a wider range of applications.

The seven largest datasets (*audikw, mou.gene, cage14, dielFilt*, and the three synthetic datasets) are treated as unsymmetric to avoid large SpGEMM output matrices C that overflow memory limits. The symmetry of each dataset is tabulated in Table 1.

3.2 Experimental Results

We first compare the performance of our SpGEMM implementation with state-of-the-art results. To do so, we consider four available implementations,

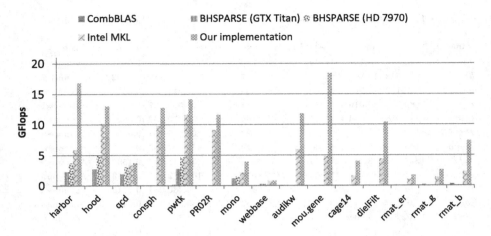

Fig. 2. Performance comparison of CombBLAS, Intel® MKL, BHSPARSE on nVidia GTX Titan GPU and on AMD Radeon HD 7970 GPU, and our implementation.

(i) the Combinatorial BLAS Library (CombBLAS v1.3, [1]), (ii) Intel® Math Kernel Library (MKL, version 11.2.1 [3]), (iii) BHSPARSE implementation on the nVidia GeForce GTX Titan GPU reported in [13], and (iv) BHSPARSE implementation on the AMD Radeon HD 7970 GPU reported in [13]. These represent some of the most recent SpGEMM publications that perform well on modern hardware [13]. We consider all 15 datasets in the comparison. However, since the GPU SpGEMM code is not available online, we used the performance results of the 6 overlapping datasets from [13]. Figure 2 shows the performance of these implementations in GFlops. As can be seen, our code is able to achieve up to 18.4 GFlops (geomean 6.6 GFlops) whereas CombBLAS, MKL, BHSPARSE on nVidia GTX Titan, and BHSPARSE on AMD Radeon HD 7970 GPU achieve up to 0.3, 11.7, 2.8, and 5.0 (geomean of 0.09, 3.6, 1.5, and 2.1) GFlops respectively. CombBLAS uses the DCSC matrix format that involves an additional layer of indirection (more cache line accesses) that leads to poor performance. MKL does not partition the columns of B and uses a static partitioning scheme that can cause performance degradation. We note that our performance results are up to 7.3X (geomean 3.9X) compared to the best BHSPARSE GPU implementation. This is despite the nearly 2× higher peak flops for the GPU cards compared to the Intel® Xeon® processor used. We attribute this to the impact of the algorithmic optimizations such as partitioning techniques, cache optimizations, and dynamic load balancing (more details are in Sect. 2).

We next demonstrate scalability using the 7 largest datasets in Table 1. Figure 3 shows the scalability of our algorithm and Intel® MKL. We ignore CombBLAS for this comparison as it is significantly slower (76X slower on average) and also the GPU implementations due to unavailability of code. Figure 3(a) and Fig. 3(b) show scaling results for our algorithm and MKL respectively. As can be seen, we achieve up to 28X speedup using 28 threads with respect to single

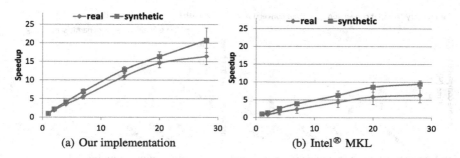

Fig. 3. Scalability of our implementation and Intel® MKL on real (geomean of largest 4) and synthetic (geomean of largest 3) datasets with {1, 2, 4, 7, 14, 20, 28} threads.

thread performance (geomean 18.2X) on our datasets (for real-world datasets: max 19.6X, and geomean of 16.4X; for synthetic datasets: max 28X, and geomean of 20.7X). MKL shows up to 9.9X speedup (geomean of 7.5X) on the same datasets (for real-world datasets:max 7.3X, and geomean of 6.3X; for synthetic datasets: max 9.9X, and geomean of 9.5X). The bar at each point shows the standard deviation on the scalability of our code as observed in our experiments. In general, scalability is better for dense datasets (*mou.gene* scales by about 20X on 28 cores); as also for more skewed datasets (*rmat_b* scales near linearly - 28X on 28 cores) where a significant portion of runtime is spent in dense areas of the matrix. For such matrices, there is more reuse of data structures and SpGEMM is more compute bound.

Figure 4(a) shows the timing breakdown in our algorithm. Among the 4 steps (memory allocation, computation, and input and output data structure conversion), computation is the dominant part and the other 3 take only 0.4 %, 2.6 %, and 0.3 %, respectively on average. For some datasets such as *mou.gene*, *rmat_g* and *rmat_b*, where there are dense regions of computation, as determined by our metric defined in Sect. 2, we partition columns of B and input data structure conversion times increase (e.g. *rmat_g* 7.9 %). This is still however small and our computation times still dominate; overall runtimes for such datasets are up to 1.4X (average 1.22X) faster with column partitioning. We verified our reasoning by counting L2 cache misses using hardware counters. Our analysis shows that for such datasets, L2 cache misses went down by 1.3-2.3X when we performed column partitioning. This ties in well with our performance gains.

We now discuss the impact of various optimizations described in Sect. 2 (Fig. 4(b)) on our SpGEMM code. We take the hash-based SpGEMM implementation as the baseline for the comparison. The main performance gain comes from using a dense array instead of hash tables during the addition phase. This yields up to 9.2X speedup (with a geomean of 6.3X). This is due to the overheads of using hash tables as explained in Sect. 2. Increasing the number of partitions improves performance by up to 49 % (with a geomean of 14.5 %). Using dynamic scheduling gives an additional 24.9 % (with a geomean of 10.2 %) performance boost. This is due to better load balancing among the parallel threads.

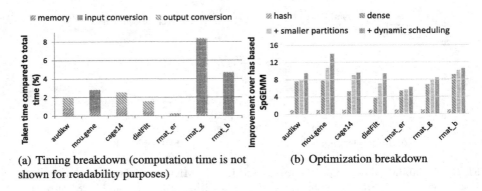

(a) Timing breakdown (computation time is not shown for readability purposes)

(b) Optimization breakdown

Fig. 4. Performance analysis of our implementation

4   Related Work

Gustavson introduced an SpGEMM algorithm with a work complexity proportional to the number of nonzeros in A, number of total flops, number of rows in C, and the number of columns in C [11]. This algorithm, and how it relates to our work, is described in detail in Sect. 2. A similar algorithm is used by Matlab, which processes a column of C at a time, and uses a dense vector with values, indices, and valid flags, for accumulating sparse partial results [9]. Buluc and Gilbert address the case of hypersparse matrices, where the number of non-zeros is less than the number of columns or rows [5]. The authors introduce the doubly compressed sparse column (DCSC) format, and two new SpGEMM algorithms to handle this case.

There have also been several efforts to optimize the performance of SpGEMM for parallel and heterogeneous hardware. Sulatycke and Ghose analyzed the cache behavior of different loop-orderings of SpGEMM with sparse A and B and dense C, and proposed a cache-efficient parallel algorithm that divided work across rows of A and C [16]. Siegel et al. created a framework for running SpGEMM on a cluster of heterogeneous (2x CPU + 2x GPU) nodes, and demonstrated a significant improvement in load-balance through dynamic scheduling as compared to a static approach [15]. Zhu et al. propose a custom hardware implementation to accelerate SpGEMM [18]. They use custom logic integrated with 3D stacked memory to retrieve columns from A, and merge intermediate results into C using content-addressable memories (CAMs). Liu and Vintner describe an SpGEMM algorithm and implementation for GPUs [13]. In this implementation, rows of C are divided into bins based on an upper-bound of the size of intermediate results and processed using different routines.

5   Conclusion and Future Work

In this paper we investigated Sparse Matrix-Matrix Multiplication (SpGEMM), an important kernel used extensively in many applications including linear solvers and graph analytics. To improve SpGEMM efficiency on multicore platforms, we performed different optimization techniques such as using dense arrays, implementing column-wise partitioning, and dynamic scheduling. We showed state-of-the-art results on both real-world and synthetic datasets. We are up to 3.8X faster than Intel® MKL and up to 257X faster than CombBLAS. We are also up to 7.3X better than the best published GPU implementation. Our code shows good scalability of 18.2X using 28 threads, as compared to MKL that achieves 7.5X speedup. In the future, we intend to extend these optimizations in a distributed setup.

References

1. Combinatorial Blas v 1.3. http://gauss.cs.ucsb.edu/~aydin/CombBLAS/html/
2. Thread affinity interface. https://software.intel.com/en-us/node/522691
3. Intel math kernel library (2015). https://software.intel.com/en-us/intel-mkl
4. Bell, N., Dalton, S., Olson, L.N.: Exposing fine-grained parallelism in algebraic multigrid methods. SIAM J. Sci. Comput. **34**(4), C123–C152 (2012)
5. Buluc, A., Gilbert, J.: On the representation and multiplication of hypersparse matrices. In: Proceedings of IPDPS, pp. 1–11, April 2008
6. Buluç, A., Gilbert, J.R.: Parallel sparse matrix-matrix multiplication and indexing: Implementation and experiments. CoRR abs/1109.3739 (2011)
7. Chan, T.M.: More algorithms for all-pairs shortest paths in weighted graphs. SIAM J. Comput. **39**(5), 2075–2089 (2010)
8. Davis, T.A., Hu, Y.: The university of florida sparse matrix collection. ACM Trans. Math. Softw. **38**(1), 1:1–1:25 (2011)
9. Gilbert, J., Moler, C., Schreiber, R.: Sparse matrices in matlab: design and implementation. SIAM J. Matrix Anal. Appl. **13**(1), 333–356 (1992)
10. Gilbert, J.R., Reinhardt, S., Shah, V.B.: High-performance graph algorithms from parallel sparse matrices. In: Kågström, B., Elmroth, E., Dongarra, J., Waśniewski, J. (eds.) PARA 2006. LNCS, vol. 4699, pp. 260–269. Springer, Heidelberg (2007)
11. Gustavson, F.G.: Two fast algorithms for sparse matrices: multiplication and permuted transposition. ACM Trans. Math. Softw. **4**(3), 250–269 (1978)
12. Kaplan, H., Sharir, M., Verbin, E.: Colored intersection searching via sparse rectangular matrix multiplication. In: Symposium on Computational Geometry, pp. 52–60. ACM (2006)
13. Liu, W., Vinter, B.: An efficient GPU general sparse matrix-matrix multiplication for irregular data. In: Proceedings of IPDPS, pp. 370–381. IEEE (2014)
14. Murphy, R.C., Wheeler, K.B., Barrett, B.W., Ang, J.A.: Introducing the graph 500. Cray User's Group (2010)
15. Siegel, J., et al.: Efficient sparse matrix-matrix multiplication on heterogeneous high performance systems. In: IEEE Cluster Computing, pp. 1–8 (2010)
16. Sulatycke, P., Ghose, K.: Caching-efficient multithreaded fast multiplication of sparse matrices. In: Proceedings of IPPS/SPDP 1998, pp. 117–123, March 1998
17. Vassilevska, V., Williams, R., Yuster, R.: Finding heaviest h-subgraphs in real weighted graphs, with applications. CoRR abs/cs/0609009 (2006)
18. Zhu, Q., Graf, T., Sumbul, H., Pileggi, L., Franchetti, F.: Accelerating sparse matrix-matrix multiplication with 3D-stacked logic-in-memory hardware. In: IEEE HPEC, pp. 1–6 (2013)

On the Design, Development, and Analysis of Optimized Matrix-Vector Multiplication Routines for Coprocessors

Khairul Kabir[1], Azzam Haidar[1(✉)], Stanimire Tomov[1], and Jack Dongarra[1,2,3]

[1] University of Tennessee Knoxville, Knoxville, USA
haider@icl.utk.edu
[2] Oak Ridge National Laboratory, Oak Ridge, USA
[3] University of Manchester, Manchester, UK

Abstract. The manycore paradigm shift, and the resulting change in modern computer architectures, has made the development of optimal numerical routines extremely challenging. In this work, we target the development of numerical algorithms and implementations for Xeon Phi coprocessor architecture designs. In particular, we examine and optimize the general and symmetric matrix-vector multiplication routines (gemv/symv), which are some of the most heavily used linear algebra kernels in many important engineering and physics applications. We describe a successful approach on how to address the challenges for this problem, starting with our algorithm design, performance analysis and programing model and moving to kernel optimization. Our goal, by targeting low-level and easy to understand fundamental kernels, is to develop new optimization strategies that can be effective elsewhere for use on manycore coprocessors, and to show significant performance improvements compared to existing state-of-the-art implementations. Therefore, in addition to the new optimization strategies, analysis, and optimal performance results, we finally present the significance of using these routines/strategies to accelerate higher-level numerical algorithms for the eigenvalue problem (EVP) and the singular value decomposition (SVD) that by themselves are foundational for many important applications.

1 Introduction

As the era of computer architectures dominated by serial processors closes, the scientific community has produced a consensus for the need to redesign numerical libraries to meet the new system design constraints and revolutionary levels of parallelism and heterogeneity. One approach, from the early days of multicore architectures, was to redesign the higher-level algorithms, e.g., LAPACK [5], to use tile operations [7–9]. To provide parallelism in these algorithms, the computation is expressed as a Directed Acyclic Graph (DAG) of tasks on small matrices/tiles with labeled edges designating data dependencies, and a runtime system schedules the DAG's execution over the cores to ensure that data

© Springer International Publishing Switzerland 2015
J.M. Kunkel and T. Ludwig (Eds.): ISC High Performance 2015, LNCS 9137, pp. 58–73, 2015.
DOI: 10.1007/978-3-319-20119-1_5

dependancies are not violated. Performance relied on fast sequential implementations of the Basic Linear Algebra Subprograms (BLAS) interface [13]. When manycore accelerators entered the HPC field, it became apparent that breaking the uniformity of the computation is not advantageous for GPUs. Instead, hybrid approaches were developed [4,17,27,28,30], where there is still a DAG and scheduling (for both GPUs and CPUs), but SIMD tasks on large data that are suitable for GPUs, e.g., GEMM, remain coarse grained and are scheduled as single tasks for parallel execution through parallel BLAS implementations. This highlighted the interest in parallel BLAS, and subsequently to parallel BLAS implementations in CUBLAS [1] and MAGMA BLAS [2]. Hybrid approaches are also suitable for the more recent many-core coprocessors, e.g., as is evident from the MAGMA MIC's extension of MAGMA for the Xeon Phi coprocessors [14,19].

The use of batched BLAS [10,11,18,20] as an extension to the parallel BLAS in many HPC applications is currently the subject of great interest. Batched algorithms address one of the significant challenges in HPC today – that numerous important applications tend to be cast in terms of a solution to many small matrix operations: they contain the large majority of computations that consist of a large number of small matrices which cannot be executed efficiently on accelerated platforms except in large groups, or "batches". Indeed, batched representations of computational tasks are pervasive in numerical algorithms for scientific computing. In addition to dense linear algebra routines and applications, batched LA can naturally express various register and cache blocking techniques for sparse computations [21], sparse direct multifrontal solvers [31], high-order FEM [12], and numerous applications in astrophysics [24], hydrodynamics [12], image processing [25], signal processing [6], and big data, to name just a few. Moreover, blocking for cache reuse - the most basic technique to accelerate numerical algorithms from the fundamental dense matrix-matrix product, to sparse matrix-vector (SpMV), to more complex linear or eigenvalue solvers – is often synonymous with a batched representation of algorithms.

To enable the effective use of parallel BLAS and batched BLAS-based computational approaches, new parallel BLAS algorithms and optimization strategies must be developed. In this work, we target the development of these foundational numerical algorithms, optimization strategies, and implementations for the Xeon Phi coprocessors, also known as Intel's many integrated core architectures (MIC). In particular, we examine and optimize the general and symmetric matrix-vector multiplication routines (gemv/symv), which are some of the most heavily used linear algebra kernels in many important engineering and physics applications. Our goal, by targeting low-level, easy to understand fundamental kernels, is to develop optimization strategies that can be effective elsewhere, and in particular for batched approaches for HPC applications on manycore coprocessors. Therefore, we developed new optimization strategies (and analysis) to obtain optimal performance. Finally, we illustrate the need and the significance of using these routines/strategies to accelerate higher-level numerical algorithms for the EVP and SVD problems that by themselves are foundational for many important applications.

2   Background and Related Work

This paper addresses two kernels – the general and the symmetric matrix-vector multiplications (gemv and symv) – which are crucial for the performance of linear solvers as well as EVP and SVD problems. A reference implementation for a generic matrix-vector multiplication kernel is straight-forward because of the data parallel nature of the computation. However, achieving performance on accelerators or coprocessors is challenging, as evident from the results on current state-of-the-art implementations. For example, even though Intel optimized dgemv in their recent release of MKL, its performance is highly nonuniform, reaching up to about 37–40 Gflop/s for only particular matrix sizes and data alignments. Performance, when the matrix size is not a multiple of the cache line (8 double precision numbers), drops by about 10 Gflop/s, or 30 % of the peak obtained. Furthermore, a sequence of calls to dgemv with "transpose" and "Non transpose" have shown a drop in the performance as well at about 10 Gflop/s. In addition to the issues for the dgemv kernel, the irregular data access patterns in the symv routine bring further challenges for its design and optimization. For example, the current MKL dsymv achieves the same performance as the dgemv ($\approx$37–40 Gflop/s) while in theory it should be twice as fast.

To the best of our knowledge, there has not been other published work on addressing the acceleration opportunities mentioned for the Xeon Phi architectures. Related algorithmic work, but for GPU architectures, is the acceleration of the symv routine in MAGMA [26]. The CUBLAS's symv, similarly to the MKL's symv for Xeon Phi, was not exploiting the symmetry of the matrix to reduce the data traffic needed, and as a result was also twice slower than theoretically expected. A new algorithm was proposed to correct this for GPUs by Nath et al. [26], which was later slightly improved for Kepler GPUs using atomic operations [3].

In this paper, we describe the optimizations performed on both the gemv and symv routines to make them reach their theoretical peak performances on coprocessors. Our gemv kernel is not affected by the matrix size or the sequence of calls. It achieves uniform performance that matches the peaks of the MKL's gemv. This improvement was important to speed up many algorithms, and in particular, the reduction to bidiagonal form which is a major component for SVD.

An optimality analysis for the symv routines shows (see Sect. 6) that this kernel should achieve twice the performance of the gemv routine. We developed an algorithm (and its implementation) that exploits cache memory to read small blocks of the matrix in cache and reuse them in the computation involving their symmetric counterparts. This implementation divides the main memory reads in half, and our experiments show that it reaches to around 50–55 Gflop/s for specific blocking sizes that allow each small block to fit into the L2 cache of a corresponding core of the coprocessor. Even though this new symv kernel brings an excellent improvement over the contemporary MKL, it is still less than what the performance bound analysis shows as being possible. This motivated us to look for further improvements that led to the development of a second algorithm (and its implementation) that reuses the data loaded into the L1 cache level, as well as from the registry, to reach to around 65 Gflop/s. We should mention that both of our symv implementations incur memory overheads of less than one percent (about 0.78%) of the matrix size. We also show the impact that this optimization has on the tridiagonal reduction, which is the most time consuming component of the symmetric eigenvalue problem.

3   Contributions to the Field

The evolution of semiconductor technology is dramatically transforming the balance of future computer systems, producing unprecedented changes at every level of the platform pyramid. From the point of view of numerical libraries, and the myriad of applications that depend on them, three challenges stand out: (1) the need to exploit unprecedented amounts of parallelism; (2) the need to maximize the use of data locality; and (3) the need to cope with component heterogeneity. Besides the software development efforts that we investigate to accomplish an efficient implementation, we highlight our main contributions related to the algorithm's design and optimization strategies aimed at addressing these challenges on the MIC architecture:

Exploit Unprecedented Amounts of Parallelism: Clock frequencies are expected to stay constant, or even decrease to conserve power; consequently, as we already see, the primary method of increasing computational capability of a chip will be to dramatically increase the number of processing units (cores), which in turn will require an increase of orders of magnitude in the amount of concurrency that routines must be able to utilize. We developed MIC-specific optimization techniques that demonstrate how to use the many (currently 60) cores of the MIC to get optimal performance. The techniques and kernels developed are fundamental and can be used elsewhere.

Hierarchical Communication Model that Maximizes the use of Data Locality: Recent reports (e.g., [16]) have made it clear that time per flop, network bandwidth (between parallel processors), and network latency are all improving, but at exponentially different rates. So an algorithm that is computation-bound and running close to peak today may be communication-bound in the near future. The same holds for communication between levels of the memory hierarchy. We demonstrate that, related to the latter, performance is indeed harder to get on new manycore architectures unless hierarchical communications are applied. Hierarchical communications to get top speed are now needed not only for Level 3 BLAS but also for Level 2 BLAS, as we show. Only after we developed and applied multilevel cache blocking, did our implementations reach optimal performance.

Performance Bounds Analysis: We study and demonstrate the maximal performance bounds that could be reached. The performance bounds allow us to ascertain the effectiveness of our implementation and how close it approaches the theoretical limit. We developed and demonstrated this use of performance bound analysis not only for the low-level kernels considered, but also for the higher-level algorithms that use them as building blocks.

4 Experimental Testbed

All experiments are done on an Intel multicore system with two 8-core Intel Xeon E5-2670 (Sandy Bridge) CPUs, running at 2.6 GHz. Each CPU has a 20 MB shared L3 cache, and each core has a private 256 KB L2 and 64 KB L1 caches. The system is equipped with 52 GB of memory. The theoretical peak in double precision is 20.8 Gflop/s per core, giving 332 Gflop/s in total. The system is equiped with one Intel Xeon-Phi KNC 7120 coprocessor. It has 15.1 GB, runs at 1.23 GHz, and yields a theoretical double precision peak of 1, 208 Gflop/s. We used the MPSS 2.1.5889-16 software stack, the icc compiler that comes with the composer_xe_2013_sp1.2.144 suite, and the BLAS implementation from MKL (Math Kernel Library) 11.01.02 [22].

5 The General Matrix-Vector Multiplication Routine gemv

Level 2 BLAS routines are of low computational intensity and therefore DLA algorithm designers try to avoid them. There are techniques that can replace Level 2 BLAS operations with Level 3 BLAS. For example, in factorizations like LU, QR, and Cholesky, the application of consecutive Level 2 BLAS operations that occur in the algorithms can be delayed and accumulated so that, at a later moment, the accumulated transformation can be applied at once as a Level 3 BLAS [5]. This approach totally removes Level 2 BLAS from Cholesky, and reduces its amount to $O(n^2)$ in LU and QR, thus making it asymptotically insignificant compared to the total $O(n^3)$ amount of operations for these factorizations. The same technique can be applied to the two-sided factorizations [15], but in contrast to the one-sided, a large fraction of the total number of floating point operations (flops) still remains Level 2 BLAS. For example, the block Hessenberg reduction has about 20 % of its flops in Level 2 BLAS, while both the bidiagonal and tridiagonal reductions have 50 % of their flops in Level 2 BLAS [29]. In practice, the flops in Level 2 BLAS do not scale well on current architectures and thus can significantly impact the total execution time. Therefore the availability of their efficient implementations is still crucial for the performance of a two sided factorization in current architectures. This section considers the Xeon Phi implementation of one fundamental Level 2 BLAS operation, namely the matrix-vector multiplication routine for general dense matrices (gemv). The gemv multiplication routine performs one of:

$$y := \alpha A x + \beta y, \quad \text{or} \quad y := \alpha A^T x + \beta y, \tag{1}$$

where A is an M by N matrix, x and y are vectors, and α and β are scalars.

5.1 Effect of the Matrix Size on the MKL gemv Performance

The gemv performance peak on the Xeon Phi coprocessor is as expected – achieving around 37–40 GFlop/s in double precision for both of its transpose and nontranspose cases, which translate to a bandwidth of about 160 GB/s. Achieving this bandwidth is what is expected on the Xeon Phi coprocessor [23]. However, this peak performance is obtained only on particular matrix sizes and data alignments. In reality, applications that rely exclusively on the gemv, e.g., the bidiagonal reduction (BRD), show much lower performance. Our analysis shows that in the case of the BRD in particular (see Eq. (7)), performance must be about twice the performance of the gemv, while experiments show that the BRD attains less than 37–40 GFlop/s. A detailed analysis of the gemv kernel shows that its performance indeed highly depends on the location of the data in the memory, and in particular, on its alignment. We benchmarked gemv on matrices of consecutively increasing sizes from 1 to 27 K, similar to the way that the BRD reduction calls it. We found out that its performance fluctuates, as shown in Fig. 1a and b (the blue curves), according to the offset from which the matrix is accessed. The performance drops by about 15 Gflop/s for the transposed case when the matrix size in the "n" dimension is not a multiple of 240 (as shown in Fig. 1a) and falls by about 10 Gflop/s for the non-transposed case when the matrix size in the m dimension is not a multiple of 8, as depicted in Fig. 1b. To resolve the dependance on the memory alignment and the matrix sizes, we developed two routines (for the transpose and non-transpose cases, respectively) that always access a matrix from its aligned data, performing a very small amount of extra work, but keeping its performance stable at its peak. The red curves in Fig. 1 show our improvement. The algorithms are described in Subsect. 5.3 below.

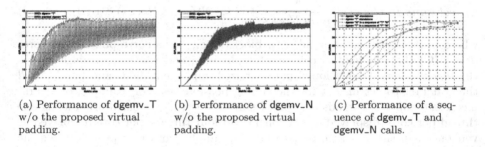

(a) Performance of dgemv_T w/o the proposed virtual padding.

(b) Performance of dgemv_N w/o the proposed virtual padding.

(c) Performance of a sequence of dgemv_T and dgemv_N calls.

Fig. 1. Performance obtained from the dgemv routine on matrices of consecutively increasing sizes (Color figure online).

5.2   Effect of the Sequence of gemv Calls

After achieving optimal performance for the gemv's transpose and non-transpose cases, as described in Sect. 5.1, we tested their use in real-world applications. For the BRD reduction for example, performance is improved for all sizes and reaches its theoretical peak for large matrix sizes. However, the performance for small sizes, in particular less than 8 K, is not as expected. The detailed experiments depicted in Fig. 1c show that performance of gemv drops by 10 Gflop/s when called in a sequence of non-transpose followed by transpose cases for matrices of size less than 8 K. We believe that this is related to the different parallelization grid used for each case of gemv (transpose vs. non-transpose), and thus this is the overhead of switching between the two different grids of cores. The overhead probably always exists for larger sizes, but its effect is less evident because the cost of the gemv is dominant. To overcome this drawback, we introduce another optimization technique and use it to develop a new gemv routine, described in detail in the following sections.

5.3   A New MAGMA MIC gemv

Transpose Matrix Case: The computation of the gemv routine for the transpose case can be parallelized in a one-dimensional (1D) block-column fashion. In this parallelization model, each thread processes its part of the gemv column by column, and thus for each column a dot product is performed. The accumulations are done in cache and the final, resulting vector y is written once. Moreover, each thread reads data that is stored consecutively in memory, which will simplify the prefetching and vectorization process. To get good performance out of a MIC core, vectorization that takes advantage of the core's 16-wide SIMD registers is essential. Each core processes one block (or multiple, if we use 1D block cyclic distribution). The number of columns in the $block_i$ can be set, for example, as:

$$columns\_in\_block_i = \frac{N}{num\_blocks} + (i < (N\%num\_blocks) \: ? \: 1 : 0), \qquad (2)$$

where num_blocks is the number of blocks (e.g., 60 to correspond to 60 cores of a MIC) that we want N columns to split into, and $i = 1, \ldots, num\_blocks$ is the block index. We developed parametrized implementations and hand-tested them at first to get insight for the tuning possibilities. For example, one parameter is number of threads per core. Figure 2 illustrates a distribution using one thread per core (displayed as version-1) and four threads per core (displayed as version-2). In this case, we found that both implementations provide the same performance. This is due to the fact that the gemv routine is memory bound and one thread per core is enough to saturate the bandwidth, thus increasing the number of threads does not affect the performance.

Non-transpose Matrix Case: Following the same strategy used for the transpose approach leads to poor performance for the non-transpose case. This is because the values of y need to be written multiple times in this case. Therefore, we can instead parallelize the algorithm in 1D block-row fashion. In this way each core processes its independent part of the gemv and thus the resulting vectors can be accumulated in cache and written to the main memory only once. To keep the blocks cache aligned, their size can be made to be a multiple of eight. For effective load balance we can think of the matrix as strips of eight, and divide the strips among the block-rows equally. In this case, the number of

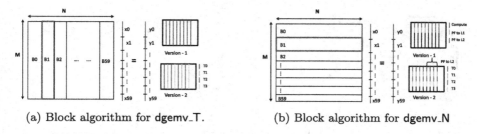

(a) Block algorithm for **dgemv_T**.   (b) Block algorithm for **dgemv_N**

Fig. 2. Basic implementation of matrix-vector multiplication on Intel Xeon Phi

rows in block$_i$ can be set as:

$$m8\_strip = (M + 7)/8$$

$$rows\_in\_block_i = [\frac{m8\_strip}{num\_blocks} + (i < (m8\_strip\%num\_blocks) \ ? \ 1 : 0)] \times 8$$

$$(3)$$

Dividing rows in block-rows like this has two advantages: first, every block except the last one will have elements that are multiples of eight, which is good for vectorization; and second, it helps keep the blocks aligned with the cache sizes which is essential to reduce memory access time. When the matrix A is not aligned for the cache size, we can increase the size of the first block in order to handle the unaligned portion, while making all the remaining blocks aligned. Compiler guided prefetching for this case is not enough to reach the same performance as for the transpose case. Prefetching to L1 and L2 cache plays an important role here.

Similarly to the transpose case, using one or four threads per core provides the same performance. Again, we developed a parametrized implementation where one parameter is the number of threads per core. Figure 2b, for example, illustrates a distribution using one thread per core (displayed as version-1) and four threads per core (displayed as version-2). The thread processes four columns together to reduce the write traffic for vector y. Before processing the eight elements (eight is the length of SIMD instruction for double precision), it prefetches the next eight elements of A from the same column to the L1 cache level and the next four columns of the same block-row to the L2 cache. In this way, when the code proceeds to process the next four columns, the data for them will be obtained from the L2 cache. Processing more than four columns does not improve the performance. For version-2 each thread handles four columns together and then the consecutive eight rows from the same column. Like version-1 each thread will prefetch its portion from the same columns to the L1 cache and from the next four columns to the L2 cache.

The blocking and prefetching technique for the transpose and non-transpose cases are described in Figs. 2a and b, respectively.

Figures 3a and b show the performance comparison of magma_dgemv *vs.* mkl_dgemv. In both the transpose and non-transpose cases the techniques presented yield better performance than the MKL's **dgemv**s.

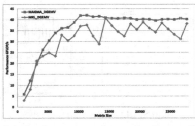

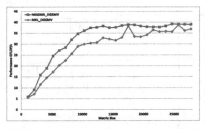

(a) Performance of magma_dgemv_T   (b) Performance of magma_dgemv_N

Fig. 3. Performance of MAGMA MIC dgemv *vs. MKL* on Intel Xeon Phi.

6   Our Proposed Symmetric Matrix-Vector Multiplication Routine symv

The symv multiplication routine performs:

$$y := \alpha A x + \beta y, \tag{4}$$

where α and β are scalars, x and y are vectors of size N, and A is an N by N symmetric matrix.

The performance of the MKL symv routine is as high as the performance of the gemv routine, and therefore can be further accelerated. Due to the fact that the symv routine accesses half of the matrix, meaning it needs only half of the data transfers, its performance (theoretically) should be twice that of the gemv. The idea behind getting this acceleration is to reuse the data from half of the matrix to perform the entire multiplication. The traditional way to attain this objective is to divide the whole matrix into small blocks so that each block fits in the cache. A symv kernel is used for the diagonal blocks, and for each of the non-diagonal blocks two calls to the gemv routine are used — one for the transpose and one for the non-transpose case. For high parallelism without the need for synchronization, each core handles a block and its resulting vector is written independently in separate locations. Thus, a summation is taken at the end to get the final y result. As each block is brought to the cache once, this technique is expected to reach close to the theoretical bound which, as mentioned, is twice the performance of gemv.

We performed a set of experiments for different block sizes. In our timing, we ignored the overhead of the summation and the launching of the threads. We illustrate in Fig. 5a the performance we obtained for different block sizes. The maximum performance achieved is around 54 Gflop/s for large matrix sizes and near 50 Gflop/s for smaller matrix sizes. When including the time for the summation, the later results decrease by about 5−10 %. This symv implementation brings an excellent improvement over the contemporary MKL (e.g., it is about 1.3 times faster). However, the performance is not optimal. This motivated us to search for other MIC-specific optimization techniques, leading to our second algorithm and implementation that adds one more level of blocking. In particular, we manage to reuse data from the L1 cache, which brings the performance up to the optimal level, i.e., twice the one for gemv.

In order to achieve the desired performance one must optimize both at the blocking and at the kernel levels. As there are sixty cores in a MIC, we divided the whole matrix into 60×60 blocks. If (i, j) is the index of a block in a two dimensional grid and block_M×block_N is the block's dimension, block_M and block_N are computed as follows:

$$n8\_strip = (N + 7)/8$$

$$block\_M = [\frac{n8\_strip}{60} + (i < (n8\_strip\%60) ? 1 : 0)] * 8 \qquad (5)$$

$$block\_N = [\frac{n8\_strip}{60} + (j < (n8\_strip\%60) ? 1 : 0)] * 8.$$

When the size of the matrix A is a multiple of 8, then both block_M and block_N are a multiple of eight as well, and all the blocks in the grid are aligned with the cache. When the size of A is not a multiple of 8, the non-aligned portion is added to block$(0, 0)$, making all the remaining blocks aligned and of sizes that are multiples of 8.

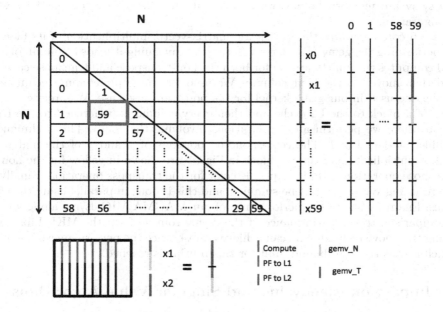

Fig. 4. Basic implementation of MAGMA symv on Intel Xeon Phi.

The symv computation is organized according to the description presented in Fig. 4. Since the diagonal blocks require special attention because their lower

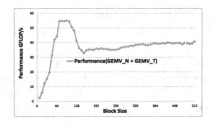
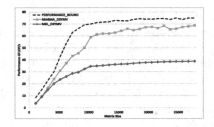

(a) Effect of the blocking size for the imple-   (b) Performance of the second approach of
mentation of the symv routine as two gemv   the symv routine.
calls.

Fig. 5. Performance of MAGMA dsymv on Intel Xeon Phi (Color figure online).

or upper portion is accessed, and in order to enforce workload balance among
the cores, we split the diagonal blocks over all the cores in a way that provides
load balance. The non-diagonal blocks are also distributed among the cores as
described in Fig. 4 in order to achieve load balance. The number inside each
block indicates which core owns and processes that block. Since the gemv and
the symv are memory bound, we found that one thread per core is the best
configuration.

Each core computes the symmetric matrix-vector multiplication of its block
by performing the gemv_N and gemv_T together, meaning it loads a column of A
and computes the multiplication for both the non-transpose and transpose cases,
and then moves to the next column. We used the same prefetching technique
as the one used in our gemv kernel for the non-transpose case. We prefetch the
data of a block to the L2 cache and then every column is prefetched to the L1
cache where we perform all computations involving that data. This technique
is illustrated in Fig. 4. The corresponding portions of x and y of the matrix-
vector multiplication of the red block in Fig. 5b are shown in yellow for the non-
transpose operation and in the purple color for the transpose operation. Finally,
the resulting vector y_i must be summed, and this is done in parallel using the 60
cores. Figure 5b shows the performance of our MAGMA MIC dsymv along with
a comparison to the performance of the dsymv routine from the MKL Library.
Using the above technique we can achieve almost twice the performance of gemv,
which means that the bound limit for this routine is reached.

7   Impact on Eigenvalue and Singular Value Algorithms

Eigenvalue and singular value decomposition (SVD) problems are fundamental for many engineering and physics applications. The solution of these problems follow three phases. The first phase involves reducing the matrix to a condensed form matrix (e.g., tridiagonal form for symmetric eigenvalue problem,
and bidiagonal form for singular value decomposition) that has the same eigen/

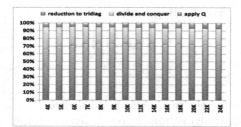 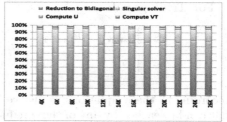

(a) Execution time profile of the symmetric eigenvalue routine dsyevd.

(b) Execution time profile of the SVD routine dgesvd.

Fig. 6. Percentage of the time spent in each of the three phases of the symmetric eigenvalue and singular value problem

singular-values as the original one. The reductions are referred to as two-sided factorizations, as they are achieved by two-sided orthogonal transformations. Then, in the second phase, an eigenvalue (or a singular value) solver further computes the eigenpairs (or, singular values and vectors) of the condensed form matrix. Finally, in the third phase, the eigenvectors (or the left and right singular vectors) resulting from the previous phase are multiplied by the orthogonal matrices used in the reduction phase. We performed a set of experiments in order to determine the percentage of time spent in each of these phases for the symmetric eigenvalue problem and the singular value decomposition problem. The results depicted in Figs. 6a, and b show that the first phase is the most time consuming portion. It consists of more than 80 % or 90 % of the total time when all eigenvectors/singular vectors or only eigenvalues/singular values are computed, respectively. These observations illustrate the need to improve the reduction phase. It is challenging to accelerate the two-sided factorizations on new architectures because they are rich in Level 2 BLAS operations, which are bandwidth limited and therefore do not scale on recent architectures. For that, we focus in this section on the reduction phase and study its limitation. Furthermore, we present the impact of our optimized kernel when accelerating it on Intel Xeon-Phi coprocessor architectures.

7.1 Performance Bound Analysis

In order to evaluate the performance behavior of the two-sided factorizations and to analyze if there are opportunities for improvements, we conduct a computational analysis of the reduction to condensed forms for the two-sided reductions (TRD and BRD). The total cost for the reduction phase can be summarized as follows:

For Tridiagonal:

$$\approx \tfrac{2}{3}n^3_{\mathsf{symv}} + \tfrac{2}{3}n^3_{\mathsf{Level\ 3}}$$

$$\approx \tfrac{4}{3}n^3.$$

For Bidiagonal:

$$\approx \tfrac{4}{3}n^3_{\mathsf{gemv}} + \tfrac{4}{3}n^3_{\mathsf{Level\ 3}}$$

$$\approx \tfrac{8}{3}n^3.$$

According to these equations we derive below the maximum performance P_{max} that can be reached by any of these reduction algorithms. In particular, for large matrix sizes n, $P_{max} = \frac{number\ of\ operations}{minimum\ time\ t_{min}}$, and thus P_{max} is expressed as:

For Tridiagonal:

$$\frac{\tfrac{4}{3}n^3}{\tfrac{2}{3}n^3 * \frac{1}{P_{symv}} + \tfrac{2}{3}n^3 * \frac{1}{P_{Level3}}}$$

$$\frac{2 * P_{Level3} * P_{symv}}{P_{Level3} + P_{symv}} \qquad (6)$$

$$\approx 2P_{symv}$$
$$when \quad P_{Level3} \gg P_{symv}.$$

For Bidiagonal:

$$\frac{\tfrac{8}{3}n^3}{\tfrac{4}{3}n^3 * \frac{1}{P_{gemv}} + \tfrac{4}{3}n^3 * \frac{1}{P_{Level3}}}$$

$$\frac{2 * P_{Level3} * P_{gemv}}{P_{Level3} + P_{gemv}} \qquad (7)$$

$$\approx 2P_{gemv}$$
$$when \quad P_{Level3} \gg P_{gemv}.$$

The performance of the Level 2 BLAS routines, such as the matrix-vector multiplication (symv or gemv), is memory bound and very low compared to the Level 3 BLAS routines which can achieve close to the machine's peak performance. For example, on the Intel Xeon Phi system the performance of dgemv is about 40 Gflop/s, while for dgemm is about 1000 Gflop/s. Thus, one can expect from Eqs. (6, 7) that the performance of the reduction algorithms are bound by the performance of the Level 2 BLAS operations. This proves that the performance behavior for these algorithms is dictated by the matrix-vector Level 2 BLAS routines, and this is one example of why it is very important to optimize them.

7.2   Impact on the Tridiagonal Reduction

Figure 7a shows the performance for the tridiagonal reduction using the Xeon Phi. The MAGMA implementation using the MKL symv routine is much slower than when using our proposed symv implementation. In particular MAGMA with the new symv optimization is about 1.6× faster than MAGMA using the MKL symv, and reaches 78 % of the theoretical performance bound derived from Eq. 6.

7.3   Impact on the Bidiagonal Reduction

Figure 7b shows the performance for the bidiagonal reduction on the Xeon Phi. Similarly to the tridiagonal factorization, the MAGMA bidiagonal reduction using our proposed gemv shows better performance than when using the gemv

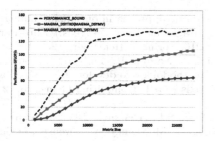
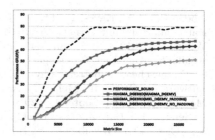

(a) Performance of MAGMA Tridiagonal Reduction Routine **dsytrd**.

(b) Performance of MAGMA Bidiagonal Reduction Routine **dgebrd**.

Fig. 7. Impact of the proposed symv and gemv routine on the reduction algorithms for eigenvalue and singular value problems.

routine from the MKL library combined with our proposed fix described in Sect. 5.1. In particular we are reaching 85 % of the theoretical performance bound that we derived in Eq. 7.

8 Conclusions

We developed MIC-specific optimization techniques that demonstrate how to use the many (currently 60) cores of the Intel Xeon Phi coprcessor to obtain optimal performance. The techniques and kernels developed are fundamental and can be used elsewhere. For example, we showed that hierarchical communications to obtain top speed are now needed not only for Level 3 BLAS but also for Level 2 BLAS – indeed, only after we developed and applied multilevel cache blocking, our implementations reached optimal performance. Further, the new gemv kernel handles unaligned general matrices efficiently and its use in higher-level routines, like the bidiagonal reduction, does not require additional optimization techniques, like padding for example. The impact of our optimizations are clearly visible in the performance of the bidiagonal reduction. Finally, our new symv is almost 2× faster than MKL's symv. Optimization in symv makes the tridiagonal reduction 1.6× faster than using MKL's symv.

Acknowledgments. This material is based upon work supported by the National Science Foundation under Grant No. ACI-1339822, the Department of Energy, and Intel. The results were obtained in part with the financial support of the Russian Scientific Fund, Agreement N14-11-00190.

References

1. CUDA Cublas Library. https://developer.nvidia.com/cublas
2. MAGMA. http://icl.cs.utk.edu/magma/

3. Abdelfattah, A., Keyes, D., Ltaief, H.: Systematic approach in optimizing numerical memory-bound kernels on GPU. In: Caragiannis, I., et al. (eds.) Euro-Par Workshops 2012. LNCS, vol. 7640, pp. 207–216. Springer, Heidelberg (2013)
4. Agullo, E., Augonnet, C., Dongarra, J., Ltaief, H., Namyst, R., Thibault, S.,Tomov, S.: Faster, cheaper, better - a hybridization methodology to develop linear algebra software for GPUs. In: Mei, W., Hwu, W. (eds.) GPU Computing Gems, vol. 2. Morgan Kaufmann, September 2010
5. Anderson, E., Bai, Z., Bischof, C., Blackford, S.L., Demmel, J.W., Dongarra, J.J., Croz, J.D., Greenbaum, A., Hammarling, S., McKenney, A., Sorensen, D.C.: LAPACK User's Guide, 3rd edn. Society for Industrial and Applied Mathematics, Philadelphia (1999)
6. Anderson, M.J., Sheffield, D., Keutzer, K.: A predictive model for solving small linear algebra problems in gpu registers. In: IEEE 26th International Parallel Distributed Processing Symposium (IPDPS) (2012)
7. Bosilca, G., Bouteiller, A., Danalis, A., Hérault, T., Lemarinier, P., Dongarra, J.: DAGuE: a generic distributed DAG engine for high performance computing. Parallel Comput. **38**(1–2), 37–51 (2012)
8. Buttari, A., Langou, J., Kurzak, J., Dongarra, J.: A class of parallel tiled linear algebra algorithms for multicore architectures. Parallel Comput. **35**(1), 38–53 (2009)
9. Chan, E., Quintana-Orti, E.S., Quintana-Orti, G., van de Geijn, R.: Supermatrix out-of-order scheduling of matrix operations for smp and multi-core architectures. In: Proceedings of the Nineteenth Annual ACM Symposium on Parallel Algorithms and Architectures, SPAA 2007, pp. 116–125. ACM, New York (2007)
10. Dong, T., Haidar, A., Luszczek, P., Harris, A., Tomov, S., Dongarra, J.: LU Factorization of small matrices: accelerating batched DGETRF on the GPU. In: Proceedings of 16th IEEE International Conference on High Performance and Communications (HPCC 2014), August 2014
11. Dong, T., Haidar, A., Tomov, S., Dongarra, J.: A fast batched Cholesky factorization on a GPU. In: Proceedings of 2014 International Conference on Parallel Processing (ICPP-2014), September 2014
12. Dong, T., Dobrev, V., Kolev, T., Rieben, R., Tomov, S., Dongarra, J.: A step towards energy efficient computing: Redesigning a hydrodynamic application on CPU-GPU. In: IEEE 28th International Parallel Distributed Processing Symposium (IPDPS) (2014)
13. Dongarra, J., Du Croz, J., Duff, I., Hammarling, S.: Algorithm 679: a set of level 3 basic linear algebra subprograms. ACM Trans. Math. Soft. **16**(1), 18–28 (1990)
14. Dongarra, J., Gates, M., Haidar, A., Jia, Y., Kabir, K., Luszczek, P., Tomov, S.: Portable HPC programming on intel many-integrated-core hardware with MAGMA port to Xeon Phi. In: Wyrzykowski, R., Dongarra, J., Karczewski, K., Waśniewski, J. (eds.) PPAM 2013, Part I. LNCS, vol. 8384, pp. 571–581. Springer, Heidelberg (2014)
15. Dongarra, J.J., Sorensen, D.C., Hammarling, S.J.: Block reduction of matrices to condensed forms for eigenvalue computations. J. Comput. Appl. Math. **27**(1–2), 215–227 (1989). Special Issue on Parallel Algorithms for Numerical Linear Algebra
16. Fuller, S.H., Millett, I. (eds.): The Future of Computing Performance: Game Over or Next Level?. The National Academies Press, Washington (2011)
17. Haidar, A., Cao, C., Yarkhan, A., Luszczek, P., Tomov, S., Kabir, K., Dongarra, J.: Unified development for mixed multi-gpu and multi-coprocessor environments using a lightweight runtime environment. In: Proceedings of the 2014 IEEE 28th

International Parallel and Distributed Processing Symposium, IPDPS 2014, pp. 491–500. IEEE Computer Society, Washington, DC (2014)

18. Haidar, A., Dong, T., Luszczek, P., Tomov, S., Dongarra, J.: Batched matrix computations on hardware accelerators based on GPUs. Int. J. High Perform. Comput. Appl. February 2015. doi:10.1177/1094342014567546

19. Haidar, A., Dongarra, J., Kabir, K., Gates, M., Luszczek, P., Tomov, S., Jia, Y.: Hpc programming on intel many-integrated-core hardware with magma port to xeon phi. Scientific Programming, 23, January 2015

20. Haidar, A., Luszczek, P., Tomov, S., Dongarra, J.: Towards batched linear solvers on accelerated hardware platforms. In: Proceedings of the 20th ACM SIGPLAN Symposium on Principles and Practice of Parallel Programming, PPoPP 2015. ACM, San Francisco, February 2015

21. Im, E.-J., Yelick, K., Vuduc, R.: Sparsity: Optimization framework for sparse matrix kernels. Int. J. High Perform. Comput. Appl. **18**(1), 135–158 (2004)

22. Intel. Math kernel library. https://software.intel.com/en-us/en-us/intel-mkl/

23. John McCalpin. STREAM: Sustainable Memory Bandwidth in High Performance Computers. (http://www.cs.virginia.edu/stream/)

24. Messer, O.E.B., Harris, J.A., Parete-Koon, S., Chertkow, M.A.: Multicore and accelerator development for a leadership-class stellar astrophysics code. In: Manninen, P., Öster, P. (eds.) PARA. LNCS, vol. 7782, pp. 92–106. Springer, Heidelberg (2013)

25. Molero, J.M., Garzón, E.M., García, I., Quintana-Ortí, E.S., Plaza, A.: Poster: a batched Cholesky solver for local RX anomaly detection on GPUs, PUMPS (2013)

26. Nath, R., Tomov, S., Dong, T., Dongarra, J.: Optimizing symmetric dense matrix-vector multiplication on GPUs. In: Proceedings of International Conference for High Performance Computing. Networking, Storage and Analysis, Nov 2011

27. Tomov, S., Dongarra, J., Baboulin, M.: Towards dense linear algebra for hybrid gpu accelerated manycore systems. Parellel Comput. Syst. Appl. **36**(5–6), 232–240 (2010)

28. Tomov, S., Nath, R., Ltaief, H., Dongarra, J.: Dense linear algebra solvers for multicore with GPU accelerators. In: Proceedings of the 2010 IEEE International Parallel & Distributed Processing Symposium, IPDPS 2010, pp. 1–8. IEEE Computer Society, Atlanta, 19–23 April 2010. http://dx.doi.org/10.1109/IPDPSW. 2010.5470941. doi:10.1109/IPDPSW.2010.5470941

29. Tomov, S., Nath, R., Dongarra, J.: Accelerating the reduction to upper Hessenberg, tridiagonal, and bidiagonal forms through hybrid GPU-based computing. Parallel Comput. **36**(12), 645–654 (2010)

30. Volkov, V., Demmel, J.: Benchmarking GPUs to tune dense linear algebra. In: Supercomputing 2008. IEEE (2008)

31. Yeralan, S.N., Davis, T.A., Ranka, S.: Sparse mulitfrontal QR on the GPU. Technical report, University of Florida Technical Report (2013)

Large-Scale Neo-Heterogeneous Programming and Optimization of SNP Detection on Tianhe-2

Yingbo Cui[1], Xiangke Liao[1], Shaoliang Peng[1(✉)], Yutong Lu[1], Canqun Yang[1], Bingqiang Wang[2], and Chengkun Wu[1]

[1] School of Computer Science, National University of Defense Technology, Changsha, China
pengshaoliang@nudt.edu.cn
[2] National Supercomputing Center in Shenzhen, Shenzhen, China

Abstract. SNP detection is a fundamental procedure in genome analysis. A popular SNP detection tool SOAPsnp can take more than one week to analyze one human genome with a 20-fold coverage. To improve the efficiency, we developed mSNP, a parallel version of SOAPsnp. mSNP utilizes CPU cooperated with Intel® Xeon Phi™ for large-scale SNP detection. Firstly, we redesigned the key data structure of SOAPsnp, which significantly reduces the overhead of memory operations. Secondly, we devised a coordinated parallel framework, in which CPU collaborates with Xeon Phi for higher hardware utilization. Thirdly, we proposed a read-based window division strategy to improve throughput and parallel scale on multiple nodes. To the best of our knowledge, mSNP is the first SNP detection tool empowered by Xeon Phi. We achieved a 45x speedup on a single node of Tianhe-2, without any loss in precision. Moreover, mSNP showed promising scalability on 4,096 nodes on Tianhe-2.

Keywords: SNP detection · SOAPsnp · Parallelized algorithm · Xeon Phi · Many Integrated Core (MIC) Coprocessor · Tianhe-2

1 Introduction

For DNA sequence analysis, reads are segments of DNA sequence generated by sequencer. Just like string matching in computer science, reads will usually be mapped back to a reference DNA sequence to locate their positions in the reference, which are called aligned reads. SNP (Single Nucleotide Polymorphism) detection is a fundamental and essential process in whole genome analysis. It takes aligned reads, the reference sequence, and sometimes curated database like dbSNP [1] as input, detects the information of aligned reads and reference site by site, and generates a list of SNP sites. Constrained by the memory size, the reference is usually divided into multiple windows with even size. SNPs are detected window by window. However, the division may separate one read into two different windows, generating overlapped bases. As a result, the previous window has to share the information of overlapped bases with the next window when switching windows.

© Springer International Publishing Switzerland 2015
J.M. Kunkel and T. Ludwig (Eds.): ISC High Performance 2015, LNCS 9137, pp. 74–86, 2015.
DOI: 10.1007/978-3-319-20119-1_6

SOAPsnp [2] is a popular SNP detection tool developed by BGI as a member of its SOAP (Short Oligonucleotide Analysis Package) series analysis tools [3]. The software adopts a Bayesian model to call consensus genotype by carefully considering the data quality, alignment and recurring experimental errors. All these information is integrated into a single quality score for each base to measure the calling accuracy. SOAPsnp usually costs several days to analyze one human genome with sequencing depth of 20X, which may account for more than 50 % time at most of a commonly used genome analysis pipeline. The low efficiency calls for a performance boost by advanced computing technologies.

Intel Xeon Phi coprocessor [4] is becoming prevailing with a number of potential applications in accelerating various computations, such as sparse matrix-vector multiplication [5], 1D FFT computations [6], Linpack Benchmark calculation [7], molecular dynamics [8], computational biology [9], and so on.

We performed an in-depth dynamic test of SOAPsnp with gprof [10] and VTune [11], and located the limiting factors that deter its performance. One of those is that the core input data (aligned bases) is stored as a highly sparse matrix, which results in a large amount of redundant computation and huge overhead of switching windows. Moreover, the current version of SOAPsnp is a CPU-based single-threaded program although SNP detections between different DNA sites are independent. In this paper, we aim to improve the efficiency of SNP calling algorithm and develop a high performance version of SOAPsnp utilizing Xeon Phi. The ultimate goal is to apply the improved tool in large-scale SNP detection of human or other complex species genome.

To realize the above objectives, we proposed a series of optimization strategies:

(1) We proposed a space-efficient data structure to replace the original inefficient sparse matrix in SOAPsnp. The new structure can dramatically reduce memory overhead and improves operation efficiency.
(2) We transported the Bayesian model to Xeon Phi with offload mode and developed a coordinated parallel framework utilizing both CPU and Xeon Phi.
(3) For large scale parallelism, we proposed a read-based window division (RWD) strategy, which enables parallel file reading for different processes. RWD efficiently improves the throughput and parallel scale of mSNP.

mSNP is freely available from https://github.com/lemoncyb/mSNP under GPL license. We evaluated our work on the Tianhe-2 supercomputer [12], where each compute node (see Table 2) is equipped with two Xeon E5-2692 v2 2.2 GHz CPUs and three Xeon Phi 31S1P coprocessors. On one compute node of Tianhe-2, mSNP managed to finish the analysis of one 20X human genome within two hours, whereas the original CPU-based SOAPsnp used several days. The software maintains promising scalability on 4,096 nodes (98,304 CPU cores and 688,128 MIC cores). Our experiments demonstrated that mSNP is an efficient and scalable software for large-scale SNP detection of human genome. The details of evaluation are presented in Sect. 5.

The remaining of this paper is organized as follows. Section 2 presents related work. Section 3 presents the analysis of our work. Section 4 describes the architecture of mSNP. Performance evaluation is presented in Sect. 5. Section 6 concludes the paper.

2   Related Work

In this section, we survey most of the popular SNP detection tools and related optimization work. We also introduce the Intel Xeon Phi coprocessor, which has been deployed as the primary accelerator on Tianhe-2.

2.1   SNP Detection Tools

SNP detection tools take aligned reads, a reference sequence, in some cases dbSNP as input to detect SNPs. Web-based tools, such as HaploSNPer [13] and SNi-Play [14], were deployed on web servers that can be accessed from anywhere conveniently via a web page. However, the data security and uploading time prevents them from performing large-scale analysis. Therefore, stand-alone tools like QualitySNP [15], SAMtools [16], SOAPsnp [2], GATK [17] and Illuminas Isaac [18] etc. were developed.

SNP detection is time-consuming; as a result, some optimization efforts have been carried out to improve the performance. Crossbow [19] is a parallel solution using Hadoop [20] and accelerates detection with cloud computing. Rainbow [21] optimizes Crossbow for larger sequencing datasets. GSNP [22] accelerates SNP detection with GPU (graphics processing unit) to achieve better performance. Mucahid adopts cluster for computation and achieves a good load balance [23]. To the best of our knowledge, mSNP is the first SNP detection tool powered by Intel Xeon Phi.

2.2   Intel Xeon Phi Coprocessor

Intel announced its Xeon Phi coprocessor based on Many Integrated Core (MIC) architecture in November 2012 [4]. The coprocessor is equipped with 50+ cores clocked at about 1 GHz and 6 GB or more on-card memory. Each core supports 4 hardware threads. The double precision peak performance of each coprocessor is higher than 1 TFlops. The architecture of MIC is x86-compatible, which alleviates the efforts needed to transport applications to Xeon Phi compared to its counterpart GPU. Some simple applications can even run directly on Xeon Phi simply after re-compiling. There are two major modes to employ Xeon Phi in applications:

(1) native mode, where Xeon Phi has one copy of the application and runs the application natively like a compute node.
(2) offload mode, where the application runs as a master thread on CPU and offloads some selected work to Xeon Phi, treating Xeon Phi as a coprocessor [24].

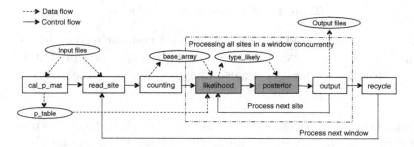

Fig. 1. Workflow of SOAPsnp. The dash lines illustrate data flow, and the real lines illustrate control flow.

As mentioned in Sect. 1, more and more applications are accelerated by Xeon Phi, from basic scientific computation to biology application [5–9]. Xeon Phi is showing great potential in parallel computing.

3 Performance Profiling Analysis of SOAPsnp

In this section, we will present our analysis of the workflow and bottleneck profiling of SOAPsnp.

3.1 Workflow of SOAPsnp

Figure 1 illustrates the workflow of SOAPsnp. SOAPsnp takes aligned reads, a reference genome, and in some cases dbSNP as input. The output is consensus genotype information. SOAPsnp mainly contains seven modules: *cal_p_mat*, *read_site*, *counting*, *likelihood*, *posterior*, *output*, and *recycle* (italics bold font represents function module, italics font represents data structure). The core data structures include *p_matrix*, *base_info*, and *type_likely* (the oval block of Fig. 1).

cal_p_mat module takes input reads and generates a calibration matrix *p_matrix* for *likelihood* computation. *p_matrix* is a four-dimensional matrix ($256 \times 256 \times 4 \times 4 = 1,048,576$) with a size of 8 MB. Constrained by the memory size, SOAPsnp divides the reference into multiple windows with even size. In each window, SNP calling is performed site by site. The *read_site* module loads a fixed number of sites (a window size) from input file. Then *counting* collects the information of aligned bases for each site and stores the information in *base_info*. *likelihood* takes *base_info* and *p_matrix* as inputs, calculates the likelihood and stores it in *type_likely*. After posterior calculation, calling results of one site are written to the output file. Then the next site of the current window will be processed from *likelihood* too. The *recycle* module switches windows by dealing with the overlapped bases and re-initializes buffers for new window.

base_info is a four dimensional matrix ($4 \times 64 \times 256 \times 2$, corresponding to *base* $\times$ *score* $\times$ *coord* $\times$ *strand*), storing the information of bases aligned to each

Table 1. Time breakdown of SOAPsnp

Module	cal_p_matrix	read_site	couting	likelihood	posterior	recycle	output
Time/s	16.73	2.35	40.59	1478.36	23.47	210.19	752.98
%	0.66 %	0.09 %	1.59 %	57.93 %	0.92 %	29.50 %	8.42 %

DNA site. The dimensions stand for four aspects of an aligned base: the base type, the sequencing quality score, the coordinates on read and the strand of read.

3.2   Bottleneck Profiling

To identify the performance bottleneck of SOAPsnp, we analyzed the code of SOAPsnp and divided it into seven main modules, as described in Subsect. 3.1. Then we timed each module and obtained a time breakdown, as listed in Table 1. *likelihood* is the most time-consuming module, which takes about 58 % of the total processing time. The second is *recycle* taking 30 % percentage. *output* is ranked third with 8.4 %. Then we investigated further with Intel VTune [11] to detect the most time-consuming operations in *likelihood* and *recycle*. Further code analysis shows large amounts of these operations are memory accesses, especially the accesses to *base_info* data structure storing information of aligned reads. As mentioned in Subsect. 3.1, *likelihood* traverses *base_info* to fetch aligned reads. *recycle* module copies the information of aligned reads across adjacent windows. The optimization strategy to *base_info* is described in Subsect. 4.1.

4   Design and Implementation of mSNP

In this section, we will describe the design and implementation of mSNP in detail.

4.1   Consolidating Sparse Matrix

SOAPsnp detects SNP site by site. For each site computation, every element of *base_info* will be accessed exactly once (including zero elements), which would generate a total number of $131,072 (= 4 \times 64 \times 256 \times 2)$ memory accesses. That is, 393 trillions memory accesses will be made for a whole human genome with about 3 billion sites.

One notable fact is that, *base_info* is a highly sparse matrix. Each element of *base_info* stands for a combination of four dimensions ($base \times score \times coord \times strand$) and is initialized with zero. The element value will increase by one if a base in a read matches the combination. However, sequencing depth is usually smaller than 100X, and the bases in one human genome are relatively fixed, so most elements in *base_info* are zero. We tested several human genomes and found that only less than 0.08 % of *base_info* elements are non-zero. This means that most memory accesses to the matrix are in vain.

base: 2 bits   coord: 8 bits

17 bits   score: 6 bits   strand: 1 bit

Fig. 2. Bit composition of *base_array*.

To reduce the amount of unnecessary memory accesses, we design a space-efficient data structure *base_array* to store the information of each DNA site. The *base_array* only stores the dimensions information of non-zero elements. As illustrated in Fig. 2, the four dimensions (*base × score × coord × strand*) are integrated into 17 bits in one word (32 bits) by bit operations. For repeated bases, *base_array* stores multiple copies of the same coordinates. Thus, all information is maintained and the space complexity of *base_info* is significantly reduced, as the percentage of non-zero elements of *base_info* is only 0.08 %.

By analyzing the source code, we discovered that recycle module produces a large amount of memory copy operations when switching windows, especially the copy of *base_info* with a size of 13MB. With the introduction of *base_array*, the cost of windows switching is reduced by three orders of magnitude too.

4.2 Coordinated Parallelism Between CPU and Xeon Phi

As described in Subsect. 3.1 and illustrated in Fig. 1, SOAPsnp divides the SNP calling of one genome into multiple windows. In each window, SNP detection is performed site by site. Theres no dependency between sites. We parallelize the procedure by multi-threading on both CPU and Xeon Phi, where each thread handles one site.

Due to Xeon Phi's weak ability of file operation in native mode, mSNP adopts the offload mode of Xeon Phi. In the naive offload mode, CPU will have to pause and wait for the results to be returned from Xeon Phi, which results in a waste of the CPU computing power. In mSNP, we make the data transfer between CPU and Xeon Phi asynchronous, which allows CPU to take on other job immediately after launching the offload region, as illustrated in Fig. 3. When the offload region is finished, CPU retrieves results from Xeon Phi and resumes other operations.

4.3 Collaborated Parallel Window Division

As described in Subsect. 4.2, mSNP parallelizes the SNP detections of different sites in a window with multi-thread. While the computing power of one computing node is limited, to achieve higher performance, we have to parallelize SOAPsnp across nodes.

SOAPsnp performs SNP calling window by window. One straightforward strategy to parallelize SOAPsnp across nodes is to assign each node at least one window. Different nodes call SNPs of different windows simultaneously.

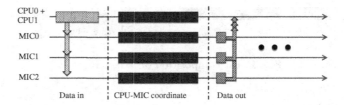

Fig. 3. Coordinated parallelism between CPU and Xeon Phi. Data in stands for CPU transfers input data to MICs. CPU-MIC coordinate means CPU and MIC perform computation simultaneously. Data out denotes MICs transfer results back to CPU.

SOAPsnp divides windows evenly according to the coordinates of base on reference sequence, denoted as coordinate-based window division (CWD) as illustrated in Fig. 4. The coordinate of base is stored in the aligned reads file, as attached information to each read. The coordinate is not known until the read sequence is loaded into memory. It's impossible to locate a read with given nonzero coordinate beforehand. That is to say, it's impossible for different processes to load reads from the start of any window simultaneously. To parallelize the SNP calling of different windows, we have to choose a master-slave mode. The master process loads reads into memory sequentially, prepares base information for each window, and sends window task to idle slave processes. For the master-slave mode, the throughput and parallel scale are limited by the master process, where all input data come from. Different processes cannot load reads simultaneously.

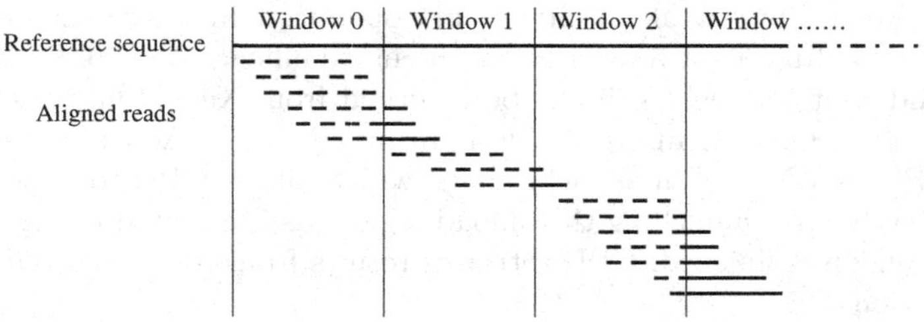

Fig. 4. Coordinate-based window division of SOAPsnp. The dash lines denote aligned reads. The real zones of dash lines represent the bases that belong to the next window, but are loaded by the previous window, that is overlapped bases.

To improve the parallel scale across nodes, we designed a read-based window division (RWD) strategy. As illustrated in Fig. 5, windows are divided by the number of reads, each window containing almost equal number of reads. As each aligned read occupies four lines in file, the RWD strategy actually divides windows by file lines. Different processes can load reads from different lines of input file simultaneously.

Another problem of RWD strategy is to deal with overlapped reads which belong to the next window, but are loaded by the previous window, responding to the real lines in Figs. 4 and 5. SOAPsnp detects SNP site by site. In order to maintain the completeness of each site, the information of overlapped bases has to be transferred to the next window before the next window launches. To realize this, two adjacent processes P_n and P_{n+1} have to send one message to each other. As illustrated in Fig. 5, P_{n+1} sends the position of its first site Pos_1 to P_n, P_n sends the information of sites after Pos_1 (overlapped bases) to P_{n+1}. Different processes accomplish loading step evenly at the same time, because the number of assigned reads is evenly equal. Then all processes communicate with each other at the same time. When communication finishes, all processes start SNP calling even simultaneously. Based on the above description, the throughput and parallel scale of mSNP improve efficiently compared with SOAPsnp. Moreover, for each process is assigned evenly equal number of reads, different processes can get a better load balance.

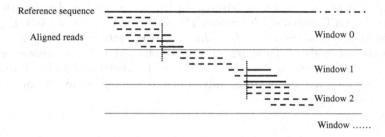

Fig. 5. Read-based window division (RWD) of mSNP. The dash lines illustrate aligned reads. The real zones of dash lines mean the bases that belong to the next window, but are read by the previous window, that is overlapped bases.

5   Evaluation

We evaluated the performance of mSNP from four aspects: effectiveness of space-efficient format *base_array*, CPU and Xeon Phi cooperation, RWD performance and scalability.

5.1   Experimental Setup

We evaluated our work on the Tianhe-2 supercomputer in the National Super Computer Center in Guangzhou (NSCC-GZ) [12]. The configuration of Tianhe-2 is described in Table 2. The whole system consists of 16,000 compute nodes.

The latest version of SOAPsnp is v1.03, which is available from it's website[1]. SOAPsnp v1.03 is a CPU-based single thread program. In consideration of

---

[1] SOAPsnp website: http://soap.genomics.org.cn/soapsnp.html.

equality, we chose different baselines for different evaluations, and the details are described in the subsections. We prepared three datasets for evaluation: 3.2 GB, 73 GB and 542 GB. The details are described in the subsections too.

Table 2. Configuration of Tianhe-2's compute node

	Xeon® E5-2692 v2 CPU	Xeon® Phi™ 31S1P
Sockets × Cores × Threads	2 × 12 × 2	3 × 57 × 4
Clock Frequency (GHz)	2.20	1.10
L1/L2/L3 Cache (KB)	32/256/30,720	32/512/-
Memory Size (GB)	64	6

5.2   Dimension Reduction of Sparse Matrix

We adopted SOAPsnp v1.03 as baseline in this evaluation and the optimized version is also CPU-based single thread. The size of test data is 3.2 GB. Figure 6 shows the time consumptions of *likelihood* and *recycle* before and after optimization on one node of Tianhe-2. Our space-efficient new representation format *base_array* outperforms *base_info* 32+ times in *likelihood* and 56+ times in *recycle* function. *base_array* stores only non-zero elements to avoid unnecessary memory accesses.

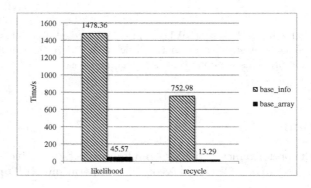

Fig. 6. Performance of *likelihood* and *recycle* before and after optmization

Table 3 shows the time breakdown of the CPU-based optimized single thread version of SOAPsnp. The main two modules optimized are *likelihood* and *recycle*. After optimization, for a 3.2 GB dataset, the percentage of *likelihood* is 5.10 %, and that of *recycle* is 1.49 %. The two modules are no longer the bottlenecks. *output* becomes the most time-consuming module taking more than 84 % and turns into the big bottleneck. It's hard to parallelize output in multi-threads, while possible in multi-processes.

Table 3. Time breakdown of CPU-based optimized version of SOAPsnp

Module	cal_p_matrix	read_site	couting	likelihood	posterior	recycle	output
Time/s	17.05	2.13	41.21	45.57	22.64	13.29	750.88
%	1.91 %	0.24 %	4.62 %	5.10 %	2.54 %	1.49 %	84.11 %

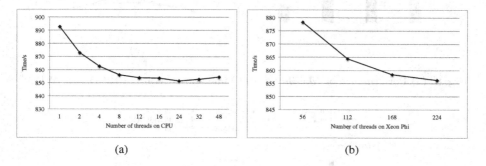

(a)   (b)

Fig. 7. (a) Performance of mSNP on CPU. (b) Performance of mSNP on Xeon Phi.

5.3   CPU and Xeon Phi Cooperation

mSNP supports coordinated computation between CPUs and MICs. We tested mSNP under different number of CPUs and MICs on one node of Tianhe-2. To determine the proper number of threads launched in CPU and MIC, we evaluated the performance of mSNP with the number of threads varying first. We adopted 3.2 GB dataset in the tests. Figure 7(a) illustrates the performance of mSNP on CPU. There are two sockets 12-core CPUs in each compute node. The time decreases with the number of threads increasing, and the peak performance is obtain in 24 threads, 1 core assigned with 1 thread. After 24 threads, the performance drops gradually. Figure 7(b) shows the performance on Xeon Phi. The peak performance is obtained in 224 threads, 1 core assigned with 4 threads. Thus, we launched 24 threads on CPUs and 224 threads on one Xeon Phi for the later tests.

The smooth varieties in Fig. 8 are contributed by the big proportion of output in mSNP (Table 3). It's hard to parallelize output in multi-thread. To make the illustration for CPU-Phi cooperation distinct, we chose 73 GB dataset and presented the time of *likelihood* only, because other modules of mSNP are not parallelized by multi-thread. Figure 8(a) shows the performance of *likelihood* for CPUs cooperating with Phis. As illustrated, for SNP detection, the computing power of one Xeon Phi corresponds to that of two CPUs in Tianhe-2. The high accelerator speedup comes from the massively parallelism on Xeon Phi. There's no other communication, except for transferring input data to Phi and getting results from Phi to CPU. Thus, the performance increases nearly linearly as the number of Phi increases.

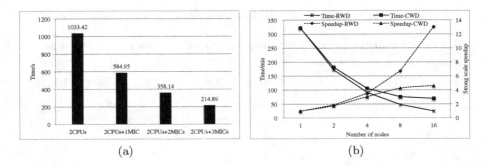

Fig. 8. (a) Performance of *likelihood*. (b) Time and speedup of RWD vs. CWD.

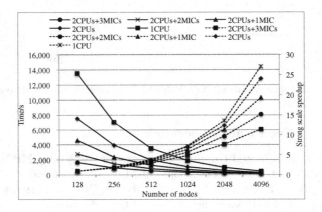

Fig. 9. Strong scale speedup of mSNP

5.4 RWD Performance

Figure 8(b) shows the performance and strong scale speedup of RWD vs. CWD
from 1 to 16 nodes on Tianhe-2. All two CPUs with 24 threads and three MICs
with 224 threads per Phi are used in each compute node. The size of dataset is
73 GB. RWD and CWD achieve evenly equal speedup before 4 nodes. After 4
nodes, the performance of RWD exceeds CWD more and more. The speedup of
CWD increases slower and slower after 4 nodes. CWD only obtains about 4.2
folds speedup on 16 nodes, while RWD achieves about 13 folds speedup, which is
over 3 folds faster. The good scalability is contributed by RWD's parallel reading
capability.

5.5 Scalability

We tested the scalability of mSNP from 128 nodes to 4,096 nodes on Tianhe-
2. Figure 9 presents the strong scale speedup of mSNP. The dash lines indicate speedup and the real lines indicate time. The size of test data is 542 GB.

For a better presentation, we used the performance achieved on 128 nodes as baseline. The lines in the figure stand for the number of processors (CPU, MIC) used in each compute node of Tianhe-2. We observed a speedup of about 27.5 from 128 nodes to 4,096 nodes with 2CPUs+3MICs, and a speedup of 24 with 2CPUs+2MICs, a speedup of about 19 with 2CPUs+1MIC, about 15 folds speedup with 2CPUs, about 11.5 folds speedup with 1CPU. These results demonstrate a promising result for strong scalability on the large scale CPU-MIC heterogeneous system, Tianhe-2.

6 Conclusion

In this paper, we presented mSNP, which a large-scale parallel SNP detection tool accelerated by Intel Xeon Phi. Firstly, we proposed a space-efficient representation format that can substantially reduces the amount of memory accesses and overhead of switching windows. Secondly, we developed a coordinated parallel framework using CPU and Xeon Phi, which optimized hardware utilization. Thirdly, we proposed a read-based window division strategy to improve data throughput and parallel scale across nodes. We evaluated our work on Tianhe-2 supercomputer. It achieves about 45x speedup on one node and exhibits strong scalability on 4,096 nodes. The algorithm optimization, parallelization on both CPU and Xeon Phi lead to a significant reduction of computing time.

Acknowledgments. We would like to thank Mr. Yingrui Li from BGI for providing the source code of SOAPsnp and Dr. Jun Wang from BGI for providing related test data. We would also like to thank Prof. Hans V. Westerhoff from University of Manchester for discussions of the human genome re-sequencing analysis problem and thus improving our own understanding. This work is supported by NSFC Grant 61272056, U1435222, 61133005, 61120106005, 91430218 and 61303191.

References

1. National Center for Biotechnology Information. http://www.ncbi.nlm.nih.gov/SNP/
2. Li, R., Li, Y., Fang, X.: SNP detection for massively parallel whole-genome resequencing. Genome Res. **19**(6), 1124–1132 (2009)
3. Short Oligonucleotide Analysis Package Sites. http://soap.genomics.org.cn/index.html
4. James, J., Reinders, J.: Intel Xeon Phi Coprocessor High Performance Programming. Morgan Kaufmann, Newnes (2013)
5. Liu, X., Smelyanskiy, M., Chow, E., Dubey, P.: Efficient sparse matrix-vector multiplication on x86-based many-core processors. In: Proceedings of the 27th International ACM Conference on International Conference on Supercomputing, pp. 273–282. ACM (2013)
6. Park, J., Bikshandi, G., Vaidyanathan, K., Tang, P.T.P., Dubey, P., Kim, D.: Tera-scale 1D FFT with low-communication algorithm and Intel® Xeon Phi™ coprocessors. In: Proceedings of SC13: International Conference for High Performance Computing, Networking, Storage and Analysis, p. 34. ACM (2013)

7. Heinecke, A., Vaidyanathan, K., Smelyanskiy, M., Kobotov, A., Dubtsov, R. et al.: Design and implementation of the linpack benchmark for single and multi-node systems based on intel® Xeon Phi coprocessor. In: 2013 IEEE 27th International Symposium on Parallel & Distributed Processing (IPDPS), pp. 126–137. IEEE (2013)

8. Pennycook, S.J., Hughes, C.J., Smelyanskiy, M., Jarvis, S.A.: Exploring SIMD for molecular dynamics, using intel® Xeon® processors and intel® Xeon Phi coprocessors. In: 2013 IEEE 27th International Symposium on Parallel & Distributed Processing (IPDPS), pp. 1085–1097. IEEE (2013)

9. Misra, S., Pamnany, K., Aluru, S.: Parallel mutual information based construction of whole-genome networks on the intel® Xeon PhiTM coprocessor. In: 2014 IEEE 28th International Parallel and Distributed Processing Symposium, pp. 241–250. IEEE (2014)

10. Graham, S.L., Kessler, P.B., McKusick, M.K.: Gprof: a call graph execution profiler. ACM SIGPLAN Not. **39**(4), 49–57 (2004)

11. Wikipedia Sites of VTune. http://en.wikipedia.org/wiki/VTune

12. TOP500 Supercomputer Sites. http://www.top500.org/system/177999

13. Tang, J., Leunissen, J.A.M., Voorrips, R.E.: HaploSNPer: a web-based allele and SNP de-tection tool. BMC Genet. **9**(1), 23 (2008)

14. Dereeper, A., Nicolas, S., Le Cunff, L.: SNiPlay: a web-based tool for detection, management and analysis of SNPs. Application to grapevine diversity projects. BMC Bioinform. **12**(1), 134 (2011)

15. Tang, J., Vosman, B., Voorrips, R.E.: QualitySNP: a pipeline for detecting single nucleotide polymorphisms and insertions/deletions in EST data from diploid and polyploid species. BMC Bioinform. **7**(1), 438 (2006)

16. Li, H., Handsaker, B., Wysoker, A.: The sequence alignment/map format and SAMtools. Bioinformatics **25**(16), 2078–2079 (2009)

17. DePristo, M.A., Banks, E., Poplin, R.: A framework for variation discovery and genotyping using next-generation DNA sequencing data. Nature Genet. **43**(5), 491–498 (2011)

18. Raczy, C., Petrovski, R., Saunders, C.T.: Isaac: ultra-fast whole-genome secondary analysis on Illumina sequencing platforms. Bioinformatics **29**, 2041–2043 (2013). btt314

19. Langmead, B., Schatz, M.C., Lin, J.: Searching for SNPs with cloud computing. Genome Biol. **10**(11), R134 (2009)

20. Shvachko, K., Kuang, H., Radia, S., The hadoop distributed file system. IEEE 26th Symposium on Mass Storage Systems and Technologies (MSST), pp. 1–10. IEEE (2010)

21. Zhao, S., Prenger, K., Smith, L.: Rainbow: a tool for large-scale whole-genome sequencing data analysis using cloud computing. BMC Genomics **14**(1), 425 (2013)

22. Lu, M., Zhao, J., Luo, Q.: GSNP: a DNA single-nucleotide polymorphism detection system with GPU acceleration. In: 2011 International Conference on Parallel Processing (ICPP), pp. 592–601. IEEE (2011)

23. Kutlu, M., Agrawal, G.: Cluster-based SNP calling on large-scale genome sequencing data. In: 2014 14th IEEE/ACM International Symposium on Cluster, Cloud and Grid computing (CCGrid), pp. 455–464. IEEE (2013)

24. Cui, Y., Liao, X., Zhu, X.: mBWA: a massively parallel sequence reads aligner. In: Saez-Rodriguez, J., Rocha, M.P., Fdez-Riverola, F., De Paz Santana, J.F. (eds.) PACBB 2014. AISC, vol. 294, pp. 113–120. Springer, Heidelberg (2014)

ACCOLADES: A Scalable Workflow Framework for Large-Scale Simulation and Analyses of Automotive Engines

Shashi M. Aithal$^{(\boxtimes)}$ and Stefan M. Wild

Argonne National Laboratory, Argonne, IL 60439, USA
{aithal,wild}@anl.gov

Abstract. Analysis and optimization of simulation-generated data have myriads of scientific and industrial applications. Fuel consumption and emissions over the entire drive cycle of a large fleet of vehicles is an example of such an application and the focus of this study. Temporal variation of fuel consumption and emissions in an automotive engine are functions of over twenty variables. Determining relationships between fuel consumption or emissions and the dependent variables plays a crucial role in designing an automotive engine. This paper describes the development of ACCOLADES (Advanced Concurrent COmputing for LArge-scale Dynamic Engine Simulations), a scalable workflow framework that exploits the task parallelism inherent in such analyses by using large-scale computing. Excellent weak scaling is observed on 4,096 cores of both an Intel Sandy Bridge-based cluster and a Blue-Gene/Q supercomputer.

Keywords: Workflow management · Industrial simulations · Large-scale vehicle simulations · Task parallelism

1 Introduction

Discrete time series occur in many scientific and industrial applications [7, 9, 11, 13]. Examples of these applications include solar radiation, temporal variations of the load requirements on a power-grid, temperature variation of power-generating equipment and variation in the price of a commodity, among others. An observed value of a time series is typically a function of several variables; developing an understanding of the effect of the variables on the observed value is a computationally intensive task. Furthermore, optimization of time-averaged or integrated values of these functions often requires analyses of large datasets.

Fuel consumption and emissions over the entire drive cycle of a large fleet of cars is an example of such a problem, and hence the focus of this study. Temporal variation of fuel consumption and emissions in an automotive engine

This material is based upon work supported by the U.S. Department of Energy, Office of Science, under Contract DE-AC02-06CH11357.

J.M. Kunkel and T. Ludwig (Eds.): ISC High Performance 2015, LNCS 9137, pp. 87–95, 2015.
DOI: 10.1007/978-3-319-20119-1_7

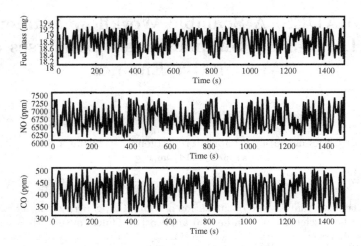

Fig. 1. Typical time series data for fuel mass (*top*), NO emissions (*middle*), and CO emissions (*bottom*) as generated by pMODES over a single drive cycle.

can be functions of over twenty independent variables, including engine speed (i.e., RPM), torque, type of fuel/additive, air-to-fuel ratio, ambient temperature, inlet pressure, humidity, ignition and valve timings, and driving conditions (e.g., city or highway). Deriving correlations between the observed values (such as fuel consumption and emissions) and the independent variables plays a crucial role during the design and development stages of an automotive engine. For instance, a study on the effect of the inflow air temperature on the fuel consumption and (NO, CO, soot, and unburned hydrocarbons) emissions might consist of four different drive cycles and five different temperatures (e.g., expressed as a percentage of the nominal temperature). Such a study would result in twenty different time series for fuel consumption and eighty time series for emissions (i.e., one for each type of emission). A typical drive cycle of an automotive engine has a duration of 25–30 min; for data sampled every second, one obtains approximately 1,500 data points per drive cycle. Dynamometer testing and measurements (called "dyno testing") are usually conducted to obtain data for engine performance and emissions. Numerical simulations can be used to complement dyno data or to estimate engine performance and emissions during the engine design process.

Figure 1 shows an instance of the temporal variation of fuel flow along with the computed temporal variation of nitric oxide (NO) and carbon monoxide (CO) emissions. For each sampled data point, which represents one (compression and expansion) engine cycle, engine state variables (e.g., temperature, pressure, andfuel-air mixture combination) are computed over 360 crank angle degrees (CAD) in intervals of roughly 0.5 CAD. These engine state variables are needed in order to compute the engine performance (e.g., torque and power) and engine-out emissions (e.g., NO and CO). Hence, each drive cycle requires the evaluation of over a million engine ($\approx$1,500 $\times$ 720) CAD.

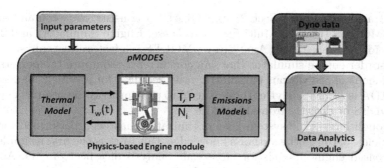

Fig. 2. Block diagram showing the structure of ACCOLADES.

The above example represents a simplified case wherein the effect of variation of a single parameter on the engine performance and emissions is studied. Typical fleet studies require the simultaneous variation of multiple design variables over specified ranges for a larger number of drive cycles, resulting in a large set of input configurations. For instance, if one were to consider the effect of variation of four design parameters (e.g., inlet pressure, inlet temperature, humidity, and engine RPM) with four different values for each of these design parameters over sixteen different drive cycles, one would need ($4^4 \times 16 = 4,096$) different independent cases. Each of these 4,096 cases would require 1,500 engine-cycle evaluations. Conducting large parametric sweeps on the drive cycles of a fleet of cars with varying combinations of operating conditions places stringent demands on the required computational resources. Furthermore, analyses of the results of these large-scale simulations present significant challenges from a data-analytics standpoint. Transient multidimensional numerical simulation of a single engine cycle (360 CAD) running on 24 to 48 cores (approaching the strong scaling limit for physically meaningful grid sizes) can take several hours to days, depending on the complexity of the physical models used. Hence, conducting multi-cycle simulations for the scenario described above would require enormous computational resources, and thus precluding their use for initial design/development studies or analyses of large transients.

Physics-based reduced-order models, which capture the temporal variation, for example, of average engine temperature, pressure, and mixture composition, are ideally suited for such large-scale studies. Given the wide range of operating conditions (engine speed, load, equivalence ratio, etc.) the reduced-order models have to be robust and fast in order to compute emissions and performance at real-time speeds. Real-time analysis would require a typical data point in any given drive cycle to be computed in approximately 250–30 ms.

This paper describes the development of ACCOLADES (Advanced Concurrent COmputing for LArge-scale Dynamic Engine Simulations), a scalable workflow management framework that enables automotive design engineers to exploit the task parallelism inherent in the study of such systems using large-scale computing (e.g., GPGPUs, multicore architectures, or the cloud). As shown in Fig. 2 and detailed in Sect. 2, ACCOLADES consists of two main components, pMODES (parallel Multi-fuel Otto Diesel Engine Simulator) and TADA (Toolkit for Advanced Data Analytics). pMODES is a fast, robust, physics-based reduced-order engine simulator that can concurrently compute the performance and emissions of the various parametric cases required for a vehicle fleet simulation. TADA is a data analytics toolbox used to post-process the results generated by pMODES or directly from dyno data.

Although large-scale system-level optimization has been performed for military vehicles [5,10], to the author's knowledge, this work is the first to implement physics-based engine models for large-scale analysis of a fleet of cars. As illustrated by our results in Sect. 3, ACCOLADES can be used in the design and conceptual analyses phase of new engine systems and can streamline workflow management in the analyses of large amounts of data obtained in dyno tests for various engine operating conditions.

2   Main Components of ACCOLADES

ACCOLADES consists of the reduced-order engine simulator p-MODES and the data analytics toolbox TADA.

2.1   pMODES

pMODES is used to compute the temporal variation of various engine parameters such as pressure, temperature and mixture composition for each CAD over an entire drive cycle. The energy equation shown in Eq. (1) describes the relationship between the engine crank-angle θ and pressure.

$$\frac{dP(\theta)}{d\theta} = \frac{\gamma - 1}{V(\theta)}(Q_{in} - Q_{loss}) - \gamma \frac{P(\theta)}{V(\theta)}\frac{dV}{d\theta} \qquad (1)$$

Solution of this equation yields the temporal variation of cylinder pressure for a given set of operating conditions (such as load, combustion duration, fuel type, engine RPM, etc). The instantaneous values of temperature and composition of the burned and unburned gas zones can be obtained from the instantaneous value of computed pressure. Knowing the instantaneous temperature, pressure and composition of the burned zone enables the computation of emissions such as NO, CO, soot, and unburned hydrocarbons using simplified reduced chemistry models. Details of these models and the solution procedure are discussed in Ref. [2]. Instantaneous values of equilibrium concentrations of the combustion products are needed to compute various emissions. Computation of these equilibrium concentrations pose serious numerical challenges on account of the stiffness of the system of nonlinear equations describing the formation of combustion products. References [1,3] discuss the details of the computation procedure and steps taken to ensure a fast, robust solution. Following the solution procedure discussed above enables one to obtain temporal variation of emissions such as NO and CO for a given fuel input profile. Figure 1 shows the NO and CO emissions for a single-cylinder gasoline engine obtained using pMODES.

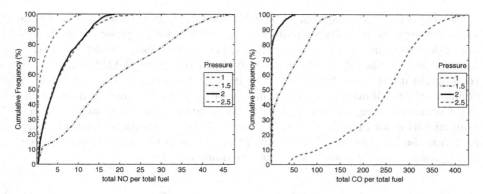

Fig. 3. Cumulative distributions of NO (*left*) and CO (*right*) emissions for different initial cylinder pressure conditions. Each curve shows the percentage of drive cycle runs for which the NO/CO is at or below the value given on the horizontal axis.

2.2 TADA

The Toolkit for Advanced Data Analytics (TADA) provides a framework for post-processing of experimental- and simulation-generated time series data. Here we overview some of the operations possible with TADA.

Whether from physical experiment or numerical simulation, TADA takes as input time series data $\{f_o(x; t; \theta_t(x)) : o = 1, \ldots, O; t = 1, \ldots, T\}$, where o indexes O different dependent variable outputs, t indexes T time periods $\tau_1 < \tau_2 < \cdots < \tau_T$, $x \in \mathbb{R}^n$ parameterizes the independent design and operational variables, and $\theta_t(x) \in \mathbb{R}^m$ denotes the state variables at time τ_t with input x.

Typical data analysis operations on these sets of time series data include

Filtering to extract basic statistics and identify input configurations of interest. For example, one can determine peak temperatures and pressures in order to characterize engine damage; peaks can be computed for each configuration, or all peaks above a threshold can be extracted.

Empirical distribution characterization to provide cross-configuration information. Such distributions can be used, for example, to determine fleet-wide fuel economy [12] or to characterize emissions as a function of ambient pressure as is done in Fig. 3 for the case study in Sect. 3.

Sensitivity analysis to analyze how operating conditions or other independent variables effect observables of interest. Sensitivity analysis can be used, for example to determine fleet-wide implications for performance and emissions of increased adoption of novel fuel types or additives.

Tradeoff visualization and analysis can be used to flag a configuration that is worse in all metrics of interest than some other configuration. Such analyses can also be used, for example, to identify vehicle configurations that sacrifice little in terms of performance while providing substantial gains in fuel economy.

We expect that the capabilities in TADA will be fully used as one "closes the loop" between the pMODES simulation and analysis for purposes of simulation-based design optimization [4] or optimal experimental design to determine configurations that should be tested on a dyno. In this view, TADA can be used to generate input configurations and/or in order to optimize a design objective of interest. Distributional information can be used to generate scenarios (e.g., ambient or operating conditions, drive cycle variations) for use in sample average approximation for optimization under uncertainty [8]. Similarly, tradeoff analysis forms the basis for simultaneously optimizing multiple conflicting objectives [6,14], such as performance and engine lifetime/reliability.

3   Results and Discussions

As an illustrative example, we discuss the simulation of a single-cylinder gasoline engine operating at 1,100 RPM, wherein the inlet gas temperature, air humidity, initial cylinder pressure, and exhaust gas recirculation (EGR) fraction are varied for realistic engine operating conditions. Each of the parameters have four values and for each configuration sixteen different drive cycles are considered, leading to 4,096 individual configurations (or parametric cases). The inlet gas temperature is varied from 28 to 31 °C in steps of 1 °C, the initial cylinder pressure is varied from 0.88 atm to 1.0 atm, the relative humidity is varied from 0 to 100 %, and the EGR fraction is varied from 0 to 3 %. These 4,096 parametric cases, each with 1,500 temporal data points in the drive cycle, were run on IBM Blue Gene/Q (BG/Q) and Sandy Bridge clusters at Argonne National Laboratory. The BG/Q supercomputer (called "Mira") is equipped with 786,432 cores, 768 TB of memory and has a peak performance of 10 petaflops. Each compute node has a PowerPC A2 1600 MHz processor containing 16 cores, each with 4 hardware threads, running at 1.6 GHz, and 16 GB of DDR3 memory. The Sandy Bridge cluster (called "Blues") is a 2.6 GHz, 4960 processors system with 16 cores per compute node and 4 GB memory per core. These systems were chosen to ensure portability of the code on different architectures (and compilers) and also to compare and contrast the relative performance of ACCOLADES on these machines. Each of the cases considered in the study was assigned to one MPI rank on the machine. Each MPI rank read its input data (i.e., operating conditions such as initial pressure, humidity, inlet air temperature, and EGR fraction) from a separate input file and wrote two different files: (a) the computed solution (e.g., emissions, maximum temperature, pressure, exhaust temperature and pressure, peak ion current, location of peak ion current) and (b) operating conditions to its own uniquely named file. This methodology was chosen to ensure no communication between different case configurations (thus ensuring task parallelism), and also to facilitate data analytics by TADA. A typical case's solution file was 306 kB while the file containing information about each of 1,500 data points was 351 kB. Since each of the parametric cases are independent of the others, increasing the number of cases directly proportional to the number of cores yields a weak scaling study. The study was run both with no optimization

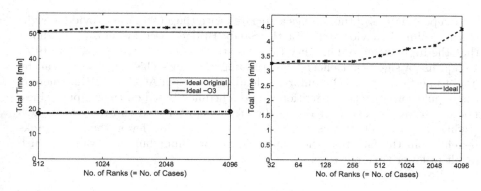

Fig. 4. Weak scaling results on the BlueGene/Q machine Mira (*left*) and the Sandy Bridge-based machine Blues (*right*).

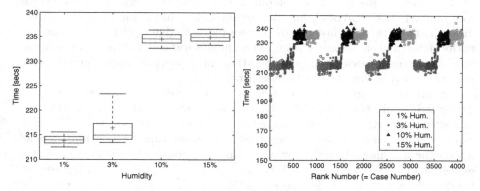

Fig. 5. Case timings on Sandy Bridge-based machine Blues: (*left*) global sensitivity analysis (outliers removed) demonstrating effect of humidity input on per case timing; (*right*) case timings as a function of rank number show a cyclic pattern associated with varying humidity input.

and with 'O3' optimization option on both machines. The Intel 13.1 compiler was used on Blues whereas the xl.legacy.ndebug (libraries with MPICH compiled with the XL compilers) was used on Mira.

Figure 4 shows the scaling for Blues and Mira (with and without optimization). Excellent weak scaling is seen on both machines. It was seen that the optimization level did not change the overall compute time on Blues (hence it is not shown in Fig. 4), whereas using -O3 level optimization on Mira reduced the computational time by a factor of nearly 2.7. We attribute the slight increase in overall computational time as the number of cores (and thus cases) increases primarily to imbalances in individual case solution times and to increased contention for the I/O operations. Furthermore, we see greater imbalances across cases for Blues than for Mira.

Deeper analysis of the timings associated with the 4,096 cases provides insight to the scaling behavior seen. For the Sandy Bridge-based system, Fig. 5 shows that the input value of humidity (for this study, selected from $\{1\%, 3\%, 10\%, 15\%\}$) has a significant effect on the timing of a run. This information can be used to perform application-informed load balancing in ACCOLADES, whereby the population of tasks is partitioned and scheduled based on their input values. For the study presented in Fig. 4, the cases were selected as ordered in Fig. 5 (right). As a result of this ordering, the results using fewer than 512 ranks benefit from the fact that they only involve low input humidity values, which result in lower time per case.

4   Conclusions

In this work, we discuss the development of a parallel design and data analysis tool, named ACCOLADES, for conducting large-scale parametric studies of a fleet of cars. A parallel, fast robust physics-based engine model used to compute performance and emissions of automotive engines was coupled to a data-analytics module to enable a wide range of operations in support of design- and decision-makers as well as vehicle experimentalists.

An illustrative example consisting of 4,096 parametric cases was run on a Sandy Bridge cluster and an IBM BG/Q supercomputer. It was shown that the emission and performance characteristics of a 25-min-long synthetic drive cycle can be obtained numerically in acceptable computing time ($\approx$ 4–20 min, depending on the machine). Excellent weak scaling was observed on both machines as expected in such inherently task parallel problems. Although no serious I/O bottlenecks were observed for the simulations considered in this work, we expect that additional care will need to be taken when performing I/O operations for massively parallel studies (e.g., involving a million cases) in order avoid overloading a parallel file system.

Acknowledgments. We gratefully acknowledge the computing resources provided by the Argonne Leadership Computing Facility and the Laboratory Computing Resource Center at Argonne National Laboratory.

References

1. Aithal, S.M.: Analysis of the current signature in a constant-volume combustion chamber. Combust. Sci. Technol. **185**, 336–349 (2013)
2. Aithal, S. M.: Development of an integrated design tool for real-time analyses of performance and emissions in engines powered by alternative fuels. In: Proceedings of the SAE 11th International Conference on Engines and Vehicles (2013). SAE Paper 2013-24-0134
3. Aithal, S.M.: Prediction of voltage signature in a homogeneous charge compression ignition (HCCI) engine fueled with propane and acetylene. Combust. Sci. Technol. **185**, 1184–1201 (2013)

4. Aithal, S.M., Wild, S.M.: Development of a fast, robust numerical tool for the design, optimization, and control of IC engines. In: Proceedings of the SAE 11th International Conference on Engines and Vehicles (2013). SAE Paper 2013–24-0141
5. Belludi, N., Receveur, J., Raymond, J.: High-performance grid computing for cummins vehicle mission simulation: architecture and applications. In: Proceedings of the SAE 2011 Commercial Vehicle Engineering Congress (2011). SAE Paper 2011–01-2268
6. Ehrgott, M.: Multicriteria Optimization, 2nd edn. Springer-Verlag, Heidelberg (2005)
7. Fu, T.-C.: A review on time series data mining. Eng. Appl. Artif. Intell. **24**, 164–181 (2011)
8. Homem-de-Mello, T., Bayraksan, G.: Monte Carlo sampling-based methods for stochastic optimization. Surv. Oper. Res. Man. Sci. **19**, 56–85 (2014)
9. Kieckhafer, K., Walther, G., Axmann, J., Spengler, T.: Integrating agent-based simulation and system dynamics to support product strategy decisions in the automotive industry. In: Proceedings of the Winter Simulation Conference (2009), pp. 1433–1443
10. Lamb, D.A., Gorsich, D., Krayterman, D., Choi, K.K., Hardee, E., Du, L., Youn, B.D., Bettig, B., Ghiocel, D.: System level RBDO for military ground vehicles using high performance computing. In: Proceedings of the SAE 2008 World Congress and Exhibition. SAE Technical Paper 2008–01-0543 (2008)
11. Liu, Y., Wang, Z., Liang, J., Liu, X.: Synchronization and state estimation for discrete-time complex networks with distributed delays. IEEE Trans. Syst. Man Cybern. B **38**, 1314–1325 (2008)
12. Moawad, A., Balaprakash, P., Rousseau, A., Wild, S.M.: Novel large scale simulation process to support DOT's CAFE modeling system. In: Proceedings of the International Electric Vehicle Symposium and Exhibition, May 2015
13. Thornton, P.E., Running, S.W.: An improved algorithm for estimating incident daily solar radiation from measurements of temperature, humidity, and precipitation. Agric. For. Meteorol. **93**, 211–228 (1999)
14. Vijayagopal, R., Sharer, P., Wild, S.M., Rousseau, A., Chen, R., Bhide, S., Dongarkar, G., Zhang, M., Meier, R.: Using multi-objective optimization for HEV component sizing. In: Proceedings of the International Electric Vehicle Symposium and Exhibition, no. EVS28_0153, May 2015

Accelerating LBM and LQCD Application Kernels by In-Memory Processing

Paul F. Baumeister[1], Hans Boettiger[2], José R. Brunheroto[3],
Thorsten Hater[1]([✉]), Thilo Maurer[2], Andrea Nobile[4], and Dirk Pleiter[1]

[1] Jülich Supercomputing Centre, Forschungszentrum Jülich, 52425 Jülich, Germany
t.hater@fz-juelich.de
[2] IBM Deutschland Research and Development GmbH, 71032 Böblingen, Germany
[3] IBM T.J. Watson Research Center, Yorktown Heights, NY 10598, USA
[4] Institute for Advanced Simulation, Forschungszentrum Jülich,
52425 Jülich, Germany

Abstract. Processing-in-memory architectures promise increased computing performance at decreased costs in energy, as the physical proximity of the compute pipelines to the data store eliminates overheads for data transport. We assess the overall performance impact using a recently introduced architecture of that type, called the Active Memory Cube, for two representative scientific applications. Precise performance results for performance critical kernels are obtained using cycle-accurate simulations. We provide an overall performance estimate using performance models.

1 Introduction

With increasing complexity the performance of modern HPC architectures becomes increasingly communication limited. The resulting need for improving efficiency of data transport and eliminating the associated overheads in terms of time and energy can be addressed by integrating compute pipelines close to the data stores, which is achieved, e.g., by processing-in-memory (PIM) designs. For various reasons none of the proposed PIM designs have resulted in products which could be integrated into HPC architectures. There are good arguments for expecting PIMs to enter system roadmaps, see [2] for an extended discussion. Besides a growing need for such approaches there are new opportunities for realizing such architectures due to novel 3-dimensional stacking technologies.

In this paper we assume that PIM technologies will become part of future massively-parallel HPC architectures to address the following question: How efficiently could such an architecture be exploited by relevant scientific applications?

For our work we selected two representative applications, namely computational fluid-dynamics calculations based on the Lattice Boltzmann Method and simulations of the theory of strong interactions, i.e. Lattice Quantum Chromodynamics. We have implemented performance relevant kernels on the IBM Research Active Memory Cube (AMC) architecture [14] to allow for cycle-accurate simulations. Performance models are used to assess the overall performance for different proxy architectures. This approach allows us to make the following contributions:

© Springer International Publishing Switzerland 2015
J.M. Kunkel and T. Ludwig (Eds.): ISC High Performance 2015, LNCS 9137, pp. 96–112, 2015.
DOI: 10.1007/978-3-319-20119-1_8

- We present and discuss our implementation of applications on AMC and analyse the observed performance.
- Based on this performance analysis we conduct an architectural evaluation of AMC for the considered application kernels.
- To assess the overall performance based on performance models for different variants of a proxy architecture.
- Finally, we report on feedback on future applications' roadmaps which we initiated to assess future application needs.

In Sects. 2 and 3 we provide an overview on the AMC architecture and the applications considered for this paper. We continue with a presentation of details of application kernels on AMC and performance analysis results in Sects. 4 and 5, respectively. In Sect. 6 we explore features and parameters of the AMC architecture and its suitability for the given application kernels. Finally in Sect. 7, we introduce a performance model approach for assessing the overall performance for HPC architectures that integrate AMCs.

2   Active Memory Cubes

Recently a new, 3-dimensional packaged memory architecture, Hybrid Memory Cube (HMC) [11], was introduced, where a set of memory dies are stacked on top of a logic die. In the HMC architecture the logic die implements a memory controller and a network interface via which the processor can access the memory. In the IBM Research Active Memory Cube (AMC) [14] architecture 32 computational lanes are added to the logic die, which also have access to the memory. The most important hardware performance parameters are listed in Table 1.

Each lane is composed of a control unit and 4 computation slices, which each comprise a memory-access and an arithmetic pipeline. Each slice contains multiple register files which include 32 scalar plus 16 vector computation registers. The latter are composed of 32 elements. All registers are 64-bit wide. Overall, AMC enabled nodes offer a significant amount of parallelism, comparable to GPU-accelerated architectures. Nodes are expected to contain multiple AMCs, in the order of sixteen devices. Each AMC possesses 32 lanes, multiplied by four slices.

The computational lanes are micro-coded and each can process in every clock cycle one Very Long Instruction Word (VLIW), mapping to 1 Control + 4 · (1 ALU + 1 LSU) instructions for a total of nine. To reduce the number of VLIWs a static or dynamic repeat counter can be specified following a temporal single-instruction-multiple-data (SIMD) paradigm. Instructions can be repeated up to 32 times and access, e.g., during each iteration consecutive elements of vector registers. The VLIWs are read from a buffer which can hold up to 512 entries.

The arithmetic pipelines take 64-bit input operands and can complete in each clock cycle one double-precision or a 2-way SIMD single-precision multiply-add.

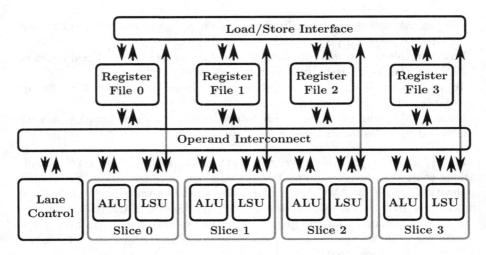

Fig. 1. Sketch of the AMC lane architecture. For more details see [14].

Table 1. Summary of AMC performance characteristics.

Clock frequency	$f = 1.25\,\text{GHz}$
Floating-point performance per lane	$B_{\text{fp}} = 8\,\text{Flop/cycle} = 10\,\text{GFlop/s}$
Memory bandwidth per lane	$B_{\text{mem}} = 8\,\text{Byte/cycle} = 10\,\text{GByte/s}$
Memory capacity per lane	$C_{\text{mem}} = 0.25\,\text{GByte}$
Number of lanes per AMC	$N_{\text{lane}} = 32$

Thus up to 8 double-precision floating-point operations can be completed per clock cycle and lane. The peak performance of one AMC running at a clock speed of 1.25 GHz is 320 GFlop/s. As one slice can read the vector registers of the other slices, double-precision complex arithmetic can be implemented without the need for data re-ordering instructions. The same holds for single-precision complex arithmetic thanks to special 2-way SIMD instructions.

Like in the HMC architecture the memory is organized into vaults. Each of the 32 vaults in the AMC architecture is functionally and operationally independent. Each vault has a memory controller (also called vault controller) which like the lanes is attached to the internal interconnect. Load/store requests issued by a lane are buffered in the lane's load-store queue which has 192 entries. A lane can load or store 8 Byte/cycle from or to the internal interconnect, i.e. the ratio of floating-point performance versus memory bandwidth is 1 and thus significantly larger than in typical processor architectures. The memory access latency depends on the distance between lane and vault as well as on whether the data is already buffered by the vault controller. The minimum access latency is 24 cycles, i.e. load operations have to be carefully scheduled to avoid stalls due to data dependencies.

Each AMC features a network interface with a bandwidth of 32 GByte/s to connect it to a processor and multiple devices may be chained to share a link to the processor. The execution model foresees main programs to be executed on the processor with computational lanes being used for off-loading small kernels. Assuming a design based on 14 nm technology, the power consumption is expected to be around 10 W.

Architectures based on AMC would feature multiple levels of parallelism with 4 slices per lane, 32 lanes per AMC, N_{AMC} AMCs per processor and possibly multiple processors per node and many nodes per system.

3   Applications and Application Roadmaps

3.1   Lattice Boltzmann Method

The Lattice Boltzmann method (LBM) is an approach to computational fluid dynamics based on a discrete approximation to the Boltzmann equation in terms of the distribution functions f_α in phase space

$$f_\alpha(\boldsymbol{x} + \boldsymbol{c}_\alpha \Delta t, t + \Delta t) = f_\alpha(\boldsymbol{x}, t) + \omega \left(f_\alpha(\boldsymbol{x}, t) - f_\alpha^{\mathrm{eq}} \right). \tag{1}$$

Here, spatial position $\boldsymbol{x}$, velocity $\boldsymbol{c}_\alpha$ and time t only take discrete values. The update process can be implemented in two separate steps: First, the local update on the right hand side, describing changes in the distribution due to particle interactions (*collide*). Second, distributing the update to adjacent sites according to a stencil with a range of three sites, equivalent to the fluid advection (*propagate*).

There are various LBM models which differ in number of spatial dimensions and velocities. In this work we considered an application which implements the *D2Q37* model , utilizes 37 populations in two spatial dimensions [17]. Parallelisation of the application is based on a domain decomposition in 1 or 2 dimensions. For typical runs and architectures the time spent in the collide and propagate kernel corresponds to about 90 % and 10 % of the overall execution time, respectively. The propagate step involves communication between tasks processing adjacent domains to update a halo. Communication can typically be overlapped with updating the bulk region. The collide step requires 5784 floating-point operations per site at $37 \cdot 8$ Bytes of input and output, whereas propagate does not involve any computation. Given this high arithmetic intensity we expect the collide step to be compute performance limited on the AMC architecture, while the propagate step will be limited by the memory bandwidth on any architecture. This split into two central tasks with distinct performance characteristics makes D2Q37 an interesting choice for evaluating the AMC architecture.

Future Requirements. The D2Q37 model is used to study fluid turbulence using lattices of size L^2 with $L = \mathcal{O}(1000\ldots10000)$. These studies will have to be extended to 3 dimensions. Studies on lattices of size $L^3 = 4000^3$ are expected to require 64 days of computing time on a machine with 100 PFlop/s peak performance assuming an efficiency of about 20 % [18]. The number of floating-point operations, which have to be executed per site and update, would increase from about 6000 to about 50000, while the memory footprint per site increases by a factor of about 3.

3.2 Lattice QCD

Quantum Chromodynamics (QCD) is a theory for describing strong interactions, e.g. the interaction between key constituents of matter like quarks. Lattice QCD (LQCD) refers to the formulation of QCD on a 4-dimensional discrete lattice. LQCD opens the path for numerical simulations of QCD.

The computational challenge in LQCD computations consists of repeatedly solving very large sparse linear systems. Iterative solver algorithms result in a very large number of multiplications of a matrix D and a vector ψ, which thus becomes the most performance critical computational tasks. In this paper we focus on a particular formulation of LQCD with so-called Wilson-Dirac fermions where this task takes the following form:

$$D\psi(\boldsymbol{x}) = m\psi(\boldsymbol{x}) + \sum_{\pm\mu}(1 \pm \hat{\gamma}^{\mu}) \otimes U_{\mu}^{\pm\dagger}(\boldsymbol{x})\psi(\boldsymbol{x} \pm \hat{\mu}). \qquad (2)$$

The index μ runs over all four dimensions of space-time.

Modern solvers (see, e.g., [8]) allow for a mixed precision approach where majority of the floating-point operations can be performed in single-precision, without compromising on the double-precision solution.

The operator D consists of a real, scalar on-site term m and eight links towards the Cartesian nearest-neighbour lattice sites in the four-dimensional discretised space-time. Spinor fields ψ are represented by one element per lattice site, where each element lives in the product space of 3 colours and 2×2 spins and thus comprises 12 complex numbers. Gauge fields U are represented by vectors with one element per lattice link, where each element acts as a SU(3)-rotation onto the colour-space. These are typically represented by a 3×3 complex matrix, however, the full information can be encoded in just 8 real numbers. The spin space is invariant with respect to the link rotations, but sensitive to the link-direction.

The spin projection operators $(1 \pm \hat{\gamma}^{\mu})$ commute with the link matrices U due to operating on different dimensions. A closer look at the 4×4 operators $(1 \pm \hat{\gamma}^{\mu})$ reveals that their matrix representation is of rank 2 rather than rank 4. This enables us to separate the operators into two parts, henceforth called spin deflation $P_{\pm\mu} \in \mathbb{C}^{2\times4}$ and spin inflation $J_{\pm\mu} \in \mathbb{C}^{4\times2}$. This reduces the number of necessary operations by performing the SU(3)-rotations in the deflated subspace. The computational task now takes the following form:

$$D\psi(\boldsymbol{x}) = m\psi(\boldsymbol{x}) + \sum_{\pm\mu} J_{\pm\mu} U_{\mu}^{\pm\dagger}(\boldsymbol{x}) P_{\pm\mu}\psi(\boldsymbol{x} \pm \hat{\mu}) \qquad (3)$$

Usually, data parallelism is exploited by decomposing the lattice into cubic sub-domains in a one to four dimensional scheme. The main source of communication

Table 2. Implementation characteristics of the three kernels per lattice site.Shown are the volumes of data loaded and stored, the number of required floating point operations (FP) and the percentage of operations which could be mapped to multiply-add type instructions (MA). We further give the resulting arithmetic intensity (AI) and the number of VLIWs in the kernel.

	Load (Byte)	Store (Byte)	FP (% MA)	AI	VLIWs
LQCD	1152	480	1368 (89 %)	0.8	63
LBM collide	765	296	5784 (80 %)	5.5	163
LBM propagate	296	296	-	0.0	26

is the surface exchange with the nearest neighbours in the respective dimensions. Therefore an appropriate torus topology is preferred. In order to minimise the impact of the communication, the operator computation is split into the forward and backward directions. This allows for transferring partial results of the latter and meanwhile computing the former, thus overlapping computation and communication. Then the procedure is reversed and the final result is computed.

Future Requirements. The performance of future algorithms are expected to be dominated by similar computational tasks as considered in this paper. With more computational resources becoming available, the lattice sizes are expected to grow during the next couple of years to $L^3 \cdot T = 128^3 \cdot 256$ [13]. Currently, even larger lattices are only expected to be required for relatively special cases.

4   Implementation on AMC

We describe our implementations of the collide and propagate kernels of the D2Q37 LBM code and the Dirac operator from the LQCD code. As the experiments were performed at an early stage of the development of this technology, neither compilers for high-level languages nor assemblers were available. Consequently, the implementation was done directly at the level of AMC micro-code supported by a set of ad-hoc tools. Thus programming involved scheduling of instruction and their allocation to slices as well as the allocation of registers.

The focus of the dicussion lies on the features of the instruction set and AMC architecture that support the implementation, rather than providing a full overview on our implementations.

4.1   LBM D2Q37 Model

Collide. For this kernel, we implemented a vectorised version over 32 elements, using the temporal SIMD paradigm, but neglected the traversal of the lattice. For a full version, this infrastructure would have to be added. An efficient, static work sharing scheme, based on partitioning the lattice, can be applied. In this case, we did not use the four slices for additional parallelisation, in order to avoid further constraint on the input. The operation is divided in four sub-steps:

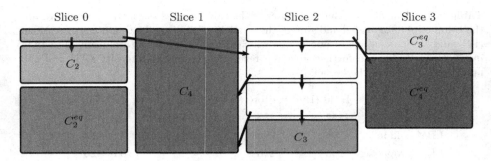

Fig. 2. Distribution of collide central loop body over the slices. Similar colours match coefficients of f and f^{eq}, white signifies auxiliary terms.

computing bulk properties, applying a non-linear transformation, computing the update on the transform and, finally, reverting to the original representation. The last three steps require the computation of six terms of differing length. These computations are distributed carefully over the four slices, resulting in a very dense packing where 92 % of the instructions are floating point computations. The six coefficients are computed in pairs matched for even length in three of the slices, while the fourth supplies intermediate terms. Common sub-terms are preferably computed in this auxiliary slice, which further increases efficiency.

Propagate. We implemented the full kernel, including traversal of the lattice, loading from the input array and storing to a different output array. Exploiting our freedom in choosing an optimal data layout, we sub-divide the lattice into rows and distribute those evenly over the participating lanes. Each lane iterates over the assigned rows handing one quarter of the row to each of its slices.

The capabilities of the LSU instructions are exploited to map the requirements to efficient code. We load the local site in linear fashion, using two VLIWs to capture the 37 populations. The LSU is capable of automatically incrementing the source address. Further, the store instruction is supplied with a vector register holding the stencil and applies this to the relevant elements of the stored data. Thus, the loop body of the kernel consist of just five VLIWs.

4.2 LQCD

In order to hide communication required when parallelising the matrix-vector multiplication, the computation of the forward and backward part is overlapped as described in Sect. 3.2. We re-produce this structure to keep our implementation close to the original memory access pattern, but do not implement inter-task communication. Further, we simplify the kernel by only mocking up the indirection infrastructure for storing the results. Therefore, the simulation results have to be understood as being approximative.

We took advantage of the temporal SIMD capabilities of the AMC by vectorising over eight lattice sites, utilising 24 out of 32 vector register elements.

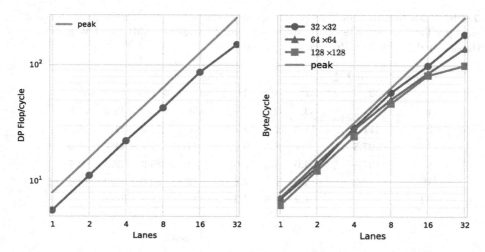

Fig. 3. Weak-scaling of the collide kernel performance for 32×32 lattice sites per lane as a function of the number of used lanes (left pane) and strong-scaling of the propagate kernel (right pane). The lines indicate the theoretical peak performance of 8 Flop/cycle/lane (left) and 8 Byte/cycle/lane (right).

By this we ensure that load latencies are mostly hidden. All necessary operations are performed on complex numbers in single precision. Specialised instructions have been added to the AMC ISA to efficiently implement complex multiply-add operations using 8-Byte complex numbers and only 2 instructions. This corresponds to a throughput of 1 single-precision complex multiply-add, i.e. 8 floating-point operations, per 2 cycles per slice. Each of the four slices operates on one of the four link dimensions. The requirements of the kernel are summarised in Table 2. Ultimately, the performance is limited by the memory bandwidth. However, while the first part executes one arithmetic operation per Byte loaded and stored, the second is imbalanced by a larger initially loaded segment. Thus, it incurs an additional start-up overhead.

5   Performance Analysis

We now proceed by presenting performance results for the kernels, for which implementation was discussed in the previous section. The results have been obtained on a cycle-accurate simulator for a full AMC including memories.

5.1   LBM

Collide. We start with a weak-scaling analysis of the collide kernel. Each instance of the kernel is executed on a single lane and operates on an individual set of 32 lattice sites. From the analysis of the kernel in terms of floating-point operations per memory access, we expect the kernel to operate close to the maximum floating-point performance. We present the relevant metric, the number of

Table 3. Median time per lattice site spent in the collide (t_{coll}, weak scaling: $l = 32$ sites per lane), propagate (t_{prop}, strong scaling: L^2 sites per AMC) and Wilson-Dirac (t_{comp}, weak scaling: l^4 sites per lane) kernel.

Lanes	t_{coll} (ns)	t_{prop} (ns)			t_{comp} (ns)			
	l | 32	L^2 | 32^2	64^2	128^2	l^4 | 2^4	4^4	8^4	16^4
1	821.2	33.7	32.9	37.9	158.5	141.0	142.9	143.8
2	411.4	17.9	16.5	19.1	90.2	76.5	81.1	81.4
4	207.5	8.1	8.4	9.6	64.0	41.7	41.7	42.9
8	107.5	4.0	4.6	5.0	58.9	25.9	23.3	23.7
16	53.2	2.3	2.7	2.8	47.3	20.0	15.2	14.4
32	30.7	1.2	1.6	2.3	41.7	13.2	10.7	-

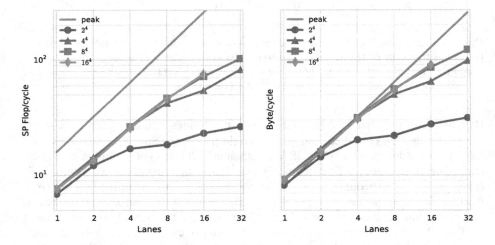

Fig. 4. LQCD operator weak scaling on AMC over the number of lanes in use.

floating-point operations performed per cycle, along with the speed-up over a single lane in Fig. 3. Across all numbers of lanes up to 32, we can exploit above 60 % of the peak floating-point performance. On a single lane, the implementation reaches 70 % of peak. We observe a small negative impact of utilising more than a single lane, despite operating on disjunct blocks of memory.

Propagate. The performance of the propagate kernel completely depends on memory access performance. In Fig. 3 (right pane) we show strong scaling results.

Out of the theoretical maximum of 320 GByte/s bandwidth, propagate can sustain 125 GByte/s on a lattice of 128^2, or 39 % of peak. The simulations show that for larger number of lanes memory accesses take longer to complete, which could be result of congestion or non-optimal access patterns.

5.2 LQCD

We investigated the performance of the partial implementation of the Wilson-Dirac operator D in a weak scaling study. The extracted kernel is run on multiple lanes, each processing a private lattice of extent L^4 where $L = 2, 4, 8, 16$. The results are summarised in Fig. 4 as performance in floating-point operations and memory bandwidth. For all lattice sizes, the best performance was achieved at the maximum of 32 lanes. From $L = 2$, the overall performance increases up to the case $L = 8$, where it is virtually identical to $L = 16$. The optimum sustained bandwidth on 32 lanes is 107 GByte/s, or 33 % of the peak value.

From Fig. 4 we can derive the optimum local lattice size per lane, namely 2^4 for two lanes, 8^4 for eight lanes and 16^4 for sixteen or more lanes.

6 Discussion of AMC Architecture

Based on our analysis of different application kernels we are now able to analyse selected hardware aspects and parameters and explore possible impact on the kernel's performance.

Instruction Set. The given set of application kernels could be mapped well on the instruction set architecture (ISA) of the Active Memory Cube (AMC). Specific ISA features which have been exploited include flexible load/store instructions and the availability of specialised single precision complex operations. The architecture allows for an efficient implementation of complex arithmetics. For the Dirac kernel the upper bound of the floating point efficiency as determined only by instruction selection and dependence lies at 94 %.

Temporal SIMD and Register File. For all kernels the temporal SIMD could be extensively exploited. The penalty of not using all elements of a vector register was found to be small. The collide kernel utilises near the maximum of scalar and vector registers on all slices. The propagate kernel uses three vectors per slice and about ten scalars. The Wilson-Dirac operator makes use of 14 out of 16 vector registers and 23 out of 32 scalar registers. The register file size was in all three cases found to be adequate for holding data or staging data loaded from memory. Sharing of vector registers between slices proved to be a crucial feature for efficient mapping of the application kernels on this architecture.

Instruction Buffer Size. The overall number of VLIWs needed to implement the (most important parts) of the kernels was found to be small (see Table 2) such that at most 32 % of the instruction buffer was filled.

Memory Bandwidth. Although the memory bandwidth is high compared to the compute performance, the Dirac and propagate kernels are nevertheless limited by the memory bandwidth on the AMC.

Memory Access Latency. Due to the size of the register file, load operations can be scheduled such that memory access latencies are largely hidden. For a strictly in-order design timely scheduling of such instructions can have significant performance impact. From our simulations we find memory access latencies to grow significantly when increasing the number of used lanes, resulting in a loss of efficiency.

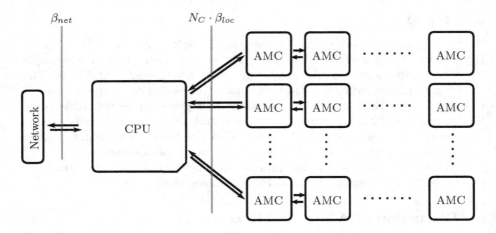

Fig. 5. Proxy architecture for AMC enabled nodes.

Table 4. Key parameters of our node proxy architecture.

Description	Parameter	Default value
Number of AMC	N_{AMC}	16
Number of chains	N_{C}	8
AMC memory capacity	C_{mem}	8 GByte
Inter-AMC link performance	$(\lambda_{\mathrm{mem}}, \beta_{\mathrm{mem}})$	$(1\,\mu\mathrm{s}, 32\,\mathrm{GByte/s})$
Network link performance	$(\lambda_{\mathrm{net}}, \beta_{\mathrm{net}})$	$(1\,\mu\mathrm{s}, 100\,\mathrm{GByte/s})$

Load/Store Queue (LSQ). The LSQ size is limited to 192 entries and holds both load and store requests. Its particular size has not been critical for neither the propagate nor the collide kernel. For the Wilson-Dirac operator, however, the majority of stalled cycles are due to a filled LSQ. Based on the memory access pattern we do not expect a larger LSQ to improve performance.

7   System Performance Modelling

For assessing the characteristics of the full applications on an AMC enabled node architecture, we define a proxy node architecture [1]. The basic structure of this architecture, as shown Fig. 5, comprises a CPU with a set of AMCs, which are organised in chains of equal length, plus a network interface attached. We assume that various parameters of this architecture as listed in Table 4 can be varied. To obtain quantitative results we use a specific choice guided by the node architecture proposed in [14].

To model the system performance for the kernels considered in this paper we assume that all calculations are performed on the AMC, for which we can use the cycle accurate simulator results presented in the previous sections.

To assess the overall performance we have to model the time needed to perform the necessary data exchange when application kernels are parallelised over multiple AMCs per node and multiple nodes. We assume that time for point-to-point communications can be described by a latency-bandwidth model, i.e.

$$T_{\text{comm}} = \lambda + \frac{I}{\beta}, \tag{4}$$

where I is the amount of communicated data and (λ, β) are the start-up latency and asymptotic bandwidth, respectively. We, furthermore, make the following assumptions:

- All links between components are bi-directional and can be described by the same parameters in both directions.
- All data transfers can be overlapped, therefore, the simulator results are valid for node level implementations.
- One task is executed per AMC and care is taken to achieve optimal placement.

7.1 LBM

The LBM application has, apart from collide and propagate, only one relevant step in performing a lattice update, the communication between different tasks. We model this part to estimate the performance on an AMC-enabled system.

As mentioned before, the lattice is distributed over multiple tasks using a one dimensional decomposition. Each task, and equivalently each AMC, holds a tranche with extent $L_x \cdot L_y$. A layer of three halo columns is introduced to exchange boundaries, necessitating a transfer of

$$I = 3 \cdot 2 \cdot L_x \cdot 37 \cdot 8 \, \text{Byte} = L_x \cdot 1776 \, \text{Byte} \tag{5}$$

per sub-domain. We assume L_x to be sufficiently large to allow execution of the propagate kernel and the halo exchange to be perfectly overlapped. We can therefore estimate the time required for an update step as follows:

$$T_{\text{step}} = \max(L_x \cdot L_y \cdot t_{\text{prop}}, T_{\text{comm}}) + L_x \cdot L_y \cdot t_{\text{coll}}, \tag{6}$$

where t_{coll} and t_{prop} are the measured execution time for collide and propagate kernel, respectively. They depend on the problem size as well as the number of used lanes. In the following we will consider only the case $N_{\text{lane}} = 32$.

Assuming that data communication performance is limited either by the link connecting the CPU and the first AMC within a chain as well as the network bandwidth, we obtain the following estimate for the time required for data communication:

$$T_{\text{comm}} = \max\left(T_{\text{ex}}^{\text{mem}}, T_{\text{ex}}^{\text{net}}\right) = \max\left(\lambda_{\text{mem}} + \frac{I \cdot N_{\text{AMC}}}{N_{\text{C}} \cdot \beta_{\text{mem}}}, \lambda_{\text{net}} + \frac{I \cdot N_{\text{AMC}}^{\frac{3}{4}}}{\beta_{\text{net}}}\right), \tag{7}$$

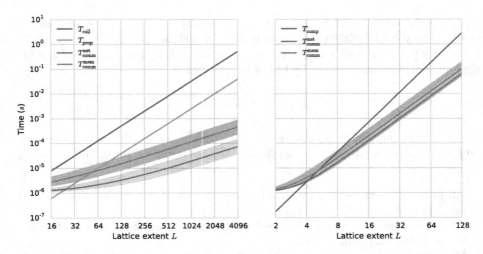

Fig. 6. Performance model for LBM (**left**) and LQCD (**right**), using the selected parameters for the proxy architecture as a function of the lattice size per AMC. Shaded areas indicate the effect of halving/doubling the respective bandwidth.

Considering square sub-domains per AMC, the minimal local size at which the kernels can utilise the AMC efficiently is about 32^2 from our experiments and maximally 3500^2 due to memory constraints.

For exploring execution time as a function of the lattice size per AMC we use the maximum execution times per lattice site observed when using $N_{\mathrm{lane}} = 32$ lanes (see Table 3): $t_{\mathrm{coll}} = 30.7\,\mathrm{ns}$, $t_{\mathrm{prop}} = 2.37\,\mathrm{ns}$. The results are shown in Fig. 6. We find that lattice size beyond 128^2 yield performance numbers that are dominated by the computations as opposed to boundary exchange. Specifically for $L_x = L_y = 128$ we obtain the following results: $T_{\mathrm{coll}} = 502\,\mu s$ and $T_{\mathrm{step}} = 542\,\mu s$.

7.2 LQCD

To model the performance of a parallelised matrix-vector multiplication we apply the same methodology as in the previous section. We assume that computation and communication can be perfectly overlapped such that

$$T^{\mathrm{Dirac}} = \max(T_{\mathrm{comp}}, T_{\mathrm{comm}}).$$

We assume a four dimensional domain decomposition into one sub-domain per task. Let L^4 be the lattice size per AMC, where the assumed memory capacity C_{mem} limits us to $L \leq 64$. The performance results shown in Table 3 indicate that a lattice with $L \geq 8$ should be used. Time for computation $T_{\mathrm{comp}} = L^4 \cdot t_{\mathrm{comp}}$ with $t_{\mathrm{comp}} = 10.7\,\mathrm{ns}$ is obtained from simulations (see Table 3).

A halo of thickness one, containing matrices comprising 12 single-precision complex numbers is exchanged with each neighbour, resulting in a data volume of

$$I = L^3 \cdot 2 \cdot 4 \cdot 12 \cdot 8\,\text{Byte} = L^3 \cdot 768\,\text{Byte} \tag{8}$$

per task. On the grounds of optimal task placement, we can argue that the amount of data exchanged by a node over the network is $I \cdot N_{\text{AMC}}^{\frac{3}{4}}$. The time consumed by the communication is then given by

$$T_{\text{comm}} = \max\left(T_{\text{ex}}^{\text{mem}}, T_{\text{ex}}^{\text{net}}\right) = \max\left(\lambda_{\text{mem}} + \frac{I \cdot N_{\text{AMC}}}{N_C \cdot \beta_{\text{mem}}}, \lambda_{\text{net}} + \frac{I \cdot N_{\text{AMC}}^{\frac{3}{4}}}{\beta_{\text{net}}}\right),$$
$$\tag{9}$$

where the local exchange has an extra factor N_{AMC}/N_C since all AMCs in a chain share the bandwidth to the CPU.

We investigate the resulting timing in Fig. 6. We conclude that even with half the available bandwidth, a lattice extent of $L = 16$ yields timings that are determined solely by the computation. At this setting we expect $T_{\text{Dirac}} = T_{\text{op}} = 0.7\,\text{ms}$ for a lattice update step, using 8192 tasks on 512 nodes. The total peak performance of such a partition is 2.6 PFlop/s. Halving the local extent to $L = 8$ is the point at which the time for local exchange (at slightly more than the half effective bandwidth) is equal to T_{op}. At this point we are using 8192 nodes (42 PFlop/s) and expect an operator evaluation every $T_{\text{Dirac}} \simeq 44\,\mu s$.

8   Related Work

Performance analysis of Lattice Boltzmann Methods have been investigated in detail in various papers. For instance, the 2-dimensional D2Q37 model has been explored extensively for different processor and accelerator architectures including IBM PowerXCell 8i [3], Intel Xeon [4], GPUs and Xeon Phi [6]. Recently an increasing number of publications focus on the 3-dimensional D3Q19 model, concentrating on optimising memory hierarchies [15,20].

With advances in research on Lattice Quantum Chromodynamics (LQCD) strongly linked to progress in available compute resources, there exists a large number of publications where performance characteristics of LQCD applications are studied and results from performance analysis for different architectures are presented. Recent examples include the performance analysis for LQCD solvers on Blue Gene/Q [5] and architectures comprising GPUs and Xeon Phi [10,21].

Starting in the 90 s different processing-in-memory (PIM) architectures have been proposed and explored, including Computational RAM [7], Intelligent RAM [16], DIVA [9], and FlexRAM [12]. The initial enthusiasm decreased lacking a perspective of PIM architectures being realised. For a brief but more comprehensive overview on different projects see [19]. Different application kernels have been mapped to these architectures to explore their performance, with focus on kernels that feature irregular memory access patterns. To the best of our knowledge no results from a performance analysis for large-scale scientific applications on massively-parallel architectures comprising PIM modules has been published.

9 Summary and Conclusions

Studying two applications on the IBM Research Active Memory Cube (AMC) processing-in-memory architecture yielded promising results. Both applications are representative for many simulation codes, which are similarly structured, so conclusions can be expected to be transferable to those applications. We could demonstrate that compared to peak floating-point performance efficiencies could be reached which are mostly larger than those for processors and accelerators available today. By keeping most of the data transfer local within the memory, the need for data transport outside the memory could be significantly reduced.

Our results for kernel execution times allows to estimate energy efficiency. Assuming a power consumption of $10\,W$ the costs of the D2Q37 LBM collide kernel per lattice site is $0.3\,\mu J$. This compares favourably to NVIDIA K20x GPUs with an energy consumption of $2.6\,\mu J$ per lattice site [6], even if one takes into account that these measurements were done on a technology which became available in 2012.

While optimal exploitation of the AMC architecture requires the programmer to take data locality and access patterns into consideration, the resulting benefit to the user is a power efficiency distinctly better than alternative platforms.

Acknowledgements. We thank the AMC team at IBM Research, in particular J. Moreno, for sharing their knowledge on the AMC and continued help on this project including many fruitful discussions. Furthermore, we gratefully acknowledge F.S. Schifano and R. Tripiccione (INFN/University of Ferrara) for making a mini-application version of their D2Q37 code available and for discussing their future roadmaps [18]. We also thank G. Koutsou, S. Krieg, and H. Simma from the Simulation Lab LQCD at Cyprus Institute/DESY/JSC for discussing the future requirements of LQCD [13]. Finally, we thank A. Frommer and S. Krieg for making their implementation of their AMG solver [8] available.

References

1. Ang, J.A., Barrett, R.F., Benner, R.E., Burke, D., Chan, C., Cook, J., Donofrio, D., Hammond, S.D., Hemmert, K.S., Kelly, S.M., Le, H., Leung, V.J., Resnick, D.R., Rodrigues, A.F., Shalf, J., Stark, D., Unat, D., Wright, N.J.: Abstract machine models and proxy architectures for exascale computing. In: Proceedings of the 1st International Workshop on Hardware-Software Co-Design for High Performance Computing (Co-HPC 2014), pp. 25–32. IEEE Press, Piscataway (2014). http://dx.doi.org/10.1109/Co-HPC.2014.4
2. Balasubramonian, R., Chang, J., Manning, T., Moreno, J.H., Murphy, R., Nair, R., Swanson, S.: Near-data processing: insights from a MICRO-46 workshop. IEEE Micro **34**(4), 36–42 (2014)
3. Biferale, L., Mantovani, F., Pivanti, M., Sbragaglia, A., Schifano, S., Toschi, F., Tripiccione, R.: Lattice Boltzmann fluid-dynamics on the QPACE supercomputer. Procedia Comput. Sci. **1**(1), 1075–1082 (2010). http://www.sciencedirect.com/science/article/pii/S1877050910001201, ICCS 2010

4. Biferale, L., Mantovani, F., Pivanti, M., Pozzati, F., Sbragaglia, M., Scagliarini, A., Schifano, S.F., Toschi, F., Tripiccione, R.: Optimization of multi-phase compressible lattice Boltzmann codes on massively parallel multi-core systems. Procedia Comput. Sci. **4**, 994–1003 (2011). http://www.sciencedirect.com/science/article/pii/S1877050911001633, Proceedings of the International Conference on Computational Science, ICCS 2011

5. Boyle, P.A., Christ, N.H., Kim, C.: Co-design of the IBM BlueGene/q level 1 prefetch engine with QCD. IBM J. Res. Dev. **57**(1/2), 13:1–13:10 (2013)

6. Calore, E., Schifano, S.F., Tripiccione, R.: A portable OpenCL lattice Boltzmann code for multi- and many-core processor architectures. Procedia Comput. Sci. **29**, 40–49 (2014). http://www.sciencedirect.com/science/article/pii/S1877050914001811, 2014 International Conference on Computational Science

7. Elliott, D., Snelgrove, W., Stumm, M.: Computational ram: a memory-simd hybrid and its application to dsp. In: Proceedings of the IEEE 1992 on Custom Integrated Circuits Conference, pp. 30.6.1–30.6.4, May 1992

8. Frommer, A., Kahl, K., Krieg, S., Leder, B., Rottmann, M.: Adaptive aggregation based domain decomposition multigrid for the lattice Wilson Dirac operator. SIAM J. Sci. Comput. **36**, A1581–A1608 (2014)

9. Hall, M., Kogge, P., Koller, J., Diniz, P., Chame, J., Draper, J., LaCoss, J., Granacki, J., Brockman, J., Srivastava, A., Athas, W., Freeh, V., Shin, J., Park, J.: Mapping irregular applications to DIVA, a PIM-based data-intensive architecture. In: ACM/IEEE 1999 Conference on Supercomputing, pp. 57–57, November 1999

10. Heybrock, S., Joó, B., Kalamkar, D.D., Smelyanskiy, M., Vaidyanathan, K., Wettig, T., Dubey, P.: Lattice QCD with domain decomposition on intel xeon phi coprocessors. In: Proceedings of the International Conference for High Performance Computing, Networking, Storage and Analysis (SC 2014), pp. 69–80. IEEE Press, Piscataway (2014). http://dx.doi.org/10.1109/SC.2014.11

11. Hybrid Memory Cube Consortium: Hybrid Memory Cube Specification (2013)

12. Kang, Y., Huang, W., Yoo, S.M., Keen, D., Ge, Z., Lam, V., Pattnaik, P., Torrellas, J.: FlexRAM: toward an advanced intelligent memory system. In: International Conference on Computer Design (ICCD 1999), pp. 192–201 (1999)

13. Koutsou, G., Krieg, S., Pleiter, D., Simma, H.: EIC co-design questionnaire: lattice QCD (unpublished, 2013)

14. Nair, R., Antao, S.F., Bertolli, C., Bose, P., Brunheroto, J.R., Chen, T., Cher, C.-Y., Costa, C.H.A., Evangelinos, C., Fleischer, B.M., Fox, T.W., Gallo, D.S., Grinberg, L., Gunnels, J.A., Jacob, A.C., Jacob, P., Jacobson, H.M., Karkhanis, T., Kim, C., Moreno, J.H., O'Brien, J.K., Ohmacht, M., Park, Y., Prener, D.A., Rosenburg, B.S., Ryu, K.D., Sallenave, O., Serrano, M.J., Siegl, P.D.M., Sugavanam, K., Sura, Z.: Active memory cube: a processing-in-memory architecture for exascale systems. IBM J. Res. Dev. **59**(2/3), 17:1–17:14 (2015)

15. Nguyen, A., Satish, N., Chhugani, J., Kim, C., Dubey, P.: 3.5-d blocking optimization for stencil computations on modern cpus and gpus. In: International Conference for High Performance Computing, Networking, Storage and Analysis (SC 2010), pp. 1–13, November 2010

16. Patterson, D., Anderson, T., Cardwell, N., Fromm, R., Keeton, K., Kozyrakis, C., Thomas, R., Yelick, K.: A case for intelligent RAM. IEEE Micro **17**(2), 34–44 (1997)

17. Scagliarini, A., Biferale, L., Sbragaglia, M., Sugiyama, K., Toschi, F.: Lattice Boltzmann methods for thermal flows: continuum limit and applications to compressible Rayleigh-Taylor systems. Phys. Fluids **22**(5), 055101 (2010)

18. Schifano, S.F., Tripiccione, R.: EIC co-design questionnaire: LBM (unpublished, 2013)
19. Torrellas, J.: Flexram: toward an advanced intelligent memory system: a retrospective paper. In: IEEE 30th International Conference on Computer Design (ICCD 2012), pp. 3–4, September 2012
20. Williams, S., Oliker, L., Carter, J., Shalf, J.: Extracting ultra-scale lattice Boltzmann performance via hierarchical and distributed auto-tuning. In: Proceedings of 2011 International Conference for High Performance Computing, Networking, Storage and Analysis (SC 2011), pp. 55:1–55:12. ACM, New York (2011). http://doi.acm.org/10.1145/2063384.2063458
21. Winter, F., Clark, M., Edwards, R., Joo, B.: A framework for lattice QCD calculations on GPUs. In: 2014 IEEE 28th International Parallel and Distributed Processing Symposium, pp. 1073–1082, May 2014

On Quantum Chemistry Code Adaptation
for RSC PetaStream Architecture

Vladimir Mironov[1], Maria Khrenova[1],
and Alexander Moskovsky[2](✉)

[1] Chemistry Department, Lomonosov Moscow State University,
Moscow, Russia
{vmironov,mkhrenova}@lcc.chem.msu.ru
[2] ZAO "RSC Technologies", Moscow, Russia
moskov@rsc-tech.ru

Abstract. Molecular simulations with quantum chemistry methods consume a large portion of CPU cycles in modern high-performance computing centers. Evolution of modern processors and HPC architectures necessitates adaptation of software to new hardware generations. The present work concentrates on the optimization of the widely used GAMESS code to Intel Xeon Phi architecture and recently devised RSC PetaStream platform. Since improvement in parallelization is required, the most frequently used Hartree-Fock and DFT methods are explored for additional parallelization options. The Xeon Phi requires vectorization that is important for electron-repulsion integrals (ERI) calculations to achieve good performance.

Keywords: Quantum chemistry · Hartree-Fock · Density functional theory · Intel xeon phi, GAMESS

1 Introduction

In 2012, Intel Many Integrated Cores (MIC) architecture [1] has been introduced as an answer to mounting challenges in building scalable and efficient high-performance computing systems. To achieve energy efficiency of computation, Intel MIC has more than 60 computational cores, each capable to execute AVX instructions. This new hardware requires new level of parallelization and vectorization from the application software for efficient performance.

Quantum chemistry algorithms were being adapted for parallel hardware for many decades. However, most popular codes "as is" don't demonstrate good performance efficiency on the Intel MIC hardware platform. In most cases, code is not vectorized, while required thread parallelism level is not achieved. For example, GAMESS(US) [2, 3] package has been parallelized for decades by now, but its code lacks vectorization and enough thread-level parallelism of important pieces of algorithm even for widely used Hartree-Fock and Density Functional Theory calculations. Intel Xeon Phi 5120D requires as many as 240 threads to be run to achieve best performance in many algorithms [4]. Attempts to run few hundred processes of GAMESS application instead of more lightweight threads overwhelm memory subsystem with dramatic performance decrease.

© Springer International Publishing Switzerland 2015
J.M. Kunkel and T. Ludwig (Eds.): ISC High Performance 2015, LNCS 9137, pp. 113–121, 2015.
DOI: 10.1007/978-3-319-20119-1_9

The Intel MIC set new performance per watt level for x86-compatible systems. While MIC is available as Intel Xeon Phi PCI express co-processor cards, it supports "Native" mode of application execution, where each Xeon Phi is visible to application as an independent manycore machine. The next generation of Intel MIC technology – Intel Knights Landing [5] – will be self-sufficient manycore bootable systems. Already existing RSC PetaStream architecture [6] leverages efficient co-processor-to-co-processor communication, providing realistic model of future Intel KNL supercomputers, where "native" mode of parallelization is the most natural and effective. Each node runs its own Linux-based OS image of operating system, and Linux OS is run on host. Majority of PetaStream computation power comes from Xeon Phi chips, therefore it make sense to run application on Intel Xeon Phi cards, and use the host's CPU for support and service functions; application is run on uniform field of Xeon Phi nodes – at least one MPI rank per node – compatible with "native" mode for Xeon Phi. In case of offload-like work sharing is efficient for an application and it is possible to harness both CPU and MIC nodes. RSC PetaStream system uses Intel Node Manager Technology to control and monitor node power consumption of every node, that mechanism can be used to implement flexible power energy and optimization strategies to help HPC sites save power and reduce operational costs. An example of the supercomputing system where both types of nodes co-exist in the same fabric is St. Petersburg Polytechnic University supercomputing center, with over 800 nodes on Intel Xeon E5v3 - 2697 (Haswell) share Infiniband FDR fabric with 256 nodes on Intel Xeon Phi 5120D.

The most common approaches in quantum chemistry are Hartree-Fock method (HF) and density functional theory (DFT). The major steps of these methods are construction and diagonalization of the Fock (Kohn-Sham) matrix [7]. For practically interesting systems computational power required is usually of supercomputer scale. The computational effort for the first step is dominated by the calculation of two-electron integrals corresponding to the Coulomb repulsion of electron pairs (and therefore frequently called electron repulsion integrals, ERI) and, in case of DFT, also by calculation of numerical quadrature of the exchange-correlation contribution to energy. The two-electron integral calculation has theoretical $O(N^4)$ computational complexity, where N is a number of basis functions used to characterize the system. However, many of these integrals are small enough and may be neglected. It is possible to reduce number of operations down to $O(N^{2 \div 3})$ using cutoffs and also some approximations, especially for very large systems. In that case a speed of Fock (or Kohn-Sham) matrix diagonalization ($O(N^3)$) significantly affects the performance of HF (DFT) method. However, for the majority of practically important molecular systems a construction of Fock (Kohn-Sham) matrix dominates overall computational cost. Also, matrix diagonalization is a pure linear algebra calculation with a great scalability, so the efficient two-electron integral code is crucial to achieve the performance in HF and DFT methods. We therefore targeted the Fock matrix two-electron contribution code to demonstrate the applicability of the Intel MIC platform to classical quantum chemistry problems.

The goal of the presented work is to enable migration of GAMESS(US) quantum chemistry code [2, 3] to novel Intel MIC hardware technology. GAMESS is widely used by the scientific community, with thousands of references in the papers each year.

We intend to minimize code modification and optimize for future-proof "native" mode of Intel Xeon Phi.

2 Basics of Hartree-Fock Method

2.1 Electron Repulsion Integrals (ERIs)

ERIs are the integrals of type:

$$I_{ijkl} = (i,j|k,l) = \iint \frac{\chi_i(r_1)\chi_j(r_1)\chi_k(r_2)\chi_l(r_2)}{r_2 - r_1} \, dr_1 dr_2 \tag{1}$$

where χ denotes basis functions, i, j, k, l – their indices, r_1, r_2 – coordinates of first and second electrons. An important property of ERIs is their eightfold permutation symmetry with respect to i, j, k, l indices. Commonly Cartesian Gaussians are used as basis functions:

$$\chi(r) = (x - A_x)^{a_x} (y - A_y)^{a_y} (z - A_z)^{a_z} e^{-\alpha(r-A)^2} \tag{2}$$

where A and α are center and exponent of basis function respectively, $a(a_x, a_y, a_z)$ – its angular momentum. They have practically important property that a product of two Gaussians is another Gaussian (see [8] for eq.). The Gaussian in form (2) is also called "primitive". Typically, linear combinations of Gaussian primitives which share the same center and angular momentum ("contracted" functions) are actually used as a basis functions. Contracted ERI are sum of integrals over their primitives:

$$(i,j|k,l) = \sum_a^M \sum_b^N \sum_c^O \sum_d^P C_{ai}C_{bj}C_{ck}C_{dl}(ab|cd) \tag{3}$$

where C is a matrix of contraction coefficients, M, N, O, P – degree of contraction. A set of (possibly contracted) basis functions that share the same center and same set of exponents is termed "shell". Grouping basis functions into shells reduces to some extent the number of expensive floating point operations and improves efficiency of integral screening. Primitive integrals are calculated numerically. Among the most popular approaches are McMurchie-Davidson [9], Obara-Saika [10] and Dupuis-Rys-King (DRK) [11] schemes. The effectiveness of the different schemes varies greatly for the different integral types. Quantum chemical codes often have several algorithms implemented and switch them wisely to improve performance. In this study we used only DRK integral scheme for testing purposes due to its numerical stability, relative simplicity, and uniformness for different kinds of integrals.

2.2 The Hartree-Fock Algorithm

The Hartree-Fock method is a method of finding an approximate wavefunction and energy of the model system. It is based on eigenvalue problem:

$$FC = \epsilon SC, \tag{4}$$

where F – Fock matrix, S – overlap matrix, C – matrix of molecular orbital coefficients, ϵ - diagonal matrix of orbital energies. Since F depends on C, the Eq. 4 has to be solved self-consistently. Matrix F incorporates contribution from electron-electron (V_{ee}) and electron-nuclei electrostatic interaction (V_{en}) as well as kinetic energy of electrons (T_e). It is usually represented as a sum of one-electron Hamiltonian (h), Coulomb (J) and exchange (K) matrices:

$$F = h + J - \frac{1}{2}K \tag{5}$$

$$h = V_{en} + T_e; J_{ij} = \sum\nolimits_{kl} D_{kl} \cdot I_{ijkl}; K_{ij} = \sum\nolimits_{kl} D_{kl} \cdot I_{ikjl} \tag{6}$$

where D – density matrix which is calculated from molecular orbital coefficients. Matrix h depends on the one-electron integrals and its computation scales quadratically depending of the system size. The Fock matrix construction requires calculation of all symmetry unique ERIs and has theoretical $O(N^4)$ complexity. It is worth noting that numerous ERIs are very small and their contribution to the Fock matrix is negligible. They could be avoided by applying screening techniques. It vastly reduces the number of ERIs required for calculation down to $O(N^{2+3})$ depending on the geometrical size of molecular system and the nature of atomic basis set used.

Different schemes have been proposed to calculate Fock matrix. Conventional algorithm requires all ERIs to be calculated once and stored on a disk. However, it is not very efficient for the large systems due to high requirements on the amount of available disk space for the integral storage and relatively slow disk operation speed. The advantage of this method is that each ERI is calculated only once. In the alternative approach ("direct" HF) integrals are recalculated every time as needed.

3   Implementation of the Hartree-Fock Method in GAMESS

The algorithm of direct HF method implemented in GAMESS is presented on Fig. 1. The implementation of main loop over shell coefficients corresponds to the so-called "triple-sort" order [12] when up to three symmetrically unique integrals are calculated at each cycle step. The alternative is a canonical way with slightly different index order, when only one integral is calculated at each cycle step. The disadvantage of triple-sort order is decreased granularity, which may be important on highly parallel systems.

GAMESS uses MPI parallelization to split workload during ERI calculation. It is done on the ish and jsh loops implementing static and dynamic load balance. The main drawback of this implementation is a huge memory footprint on multicore architectures, because each MPI rank has its own copy of density matrix and a partial contribution to Fock matrix that scales quadratically with job size. Straightforward OpenMP implementation also inherits this drawback; however the density matrix is read-only during ERI computation cycle and could be shared between threads. The Fock matrix is constantly updated in this cycle and in simplest case it is replicated. It is not a big problem when a large amount of memory is available. Replicated-memory MPI/OpenMP version of GAMESS was previously reported to work on Cray XT5 and further on K-computer [13]. In this algorithm each thread has its own copy of Fock matrix. Even in this case the amount of required memory reduces up to two times in comparison to original GAMESS implementation. Co-processors like MICs have large number of cores and a limited amount of on-chip memory. In this case a maximum job size is limited by the amount of available memory. A possible solution to this problem is to use distributed memory libraries like Global Arrays [14] or DDI [15]. This approach makes calculation possible even for extremely large jobs when none of these matrices could fit in a single-node memory in expense for some internode communication overhead. The distributed memory algorithms are based on the fact, that at every moment only a small amount of data from density and Fock matrix is required for the computation. Actually, only three rows of Fock matrix are updated in the innermost loop of the ERI calculation cycle. The drawback of this implementation is that inter-process communication grows, which may be quite expensive in runtime. In this study we focus on the straightforward variant of the memory problem solution.

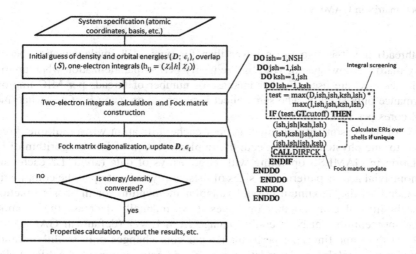

Fig. 1. Simplified algorithm of Hatree Fock implementation in GAMESS. NSH – number of shells. NSH $\leq$ 1000 for typical workloads.

First we tried both triple-sort and canonical way of integral ordering. They show nearly identical performance, however canonical order is slightly faster on medium-size problems due to smaller granularity. Further we always used canonical order of shells in the two-electron integral computational loop. It also has an advantage of the rectangular structure of second and third loop in nest, that could be used to improve load balance between threads.

The straightforward OpenMP version of GAMESS Fock matrix two-electron contribution shows quite a good performance on Xeon Phi (see Tables 1, 2, and 3). This implementation still has considerable memory footprint (Fock matrix is local to

```
!$omp parallel
  DO ish=NSH, 1
!$omp do schedule(dynamic,1) collapse(2)
    DO jsh=1, ish
      DO ksh=1, ish
        IF (ish.EQ.ksh) THEN
          lmax = jsh
        ELSE
          lmax = ksh
        ENDIF
        DO lsh=1, lmax
          test = max(D,ish,jsh,ksh,lsh) *
                 max(I,ish,jsh,ksh,lsh)
          IF (test.GT.cutoff) THEN
            calculate (ish,jsh|ksh,lsh)
              CALL DIRFCK
          ENDIF
        ENDDO
      ENDDO
    ENDDO
!$omp end do nowait
  ENDDO
!$omp end parallel
```

Fig. 2. Algorithm of OpenMP parallelization of the calculation of two-electron contribution to the Fock matrix in GAMESS.

each thread) but it is two times lower than for pure MPI implementation because density matrix is now shared. We observe nearly perfect parallelization when up to 60 threads per MIC are used. Further increase of number of threads per MIC improves performance only slightly. The same effect is observed on Xeon E5 CPU when more than 8 cores per socket are used.

One of the reasons of this effect is poor cache utilization when multiple threads are tied to one physical core. Indeed, the implementation of DRK algorithm of ERI calculation in GAMESS operating with large arrays of data (about L2 cache size) with nontrivial access pattern. The sizes of these arrays are set up at the compile time and depend on the maximum possible angular momentum for the basis functions. The scalability of code notably improves if we manually decrease the maximum angular momentum that code could manage from $L = 7$ (default in GAMESS) to $L = 4$. At the same time, the performance per core changes only slightly. Another reason for the scalability degradation is a poor vectorization of the ERI code in GAMESS.

It is worth noting that the scalability of code is unaltered if we consider benchmarks with similar thread/core affinity (Table 2). Therefore further improvement of single-core performance would increase overall performance as well.

The code on Fig. 2 could be also straightforwardly parallelized over the top loop in nest across MPI processes. The performance of the hybrid MPI/OpenMP version is presented in Table 3. The heaviest MPI communication task is a Fock matrix reduction that is performed only one time per HF iteration. We observe quite small ($\sim$ 1 % of execution time) synchronization and communication overhead in the case of multi-MIC run.

Table 1. Performance of the OpenMP parallelized Fock matrix two-electron contribution code for the C60 (6-31G) benchmark (KMP_AFFINITY = balanced).

Number of threads	Time of single Fock matrix build, seconds		
	Xeon E5-2690	Xeon Phi 7120D, L = 7	Xeon Phi 7120D, L = 4
1	370.8	–	–
2	195.5	–	–
4	105.5	–	–
8	55.0	815.2	790.2
16	48.5	409.6	396.4
32	–	215.2	211.4
60	–	109.7	106.6
120	–	75.6	69.0
180	–	–	61.5
240	–	79.6	59.2

Table 2. Thread affinity impact on the performance of the OpenMP parallelized Fock matrix two-electron contribution code for the C60 (6-31G) benchmark.

Number of cores used	Time of single Fock matrix build, seconds			
	1 thread/core	2 thread/core	3 thread/core	4 thread/core
16	393.1	256.4	227.8	216.1
30	212.1	137.6	123.2	117.1
60	104.9	69.3	61.3	59.2

Table 3. Performance of hybrid MPI/OpenMP parallelized Fock matrix two-electron contribution code on multiple Xeon Phi modules

Number of threads	Time of single Fock matrix build, seconds	
	C60 (6-31G), 540 b.f.	C60 (6-31G*), 900 b.f.
240 (1 MIC)	59.2	147.2
480 (2 MICs)	29.7	81.8
960 (4 MICs)	15.6	32.0
1920 (8 MICs)	8.2	25.8

3.1 Details of Benchmarks

As a benchmark systems we used fullerene molecule with two basis sets (6-31G and 6-31G*). The sizes of basis for these systems are 540 and 900 functions respectively. Xeon Phi benchmarks were conducted on RSC PetaStream platform. MIC results were compared to those of the RSC Tornado platform based on dual-socket Xeon E5-2690 server. Configurations of the test systems are summarized in Table 4.

Table 4. Configurations of the test systems

	RSC PetaStream	RSC Tornado
Host processors	1x Xeon E5-2697v2	2x Intel Xeon E5-2690
Co-processor	8x Xeon Phi 7120D	2x Xeon Phi SE10X
RAM amount/speed	128 GB DDR3R-1600	64 GB DDR3R-1600
Main board	Intel Server Board S1600JP	Intel Server Board S2600JFF
PM settings	cpufreq and PC6 enabled	EIST and Turbo enabled
Infiniband HCA	Connect-IB, 2-port	ConnectX-3 on-board
Host OS	CentOS 6.4	CentOS 6.2
MPSS	3.2.3	2.1.2
OFED version	3.5-rc3	1.5.4.1
Infiniband switch	Mellanox FDR MSX6025F. 1 hop between hosts	

4 Related Work

GAMESS [2, 3] is one of the most widely used software packages for quantum chemistry calculations. Existing parallelization in GAMESS is sophisticated [16], it has dynamic load balancing and distributed shared memory features.

GPU technology advances [17–19] created opportunity to take advantage of this new technology. NWChem code has been re-written initially for GPU [17] with CUDA technology, at its implementation on Xeon Phi [20] uses offload mode for harnessing Xeon Phi computational power. In this paper, implementation uses Xeon Phi native mode for better fitness to next generation architectures, with performance demonstration of multi-Phi. Existing GAMESS adaptation to GPU doesn't affect most widely used algorithms by computational chemists, and limited to some PCM model implementation. In more general contexts, only profiling work is reported [20]. In this respect, this paper constitutes an important contribution to the development of important software tools used by practicing researchers.

5 Conclusions

In this paper we present the design of parallelization scheme of GAMESS(US) code for quantum chemistry calculations, namely, Hartree-Fock and Density Function Theory (DFT) algorithms. Current work demonstrates the applicability of Xeon Phi coprocessors for the quantum chemistry problems. In this paper, we demonstrate scalability of the current implementation on Xeon Phi cores, as well as with multiple Xeon Phi chips running in native mode (OpenMP+MPI parallelization). Future work include more thorough performance characterization and additional vectorization of ERI calculation.

Acknowledgements. This work is supported by Intel Parallel Compute Center program. We thank Georg Zitzlsberg (Intel Corp.) and Klaus-Dieter Oertel (Intel Corp.) for valuable advices.

References

1. Goodwins, R.: Intel unveils many-core Knights platform for HPC. http://www.zdnet.com/article/intel-unveils-many-core-knights-platform-for-hpc/ (2010)
2. Schmidt, M.W., Baldridge, K.K., Boatz, J.A., Elbert, S.T., Gordon, M.S., et al.: General atomic and molecular electronic structure system. J. Comput. Chem. **14**, 1347–1363 (1993)
3. Gordon, M.S., Schmidt, M.W.: Advances in electronic structure theory: GAMESS a decade later. In: Dykstra, C., Frenking, G., Kim, K., Scuseria, G. (eds.) Theory And Applications Of Computational Chemistry: The First Forty Years, pp. 1167–1189. Elsevier, Amsterdam (2005)
4. Jeffers, J., Reinders, J.: Intel Xeon Phi Coprocessor High-Performance Programming. Morgan Kaufmann Publishers, San Francisco (2013)
5. Anthony, S.: Intel unveils 72-core x86 Knights Landing CPU for exascale supercomputing. http://www.extremetech.com/extreme/171678-intel-unveils-72-core-x86-knights-landing-cpu-for-exascale-supercomputing (2013)
6. Semin, A., Druzhinin, E., Mironov, V., Shmelev, A., Moskovsky, A.: The performance characterization of the rsc petastream module. In: 29th International Conference (ISC 2014), Leipzig, Germany, pp. 420–429 (2014)
7. Schlegel, H.B., Frisch, M.J.: Computational Bottlenecks in Molecular Orbital Calculations. Theor. Comput. Model. Org. Chem. **339**, 5–33 (1991)
8. Reza Ahmadi, G., Almlöf, J.: The Coulomb operator in a Gaussian product basis. Chem. Phys. Lett. **246**, 364–370 (1995)
9. McMurchie, L.E., Davidson, E.R.: One- and two-electron integrals over cartesian gaussian functions. J. Comput. Phys. **26**, 218–231 (1978)
10. Obara, S., Saika, A.: Efficient recursive computation of molecular integrals over Cartesian Gaussian functions. J. Chem. Phys. **84**, 3963 (1986)
11. Rys, J., Dupuis, M., King, H.F.: Computation of electron repulsion integrals using the rys quadrature method. J. Comput. Chem. **4**, 154–157 (1983)
12. Foster, I.T., Tilson, J.L., Wagner, A.F., Shepard, R.L., Harrison, R.J., et al.: Toward high-performance computational chemistry: i. scalable fock matrix construction algorithms. J. Comput. Chem. **17**, 109–123 (1996)
13. Ishimura, K., Kuramoto, K., Ikuta, Y., Hyodo, S.: MPI/OpenMP hybrid parallel algorithm for hartree − fock calculations. J. Chem. Theory Comput. **6**, 1075–1080 (2010)
14. Nieplocha, J.: Advances, applications and performance of the global arrays shared memory programming toolkit. Int. J. High Perform. Comput. Appl. **20**, 203–231 (2006)
15. Alexeev, Y., Kendall, R.A., Gordon, M.S.: The distributed data SCF. Comput. Phys. Commun. **143**, 69–82 (2002)
16. Fletcher, G.D., Schmidt, M.W., Bode, B.M., Gordon, M.S.: Distributed data interface in GAMESS. Comput. Phys. Commun. **128**, 190–200 (2000)
17. Sengottaiyan, S., Liu, F., Sosonkina, M.: A GPU support for large scale quantum chemistry applications. In: The 2012 International Conference on Parallel and Distributed Processing Techniques and Applications (PDPTA 2012), Las Vegas, Nevada, USA (2012)
18. Ufimtsev, I.S., Martínez, T.J.: Quantum chemistry on graphical processing units. 1. strategies for two-electron integral evaluation. J. Chem. Theory Comput. **4**, 222–231 (2008)
19. Ufimtsev, I.S., Martinez, T.J.: Quantum chemistry on graphical processing units. 2. direct self-consistent-field implementation. J. Chem. Theory Comput. **5**, 1004–1015 (2009)
20. Aprà, E., Klemm, M., Kowalski, K.: Efficient implementation of many-body quantum chemical methods on the intel® xeon phi™ coprocessor. In: Proceedings of the International Conference for High Performance Computing, Networking, Storage and AnalysisPiscataway, NJ, USA, pp. 674–684. IEEE Press (2014)

Dtree: Dynamic Task Scheduling at Petascale

Kiran Pamnany[1]([⊠]), Sanchit Misra[1], Vasimuddin Md.[2], Xing Liu[3],
Edmond Chow[4], and Srinivas Aluru[4]

[1] Parallel Computing Lab, Intel Corporation, Bangalore, India
kiran.pamnany@intel.com
[2] Department of Computer Science and Engineering,
Indian Institute of Technology Bombay, Mumbai, India
[3] IBM T.J. Watson Research Center, Yorktown Heights, NY, USA
[4] School of Computational Science and Engineering, Georgia Institute of Technology,
Atlanta, USA

Abstract. Irregular applications are challenging to scale on supercomputers due to the difficulty of balancing load across large numbers of nodes. This challenge is exacerbated by the increasing heterogeneity of modern supercomputers in which nodes often contain multiple processors and coprocessors operating at different speeds, and with differing core and thread counts. We present Dtree, a dynamic task scheduler designed to address this challenge. Dtree shows close to optimal results for a class of HPC applications, improving time-to-solution by achieving near-perfect load balance while consuming negligible resources. We demonstrate Dtree's effectiveness on up to 77,824 heterogeneous cores of the TACC Stampede supercomputer with two different petascale HPC applications: ParaBLe, which performs large-scale Bayesian network structure learning, and GTFock, which implements Fock matrix construction, an essential and expensive step in quantum chemistry codes. For ParaBLe, we show improved performance while eliminating the complexity of managing heterogeneity. For GTFock, we match the most recently published performance without using any application-specific optimizations for data access patterns (such as the task distribution design for communication reduction) that enabled that performance. We also show that Dtree can distribute from tens of thousands to hundreds of millions of irregular tasks across up to 1024 nodes with minimal overhead, while balancing load to within 2 % of optimal.

Keywords: Petascale · Dynamic scheduling · Load balance

1 Introduction

The scheduling challenge on modern supercomputers arises from the need for fine-grained parallelism in applications. Scaling to large numbers of processors requires that there be a large number of parallel tasks that can be distributed.

X. Liu—During this research, Xing Liu was affiliated with Georgia Institute of Technology.

J.M. Kunkel and T. Ludwig (Eds.): ISC High Performance 2015, LNCS 9137, pp. 122–138, 2015.
DOI: 10.1007/978-3-319-20119-1_10

This brings forth the need for efficient scheduling – to distribute tasks among all available processors so as to minimize total run time.

Applications that can be decomposed into equal-sized tasks can be scheduled simply by statically distributing the tasks evenly among the number of processors. This additionally simplifies the distribution of input data for tasks as well as routing for any required inter-task communication. For these reasons, this class of applications can be easily scaled to large supercomputers.

However, many applications exhibit irregular characteristics and require more sophisticated scheduling to prevent unbalanced computing load and the resulting unnecessary increase in total run time. Such applications vary widely, and a number of techniques have been proposed to address the diverse problems presented. We introduce our approach by classifying irregular applications according to the following characteristics:

1. Irregular tasks – individual tasks may vary in length.
2. Dynamic task pool – the set of tasks may be dynamic, i.e. new tasks may be added during application execution.
3. Locality – input and/or output data for a task may be large, i.e. the cost of movement must be considered.
4. Dependencies – there may be inter-task dependencies or communication.

There are important applications that display various combinations of one or more of these characteristics. While it is possible to design dynamic scheduling algorithms that cope with all of them, the resulting overhead may be needlessly large for applications that exhibit only few of the characteristics. Hence, many solutions in the literature focus on particular characteristics, the most common being the data locality problem.

Devine et al. [11] address load balancing entirely in the context of data partitioning. Menon and Kalé [20] target iterative applications with a synchronous load balancer, measuring load information with a gossip protocol and running sender-initiated load transfer at application synchronization points. Zheng et al. [27] also balance load periodically, but use a hierarchy of load balancing domains. These solutions share a theme in being measurement-based – which nodes are overloaded and which underutilized must be determined before load balancing decisions can be taken.

Other solutions target applications using recursive parallelism, e.g. combinatorial search or divide-and-conquer, in which the task pool is dynamic. Work stealing [8] is the dominant technique in this space [12,19] but generalized approaches can struggle with scaling beyond 6K processors due to large increases in failed steals [12]. Lifflander et al. have scaled a specialized work stealing approach for iterative applications to 163K cores [16]. Guo et al. use locality hints to improve performance and explore scheduling policies in their work stealing scheduler, SLAW [13].

Min et al. have proposed a topology-aware hierarchical work stealing strategy [21]; their implementation is in UPC [2]. Saraswat et al. extend work stealing with work sharing over lifeline graphs [24]; their system is implemented in X10 [9].

All work stealing approaches share the problem of distributed termination detection – if a node repeatedly fails to steal work, it cannot conclude that there is no work left in the system; other means of detecting quiescence must be used.

Numerous scheduling algorithms exist for applications that model inter-task dependencies as static task graphs [15]. Dependencies in applications that have dynamic task pools may be expressed as dynamic task additions and scheduled via work stealing.

For applications that do not have a data locality problem, applying a technique designed to minimize that problem is inefficient or unfeasible. Similarly, applications with static task pools cannot benefit from a technique intended to facilitate the easy addition of dynamically created tasks.

Our scheduler, Dtree, uses work sharing rather than work stealing, and further differs from other approaches in focusing on applications with independent irregular tasks in a static task pool. We decouple the task scheduling problem from the data distribution problem, focusing on balancing load by distributing tasks with minimal overhead. This allows us to demonstrate near-optimal load balance for an application that does not require data distribution. Furthermore, for an application that does require data distribution, the high efficiency of our scheduler allows us to discard application-specific optimizations designed to reduce data movement and still match the performance.

Many other approaches impose a particular programming model or framework on the application. We target the widely used and familiar hybrid MPI+X programming model (although the applications considered in this paper use OpenMP®, Dtree is agnostic to the shared memory parallelism model).

Finally, Dtree enables full utilization of heterogeneous nodes containing Intel® Xeon® processors as well as Intel® Xeon Phi™ coprocessors[1], balancing load across the different processors transparently and thereby eliminating the need for applications to manage such heterogeneity. The potential for this has been discussed in the literature, but to the best of our knowledge, ours is the first scalable solution showing experimental results.

We briefly introduced an early version of Dtree in the context of a specific application in previous work [22]. We have since significantly improved Dtree's performance and flexibility, extended it to support manycore processors and heterogeneous clusters, and evaluated it in depth, both with another large application, and with a micro-benchmark designed to find its limitations.

The remainder of this paper is organized as follows: we provide an in-depth description of Dtree in Sect. 2, followed by an analysis of Dtree's performance using a micro-benchmark to simulate a variety of workloads in Sect. 3. Sections 4 and 5 detail how we have used Dtree with a machine learning application and a quantum chemistry application, respectively, and present experimental results. We summarize and conclude in Sect. 6.

---

[1] Intel, Xeon, and Intel Xeon Phi are trademarks of Intel Corporation in the U.S. and/or other countries.

1.1 Experimental Setup

We performed all our experiments on the TACC Stampede supercomputer [3]. The Stampede nodes used in our experiments each contain two Intel Xeon E5-2680 at 2.7 Ghz, one Intel Xeon Phi SE10P coprocessor at 1.09 GHz, and 32 GB of DRAM. We compiled and ran our code using Intel Composer XE 2013 and either Intel MPI Library 4.1 or MVAPICH2 2.0b, depending on the application.

2 Dtree

A fundamental step in scaling an application is determining how work will be decomposed into a large number of independent tasks. Dtree addresses the challenge of scheduling these tasks across all available processors so as to minimize runtime.

2.1 Overview

Task Model. We follow Dinan *et al.* [12] in referring to the set of tasks as a *task pool* and requiring that all tasks in the pool are independent and able to execute till completion without blocking or waiting for results produced by any concurrently executing tasks. We further specify that a task pool may be dynamic and allow task addition during program execution, or static and contain the entire set of tasks to be completed at program start. Our approach targets static task pools.

It is possible, with a static task pool, to assign numbers to the tasks to arrange them in a total order. These *task IDs* allow a compute node to independently and uniformly identify the task, given the task ID. Dtree is agnostic to application task structure as it schedules tasks by distributing task IDs.

Task Characteristics. From the perspective of scheduling, the typical length of a task and the variance in task lengths are key characteristics of a task pool. A large number of short tasks and a smaller number of long tasks present quite different scheduling challenges. Similarly, tasks with high variance in length are difficult to balance whereas for tasks with low variance in length, the challenge is to outperform a static schedule.

Dtree's design, described in the following sub-section, addresses these challenges effectively. We validate these claims in Sect. 3.

2.2 Design

Distribution Tree. A centralized task distribution scheme offers excellent performance [7], but can face scalability problems due to the central node becoming a bottleneck. We address this with the well-known technique of arranging the nodes into a tree.

Figure 1 illustrates our approach, showing an example Dtree for 32 nodes. We arrange the tree to maximize the number of leaf nodes. The *fan-out* of the

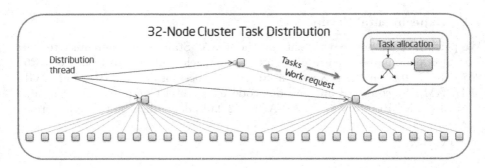

Fig. 1. Task distribution with an example Dtree for a 32 node cluster using a fan-out of 16. Observe that leaf nodes do not require a distribution thread.

tree, 16 in the example, is the maximum number of children for which a single node can be a parent, and is a function of the communication cost between a child node and a parent node. The protocol used by Dtree for task distribution is designed to minimize this communication cost, and thereby maximize the fan-out of the distribution tree.

Task Distribution. Dtree uses receiver-initiated task distribution – a node requests work from its parent in the tree and a parent node responds to requests from its children. As a parent node must listen for requests from its children, Dtree requires one thread in each parent node. All other threads in a parent node may be used for computation.

As Dtree distributes task IDs, the application need only specify T, the total number of tasks to be distributed. An important component of Dtree's efficiency is that tasks are distributed in groups identified by a range of task IDs, i.e. a start and end task ID. Initially, the root node alone holds a single task group comprised of tasks IDs 0 to $T - 1$.

Distribution Cost. A child node's request for work from its parent node takes the form of an 8-byte message. A parent node's response is a task group, sent in a 16-byte message. Thus, a request/response pair consists of two small messages.

Dtree is built on top of MPI. Running over a typical Infiniband interconnect, point-to-point MPI small messages see a one-way latency of approximately 1.31 ms, which equates to over 3 million messages per second [6]. In practice, this allows us to use a very large fan-out for the distribution tree, which minimizes the number of parent nodes required and consequently, the number of threads required by the scheduler.

Task Allocation. At program start, a node initializes its Dtree with an *init-work()* call. This returns a task group which is allocated as follows: the Dtree root node distributes $d_f \times T$ tasks to its children. All parent nodes in the tree apply the same strategy which leaves a buffer of tasks with each parent.

The number of tasks allocated to a child node is computed on the basis of the number of nodes in the child's sub-tree. In the example Dtree in Fig. 1, the left side sub-tree has 15 leaf nodes while the right side sub-tree has 14 leaf nodes. Parent nodes also work, and must be counted as part of their sub-trees for allocation purposes. Thus the left side intermediate parent node apportions 1/16 of its task allocation to each of its children and to itself. The root node must consider itself and its 2 children, which are parents themselves. Thus it computes *distribution fractions* of 1/32, 16/32, and 15/32 respectively.

When a node completes executing its initial allocation of tasks, it requests additional work from its Dtree using a *getwork()* call. This request is satisfied by applying the child's distribution fraction to the tasks remaining in the buffer. The resulting number is scaled by d_r, which controls the task drain rate, and subjected to a minimum threshold, t_{min}. When a node's task buffer is exhausted, Dtree transparently requests more work from the node's parent.

This approach results in reducing amounts of work being issued to requesting children, effectively balancing load.

Heterogeneity. A node may specify a multiplier, n_m, to its Dtree in order to indicate its performance relative to other nodes. The default multiplier is 1.0. As an example, if a cluster has two types of nodes, A and B, and a node of type B executes a task from the task pool in roughly twice the time a node of type A would take to execute that task, then nodes of type A would specify a multiplier of 2.0 while nodes of type B would specify a multiplier of 1.0.

Dtree parent nodes use node multipliers to compute distribution fractions for their children, effectively scaling task allocations. Load can be balanced effectively even if these estimates cannot be provided, however Dtree can be more efficient if they are available.

Mapping Task IDs. On receiving a task group to execute from Dtree, the application may schedule a task per thread, or use multiple (or all) threads to process the task. In either case, the task ID needs to be mapped to the input data for that task. The application must establish a swift means of translating the task IDs in the task group to the requisite task data. If this data is non-local, it may potentially be pre-fetched at this point, enabling a significant performance boost from computation and communication overlap. Global Arrays [4] may be

Table 1. Dtree parameters

F	Tree fan-out. Up to 1024, depending on network traffic
T	Total number of tasks
d_f	Size of the initial (static) distribution. 0.2 is a reasonable default
d_r	Task drain rate. 0.5 is a reasonable default
t_{min}	Minimum task allocation. Function of mean task length
n_m	Node multiplier. 1.0 is default

used effectively for data storage as task IDs (0 to $T - 1$) can be used to index them.

3 Micro-benchmark

We describe the use of Dtree with full applications in the following two sections. However, we have additionally written a micro-benchmark in order to evaluate Dtree performance and efficiency under a range of conditions. The micro-benchmark is an MPI application that uses OpenMP® for intra-node parallelism. It does not perform any actual computation – a task is simply a timed delay.

As discussed in Sect. 2.1, the key considerations for scheduling the tasks in a pool are the mean and standard deviation of the task lengths. We instrumented the execution of the ParaBLe and GTFock applications on two real datasets each, and recorded the actual lengths of the tasks. From this data, we have computed the statistics shown in Table 2.

Table 2. Measured task pool statistics in seconds

Application	Dataset	Mean	Std. Dev.
ParaBLe	<leaf,development>	0.696	0.314
	<seed,development>	0.414	0.114
GTFock	15mer	0.733	0.197
	graphene.336	0.644	0.153

We observe from the histograms of the measured task lengths that they could roughly be approximated by a Gaussian probability distribution. We apply this observation to generate task lengths for the micro-benchmark as follows: given a mean and a standard deviation, we use the Intel Math Kernel Library [1] to generate pseudo-random numbers in a Gaussian distribution. Each node uses the same seed for the generator and generates R sets of n random numbers each, where R is the number of participating nodes, and $n \times R$ is the total number of tasks specified. For each of the R sets, we vary the mean for the n numbers randomly within one standard deviation. This approach produces an artificial task pool that approximates the characteristics seen in the real applications.

In each of the following experiments, we compare the runtime and the average load imbalance of a micro-benchmark run that dynamically schedules tasks using Dtree, against the runtime and average load imbalance of a run that is statically scheduled, i.e. an equal number of tasks are distributed to each node. We run one MPI rank per node, with each rank using all 16 threads available on the two Intel Xeon processors. For the experiments involving Intel Xeon Phi coprocessors, we run one MPI rank per coprocessor, using all 240 threads available.

3.1   Scaling Experiments

The total number of tasks to be distributed is significant in evaluating scheduling efficiency. Clearly, as this number reduces, it becomes harder to balance load – at 1 task per thread, it becomes impossible for any scheduler. Our first experiment evaluates Dtree's effectiveness in this regard. We ran these tests using Intel Xeon processors only on 256 nodes with a mean task length of 0.5 s and a standard deviation of 0.125 s. In Fig. 2a, we see that even with as few as 2.5 tasks per thread (40 tasks per node with each node running 16 threads) and a total runtime of 2 s, Dtree does better than a static schedule, although we do observe a load imbalance of 13 %. For 40 tasks per thread, the load imbalance is 1.6 %.

We then perform a weak scaling experiment using only Intel Xeon processors, the results of which are shown in Fig. 2b. We ran these tests using a mean task length of 0.5 s and a standard deviation of 0.125 s with 320 tasks per node. Dtree exhibits a load imbalance of no more than 5 %.

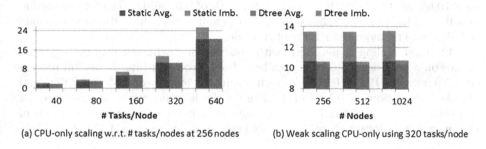

(a) CPU-only scaling w.r.t. # tasks/nodes at 256 nodes   (b) Weak scaling CPU-only using 320 tasks/node

Fig. 2. Scaling number of tasks and weak scaling with the micro-benchmark

We then performed a strong scaling experiment using only Intel Xeon processors, running 1,310,720 tasks with a mean task length of 0.5 s and a standard deviation of 0.125 s. The results are shown in Fig. 3a. Given a larger number of tasks, Dtree reduces load imbalance to no more than 1.4 % of runtime, even at 1024 nodes.

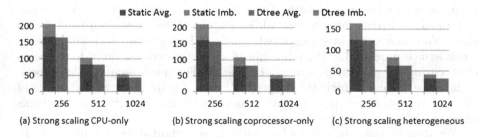

(a) Strong scaling CPU-only   (b) Strong scaling coprocessor-only   (c) Strong scaling heterogeneous

Fig. 3. Strong scaling experiments with the micro-benchmark. The X-axis is # nodes and Y-axis is time-to-solution in seconds.

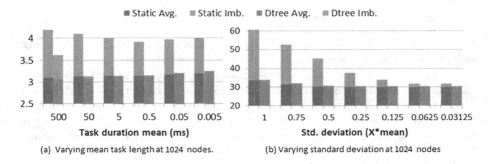

(a) Varying mean task length at 1024 nodes.   (b) Varying standard deviation at 1024 nodes

Fig. 4. Effect of task length and standard deviation. Y-axis is time-to-solution in seconds. Standard deviation for (a) is 0.125 s. Mean for (b) is 0.05 s.

We repeated the strong scaling experiment using only Intel Xeon Phi coprocessors in order to evaluate the performance of Dtree on a manycore cluster. We execute 19,660,800 tasks with a mean task length of 0.5 s and a standard deviation of 0.165 s. The results are shown in Fig. 3b. Again, we see that Dtree reduces load imbalance to no more than 1.9 % of runtime.

Our final scaling experiment with the micro-benchmark evaluates performance on a heterogeneous cluster of both Intel Xeon and Intel Xeon Phi processors. We execute 10,000,000 tasks with mean task lengths of 0.35 and 0.87 s, and standard deviations of 0.12 and 0.0.29 s for the host processor and coprocessor respectively. We see in Fig. 3c that despite the differing speeds and core counts of the processors, Dtree reduces load imbalance to no more than 3.7 % of runtime.

3.2   Task Length Experiments

Given the importance of task lengths in dynamic scheduling, we used the micro-benchmark to analyze Dtree performance for task pools with differing characteristics. In particular, we assessed the impact of changing the mean task length, and also of changing the standard deviation. We ran all these experiments on 1024 nodes, using only Intel Xeon processors.

We begin by experimenting with the mean task length. In order to maintain a roughly consistent runtime across experiments, we increase the number of tasks when we reduce the mean length. Thus, for a mean task length of 0.5 s, we run 6,400 tasks, whereas for a mean task length of 0.000005 s, we run 640,000,000 tasks. Note that as the task length reduces, thread scheduling overhead increases – this issue is unrelated to Dtree but can affect runtime considerably, to the point of obscuring the performance we are evaluating. For this reason, for this experiment alone, we use a single thread per MPI rank. Figure 4a shows the results of this experiment, clearly demonstrating that Dtree can effectively schedule tasks as short as 5 ms (13,500 processor cycles).

We then explore the effect of varying the standard deviation of the tasks in the task pool. We see in Fig. 4b that even with very small variance in task lengths, Dtree outperforms a static schedule.

4   ParaBLe

Bayesian network structure learning is an important machine learning problem. ParaBLe (Parallel Bayesian Learning) implements a parallel heuristic algorithm to solve this problem at scale [22,23]. We have modified this application to use Dtree. In this section, we provide a brief introduction to the algorithm, describe how we use Dtree, and evaluate the performance gains from doing so.

4.1   Bayesian Network Structure Learning Algorithm

A Bayesian network is represented as a directed acyclic graph in which nodes represent the set of variables of interest in the domain. Data regarding the observations of these variables are taken to estimate the joint probability distribution of the variables – a Bayesian network is the graphical representation of a factorization of the joint probability distribution. Automatically learning the structure of a Bayesian network from data is an NP-hard problem [10].

Let n denote the number of variables, X, Y, etc. denote individual variables, $\mathcal{X}$ denotes the set of all variables, and A, B, etc. denote subsets of $\mathcal{X}$. The structure learning problem can be defined as follows. Let the function $s(X, A)$ model the fitness of choosing elements of set A as the parents of X. Let $CP(X) \subseteq \mathcal{X}$ denote the set of candidate parents of a variable X. For each variable X, we need to identify $Pa(X) \subseteq CP(X)$ that maximizes $s(X, Pa(X))$. This requires computing $s(X, A)$ for all $A \subseteq CP(X)$. ParaBLe represents this computation using a hypercube of dimension $|CP(X)|$, in which each node represents a subset of $CP(X)$. Therefore, for each variable X, all the $2^{|CP(X)|}$ nodes of the corresponding hypercube have to be computed. Note that choosing $CP(X) = \mathcal{X} \setminus \{X\}$ results in exact structure learning, which has exponential complexity. ParaBLe heuristically determines much smaller $CP(X)$ sets to stem the computational complexity.

4.2   Work Decomposition

Consider the n candidate parents sets, exploring the subsets of which constitutes the total amount of work to be done. The CP sets vary significantly in size and the corresponding work varies exponentially in the size of the CP sets, therefore the required work for each variable is vastly different. The number of variables and the exponential variation in the corresponding workloads does not permit balancing the load to thousands of nodes. To more effectively distribute work, ParaBLe chooses an r-dimensional hypercube as the largest allowed unit of work, for a specific threshold r. For any variable X with $|CP(X)| > r$, the corresponding hypercube is divided into $2^{|CP(X)|-r}$ sub-hypercubes each creating a work item[2]. Any variable X with $CP(X) \leq r$ creates a work item with hypercube dimension $|CP(X)|$. This creates a sufficiently large list of work items.

---

[2] We refer to Dtree tasks as work items in this application.

4.3 Using Dtree

The work items are arranged in a global order so that using a small metadata and a bijective mapping, the ID of a work item can be mapped to the corresponding (variable, hypercube) pair. The data for learning the network is small enough to be replicated on every processor. Hence, no communication is needed to provide the data required for a work item. ParaBLe executes one work item with one thread. The results of the work items assigned to a node are accumulated on the node and reduced across all nodes on completion.

ParaBLe has optimized implementations for executing work items on both the Intel Xeon and Intel Xeon Phi processors. It uses the offload model [5] to achieve heterogeneity, running MPI only on the host processor and using a dynamic scheduling algorithm to balance load between the processors.

We modified the application to use the symmetric model, eliminating the complex offloading code and creating a simpler, truly heterogeneous version, running MPI on both the host processor and on the coprocessor, and using Dtree to balance load across all the processors and coprocessors in the cluster.

4.4 Datasets Used

ParaBLe was created to learn genome-scale networks from microarray data, a grand challenge in systems biology, and we test Dtree's performance for the same application. In this application, nodes in the Bayesian network represent genes of the underlying organism. The data comes from a large number of experiments, each of which measures quantitatively the expression level of each gene in the organism under different experimental conditions. We ran our experiments on two datasets for the plant *Arabidopsis thaliana* – one for the seedling tissue type and the other for the leaf tissue type, both classified under developmental conditions. More details on these datasets may be found in [22].

4.5 Experimental Results

We ran strong scaling experiments with ParaBLe on the two datasets over 256, 512, and 1024 heterogeneous nodes on Stampede. We measured the time-to-solution of the implementation using the offload model with static and dynamic task distribution across nodes using an earlier version of Dtree, against the implementation using the symmetric model with the improved Dtree. The graphs in Fig. 5 show the results of these experiments. We see that performance improves in all cases, up to 18 % with respect to dynamic on 1024 nodes, while load imbalance is almost completely eliminated.

5 GTFock

Fock matrix construction is an important algorithm in quantum chemistry. It is the most time consuming step in the widely used Hartree Fock (HF) algorithm

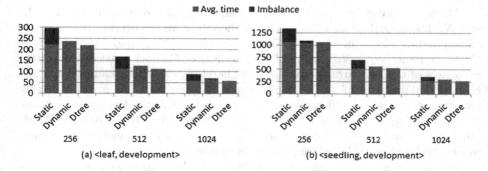

Fig. 5. ParaBLe performance (static and dynamic schedule) vs. using Dtree for 256, 512 and 1024 nodes. Y-axis is time-to-solution in seconds.

and optimizations of Fock matrix construction have been studied for decades. GTFock [17], NWChem [26], GAMESS [25], ACESIII [18] and MPQC [14] are some of the many existing computational chemistry packages that implement parallel Fock matrix construction and HF.

In this section, we provide a brief introduction to GTFock and to Fock matrix construction, describe how we use Dtree, and study the resulting performance.

5.1 Fock Matrix Construction

The Fock matrix is defined as

$$F_{ij} = H_{ij}^{core} + \sum_{kl} D_{kl}(2(kl|ij) - (ik|jl)) \tag{1}$$

where i, j, k and l are indices such that $0 \leq i,j,k,l < n_f$, where n_f is the number of basis functions. The two dimensional matrices H^{core} and D are fixed for this computation. Each $(ij|kl)$ is an element of a 4-dimensional array called an electron repulsion integral (ERI) tensor. Along each dimension, the indices are grouped into "shells" of 1 to 10 (or more) indices, which is necessary to facilitate efficient computation of ERIs in quantum chemistry programs.

GTFock defines a task[3] as computing the set of ERIs,

$$(M,:|N,:) = \{(ij|kl) \ s.t. \ i \in shell \ M, \ k \in shell \ N, 0 \leq j,l < n_f\} \tag{2}$$

and then computing contributions to the Fock matrix due to these ERIs. Here, M and N are shell indices. Some ERIs can be pre-determined to be very small, and their computation can be neglected. The ERI tensor also has 8-way symmetry, so only unique elements of $(ij|kl)$ need to be computed. Thus the number of ERIs in $(M,:|N,:)$ to be computed in each task can vary, making it hard to balance the load.

---

[3] We refer to Dtree tasks as work items, to prevent confusion with GTFock tasks.

All the tasks can be represented as a 2-dimensional task array indexed by M and N. The way the tasks are designed, there is a higher overlap between the corresponding blocks of D and F of batches $(M_1, : |N_1, :)$ and $(M_2, : |N_2, :)$ if $|M_2 - M_1|$ and $|N_2 - N_1|$ are small. Based on this, GTFock statically allocates subarrays of the task array across nodes. Therefore, each node can prefetch the required submatrices of D for all the tasks assigned to it. As a result of this partition, there is a significant overlap between the submatrices of D for tasks assigned to a node, thus greatly reducing the volume of data to be communicated. Similarly, submatrices of F can be accumulated locally first and the global copy can be updated once the entire parition is finished.

The blocks of tasks assigned to a node are divided into sub-blocks and computation is performed one sub-block at a time. When a node is done with its own quota, it uses work stealing to steal one of the sub-blocks from some other node that still has some left. It will also need to copy the corresponding blocks of D and update the corresponding blocks of F. Since this happens only towards the end, it results in only a small increase in communication while significantly balancing the load.

5.2   Using Dtree

For Dtree, the work items are defined as equal sized subarrays of the task array. When a node receives a work item, it uses the size of the blocks (S) and n_{shells}, to uniquely map the ID to the corresponding block of the task array. It then loads the corresponding blocks of D from the global copy, processes the work item, and updates the corresponding blocks of F in the global copy. Larger work items allow more overlap between the blocks of D and F within the work item and thereby reduce communication, but also make it harder to balance load.

5.3   Datasets Used

We have used two datasets to study the performance of Dtree for Fock matrix construction. The system 15mer is a 15 nucleotide strand of DNA containing 981 atoms, 4826 shells and 10498 functions. The system 1hsg is a human immunodeficiency virus (HIV) II protease complexed with a 92-atom ligand which is an HIV inhibitor. We have modified the system to include only residues 8 Angstroms from any atom in the ligand, and call this system 1hsg_80. It has 1035 atoms, 4576 shells and 9584 functions.

5.4   Experimental Results

Figure 6 shows the results of strong scaling experiments for Fock matrix construction by GTFock, using four different scheduling schemes – static, static with work stealing, using ADLB [19], and using Dtree – on the two datasets.

As expected, the static schedule has the highest amount of imbalance, but negligible communication. Adding work stealing significantly reduces the imbalance while increasing the communication only slightly. Dtree reduces imbalance

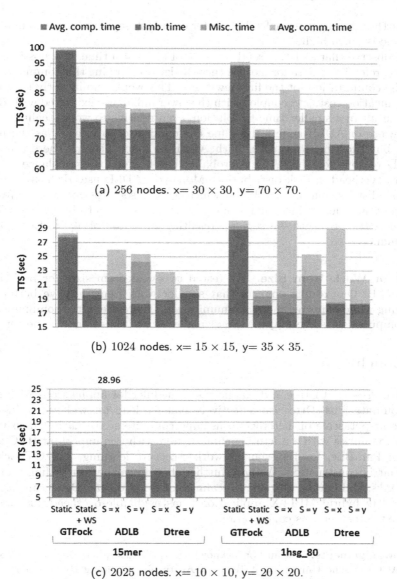

(a) 256 nodes. x= 30 × 30, y= 70 × 70.

(b) 1024 nodes. x= 15 × 15, y= 35 × 35.

(c) 2025 nodes. x= 10 × 10, y= 20 × 20.

Fig. 6. GTFock strong scaling experiment. Avg. comp. time and Avg. comm. time are averages of time spent by each node in computation and communication, respectively. Misc. time is obtained by subtracting the average computation and communication time from the average total time, and includes scheduling overhead. Imb. time is time-to-solution minus average total time and quantifies the load imbalance across nodes. The bars for ADLB do not have any imbalance since every node in effect waits for every other node before exiting the scheduler. So, for ADLB, the imbalance is included in the Misc. time. Parameters used: GTFock(# of sub-blocks = 5 × 5), ADLB(# servers = $\frac{1}{64}$(#nodes), $task\_size = 1$), Dtree($F = 256$)

even further, but as it must fetch data for each task separately, the communication time is much higher.

We observe that as Dtree sends a range of tasks at a time, it is possible for a node to prefetch the data for most of these tasks, overlapping this communication with the computation for the first few tasks. This would significantly reduce the communication cost, and coupled with the lower imbalance exhibited with Dtree, would result in a smaller time-to-solution, even relative to work stealing.

The use of ADLB suffers the same communication overheads as the use of Dtree, but the time-to-solution with ADLB is much higher. There are three possible reasons for this. ADLB probably has higher load imbalance, as well as more overhead in task distribution. Moreover, ADLB uses dedicated servers for work distribution, as a result of which it loses some performance. We have experimentally determined that 1 of every 64 nodes needs to be a server. Thus, of 1024 nodes, 16 must be servers, resulting in a loss of $\frac{1}{64} = 1.6\%$ of the performance.

Effect of Work Item Size. We tested two work item sizes for both Dtree and ADLB. Our results confirm that smaller work items achieve better load balancing while requiring more communication. Therefore, if the communication and computation is overlapped, using smaller work items might be better.

6   Conclusion

We have presented Dtree, a dynamic task scheduler for applications with irregular computations. Dtree can effectively balance load for widely varying task profiles at petascale on heterogeneous supercomputers. We have demonstrated these capabilities with a micro-benchmark, and with two important HPC applications: ParaBLe, for Bayesian network structure learning, and GTFock, for Fock matrix construction. We have further shown near-perfect scaling up to 2K MPI ranks, and find no obstacle to scaling well beyond that. Dtree can easily be deployed in hybrid MPI+X applications, has negligible overhead, and enables balanced heterogeneous computation.[4]

Acknowledgements. The authors acknowledge the Texas Advanced Computing Center (TACC) at The University of Texas at Austin for providing HPC resources that have contributed to the research results reported within this paper. URL: http://www.tacc.utexas.edu.

---

[4] Software and workloads used in performance tests may have been optimized for performance only on Intel microprocessors. Performance tests, such as SYSmark and MobileMark, are measured using specific computer systems, components, software, operations and functions. Any change to any of those factors may cause the results to vary. You should consult other information and performance tests to assist you in fully evaluating your contemplated purchases, including the performance of that product when combined with other products. For more information go to http://www.intel.com/performance.

References

1. Intel® math kernel library MKL. http://software.intel.com/en-us/intel-mkl
2. Upc consortium. upc language specifications, v1.2. Technical report LBNL-59208, Lawrence Berkeley National Lab (2005)
3. TACC Stampede supercomputer (2014). http://top500.org/system/177931
4. Global arrays webpage (2015). http://hpc.pnl.gov/globalarrays/
5. Intel mpi on intel xeon phi coprocessor systems (2015). https://software.intel.com/en-us/articles/using-the-intel-mpi-library-on-intel-xeon-phi-coprocessor-systems
6. Mvapich: Performance (2015). http://mvapich.cse.ohio-state.edu/performance/pt_to_pt/
7. Bhatele, A., Kumar, S., Mei, C., Phillips, J., Zheng, G., Kale, L.: Overcoming scaling challenges in biomolecular simulations across multiple platforms. In: IEEE International Symposium on Parallel and Distributed Processing, IPDPS 2008, pp. 1–12, April 2008
8. Blumofe, R.D., Leiserson, C.E.: Scheduling multithreaded computations by work stealing. J. ACM 46(5), 720–748 (1999). http://doi.acm.org/10.1145/324133.324234
9. Charles, P., Grothoff, C., Saraswat, V., Donawa, C., Kielstra, A., Ebcioglu, K., von Praun, C., Sarkar, V.: X10: an object-oriented approach to non-uniform cluster computing. In: Proceedings of the 20th Annual ACM SIGPLAN Conference on Object-Oriented Programming, Systems, Languages, and Applications, OOPSLA 2005, pp. 519–538. ACM, New York (2005). http://doi.acm.org/10.1145/1094811.1094852
10. Chickering, D.M., Heckerman, D., Geiger, D.: Learning Bayesian networks is NP-hard. Technical report MSR-TR-94-17, Microsoft Research (1994)
11. Devine, K.D., Boman, E.G., Heaphy, R.T., Hendrickson, B.A., Teresco, J.D., Faik, J., Flaherty, J.E., Gervasio, L.G.: New challenges in dynamic load balancing. Appl. Numer. Math. 52(2–3), 133–152 (2005). http://dx.doi.org/10.1016/j.apnum.2004.08.028
12. Dinan, J., Larkins, D.B., Sadayappan, P., Krishnamoorthy, S., Nieplocha, J.: Scalable work stealing. In: Proceedings of the Conference on High Performance Computing Networking, Storage and Analysis, SC 2009, pp. 53:1–53:11. ACM, New York (2009). http://doi.acm.org/10.1145/1654059.1654113
13. Guo, Y., Zhao, J., Cave, V., Sarkar, V.: Slaw: A scalable locality-aware adaptive work-stealing scheduler for multi-core systems. In: Proceedings of the 15th ACM SIGPLAN Symposium on Principles and Practice of Parallel Programming, PPoPP 2010, pp. 341–342. ACM, New York (2010). http://doi.acm.org/10.1145/1693453.1693504
14. Janssen, C.L., Nielsen, I.M.: Parallel Computing in Quantum Chemistry. CRC Press, Boca Raton (2008)
15. Kwok, Y.K., Ahmad, I.: Static scheduling algorithms for allocating directed task graphs to multiprocessors. ACM Comput. Surv. 31(4), 406–471 (1999). http://doi.acm.org/10.1145/344588.344618
16. Lifflander, J., Krishnamoorthy, S., Kale, L.V.: Work stealing and persistence-based load balancers for iterative overdecomposed applications. In: Proceedings of the 21st International Symposium on High-Performance Parallel and Distributed Computing, HPDC 2012, pp. 137–148. ACM, New York (2012). http://doi.acm.org/10.1145/2287076.2287103

17. Liu, X., Patel, A., Chow, E.: A new scalable parallel algorithm for Fock matrix construction. In: 2014 IEEE International Parallel & Distributed Processing Symposium (IPDPS), Phoenix, AZ (2014)
18. Lotrich, V., Flocke, N., Ponton, M., Yau, A., Perera, A., Deumens, E., Bartlett, R.: Parallel implementation of electronic structure energy, gradient, and hessian calculations. J. Chem. Phys. **128**, 194104 (2008)
19. Lusk, E.L., Pieper, S.C., Butler, R.M., et al.: More scalability, less pain: a simple programming model and its implementation for extreme computing. SciDAC Rev. **17**(1), 30–37 (2010)
20. Menon, H., Kalé, L.: A distributed dynamic load balancer for iterative applications. In: Proceedings of the International Conference on High Performance Computing, Networking, Storage and Analysis, SC 2013, pp. 15:1–15:11. ACM, New York (2013). http://doi.acm.org/10.1145/2503210.2503284
21. Min, S.J., Iancu, C., Yelick, K.: Hierarchical work stealing on manycore clusters. In: 5th Conference on Partitioned Global Address Space Programming Models (2011)
22. Misra, S., Vasimuddin, M., Pamnany, K., Chockalingam, S., Dong, Y., Xie, M., Aluru, M., Aluru, S.: Parallel Bayesian network structure learning for genome-scale gene networks. In: International Conference for High Performance Computing, Networking, Storage and Analysis, SC14, pp. 461–472, November 2014
23. Nikolova, O., Aluru, S.: Parallel Bayesian network structure learning with application to gene networks. In: Proceedings of the International Conference on High Performance Computing, Networking, Storage and Analysis, SC 2012, pp. 63:1–63:9 (2012)
24. Saraswat, V.A., Kambadur, P., Kodali, S., Grove, D., Krishnamoorthy, S.: Lifeline-based global load balancing. In: Proceedings of the 16th ACM Symposium on Principles and Practice of Parallel Programming, PPoPP 2011, pp. 201–212. ACM, New York (2011). http://doi.acm.org/10.1145/1941553.1941582
25. Schmidt, M.W., Baldridge, K.K., Boatz, J.A., Elbert, S.T., Gordon, M.S., Jensen, J.H., Koseki, S., Matsunaga, N., Nguyen, K.A., Su, S., et al.: General atomic and molecular electronic structure system. J. Comput. Chem. **14**(11), 1347–1363 (1993)
26. Valiev, M., Bylaska, E.J., Govind, N., Kowalski, K., Straatsma, T.P., Van Dam, H.J., Wang, D., Nieplocha, J., Apra, E., Windus, T.L., et al.: NWChem: a comprehensive and scalable open-source solution for large scale molecular simulations. Comput. Phys. Commun. **181**(9), 1477–1489 (2010)
27. Zheng, G., Bhatelé, A., Meneses, E., Kalé, L.V.: Periodic hierarchical load balancing for large supercomputers. Int. J. High Perform. Comput. Appl. **25**(4), 371–385 (2011). http://dx.doi.org/10.1177/1094342010394383

Feasibility Study of Porting a Particle Transport Code to FPGA

Iakovos Panourgias[1](✉), Michele Weiland[1], Mark Parsons[1],
David Turland[2], Dave Barrett[2], and Wayne Gaudin[2]

[1] EPCC, James Clerk Maxwell Building, Peter Guthrie Tait Road, Edinburgh
EH9 3FD, UK
{i.panourgias,m.weiland,m.parsons}@epcc.ed.ac.uk
[2] AWE, Aldermaston, Reading RG7 4PR, UK
{David.Turland,Dave.Barrett,Wayne.Gaudin}@awe.co.uk

Abstract. In this paper we discuss porting a particle transport code, which is based on a wavefront sweep algorithm, to FPGA. The original code is written in Fortran90. We describe the key differences between general purpose CPUs and Field Programmable Gate Arrays (FPGAs) and provide a detailed performance model of the FPGA. We describe the steps we took when porting the Fortran90 code to FPGA. Finally, the paper will present results from an extensive benchmarking exercise using a Virtex 6 FPGA.

Keywords: FPGA · Particle transport · Wavefront sweep

1 Introduction

Chimaera-2 is a particle transport code based on a wavefront algorithm. The code has been developed and maintained by the UK Atomic Weapons Establishment (AWE) and is used primarily for benchmarking during procurement processes. Chimaera-2 is written in Fortran90 and MPI/OpenMP; it scales well to thousands of cores for large problem sizes and is used to calculate nuclear criticality. It is one of the highest priority application codes in the benchmark suite used by AWE for procurement of HPC systems.

This paper will discuss the programming strategies required to port a CPU-centric HPC code to Field Programmable Gate Arrays (FPGAs) by an application developer with no prior knowledge of FPGA/embedded programming. This feasibility study will provide a detailed performance model of the FPGA implementation of Chimaera-2 and we will show how the model can forecast the runtime of an FPGA ported application. A mini-app, which closely matches the Chimaera-2 code, was implemented and used to evaluate our porting strategy and the performance model predictions. Finally, we will describe the steps we took when porting parts of the Fortran90 code to FPGA using Maxeler's FPGA solution. The limiting factors of the algorithm will be discussed and we will provide solutions for future development.

© Springer International Publishing Switzerland 2015
J.M. Kunkel and T. Ludwig (Eds.): ISC High Performance 2015, LNCS 9137, pp. 139–154, 2015.
DOI: 10.1007/978-3-319-20119-1_11

1.1 Contributions

Although writing applications for FPGAs and embedded devices dates back to the 1990s and the difficulties and steep learning curve have been mentioned in research papers feasibility studies of using new methodologies have not been sufficiently explored. This paper is amongst the first to consider new abstract methods of porting HPC CPU applications to FPGA. Furthermore, this paper studies the feasibility of an application developer with no knowledge of FPGA or embedded computing being able to port a large and complex HPC application. This paper makes the following contributions:

- We discuss and evaluate a set of techniques which enable an application developer to predict the performance characteristics of an FPGA application;
- We describe the conceptual differences between CPU and FPGA programming;
- We describe the implementation of a mini-app that closely matches Chimaera-2 to test different porting strategies and to evaluate the performance model predictions.

2   Related Previous Work

This section will discuss previous attempts of porting a particle sweep transport code to accelerators. The Denovo code [1], produced by the Scientific Computing Group at Oak Ridge National Laboratory, serves a similar purpose to Chimaera-2 – it is used for advanced nuclear reactor design and as a benchmark code. Denovo also works on a three dimensional domain, but unlike Chimaera it is written in C ++. Denovo has been ported to work with GPUs using CUDA for the three dimensional case with performances that achieve from 1 to 10 % of the peak GPU performance; however these are for three dimensional systems that parallelise more extensively, including groups (or energy levels), which expose additional levels of parallelism. Work by Gong et al. [2, 3] attempted to convert another three dimensional sweep code, Sweep3D[1], a benchmark code produced by the Los Alamos National Laboratory, to work on GPUs. Their results obtained overall performance speedups for a single NVIDIA Tesla M2050 GPU ranging from 2.56, compared to an Intel Xeon X5670 CPU, to 8.14, compared to an Intel Core Q6600 CPU with no flux fix-up (with flux fix-up on an M2050 was 1.23 times faster than on one X5670). In [4], Gong et al. go on to look at 2D problems using a "Discontinuous Finite Element – Sn" (DFE-Sn) method [5], using a 2D Lagrangian geometry. The performance speed-ups they obtain for simulations on an M2050 GPU range from 11.03 to 17.96 compared with an NTXY2D [6] on Intel Xeon X5355 and Intel Core Q6600. In their case the energy groups in the calculation are regarded as inherently independent and thus can be executed in parallel.

3   Chimaera-2

The full problem space for a Chimaera execution is a fixed uniform rectilinear 3D spatial mesh of grid points. All faces of the problem space are squares or rectangles.

---

[1] The code can be downloaded from http://wwwc3.lanl.gov/pal/software/sweep3d.

For running in parallel using MPI, Chimaera performs a simple domain decomposition of this mesh as shown in Fig. 1. The front face is divided into N rectangles (with N being the number of MPI tasks) that are projected the whole way from the front face to the back face to form 3D elongated cuboids. These 3D domains are often referred as "pencils".

Each iteration of the solver algorithm used in Chimaera-2 involves sweeping through the whole spatial mesh eight times, each of the sweeps starting at one of the eight vertices of the mesh and proceeding to the diametrically opposed vertex. As the boundaries between pencils are crossed, MPI message passing is used to transmit the updated data to adjacent pencils.

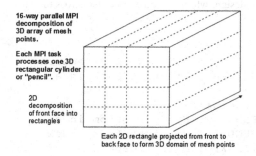

Fig. 1. Chimaera domain decomposition for a 16-way parallel run

Figure 2 shows a single pencil (MPI domain) with a 6×6 square cross section of mesh points. 10^3 geometry sizes can be used to test correctness; however, realistic problems are likely to be larger. 200^3 to 500^3 geometries are common and sizes over $1{,}000^3$ are considered very large. The sweep direction being illustrated starts at the front top-right vertex; therefore this MPI task will receive data from the pencil to its immediate right and from the one immediately above and transmit data to the left and downwards. Within the pencil, the order of computation is shown by the following code fragment in Code Listing 1.

Note that this assumes that the data in the 3D arrays are held in the same sequence as the sweep direction; that is that the front top-right element has the index (1,1,1) in Fortran syntax. With the data still in this sequence for other sweep directions, one or more of the loops end up being computed in reverse order. For example, "DO K = 1, KEND" might become "DO K = KEND,1,-1" when we compute sweep "Front, Top, Left". This is because each of the J, K, and L loops exhibits sequential dependence where every iteration depends on the previous iteration and must be computed in the order corresponding to the sweep direction.

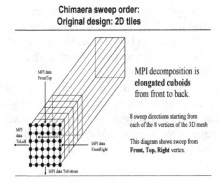

Fig. 2. Original 2D tile design, where computation order across the tile is a simple x and y pair of loops.

```
DO ISW=1,8         ! ISW: sweep direction
  DO L=1,LEND      ! L: Front/Back index
    MPI calls
    ----------Kernel
    DO K=1,KEND    ! K: Top/Bottom index
      DO J=1,JEND  ! J: Right/Left index
        DO M=1,ISNX ! M is independent of the  structure
          Computation
        ENDDO
      ENDDO
    ENDDO
    ----------
  ENDDO
ENDDO
```

Code Listing 1: Basic structure of algorithm.

Although all three spatial loops (i.e. J, K and L) have this sequential dependence, the order of nesting can be changed in any way without affecting the results (except for the complication that it has been chosen to perform the MPI communication after each iteration of the L-loop). The M-loop is concerned with the directions of the particles being tracked and is independent of the J, K and L loops. It does not have sequential dependence and can be logically nested at any point. With the above algorithm, the computational Kernel within the MPI layer processes a single 2D tile (indexed by K and J), which moves from front to back as the outer L-loop is iterated. The Chimaera-2 application is used for procurement purposes at AWE and has been maintained and optimised for the past 10 years. The algorithm has been optimised for serial, MPI, OpenMP and GPU runs.

3.1 Mini-app

Our goal was to port the computationally expensive Kernel of the Chimaera-2 application to the FPGA. However, in order to better understand the effects of porting different parts of the code using different techniques we implemented a mini-app. The mini-app uses less memory than the full Chimaera-2 application; however, the computational Kernel is identical to the full application showing the same data dependencies. It also uses the same number of arrays as input and output.

The mini-app does not implement 8 different sweeps; rather a single sweep (Front, Top, Left) is used. Furthermore, it does not use MPI or OpenMP. The initial values of the arrays are populated programmatically rather than reading an input file. The mini-app allowed us to experiment with different porting techniques and to run large simulations. Chimaera-2 uses more than 40 GBs of RAM for a 120^3 simulation; whereas, the mini-app only uses 12 GBs of RAM for a $1,000^3$ simulation.

4 Porting from CPU to FPGA

Porting to an FPGA historically required writing code in VHSIC Hardware Description Language (VHDL) or Verilog. VHDL and Verilog are hardware description languages (HDLs) and are used to describe the structure, design and operation of electronic circuits. Unlike an Application-Specific Integrated Circuit (ASIC), an FPGA is a semiconductor device that can be configured by the end user. FPGAs contain programmable logic blocks, that can perform complex Boolean logic functions or simple AND or XOR operations. These logic blocks can be connected in order to provide more complex functionalities. The logic blocks are made up of two basic components: flip-flops (FF) and lookup tables (LUT). Many logic blocks can be combined to create simple arithmetic operations (addition, multiplication) or higher math operations like *abs* or even trigonometry operations like *sin* and *cos*.

There is a growing interest in using FPGAs as energy efficient accelerators and new programming models designed to make FPGA programming more widely accessible are gradually emerging. The work presented in this paper uses Maxeler's Multiscale Dataflow solution to port Chimaera-2 to FPGA. This approach allows an application programmer to use a high-level (Java-like) language, called MaxJ, as an intermediary step before using the Maxeler tool chain to translate the code to VHDL. The VHDL files are then used by a set of third party vendor tools, which build the configuration bitstream that is uploaded to the FPGA. The FPGA used here is a Max3 solution which is based on a Xilinx Virtex-6 (V6-SXT475) FPGA with 24 GB RAM. Maxeler's solution allows an application to be split into three parts:

- Kernel(s), which implement the computational components of the application in hardware;
- Manager configuration, which connects Kernels to the CPU, engine RAM, other Kernels and other dataflow engines via MaxRing;
- CPU application, which interacts with the dataflow engines to read and write data to the Kernels and engine RAM.

– Dataflow variable type

FPGAs allow the representation of a number by using an arbitrary number of bits. It is possible to either use pre-defined primitive variable types (such as 32-bit integers or 64-bit floats) or define a custom data format. For instance, if it is known that an algorithm requires 48-bit precision a matching custom type can be created.

– Streams of data

Dataflow computing operates on windows into data streams. The data window can be held in the on-chip memory of the FPGA and thus minimises data transfer costs. We can use static or variable stream offsets to look back or forward into a stream of data. Variable stream offsets can be set once for the duration of a Kernel, or they can be modified per FPGA clock cycle.

– Loops/Counters

Loop statements are heavily used in High Performance Computing. Simple loops can be easily ported to an FPGA. A simple loop applies the same operation to a group of data elements. In an FPGA this translates to streaming data element through the same logic block. Unfortunately, not all loop statements are simple. In order to implement more complex loop statements on an FPGA it is necessary to keep track of where we are in the stream. Furthermore, many HPC applications use nested loops. We use counters to port nested or loops with boundary conditions.

– Data Dependency Loops

So far discussion has been limited to simple loops, where each iteration of the loop is using values from the incoming stream(s) and loop counters. However, many loops in HPC applications have dependencies and each iteration relies on the values calculated in previous iterations. In order to port these loops, it is necessary to either unroll the loops or create cyclic graphs. Unrolling loops is only possible if the number of iterations is known (or if it is known that the number of iterations will be N at most). Loop unrolling on the FPGA uses replicated hardware resources and the limit is therefore the size of the FPGA. Unfortunately in many HPC applications the number of iterations per loop will be large enough to consume all available hardware resources. Therefore the better option is to create a cyclic data graph, in which the output of the loop stream can be connected to the input stream. Thus, the output of a calculation is available as input.

– Scalar inputs and outputs

In addition to streaming input and output data between CPU and FPGA, it is also possible to transfer read-only configuration values at runtime.

– Boolean control logic

Since FPGA designs are built in advance, FPGA code must be able to handle all possible execution paths through the code. For every conditional "if/then/else" statement a multiplexer is created, which diverts the data streams (using multiplexers) to the correct logic block path.

5 Performance Model

Estimating the performance of a dataflow implementation is simpler than for a CPU implementation due to the static scheduling of the FPGA. The FPGA design is built out-of-band using the MaxCompiler and the FPGA vendor tools. The bitstream is then loaded on the FPGA and can be used by an HPC application. We can estimate the performance of an application with a known runtime in cycles (like Chimaera 2) executing an FPGA design. If the runtime is not known, it is still possible to model the performance of the application; as long as the application uses a regular pattern for reading and writing data to external interfaces. The FPGA has a set of well-defined external interfaces (PCIe and DRAM) with fixed performance capabilities. Furthermore, the FPGA does not create or handle any dynamic events, like interrupts. Also the FPGA does not use pre-emption for interrupting the kernels since only a specific set of kernels can be executed at one time. Finally, out of order execution and cache misses are not relevant on an FPGA. The FPGA design dictates the compute nodes that will be used and the data that will be computed.

Thus, the performance of an FPGA design depends on the following factors:

- Number of cycles per kernel
- Data read from and written to DRAM
- Data read from and written to PCIe
- Data read from and written to Network Interface

The total time that an application spends in a dataflow execution is computed by:

$$T_{Total} = \max\left(T_{compute}, T_{DRAM}, T_{PCIe}, T_{MaxRing}\right) \tag{1}$$

5.1 Model Compute

As mentioned earlier, the dataflow design uses static scheduling. Therefore $T_{COMPUTE}$ is the time that it takes the input data to run through the dataflow design:

$$T_{compute} = \frac{Cycles}{Frequency} \tag{2}$$

The frequency of the design determines the compute speed. For simple single pipe designs the number of cycles is equal to the number of inputs, i.e. 1. However, for multi-pipe designs the number of cycles is equal to the number of input divided by the number of pipes.

As an example, in order to compute the loops K, J and M (from Code Listing 1) we need to run for $K*J*M$ cycles. Thus, for the 10^3 simulation with M = 36, the FPGA will run for 3,600 cycles. Using a frequency of 150 MHz we estimate that the FPGA will run for 24 μs. If we port the L loop, the FPGA will run for $L*K*J*M$ cycles. Thus, for the 10^3 simulation the FPGA will run for 36,000 cycles or for 240 μs. However, the LKJ FPGA port will be called L fewer times than the KJ FPGA port. It is estimated that the overhead of calling the FPGA is close to 7 ms. As the size of the simulation increases, the overheads of calling the FPGA many times for small runtimes also increases.

5.2 Model PCIe

PCIe is one of the three different ways of getting data into an FPGA. PCIe is a bi-directional link which can send and receive data in parallel without sharing bandwidth. To estimate the PCIe transfer rate we can use the following formula:

$$T_{PCIe} = \max\left(\frac{BytesIn_{PCIe}}{BandwidthIn_{PCIe}}, \frac{BytesOut_{PCIe}}{BandwidthOut_{PCIe}}\right) \tag{3}$$

The number of bytes transferred to and from the FPGA is known at compile time. For the Chimaera-2 application it is known that the KJ FPGA port is streaming $Bstream = K*J*M*sizeof(double)*number\ of\ array$ bytes to the FPGA. The values for K, J and M depend on the size and configuration of the simulation. The "number of arrays" value depends on the implementation and is equal to 8 for the KJ FPGA port. The naïve implementation copies redundant data to the FPGA. This approach simplifies the logic on the FPGA, but the cost of copying more data slows down the application. The optimised version uses more logic on the FPGA in order to re-arrange arrays which hold replicated data. For example, the naïve implementation copies three 2D arrays as three 3D arrays. The optimised implementation copies three 2D arrays.

We also know that the design is streaming out to the host Bstream Bytes. The naïve approach copies all output values to the host (even if some of them are temporary and not useful). The optimised version on the other hand only copies the minimum data back to the host that is needed for future iterations. Table 1 shows the two versions:

Table 1. GBs transferred for KJ FPGA port

Size	Total naïve (GBs)	Total optimised (GBs)
10^3	0.00038	0.00014
60^3	0.01352	0.00405
500^3	0.93877	0.27142
$1,000^3$	3.75509	1.08302

The ideal PCIe bandwidth is 1.8 GBs/s; however, for our calculations we also used a non-ideal value of 1.5 GBs/s. The non-ideal bandwidth reflects real life benchmarks using Chimaera-2 and the mini-app. Table 2 shows the PCIe transfer times in seconds. It can be seen that the optimised KJ FPGA port reduces the time spend on PCIe data transfers. The reason behind the performance improvement is that the optimised KJ FPGA port transfers less data to the FPGA. The naïve KJ FPGA implementation copies superfluous data, thus spending more time on the host in order to create the data arrays and spending more time when transferring the data to/from the FPGA.

Table 2. Model KJ FPGA port PCIe performance in seconds

Size	Naïve In	Naïve Out	Optimised IN	Optimised OUT
10^3	0.00011	0.000080	0.000037	0.000034
60^3	0.00429	0.00321	0.00115	0.0011
500^3	0.29802	0.22357	0.07606	0.07472
$1,000^3$	1.19209	0.89407	0.3032	0.29847

5.3 Model DRAM

The FPGA has two different types of memory: DRAM and BRAM. The BRAM memory is a very fast close to the FPGA logic chips memory of a very limited size. The BRAM on the FPGA is less than 10 MBs in size. The FPGA also has 24 GBs of DDR3 DRAM on-board. Like any DRAM, it shares read and write bandwidth on a single bus (unlike the PCIe bus, which has different bandwidths for read and write). The time spent on writing and reading to the DRAM can be expressed by the following formula:

$$T_{DRAM} = \frac{BytesIn_{DRAM} + BytesOut_{DRAM}}{Bandwidth_{DRAM}} \tag{4}$$

The performance of writing to and reading from the DRAM is also affected by two other factors: memory frequency and memory access pattern.

Memory frequency is chosen at build time. A faster memory frequency usually yields a higher bandwidth; however, a faster memory frequency makes the design harder to build due to the stricter timing requirements imposed by the faster frequency.

Memory access patterns play a more significant role to the DRAM performance. If we try to a use a semi-random access pattern, e.g. one where the data is not located sequentially on DRAM, the performance will be very poor. The maximum bandwidth that can be achieved is expressed by the following formula:

$$Bandwidth = Bytes_{DIMM} \times No\_DIMMS \times Frequency_{DRAM} \times Efficiency \tag{5}$$

"Bytes per DIMM" is 8 Bytes on the MAX3. However, it can be configured and set during the build phase of the design. The "No_DIMMS" is based on the actual FPGA hardware that is used (in our case this is 6 DIMMS). The frequency of the DRAM controller is also set during the build phase of the design. It can vary from 606 up to 800 MHz (for both read and write). The efficiency depends on the size of the transfer and the access pattern. Assuming a perfect efficiency and using the maximum frequency for both read and write operations a MAX3 DRAM subsystem can achieve a theoretical bandwidth of 38.4 GB/s. More modern FPGAs can achieve higher frequencies and are also able to accommodate more complicated designs.

Our implementation used a streaming approach rather than copying data to the DRAM. Thus, we will not use T_{DRAM} and $T_{NETWORK}$ in our calculations. The algorithm which we used did not require the use of DRAM, however in order to inform design choices it is useful to estimate the time spent on the DRAM. As long as we know the amount of required data we can model the performance of the DRAM subsystem.

6   Results

This section discusses the performance results of porting the mini-app and Chimaera-2 to FPGA. Due to the memory requirements of the Cimaera-2 code we were able to run simulations with geometry sizes up to 120^3. The mini-app enabled us to run simulations with geometry sizes up-to $1,000^3$.

The CPU run-times were obtained on a workstation with an Intel Core i7-2600S CPU @ 2.8 GHz (3.8 GHz with turbo mode) and running CentOS release 6.6. The workstation had 32 GBs of DDR3 RAM and the mini-app and Chimaera-2 applications were using a single core. The Fortran90 code was compiled using the GNU Fortran compiler (v4.4.7) and the O3 optimisation flag. The C code was compiled using the GNU Compiler Collection compiler (v4.4.7) and the O3 optimisation flag.

Both the mini-app and Chimaera-2 code stream data to/from the FPGA. Hence, we did not use the on-board DRAM. The input data are streamed to the FPGA before the execution of the compute Kernel and the computed values are streamed back to the host. The amount of data copied to/from the FPGA depends on the port implementation (naïve or optimised) and the number of ported directional loops (KJ or LKJ).

6.1   Mini-app Naïve KJ Implementation

Using the performance model calculations it is possible to estimate $T_{COMPUTE}$ and T_{PCIe}. Based on this model, we created two versions of the application: a naïve and an optimised implementation. The first 2 columns of Table 3 show the performance in seconds for streaming data (T_{PCIe}) to/from the FPGA using the naïve implementation and using 1.8 GB/s bandwidth. The third column shows the performance (in seconds) of running the FPGA at 100 MHz. The next two columns select the maximum of each phase (T_{PCIe} to/from and $T_{COMPUTE}$) and use it to model the performance of the naïve mini-app using either 1.8 GB/s and 1.5 GB/s PCIe rates.

Table 3. Mini-app (KJ) Naive T_{PCIe}, $T_{COMPUTE}$, modelled and actual duration

Size	To FPGA	From FPGA	Compute total	Duration 1.8 GB/s	Duration 1.5 GB/s	Actual duration	Actual duration*
10^3	0.0008	0.0006	0.0736	0.0008	0.0008	0.00657	0.00453
100^3	0.895	0.5960	0.43	0.895	1.0747	1.1515	0.9213
500^3	111.80	74.51	48.50	111.80	134.16	124.56	115.37
$1,000^3$	894.22	596.05	367.00	894.22	1,073.06	963.66	950.08

Table 3 shows the naïve implementation of the mini-app is PCIe bound. For small simulations the overhead of calling the FPGA multiple times makes the runtime compute bound. However, for simulations larger than 100^3 the application becomes PCIe bound. The last two columns of Table 3 show the actual duration of the naïve mini-app in seconds (for two different designs; using 100 MHz and 170 MHz speeds). It can be seen that increasing the operation speed of the FPGA by 70 % does not affect the duration of the mini-app; since it is PCIe bound. For example, for the $1,000^3$

simulation the 100 MHz design runs for 963 s; whereas the 170 MHz design runs for 950 s (a performance improvement of 1.3 %).

Furthermore, the performance model is able to accurately predict the actual performance of the application. For the $1,000^3$ simulation, the performance model predicts a duration between 894 and 1,073 s using a speed of 1.8 GB/S and a less favourable speed of 1.5 GB/s. The actual duration is 963 and 950 s (for the 100 MHz and 170 MHz designs). The actual duration corresponds to a ~ 1.65 GB/s PCIe transfer rate.

6.2 Mini-app Optimised KJ Implementation

The optimised mini-app application reduces the need for redundant data copies to/from the FPGA. In order to reduce the amount of data that needs to be copied it is necessary to implement more logic on the FPGA. Three of the input arrays are used as read-only memory and it was possible to reduce the size of the arrays from three dimensions to two. The three read-only arrays are accessed using a constant pattern. The pattern is not the same for each array; however, it is the same for the runtime of the application. We implemented the pattern on the FPGA using logic blocks and several fast memory blocks to store the data. The effect that this reduction has on T_{PCIe} can be seen in the first two columns of Table 4. The third column shows that the optimised version of the mini-app is compute bound. Since the optimised version of the mini-app is compute bound, increasing the operational speed of the FPGA by 70 % (from 100 MHz to 170 MHz) also improves the runtime performance of the mini-app.

Table 4. Mini-app (KJ) T_{PCIe}, $T_{COMPUTE}$, modeled and actual duration

Size	To FPGA	From FPGA	T_{COMPUT}	Duration 1.8 GBs	Duration 1.5 GBs	Actual duration	Actual duration*
10^3	3.4E-4	2.8E-4	0.0736	0.07036	0.07036	0.00587	0.0041
100^3	0.306	0.2995	0.43	0.43	0.43	0.11267	0.0970
500^3	37.88	37.29	45.35	45.35	45.46	52.2	39.9
$1,000^3$	302.6	298.2	360.7	360.7	363.13	375.5	318.1

As mentioned earlier, the performance of an application on an FPGA can be improved by increasing the number of pipes that are used, which in turn increases the number of calculations per cycle. In order to perform more calculations the FPGA design increases the width between logic blocks. Instead of streaming 64 bits of data between logic blocks, multiples of 64 bits are streamed (i.e. 128 bits for 2 pipes, 256 bits for 4 pipes, and so on) using more logic blocks (such as adders or multipliers); thus, more physical space is required on the FPGA. Fortunately, there is an initial cost for each resource; however, doubling the resource usage does not double the actual hardware usage. We experienced 50 % increase of actual resource usage whenever we doubled the number of pipes.

The T_{PCIe} performance model of the "double" implementation is identical to the model of the "single", because the same amount of data is being streamed. However,

$T_{COMPUTE}$ is now reduced to 50 % as two cells are computed per cycle and the FPGA Kernel will therefore run for half the time. Unfortunately in that case the problem is again PCIe bound. Figure 3 shows a comparison between the various versions of the mini-app.

If the double pipes mini-app application was not PCIe bound a performance increase of $\sim$ 100 % could be expected. And since there is enough physical space on the FPGA to use even more pipes, a doubling of performance with each step could be expected.

Since the problem is now PCIe bound, an option is to employ compression on the host side to reduce the amount of data that needs to be transferred. Uncompressing the data on the FPGA is free in terms of compute cost. However, one has to take into account that compressing the data on the host side would increase the runtime of the host application.

6.3   Mini-app LKJ Implementation

Using the same methodology as above we model T_{PCIe} and $T_{COMPUTE}$; the results are shown in Table 5. We can see that porting the L loop, the application becomes compute bound. However, the amount of data that needs to be streamed to/from the FPGA has been reduced. For example, for the $1,000^3$ simulation the LKJ version streams 7.9 GBs and streams back 0.53 GBs (as opposed to 0.54 GBs and 0.53 GBs for the KJ version). The LKJ version streams the data only once, whereas the KJ version has to repeat the streaming operation 1,000 times.

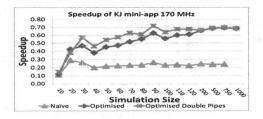

Fig. 3. Mini-app (KJ) speedup comparison

The last two columns of Table 5 show the actual duration and the modelled duration of the mini-app LKJ port. Since the mini-app LKJ port is compute bound, a speed increase from 100 MHz to 170 MHz reduces the runtime of the application.

Table 5. Mini-app (LKJ) T_{PCIe}, $T_{COMPUTE}$, modeled and actual duration

Size	To FPGA	From FPGA	T_{COMP}	Duration 1.8 GBs	Duration 1.5 GBs	Actual Duration	Actual duration*
10^3	4.0E-05	3.0E-05	0.0011	0.0011	0.0011	0.00195	0.00123
60^3	0.0020	0.00108	0.0785	0.0785	0.0785	0.07962	0.04636
500^3	0.59	0.07	45.01	45.01	45.01		
$1,000^3$	4.44	0.30	360.01	360.01	360.01		

We are not able to run simulations larger than 60^3. The M loop calculations are independent; however, the K, J and L loop calculation are not. Our design creates a cyclic loop on the K, J and L output streams in order to drive the output calculation as input for the next iteration. The Virtex FPGA allows $\sim$ 1 MB of look-back buffers per stream. For the 60^3 simulation 0.9887 MBs ($K*J*M$ entries) are used as buffer. For the 70^3 we need 1.34 MBs, which is larger than the available buffer. In order to be able to execute problems that are larger than 60^3 it is necessary to modify the algorithm and use the DRAM as a temporary buffer. Furthermore, if the size of the simulation increases to more than the available DRAM there will not enough space on the FPGA to hold the temporary data. Another option to support larger problem sizes is to modify the computational algorithm. The current algorithm computes a 2D face and then moves back in the L (Z) dimension. However, it is possible to instead compute a whole pencil in the L (Z) dimension and then move to the next pencil in the J (X) dimension. This modification would reduce the look back buffer to $L*M$ entries. Thus, we could run $3,600^3$ simulations.

6.4   Chimaera-2 Port

We implemented two versions of the K, J and M loop FPGA port for the Chimaera-2 application: the naïve and the optimised versions. The Chimaera-2 kernel uses 8 input arrays and 6 output arrays.

The first three columns of Table 6 show T_{PCIe} and $T_{COMPUTE}$ for the optimised version of Chimaera-2 kJ port, which reduces the amount of data that needs to be copied to/from the FPGA. As an example, the PCIe duration of the optimised version compared to the naïve for the 120^3 simulation dropped from 8,261 to 2,154 s, which represents an improvement of almost 4x.

Table 6. Chimaera-2 (KJ) T_{PCIe}, $T_{COMPUTE}$, modeled and actual Duration

Size	To FPGA	From FPGA	$T_{COMPUTE}$	Duration 1.8 GBs/s	Duration 1.5GBs/s	Actual Duration
10^3	1.69	1.43	3.9	3.9	3.9	10.93
60^3	305.91	292.47	248.37	305.91	367.09	403.81
100^3	1,390.41	1,345.56	1,098.66	1,390.41	1,668.50	1,588.80
500^3	169,162	166,198	133,595	169,162	202,994	
$1,000^3$	1,348,658	1,327,596	1,067,831	1,348,658	1,618,389	

The last column of Table 6 shows the actual duration of the FPGA kernel calls. For small simulation sizes the overheads cause the model to drift. However, as the simulation sizes increase the predictions of the model match the duration of the Kernel. Figure 4 (top left) shows the overall runtime of the Chimaera-2 application. The difference between the naïve and optimised approach grows larger as the simulation increases in size.

Figure 4 (top right and bottom left) show the performance improvement of reducing data transfers to/from the FPGA. The first figure shows the speedup of the overall application runtime whereas the second compares only the durations of the Kernels.

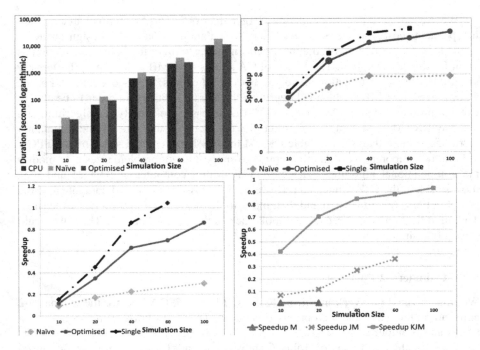

Fig. 4. Overall duration (CPU, naïve and optimised) (top left); overall speedup (naïve, optimised and single precision) compared to single core CPU run (top right); kernel only speedup (naïve and optimised) compared to single core CPU run (bottom left); speedup of M, JM and KJM loop implementations (bottom right)

Both implementations (naïve and optimised) are PCIe bound. It can be seen that as the size of the simulation increases, both implementations perform better. However, this improvement will only last until the PCIe links become saturated. Once the PCIe links are saturated performance improvements will plateau. It can be seen that the naïve implementation speedup plateaus with the 60^3 simulation.

We also implemented a version of the optimised code, which replaced double floating point numbers with single precision numbers in order to further reduce the amount of data that needs to be transferred. The single precision version is faster than the double precision implementation. However, it is not twice as fast even though data transfer is reduced by 50 %. From Table 6 it can be seen that even though the KJ optimised implementation is PCIe bound, the value of TPCIe is very close to $T_{COMPUTE}$. Thus, when using single precision TPCIe is reduced and the performance limiting factor is again $T_{COMPUTE}$.

7   Conclusions

We have shown how an application programmer with limited knowledge of FPGAs and embedded computing can port a complicated production-ready Fortran90 code to an FPGA and achieve acceptable performance. We have also seen that porting a greater proportion of the code to the FPGA improves performance. Our latest design uses around 20 % of the available resources (thus we have enough physical space on the FPGA to port more code or to use multiple pipes).

We have also shown how an application programmer can use a mini-app to test different porting strategies. We used the mini-app to implement a streaming version; a version which first copies to DRAM and then streams the data back; a version which copies to DRAM the input and output arrays and a version which copies some of the small arrays to the BRAM. Using the mini-app results, we decided to implement the data streaming version for the full application.

Figure 4 (bottom right) shows the speedups of the M, JM and KJM loop implementations. The M loop implementation clocked a "speedup" of 0.0076, whereas the KJM implementation reached 0.93 of the single CPU performance. Furthermore, as we minimise data transfers and allow the FPGA to re-use data that are already on-chip we realise that one of the most important optimisations that an application programmer can implement is to reduce data traffic. FPGAs can provide Terabytes/sec of data bandwidth between the logic blocks and BRAM. The bandwidth drops to tens of gigabytes/sec for DRAM memory. Furthermore, newer FPGAs increase the available physical space for logic blocks thus allowing even more code to be ported. Also, they run at faster speeds and include more and faster memory (BRAM and DRAM).

We plan to change the algorithm and port the L loop on the FPGA. We need to modify the algorithm due to the limited physical resources of the FPGA. The existing algorithm solves a 2D plane and then moves (backwards or forwards) to the next plane in the Z dimension. However, this approach requires "$X*Y*M$" look-back entries on several streams. We will modify the algorithm and solve a pencil of Z length before moving to the next pencil in the X plane. Thus we will reduce the amount of look-back buffer to $Z*M$ entries. If we have enough physical resources we plan to use multiple pipes in order to compute multiple cells per cycle. Since, the LKJ port will be compute bound, each extra pipe will improve performance.

In order to reduce the amount of data being copied to/from the FPGA we can use compression. We plan to measure the effects of compression and perform a cost benefit analysis to help us decide if the extra time spent on the host CPU to compress data reduces the overall runtime of the application.

Finally, once the performance of the FPGA port is on par with the performance of a compute node we plan to measure and compare the energy consumption of the FPGA and the host platform.

References

1. Joubert, W.: Oak Ridge National Laboratory. Presentation given at the OLCF Titan Summit 2011. Porting the Denovo Radiation Transport Code to Titan: Lessons Learned. http://www.olcf.ornl.gov/wp-content/uploads/2011/08/TitanSummit2011_Joubert.pdf
2. Gong, C., Liu, J., Chi, L., Huang, H., Fang, J., Gong, Z.: Accelerated simulations of 3D deterministic particle transport using discrete ordinates method. J. Comput. Phys. **230**, 6010–6022 (2011). http://www.sciencedirect.com/science/article/pii/S0021999111002348

3. Gong, C., Liu, J., Chen, H., Xie, J., Gong, Z.: Accelerating the Sweep3D for a graphic processor unit. J. Inf. Process. Syst. **7**(1), 63–74 (2011). doi:10.3745/JIPS.2011.7.1.063
4. Gong, C., Liu, J., Chi, L., Huang, H., Gong, Z.: Particle transport with unstructured grid on GPU. Comput. Phys. Commun. **183**, 588–593 (2012). http://www.sciencedirect.com/science/article/pii/S0010465511003870
5. Plimpton, S. Hendrickson, B., Burns, S., McLendon, W., Rauchwerger, L.: Parallel Sn sweeps on unstructured grids: Algorithms for prioritization, grid partitioning, and cycle detection. Nuclear Science and Engineering, vol. 150, p. 267 (2005). http://www.sandia.gov/~bahendr/papers/Rad-Transport.pdf
6. Fu, L., Yang, S.: Researches on 2-D neutron transport solver NTXY2D, Technical report, Institute of Applied Physics and Computational Mathematics, Beijing, China (1999)
7. Maxeler, MaxCompiler Tutorial, v2014.1.1

A Scalable, Linear-Time Dynamic Cutoff Algorithm for Molecular Dynamics

Paul Springer$^{(\boxtimes)}$, Ahmed E. Ismail, and Paolo Bientinesi

Aachen Institute for Advanced Study in Computational Engineering Science,
RWTH Aachen University, Schinkelstr. 2, 52062 Aachen, Germany
{springer,ismail,pauldj}@aices.rwth-aachen.de
http://hpac.rwth-aachen.de/

Abstract. Recent results on supercomputers show that beyond 65 K cores, the efficiency of molecular dynamics simulations of interfacial systems decreases significantly. In this paper, we introduce a dynamic cutoff method (DCM) for interfacial systems of arbitrarily large size. The idea consists in adopting a cutoff-based method in which the cutoff is chosen on a particle-by-particle basis, according to the distance from the interface. Computationally, the challenge is shifted from the long-range solvers to the detection of the interfaces and to the computation of the particle-interface distances. For these tasks, we present linear-time algorithms that do not rely on global communication patterns. As a result, the DCM algorithm is suited for large systems of particles and massively parallel computers. To demonstrate its potential, we integrated DCM into the LAMMPS open-source molecular dynamics package, and simulated large liquid/vapor systems on two supercomputers: SuperMuc and JUQUEEN. In all cases, the accuracy of DCM is comparable to the traditional particle-particle particle-mesh (PPPM) algorithm, while the performance is considerably superior for large numbers of particles. For JUQUEEN, we provide timings for simulations running on the full system (458, 752 cores), and show nearly perfect strong and weak scaling.

Keywords: Dynamic cutoff · Interface detection · Linear-time complexity · Scalability · Molecular dynamics · Fast sweeping method

1 Introduction

Molecular dynamics (MD) is a vital tool for computational chemistry, materials science, biophysics, and many other fields. The basic idea underpinning MD is the direct numerical integration of Newton's laws of motion, which require the frequent evaluation of forces between atomistic- or molecular-scale "particles". Although the underlying model is conceptually simple, significant challenges arise because of the enormous number of particles found even in nanoscopic systems. In this paper, we discuss the development implementation, and parallelization of a new force computation algorithm especially designed for systems

© Springer International Publishing Switzerland 2015
J.M. Kunkel and T. Ludwig (Eds.): ISC High Performance 2015, LNCS 9137, pp. 155–170, 2015.
DOI: 10.1007/978-3-319-20119-1_12

consisting of large number of particles which demand the equivalent of "Tier-0" computing resources.

Practically, MD calculations are limited by available computational resources, with typical simulations today involving anywhere from 10^4 to 10^7 particles, although simulations of 10^9 atoms or more have been reported in the literature [24, 26]. In general, larger simulations are preferable to smaller ones because smaller simulations can be affected by finite-size effects that reduce the accuracy of the calculations by introducing spurious correlations between particles [11]. Moreover, in principle, every particle can interact with every other particle, making the inherent complexity of MD $\mathcal{O}(N^2)$. Thus, a primary driver of active research in MD is reducing the algorithmic complexity of the force calculations while preserving both accuracy and scalability.

To integrate Newton's equations of motion, one needs to calculate the interaction forces among all of the particles in the system. Formally, these forces can be calculated using any scheme that correctly accounts for all forces present. Calculations are typically divided into *bonded* and *non-bonded* forces:

$$\mathbf{F} = \mathbf{F}_{\text{bonded}} + \mathbf{F}_{\text{non-bonded}}, \tag{1}$$

where bonded forces result from the topological structure of molecules, while non-bonded forces account for all other interactions (such as gravity and electromagnetic effects). Since the calculation of bonded forces already has linear complexity, our focus is on the non-bonded forces, which can have complexity up to $\mathcal{O}(N^2)$. In particular, we focus on a class of forces known as *dispersion* forces, which represent forces that exist as a result of the gravitational interaction between particles, independent of any other internal and external forces in the system. These dispersion forces are typically calculated as a sum of pairwise interactions between particles, with the strength of the interaction depending on the distance between them:

$$\mathbf{F}_{\text{disp}} = \sum_{i<j} \mathbf{F}(r_{ij}), \tag{2}$$

where $r_{ij} = |\mathbf{r}_i - \mathbf{r}_j|$ is the distance between atoms i and j.

Until recently, dispersion forces were treated using a cutoff on the distance, beyond which they were assumed to be negligible:

$$\mathbf{F}(r_{ij}) = \begin{cases} \mathbf{F}(r_ij), & r_{ij} \leq r_c \\ 0 & r_{ij} > r_c \end{cases}, \tag{3}$$

where r_c is the user-specified "cutoff" parameter. This approach, also referred to as a short-range method, reduces the complexity of the force calculation in Eq. 2 from $\mathcal{O}(N^2)$ to $\mathcal{O}(Nr_c^3)$, where N is the number of particles. Such cutoff-based methods are sufficiently accurate for homogeneous systems, whose composition is uniform throughout the simulation volume. However, in heterogeneous systems, with nonuniform spatial density that leads to the existence of interfaces, assuming isotropic behavior can cause major technical problems, as illustrated

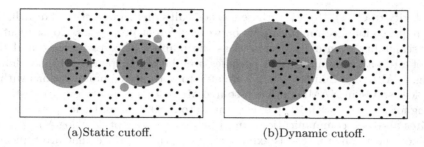

(a)Static cutoff.   (b)Dynamic cutoff.

Fig. 1. Interfacial system using a (a) static cutoff and a (b) dynamic cutoff. Gray area denotes the cutoff. The arrows represent the force acting on a particle. The yellow arrow depicts the additional force contribution due to a larger cutoff (Color figure online).

in Fig. 1a. The red particle in the right-hand circle indicates the behavior in the "bulk" part of the system, where isotropic behavior can be assumed and the errors introduced by Eq. 3 largely cancel, as can be seen from the green particles around the red particle, whose force contributions essentially negate one another. However, near the interface, such as the blue particle on the left, this cancellation of errors is impossible, as the distribution of atoms across the interface is far from isotropic. This breakdown, which can lead to completely inaccurate results, has been demonstrated by a number of different researchers [2,6,10,17]. Successful resolution of this problem is critical in a range of applications, including industrial uses such as spreading and coating of films [14] as well as modeling of the dynamics of cell membranes [4].

A naïve solution to account for the "missing" interactions in Fig. 1b would be to increase the magnitude of the cutoff r_c; doubling and even tripling the magnitude of the cutoff has been proposed [33]. Such an approach is inherently undesirable, as the $\mathcal{O}(Nr_c^3)$ complexity of the method means that doubling the cutoff leads to an eight-fold increase in the cost of the pairwise computations. In response, a number of so-called "long-range solvers" have been developed to reduce the overall complexity. Most of these approaches are based on Ewald summation methods [8], which rely on Fourier transforms to reduce the complexity of the force calcu-

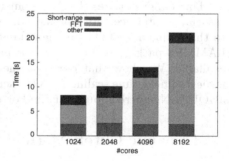

Fig. 2. Weak scaling of the PPPM long range solver (from the LAMMPS framework) for an interfacial system with 1200 particles per core (IBM BG/Q).

lations to as little as $\mathcal{O}(N \log N)$, with implementations based on the classical method [13] and mesh-based approaches such as the particle-particle particle-mesh (PPPM) [15,16] and particle mesh Ewald (PME) [30] methods. Other approaches, such as the multilevel summation algorithm [27] further reduce the complexity to $\mathcal{O}(N)$. However, these methods all suffer from a critical drawback: they require global communications between different processors. Consequently, their scalability eventually decreases as the number of cores increase and the cost of all-to-all communications becomes prohibitively expensive [15], as shown in Fig. 2. Although Sun et al. [26] were able to optimize communications within the PME solver in NAMD, an open-source MD package, to achieve good strong scaling for a system with 10^8 particles on up to 298992 cores, their approach still requires all-to-all communications and has a complexity of $\mathcal{O}(N \log N)$.

Since short-range methods exhibit errors at the interface that are typically two orders of magnitude larger than the errors for particles in the bulk phase [15], it would be helpful to direct the computational resources to where they are most needed. The approach we introduce in this paper, which we call the *dynamic cutoff method* (DCM), circumvents the need for all-to-all communications by making the cutoff a particle-dependent property. As shown in Fig. 1b, particles located in bulk regions, where the isotropic assumption is valid, can be handled with a small cutoff, while particles close to the interface are assigned a larger cutoff. Consequently, computational demands are kept to a minimum while maintaining high accuracy. The DCM is closely related to static cutoff methods [12,28] and, as a result, inherits their good properties, such as strictly local communication and good scalability. To make DCM competitive with state-of-the-art solvers, we have also developed a fast and scalable algorithm to detect interfaces. A similar method involving adaptive cutoffs, using a derived error estimate rather than the relative location of the particles to determine the cutoff, was recently proposed [29]. However, as that algorithm still relies on the use of fast Fourier transforms, its large-scale scalability remains questionable.

This paper outlines the development of the dynamic cutoff method and the associated interface detection method, which has been parallelized and extended to three dimensions. These algorithms were incorporated into the open-source LAMMPS package [9,20], one of the most widely used MD simulators currently available. We show that our implementation of the dynamic cutoff algorithm achieves linear-time scaling for interfacial systems, even when utilizing the entire JUQUEEN supercomputer at the Forschungszentrum Jülich.

2   Dynamic Cutoff Method

The core idea of the DCM is to circumvent the use of long-range solvers by adaptively choosing the cutoff on a particle-by-particle basis, using small cutoffs for particles far away from the interface and increasingly larger cutoffs as one approaches the interface. Clearly, this strategy requires knowledge of the position and the time evolution of the interface.

The computational tasks involved in one iteration of the DCM are shown schematically in Fig. 3. First, the interface is identified (box 1); for each particle, the distance from the interface is computed, and the cutoff for each atom is determined and assigned (box 2). Like classical short-range methods, the DCM builds a neighbor list (box 3), enabling each particle to access its neighbors in

$\mathcal{O}(1)$ time. Finally, pairwise forces are computed (box 4), and the positions and velocities of all particles are updated (box 5). At this point, the next iteration begins. Since in typical MD simulations the interface changes very slowly, the interface detection and neighbor-list build need not be executed every iteration.

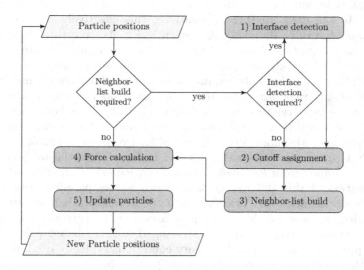

Fig. 3. Schematic overview of the dynamic cutoff method.

Before describing the individual tasks, we briefly discuss our overall parallelization strategy for distributed memory environments. Following the main scheme used by LAMMPS, the physical domain is spatially decomposed and assigned to the underlying three-dimensional grid of MPI processes. Each process p is responsible for one subdomain $L^p \subseteq L$ of the computational domain $L = L_x \times L_y \times L_z \subset R^3$, and has an average memory requirement of $\mathcal{O}(N/P)$, where N and P are the total number of particles and processes, respectively. Particles can migrate between pairs of neighboring processes [20]. As we will show, irrespective of the task performed, each process only communicates with its direct neighbors, so that global communication patterns are entirely avoided.[1] DCM exhibits a linear dependence on the number of particles in the system.

The first four tasks enumerated in Fig. 3 are covered in detail in the next subsections. The final task, responsible for the updates of the particle positions and velocities, uses velocity Verlet integration [28], the standard integration scheme in MD simulations, and is therefore not discussed further.

---

[1] With the exception of a reduction operation to identify the maximum of a scalar in the interface detection method.

2.1   Interface Detection

Our approach for a fast interface detection is inspired by algorithms for binary image segmentation. The main idea is that an interface delineates the regions of the physical domain in which the density of particles changes; with this in mind, we treat particle densities as gray-scale values and apply image segmentation techniques to the data. In three dimensions, this effectively becomes a gray-scale volume of voxels (3D pixel). As shown in Fig. 4a, to create the gray-scale volume from the particle positions, all particles are binned into small 3D $h \times h \times h$ "boxes",[2] effectively decomposing each subdomain L^p into small 3D boxes $b_{x,y,z} \subset L^p$; this operation only requires neighbor-neighbor communication.

At this stage, each box is treated as a voxel and is assigned a gray-scale value according to its relative particle density (Fig. 4b). Based on this gray-scale volume, the segmentation (Fig. 4c) can be computed as the minimization of the piecewise constant Mumford-Shah functional for two-phase segmentation [1,18]. The result is a binary classification of the boxes, differentiating high-density phases (e.g., liquid) from low-density ones (e.g., vapor). A distributed-memory implementation of this third stage boils down to the parallelization of a 3D finite-difference stencil [3,9]. Starting from the Mumford-Shah algorithm from the QuocMesh open-source library [21], an accurate 3D segmentation algorithm for shared-memory architectures, we developed an MPI-based parallelization, adding support for the periodic boundary conditions typically used in MD simulations; this algorithm is now included in QuocMesh.

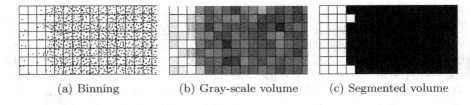

(a) Binning   (b) Gray-scale volume   (c) Segmented volume

Fig. 4. Interface detection: a 2D slice from a 3D domain.

The output of the three stages shown in Fig. 4 is a segmented volume S:

$$S = \{s_{x,y,z} \in \{0,1\} \mid 0 \leq x < N_x, 0 \leq y < N_y, 0 \leq z < N_z\}, \qquad (4)$$

where N_x, N_y and N_z are the number of local boxes on a given processor; $s_{x,y,z}$ equals 0 if the corresponding box $b_{x,y,z}$ belongs to the low-density phase, and $s_{x,y,z} = 1$ otherwise. The interface is then determined by adjacent boxes with discontinuous values (Fig. 4c). The minimization of the Mumford-Shah functional might result in the set S presenting low-density "bubbles" inside the high-density

---

[2] The edge length h determines the resolution of the interface and can be automatically chosen at the beginning of the simulation.

region and vice versa. Depending on their size, such bubbles can be interpreted as false-detections and cause a noticeable performance degradation (bubbles yield additional interfaces and hence unnecessarily large cutoffs). For this reason, we apply a parallel multi-stage filtering algorithm to identify and remove connected components smaller than a user-specified volume. This step, which again requires communication only between neighboring processes, is described in [25]. In contrast to other interface-detection methods [5,19,22], our algorithm is so fast that it does not affect the performance of an MD simulation.

2.2 Cutoff Assignment

The objective of this task is to adaptively assign a suitable cutoff to each individual particle; to this end, the set D^p of box-interface distances,[3] and from this the particle-interface distances δ are then derived. Two numerical methods for approximating the box-interface distances are the Fast Marching Method (FMM) [23] and the Fast Sweeping Method (FSM) [32]. Let N_v be the number of voxels of the system; FMM has a complexity $\mathcal{O}(N_v \log N_v)$ and is generally more accurate than FSM. However, since FSM has a preferred complexity of $\mathcal{O}(N_v)$ and in practice its accuracy is sufficient for the DCM, we adopted an FSM-based approach.

Because the cutoffs for particles vary only for particles within a given distance from the interface, we need not compute the exact distance between the interface and each box. Instead, it suffices to carry out the calculations up to a certain threshold distance r_c^{grid}, since beyond this distance, the "minimum cutoff" will be applied, regardless of the actual distance from the interface. This problem formulation makes it possible to devise a fast sweeping method that only requires local communication and the reduction of a scalar.

Zhao et al. proposed two parallel algorithms/implementations for the FSM [31]. Since scalability is one of our main concerns, we developed our own version of FSM which was specifically tailored to the needs of our problem. Henceforth we call our implementation a cutoff-based fast sweeping method (CFSM).

As shown in Algorithm 1, the CFSM propagates box-interface distances outwards until the distance is larger than the threshold r_c^{grid}.[4] Visually, the algorithm unfolds as a wave that starts at the interface and flows outwards until it has traveled the maximum distance r_c^{grid}. The set of box-interface distances D^p, local to process p, is initialized such that boxes at the interface and in the low-density region are assigned a distance of 0, while boxes in the high-density region are assigned a distance of $+\infty$ (line 1). All boxes adjacent to the interface and have nonzero distance are added to queue Q, which keeps track of the remaining boxes to be processed. After initialization, Q is processed breadth-first. For each box, indexed as (x, y, z), the distance to the interface is computed using a

---

[3] $D^p = \{d_{x,y,z} \in \mathbb{R} \,|\, 0 \leq x < N_x, 0 \leq y < N_y, 0 \leq z < N_z\}$; the superscript p indicates that this set is computed on each process, in parallel.

[4] The exact value for the threshold is not important here. More information is provided in [25].

Algorithm 1. Distributed cutoff-based fast sweeping method.

```
 1: initialize($D^p$, $Q$)                                           ▷ Add interfacial boxes to $Q$
 2: for $0 \leq$ iter $<$ iter$^{\mathrm{max}}$ do
 3:     for all boxes $(x, y, z) \in Q$ do
 4:         $d^{new} \leftarrow$ solveDistance($D^p$, $(x, y, z)$)                        ▷ local FSM
 5:         if $d^{new} \leq r_c^{\mathrm{grid}}$ then
 6:             if $|d_{x,y,z} - d^{new}| > \Delta e$ then
 7:                 $\Delta e \leftarrow |d_{x,y,z} - d^{new}|$
 8:             $d_{x,y,z} \leftarrow d^{new}$
 9:             addNeighborsToQueue($\widetilde{Q}$, $(x, y, z)$)
10:     swapQueues($Q$, $\widetilde{Q}$)
11:     emptyQueue($\widetilde{Q}$)
12:     $\Delta e \leftarrow$ MPI_Allreduce($\Delta e$, MAXIMUM)
13:     if $\Delta e < \epsilon$ then
14:         break
15:     ghostExchange($D^p$)                                        ▷ Local communication
16:     addModifiedBoundariesToQueue($D^p$, $Q$)
```

FSM on the local subdomain (line 4), the distance of box $b_{x,y,z}$ is updated (line 8), and all its adjacent boxes are added to the auxiliary queue $\widetilde{Q}$ (line 9). Once all boxes in Q have been processed, the queues Q and $\widetilde{Q}$ are swapped (line 10), and the maximum difference Δe between the old and new distances (line 7) is reduced among all processes (line 12). If $\Delta e < \epsilon$ for some threshold ϵ (line 13), all processes terminate; otherwise, each process communicates its boundary boxes to its neighbors (line 15), adds the received boundary to Q (line 16), and enters a new iteration. Typically, two to four iterations suffice for convergence. For completeness, we point out that for any box within the threshold r_c^{grid}, this implementation yields the same results as the algorithms proposed by Zhao et al. [31].

From the set of computed box-interface distances D^p, the particle–interface distances $\delta_i \in \mathbb{R}$, $i \in [1, \ldots, N]$, can be estimated via trilinear interpolation. The cutoff r_c of each particle is then chosen as a function of δ_i.[5] In all cases, particles at the interface or within the low-density phase are assigned a larger cutoff, up to r_c^{max}, than particles further away; beyond a given distance from the interface, particles in the high-density phase are assigned the minimum cutoff r_c^{min}.

2.3   Neighbor-List Build

Neighbor lists in MD simulations allow particles to access all of their neighbors in constant time. Hockney et al. [12] introduced the *linked-cell* method, which bins particles into cells of edge r_c, thereby restricting the search for neighbors of particle i to the cell containing particle i and its 26 neighbors. An alternative technique, introduced by Verlet [28], uses a neighbor (or Verlet) list for each particle i: the indices of all particles that interact with particle i are stored (i.e., $r_{ij} \leq r_c$) (Algorithm 2). In practice, a skin distance $r_s > 0$ is introduced, so that

---

[5] Possible interpolation functions and the resulting accuracy are discussed in [25].

particles with $r_{ij} \leq r_c + r_s$ are stored; this allows reuse of the neighbor list over multiple timesteps. A drawback of this technique is that the neighbor list must be updated frequently [7]. Currently, the most common approach combines these techniques and bins all particles only when a neighbor-list build is required.

Algorithm 2 outlines the steps needed to build a neighbor list in the specific context of the DCM; it is assumed that all particles are already spatially sorted into bins. For each particle i, the algorithm loops over all particles j in the neighboring bins $jBin$ and adds j to the neighbor list of particle i if r_{ij} is less than the cutoff $r_c[i]$ of atom i.

Algorithm 2. Neighbor-list build.
1: **for all** local atoms i **do**
2:     nNbrs$[i] \leftarrow 0$
3:     iBin $\leftarrow$ getBin(i)
4:     **for all** jBin $\in$ neighbors(iBin) **do**
5:         **for all** atoms j of jBin **do**
6:             $r_{ij} \leftarrow r_i - r_j$
7:             **if** $|r_{ij}| < r_c[i]$ **and** $i \neq j$ **then:**
8:                 nbrs$_i$[nNbrs$[i]] \leftarrow j$
9:                 nNbrs$[i] \leftarrow$ nNbrs$[i] + 1$

Algorithm 3. Force calculation.
1: **for all** atoms i **do:**
2:     $f_i \leftarrow 0$
3:     **for all** neighbors k of i **do**
4:         $j \leftarrow$ nbrs$_i[k]$
5:         $r_{ij} \leftarrow r_i - r_j$
6:         **if** $|r_{ij}| < r_c[i]$ **then:**
7:             $f \leftarrow$ forceLJ$(|r_{ij}|)$
8:             $f_i \leftarrow f_i - f \times r_{ij}$
9:         force$[i] \leftarrow$ force$[i] + f_i$

The varying cutoffs of DCM pose additional challenges for efficient implementation of the neighbor-list build. With a static cutoff, all particles traverse the same stencil of neighboring cells. If applied to the DCM, this static approach would result in poor performance because particles with a small cutoff traverse the same volume as particles with the maximum cutoff. For instance, assuming $r_c^{min} = \frac{1}{2} r_c^{max}$ and a typical skin distance $r_s = 0.1 r_c^{max}$, all particles would traverse a volume $V_{cube} = (3(r_c^{max} + r_s)^3)$ to find their neighbors. However, particles assigned the minimum cutoff have their neighbors within the much smaller volume $V_{min} = \frac{4}{3} \pi r_c^{min^3}$. Thus, only $V_{min}/V_{cube} \approx 1.5\%$ of all particle-particle calculations would contribute to the neighbor-list build (i.e., Line 7 of Algorithm 2 would return **false** 98.5% of the time). Since the neighbor-list build is memory-bound, this approach would nullify any performance benefit gained using dynamic cutoffs.

The solution lies in the choice of the bins' edge length: instead of $l^{max} = r_s + r_c^{max}$, we use an edge length of $l^{min} = r_s + r_c^{min}$ or smaller. While this results in having to traverse a slightly larger stencil of neighboring cells, the traversed volume is considerably smaller than V_{cube} and results in many fewer spurious distance calculations. Note that the complexity of this improved neighbor-list build is hidden in Line 4 of Algorithm 2. This optimization yields a 4× to 6× speedup of the neighbor-list build over the binning with edge length l^{max}.

2.4   Force Calculation

Compared to classical short-range methods, the force calculations within the DCM (Algorithm 3) show two striking differences: a particle-dependent cutoff (shown in red), and the inapplicability of Newton's third law of motion[6] (henceforth called N3). Since the cutoff is independently assigned to each particle, the fact that particle j is "influenced" by particle i does not imply that particle i is influenced by particle j. Effectively, neglecting N3 means that the update $\mathbf{f_j} \leftarrow \mathbf{f_j} + f \times \mathbf{r_{ij}}$, which would appear in Algorithm 3 right after Line 8, is not performed. Computationally, this results in twice as many force calculations, but also allows a better memory access pattern, since costly scattered memory accesses for $\mathbf{f_j}$ are avoided.[7]

Our DCM implementation is based on the existing short-range Lennard-Jones solver in LAMMPS. We developed both a pure MPI implementation, as well as a hybrid MPI + OpenMP-based shared-memory parallelization that allows us to start multiple threads per MPI rank, reducing both the memory requirements and communication overhead. While the shared-memory implementation consists of simple OpenMP directives—for instance, (**#pragma omp for schedule**(dynamic,20)) before the outermost loops of Algorithms 2 and 3 suffices to distribute the loops across multiple threads—we stress that the default static schedule would result in severe load imbalance (due to different cutoffs for different particles). By contrast, a dynamic schedule, using tasks of about 20 particles, results in almost perfectly load-balanced simulations. The benefits of dynamic scheduling become more apparent as more threads are involved. Simulations with 256 MPI ranks and 16 threads per rank[8] show a speedup of 1.4× for the neighbor list and 2.2× for the force-calculation kernels over static scheduling.

3   Simulation Methodology

We present performance results for two interfacial systems: one with a planar interface (Fig. 5a) and another with a non-planar interface (Fig. 5b). As the processor count increases, the area of the interface in the planar system is scaled proportionally in two dimensions (i.e., creating a large plane), and in the non-planar system is extended along its cylindrical axis.

Both accuracy and performance are compared to the particle-particle particle-mesh solver (PPPM), a state-of-the-art long-range algorithm included in the LAMMPS package. Specifically, the measurements for the static cutoff method and PPPM are obtained using LAMMPS, version *30Oct14*, with the OpenMP user-package installed. For all experiments, the settings for PPPM are chosen according to [16] and are considered to be optimal. Unless otherwise specified, the minimum and maximum cutoff of DCM are respectively set to $r_c^{min} = 3.0$ and $r_c^{max} = 8.0$, such that the resulting accuracy is comparable to that of PPPM. The experiments were carried out on two different supercomputing architectures: SuperMuc and JUQUEEN.

---

[6] If a body i exerts a force f onto another body j, then j exerts a force $-f$ on i.

[7] This is why most GPU implementations of force calculations also neglect N3.

[8] Running on 1024 cores on the BlueGene/Q supercomputer with simultaneous multi-threading enabled for four threads per core.

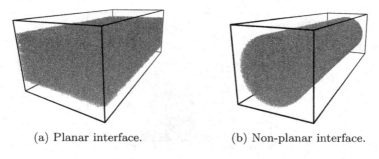

(a) Planar interface.   (b) Non-planar interface.

Fig. 5. The two interfacial systems used in this publication.

SuperMUC. The SuperMUC supercomputer at the Leibniz Supercomputing Centre is based on Intel's Sandy Bridge architecture, with 147.456 cores and 288 TB of main memory arranged in 18 "islands" of 512 nodes each. A node consists of two Intel Xeon E5-2680 CPUs with a total of 16 cores. We used Intel's C++ compiler *icpc 14.0.3* with compiler flags *-O3 -restrict -ip -unroll0 -openmp -xAVX*.

JUQUEEN. The JUQUEEN supercomputer at Forschungszentrum Jülich is a IBM Blue Gene/Q machine with 28.672 nodes organized in 28 racks, each comprising 1024 nodes. A node consists of 16 IBM PowerPC A2 cores, and 16GBs of DDR3 memory, for a total of 458.752 cores and 448 TB of main memory. We used IBM's C compiler *xlc++ 12.01* with compiler flags *-O3 -qarch=qp -qtune=qp - qsmp=omp -qsimd=auto -qhot=level=2 -qprefetch -qunroll=yes*.

4 Performance and Accuracy Results

4.1 Accuracy

As discussed in Sect. 1, every physical property (e.g., pressure, density) in a molecular dynamics simulation relies on accurate force calculations. We therefore choose to measure the per-particle error in the forces perpendicular to the interface (in these experiments, along the z-direction) to validate the correctness of DCM. A detailed accuracy analysis of DCM is beyond the scope of this paper. The error Δf_{i_z} of particle i is computed as follows:

$$\Delta f_{i_z} = f_{i_z}^* - f_{i_z} \tag{5}$$

where $f_{i_z}^*$ denotes the correct force for particle i along the z-direction.[9] We only show the component of the error perpendicular to the interface because this is much larger than the error along either of the other directions.

Figure 6 shows the error in the z-component of the forces for the *planar* system with 19.200 particles for PPPM and DCM with different maximum cutoffs.

---

[9] $f_{i_z}^*$ is computed by the accurate (but expensive) Ewald long-range solver.

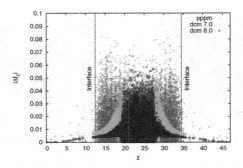

Fig. 6. Absolute error in the z-direction (i.e., perpendicular to the interface) for the planar system with $19,200$ particles. Each cross corresponds to a single particle. DCM uses a minimum cutoff of $r_c^{min} = 3.0\sigma$.

Table 1. Speedup of DCM over a static cutoff with $r_c = r_c^{max}$ for the planar system with 12 million particles. The DCM setting reads as r_c^{min}/r_c^{max}. The experiments were run on JUQUEEN using 1024 cores (256 MPI ranks and 16 threads per rank).

DCM setting	3.0/7.0	3.0/8.0	3.5/8.0	3.0/9.0	3.5/9.0
Speedup	2.31	2.66	2.38	2.42	2.23

First, we note that the errors of DCM and PPPM are comparable in magnitude. Second, larger cutoffs for DCM lead to more accurate results, as expected. Third, in DCM the errors are smaller at the interface; this is critical, as the error strongly influences the physical behavior [15, 16, 25]. Finally, as the dashed lines indicate, one can see that our interface detection method correctly identifies the interface.

4.2   Performance

We compare the performance of DCM with the static cutoff method and PPPM on two different architectures. Table 1 shows the speedup of DCM over its static counterpart forthe planar system. The simulation was run on JUQUEEN, on 1024 cores with 1200 particles per core. The static cutoff is set to the maximum DCM cutoff: $r_c = r_c^{max}$.Despite not exploiting Newton's third law, the DCM outperforms the static cutoff version by at least a factor of 2.2. We note that these speedups are highly dependent on the ratio between the number of particles at the interface and away from the interface; depending on this ratio, even higher speedups can be expected by incorporating Newton's third law.

Figure 7 presents the strong and weak scalability on SuperMUC for the non-planar system and on JUQUEEN for the planar system. On both architectures, the weak scaling experiments were performed with 1200 particles per core, while the strong scaling experiments use a system with roughly 4×10^7 particles.

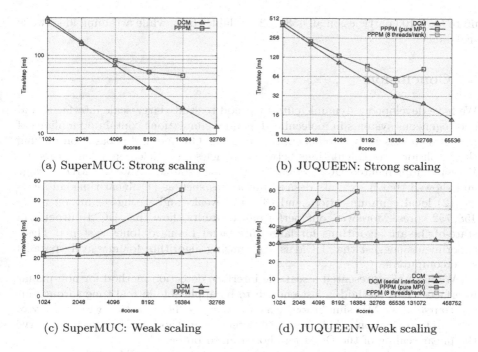

(a) SuperMUC: Strong scaling   (b) JUQUEEN: Strong scaling

(c) SuperMUC: Weak scaling   (d) JUQUEEN: Weak scaling

Fig. 7. Strong (a, b) and weak (c, d) scalability for PPPM and DCM.

Figure 7a and b show a head-to-head comparison between DCM and PPPM in terms of strong scalability. The results for the pure MPI version of PPPM expose a degradation in scalability starting from 4 k and 8 k cores on Super-MUC and JUQUEEN, respectively. On JUQUEEN, we also ran an hybrid multithreaded+MPI version of PPPM, using 8 threads per MPI rank; this configuration attained somewhat better timings than the pure MPI version, but consistently crashed on 32 k cores or more. The DCM achieved convincing (nearly-linear) scalability on both systems.

The weak scalability behaviour of DCM and PPPM is illustrated in Fig. 7c and d. On both systems, the trend of PPPM (red line) matches exactly the behaviour presented in Fig. 2: use of FFTs causes the scalability to progressively deteriorate as the number of cores increases. This phenomenon is only delayed in the hybrid multithreaded + MPI version of PPPM (orange line in Fig. 7d), which eventually follows the same diverging trend. The results for the DCM on JUQUEEN clearly indicate the need for a parallel interface detection method, since the serial implementation (blue line), although extremely fast, eventually becomes the bottleneck for the entire DCM. Finally, we direct our attention to the DCM (green line) with parallel interface detection (as described in Sect. 2.1): for both the planar and the nonplanar systems, scalability is nearly perfect. Indeed, Fig. 7d reveals that on JUQUEEN it was possible to scale the system up to 5.5×10^8 particles on all $458,752$ available cores, while attaining ideal weak scalability.

5 Conclusion

We have developed a dynamic cutoff method to study large-scale interfacial and heterogeneous systems in molecular dynamics simulations containing millions of particles on massively parallel supercomputers. Our method is based on making the cutoff for force calculations between particles a particle-dependent property. We have implemented DCM as part of the open-source LAMMPS MD package and showed that it exhibits desired properties such as (1) linear-time complexity, (2) local communication, and (3) ideal weak- and strong-scaling on up to $458,752$ cores. Moreover, our performance results show that DCM outperform state-of-the-art algorithms for large interfacial Lennard-Jones systems. These experiments suggest that DCM is a promising algorithm for massively parallel supercomputers.

We have also presented a scalable interface detection method for non-planar interfaces. This method is fast enough to be applicable in real time throughout the course of an MD simulation, which may open the door to a wide variety of new MD applications. This interface detection method enabled us to preserve the linear scaling of the DCM for short-ranged potentials.

Even though not investigated further in this paper, DCM can be used as a replacement for short-range calculations within mesh-based Ewald solvers (e.g., PPPM). This allows to shift computational workload from the FFTs to the short-range calculations and therefore should improve the scalability of these solvers as well.

Acknowledgments. The authors gratefully acknowledge financial support from the Deutsche Forschungsgemeinschaft (German Research Association) through grant GSC 111, computing resources on the supercomputer JUQUEEN at Jülich Supercomputing Centre (JSC) (project ID: e5430301) and the Gauss Centre for Supercomputing/Leibniz Supercomputing Centre (project ID: pr84za), and Edoardo Di Napoli and Benjamin Berkels for helpful discussions.

References

1. Berkels, B.: An unconstrained multiphase thresholding approach for image segmentation. In: Tai, X.-C., Mørken, K., Lysaker, M., Lie, K.-A. (eds.) SSVM 2009. LNCS, vol. 5567, pp. 26–37. Springer, Heidelberg (2009)
2. Blokhuis, E., Bedeaux, D., Holcomb, C., Zollweg, J.: Tail corrections to the surface tension of a lennard-jones liquid-vapour interface. Mol. Phys. **85**(3), 665–669 (1995)
3. Bohlen, T.: Parallel 3-d viscoelastic finite difference seismic modelling. Comput. Geosci. **28**(8), 887–899 (2002)
4. Bradley, R., Radhakrishnan, R.: Coarse-grained models for protein-cell membrane interactions. Polymers **5**(3), 890–936 (2013)

5. Bresme, F., Chacón, E., Tarazona, P.: Molecular dynamics investigation of the intrinsic structure of water-fluid interfaces via the intrinsic sampling method. Phys. Chem. Chem. Phys. **10**(32), 4704–4715 (2008)
6. Chapela, G.A., Saville, G., Thompson, S.M., Rowlinson, J.S.: Computer simulation of a gas-liquid surface. Part 1. J. Chem. Soc. Faraday Trans. 2: Mol. Chem. Phys. **73**(7), 1133–1144 (1977)
7. Chialvo, A.A., Debenedetti, P.G.: On the use of the verlet neighbor list in molecular dynamics. Comput. Phys. Commun. **60**(2), 215–224 (1990)
8. Ewald, P.: Die berechnung optischer und elektrostatischer gitterpotentiale. Annalen der Physik **369**, 253–287 (1921)
9. Griebel, M., Knapek, S., Zumbusch, G.: Numerical Simulation in Molecular Dynamics. Springer, Heidelberg (2007)
10. Guo, M., Peng, D.-Y., Lu, B.C.-Y.: On the long-range corrections to computer simulation results for the Lennard-Jones vapor-liquid interface. Fluid Phase Equilib. **130**(1), 19–30 (1997)
11. Hill, T.L.: Thermodynamics of Small Systems. Dover Publications, Mineola (2013)
12. Hockney, R., Goel, S., Eastwood, J.: Quiet high-resolution computer models of a plasma. J. Comput. Phys. **14**(2), 148–158 (1974)
13. in 't Veld, P.J., Ismail, A.E., Grest, G.S.: Application of ewald summations to long-range dispersion forces. J. Chem. Phys. **127**, 144711 (2007)
14. Isele-Holder, R.E., Ismail, A.E.: Atomistic potentials for trisiloxane, alkyl ethoxylate, and perfluoroalkane-based surfactants with tip4p/2005 and application to simulations at the airwater interface. J. Phys. Chem. B **118**(31), 9284–9297 (2014)
15. Isele-Holder, R.E., Mitchell, W., Hammond, J.R., Kohlmeyer, A., Ismail, A.E.: Reconsidering dispersion potentials: reduced cutoffs in mesh-based ewald solvers can be faster than truncation. J. Chem. Theory Comput. **9**(12), 5412–5420 (2013)
16. Isele-Holder, R.E., Mitchell, W., Ismail, A.E.: Development and application of a particle-particle particle-mesh ewald method for dispersion interactions. J. Chem. Phys. **137**(17), 174107 (2012)
17. Ismail, A.E., Tsige, M., in 't Veld, P.J., Grest, G.S.: Surface tension of normal and branched alkanes. Mol. Phys. **105**(23–24), 3155–3163 (2007)
18. Mumford, D., Shah, J.: Optimal approximations by piecewise smooth functions and associated variational problems. Commun. Pure Appl. Math. **42**(5), 577–685 (1989)
19. Pártay, L.B., Hantal, G., Jedlovszky, P., Vincze, Á., Horvai, G.: A new method for determining the interfacial molecules and characterizing the surface roughness in computer simulations. Application to the liquid-vapor interface of water. J. Comput. Chem. **29**(6), 945–956 (2008)
20. Plimpton, S.: Fast parallel algorithms for short-range molecular dynamics. J. Comput. Phys. **117**(1), 1–19 (1995)
21. Rumpf, A.G.: Quocmesh software library. Institute for Numerical Simulation, University of Bonn. http://numod.ins.uni-bonn.de/software/quocmesh/
22. Sega, M., Kantorovich, S.S., Jedlovszky, P., Jorge, M.: The generalized identification of truly interfacial molecules (ITIM) algorithm for nonplanar interfaces. J. Chem. Phys. **138**(4), 044110 (2013)
23. Sethian, J.A.: A fast marching level set method for monotonically advancing fronts. Proc. Nat. Acad. Sci. **93**(4), 1591–1595 (1996)
24. Shekhar, A., Nomura, K.-I., Kalia, R.K., Nakano, A., Vashishta, P.: Nanobubble collapse on a silica surface in water: Billion-atom reactive molecular dynamics simulations. Phys. Rev. Lett. **111**, 184503 (2013)

25. Springer, P.: A scalable, linear-time dynamic cutoff algorithm for molecular simulations of interfacial systems (2013). arXiv:1502.0323
26. Sun, Y., Zheng, G., Mei, C., Bohm, E.J., Phillips, J.C., Kalé, L.V., Jones, T.R.: Optimizing fine-grained communication in a biomolecular simulation application on cray xk6. In: 2012 International Conference on High Performance Computing, Networking, Storage and Analysis (SC), pp. 1–11. IEEE (2012)
27. Tameling, D., Springer, P., Bientinesi, P., Ismail, A.E.: Multilevel summation for dispersion: a linear-time algorithm for r^{-6} potentials. J. Chem. Phys. **140**(2), 024105 (2014)
28. Verlet, L.: Computer "experiments" on classical fluids. I. thermodynamical properties of Lennard-Jones molecules. Phys. Rev. **159**, 98–103 (1967)
29. Wang, H., Schütte, C., Zhang, P.: Error estimate of short-range force calculation in inhomogeneous molecular systems. Phys. Rev. E **86**(2), 026704 (2012)
30. Wennberg, C.L., Murtola, T., Hess, B., Lindahl, E.: Lennard-Jones lattice summation in bilayer simulations has critical effects on surface tension and lipid properties. J. Chem. Theory Comput. **9**, 3527–3537 (2013)
31. Zhao, H.: Parallel implementations of the fast sweeping method. J. Comput. Math. **25**(4), 421–429 (2007)
32. Zhao, H.-K., Osher, S., Merriman, B., Kang, M.: Implicit and nonparametric shape reconstruction from unorganized data using a variational level set method. Comput. Vis. Image Underst. **80**(3), 295–314 (2000)
33. Zubillaga, R.A., Labastida, A., Cruz, B., Martínez, J.C., Sánchez, E., Alejandre, J.: Surface tension of organic liquids using the OPLS/AA force field. J. Chem. Theory Comput. **9**, 1611–1615 (2013)

BWTCP: A Parallel Method for Constructing BWT in Large Collection of Genomic Reads

Heng Wang, Shaoliang Peng$^{(\boxtimes)}$, Yutong Lu, Chengkun Wu, Jiajun Wen, Jie Liu, and Xiaoqian Zhu

School of Computer Science, National University of Defense Technology,
Changsha 410073, People's Republic of China
{pengshaoliang,zhu_xiaoqian}@nudt.edu.cn

Abstract. Short-read alignment and assembly are fundamental procedures for analyses of DNA sequencing data. Many state-of-the-art short-read aligners employ Burrows-Wheeler transform (BWT) as an in-memory index for the reference genome. BWT has also found its use in genome assembly, for indexing the reads. In a typical data set, the volume of reads can be as large as several hundred Gigabases. Consequently, fast construction of the BWT index for reads is essential for an efficient sequence processing. In this paper, we present a parallel method called BWTCP for BWT construction at a large scale. BWTCP is characterized by its ability to harness heterogeneous computing power including multi-core CPU, multiple CPUs, and accelerators like GPU or Intel Xeon Phi. BWTCP is also featured by its novel pruning strategy. Using BWTCP, we managed to construct the BWT for 1 billion 100bp reads within 30 m using 16 compute nodes (2 CPUs per node) on Tianhe-2 Supercomputer. It significantly outperforms the baseline tool BCR, which would need 13 h to finish all processing for the same dataset. BWTCP is freely available at https://github.com/hwang91/BWTCP.

Keywords: BWT · Genome assembly · BWTCP · BCR · CX1 · Radix sort · Parallel computing

1 Introduction

Short-read alignment and assembly are fundamental problems in genomics [1–5]. Burrows Wheeler Transform (BWT) [6] was used to index a reference genome in some state-of-the-art short-read aligners, for instance, BWA [7], Bowtie2 [8] and MICA [9]. These short-read aligners store the BWT of the reference genome in main memory to allow efficient mapping of short-reads. Recently, Simpson and Durbin [10] reported that BWT of reads could also be used to accelerate genome assembly. While BWT construction for aligning only involves one reference genome, constructing BWT for a large collection of short reads is far more complicated and computationally expensive. In a typical sequencing run,

---

H. Wang, S. Peng, and X. Zhu—Joint first authors.

© Springer International Publishing Switzerland 2015
J.M. Kunkel and T. Ludwig (Eds.): ISC High Performance 2015, LNCS 9137, pp. 171–178, 2015.
DOI: 10.1007/978-3-319-20119-1_13

the amount of short reads generated is usually ten times larger than the size of the reference genome. For instance, human genome with 30X depth can produce about 100 Gigabases, or equivalently about 1 billion reads of length 100. Many existing BWT construction methods utilize suffix arrays as an intermediate data structure, which occupies even more memory. For a collection of 1 billion reads of length 100, it takes 800 GB memory to store its suffix array. Hence, these methods are impractical for the BWT construction of large collection of short reads. In 2013, Bauer et al. [11] presented a method, embodied in BCR, to construct BWT of a large string collection with a small memory footprint with a sacrifice in time efficiency. It takes up to 13 hours to construct the BWT of one billion reads with a length of 100 using BCR. This makes it reasonable to accelerate BCR with parallelization. However, as BCR constructs partial BWT of substrings of length 0 to length k in a sequential order, it's non-trivial to parallelize BCR for acceleration.

Liu et al. [12] proposed a parallel algorithm named CX1 to construct the BWT of a large collection of reads utilizing GPU. CX1 construct the BWT of $R = \{S_1, S_2, \ldots, S_m\}$ by its definition: sorting suffixes in R. Firstly, CX1 find a set of splitters $P_0, P_1, \cdots, P_u$, which are strings over Σ satisfying $P_0 < P_1 < \cdots < P_u$ (they are not necessarily suffixes in R). Then it uses those splitters to partition the suffixes in R. Each partition gives a portion of the BWT, which can be simply concatenated together to form the complete BWT. The splitters are chosen such that the suffixes in each partition can be sorted within the GPU memory limit. Then CX1 sort the partitions on GPU by means of LSD (least significant digit) radix sort. CX1 managed to construct the BWT of one billion reads with a length of 100 in 2 h using a machine equipped with an Intel Xeon i7-3930K (Hexa-core) 3.2 GHz processor and an NVIDIA GeForce GTX 680 GPU.

One notable fact is that both BCR and CX1 are sensitive to the length of reads while modern sequencers are producing longer reads, which can be as long as several kilobases. For instance, when processing the same amount of reads, BCR spent about 290 % more time on reads of length 400 than those of length 100. 150 % more time is needed for CX1.

In this paper, we proposed a more efficient method based on CX1, named BWTCP (BWT Construction in Parallel), to construct the BWT of a large collection of reads in parallel. By adopting a different sorting algorithm together with an optimized pruning strategy, BWTCP can build the BWT of one billion reads of length 100 within 30 m using 16 compute nodes on Tianhe-2 supercomputer. Each compute node on Tianhe-2 is equipped with 2 Intel Xeon E5 CPUs. As conducted in [12], we tested BWTCP on 100M 100-bp reads and 25M 400-bp reads, which used 197s and 201s respectively. BWTCP is far more efficient on longer reads than existing tools.

2   Preliminaries

Burrows-Wheeler transform (BWT) was introduced in [6] and originally used to conduct data compression. Ferragina and Manzini found in [13] that BWT could be used to construct full-text indices, which could be used to accelerate sequence alignment. BWT originally works for a single string, but the definition can be easily extended to a collection of strings. A detailed discussion of BWT can be found in [6].

Let $\Sigma = \{c_1, c_2, \ldots, c_\sigma\}$ be a finite alphabet, and c_i is lexicographically less than c_j for $1 <= i < j <= \sigma$. Given a string $S = s_0 s_1 \ldots s_{m-1}$ over Σ, we denote the substring $s_i s_{i+1} \ldots s_j$ by $S[i, j]$, for $0 <= i <= j <= m - 1$. A substring of type $S[0, i]$ is called a prefix while a substring of type $S[i, m - 1]$ is called a suffix of S. Generally, when constructing BWT of a string, a special end-marker symbol $ is firstly appended to the string, where $ is lexicographically smaller than every symbol in Σ. We define the BWT code of a suffix as the character just before the start position of the suffix, and for suffix start from 0, the BWT code is defined as end-marker $.

Let $R = \{S_1, S_2, \ldots, S_n\}$ be a collection of n strings. Each of the strings S_i is of length $m + 1$ with $S_i[k] \in \Sigma (0 <= k <= m)$ and $S_i[m] = \$_j$, with $\$_i < \$_j$ for $0 <= i < j <= n$. BWT of R is similar to that of a single string. Firstly, we lexicographically sort the suffixes of all strings in R. Each string has $m + 1$ suffixes, thus the sorted list contains $n(m+1)$ different suffixes. Once the sorted list L is generated, we can define the BWT of R, denoted by B_R, as a string of length $n(m + 1)$, such that $B_R[i]$ is the BWT code of the suffix $L[i]$, for $0 <= i <= n(m + 1)$.

3   Method - BWTCP

Similar to CX1, we sort all suffixes of reads in R to construct the BWT of R. However, given a large amount of genomic reads, it's impractical to sort all suffixes in memory. Consider that the BWT construction of 1 billion reads of length 100. Each read has 100 non-empty suffixes with length ranging from 1 to 100. If we explicitly enumerate all the suffixes of the 1 billion reads, there will be about 5 trillion characters. It requires at least 1250 gigabytes to store all these characters, using the canonical 2-bit-per-character representation for DNA strings. Obviously, such requirement is far beyond the memory capacity of most PCs or commodity servers. To be memory efficient, we adopt a strategy similar to block-wise suffix sorting proposed in [12, 14]. BWTCP mainly involves two steps: partitioning and sorting. The workflow is illustrated in Fig. 1.

3.1   Partitioning

As mentioned above, it is impractical to list all the suffixes of a large collection of reads in memory. Splitting the suffixes list to smaller partitions is an obvious approach, which was employed in CX1. We adopt the same strategy. $l - mers$ (string of length l) are chosen as splitters, i.e. the suffixes with same l-prefix, or in other words, suffixes share the same l characters at their beginning, will be placed into same partition (Suffixes shorter than l require special but easy handling). Thus the order of suffixes from different partition is absolutely determined by the partition they belong to, and we can sort each partition separately and simply

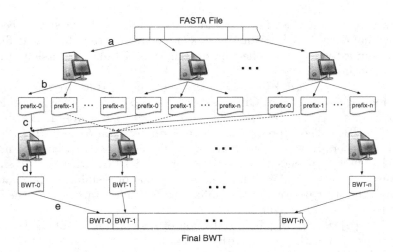

Fig. 1. Workflow of BWTCP. (a) several processors load different part of the reads contained in a fasta file; (b) suffixes are partitioned and placed into a number of files by their l-prefix; (c) several processors load and sort the suffixes with same l-prefix; (d) the BWT codes of each partition is outputted into temporary files; (e) concatenate the temporary files to get the final BWT.

concatenate the sorted partitions to form the sorted list of all suffixes. The value of l is a parameter dependent on the amount of available memory. A larger l simply means more partitions but less memory is needed to sort each partition. We observed that it costs about 15 m merely to load 1 billion reads of length 100 from hard disk to main memory. To accelerate the loading process, we load the reads in parallel as follows. Consider the scenario of loading a file with n reads using p processors. We can evenly partition n reads into p parts, each part containing n/p reads. The p parts are then loaded into the main memory of p processors simultaneously. After that, we perform the partitioning process on each processor concurrently. On each processor, we simply scan all suffixes of reads loaded and σ^l files each containing suffixes with specific l-prefix would be written to hard disk. Next, suffixes in these files will be sorted in parallel.

3.2   Hybrid Radix Sorting

Suffixes Representation. Note that DNA sequences are strings over the alphabet {A, C, G, T}, so each character can be represented by 2 bits, with A, C, G, T represented by 00, 01, 10 and 11 respectively. We store the suffix in units of byte, i.e. every four adjacent characters are stored in one byte. For convenience in sorting, all suffixes will be stored in same length of $k/4$, where k is the length of reads. Suffixes with a length less than k will be padded with 0. Note that suffixes in same partition share same l-prefix, so we need not store the first l bits of the suffix. Instead, we keep the BWT code of the suffix in the l bits for further acceleration.

Table 1. Representation of suffixes. For no more than 4G reads of length 100 and splitters set as 4-prefixes, each suffix occupies 30 byte: 1 for BWT code, 24 for suffix content excluding the first byte, 1 byte for the start position and 4 byte for the ID of the read the suffix belongs to.

BWT Code	Suffix excluding l-prefix	Suffix start position	Read ID

To make each suffix unique (so we can adopt all sorting strategies, stable or not), we append the start position of each suffix and ordinal number of the original read. As we have stored start positions of suffixes, we can skip storing the end-marker $ for each read. Thus, for suffixes of reads with length less than 256 and number of reads less than 4G, we store each suffix with $k/4 + 5$ bytes. For longer or larger collection of reads, we just need to modify the number of bytes used to store start position or ordinal number of the reads. Table 1 presents a template of how the suffixes are stored.

Suffixes Sorting. Radix sort is efficient for sorting large byte arrays. We optimized radix sort using strategies as described in [15]. The idea of radix sort is as follows. Firstly, classify the suffixes into piles by their first several, say, 4 characters. One pile gets all the suffixes that begin with $AAAA$, another pile gets suffixes begin with $AAAC$, and so on. Split these piles recursively on succeeding 4-character substrings until the suffixes end. When there are no more piles to split, pick up all the piles in order. Then the suffixes are sorted.

However, radix sorting is most advantageous for large arrays, so when the piles get smaller than a pre-determined threshold, we just sort it with comparison-based sorting algorithms such as insertion or quicksort. Referring to [15] and simple experiment results, an empirical threshold is set as 25.

Pruning Strategy. From the definition of BWT we can see that a strictly sorted list of the suffixes is not our final goal. Once the suffixes are sorted, we take a further step to collect the BWT code of each suffix. CX1 adopts LSD radix sorting method, which sorts from the last digit to the first one for all suffixes. Actually it's not necessary to compare all the digits. As described above, we store the BWT code in the suffix representation and when the suffixes in a pile share the same BWT code, we need not to sort the pile any longer. Repeated patterns in genomes are commonly seen, there would be pretty many piles sharing the same BWT code and this strategy could save a lot of time. Actually, the suffix sorting part only represents 30 % of the total runtime of BWTCP, while CX1 spent 86 % of total runtime on sorting, both in the case of BWT construction of 1 billion 100-length reads.

3.3   Parallelism

BWTCP can be highly parallelized, either in the partitioning part or the sorting part. Note that to avoid missing some suffixes, the sorting part should not be invoked until the partitioning part has finished. Given that the reads collection is evenly split, partitioning time on each part only differs very slightly, so the waiting time is quite short (For 1 billion 100-bp reads, the waiting time is less than 30 s. Note that the total running time is 1778 s).

In the partitioning part, the speedup is almost linear to the number of processors employed (Simple experiment shows that comparing to employing one processor, a speedup of 15.4X speedup was achieved when employing 16 processors). However, there exists a concern that when too many processors are writing on the same hard disk, the I/O performance will be limited by the writing speed of the hard disk. One possible solution is to use more hard disks to avoid writing jam. While in the sorting part, the degree of parallelism is as high as the number of the partitions of suffixes, i.e. σ^l, with σ being the alphabet size and l being the length of splitter when partition the suffixes. More partitions straightly mean higher degree of parallelism.

4   Experiments and Results

BWTCP was implemented in C. We tested BWTCP with the Asian YH short reads dataset presented in [16] on Tianhe-2 supercomputer. The results were compared against CX1 and BCR (version 0.6.0). The evaluation of BWTCP was carried out on 32 Intel Xeon E5-2692V2 CPUs connected by Gigabit Ethernet in Tianhe-2 supercomputer system, each equipped with 64 GB memory. As Tianhe-2 is not equipped with GPU, We previously tested BCR and CX1 on a machine with an Intel Xeon i7- 3930K (Hex-core) 3.2 GHz processor and 64 GB of memory. A comparison of Intel E5-2692V2 and Intel Xeon i7-3930K can be found at [17]. The machine was also equipped with an NVIDIA GeForce GTX 680 graphics card with 4 GB of global memory.

We prepared three input data sets with 100 million, 500 million, and 1 billion reads respectively. For each data set, we randomly selected a subset of the YH short reads of the required size. Each read contains 100 bases of A, C, G, T. Then we invoked BWTCP, CX1 and BCR to construct the BWT of the selected reads. The BWT was outputted in ASCII format. All parameters and options of CX1 and BCR are set as default, except I/O formats and algorithm of BCR (which was set to BCR).

4.1   Time and Memory

Table 2 lists the construction time and memory consumption of BWTCP, CX1 and BCR on the three datasets. Note that the memory consumption of BWTCP is the maximum value on all the processors employed. From Table 2 we can see that BWTCP is way faster than BCR and CX1 both on small dataset and big ones. BWTCP employed many processors in order to release memory pressure and the improvement is evident in Table 2.

Table 2. Time (sec) and memory consumption by the three tools.

Tools	$100M \times 100bp$	$500M \times 100bp$	$1000M \times 100bp$
BCR	6141 (3.3 GB)	23094 (17.6 GB)	46899 (33.3 GB)
CX1	565 (45.0 GB)	3108 (57.0 GB)	6886 (57.0 GB)
BWTCP	197 (2.2 GB)	883 (10.7 GB)	1778 (22.1 GB)

4.2   Impact of Read Length

Table 3 illustrates the impact of read length on BCR, CX1 and BWTCP. As performed in [12], data sets of length-200 reads and length-400 reads were created based on the 100 M data set by concatenating adjacent 100-bp reads. We can see from Table 3 that the performance of BCR and CX1 dropped sharply on longer reads. On the contrary, BWTCP was robust to read length variation. This is mainly because that the sorting procedure in BWTCP would be terminated as early as possible, when all suffixes in a pile share the same BWT code.

Table 3. Construction time (sec) for different length of reads.

Tools	$100M \times 100\,bp$	$50M \times 200bp$	$25M \times 400bp$
BCR	6141	9334	23950
CX1	565	724	1269
BWTCP	197	183	201

5   Conclusion

We presented an efficient method, BWTCP, for constructing the BWT of a large string collection in parallel. BWTCP employs multiple nodes to cut down memory footprint on single node and enhance speed performance. As supported by our experiments, our method is more efficient (both on time and space performance) compared to existing tools, especially on longer reads. Similar to BCR, our method is also I/O bound. So BWTCP can be even faster on processors equipped with SSD.

We carried out a performance test on 1 billion reads of length 100 with 16 nodes of Tianhe-2 Supercomputer system. This implies the possibility that BWTCP can be scaled up to process larger read volumes by employing more nodes (16,000 nodes are available on Tianhe-2).

In addition, BWTCP is theoretically portable. One can take advantage of accelerators like GPU or Intel Xeon Phi to construct BWT of reads with simple modification to BWTCP.

Acknowledgement. We acknowledge Prof. T.W. Lam, Project Manager Ruibang Luo and C.M. Liu in BAL lab, Department of Computer Science, The University of

Hong Kong for providing the source codes, related data and constructive advice both in designing and testing of BWTCP. And this work is supported by NSFC Grant 61272056, U1435222, 61133005, 61120106005 and 91432018.

References

1. Deshpande, V., Fung, E.D.K., Pham, S., Bafna, V.: Cerulean: a hybrid assembly using high throughput short and long reads. In: Darling, A., Stoye, J. (eds.) WABI 2013. LNCS, vol. 8126, pp. 349–363. Springer, Heidelberg (2013)
2. Deshpande, V.: Sequencing, assembling, and annotating a mid-sized genome. In: Plant and Animal Genome XXII Conference. Plant and Animal Genome (2014)
3. Huang, L., Popic, V., Batzoglou, S.: Short read alignment with populations of genomes. Bioinformatics **29**(13), i361–i370 (2013)
4. Blazewicz, J., Frohmberg, W., Gawron, P., et al.: DNA sequence assembly involving an acyclic graph model. Found. Comput. Decis. Sci. **38**(1), 25–34 (2013)
5. Li, B., Fillmore, N., Bai, Y., et al.: Evaluation of de novo transcriptome assemblies from RNASeqdata. bioRxiv (2014)
6. Burrows, M., Wheeler, D.J.: A block-sorting lossless data compression algorithm (1994)
7. Li, H., Durbin, R.: Fast and accurate short read alignment with Burrows Wheeler transform. Bioinformatics **25**(14), 1754–1760 (2009)
8. Langmead, B., Salzberg, S.L.: Fast gapped-read alignment with Bowtie 2. Nat. Methods **9**(4), 357–359 (2012)
9. Chan, S.H., Cheung, J., Wu, E., et al.: MICA: a fast short-read aligner that takes full advantage of intel many integrated core architecture (MIC) (2014). arXiv preprint arXiv:1402.4876
10. Simpson, J.T., Durbin, R.: Efficient de novo assembly of large genomes using compressed data structures. Genome Res. **22**(3), 549–556 (2012)
11. Bauer, M.J., Cox, A.J., Rosone, G.: Lightweight algorithms for constructing and inverting the BWT of string collections. Theoret. Comput. Sci. **483**, 134–148 (2013)
12. Liu, C.M., Luo, R., Lam, T.W.: GPU-accelerated BWT construction for large collection of short reads (2014). arXiv preprint arXiv:1401.7457
13. Ferragina, P., Manzini, G.: Opportunistic data structures with applications. In: Proceedings of the 41st Annual Symposium on Foundations of Computer Science, p. 390–398. IEEE (2000)
14. Kärkkäinen, J.: Fast BWT in small space by blockwise suffix sorting. Theoret. Comput. Sci. **387**(3), 249–257 (2007)
15. Mcllroy, P.M., Bostic, K., Mcllroy, M.D.: Engineering radix sort. Comput. Syst. **6**(1), 5–27 (1993)
16. Luo, R., Liu, B., Xie, Y., et al.: SOAPdenovo2: an empirically improved memory-efficient short-read de novo assembler. Gigascience **1**(1), 18 (2012)
17. http://www.cpu-world.com/Compare/501/Intel_Core_i7_i7-3930K_vs_Intel_Xeon_E5-2692_v2.html

Lattice-CSC: Optimizing and Building an Efficient Supercomputer for Lattice-QCD and to Achieve First Place in Green500

David Rohr[1]([✉]), Matthias Bach[1], Gvozden Nešković[1], Volker Lindenstruth[1,2], Christopher Pinke[3], and Owe Philipsen[3]

[1] Frankfurt Institute for Advanced Studies, Department for High Performance Computing, Goethe University Frankfurt, Ruth-Moufang-Str.1, 60438 Frankfurt, Germany
rohr@fias.uni-frankfurt.de
[2] GSI Helmholtz Center for Heavy Ion Research, Planckstraße 1, 64291 Darmstadt, Germany
[3] Institute for Theoretical Physics, Goethe University Frankfurt, Max-von-Laue-Str.1, 60438 Frankfurt, Germany

Abstract. In the last decades, supercomputers have become a necessity in science and industry. Huge data centers consume enormous amounts of electricity and we are at a point where newer, faster computers must no longer drain more power than their predecessors. The fact that user demand for compute capabilities has not declined in any way has led to studies of the feasibility of exaflop systems. Heterogeneous clusters with highly-efficient accelerators such as GPUs are one approach to higher efficiency. We present the new L-CSC cluster, a commodity hardware compute cluster dedicated to Lattice QCD simulations at the GSI research facility. L-CSC features a multi-GPU design with four FirePro S9150 GPUs per node providing 320 GB/s memory bandwidth and 2.6 TFLOPS peak performance each. The high bandwidth makes it ideally suited for memory-bound LQCD computations while the multi-GPU design ensures superior power efficiency. The November 2014 Green500 list awarded L-CSC the most power-efficient supercomputer in the world with 5270 MFLOPS/W in the Linpack benchmark. This paper presents optimizations to our Linpack implementation HPL-GPU and other power efficiency improvements which helped L-CSC reach this benchmark. It describes our approach for an accurate Green500 power measurement and unveils some problems with the current measurement methodology. Finally, it gives an overview of the Lattice QCD application on L-CSC.

1 Introduction and Contribution of This Paper

In order to cope with today's scientific challenges, supercomputers are of paramount importance. For a long time now, performance has grown exponentially. A fraction of this increase has been acquired through higher power consumption.

© Springer International Publishing Switzerland 2015
J.M. Kunkel and T. Ludwig (Eds.): ISC High Performance 2015, LNCS 9137, pp. 179–196, 2015.
DOI: 10.1007/978-3-319-20119-1_14

With data centers draining tens of megawatts of electricity, we have reached a point where this increase of power consumption has to stop. It is our obligation as a society to use our resources as carefully as possible, which means that supercomputers must become more efficient. One approach to improving supercomputer power efficiency is the usage of accelerator cards such as **GPUs** (**G**raphics **P**rocessing **U**nits), which have already shown great power efficiency [1].

The **L-CSC** (**L**attice **C**omputer for **S**cientific **C**omputing) is a new compute cluster dedicated to simulations in the field of the strong interactions between quarks and gluons, which is under investigation both experimentally and theoretically. The cluster is installed at the GSI Helmholtz Center for Heavy Ion Research in Darmstadt, Germany[1]. The theory of the strong interaction is an SU(3) gauge theory called **Q**uantum **C**hromo **D**ynamics (**QCD**). In general, QCD is non-perturbative and the only approach to study it from first principles is **Lattice QCD** (**LQCD**) [2]. Here, space time is discretized on a four-dimensional lattice, allowing numerical evaluation of the theory. Due to the large computational demands, state-of-the-art LQCD simulations require **H**igh **P**erformance **C**omputing (HPC). LQCD applications are always memory bandwidth limited. Accordingly, GPUs, which offer a much higher peak memory bandwidth compared to traditional CPUs, have become a vital ingredient to modern LQCD applications [3]. In addition, with respect to both peak performance and peak memory bandwidth, GPUs are much more power-efficient than traditional CPUs. Hence, GPUs can increase the power efficiency significantly for applications that can harness their capabilities. L-CSC features a multi-GPU design, providing a huge aggregate global memory bandwidth and superior power efficiency.

For LQCD computations we use the CL^{2}QCD application [4–7]. It utilizes GPUs through OpenCL, which is a vendor independent **API** (**A**pplication **P**rogramming **I**nterface) for GPU programming [8]. In particular, it can run on different architectures independent of the hardware vendor, as opposed to most other modern LQCD applications, which are bound to NVIDIA's CUDA [9].[2] CL^{2}QCD has been shown to give significant speedups on the predecessors of L-CSC, LOEWE-CSC and Sanam (see below) [4–6], compared to CPU systems and literature values. It has been successfully applied in physical studies [10,11].

Linpack [12] is the standard tool for measuring the compute performance of supercomputers and it is the basis for the semi-annual **Top500** list of the fastest supercomputers [13]. The standard implementation of Linpack is **HPL** (**H**igh **P**erformance **L**inpack). We have presented an adapted version called **HPL-GPU** that can run on GPUs [14,15]. The **Green500** list [16,17] awards the most power-efficient supercomputers worldwide, ranked according to performance per watt achieved in Linpack. We have tuned L-CSC for power efficiency, and we optimized HPL-GPU for the best Green500 result. In November 2014, L-CSC was awarded 1st place for the most power-efficient supercomputer in the world.

---

[1] See http://www.gsi.de.

[2] See e.g. http://lattice.github.io/quda/.

The design of the L-CSC cluster continues the approach of the predecessors **LOEWE-CSC** [18] and **Sanam** [1]. We give some details on L-CSC hardware selection in [19]. In summary, L-CSC consists of 160 compute nodes interconnected by 56 GBit **FDR** (**F**ourteen **D**ata **R**ate) **InfiniBand** with half bisectional bandwidth. Each node offers two 10-core Ivy-Bridge-EP Xeon CPUs, 256 GB RAM, and four AMD FirePro GPUs. 148 nodes feature the FirePro S9150 card while 12 nodes also feature the S10000 dual GPU, for a total of eight GPU chips per node. The two different GPU models are chosen to serve different types of QCD problems [19]. An important aspect related to power efficiency, which is not considered in the Green500 ranking, is the data center itself. L-CSC inherits the cooling principles from Sanam and LOEWE-CSC, which use passive water cooling heat exchangers in the racks' back doors. The only active cooling components, aside from the fans inside the servers, are the water pumps and cooling towers yielding a **P**ower **U**sage **E**ffectiveness (**PUE**) of 1.05, i. e. only 5 % cooling overhead, which is significantly lower than in most data centers [18].

This paper is structured as follows: After Sect. 2 gives an overview of other power-efficient clusters, Sect. 3 presents the optimizations for HPL-GPU. Section 4 illustrates other power efficiency improvements mostly related to the hardware. We describe our efforts to achieve an accurate power measurement in Sect. 5. Finally, Sect. 6 gives an overview of the LQCD application on L-CSC.

2 Related Work

A newcomer to the November 2014 Green500 list, the ExaScaler-1 Cluster at the High Energy Accelerator Research Organization KEK [20], employs PEZY-SC [21] many-core coprocessors. It is ranked at 2nd place. Each node of the ExaScaler-1 uses two Intel Xeon E5-2660v2 CPUs, 256 GiB RAM and eight PEZY-SC coprocessors. The ExaScaler-1 cluster is comprised of eight nodes and uses FDR InfiniBand for interconnect. PEZY-SC contains 1024 logical cores running at 733 MHz, having a theoretical double precision floating point peak performance of 1.5 TFLOPS and 1533.6 GiB/s memory bandwidth. Altogether, the ExaScaler-1 cluster achieves power efficiency of 4945.63 MFLOPS/W.

Current 2nd (ExaScaler-1) and 3rd (TSUBAME-KFC [22]) place systems in the Green500 list are using liquid submersion cooling. In contrast to our solution, this approach directly cools the components by circulating dielectric liquid. Components are submerged in large tanks of liquid. Pumps and heat exchangers are used to remove heat away from components, eliminating the need for server fans. Regardless, our passive water cooling solution still achieves comparable PUE while enabling the use of commodity hardware without any modifications. It is worth mentioning that many of the top Green500 systems in 2014 are commodity hardware HPC clusters. This approach, which extends upon Beowulf clusters [23] concept, proves to be highly energy and cost-effective.

We present related work to the LQCD application directly in Sect. 6.

3   Optimizing the Linpack Benchmark

The HPL-GPU software itself is already quite optimized. Thus, there is no single new feature that leads to the good result on its own. Instead, tuning the software at multiple places for small improvements of 1 % – 5 % each leads to the overall improvement. This process increased matrix multiplication performance on a quad-S9150 server from about 4 TFLOPS to 7.8 TFLOPS and power efficiency from 3680.3 MFLOPS/W to 5367.8 MFLOPS/W. We give a short introduction to the terminology first and then present a selection of these new improvements.

Linpack solves a dense system of linear equations iteratively. Every iteration consists of many steps: the large **Update-DGEMM** (matrix-matrix multiplication), the **Update-DTRSM** (solving a triangular matrix), **LASWP**, **Factorization**, and **Broadcast**. The factorization is a complex step involving many substeps, among them smaller DGEMM tasks. The most compute-intense step is DGEMM. GPUs are ideally suited for DGEMM calculations because DGEMM can load the GPUs' **FMA** (**F**used **M**ultiply **A**dd) ALUs almost to the full extent, which most tasks cannot do. DGEMM on GPUs can achieve around 90 % of the theoretical peak performance [14]. Hence, HPL-GPU attempts to run DGEMM on the GPU 100 % of the time. It leaves the other steps on the processor, and hides them behind DGEMM execution on the GPU. In addition, HPL-GPU can use the remaining compute capabilities of the CPU to assist the GPU at the DGEMM task. It can work with static workload distribution (**static scheduler**) and dynamic workload distribution (**dynamic scheduler**), the latter one yielding better CPU utilization but larger scheduling overhead. Hiding CPU tasks behind DGEMM is facilitated by a feature called **Lookahead**, which runs the CPU tasks of the next iteration concurrent to the large Update-DGEMM of the current iteration. Lookahead adds an additional step to each iteration: a **Preparatory-DGEMM**, which is executed on the CPU to simplify the scheduling. We use the Intel MKL BLAS library [24] for the CPU and a custom GPU DGEMM kernel. HPL-GPU offers two operating modes: a **performance-optimized mode**, and an alternative **efficiency-optimized mode** that sacrifices a small fraction of the performance for a better net power efficiency. The first mode yields better results for the Top500 list, the second mode for the Green500 list. During an HPL run, the trailing matrix gets consecutively smaller and the computational effort for DGEMM shrinks faster than the workload for the other CPU tasks. This shifts the workload to the CPUs and at a certain point the minimum CPU time exceeds the GPU time. From this time forward, the GPU idles regularly. Formerly, e. g. on LOEWE-CSC, this was no problem because the GPUs were not that much faster than the CPUs. Usually, the performance of each new GPU-generation improves by a larger factor than for the corresponding CPU-generation. It becomes more difficult with every new generation of GPUs to overlap computations on GPU and CPU. On Sanam this became a relevant problem [1], and on L-CSC the discrepancy between CPU performance and GPU performance prohibits the original approach.

In the following, we present the new features we have added to HPL-GPU for Lattice-CSC, in order to cope with these inefficiencies. An asynchronous

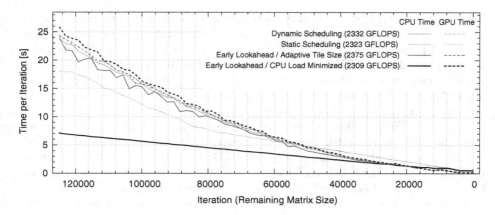

Fig. 1. Computation time of CPU and GPU during HPL runs with different settings on a node with two S10000 cards. The upper three versions are optimized for compute performance and try to use the CPU to the full extent, the lower version (CPU Load Minimized) is optimized for energy efficiency and tries to keep the CPU idle. Hence, its CPU execution time is shorter and its GPU execution time longer.

GPU command queue allows a **dynamic offload** of other CPU tasks onto the GPU. Due to full-duplex DMA transfer, there is only little influence on the Update-DGEMM performance of the GPU. Three CPU tasks are worthwhile for dynamic offload: the Preparatory-DGEMM, the small DGEMM steps during the factorization, and the Update-DTRSM. Offloading the Preparatory-DGEMM for lookahead is called **Early Lookahead** and analyzed in Fig. 1 in Sect. 3.1, offloading the other tasks is handled afterward in Sect. 3.2. Another modification is an **adaptive tile size**. It allows a more fine-grained selection of the matrix splitting ratios for the static scheduler [14].

3.1 Early Lookahead / Adaptive Tile Size

Figure 1 shows GPU and CPU runtime during an HPL run with two S10000 GPUs for different settings in HPL-GPU. The X-axis shows the remaining workload (matrix size) whereas the Y-axis shows the time needed for the related iteration. Two curves, one for the CPU runtime (solid) and a second for the GPU runtime (dashed), show the time contribution of both processor types in each iteration. All curves in the plot are falling, since matrix size becomes smaller towards the right side. The GPU curves fall faster, because the DGEMM workload shrinks faster than the CPU steps' workload. The graph shows whether the CPU or the GPU generates the bottleneck in each iteration. (The CPU is the bottleneck if and only if the CPU curve is above the GPU curve.) The wasted GPU time, when the CPU is still working but GPU has finished the iteration, is directly visible as the integral between the curves for GPU and CPU.

The figure compares (among others) the versions with static and dynamic GPU / CPU scheduling. The dynamic one utilizes the processor almost to the full extent (the CPU curve is very close to the GPU curve). The benefit compared to the static one is small since the CPU contributes only little to the combined performance. The version with adaptive tile size and static scheduler has a slightly shorter CPU active period compared to the dynamic scheduler, but the performance is better due to less scheduling overhead. (See "Early Lookahead / Adaptive Tile Size" in Fig. 1.) Early lookahead reduces the minimum CPU runtime such that the CPU dominated period of HPL-GPU begins later.

In terms of power efficiency, it is better to move as much DGEMM workload from the CPU to the GPU because the latter is the more efficient chip. The efficiency optimized operation mode of HPL-GPU performs the entire Update-DGEMM step on the GPU, and does not split this workload between CPU and GPU. (See "Early Lookahead / CPU Load Minimized" in Fig. 1.) This creates a small performance penalty but improves the net power efficiency by 2 %. Consequently, this approach increases the duration of the GPU computation.

3.2 Dynamic Offload of CPU Steps to GPU

The previous section showed that offloading the Preparatory-DGEMM onto GPU is better in any case. Offloading the DGEMM substeps during the factorization and the Update-DTRSM is more complex, as they run less efficiently on the GPU than the other DGEMM tasks. (DGEMM inside the factorization has matrices that are too small and DTRSM is limited by PCIe bandwidth.)

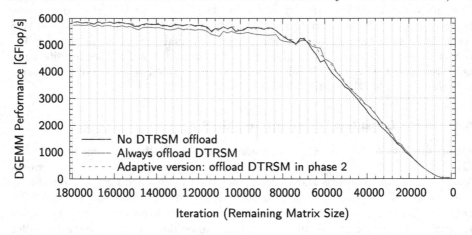

Fig. 2. Performance of HPL-GPU during the iterations of a Linpack run different settings for DTRSM offload.

Due to the non-constant ratio of CPU and GPU workload in a Linpack run, the optimal settings during such a run can change with every iteration [1]. In the following, **phase 1** denotes the GPU dominated period at the beginning and **phase 2** refers to the period at the end with the CPU being the bottleneck. Figure 2 shows the performance achieved during every iteration of the Linpack run (with the iteration on the x-axis) with and without DTRSM offload. It turns out the version without DTRSM offload is faster at the beginning, but the version with DTRSM offload is faster at the end. Hence, an adaptive version switches the setting when the curves intersect to ensure optimal performance in every iteration. Offloading the smaller DGEMMs shows a similar behavior. As mentioned before, it is possible that optimal settings with respect to performance and with respect to energy efficiency are different. Section 4.1 presents a way to obtain optimal settings for best efficiency. Table 1 gives an overview of which HPL-GPU mode performs which offloads.

Table 1. Dynamic Offload of CPU steps onto GPU.

Step	Performance Mode	Efficiency Mode
Preparatory-DGEMM	Always Offload	Always Offload
DGEMM during factorization	Offload in phase 2	Always Offload
Update-DTRSM	Offload in phase 2	Offload in phase 2

3.3 DMA Optimizations and OpenCL

We have already shown that system memory bandwidth can become a serious bottleneck for HPL in multi-GPU configurations [15,25]. A large blocking factor N_b in HPL can compensate this to some degree [15], but this approach encounters a principle limit at around $N_b = 2048$. The factorization workload goes with N_b^3. Since, as shown in the previous sections, the CPU-based factorization workload creates a bottleneck, N_b should not be increased further.

Due to limits in the DMA capabilities of former GPU programming APIs like AMD CAL[3] or older versions of CUDA, HPL-GPU had to copy data to intermediate host buffers before performing a DMA transfer to the GPU and vice versa. The problem lies in the limited size of GPU-accessible host memory. Meanwhile, both OpenCL and CUDA allow the allocation of large GPU-accessible host buffers. HPL-GPU has been modified to be platform independent supporting CAL, OpenCL, and CUDA as GPU APIs but also pure CPU systems. If the platform provides sufficient DMA support, HPL-GPU can do direct DMA transfers in any case avoiding all intermediate host buffers, which halves the system memory load [25]. Since no GPU exceeded 1 TFLOPS DGEMM performance at that time, we used a simulation in [25] to show that the DMA framework of HPL-GPU can keep step with a quad-GPU system achieving 2 TFLOPS DGEMM performance per GPU. The new S9150 GPU of L-CSC achieves real 2 TFLOPS DGEMM kernel performance and the final DGEMM performance achieved by HPL-GPU in the system is in complete accordance with the simulations.

HPL-GPU comes with GPU assembler CAL DGEMM kernels for Cypress, Cayman, and Tahiti GPU families. Today, OpenCL compilers have matured and it is possible to write fast DGEMM kernels in OpenCL. In order to use proprietary DGEMM kernels offered by vendors, HPL-GPU can load binary

---

[3] **C**ompute **A**bstraction **L**ayer is the assembler language of former AMD GPUs.

kernels from a shared binary library. AMD provided such a library with an OpenCL DGEMM kernel which achieves more than 2050 GFLOPS (approx. 80 % of the GPU peak performance) on S9150 (Hawaii family). HPL-GPU makes around 98 % of this DGEMM kernel performance available to the host.

4   Power Optimizations

Besides the optimizations to HPL-GPU, it is possible to tune the compute nodes to drain less power. Deactivation of hardware components are immediate measures. Universal Serial Bus (**USB**) can drain up to 16 W [1]. Disabling USB completely has the exact same effect as enabling USB auto suspend in Linux. Hence, L-CSC employs the second option. Hard disks and SATA controllers can be eliminated by booting an **NFS** (**N**etwork **F**ile **S**ystem) root system from LAN. Since InfiniBand is used anyway as a high performance network, L-CSC boots directly via InfiniBand which allows switching off the Ethernet ports completely. These steps yield an additional saving of 7 W.

CPU as well as GPU voltage and frequency play an important role. Power consumption goes with the voltage squared. Hence, it can be beneficial to reduce the frequency a bit, which allows a voltage reduction as well. Voltage should be minimal to ensure stable operation at the chosen frequency, and the best sweet spot in terms of frequency is determined experimentally.

4.1   CPU Voltage / Frequency

HPL-GPU can internally alter CPU frequencies via **libCPUFreq** [26]. This library forces the CPU to a lower **P-State** [27], lowering the processor's voltage accordingly. As the ratio of CPU and GPU workload in Linpack is not constant, the optimal CPU frequency is likely to change during the run. A lower frequency should yield better power efficiency during phase 1 at the beginning of Linpack while phase 2 is supposed to favor higher frequencies. Naturally, the performance-optimized HPL-GPU mode will always favor the faster CPU with high clocks, hence the following discussion applies only to the efficiency-optimized mode.

We use a technique similar to that in Fig. 2 to find the best settings with respect to efficiency. Production of the plot is a bit more complex than for pure performance analysis. The number of compute operations C_i per Linpack iteration i is constant and straightforward to compute. Hence, the energy efficiency E_i during the iteration i is given by C_i divided by the total power consumed during the iteration. The power meter integrates the power continuously and provides power values in configurable intervals, but a Linpack iteration does not coincide with one or multiple intervals. Consider that in particular between two iterations, power consumption can change significantly, e. g. because of lookahead reinitialization (See the fluctuating power measurement in Fig. 4.) We estimate the actual power by accumulating all power meter intervals completely within the iteration's duration, and scaling this power value linearly to the duration of the iteration. Figure 3 shows such a plot for two Linpack runs with different

CPU frequencies, which matches the expectations exactly. Due to the above-explained estimation, the curves are a bit noisy, but the trend is clearly visible. HPL-GPU on L-CSC varies CPU frequencies gradually from 1.2 GHz to 3 GHz with changeover points determined by the technique presented in Fig. 3.

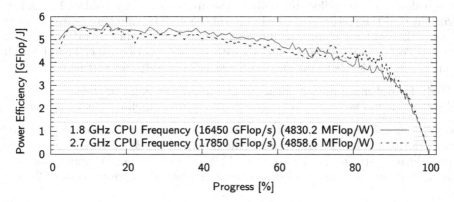

Fig. 3. Power efficiency of HPL-GPU during the iterations of a Linpack run with different CPU frequencies.

4.2   GPU Voltage / Frequency

Most programs cannot utilize all GPU ALUs to the full extent. (The same holds true for CPUs.) Hence, vendors such as AMD, Intel, or NVIDIA have implemented a **Turbo Mode**, where the chips run at higher frequencies, which can exceed the **TDP** (**T**hermal **D**esign **P**ower) under full load. The FirePro GPUs of L-CSC have an intelligent power management, which monitors the power consumption, and lowers the clocks if needed in order to stay within thermal and power limits. A GPU oscillating between a high turbo frequency and a lower frequency to maintain the TDP is roughly as fast as a GPU running at the middle frequency, but it runs less effectively. Compared to the middle frequency, the turbo mode drains more power than the low frequency saves. During Linpack on L-CSC, this feature is disabled via the AMD ADL library (**AMD D**isplay **L**ibrary), temperature and power consumption are monitored manually, and the optimal combination of voltage and frequency is fixed.

We investigated the efficiency with different frequency/voltage settings during the Linpack run. It turned out that in different phases of Linpack, different settings are optimal. During phase 1 the GPUs harness the full potential of their maximum clocks, while in phase 2 they are limited by the CPU. Hence, in the other way around as for the CPU, phase 1 favors high GPU clocks while phase 2 shows better efficiency with lower clocks. AMD provided a custom BIOS with several custom performance levels (voltage/frequency settings) and a tool that can switch between these performance levels during runtime. This enables operation of the GPUs with optimal efficiency at every point in time. This approach can also improve the performance in the case when the GPU hits the TDP limit, because in that situation performance and efficiency are linked linearly.

In addition, the pipeline reinitialization in HPL-GPU introduces short time periods (some tenths of milliseconds) where the GPU is not used. These periods are too short to be handled manually in the above-described fashion. Instead, it turns out that the power saving technique of the AMD PowerTune feature, based on an SVI2 regulator chip, can efficiently reduce voltage (in 6.25 mV steps) and frequency on demand for short periods with 10 ms transition time. Therefore, all the performance levels in the custom BIOS have exactly two settings:

- High: for optimal Linpack efficiency at the current point in time.
- Low: minimum voltage / clocks save power during pipeline reinitialization.

Overall, our software performs the coarse-grain switching by selecting the correct performance level, while PowerTune does the fine-grain switching to save power during pipeline reinitialization. Voltage and frequency tuning was the most important step and yielded a net energy efficiency improvement of 22 %.

5   Power Efficiency Results

Since L-CSC was assembled in October 2014, the full system was not yet ready for the Linpack run for the November Green500 submission. Instead, we used only a subsystem of 56 nodes. All results in this section refer to these 56 nodes.

The EEHPC Power Measurement Methodology [28] defines the procedure to obtain the power measurements for the Green500 list. It specifies three levels for the measurement. Level 1 is the basic level which requires the least effort, but has the least accuracy. The higher levels have stricter rules on the procedure and have higher demands on the measurement equipment, resulting in higher accuracy of the measurement. For instance, a level 1 measurement may measure only a small fraction of the cluster and scale the power consumption linearly to the full size (i. e. all nodes which participated in the Linpack run.) Level 2 requires a larger fraction and level 3 the full cluster. The power meter used for L-CSC is an LMG95 [29] revenue-grade power meter qualified for level 3 measurements with an accuracy of 0.025 %, but the total power it can measure did restrict the L-CSC submission to level 1. All other aspects of the L-CSC measurement are valid for level 3 and by screening the nodes to select ones with middle power consumption for the submission, we estimate an inaccuracy compared to a full level 3 measurement of less than 1.2 % [19].

Compared to the higher levels, there are three main factors which can distort a level 1 measurement. It is possible to exploit them, in order to obtain a higher power efficiency than actually achieved. These factors are:

- The measurement only has to cover a fraction of the cluster ($\frac{1}{64}$ for level 1).
- The duration of the measurement only has to cover at least 20 % of the middle 80 % of the core phase of Linpack [28].
- Level 1 requires only a measurement of the compute nodes which ignores other components such as network and infrastructure nodes.

The remainder of this section discusses how the L-CSC power measurement dealt with the above aspects and illustrates how exploiting these points leads to a false but higher power efficiency, which is still compliant to level 1 specifications.

5.1 Number of Measured Nodes

Compute nodes identical in construction can show significant node variability in power consumption. It is possible to screen the compute nodes for the most efficient ones and measure only them. Scaling this result to the full size gives a false result if the measured nodes are more efficient than the average.

The node variability in terms of power efficiency of $\pm 1.2\%$ on L-CSC [19] is small and in fact than we expected. Still, measuring the best nodes would improve the result by 1.2%. However, it can be quite challenging to measure 1 MW or more, which is drained by large installations, with high accuracy. Hence, we consider the approach to scale up a smaller measurement reasonable. A pre-screening and selection of average nodes can improve the measurement. In case of L-CSC, this leads to an estimated error of less than 1.2%.

Table 2. Linpack power efficiency in GFLOPS/W on Sanam and L-CSC clusters.

Cluster	1 Node	4 Nodes	Full Cluster
Sanam	2432.4	2318.7	2346.8
L-CSC	5367.8	5183.4	5293.4

Linpack may run on fewer nodes than available. Obviously, this deteriorates Linpack performance and Top500 ranking. But, such a small configuration usually yields better per-node performance, as it involves less communication. On the one hand, it seems self-suggesting that such a small configuration could also lead to better efficiency. On the other hand, the more nodes participate the more dominant is the GPU DGEMM workload, which is the most efficient one. Hence, the best option is not apparent. Table 2 shows that on both the Sanam [30] and the L-CSC clusters the efficiency is almost independent from the number of nodes. The single-node configurations have a small advantage as they do not need communication at all, but results with four and many nodes are similar. This demonstrates how well HPL-GPU hides the communication phases with its lookahead feature and how well it scales to many nodes.

5.2 Duration of Power Measurement

Figure 4 shows the measured power consumption over the time of the final Linpack run on L-CSC submitted to Green500. The red vertical lines mark the core phase of Linpack. This is the duration relevant for computing the FLOPS for the performance, so it should also be the duration of the power measurement. Levels 2 and 3 require this, but level 1 allows measuring a shorter duration for facilities with less advanced power measurement equipment. L-CSC's

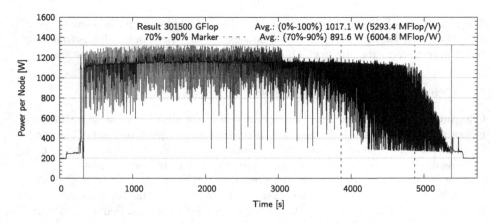

Fig. 4. Power consumption measurement during the Green500 Linpack run of L-CSC.

result submitted to the Green500 list uses the measurement of the full run with 5293.4 MFLOPS/W for the compute nodes. The following paragraphs illustrate false but higher efficiency measurements allowed by the level 1 specification. A level 1 measurement may select the best 20 % out of the middle 80 %, which is usually the period 70 % – 90 %. The power consumption steadily reduces towards the end of the run, because in this phase 2 of Linpack the computation is CPU-dominated and the GPU load becomes ever smaller.

The figure shows clearly that by simply redefining the power measurement interval from 0 % – 100 % to 70 % – 90 %, the measured power consumption drops from 1017 W to 892 W boosting the obtained efficiency from 5293 MFLOPS/W to 6005 MFLOPS/W. In this figure the 70 % – 90 % interval does not cover the period with very low power consumption at the very end. The power consumption at a time depends more or less only on the remaining matrix size. Starting with a smaller matrix does reduce performance but shifts the 70 % – 90 % interval to the smaller matrix sizes on the right. Thus, it enables harnessing a large fraction of the period with significantly lower power consumption.

Figure 5 shows the power consumption during such a shorter run. The completely ironic fact is that the short run achieves worse efficiency than the long run in the full measurement (4907 MFLOPS/W versus 5293 MFLOPS/W for 0 % – 100 % measurement). However, selecting an "optimal" interval boosts the efficiency further to 6899.6 MFLOPS/W. And theoretically, by using dynamic voltage and frequency adjustment, it is possible to reduce the power consumption much further for exactly the interval that is measured. This would reduce the performance, but only during 20 % of the time, and would lead to even higher results beyond 10000 MFLOPS/W. The period of measurement has by far the largest influence on the result. Therefore, it should be required to measure the full run, in particular because the additional effort is negligible.

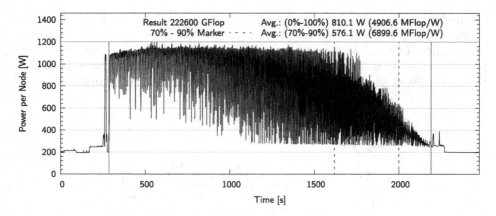

Fig. 5. Power consumption during a short Linpack run on L-CSC. Matrix size is tuned such that the 70 % – 90 % measurement yields the highest efficiency.

5.3 Measured Components

The above measurements covered only the compute nodes. In principle, a level 1 measurement could leave the other components out, which would improve the efficiency slightly. L-CSC can run from an InfiniBand NFS network root file system served by a single SSD. Mass storage and login nodes are not required for the Linpack run. Hence, the only other significant contribution comes from the three InfiniBand switches, arranged in a ring-configuration. The measured total power of all InfiniBand switches is 256.8 W while idle and 257.5 W during Linpack. It came as a surprise to us that the InfiniBand power consumption is so low and in particular that there is literally no difference between idle and load. Adding this power consumption to the measurement of the compute nodes yields the final result of **5271.8 MFLOPS/W** submitted to the November 2014 list.

6 Quantum Chromo Dynamics on L-CSC with CL²QCD

The main application on L-CSC is CL²QCD, used for QCD studies. Hence, good performance of CL²QCD on L-CSC is important and will be elucidated in the following. On the lattice, physical values are measured by means of evaluating operators over a representative sample of the phase space. One method to generate such samples is the **Hybrid Monte-Carlo (HMC)** algorithm, which integrates a virtual molecular-dynamic system corresponding to a system of quarks and gluons. The lattice action, which must be evaluated for these calculations, contains the inverse of the Dirac operator (a large sparse matrix). The off-diagonal part of this Dirac operator is called $\not{D}$. It implements a matrix-vector multiplication and is by far the most compute-intensive part [31] and is hence the core routing of the application.

The lattice spacing must be decreased to infinitesimal values to remove the discretization again. However, a lattice of 30^4 points, merely enough for a cube of 3 fm linear extent, already requires a large amount of TFLOPS. Improving the resolution by a factor of two increases the number of lattice points by a factor of 2^4. Thus, LQCD has already led to the development of dedicated compute platforms like APE [32], QCDOC [33] and QPACE [34], as well as influenced the development of high-performance systems like the BlueGene family [35].

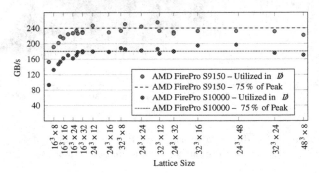

Fig. 6. Memory bandwidth achieved in $\rlap{/}{D}$ kernel on L-CSC.

CL^{2}QCD is a major application on LOEWE-CSC (one Radeon HD 5870 per node), and it has shown convincing performance on the Sanam cluster (two S10000 dual-GPUs per node). The core routine $\rlap{/}{D}$ achieves 100 GFLOPS per chip on the S10000 dual-GPU [1] and 135 GFLOPS on the S9150, i. e. 8×100 GFLOPS and 4×135 GFLOPS respectively per L-CSC node. The speedup compared to older GPUs (e. g. on LOEWE-CSC) and especially to CPUs is significant [4]. The aggregate $\rlap{/}{D}$ performance on the entire L-CSC cluster for parallel individual jobs is 89.5 TFLOPS. CL^{2}QCD is currently optimized for S10000 and achieves the excellent S9150 performance out of the box. Fine-tuning for the new card should further improve this result. Since LQCD is memory-bound, these performance numbers cannot reach the peak performance. Instead, Fig. 6 puts the achieved memory throughput during the $\rlap{/}{D}$ kernel into relation with the theoretical peak memory bandwidth. The figure reveals that CL^{2}QCD utilizes the available bandwidth to a great extent, leaving little room for improvements. We want to put the performance on L-CSC into relation to its predecessors LOEWE-CSC and Sanam. A single GPU chip of one S10000 GPU is twice as fast as a LOEWE-CSC GPU. The S9150 is roughly 35 % faster than one S10000 chip. Considering the aggregate processing throughput, an S9150 L-CSC node outperforms a Sanam node by 35 % and a LOEWE-CSC node by a factor of 10.8. The S10000 L-CSC nodes outperform the Sanam nodes by a factor 2 and the LOEWE-CSC nodes by a factor 16. To put our results into perspective, we quote some recent $\rlap{/}{D}$ performances on CPUs and GPUs. Smelyanskiy et al. [36] have reached 75 GFLOPS on an Intel Xeon X5680 CPU with a single precision $\rlap{/}{D}$ for problem sizes that fit into the last-level cache. For realistic problem sizes their performance drops to 42 GFLOPS, effectively reaching the throughput limit of the main memory. A variant that merges multiple $\rlap{/}{D}$ invocations (as they usually show up in applications) manages to exceed the data rate limit and achieve 53 GFLOPS on that same CPU. In single-precision, current NVIDIA GPUs achieve about 250 GFLOPS in $\not{D}$ [38]. In double precision, an NVIDIA GTX 280 can achieve 40 GFLOPS [31]. The NVIDIA GTX 480 reaches slightly more than 50 GFLOPS. Current results on NVIDIA k20m GPUs achieve close to 90 GFLOPS [37]. Note that these quoted values use a slightly different discretization than our implementation. The excellent $\not{D}$ performances translate very well to the full HMC application, where similar speedups are observed.

The 1 GB of memory of the older AMD Radeon HD 5870 on LOEWE-CSC limits the maximum possible lattice size severely. The 3 GB memory of the Sanam GPUs can handle many state-of-the-art finite temperature lattice sizes such as ($32^3 \times 12$), but are still subject to limitations. Both GPU types used in L-CSC have more memory (6 GB per chip on the new L-CSC S10000 cards and 16 GB on S9150), which removes most limitations. CL²QCD can also utilize four GPUs in a single process [5]. While the communication overhead reduces the aggregate system throughput for small lattices by around 20 %, this approach diminishes the wall time for individual jobs. In addition, it enables processing of larger lattices utilizing the accumulated GPU memory of 64 GB (e. g. $48^3 \times 96$ for zero temperature) which exceeds the capacity of a single GPU. With 64 GB we are able to process all lattices of interest without the additional development time and the penalties of inter-node communication. In many cases we process multiple individual smaller lattices which fit into 6 GB of memory. Requiring no communication at all, this is the most efficient configuration. The S10000 nodes are ideally suited for this. Hence, L-CSC provides an optimal execution environment for a broad variety of LQCD problems [19]: the S10000 nodes offer the highest aggregate throughput, while the S9150 nodes can process larger lattices and are faster for single jobs. We will still have to scale over multiple nodes, as Babich et al. [3] already showed, to further speed up individual compute-intensive jobs.

Multiple GPUs in a single server can improve energy efficiency. A single AMD FirePro S10000 chip is about four times as fast as a pure CPU system. Therefore, the four AMD FirePro S10000 dual-GPUs provide 32 times the throughput of an equivalent CPU system. Still, the GPUs raise the TDP of the system only by 1500 W. 31 additional systems are necessary to achieve the same throughput increase by use of CPUs. Their idle power-consumption already adds up to more than 1500 W. Even if the pure CPU systems could run LQCD at 200 W each, their combined energy consumption would be 6,400 W. This is more than four times the TDP of the four AMD FirePro S10000. Spread over multiple systems, the GPUs still have the same performance benefit. However, additional servers add additional power consumption, reducing overall energy efficiency.

7   Conclusions

The L-CSC cluster is a great success. It was awarded 1st place in November 2014 Green500 list for its energy efficient design and software as the most power efficient cluster in the world. The presented optimizations to the HPL-GPU software and in particular the tuning of clocks and voltage yield a significant boost in performance and power efficiency. It was shown that the software scales perfectly from few nodes to large systems. The cluster is dedicated to physics simulations, in particular of Lattice QCD investigations. The previously developed LQCD application CL^2QCD makes great usage of the hardware and performs very well. It achieves more than 75 % of the global GPU memory bandwidth, leaving only very little possibility for improvement because LQCD is memory-bound.

Acknowledgments. We would like to thank Advanced Micro Devices, Inc. (AMD) and ASUSTeK Computer Inc. (Asus) for their support.

References

1. Rohr, D., Kalcher, S., Bach, M., Alaqeeli, A., Alzaid, H., et al.: An energy-efficient multi-GPU supercomputer. In: Proceedings of the 16th IEEE International Conference on High Performance Computing and Communications, IEEE, Paris, France (2014)
2. Gupta, R.: Introduction to Lattice QCD (1998). http://arxiv.org/abs/hep-lat/9807028
3. Babich, R., Clark, M., Joó, B., Shi, G., Brower, R. C., Gottlieb, S.: Scaling lattice QCD beyond 100 GPUs. In: SC 2011 Proceedings of 2011 International Conference for High Performance Computing, Networking, Storage and Analysis, pp. 70:1–70:11 (2011)
4. Bach, M., Lindenstruth, V., Philipsen, O., Pinke, C.: Lattice QCD based on OpenCL. Comput. Phys. Commun. **184**, 2042–2052 (2013)
5. Bach, M., Lindenstruth, V., Pinke, C., Philipsen, O.: Twisted-Mass Lattice QCD using OpenCL. In: PoS LATTICE2013, p. 032 (2013)
6. Philipsen, O., Pinke, C., Sciarra, A., Bach, M.: CL2QCD - lattice QCD based on OpenCL. In: PoS LATTICE2014, p. 038 (2014)
7. http://code.compeng.uni-frankfurt.de/projects/clhmc
8. Khronos OpenCL Registry, OpenCL API and C Language Specifications. https://www.khronos.org/registry/cl/
9. NVIDIA, CUDA Toolkit Documentation. http://docs.nvidia.com/cuda/index.html
10. Philipsen, O., Pinke, C.: The nature of the Roberge-Weiss transition in $N_f = 2$. Phys. Rev. D **89**(9), 094504 (2014)
11. Philipsen, O., Bach, M., Lindenstruth, V., Pinke, C.: The thermal quark hadron transition in lattice QCD with two quark flavours. In: Proceedings of Conference: C14-02-12.1, pp. 33–40
12. Dongarra, J., Luszczek, P., Petitet, A.: The LINPACK benchmark: past, present and future. Concurrency Comput.: Pract. Experience **15**(9), 803–820 (2003)
13. TOP500 Supercomputer Sites. http://www.top500.org
14. Bach, M., Kretz, M., Lindenstruth, V., Rohr, D.: Optimized HPL for AMD GPU and multi-core CPU usage. Comput. Sci. - Res. Dev. **26**(3–4), 153–164 (2011)
15. Rohr, D., Bach, M., Kretz, M., Lindenstruth, V.: Multi-GPU DGEMM and HPL on highly energy efficient clusters. In: IEEE Micro, Special Issue, CPU, GPU, and Hybrid Computing (2011)
16. Sharma, S., Hsu, C., Feng, W.: Making a case for a Green500 list. In: Proceedings of the 20th IEEE International Parallel Distributed Processing Symposium p. 343 (2006)
17. The Green500 List. http://www.green500.org

18. Bach, M., De Cuveland, J., Ebermann, H., Eschweiler, D., Kretz, M., et al.: The LOEWE-CSC: a comprehensive approach for a power efficient general purpose supercomputer. In: 21st Euromicro International Conference on Parallel, Distributed and Network-Based Processing (2013)
19. Rohr, D., Nescovic, G., Radtke, M., Lindenstruth, V.: The L-CSC cluster: greenest supercomputer in the world in Green500 list of November 2014. In: Proceedings of Supercomputing Frontiers (2015)
20. High Energy Accelerator Research Organization. http://www.kek.jp
21. PEZY Computing, PEZY-SC Many Core Processor (2014). http://www.pezy.co.jp/en/products/pezy-sc.html
22. http://www.gsic.titech.ac.jp/tsubame
23. Sterling, T.L.: How to Build a Beowulf: A Guide to the Implementation and Application of PC Clusters. MIT Press, Cambridge (1999)
24. Intel Corporation, Intel MKL BLAS Library. https://software.intel.com/en-us/intel-mkl
25. Rohr, D., Lindenstruth, V.: A flexible and portable large-scale DGEMM library for linpack on next-generation multi-GPU systems. In: 23rd Euromicro International Conference on Parallel, Distributed and Network-Based Processing (2015)
26. https://www.kernel.org/pub/linux/utils/kernel/cpufreq/
27. Kidd, T.I.: What exactly is a P-state? (2008). https://software.intel.com/en-us/blogs/2008/05/29/what-exactly-is-a-p-state-pt-1
28. EEHPC Working Group: Energy Efficient High Performance Computing Power Measurement Methodology v1.2 RC 2
29. ZES Zimmer: LMG95 1 Phase Power Analyzer. http://www.zes.com/en/Products/Precision-Power-Analyzer/LMG95
30. Rohr, D.: On Development, Feasibility, and Limits of Highly Efficient CPU and GPU Programs in Several Fields. Dissertation Thesis (2013)
31. Clark, M.A., Babich, R., Barros, K., Brower, R.C., Rebbi, C.: Solving lattice QCD systems of equations using mixed precision solvers on GPUs. Comput. Phys. Commun. 181, 1517–1528 (2010)
32. Battista, C., Cabasino, S., Marzano, F., Paolucci, P., Pech, J., et al.: APE-100 computer: (i) the architecture. Int. J. High Speed Comput. 05(04), 637–656 (1993)
33. Boyle, P. A., Chen, D., Christ, N. H., Clark, M. A., Cohen, S. D., et al.: QCDOC: a 10 teraflops computer for tightly-coupled calculations. In: SC 2004 Proceedings of 2004 International Conference for High Performance Computing, Networking, Storage and Analysis (2004)
34. Baier, H., Boettiger, H., Drochner, M., Eicker, N., Fischer, U.: QPACE - a QCD parallel computer based on cell processors. In: Proceedings of Science, p. 21, November 2009
35. Vranas, P.: QCD and the BlueGene. J. Phys.: Conf. Ser. 78, 012080 (2007)
36. Smelyanskiy, M., Vaidyanathan, K., Choi, J., Joó, B., Chhugani, J., et al.: High-performance lattice QCD for Multi-Core based parallel systems using a cache-friendly hybrid threaded-MPI approach. In: SC 2011 Proceedings of 2011 International Conference for High Performance Computing, Networking, Storage and Analysis (2011)

37. Winter, F. T., Clark, M. A., Edwards, R. G., Joó, B.: A framework for lattice QCD calculations on GPUs. In: Proceedings of the 2014 IEEE 28th International Parallel and Distributed Processing Symposium, pp. 1073–1082 (2014)
38. Joó, B., Kalamkar, D.D., Vaidyanathan, K., Smelyanskiy, M., Pamnany, K., et al.: Supercomputing. In: Kunkel, J.M., Ludwig, T., Meuer, H.W. (eds.) ISC 2013. Lecture Notes in Computer Science, vol. 7905, pp. 40–54. Springer, Heidelberg (2014)

An Efficient Clique-Based Algorithm of Compute Nodes Allocation for In-memory Checkpoint System

Xiangke Liao$^{(\boxtimes)}$, Canqun Yang, Zhe Quan, Tao Tang, and Cheng Chen

College of Computer Science, National University of Defense Technology,
Changsha 410073, China
{xkliao,canqun,zhequan,taotang84,chengchen}@nudt.edu.cn

Abstract. Fault-tolerant is an essential technology for high-performance computing systems. Checkpoint/Restart (C/R) is the most popular fault-tolerant technique in which the programs save their states in stable storage, typically a global file system, and recover from the last checkpoint upon a failure. Due to the high-cost of global file system, node-local storage based checkpoint techniques are now getting more and more interests, where checkpoints are saved in local storage, such as DRAM. Typically, computing nodes are divided into groups and the checkpoint data is redundantly saved on a specified another node or is distributed among all other nodes in the same group, according to different cross-node redundancy schemes, to overcome the volatility of node-local storage. As a result, multiple simultaneous failures within one group often cannot be withstood and the strategy of node grouping is consequently very important since it directly impacts the probability of multi-node-failure within one group. In this paper, we propose a novel node allocation model, which takes the topological structure of high-performance computing systems into account and can greatly reduce the probability of multi-node-failure within a group, compared with traditional architecture-neutral grouping algorithms. Experimental results obtained from a simulation system based on TianHe-2 supercomputer show that our method is very effective on random simulative instances.

Keywords: Fault-tolerance · In-memory checkpoint · Algorithm

1 Introduction

In high performance computing (HPC) systems, the probability of overall failure increases over the computing time and the number of compute nodes due to more involved components. The mean time between failures (MTBF) of toady's systems have decreased to only a few hours [5, 6, 14] because of hardware and/or software errors [8, 15]. As a result, fault-tolerant has become a well-known issue in HPC area [11].

One commonly used fault-tolerant technique is Checkpoint/Restart (C/R) [1]. In a C/R-based method, the state of an application, known as a checkpoint,

© Springer International Publishing Switzerland 2015
J.M. Kunkel and T. Ludwig (Eds.): ISC High Performance 2015, LNCS 9137, pp. 197–211, 2015.
DOI: 10.1007/978-3-319-20119-1_15

is periodically saved to stable storages, typically the global file system. Once a failure occurs, the program can be restarted from the latest saved checkpoint. The critical issue of C/R-based methods is the high-cost of checkpoint access from global file system, especially for those large-scale systems, in which the I/O bandwidth will become the performance bottleneck [7,13]. Consequently, many local-storage based C/R methods have emerged [3,4,12,16]. In this paper, we focus on one that takes host memory as the storage to save checkpoints. It should be noted that local storage based C/R method is usually adopted as a supplement to the disk based C/R, to reduce the frequency of global file system access. This is also known as multi-level checkpoint technique [10].

The performance benefit of local storage based C/R derives from the linearly increasing checkpoint access bandwidth and at least an order of magnitude lower access latency compared with disks. However, local storage is usually supposed to be unstable. For example, DRAM is volatile and the data will be lost once the power is off. Consequently, the checkpoint of one node has to be redundantly saved in other nodes, so as to recover the node failure. The most common strategy is dual-redundancy. To be more specific, local storage based C/R typically divides compute nodes into groups, and only duplicates a checkpoint onto another node in the same group (usually called *partner node*). Upon a node failure, the execution state can be recovered by the checkpoint saved on its partner node. The dual-redundancy strategy means that a given node and its partner cannot fail at the same time, otherwise the execution cannot be recovered. To reduce the data amount of checkpoint, another commonly used scheme is XOR, which calculates a parity of redundant data from all checkpoints and then distributes it among all nodes in the same group. In this case, two nodes from the same group cannot fail at the same time.

How to group the compute nodes has a direct impact on the fault-tolerant effect of these local storage based C/R techniques, since different grouping strategies often lead to different probabilities of multi-node-failure in a group. In traditional methods, grouping strategy is relatively intuitive. For instance, in the Scalable Checkpoint/Restart (SCR) library [9], a multi-level checkpointing system, the nodes can be grouped by continuous node ID or a specified stride. This strategy is straightforward to implement, while the architecture of system is ignored. In real-world large-scale parallel computing systems, multiple simultaneous failures occur with higher probability in some set of nodes than others. For instance, by omitting other factors, two nodes that share the same electricity supply module are more likely to fail simultaneously than two isolated nodes due to the possible power failure. Generally, two nodes with larger logic distance may have lower probability of failing simultaneously.

Based on these observations, we propose a new algorithm in this paper, to group the computing nodes with the topological structure of a parallel computing system taken into account. Our method transfers the computing nodes with the probability of failure into a complete weighted undirected graph and uses clique technology to improve the nodes groups. Compared with intuitive grouping strategies, our algorithm can effectively reduce the probability of multiple simultaneous intragroup failures, in which case high-cost global C/R system has to be invoked. To evaluate our method, we build a simulation system based on TianHe-2 [2], the world's fastest supercomputer in the latest TOP500 list, which has more than 16,000 nodes. The topological structure and the essential parameters of the simulation system are extracted from this real system, and can also be modified easily to simulate other systems. The experimental results obtained show that the approach is very effective on random instances, especially for hard instances.

The remainder of this paper is organized as follows: Sect. 2 introduces the background. We propose our model and algorithm in detail in Sects. 3 and 4 respectively. Section 5 evaluates the performance of this model and conclusions are given in Sect. 6.

2 Background

In-memory checkpoint system is the most important local-storage based checkpoint technique. Generally, memory access speed is at least an order of magnitude faster than the file system. In addition, the capacity and bandwidth of memory can expand linearly with system scale from the view of the whole system. The major problem of takeing memory as checkpoint storage is its volatility. Note that in this paper we assume a fail-stop fault model, which means once an error occurs, the node stops responding and need to be replaced. Thus, we need a redundancy scheme to ensure that checkpoint data can be retrieved after the node failure. One common scheme is dual-redundancy (also called mirror scheme in some literatures), as illustrated in Fig. 1. Each node has a partner node, where its checkpoint data is stored redundantly.

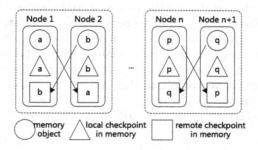

Fig. 1. Scheme of in-memory dual-redundancy checkpoint system

This dual-redundancy scheme demands that one node cannot fail simultaneously with its partner node, otherwise the checkpoint data will be lost. In practise, nodes are divided into groups and each node is assigned a partner node within the group. The strategy of node grouping is intuitive in existing checkpoint system, i.e., dividing nodes according to node's ID. Users can assign a hop distance so as to avoid adjacent nodes being allocated into the same group. Besides, a so-called XOR-scheme is another option, in which all nodes in a group collectively calculate a parity redundancy data according to their own checkpoints and then evenly distribute the parity redundancy data among all nodes in the group. Upon a node failure, other nodes in the group can recover the checkpoint according to their segments of the parity redundancy data. Compared with the dual-redundancy scheme, XOR-scheme demands less memory storage to save checkpoint data, while introducing extra computations. The XOR-scheme can withstand node failures as long as two or more nodes from the same group do not fail simultaneously.

We can see that in-memory checkpoint system is sensitive to simultaneous failures within a group. As a result, it is often taken as a complement of the global checkpoint system. That is, upon the failures that in-memory checkpoint system cannot withstand, the global checkpoint system is invoked. Notice that global checkpoint system is high-cost and thus the overall fault tolerance overhead can be reduced if we can lower the probability of simultaneous node failure within a group. This is also the object of the node allocation model we propose in this paper.

3   Node Allocation Model

3.1   Assumptions and Errors

Due to the complexity of organization structure, the fault model of high performance computing system can be very complicated, thus requiring some assumptions and simplifications when modeling the fault-tolerant system. We believe that these assumptions can cover the majority of actual situations.

- First, we assume errors follow a fail-stop model. Upon a node crash, all data on that node are supposed to be lost and we have to migrate its working state to a new node. The crashed node can be allocated again after repaired.
- We assume node failures are completely independent. In other words, a node failure does not increase or decrease the failure probability of other nodes.
- We assume that all kinds of failures have constant probabilities, including single node failure, power supply module failure, fan system failure, air condition system failure and water cooling system failure. We assume that these probabilities do not vary by time or utilization frequency.

3.2   Probability Function

As mentioned in Sect. 2, the uppermost reason that in-memory checkpoint system fails is simultaneous node failure within the same group, and the probability of that is closely related to the scheme of node grouping in a given system. So, we first calculate the simultaneous failure probability of any two given nodes before we propose the node group model in next section.

We take TianHe-2 high performance system as platform in this paper, which has a typical hierarchy architecture of large-scale parallel computing system.

As shown in Fig. 2, two nodes are integrated on a mainboard and share a power supply module. Several mainboards, then form a chassis, which is equipped with a standalone fan system. Each cabinet consists of several chassis and has its own air condition system. Finally, a row of cabinets share a water cooling system. In such a hierarchy architecture, different node grouping schemes will result in different probability of simultaneous node failure within the same group.

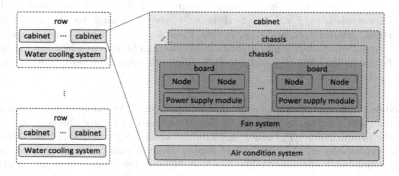

Fig. 2. Organization structure of TianHe-2

Below, we will discuss in detail the probability function of simultaneous failure of node i and j (denoted as P_i^j). The probability can be calculated according to the coordinates of the two nodes involved. We take the ratios of five kinds of failures into account when calculating the probability: single node failure, power supply failure, fan failure, air condition failure and water cooling system failure.

Single node failure ratio P_n is commonly considered as the reciprocal of the mean time between failure of node $MTBF_n$:

$$P_n = \frac{1}{MTBF_n}.$$

In the same way, the probability of power supply module failure P_m is equal to the reciprocal of the mean time between failure of power supply module $MTBF_m$:

$$P_m = \frac{1}{MTBF_m}.$$

As mentioned above, nodes on the same board share a single power supply module. In other words, the failure of the power supply module will directly result in the failure of all nodes on that board. Thus, without regard to other factors, the probability of two simultaneous node failures (on the same board) caused by power supply module failure is equal to P_m. Similarly, nodes within the same chassis share a unique fan system and will fail together due to the high temperature if the fan system stops working. Consequently, the probability of two simultaneous node failures (in the same chassis) caused by fan system failure is equal to the probability of fan failure P_f, which is equal to the reciprocal of the mean time between failure of fan $MTBF_f$:

$$P_f = \frac{1}{MTBF_f}.$$

For nodes within the same cabinet (sharing a unique air condition system) and the same row (sharing a unique water cooling system), the probabilities of two simultaneous failures caused by the air condition cooling system (P_c) and water cooling system (P_l) failures are the mean time between failure of each cooling system:

$$P_c = \frac{1}{MTBF_c}, \quad P_l = \frac{1}{MTBF_l}.$$

Now we consider the simultaneous failure probability of any two nodes i and j. Let symbol $m/f/c/l$ be 1 if node i and j belong to the same mainboard/chassis/cabinet/row, and 0 otherwise. First we only consider the factor of node failure. As mentioned above, all failures are assumed to be independent. So the simultaneous failure probability of i and j is P_n^2. To simplify the representation, we denote it as $P_i^j|_n$, that is,

$$P_i^j|_n = P_n^2.$$

Based on $P_i^j|_n$, we further take the power supply module into account. When i and j are on the same mainboard ($m = 1$), the simultaneous failure probability is the sum of P_m and the product of $1 - P_m$ and $P_i^j|_n$. That is because both nodes will fail definitely (with the probability of 1) if the power supply module fails (with the probability of P_m); otherwise (with the probability $1 - P_m$), the simultaneous failure probability is $P_i^j|_n$. When i and j are on different mainboards ($m = 0$), however, their failure are independent and the probability is the product of each one's failure probability, which is $P_m + (1 - P_m)P_n$. We denote the probability of single node failure considering node failure and power supply module failure as P_{nm}. Consequently, the simultaneous failure probability of i and j with node failure and power supply module failure considered (denoted as $P_i^j|_{nm}$) is

$$P_i^j|_{nm} = \begin{cases} P_m + (1 - P_m)P_i^j|_n, m = 1 \\ P_{nm}^2, \quad otherwise \end{cases}$$

In the same way, we take the fan system failure into account based on the equation above. When i and j are in the same chassis ($f = 1$), the simultaneous failure probability is the sum of P_f and the product of $1 - P_f$ and $P_i^j|_{nm}$, and otherwise ($f = 0$) is the product of each one's failure probability considering node failure, power supply module failure and fan system failure. We denote the latter one as P_{nmf}, which can be calculated as

$$P_{nmf} = P_f + (1 - P_f)P_{nm}.$$

So, we have

$$P_i^j|_{nmf} = \begin{cases} P_f + (1 - P_f)P_i^j|_{nm}, f = 1 \\ P_{nmf}^2, \quad otherwise \end{cases}$$

After all factors are involved, we can get the final probability equation as follows:

$$P_i^j|_{nmfcl} = \begin{cases} P_l + (1 - P_l)P_i^j|_{nmfc}, l = 1 \\ P_{nmfcl}^2, \quad otherwise \end{cases} \qquad (1)$$

We can see that Eq. 1 is a recursion function and can be easily extended to a failure model with more organization hierarchies. Generally, for an S-level model, the simultaneous failure probability of i and j considering all S kinds of failures (denoted as $P_i^j|_{1\sim S}$) is

$$P_i^j|_{1\sim S} = \begin{cases} P_S + (1 - P_S)P_i^j|_{1\sim(S-1)}, T_S = 1 \\ P_{1\sim S}^2, \quad otherwise \end{cases}$$

where T_S represents whether the two nodes are in the same set at level S and $P_{1 \sim S} = P_S + (1 - P_S) P_{1 \sim (S-1)}$. $P_i^j |_{1 \sim 1}$ means the probability of simultaneous failure considering the factor of level 1 failure (node failure) only, which is P_1^2. Given P_k and T_k ($1 \leq k \leq S$), we can get the simultaneous failure probability of any two nodes.

3.3 Model Overview

Based on the probability function, we propose a node allocation model, to find the optimal node grouping scheme for a given node set, a given probability function and a given group size, so that the probability of simultaneous node failure within the same group is minimal.

In the paper, we abstract the allocation model as a weighted undirected graph, where vertices represent the computer nodes and the weight on the edge indicates the probability that the two connected nodes fail simultaneously. Figure 3 shows a partial view of a basic model with 3 individual computing nodes 1,2 and 3. The position of Node in the system is denoted by its coordinate x_i, y_i, z_i, k_i. The value P on the edge is the weight.

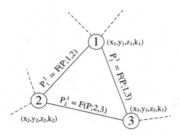

Fig. 3. A weighted undirected graph

It should be explained that (x_i, y_i, z_i, k_i) indicates the specific position of node i in the system, where x_i, y_i, z_i and k_i denote the number of board, the number of chassis, the number of cabinet and the number of row where node i is located in respectively.

Consequently, we abstract the node allocation model as a graph problem. For a given system, we use a graph to represent any given set of nodes. According to the probability function proposed above, the weight of each edge in the graph can be calculated. Then, the problem is to find a graph partition scheme with a given group size so that the probability of system failure due to two simultaneous node failures in a group is minimal. In the next section, we propose a novel algorithm to solve this problem.

4 Node Allocation Algorithm Based on Clique

SCR uses hop algorithm to divide compute nodes to groups, and hops are generally selected to be 1 in many systems. Our model, however, transfers the compute nodes into a weighted undirected graph, and tries to find an optimal combination checkpoint sets of nodes with the minimal weight. Given the positions of nodes, we can use Eq. 1 to calculate the simultaneous failure probability of every two nodes in the node set.

Table 1. Probabilities of simultaneous failure

Node	1	2	3	4	5	6
1	-	0.18	0.1	0.18	0.18	0.18
2	0.18	-	0.85	0.18	0.1	0.1
3	0.1	0.85	-	0.1	0.1	0.36
4	0.18	0.18	0.1	-	0.1	0.25
5	0.18	0.1	0.1	0.1	-	0.85
6	0.18	0.1	0.36	0.25	0.85	-

For instance, we assume a task that occupies 6 compute nodes: {1,2,3,4,5,6}, and the simultaneous failure probabilities are listed in Table 1:

As shown in Fig. 4, these nodes can be transferred into a complete weighted undirected graph, where the weight of edge denotes the simultaneous failure probability of these two nodes.

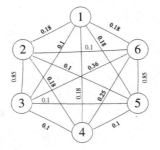

Fig. 4. A complete weighted undirected graph.

Consider a weighted undirected graph $G = (N, E, W)$, where N is a set of nodes $\{n_1, n_2, ..., n_n\}$, and E and W are the edge and weight sets respectively, we have:

Definition 1. *Given a node n in G, the number of its neighbor nodes is called the degree of n.*

Definition 2. *Given a graph G, a subset of N is called a clique if every two nodes in the subset are connected by an edge in G.*

The problem is then attributed to find a clique partition of the graph with specified size, so as to minimize the probability of system failure due to two simultaneous node failures in a clique.

Algorithm 1 shows the pseudo-code of a basic algorithm for node allocation. The algorithm based on clique(*CB algorithm* for short) finds all cliques of specified size in a set of compute nodes N. Given a set N, clique size s and the probability function of simultaneous failure P, the algorithm will find a clique sets $C : \{C_1, C_2, C_3, ..., C_n\}$. In line 5, the function $BuildProbMatrix(N, P)$ calculates the simultaneous failure probability of every two nodes in N based on function P (i.e., Formula 1). The function *AddEdges* in line 12 adds new edges with minimal weight for nodes in the latest graph G. Note that there may be multiple edges added at one time since they have the same weight. We start with minimal weight edges to make the weight of clique as small as possible. Lines 13–24 search all cliques in the current graph. We travel the node set N in ascending order of node degree since node with small degree has less opportunity to form cliques with other nodes, so as to get as more cliques with minimal weight as possible.

Algorithm 1. Find all cliques

Input: nodes set N, clique size s, probability function P
Output: clique set C

1. $C \leftarrow \emptyset$
2. $G \leftarrow \{N, \emptyset, \emptyset\}$
3. $W \leftarrow BuildProbMatrix(N, P)$
4. *while* $N \neq \emptyset$ *do*
5.   *if* $(\#N) \leq s$ *then*
6. $c \leftarrow N$
7. $C \leftarrow C + \{c\}$
8.   *return* C
9.   *end if*
10. $G \leftarrow AddEdges(G, W)$ // *edges with minimal weight for nodes in current* G
11. $N' \leftarrow N$
12.   *while* $N' \neq \emptyset$ *do*
13.   Let $v \in N'$ be the node with minimal degree in current G
14. $c \leftarrow FindAClique(G, v, s)$
15.   *if* $c \neq \emptyset$ *then*
16. $C \leftarrow C + \{c\}$
17. $N \leftarrow N - c$ // *also remove all edges connected to c in G*
18. $N' \leftarrow N' - c$
19.   *else*
20. $N' \leftarrow N' - \{v\}$
21.   *end if*
22.   *end while*
23. *end while*
24. *return* C

The function *FindAClique* in line 16 is used to find a clique that contains node v with size s in graph G. It uses a basic branch-and-bound algorithm to search for a clique. Once a clique is found, we add it into the clique set C (line 18), remove the nodes from original graph G (line 19), and also remove all edges connected to these nodes. After the while-loop finishes (line 24), all possible cliques are generated and removed from the current graph. Then some new edges with minimal weight should be added and the search is redone until the graph is empty. Note that if the number of nodes in current graph is no more than s, i.e., the clique size, we directly output it as the last clique and quit (lines 7–11). This works for the situations that the number of nodes is not divisible by s.

For the instance with 6 compute nodes given in Fig. 4, traditional hop algorithm will divide them into two groups: $\{1, 2, 3\}$ and $\{4, 5, 6\}$ (assume that hop distance is 1 and group size is 3). Based on the probabilities in Table 1, the failure probability of the system will be 0.9888.

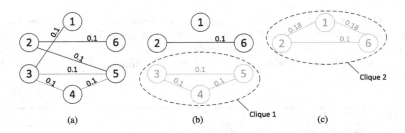

Fig. 5. An example of the algorithm.

The CB algorithm, however, tries to find all cliques of size 3 with minimal weight. First, all edges with weight 0.1 are added to the graph, as shown in Fig. 5(a), and we travel the graph in the order $1 \rightarrow 6 \rightarrow 2 \rightarrow 4 \rightarrow 3 \rightarrow 5$ according to the node degree. The function *FindAClique* will find the first clique ($\{3, 4, 5\}$) when $v = 4$. Then, the clique and all related edges are removed, as shown in Fig. 5(b). New edges with weight 0.18 are added after that because no more clique of size 3 can be found in the left graph. Actually, in this example, ($\{1, 2, 6\}$) can be directly denoted as a clique without search since the number of left nodes is 3, which is equal to the clique size. The failure probability of whole system in this solution is 0.5588, which is only 56.51 % of that in the hop algorithm.

As mentioned before, the "short-plate" of in-memory checkpoint system is probability of failure of any two nodes from the same group. The CB algorithm takes probabilistic model as a guide, initiatively avoids the allocation of checkpoint set with high simultaneous failure probability, and makes each "short-plate" as long as possible. Consequently, it reduces the frequency of using file system checkpoints, which means the cost of fault tolerance will be decreased.

5   Experimental Results

We have compared the performance of our algorithm with hop algorithms from the state-of-the-art fault-tolerant library. In practice, the execution time of application could be very long (up to days or months), and the overhead of grouping algorithm is negligible; so we only compare the probability of simultaneous failure, in which case the in-memory checkpoint system cannot recover the execution and higher level fault-tolerant system with much higher cost has to be involved.

Table 2 lists the probabilities of simultaneous failure of our algorithm and hop algorithm. P_{CB} represents the probability of our clique algorithm, P_{HOP} represents the best result of the hop algorithm, and *ratio* represents the difference between them. As mentioned in Sect. 3.2, the system has a total of 16,000 nodes, and we choose a random subset of nodes in this experiment. It can be seen obviously in Table 2 that clique allocation algorithm is very efficient when the size of XOR set is small, especially with size of 2. The ratio between the two algorithms becomes smaller as the size of XOR set increases, and the solutions of two algorithms will become identical when the size is equal to (or larger than) the number of computing nodes. This tendency is more clearly illustrated in Fig. 6.

To be more clear, Fig. 7 gives the simultaneous failure probabilities of two algorithms when #Node is 2048. We can see from the figure that the probability of the

Table 2. Probabilities of simultaneous failure with different node numbers and group sizes

#Node	$Size_{XOR}=2$			$Size_{XOR}=4$			$Size_{XOR}=8$			$Size_{XOR}=16$		
	P_{CB}	P_{HOP}	ratio	P_{CB}	P_{HOP}	ratio	P_{CB}	P_{HOP}	ratio	P_{CB}	P_{HOP}	Ratio
64	1E-09	0.00031	114959	3.97E-05	0.00113	67.87	0.00034	0.00296	13.50	0.00465	0.00684	1.52
128	1E-08	0.00090	167483	3.19E-05	0.00245	88.53	0.00032	0.00589	18.90	0.00595	0.01295	2.27
256	1E-08	0.00170	145818	6.64E-05	0.00526	117.40	0.00059	0.01204	20.30	0.00912	0.02551	2.90
512	2E-08	0.00327	139793	0.00015	0.00981	148.50	0.00120	0.02288	19.10	0.01211	0.04923	4.21
1024	5E-08	0.00668	145621	0.00017	0.02010	207.60	0.00242	0.04596	19.10	0.02112	0.09744	4.81
2048	9E-08	0.01401	152651	0.00016	0.04020	411.70	0.00480	0.09059	18.90	0.03186	0.18509	6.06
4096	1.8E-07	0.00730	39570	0.00040	0.03976	287.50	0.00962	0.13239	13.80	0.04554	0.30447	6.73
8192	3.7E-07	0.01442	39092	0.00025	0.03938	154.50	0.01913	0.16271	8.51	0.07993	0.45199	5.65
16384	7.4E-07	0.12184	165302	0.00177	0.29667	167.20	0.03818	0.57240	15.00	0.71965	0.80620	1.12

#Node	$Size_{XOR}=32$			$Size_{XOR}=64$			$Size_{XOR}=128$			$Size_{XOR}=256$		
	P_{CB}	P_{HOP}	ratio	P_{CB}	P_{HOP}	ratio	P_{CB}	P_{HOP}	ratio	P_{CB}	P_{HOP}	Ratio
64	0.01114	0.01392	1.25	0.02705	0.02705	1.00	0.02705	0.02705	1.00	0.02705	0.02705	1.00
128	0.01989	0.02613	1.32	0.05203	0.05263	1.02	0.10208	0.10208	1.00	0.10208	0.10208	1.00
256	0.03645	0.05126	1.41	0.09059	0.10132	1.12	0.19173	0.19381	1.01	0.35117	0.35117	1.00
512	0.06925	0.10048	1.45	0.19105	0.19369	1.02	0.32208	0.34899	1.08	0.53657	0.57689	1.08
1024	0.13777	0.19352	1.41	0.30183	0.35450	1.18	0.56614	0.58503	1.03	0.74841	0.82544	1.10
2048	0.25198	0.34635	1.37	0.47044	0.58109	1.24	0.77218	0.82778	1.07	0.87476	0.97030	1.11
4096	0.43440	0.55524	1.28	0.67615	0.81967	1.21	0.87961	0.96930	1.10	0.89930	0.99908	1.11
8192	0.65864	0.77372	1.17	0.84162	0.96272	1.14	0.89956	0.99894	1.11	0.89999	0.99999	1.11
16384	0.86865	0.96454	1.11	0.89906	0.99890	1.11	0.89999	0.99999	1.11	0.90000	0.99999	1.11

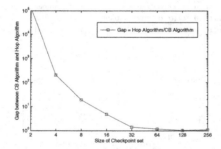

Fig. 6. Gap between two algorithms when #Node=1024.

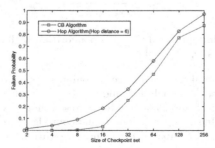

Fig. 7. Simultaneous failure probabilities of the two algorithms when #Node=2048.

simultaneous failure is always larger in hop algorithm than in our algorithm with all set sizes.

Tables 3 and 4 compare the simultaneous failure probabilities of two algorithms when $size_{XOR} = 3$ and $size_{XOR} = 4$ respectively, where we vary the hop distance in the hop algorithm within different ranges. The results show that the probability in the hop algorithm is not affected by the hop distance evidently. We can also see that our algorithm obtains much lower simultaneous failure probabilities than the hop algorithm in all cases. Figure 8 illustrates this result more clearly and intuitively.

Table 3. Probabilities of simultaneous failure with small hops in hop algorithm when $size_{XOR} = 3$.

#Node	P_{HOP}										P_{CB}
	hop=1	hop=2	hop=3	hop=4	hop=5	hop=6	hop=7	hop=8	hop=9	hop=10	
1000	0.01058	0.01574	0.01511	0.01430	0.01120	0.01414	0.01405	0.01167	0.01414	0.01272	**1.01E-05**
6000	0.13404	0.02085	0.02418	0.02445	0.02534	0.02562	0.02605	0.01772	0.01866	0.03975	**5.99E-07**
10000	0.31091	0.03400	0.03196	0.03063	0.03286	0.04901	0.07563	0.11029	0.10535	0.07420	**1.1E-05**
15000	0.54986	0.05346	0.05140	0.04826	0.04553	0.04403	0.04140	0.04100	0.04892	0.08605	**1.5E-06**

Table 4. Probabilities of simultaneous failure with large hops in hop algorithm when $size_{XOR} = 4$.

#Node	P_{HOP}										P_{CB}
	hop=1	hop=17	hop=33	hop=49	hop=65	hop=81	hop=97	hop=113	hop=121	hop=136	
1024	0.01853	0.02186	0.01971	0.02012	0.01971	0.02070	0.01971	0.01925	0.01981	0.01930	**0.00018**
2048	0.03534	0.04087	0.04171	0.04143	0.03893	0.04063	0.04042	0.04023	0.04054	0.04002	**0.00017**
8192	0.06354	0.04198	0.04047	0.04210	0.03984	0.03963	0.04264	0.03842	0.03951	0.03889	**0.00026**
16384	0.66958	0.15221	0.08228	0.33279	0.21335	0.38715	0.21852	0.28729	0.20119	0.33215	**0.00177**

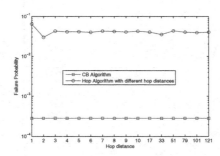

Fig. 8. Simultaneous failure probabilities of hop algorithm with different hop distances when #Node=8192 and $size_{XOR} = 4$.

Figure 9 shows the simultaneous failure probabilities with different hop distances and checkpoint set sizes. As concluded above, hop distance has little influence on probability in the hop algorithm. Those curves represent hop algorithm almost coincide in this figure. Also, the blue curve, which represents our algorithm, shows better results with all checkpoint set sizes compared to the hop algorithm.

Table 5 collects the times that our algorithm outperforms the hop algorithm in 1,000 random experiments. Since our algorithm is heuristic, the search result is not necessarily the optimum solution, and the hop algorithm gets chance to obtain better

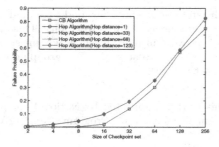

Fig. 9. Simultaneous failure probabilities of the two algorithms with different hop distances and $size_{XOR}$s when #Node=1024

result due to the randomness of the node set we choose. However, we can notice in the table that for most situations, our method can outperform the hop algorithm in all 1,000 random tests. We can also see that with a fixed checkpoint set size, the times that our method win decrease mildly when the number of nodes gets larger. That is because when almost all nodes in the system are involved, the topology of these nodes is also pretty much fixed, in which case, the hop algorithm can decrease simultaneous node failure probability easily by assigning a hop distance large enough.

Table 5. Times that our algorithm outperforms the hop algorithm in 1,000 random experiments.

#Node	$size_{XOR}$				#Node	$size_{XOR}$			
	2	4	64	256		3	5	65	257
512	1000	1000	1000	1000	500	1000	1000	1000	1000
1024	1000	1000	1000	999	1000	1000	1000	1000	1000
8192	1000	1000	998	992	10000	1000	1000	996	988
16384	1000	1000	990	978	15000	1000	1000	991	976

Experimental results above show that our clique-based algorithm is very efficient, especially for small size of checkpoint set. The probability of simultaneous node failure is far below the hop algorithms, which means we can greatly reduce the chance to invoke the high-cost global checkpoint system.

6 Conclusion and Future Work

We build a new node allocation model based on the architecture of TianHe-2 and propose a new algorithm to decrease the probability that in-memory checkpoint system cannot work. We calculate the probability of simultaneous failure of any two nodes, transfer it into a complete weighted undirected graph, use a heuristic algorithm to find clique in the graph, and then rationally divide the compute nodes into groups to decrease the in-group simultaneous failure probability. The experimental results performed based on the probability model abstracted from TianHe-2 show that, compared to the traditional node distribution scheme, our model can find near optimal combination of nodes with lower simultaneous failure probability. This also means that we can greatly reduce the cost of recovery in multi-level checkpoint system. In the future, we will take the communication cost into account when grouping the nodes based on the topology of the interconnect network.

Acknowledgment. This work is supported by National High Technology Research and Development Program of China (863 Program) No.2012AA01A301 and 2012A A01A309.

References

1. http://source-forge.net/projects/scalablecr/scalable-checkpoint/restart-library
2. http://www.netlib.org/utk/people/jackdongarra/papers/tianhe-2-dongarra-report.pdf
3. Daly, J.: A higher order estimate of the optimum checkpoint interval for restart dumps. Future Gener. Comput. Syst. **22**(3), 303–312 (2006)
4. Duda, A.: The effects of checkpointing on program execution time. Inf. Process. Lett. **16**(5), 221–229 (1983)
5. Vivek Sarkar, E.: Exascale software study: Software challenges in exascale systems (2009)
6. Glosli, J.N., Caspersen, K.J., Gunnels, J.A., Rudd, D.F.R.A.E., Streitz, F.H.: Extending stability beyond cpu millennium: a micron-scale atomistic simulation of kelvin-helmholtz instability. In: Proceedings of the 2007 ACM/IEEE Conference on Supercomputing (SC), pp. 1–11 (2007)
7. Iskra, K., Romein, J.W., Yoshii, K., Beckman, P.: Zoid: I/o-forwarding infrastructure for petascale architectures. In: PPoPP 2008: Proceedings of the 13th ACM SIGPLAN Symposium on Principles and Practice of Parallel Programming, pp. 153–162 (2008)
8. Michalak, S.E., Harris, K.W., Hengartner, N.W., Takala, B.E., Wender, S.A.: Predicting the number of fatal soft errors in los alamos national laboratory's ASC Q supercomputer. IEEE Trans. Device Mater. Reliab. **5**(3), 329–335 (2005)
9. Moody, A.: The scalable checkpoint/restart (scr) library, user manual version 1.1-6 (2010)
10. Moody, A., Bronevetsky, G., Mohror, K., de Supinski, B.R.: Design, modeling, and evaluation of a scalable multi-level checkpointing system. In: Proceedings of the International Conference for High Performance Computing, Networking, Storage and Analysis(SC), pp. 13–29, November 2010
11. Naksinehaboon, N., Liu, Y., Leangsuksun, C.B., Nassar, R., Paun, M., Scott, S.L.: Reliability-aware approach: an incremental checkpoint/restart model in hpc environments. In: Proceedings of the 2008 Eighth IEEE International Symposium on Cluster Computing and the Grid (CCGRID), pp. 783–788 (2008)
12. Plank, J.S., Thomason, M.G.: Processor allocation and checkpoint interval selection in cluster computing systems. J. Parallel Distrib. Comput. **61**(11), 1570–1590 (2001)
13. Ross, R., Moreira, J., Cupps, K., Pfeiffer, W.: Parallel i/o on the ibm blue gene/l system. Blue Gene/L Consortium Quarterly Newsletter. Technical report (2006)

14. Schroeder, B., Gibson, G.: Understanding failure in petascale computers. J. Phys. Conf. Series: SciDAC **78**, 012–022 (2007)
15. Schroeder, B., Gibson, G.A.: A large-scale study of failures in high-performance computing systems. In: Proceedings of the International Conference on Dependable Systems and Networks (DSN), pp. 249–258 (2006)
16. Young, J.W.: A first order approximation to the optimum checkpoint interval. Commun. ACM **17**(9), 530–531 (1974)

A Scalable Algorithm for Radiative Heat Transfer Using Reverse Monte Carlo Ray Tracing

Alan Humphrey[✉], Todd Harman, Martin Berzins, and Phillip Smith

University of Utah, Salt Lake City, USA
ahumphrey@sci.utah.edu

Abstract. Radiative heat transfer is an important mechanism in a class of challenging engineering and research problems. A direct all-to-all treatment of these problems is prohibitively expensive on large core counts due to pervasive all-to-all MPI communication. The massive heat transfer problem arising from the next generation of clean coal boilers being modeled by the Uintah framework has radiation as a dominant heat transfer mode. Reverse Monte Carlo ray tracing (RMCRT) can be used to solve for the radiative-flux divergence while accounting for the effects of participating media. The ray tracing approach used here replicates the geometry of the boiler on a multi-core node and then uses an all-to-all communication phase to distribute the results globally. The cost of this all-to-all is reduced by using an adaptive mesh approach in which a fine mesh is only used locally, and a coarse mesh is used elsewhere. A model for communication and computation complexity is used to predict performance of this new method. We show this model is consistent with observed results and demonstrate excellent strong scaling to 262 K cores on the DOE Titan system on problem sizes that were previously computationally intractable.

Keywords: Uintah · Radiation modeling · Parallel · Scalability · Adaptive mesh refinement · Simulation science · Titan

1 Introduction

Our study is motivated primarily by the target problem of the University of Utah Carbon Capture Multi-Disciplinary Simulation Center (CCMSC). This project aims to eventually simulate a 350 MWe clean coal boiler being developed by Alstom Power during the next five years, by using large parallel computers in a scalable manner for reacting, large eddy simulations (LES)-based codes within the Uintah open source framework, and to use accelerators at large scale.

Within the boiler, the hot combustion gases radiate energy to the boiler walls and to tubes carrying water and steam that is superheated to a supercritical fluid. This steam acts as the working fluid to drive the turbine for power generation. The residual energy in the mixture passes through a convective heat exchange system to extract as much of the remaining energy as possible into the working

© Springer International Publishing Switzerland 2015
J.M. Kunkel and T. Ludwig (Eds.): ISC High Performance 2015, LNCS 9137, pp. 212–230, 2015.
DOI: 10.1007/978-3-319-20119-1_16

fluid. This radiative flux depends on the radiative properties of the participating media and temperature. The mixture of particles and gases emits, absorbs and scatters radiation, the modeling of which is a key computational element in these simulations. The radiation calculation, in which the radiative-flux divergence at each cell of the discretized domain is calculated, can take up to 50 % of the overall CPU time per timestep using the discrete ordinates method (DOM), one of the standard approaches to computing radiative heat transfer. This method, which Uintah currently uses, is computationally expensive, involves multiple global, sparse linear solves and presents challenges both with the incorporation of radiation physics such as scattering and to the use of parallel computers at very large scales. Reverse Monte Carlo ray tracing (RMCRT), the focus of this work, is one of the few numerical techniques that can accurately solve for the radiative-flux divergence while accounting for the effects of participating media, naturally incorporates scattering physics, and lends itself to scalable parallelism. The principal challenges with our initial, single fine mesh (single-level) RMCRT approach are the all-to-all communication requirements and on-node memory constraints. To address these challenges, our study explores a multi-level, adaptive mesh refinement (AMR) approach in which a fine mesh is only used close to each grid point and a successively coarser mesh is used further away. The central question of our study will be to determine if our AMR approach can scale to large core counts on modern supercomputers, and if our communication and computation models can accurately predict how this approach to radiation scales on current, emerging and future architectures.

In what follows, Sect. 2 provides an overview of the Uintah software, while Sect. 3 describes our RMCRT model in detail and provides an overview of the key RMCRT approaches considered and used within Uintah. Section 4 details our model of communication and computation for our multi-level AMR approach. Section 5 provides strong scaling results over a wide range of core counts (up to 262 K cores) for this approach, and an overview of related work is given in Sect. 6. The paper concludes in Sect. 7 with future work in this area.

2   The Uintah Code

The Uintah open-source (MIT License) software has been widely ported and used for many different types of problems involving fluids, solids and fluid-structure interaction problems. The present status of Uintah, including applications, is described by [4]. The first documented full release of Uintah was in July 2009 and the latest in January 2015 [37]. Uintah consists of a set of parallel software components and libraries that facilitate the solution of partial differential equations on structured adaptive mesh refinement (AMR) grids. Uintah presently contains four main simulation components: (1.) the multi-material ICE [20] code for both low and high-speed compressible flows; (2.) the multi-material, particle-based code MPM for structural mechanics; (3.) the combined fluid-structure interaction (FSI) algorithm MPM-ICE [12] and (4.) the ARCHES turbulent reacting CFD component [19] that was designed for simulating turbulent reacting flows with participating media radiation. Uintah is highly scalable [6,24], runs on many National Science Foundation (NSF), Department of Energy (DOE) and Department of Defense (DOD) parallel computers (Stampede, Mira, Titan, Vulcan, Vesta, Garnet, Kilraine, etc.) and is also used by many NSF, DOE and DOD projects in areas such as angiogenesis, tissue engineering, green urban modeling, blast-wave simulation, semi-conductor design and multi-scale materials research [4].

Uintah is unique in its combination of the MPM-ICE fluid-structure-interaction solver, ARCHES heat transfer solver, AMR methods and directed acyclic graph (DAG)-based runtime system. Uintah is one of the few codes that uses a DAG approach as part of a production strength code in a way that is coupled to a runtime system. Uintah also provides automated, large-scale parallelism through a design that maintains a clear partition between applications code and its parallel infrastructure, making it possible to achieve great increases in scalability through changes to the runtime system that executes the taskgraph, *without changes to the taskgraph specifications themselves*. The combination of the broad applications class and separation of the applications problems from a highly scalable runtime system has enabled engineers and computer scientists to focus on what each does best, significantly lowering the entry barriers to those who want to compute a parallel solution to an engineering problem. Uintah is open source, freely available and is the only widely available MPM code. The broad international user-base and rigorous testing ensure that the code may be used on a broad class of applications.

Particular advances made in Uintah are scalable adaptive mesh refinement [25] coupled to challenging multiphysics problems [5]. A key factor in improving performance has been the reduction in MPI wait time through the dynamic and even out-of-order execution of task-graphs [29]. The need to reduce memory use in Uintah led to the adoption of a nodal shared memory model in which there is only one MPI process per multicore node, and execution on individual cores is through Pthreads [27]. This has made it possible to reduce memory use by a factor of 10 and to increase the scalability of Uintah to 768 K cores on complex fluid-structure interactions with adaptive mesh refinement. Uintah's thread-based runtime system [27,30] uses: decentralized execution [29] of the task-graph, implemented by each CPU core requesting work itself and performing its own MPI. A shared memory abstraction through Uintah's data warehouse hides message passing from the user but at the cost of multiple cores accessing the warehouse originally. A shared memory approach that is lock-free [30] was implemented by making use of atomic operations (supported by modern CPUs) and thus allows efficient access by all cores to the shared data on a node. Finally, the nodal architecture of Uintah has been extended to run tasks on one or more on-node accelerators [15]. This unified, heterogeneous runtime system [28] makes use of a multi-stage queue architecture (two sets of task queues) to organize work for CPU cores and accelerators in a dynamic way, and is the focus of current development.

2.1   The ARCHES Combustion Simulation Component

The radiation models in Uintah have previously been a part of the ARCHES component, which was designed for the simulation of turbulent reacting flows with participating media. ARCHES is a three-dimensional, large eddy simulation (LES) code that uses a low-Mach number variable density formulation to simulate heat, mass, and momentum transport in reacting flows. The LES algorithm solves the filtered, density-weighted, time-dependent coupled conservation equations for mass, momentum, energy, and particle moment equations in a Cartesian coordinate system [19]. This set of filtered equations is discretized in space and time and solved on a staggered, finite volume mesh. The staggering scheme consists of four offset grids, one for storing scalar quantities and three for each component of the velocity vector. Stability preserving, second order explicit time-stepping schemes and flux limiting schemes are used to ensure that scalar values remain bounded. ARCHES is second-order accurate in space and time and is highly scalable through Uintah and its coupled solvers like hypre [10] to 256 K cores [36]. Research using ARCHES has been done on radiative heat transfer using the parallel discrete ordinates method and the P1 approximation to the radiative transport equation [22]. Recent work has shown that RMCRT methods are potentially more efficient [17, 39].

3   RMCRT Model

Scalable modeling of radiation is currently one of the most challenging problems in large-scale simulations, due to the global, *all-to-all* nature of radiation [31]. To simulate thermal transport, two fundamental approaches exist: random walk simulations, and finite element/finite volume simulations, e.g., discrete ordinates method (DOM) [3], which involves solving many large systems of equations. Accurate radiative-heat transfer algorithms that handle complex physics are inherently computationally expensive [16], particularly when high-accuracy is desired in cases where spectral or geometric complexity is involved. They also have limitations with respect to scalability, bias and accuracy.

The Uintah ARCHES component is designed to solve the mass, momentum, mixture fraction, and thermal energy governing equations inherent to coupled turbulent reacting flows. ARCHES has relied primarily on a legacy DOM solver to compute the radiative source term in the energy equation [19]. Monte Carlo ray tracing (MCRT) methods for solving the radiative transport equation offer higher accuracy in two key areas where DOM suffers: geometric fidelity and spectral resolution. In applications where such high accuracy is important, MCRT can become more efficient than DOM approaches. In particular, MCRT can potentially reduce the cost significantly by taking advantage of modern hardware on large distributed shared memory machines [14], and now on distributed memory systems with on-node graphics processing unit (GPU) accelerators, using a prototype GPU implementation of the single-level RMCRT [15], written using NVidia CUDA.

3.1   Radiation and Ray Tracing Overview

The heat transfer problems arising from the clean coal boilers being modeled by the Uintah framework has thermal radiation as a dominant heat transfer mode and involves solving the conservation of energy equation and radiative heat transfer equation (RTE) simultaneously. Thermal radiation in the target boiler simulations is loosely coupled to the computational fluid dynamics (CFD) due to time-scale separation and is the rightmost source term in the conservation of energy equation shown by:

$$c_v \frac{DT}{Dt} = -\nabla \cdot (\kappa \nabla T) - p\nabla \cdot v + \Phi + Q''' - \nabla \cdot q_r \qquad (1)$$

where c_v is the specific heat, T is the temperature field, p is the pressure, k is the thermal conductivity, c is the velocity vector, Φ is the dissipation function, Q''' is the heat generated within the medium, e.g. chemical reaction, and $\nabla \cdot q_r$ is the net radiative source. The energy equation is then conventionally solved by ARCHES (finite volume) and the temperature field, T is used to compute net radiative source term. This net radiative source term is then fed back into energy equation (for the ongoing CFD calculation) which is solved to update the temperature field, T.

A radiatively participating medium can emit, absorb and scatter thermal radiation. The RTE (2) as shown in [41], is the equation describing the interaction of absorption, emission and scattering for radiative heat transfer and is an integro-differential equation with three spatial variables and two angles that determine the direction of $\hat{s}$ [41].

$$\begin{aligned} \frac{dI_\eta(\hat{s})}{ds} &= \hat{s}\nabla I_{\eta(\hat{s})} \\ &= k_\eta I_\eta - \beta_\eta I_\eta(\hat{s}) \\ &+ \frac{\sigma_{s\eta}}{4\pi} \int_{4\pi} I_\eta(\hat{s})\Phi_\eta(\hat{s}_i, \hat{s})d\Omega_i, \end{aligned} \qquad (2)$$

In (2), k_η is the absorption coefficient, $\sigma_{s\eta}$ is the scattering coefficient (dependent on the incoming direction s and wave number η), β_η is the extinction coefficient that describes total loss in radiative intensity, I_η is the change in intensity of incoming radiation from point s to point $s + ds$ and is determined by summing the contributions from emission, absorption and scattering from direction $\hat{s}$ and scattering into the same direction $\hat{s}$ at wave number η. $\Phi_\eta(\hat{s}_i, \hat{s})$ is the phase function that describes the probability that a ray coming from direction s_i will scatter into direction $\hat{s}$ and integration is performed over the entire solid angle Ω_i [32,41].

DOM, MCRT and RMCRT all aim to approximate the radiative transfer equation. In the case of RMCRT, a statistically significant number of rays (photon bundles) are traced from a computational cell to the point of extinction. This method is then able to calculate energy gains and losses for every element in the computational domain. The process is considered "reverse" through the

Helmholtz Reciprocity Principle, e.g. incoming and outgoing intensity can be considered as reversals of each other [13]. Through this process, the divergence of the heat flux for every sub-volume in the domain (and radiative heat flux for surfaces, e.g., boiler walls) is computed by Eq. 3, as rays accumulate and attenuate intensity (measured in watts per square meter, SI units based on the StefanBoltzmann constant) according to the RTE for an absorbing, emitting and scattering medium.

$$\nabla \cdot q \ = \ \kappa(4\pi I_{emmited} - \int_{4\pi} I_{absorbed}\mathrm{d}\Omega), \tag{3}$$

where the rightmost term, $\int_{4\pi} I_{absorbed}\mathrm{d}\Omega$ is represented by the sum $\sum_{r=1}^{N} I_r \frac{4\pi}{N}$ for each ray r up to N rays. The integration is performed over the entire solid angle Ω. Ray origins are randomly distributed throughout a given computational cell. In our implementation, the Mersenne Twister random number generator [26] is used to generate ray origins. The ray marching algorithm proceeds in a similar fashion to that shown by [1].

Within the Uintah RMCRT module, rays are traced backwards from the detector, thus eliminating the need to track ray bundles that never reach the detector [32]. Rather than integrating the energy lost as a ray traverses the domain,

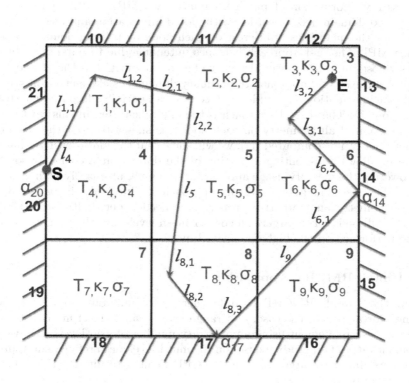

Fig. 1. 2D Outline of reverse Monte Carlo ray tracing [15]

RMCRT integrates the incoming intensity absorbed at the origin, where the ray was emitted. RMCRT is more amenable to domain decomposition, and thus Uintah's parallelization scheme due to the backward nature of the process [38], and the mutual exclusivity of the rays themselves. Figure 1 shows the back path of a ray from **S** to the emitter **E**, on a nine cell structured mesh patch. Each ith cell has its own temperature T_i, absorption coefficient κ_i, scattering coefficient σ_i and appropriate pathlengths $l_{i,j}$ [15]. In each case the incoming intensity is calculated in each cell and then traced back through the other cells. The Uintah RMCRT module computes how much of the outgoing intensity has been attenuated along the path. When a ray hits a boundary, as on surface 17 in Fig. 1, the incoming intensities will be partially absorbed by the surface. When a ray hits a hot boundary surface, its emitted surface intensity contributes back to point **S**. Rays are terminated when their intensity is sufficiently small [15].

RMCRT uses rays more efficiently than forward MCRT, but it is still an *all-to-all* method, for which all of the geometric information and radiative properties (temperature T, absorption coefficient κ, and cellType (boundary or flow cell)) for the entire computational domain must be accessible by every ray [38]. When using a ray tracing approach (forward or backward), two approaches for parallelizing the computation are considered when using structured grids, 1.) parallelize by patch-based domain decomposition with local information only and pass ray information at patch boundaries via MPI, and 2.) parallelize by patch-based domain decomposition with global information and reconstruct the domain for the quantities of interest on each node by passing domain information via MPI. The first approach becomes untenable due to potentially billions of rays whose information would need to be communicated as they traverse the domain. In the second approach the primary difficulty is efficiently constructing the global information for millions of cells in a spatially decomposed (patch-based) domain. The second approach is the one taken used in this work. While reconstruction of all geometry on each node has shown to limit the size of the problem that can be computed [17], we will show that the multi-level mechanisms in Uintah allows representing a portion of the domain at a coarser resolution, thus lowering the memory usage and message volume, ultimately scaling to over 256 K CPU cores. The hybrid memory approach of Uintah also helps as only one copy of geometry and radiative properties is needed per multi-core node [30]. RMCRT will be invoked largely on coarser mesh levels and the CFD calculation will be performed on the highest resolved mesh.

3.2   Uintah RMCRT Approaches

Within the Uintah RMCRT module there are numerous approaches, each designed for a specific use case, and range from a single-level method to a full adaptive mesh refinement using an arbitrary number of grid levels with varying refinement ratios. Our study focuses on the multi-level mesh refinement approach and its scalability to large core counts. CPU Scaling results for this approach are shown in Sect. 5.

Single-Level RMCRT: The single level RMCRT approach was initially implemented as a proof-of-concept to begin comparisons against the legacy DOM solver within the Uintah ARCHES component. This approach focused on the benchmark problem described by Burns and Christen in [9]. In this approach, the quantity of interest, the divergence of the heat flux, ∇q is calculated for every cell in the computational domain. The entire domain is replicated on every node (with all-to-all communication) for the following quantities; κ, the absorption coefficient, a property of the medium the ray is traveling through, σT^4, a physical constant σ· temperature field, T^4 and, *cellType*, a property of each computational cell in the domain to determine if along a given path, a ray will reflect or stop on a given computational cell. These three properties are represented by 1 double, 1 double and 1 integer value respectively.

For N_{total} mesh cells, the amount of data communicated is $\mathcal{O}(N^2)$. While accurate and effective at lower core counts, the volume of communication in this case overwhelms the system for large problems in our experience. Calculations on domains up to 512^3 cells are possible on machines with at least 2 GB RAM per core and only when using Uintah's multi-threaded runtime system, described in Sect. 2. Strong scaling breakdown for the single-level approach occurs around 8-10 K CPU cores for a 384^3 domain. Currently, Uintah has a production-grade GPU implementation of this single-level approach that delivers a 4-6X speedup[1] in mean time per timestep for this benchmark with a domain size of 128^3 cells. The work done to achieve accelerator task scheduling and execution is detailed in [15]. Initial scalability and accuracy studies of the single-level RMCRT algorithm are also shown in [17] which examines the accuracy of the computed divergence of the heat flux as compared to published data and reveals expected Monte-Carlo convergence.

Multi-level Adaptive Mesh Refinement: In this adaptive meshing approach, a fine mesh is used locally and only coarser representations of the entire domain are replicated on every node (with all-to-all communication) for the radiative properties, T, κ *cellType*. The fine level consists of a collection of patches where each patch is considered a region of interest and individually processed using a local fine mesh and underlying global coarse mesh data. Figure 2 illustrates a three-level mesh coarsening scheme and how a ray might traverse this multi-level domain. Surrounding a patch is a halo region which effectively increases the size (at the finest resolution) of each patch in each direction, x, y and z. This distance is user specified. An arbitrary number of successively coarser levels (received by each node during the all-to-all communication phase) reside beneath the fine level for the rays to travel across once they have left the fine level. Each ray first traverses a fine level patch until it moves beyond the boundary and surrounding halo of this fine-level patch. At this point, the ray moves to a coarser level. Once outside this coarse level, the ray moves again to a coarser level. The rays move from level to level, similar to stair stepping, until the coarsest level is reached. Once on the coarsest level, a ray cannot move to a finer level. The key goal of this approach is to achieve a reduction in both

---

[1] 1-NVIDIA K20 GPU vs. 16-Intel Xeon E5-2660 CPU cores @2.20 GHz.

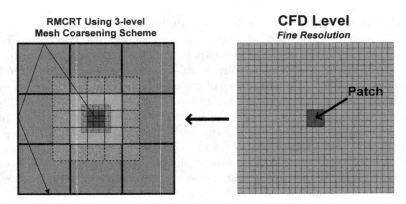

Fig. 2. RMCRT - 2D diagram of three-level mesh refinement scheme, illustrating how a ray from a fine-level patch (right) might be traced across a coarsened domain (left).

communication and computation costs as well as memory usage. This approach is fundamental to our target problem, the 350 MWe boiler predictive case where the entire computational domain needs to be resolved to adequately model the radiative heat flux.

Initial scalability results on a two-level methane jet problem are shown in [31]. This problem was run on the the DOE Titan, Mira and NSF Stampede systems with 10 rays per cell, two grid levels, a refinement ratio of four and a problem size of 256^3 cells on the highest resolved mesh. These results provided an excellent starting point by showing scaling to 16 K CPU cores. Scaling results beyond 16 K cores at the time was not possible due to algorithmic issues, which were ultimately resolved in this work and are detailed in Sect. 5.

4   Complexity Model

In this section we generalize the somewhat simplistic analysis given in [31] (as suggested there) of the two-level scheme of [17] to a detailed discussion of both the computational and communications costs of a multiple mesh level approach. Initially our approach involves replicating the geometry of the target problem and constructing an adaptive mesh for the radiation calculations. The adaptive mesh used by the radiation calculation may be constructed directly from the efficient mesh data structure used to describe the whole mesh. This is a one-time procedure and so is not analyzed further here.

We suppose that on N_{nodes}^3 compute nodes there is a global fine mesh of n_{mesh}^3 cells in n_{patch}^3 mesh patches. Define $n_{local} = n_{mesh}/N_{nodes}$, and defines $n_{plocal} = n_{patch}/N_{nodes}$ so that each node has n_{local}^3 fine mesh cells in n_{plocal}^3 patches. In the ray tracing algorithm, each compute node then has to compute the heat fluxes, ∇q on its local mesh by ray tracing **and** to export the temperatures T and and the absorption coefficient κ on the original mesh to neighbouring "halo" nodes, or in a coarsened form (possibly at multiple levels) to other nodes.

Finally the coarsest mesh representations are distributed to all the other nodes. The amount of information per cell transmitted is two doubles $\kappa, \sigma T^4$ and one integer, *cell_type*.

To assess the complexity of RMCRT on a fixed fine mesh, computational experiments to measure the per cell and per ray cost of the RMCRT:CPU implementation were conducted on a single CPU with a single-level grid. Ray scattering and reflections were not included in these experiments. In both experiments the absorption coefficient was initialized according to the benchmark of Burns & Christen [9] with a uniform temperature field. A grid with a single patch and 1 MPI process was used, thus eliminated any communication costs. The grid resolution varied from $16^3, 32^3, 64^3$ to 128^3 cells with each cell using emitting 25 rays. The mean time per timestep (MTPTS) was computed using 7 timesteps. The code was instrumented to sum the number of cells traversed during the computation and it was shown that $MTPTS = (n_{mesh}^3)^{1.4}$. In the second experiment the number of grid cells in the domain was fixed at 41^3 and the number of rays, n_{ray} per cell varied. The MTPTS was computed over 47 timesteps. Here it was shown that the MTPTS varies linearly with the number of rays per cell. Based on these experiments, the cost for a single patch, without any communication, is approximately given by

$$T_{rmcrt}^{global} = C^* n_{rays} n_{mesh}^3{}^{4/3}, \tag{4}$$

where C^* is a constant. This result may be interpreted as saying that the rays from each of the n_{mesh}^3 cells travel a distance of n_{mesh} cells on average. In the case of a fine mesh on a node and a coarse representation of the rest of the mesh.

$$T_{rmcrt}^{local} = C^* n_{rays} \left[n_{local}^3{}^{4/3} + (n_{mesh}2^{-m})^3)^{4/3} \right] \tag{5}$$

where 2^m is the refinement ratio used to obtain the coarse mesh. It is possible to extend this analysis to more mesh refinement levels.

Communications Costs: The main step with regard to communication is to update the temperatures T and and the absorption coefficients κ every timestep. On a uniform fine mesh this is done by each node sending out the values of these quantities to all the other compute nodes, and in a multiple mesh level approach this is done by each node sending out the values of these quantities on the coarse mesh and fine mesh values locally.

Fine Mesh Global Communications: Each node has to transmit $(N_{nodes}^3 - 1)$ messages of size $(n_{local})^3 \cdot 3$. This is currently done by a series of asynchronous sends but could be done with an MPI_Allgather. This has a complexity of $\alpha 3log(N_{nodes}) + \beta \frac{N_{nodes}^3 - 1}{N_{nodes}^3}(n_{local})^3$ for N_{nodes}^3 nodes with n_{local}^3 elements per mesh patch, where α is the latency and β is the transmission cost per element [40]. This result applies for both the recursive doubling and Bruck algorithms [40]. Other recursive doubling algorithms result in a complexity of $\alpha 3log(N_{nodes}) + \beta(N_{nodes}^3 - 1)(n_{local})^3$, so the cost may be dependent on the MPI implementation used.

Coarse Mesh All-to-All: In the case of using a coarse mesh in which the mesh is refined by a factor of 2^m in each dimension, each node has to transmit $(N_{nodes}^3 - 1)$ messages of size $(n_{local}2^{-m})^3 * 3$. Thus reducing the communications volume, but not the number of messages, by a factor of 2^{3m} overall.

Multi-level Adaptive Mesh Refinement: This approach considers each fine level patch (individually) in the domain as a region of interest (ROI) and for each fine level patch, the highest resolved CFD mesh is used. Figure 2 illustrates one patch being such a region of interest. In the case of a region of interest consisting of P_{int} patches, the compute node must transmit the fine mesh information to all the local nodes close to the ROI. In this context let L_i be the nodes that are i levels of nodes removed from node containing the region of interest. There will then be 26 level-1 nodes and 98 level-2 nodes. Of course at the edges of a spatial simulation domain or in the case of a small domain of interest each node will only have to communicate fine mesh values of $\kappa, \sigma T^4$ to a fraction of the nodes. In this case let $L_{active}^{i,j}$ be the number of active nodes (halo-level nodes) at level j, where $j < N_{levels}$, active for the ith level of interest, where active nodes are the local halos from the fine mesh. Furthermore let the refinement factor be $\frac{1}{2^{m(i,j)}}$ active at this level. Then the fine mesh communication associated with this region of interest is given by

$$Com_{fhalo} = \sum_{j=1}^{N_{levels}} L_{active}^{i,j}(\alpha + \beta(n_{local}2^{-m(i,j)})^3 * 3) \qquad (6)$$

This means that the ratio of communications to computations R_{atio} is now be given as:

$$R_{atio} = \frac{((N_{nodes}^3 - 1))(\alpha + \beta(n_{local}2^{-m})^3 * 3) + Com_{fhalo}}{T_{rmcrt}^{local}}, \qquad (7)$$

where α and β are defined above and scaled by the cost of a FLOP. Overall this expression allows us to analyze the relationship between computation and communications.

Strong scaling of RMCRT does not change the overall volume of data communicated. Increasing the number of N_{nodes} by a factor of two simply reduces n_{local} by two. This does mean that the number of messages increases even with the total communications value being constant. Moving to MPI_Allgather also has the same issue but the factor of $3logN_{nodes}$ also increased by adding 3. Thus for enough rays n_{rays} with enough refinement by a factor of 2^m on the coarse radiation mesh, the computation will likely dominate. A key challenge is that storage of $O(n_{mesh}2^{-m})^3)$ is required on a multicore node and that an AMR mesh representation is needed at very large core counts. Some aspects of this analysis are not dissimilar to earlier work by one of us on PDE solvers with global coarse mesh operations [11] using algorithms related to those of [8]. The results of this analysis will make it possible to prioritize subsequent serial and parallel performance tuning and and also perhaps to make projections regarding performance on forthcoming petascale and exascale architectures.

5   Scaling Studies

In this section, we show strong scalability results on the DOE Titan XK7[2] system for the Burns and Christen [9] benchmark problem using the multi-level mesh refinement approach. We define strong scaling as a decrease in execution time when a fixed size problem is solved on more cores. This work focuses on using all CPU cores available on Titan. Subsequent work will focus on additionally using all of Titan's GPUs in addition to its CPUs, following our prototype work on a single mesh in [15, 31].

The scaling challenges faced in this work have only become apparent by running this challenging problem at such high core counts, stressing areas of infrastructure code in ways never before seen, specifically Uintah's task-graph compilation phase. With Uintah's directed acyclic graph (DAG)-based design [31], during an initial simulation timestep, the initial timestep of a restart, or when the grid layout or its partition changes, a new task graph needs be to created and compiled. Task-graph compilation is a complex operation with multiple phases, including creation and scheduling of tasks themselves on local and neighboring patches (for halo exchange), keeping a history of what these tasks require and compute, setting up connections between tasks (edges in the DAG), and finally assigning MPI message tags to dependencies.

As the RMCRT ray trace task requests ghost cells across the entire domain (a global halo) for ray marching, Uintah's task-graph compilation algorithm was overcompensating when constructing lists of neighboring patches for local halo exchange. The cost of this operation grew despite the number of patches per node remaining constant, resulting in task-graph compilation times of over four hours at 32 K cores with 32,000 total patches. This necessitated extensive algorithmic improvements to the task-graph compilation algorithm. The original complexity of this operation was $\mathcal{O}(n_1 \cdot log(n_1) + n_2 \cdot log(n_2))$, and after optimization became $\mathcal{O}(n_1 \cdot log(n_1)) + \mathcal{O}\left(\frac{n_2}{p} \cdot log(n_2)\right)$, where n_1 is the number of patches on coarse level, n_2 is the number of patches on fine level, and p is the number of processor cores. This reduced the four hour task-graph compilation time to under one minute at 32 K cores, thus making possible the results presented here.

5.1   CPU Strong Scaling of Multi-level Adaptive Mesh Refinement, RMCRT

Our scaling study focuses on a two-level AMR problem based on benchmark described in [9], which exercises all of the main features of the AMR support

---

[2] Titan is a Cray KX7 system located at Oak Ridge National Laboratory, where each node hosts a 16-core AMD Opteron 6274 processor running at 2.2 GHz, 32 GB DDR3 memory and 1 NVIDIA Tesla K20x GPU with 6 GB GDDR5 ECC memory. The entire machine offers 299,008 CPU cores and 18,688 GPUs (1 per node) and over 710 TB of RAM. Titan uses a Cray Gemini 3D Torus network, 1.4 μs latency, 20 GB/s peak injection bandwidth, and 52 GB/s peak memory bandwidth per node.

Table 1. Total number of MPI messages and average number of messages per MPI rank for each problem size, 128^3, 256^3 and 512^3 (fine mesh)

Cores	256	1 K	4 K	8 K	16 K	32 K	64 K	128 K	256 K
128^3 total msgs	1001	5860	36304						
avg msgs/node	62.5	91.6	141.8						
256^3 total msgs		9843	52.1 K	105.2 K	212.1 K	437.7 K			
avg msgs/node		153.8	203.3	205.6	207.0	213.7			
512^3 total msgs				338.2 K	673.8 K	1.36 M	2.71 M	5.42 M	10.88 M
avg msgs/node				660.5	658.0	663.65	662.6	661.36	662.83

within Uintah in addition to the radiation physics required by our target problem. A fine level halo region of four cells in each direction, x, y, z was used. The AMR grid consisted of two levels with a refinement ratio of four, the CFD mesh being four times more resolved than the radiation mesh. For three separate cases, the total number of cells on the highest resolved level was 128^3, 256^3 and 512^3 (green, red and blue lines respectively in Fig. 3), with 100 rays per cell in each case. The total number of cells on the coarse level was 32^3, 64^3 and 128^3. In all cases, each compute core was assigned at least 1 fine mesh patch from the CFD level. Figure 3 shows excellent strong scaling characteristics for our prototype, two-level benchmark problem [9]. The eventual breakdown in scaling in each problem size is due to diminishing work, when a patch's MPI messages begins to exceed the cost of its computation, and hence the runtime system cannot overlap computation with communication. Figure 4 additionally shows the MPI wait associated with the global and local communications for this calculation along side the execution times for each of the three cases above.

Though the actual communication patterns for this problem are perhaps more complicated than our predictive model, due to MPI message combining and packing done by Uintah, both Table 1 and Fig. 4 illustrate points made in Sect. 4, that global communications dominate and that the local communications do not have a significant impact, and for enough rays and enough refinement on the coarse radiation mesh, the computation does in fact dominate (Eq. 7 of our predictive model). These results also show how the number of MPI messages grows with the number of cores. A key point to note, as is evidenced by the dominating global communications, is that the refinement ratio of four reduces the global communication phase by a factor of 64 (ignoring communications latency for large messages) over a fine mesh all-to-all. If this communications phase took 8–64 times as long it would destroy scalability.

5.2 Multi-Level Accuracy Considerations

To quantify the error associated with coarsening the radiative properties (temperature T, absorption coefficient κ, and cellType (boundary or flow cell)), an error analysis was performed using a simplified version of the adaptive-meshing approach described in Sect. 3. The grid consisted of a fine and coarse mesh and

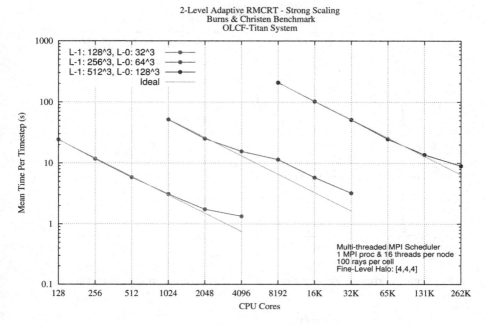

Fig. 3. Strong scaling of the two-level benchmark RMCRT problem on the DOE Titan system. L-1 (Level-1) is the fine, CFD mesh and L-0 (Level-0) is the coarse, radiation mesh.

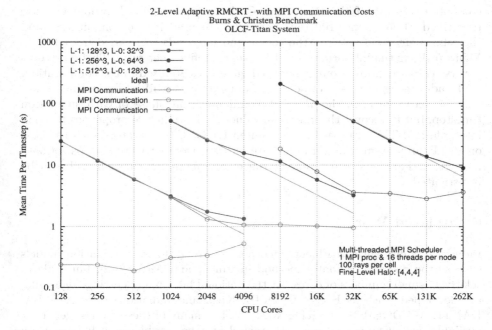

Fig. 4. Strong scaling with communication costs of the two-level benchmark. L-1 (Level-1) is the fine, CFD mesh and L-0 (Level-0) is the coarse, radiation mesh

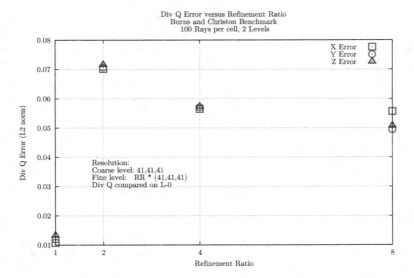

Fig. 5. L2 norm error of ∇q vs refinement ratio, The error in each direction (x,y,z) is shown.

during a radiation timestep the quantities necessary to compute ∇q were interpolated to the coarser grid level. The radiation calculation was performed on the coarse level including all ray tracing. The ∇q was then compared using the computed solution of the Burns and Christen [9] benchmark problem at the prescribed 41 locations. 100 rays per cell were used in the computation and the refinement ratio between the coarse and fine grids was varied from 1 to 8. Figure 5 shows the L2 norm error of ∇q versus refinement ratio. This represents a worse case scenario, as only coarsened quantities are used in the computation.

In addressing the issue of accuracy, our approach will be to continue sending the coarse mesh in the *all-to-all* communication phase of each simulation timestep, but to recover the fine mesh values of the radiative properties through interpolation. This approach is well suited for GPU accelerators such as those on the Titan system, where FLOPS are inexpensive relative to the cost of data movement. Further compression of the coarse mesh information will also be investigated.

6   Related Work

Industrial codes, such as Fluent, incorporate straightforward radiation models such as the discrete ordinates method in Fluent and Airpack [2], but scale to relatively small numbers of cores. At the national labs, many cutting edge codes are developed, such as Fuego, CFDLIB, Kiva, and radiation codes ATTILA, DANTE, WEDGEHOG, PARTISN [21,23], but many of these are not generally available, are unsupported, or are targeted at other problems such as neutron transport. There are also radiation transport problems that use CFD codes and AMR techniques [18, 34], however, a broad range of problems exist that require the concept of tracing rays or particles, such as the simulation of light transport and electromagnetic waves. In the case of adaptive mesh codes there are many such solvers. Specific examples of these codes are the Flash code [7, 35] based on adaptive oct-tree meshes and the physics AMR code Enzo [33, 42]. These examples are perhaps closest as these combine AMR and radiation, but for very different problem classes. Most of these codes do not target the problems that Uintah has been designed for, with large deformations, complex geometries, high degrees of parallelism and now radiation.

7   Conclusions and Future Work

We have demonstrated that through leveraging the multi-level AMR infrastructure provided by the Uintah framework, we have developed a scalable approach to radiative heat transfer using reverse Monte Carlo ray tracing. The scaling and communication cost results shown in Sect. 5 provide a promising alternative to approaches to radiation modeling such as discrete ordinates. Using our cost model for communication and computation, we can predict how our approach to radiation modeling may scale and perform on current, emerging and future architectures.

The addition of a scalable, hierarchical radiation solver within Uintah will also benefit the general computational science engineering community in applications areas such as turbulent combustion simulation and other energy-related problem. The broader impact of our work may ultimately include algorithmic developments for related problems with pervasive all-to-all type communications in general, such as long-range electrostatics in molecular dynamics, and will be of importance to a broad class of users, developers, scientists and students for whom such problems are presently a bottleneck.

Our primary focus in moving beyond this study will be continued development of RMCRT capabilities explored here, to provide support for several additional energy-related problems within the scope of the Utah CCMSC. The relationship between accuracy, number of rays cast, refinement ratios between grid levels and extent of the fine-level halo region is being explored as part of the ongoing research goals. The calculations demonstrated in this work are ideal candidates for large-scale accelerator use, employing large numbers of rays for every cell in the computational domain. As such, implementation of a multi-level GPU:RMCRT module is now underway with the aim of using the whole of machines like Titan with accelerators.

Acknowledgments. This material is based upon work supported by the Department of Energy, National Nuclear Security Administration, under Award Number(s) DE-NA0002375, and by DOE ALCC award CMB109, "Large Scale Turbulent Clean Coal Combustion", for time on Titan. This research used resources of the Oak Ridge Leadership Computing Facility, which is a DOE Office of Science User Facility supported under Contract DE-AC05-00OR22725. We would also like to thank all those involved with Uintah past and present, Isaac Hunsaker and Qingyu Meng in particular.

References

1. Amanatides, J., Woo, A.: A fast voxel traversal algorithm for ray tracing. Eurographics **87**, 3–10 (1987)
2. Ansys, I.: Fluent Web Page (2014). http://www.ansys.com/Products/
3. Balsara, D.: Fast and accurate discrete ordinates methods for multidimensional radiative transfer. part i, basic methods. J. Quant. Spectr. Radiative Trans. **69**(6), 671–707 (2001). http://www.sciencedirect.com/science/
4. Berzins, M.: Status of release of the Uintah computational framework. Technical report, UUSCI-2012-001, Scientific Computing and Imaging Institute (2012). http://www.sci.utah.edu/publications/SCITechReports/UUSCI-2012-001.pdf
5. Berzins, M., Luitjens, J., Meng, Q., Harman, T., Wight, C., Peterson, J.: Uintah - a scalable framework for hazard analysis. In: TG 2010: Proceedings of 2010 TeraGrid Conference. ACM, New York (2010)
6. Berzins, M., Meng, Q., Schmidt, J., Sutherland, J.C.: DAG-based software frameworks for PDEs. In: Alexander, M., D'Ambra, P., Belloum, A., Bosilca, G., Cannataro, M., Danelutto, M., Di Martino, B., Gerndt, M., Jeannot, E., Namyst, R., Roman, J., Scott, S.L., Traff, J.L., Vallée, G., Weidendorfer, J. (eds.) Euro-Par 2011, Part I. LNCS, vol. 7155, pp. 324–333. Springer, Heidelberg (2012)
7. Fryxell, B., Olson, K., Ricker, P., Timmes, F.X., Zingale, M., Lamb, D.Q., Macneice, P., Rosner, R., Truran, J., Tufo, H.: FLASH an adaptive mesh hydrodynamics code for modeling astrophysical thermonuclear flashes. Astrophys. J. Suppl. Ser. **131**, 273–334 (2000)
8. Brandt, A., Lubrecht, A.: Multilevel matrix multiplication and fast solution of integral equations. J. Comput. Phys. **90**(2), 348–370 (1990). http://www.sciencedirect.com/science/article/pii/002199919090171V
9. Burns, S.P., Christen, M.A.: Spatial domain-based parallelism in large-scale, participating-media, radiative transport applications. Numer. Heat Trans., Part B: Fundam. **31**(4), 401–421 (1997)
10. Falgout, R., Jones, J., Yang, U.: The design and implementation of hypre, a library of parallel high performance preconditioners. In: Numerical Solution of Partial Differential Equations on Parallel Computers, UCRL-JRNL-205459, vol. 51, pp. 267–294. Springer (2006)
11. Goodyer, C.E., Berzins, M.: Parallelization and scalability issues of a multilevel elastohydrodynamic lubrication solver. Concurrency Comput.: Pract. Experience **19**(4), 369–396 (2007). http://dx.doi.org/10.1002/cpe.1103
12. Guilkey, J.E., Harman, T.B., Xia, A., Kashiwa, B.A., McMurtry, P.A.: An Eulerian-Lagrangian approach for large deformation fluid-structure interaction problems, part 1: algorithm development. In: Fluid Structure Interaction II. WIT Press, Cadiz (2003)
13. Hapke, B.: Theory of Reflectance and Emittance Spectroscopy. Cambridge University Press, Cambridge (1993). http://dx.doi.org/10.1017/CBO9780511524998. cambridge Books Online
14. Howell, J.R.: The monte carlo in radiative heat transfer. J. Heat Trans. **120**(3), 547–560 (1998)

15. Humphrey, A., Meng, Q., Berzins, M., Harman, T.: Radiation modeling using the Uintah Heterogeneous CPU/GPU runtime system. In: Proceedings of the 1st Conference of the Extreme Science and Engineering Discovery Environment (XSEDE 2012). ACM (2012)

16. Hunsaker, I.: Parallel-distributed, Reverse Monte-Carlo radiation in coupled, Large Eddy combustion simulations. Ph.D. thesis, Department of Chemical Engineering, University of Utah (2013)

17. Hunsaker, I., Harman, T., Thornock, J., Smith, P.: Efficient parallelization of RMCRT for large scale LES combustion simulations, paper AIAA-2011-3770. In: 41st AIAA Fluid Dynamics Conference and Exhibit (2011)

18. Jessee, J.P., Fiveland, W.A., Howell, L.H., Colella, P., Pember, R.B.: An adaptive mesh refinement algorithm for the radiative transport equation. J. Comput. Phys. **139**(2), 380–398 (1998)

19. J. Spinti, Thornock, J., Eddings, E., Smith, P., Sarofim, A.: Heat transfer to objects in pool fires. In: Transport Phenomena in Fires. WIT Press, Southampton (2008)

20. Kashiwa, B., Gaffney., E.: Design basis for cfdlib. Technical report, LA-UR-03-1295, Los Alamos National Laboratory (2003)

21. Kerbyson, D.: A look at application performance sensitivity to the bandwidth and latency of infiniband networks. In: 20th International Parallel and Distributed Processing Symposium, IPDPS 2006, p. 7, April 2006

22. Krishnamoorthy, G., Rawat, R., Smith, P.: Parallelization of the P-1 radiation model, numerical Heat Transfer. Part B: Fundamentals **49**(1), 1–17 (2006)

23. Los Alamos National Security, L.: Los Alamos National Laboratory Transport Packages (2014). http://www.ccs.lanl.gov/CCS/CCS-4/codes.shtml

24. Luitjens, J., Berzins, M.: Improving the performance of Uintah: A large-scale adaptive meshing computational framework. In: Proceedings of the 24th IEEE International Parallel and Distributed Processing Symposium (IPDPS10) (2010). http://www.sci.utah.edu/publications/luitjens10/Luitjens_ipdps2010.pdf

25. Luitjens, J., Berzins, M.: Scalable parallel regridding algorithms for block-structured adaptive mesh refinement. Concurrency and Comput.: Pract. Experience 23(13), 1522–1537 (2011). http://dx.doi.org/10.1002/cpe.1719

26. Matsumoto, M., Nishimura, T.: Mersenne twister: A 623-dimensionally equidistributed uniform pseudo-random number generator. ACM Trans. Model. Comput. Simul. **81**(3), 3–30 (1998). http://doi.acm.org/10.1145/272991.272995

27. Meng, Q., Berzins, M., Schmidt, J.: Using hybrid parallelism to improve memory use in the Uintah framework. In: Proceedings of the 2011 TeraGrid Conference (TG11), Salt Lake City, Utah (2011)

28. Meng, Q., Humphrey, A., Berzins, M.: The Uintah framework: a unified heterogeneous task scheduling and runtime system. In: Digital Proceedings of Supercomputing 2012 - WOLFHPC Workshop. IEEE (2012)

29. Meng, Q., Luitjens, J., Berzins, M.: Dynamic task scheduling for the uintah framework. In: Proceedings of the 3rd IEEE Workshop on Many-Task Computing on Grids and Supercomputers (MTAGS 2010) (2010). http://www.sci.utah.edu/publications/meng10/Meng_TaskSchedulingUintah2010.pdf

30. Meng, Q., Berzins, M.: Scalable large-scale fluid-structure interaction solvers in the Uintah framework via hybrid task-based parallelism algorithms. In: Concurrency and Computation: Practice and Experience (2013). http://dx.doi.org/10.1002/cpe.3099

31. Meng, Q., Humphrey, A., Schmidt, J., Berzins, M.: Investigating applications portability with the uintah dag-based runtime system on petascale supercomput-

ers. In: Proceedings of the International Conference on High Performance Computing, Networking, Storage and Analysis, SC 2013, pp. 96:1–96:12. ACM, New York (2013). http://doi.acm.org/10.1145/2503210.2503250

32. Modest, M.F.: Backward Monte Carlo simulations in radiative heat transfer. J. Heat Trans. 125(1), 57–62 (2003). http://link.aip.org/link/JHTRAO/v125/i1/p57/s1&Agg=doi

33. O'Shea, B., Bryan, G., Bordner, J., Norman, M., Abel, T., Harkness, R., Kritsuk, A.: Introducing Enzo, an amr cosmology applications. In: Plewa, T., Linde, T., Gregory Weirs, V. (eds.) Adaptive Mesh Refinement - Theory and Application. Lecture Notes in Computational Science and Engineering, vol. 41, pp. 341–350. Springer, Heidelberg (2005)

34. Pernice, M., Philip, B.: Solution of equilibrium radiation diffusion problems using implicit adaptive mesh refinement. SIAM J. Sci. Comput. 27(5), 1709–1726 (2005)

35. Rijkhorst, E.J., Plewa, T., Dubey, A., Mellema, G.: Hybrid characteristics: 3d radiative transfer for parallel adaptive mesh refinement hydrodynamics. Astron. Astrophys. 452(3), 907–920 (2006)

36. Schmidt, J., Berzins, M., Thornock, J., Saad, T., Sutherland, J.: Large scale parallel solution of incompressible flow problems using Uintah and hypre. In: Proceedings of CCGrid 2013. IEEE/ACM (2013)

37. Scientific Computing and Imaging Institute: Uintah Web Page (2015). http://www.uintah.utah.edu/

38. Sun, X.: Reverse Monte Carlo ray-tracing for radiative heat transfer in combustion systems. Ph.D. thesis, Department of Chemical Engineering, University of Utah (2009)

39. Sun, X., Smith, P.J.: A parametric case study in radiative heat transfer using the reverse monte-carlo ray-tracing with full-spectrum k-distribution method. Journal of Heat Transfer 132(2) (2010)

40. Thakur, R., Rabenseifner, R., Gropp, W.D.: Optimization of collective communication operations in mpich. Int. J. High Perform. Comput. Appl. 19(1), 49–66 (2005)

41. Viswanath, K., Veljkovic, I., Plassmann, P.E.: Parallel load balancing heuristics for radiative heat transfer calculations. In: CSC, pp. 151–157 (2006)

42. Wise, J.H., Abel, T.: enzo+moray: radiation hydrodynamics adaptive mesh refinement simulations with adaptive ray tracing. Monthly Notices of the Royal Astronomical Society 414(4), 3458–3491 (2011). http://dx.doi.org/10.1111/j.1365-2966.2011.18646.x

Optimizing Processes Mapping for Tasks with Non-uniform Data Exchange Run on Cluster with Different Interconnects

Victor Getmanskiy[1]($\boxtimes$), Vladimir Chalyshev[1], Dmitriy Kryzhanovsky[1],
Igor Lopatin[2], and Evgeny Leksikov[2]

[1] Singularis Lab Ltd., Lenina Av. 86, 400005 Volgograd, Russia
{victor.getmanskiy,vladimir.chalyshev,
dmitry.kryzhanovsky}@singularis-lab.com
http://www.singularis-lab.com

[2] Intel Inc., Turgeneva 30, 603950 Nizhniy Novgorod, Russia
http://www.intel.com

Abstract. The problem of mapping the parallel task to the nodes of computing cluster is considered. MPI software with non-uniform communication and heterogeneous interconnect of computing cluster could run faster using custom parallel processes mapping for optimization of data exchange. The graph mapping algorithm is developed. It uses parallel program representation as a task graph and cluster topology representation as system graph. The proposed optimization technique is tested on synthetic benchmark and on CORAL QBox software to study its efficiency on large number of computing cores. The positive results of optimization are achieved and the summary is presented in the paper.

Keywords: Task mapping · Communication graph · Cluster · MPI

1 Introduction

Efficient heterogeneous computing requires some approaches and methods of appropriate mapping of parallel processes into computing hardware. Majority of these approaches uses task graph and system graph model [1–3,7,8,11]. There are different optimization methods for solving NP-full problem of mapping task graph to system graph, include heuristic [8,10], clustering [11], genetic [7] and profile-based greedy [3] strategies. Common issue in heterogenous cluster system is the bandwidth and latency of interconnect which affects the performance in case of intensive non-uniform data exchange between parallel processes [9].

In considered approaches task graph is an undirected graph in which vertices represent parallel processes and edges are weighted by data sizes sent between processes. In scientific simulation software task graph can have a non-uniform edges configuration. The width of the edge lines is selected according to the amount of exchanged data.

© Springer International Publishing Switzerland 2015
J.M. Kunkel and T. Ludwig (Eds.): ISC High Performance 2015, LNCS 9137, pp. 231–239, 2015.
DOI: 10.1007/978-3-319-20119-1_17

System graph represents the computing cluster topology taking into account the performance of different interconnect channels. Edges of system graph are weighted by factors representing the ratio between inter node and intra node sending time. Modern cluster hardware consists of several CPUs and coprocessors such as GPGPU FPGA or Intel$^{\circledR}$ Xeon Phi^{TM}. Interconnect between nodes can also have a different speed (InfiniBand^{TM} and Ethernet). So the cluster graph also can have a complex non-uniform structure (Fig. 1).

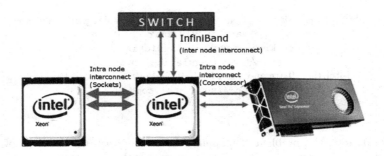

Fig. 1. Heterogeneous cluster node configuration

1.1   Problem Formulation

The main assumption in this work is that the exchange will be performed faster if the task graph nodes are mapped to system graph nodes in such a way that the heavy edges of task graph are mapped to the fastest interconnect edges in system graph. The problem described is reduced to the following optimization problem. Let us specify the task graph as

$$G_1(P, L), L_i = (n_i, d_i), i = 1, \ldots, N$$

where P–set of vertices (parallel processes), L–set of edges (processes communications), n_i–data exchange frequency, d_i–amount of data exchanged, N–number of edges. Let us specify the system graph as

$$G_2(V, D), D_j = (l_j, b_j), j = 1, \ldots, M$$

where V–set of vertices (computing cores), D–set of edges (communication links), l_j–latency, b_i–bandwidth, M–number of edges. In first assumption any pair of nodes cluster nodes could exchange data through interconnect, so G_2 is a complete graph and $N \leq M$. The required mapping can be described as:

$$G_1 \to G_2(P \to V) : L_i \to D_j, F(D, L) \to min$$

Objective function to be minimized if as follows:

$$F(D, L) = \sum_{k=1}^{N} T_k, T_k(D_i, L_j) = l_i n_j + d_j/b_i, F \to min$$

The simplified formulation is used for the developed prototype. Task graph weight is an amount of exchanged data and system graph edges weight is data exchange "speed" ratio r_i:

$$\tilde{F}\,(\tilde{D}, L) = \sum_{k=1}^{N} \tilde{T}_k, \tilde{T}_k(\tilde{D}_i, L_j) = r_i d_j, \tilde{D}_i = (r_i), \tilde{F} \rightarrow min$$

2   Mapping Algorithm

Two algorithms were developed. The first one is based on brute force and the second one is a greedy algorithm. The first algorithm gives exact solution but requires a lot of computation and suits only for small graphs with up to 10 vertices. The greedy solution is practically used and provides the optimal solution in most cases.

The greedy solution is based on paper [3]. The main difference with our modification is that the paper examines a vertexes number in the cluster graph equal to a vertex number in the task graph. The general scheme is as follows:

1. We find the first approximation. At the prototype stage we use the mapping of the i-th cluster graph vertex to the i-th task graph vertex.
2. After that we try to improve the result iteratively:
   (a) Take two vertexes of the task graph and change their destinations, that is, if we had the mapping $a \rightarrow p$, $b \rightarrow q$, it will become $a \rightarrow q$, $b \rightarrow p$ as proposed in paper [3].
   (b) Take any vertex and assign it to another system node (for example, $a \rightarrow p$, $a \rightarrow q$).

The method complexity is $O(IE(M + N))$, where I is the iterations number, E is the edges number in the task graph, M is the vertexes number in the task graph, N is the vertexes number in the cluster graph. The greedy algorithm converges quite fast, approximately within 100 iterations. The main drawback of the algorithm is in finding suboptimal solutions, not truly optimal, but in many cases the solution gives the mapping that improves the performance of MPI software.

3   Synthetic Test Description

Synthetic test is a data exchange benchmark with different amount and intensity. It represents a best-for-optimization test case of task graph. There are two types of communication:

1. Groups of parallel processes with tight communication (Intragroup communication).
2. Intergroup communications.

Tight interaction blocks count is specified as N_{bl}. Number of processes in block is specified as N_{perbl}. In each block processes communicate with each other (fully connected sub graph) but inter-block communication is performed only between the last process in i-th block and the first (see Fig. 2). Iteration skipping is specified (inter-block exchanges are not at each iteration). Process numbers are mixed randomly (with constant Seed for random generator).

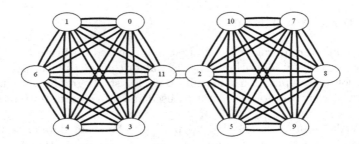

Fig. 2. Task graph example for 2 blocks with 6 processes in each

Synthetic test is also parameterized by intra-group data volume amount D, and inter-block data amount D_{bl}, and iteration skipping N_{skip}. The offset and length linear arrays are constructed at each iteration for collective MPI communication routine MPI_AllToAllv [4]. These arrays are complemented at each $1+N_{skip}$ iteration by inter-block exchange data. For example, in case of $N_{skip} = 2$ the arrays are filled as shown at Table 1.

Table 1. Synch table

Target process id		0	1	2	3	4	5	6	7	8	9	10	11
Iter. 3k, 1 + 3k	offset	0	0	0	0	0	0	D	D	2D	3D	4D	5D
Process id 2	length	0	0	0	0	0	D	0	D	D	D	D	D
Iter. 3k, 1 + 3k	offset	0	D	2D	2D	3D	4D	5D	5D	5D	5D	5D	5D
Process id 11	length	D	D	0	D	D	0	D	0	0	0	0	0
Iter. 2 + 3k	offset	0	0	0	0	0	0	D	D	2D	3D	4D	5D
Process id 2	length	0	0	0	0	0	D	0	D	D	D	D	D_{bl}
Iter. 2 + 3k	offset	0	D	2D	2D+ D_{bl}	3D+ D_{bl}	4D+ D_{bl}	4D+ D_{bl}	5D+ D_{bl}	5D+ D_{bl}	5D+ D_{bl}	5D+ D_{bl}	5D+ D_{bl}
Process id 11	length	D	D	D_{bl}	D	D	0	D	0	0	0	0	0

The exchange data array is filled according to the table for process 2 and process 11 at inter-group exchange iterations (Iteration number $0 + 3k$, $1 + 3k$) and intra-group exchange iterations (Iteration number $2 + 3k$). For processes without intra-group communications the tables are similar but without additional D_{bl} at intra-group exchange iterations. So D_{bl} exchange data block is inserted to data offset and length arrays of the 2-nd and 11-th processes in every three iterations. Thus the synthetic test routine is parameterized by following parameters: N_{bl}–number of blocks, N_{perbl}–number of processes in block, D–intra-block data volume amount, D_{bl}–inter-block data amount, N_{skip}–iteration skipping step for inter-block communication. Synthetic test allows setting arbitrary configuration of task suitable for custom CPUs with different number of cores and loading the interconnect with different data amount and different inter-node exchange intensity. The simulated data exchange is used to build task graph by Intel$^{\circledR}$ MPI Library statistics (generated using I_MPI_STATS environment variable) [4]. So the synthetic test allows simulating the data exchange suitable for cluster with groups of computing cores linked by interconnect by a specifying number of processes in group equal to number of cores per node in cluster. After processes are randomized, the optimization algorithm must find the solution that maps these groups on cluster nodes.

4   Benchmarking

Benchmarks run using Intel$^{\circledR}$ MPI Library [4] launcher mpirun. A convenient way to pass a lot of parameters to MPI launcher is through using the configuration file and –configfile key. So the run command is

```
mpirun --configfile config.txt
```

The tool for generating configuration files is developed. It uses a host list file for input The first step is running small time test collecting MPI statistics. Input data for generating configuration file (config.txt) is a host list with names of node machines in cluster and number of cores in each node (hostlist.txt). Config file for 4-nodes cluster with 4-cores CPU in each node is as follows:

```
-env I_MPI_STATS 4 -env I_MPI_STATS_FILE stat -n 4 -host node1 app
-env I_MPI_STATS 4 -env I_MPI_STATS_FILE stat -n 4 -host node2 app
-env I_MPI_STATS 4 -env I_MPI_STATS_FILE stat -n 4 -host node3 app
-env I_MPI_STATS 4 -env I_MPI_STATS_FILE stat -n 4 -host node4 app
```

Running the MPI program using this config.txt file launches application profiles it and generates stats.txt file with data exchange statistics between each pair of processes. After that tool generates task graph for G_1 which edges are weighted by amount of exchanged data from stats.txt. Then tool generates full system graph G_2 based on hostlist.txt creating groups of vertices coresponded to each host (row in hostlist.txt). Vertices in each group are connected with "fast" edges weighted by constant 1 and vertices between groups are connected with "slow" edges weighted by constant 2. For the second run the tool uses stats.txt file and hostlist.txt as input and generates optimized config.txt file. It generates a config.txt file with properly ordered tasks so that they are mapped to computing cores in the optimal way. The generated config.txt file for optimized run maps the tasks to hosts.

```
-n 2 -host node1 /path/to/application
-n 2 -host node4 /path/to/application
-n 1 -host node2 /path/to/application
...
```

The optimized configuration file is used for a long running benchmark. Benchmarking methodology is to measure long running benchmark time with default configuration file (T, sec.) and with optimized configuration file (T_{opt}, sec.). The efficiency metric is an actual speedup calculated as $S = T/T_{opt}$.

All benchmarks were launched on remote Tornado SUSU cluster [6]. Cluster has the following configuration. Hardware: 50–400 nodes: 2 x Intel® Xeon™ X5680 CPUs, Intel® Xeon Phi™ SE10X, 2 Gb DDR3-1333 RAM per node, QDR InfiniBand™, Software: Linux CentOS 6.2, Software: Intel MPI 4.1.3.045, CORAL QBox 1.40b. (default parameters; built with Intel C++ Compiler XE 14.0.1 for Linux).

4.1 Synthetic Benchmark on Two Intel® Xeon Phi™ Nodes

Benchmark was launched in two nodes with 60-cores Intel® Xeon Phi™ in native mode. Synthetic benchmark consists of K process groups with M processes in each and $K \cdot M = 120$. Intra-group communication data volume is much greater than inter-node. Benchmark results are presented in Table 2.

Table 2. Synch table

K	M	T, sec	T_{opt}, sec	S
2	60	660.847	84.125	7.855
4	30	320.938	153.668	2.088
8	15	165.581	34.700	4.771
15	8	93.015	39.100	2.378
20	6	68.347	30.007	2.277

4.2 Synthetic Benchmark for 10 Nodes Cluster

Benchmarking is performed on CPUs of 10 nodes using various exchanged data amount and a number of exchange iterations (N_{iter}) according to Table 3. Amount of exchanged data is defined in 64-bit doubles which means that for 100000000 doubles the data volume is about 800 Mb per node. 10 groups with 12 processes in each are used in synthetic benchmark so there are 120 parallel processes. The benchmarks were performed with fixed amount of total exchanged data. Number of exchange iteration differs. Data size in doubles for inter group (V_{inter}) and intra group (V_{intra}) communication also differs, and $V_{intra} = 1000V_{inter}$.

The results prove that the higher exchange intensity of smaller amount of data benchmark case gives better optimization results.

Table 3. Synthetic benchmark results for 10-nodes CPU cluster

N_{iter}	V_{inter}	V_{intra}	$T, sec.$	$T_{opt}, sec.$	S
100	1000	1000000	1755	880	1.99
1000	100	100000	23.21	9.56	2.42
10000	10	10000	5.96	1.01	5.9

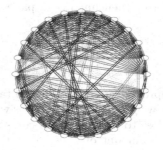

Fig. 3. Task graph for QBox run on 2 nodes

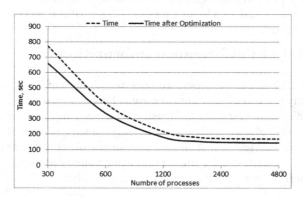

Fig. 4. Time and optimization time of QBox benchmark

4.3   CORAL QBox Software Benchmark on Remote Cluster

The benchmarks were launched on up to 400 nodes. CORAL QBOX [5] benchmark is a molecular dynamics code. The method has $O(N^3)$ computational complexity, where N is the total number of valence electrons in the system. Task graph for large amount of nodes is quite general. But two nodes communication graph (Fig. 3) demonstrates two clusters of nodes with tight communication. And the ordering of nodes in each group corresponds to cores on nodes. QBox benchmark was selected for better performance with grid dimensions 2512 for 25 nodes and 50×12, 100×12, 150×12, 200×12, 400×12 for 50–400 nodes (benchmark was performed on 300–4800 cores). Optimized benchmark configuration file is obtained using ration of 2 inter-nodes edges weight to intra-nodes edges weight. The result of optimization is steady increasing effect with increasing number of nodes and on 100 nodes it gives 20 % performance gain. Also QBox benchmark has a high scalability but at some point the time converges to some constant value as shown in Fig. 4. So the prediction of scalability to higher number of nodes made by extrapolating the data for considered QBox benchmark is the constant effect of optimization and constant run time of benchmark. The considered QBox benchmark has a good scalability up to 100 nodes. On larger task scalability is better (benchmarks in paper [5]) and it is possible to get better results.

5   Conclusions

The proposed approach improves the performance if task graph of MPI application has non-uniform edges weighting and subgraphs with tight communications and the number of nodes close to the number of cores per cluster node. Positive effect is obtained on a large amount of nodes for QBox benchmark because it has non-uniform collective communications between processes and high scalability. The task mapping method can be improved taking into account the cluster topology and latency and bandwidth characteristics of interconnect.

6   Product and Performance Information

Software and workloads used in performance tests may have been optimized for performance only on Intel® microprocessors. Performance tests, such as SYSmark and MobileMark, are measured using specific computer systems, components, software, operations, and functions. Any change to any of those factors may cause the results to vary. You should consult other information and performance tests to assist you in fully evaluating your contemplated purchases, including the performance of that product when combined with other products.

Configuration. Hardware: 50–400 nodes: 2 x Intel® Xeon™ X5680 CPUs, Intel® Xeon Phi™ SE10X, 2 Gb DDR3-1333 RAM per node, InfiniBand™ QDR, Software: Linux CentOS 6.2, Software: Intel MPI 4.1.3.045, CORAL QBox 1.40b. (default parameters; built with Intel C++ Compiler XE 14.0.1 for Linux).

Optimization Notice. Intel's compilers may or may not optimize to the same degree for non-Intel microprocessors for optimizations that are not unique to Intel microprocessors. These optimizations include SSE2, SSE3, and SSSE3 instruction sets and other optimizations. Intel does not guarantee the availability, functionality, or effectiveness of any optimization on microprocessors not manufactured by Intel. Microprocessor-dependent optimizations in this product are intended for use with Intel microprocessors. Certain optimizations not specific to Intel microarchitecture are reserved for Intel microprocessors. Please refer to the applicable product User and Reference Guides for more information regarding the specific instruction sets covered by this notice. Notice revision #20110804.

References

1. Karlsson, C., Davies, T., Chen, Z.: Optimizing process-to-core mappings for application level multi-dimensional MPI communications. In: IEEE International Conference on Cluster Computing (CLUSTER 2012), pp. 486–494, 24–28 September 2012

2. Zhang, J., Zhai, J., Chen, W., Zheng, W.: Process mapping for MPI collective communications. In: Sips, H., Epema, D., Lin, H.-X. (eds.) Euro-Par 2009. LNCS, vol. 5704, pp. 81–92. Springer, Heidelberg (2009)

3. Chen, H., Chen, W., Huang, J., Robert, B., Kuhn, H.: MPIPP: an automatic profile-guided parallel process placement toolset for SMP clusters and multiclusters. In: Proceedings of the 20th Annual International Conference on Supercomputing, ICS 2006, pp. 353–360, June 2006

4. Intel® Library Reference Manual (2014)

5. Gygi, F., Yates, R.K., Lorenz, J., Draeger, E.W., Franchetti, F., Ueberhuber, C., Supinski, B., Gunnels, S., Sexton, J.: Large-scale first-principles molecular dynamics simulations on the BlueGene platform using the Qbox code. In: Proceedings of the ACM/IEEE SC 2005, p. 24, 12–18 November 2005

6. Tornado SUSU Supercomputer (2014). http://supercomputer.susu.ac.ru/en/computers/tornado/

7. Sanyal, S., Jain, A., Das, S.K., Biswas, R.: A hierarchical and distributed approach for mapping large applications to heterogeneous grids using genetic algorithms. In: CLUSTER, pp. 496–499. IEEE Computer Society (2003)

8. Kafil, M., Ahmad, I.: Optimal task assignment in heterogeneous distributed computing systems. IEEE Concurrency **6**(3), 42–50 (1998)

9. Martin, R., Vahdat, A., Culler, D., Anderson, T.: Effects of communication latency, overhead, and bandwidth in a cluster architecture. In: Proceedings of the 24th Annual International Symposium on Computer Architecture (ISCA), pp. 85–97, June 1997. Graph with spatial structure like mesh

10. Bhatele, A., Kale, L.V.: Heuristic-based techniques for mapping irregular communication graphs to mesh topologies. In: 2011 IEEE 13th International Conference on High Performance Computing and Communications (HPCC), pp. 765–771, 2–4 September 2011

11. Eshaghian, M.M.: Mapping arbitrary heterogeneous task graphs onto arbitrary heterogeneous system graph. Int. J. Found. Comput. Sci. **12**(05), 599–628 (2001)

Dynamically Adaptable I/O Semantics for High Performance Computing

Michael Kuhn[(✉)]

University of Hamburg, Hamburg, Germany
michael.kuhn@informatik.uni-hamburg.de

Abstract. While an input/output (I/O) interface's syntax describes the available operations, its semantics determines how these operations behave and which assumptions developers can make about them. There are several different interface standards in existence, some of them dating back decades and having been designed for local file systems; one such representative is POSIX. Many parallel distributed file systems implement a POSIX-compliant interface to improve portability. All currently available interfaces follow a fixed approach regarding semantics, making them only suitable for a subset of use cases and workloads. While the interfaces do not allow application developers to influence the I/O semantics, applications could benefit greatly from the possibility of being able to adapt them to their requirements.

The work presented in this paper includes the design of a novel I/O interface and a file system called JULEA. They offer support for dynamically adaptable semantics and are suited specifically for HPC applications. The introduced concept allows applications to adapt the file system behavior to their exact I/O requirements instead of the other way around. The general goal is an interface that allows developers to specify *what* operations should do and *how* they should behave – leaving the actual realization and possible optimizations to the underlying file system.

JULEA has been evaluated using both synthetic benchmarks and real-world applications. Overall, JULEA provides data and metadata performance comparable to that of other established parallel distributed file systems. However, in contrast to the existing solutions, its flexible semantics allows it to cover a wider range of use cases in an efficient way. The results demonstrate that there is need for I/O interfaces that can adapt to the requirements of applications. Even though POSIX facilitates portability, it does not seem to be suited for contemporary HPC demands.

Keywords: I/O semantics · I/O interface · Parallel file system

1 Introduction

Throughout their history, the computational power of supercomputers has been increasing exponentially, doubling roughly every 14 months [20]. While this computational power has allowed more accurate simulations to be performed, this

© Springer International Publishing Switzerland 2015
J.M. Kunkel and T. Ludwig (Eds.): ISC High Performance 2015, LNCS 9137, pp. 240–256, 2015.
DOI: 10.1007/978-3-319-20119-1_18

has also caused the simulation results to grow in size. Due to the large amounts of data produced by parallel applications, high performance I/O is an important aspect because storing and retrieving such large amounts of data can greatly affect the overall performance of these applications.

However, the I/O requirements of parallel applications can vary widely: While some applications process large amounts of input data and produce relatively small results, others might work using a small set of input data and output large amounts of data; additionally, the aforementioned data can be spread across many small files or be concentrated into few large files. Naturally, any combination thereof is also possible. These different requirements can make high demands on supercomputers' storage systems.

Parallel distributed file systems provide one or more I/O interfaces that can be used to access data within the file system. Usually at least one of them is standardized, while additional proprietary interfaces might offer improved performance at the cost of portability. Popular interface choices include POSIX [9], MPI-IO [16], HDF [19] and NetCDF [18]. Almost all the I/O interfaces found in HPC today offer simple byte- or element-oriented access to data and thus do not have any a priori information about what kind of data the applications access and how the high-level access patterns look like. However, this information can be very beneficial for optimizing the performance of I/O operations.

While the I/O interface defines which I/O operations are available, the I/O semantics describes and defines the behavior of these operations. Usually each I/O interface is accompanied by a set of I/O semantics, tailored to this specific interface. The POSIX I/O semantics is probably both the oldest and the most widely used semantics, even in HPC. However, due to being designed for traditional local file systems, it imposes unnecessary restrictions on today's parallel distributed file systems. POSIX's very strict consistency requirements that require write operations to be propagated to all other clients immediately are one of these restrictions and can lead to performance bottlenecks in distributed environments [21]. Parallel distributed file systems often implement the strict POSIX I/O semantics to accommodate applications that require it or simply expect it to be available for portability reasons. However, this can lead to suboptimal behavior for many use cases because its strictness is often not necessary. Even though application developers usually know their applications' requirements and could easily specify them for improved performance, current I/O interfaces and file systems do not provide appropriate facilities for this task.

Performing I/O efficiently is becoming an increasingly important problem. CPU speed and HDD capacity have roughly increased by factors of 500 and 100 every 10 years, respectively [20,24]. The speed of HDDs, however, has only grown by a factor of 10 every 10 years [23]; even newer technologies such as SSDs only offer a factor of 18. Although it is theoretically possible to compensate for this fact in the short term by simply buying more storage hardware, the ever increasing gap between the exponentially growing processing power on the one hand and the stagnating storage capacity and throughput on the other hand, requires new approaches to use the storage infrastructure as efficiently as possible.

The goal of this paper is to explore the usefulness of additional semantical information in the I/O interface. The JULEA framework introduces a newly designed I/O interface featuring dynamically adaptable semantics that is suited specifically for HPC applications. It allows application developers to specify the semantics of I/O operations at runtime and supports batch operations to increase performance. The overall goal is to allow the application developer to specify the desired behavior and leave the actual realization to the I/O system.

This paper is structured as follows: The most important design aspects of the JULEA I/O interface are elaborated in Sect. 2, focusing on the differences to traditional I/O interfaces and file systems. Section 3 covers related work and compares JULEA's design with existing approaches. Section 4 contains an analysis of the behavior of different file systems using synthetic benchmarks. A conclusion and future work are given in Sect. 5.

2   Interface and File System Design

JULEA's general architecture closely follows that of established parallel distributed file systems such as Lustre [5] and OrangeFS [4]. Machines can have one or several of three different roles: client, data server or metadata server. While it is possible to have a machine perform all three roles simultaneously, it is recommended to separate the clients from the servers to provide stable performance. JULEA supports multiple data and metadata servers and allows data and metadata to be distributed among them; it is possible to influence the actual distribution of data using distributions.

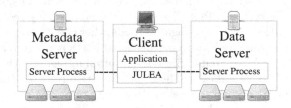

Fig. 1. JULEA's file system components

A very brief general view of JULEA's different components and their interactions with each other are shown in Fig. 1. Applications are able to use JULEA's I/O interface that talks directly to the data and metadata servers by linking against its client library `libjulea.so`; it abstracts all the internal details and provides a convenient interface for developers. The metadata and data servers run on dedicated machines with attached storage hardware. While the metadata servers make use of the MongoDB database system, the data servers run a user space daemon called `julea-daemon` that handles all I/O on behalf of the clients.

Figures 2a and b show a comparison of an exemplary HPC I/O stack and the proposed JULEA I/O stack. In addition to the logical layers, the separation

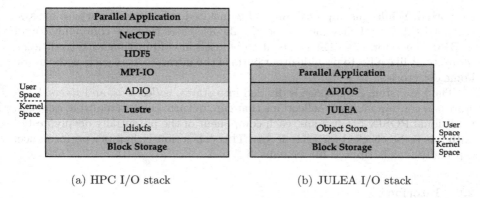

(a) HPC I/O stack   (b) JULEA I/O stack

Fig. 2. Current HPC I/O stack and proposed JULEA I/O stack

between kernel and user space is shown. All kernel space layers are either implemented directly inside the kernel or as kernel modules; the user space layers are either normal applications or libraries. As can be seen, JULEA's architecture features less layers, which makes it easier to analyze the actual I/O behavior of applications. It also allows concentrating all optimizations into a single layer, reducing the implementation and runtime overhead.

The current I/O stack's design results in several transformations of the data as it is being transported through the different layers. The parallel application's data types are stored in NetCDF that in turn stores its data in HDF's datasets and groups. This data is then transformed into a byte stream for MPI-IO. It then stores the data in the actual parallel distributed file system that splits up the data and stripes it across its servers, potentially storing it in yet another underlying local file system.

An important design goal of JULEA is to remove the duplication of functionality found in the traditional HPC I/O stack. Because many distributed file systems use an underlying local POSIX file system to store the actual data and metadata, a lot of common file system functionality such as path lookup and permission checking is duplicated. This can be achieved by completely eliminating the underlying POSIX file systems and using suitable object stores.

Because it is often unreasonable to port applications to new and experimental I/O interfaces due to their size and complexity, it makes sense to leverage a layer providing compatibility for existing applications. ADIOS is an established I/O interface and specifically allows implementing different backends. To minimize the overhead, ADIOS could be used as a relatively thin layer on top of JULEA to provide convenient access for application developers.

2.1   File System Namespace

Traditional file systems allow deeply nested directory structures. To avoid the overhead caused by this, only a restricted and relatively flat hierarchical namespace is supported. While this approach might be unsuited for a general purpose file system, JULEA is explicitly focused on specific use cases that are commonly found in HPC. Therefore, JULEA is meant to be used in conjunction with traditional file systems like NFS to provide other parts of the infrastructure such as the users' home directories.

The file system namespace is divided into *stores*, *collections*, and *items*. Each store can contain multiple collections that can, in turn, contain multiple items. In traditional POSIX file systems, each component of the potentially deeply nested path has to be checked for each access. This can seriously hamper performance, especially for distributed file systems.

2.2 Interface

JULEA's interface has been designed from scratch to offer simplicity of use while still meeting the requirements of high performance and dynamically adaptable semantics. Its functionality can be subdivided into five groups:

1. **Batches:** Multiple operations can be batched explicitly to improve performance by reducing network overhead.
2. **Distributions:** It is possible to influence the distribution of data directly to optimize its placement on the data servers if necessary.
3. **Namespace:** The file system namespace is accessible using a convenient abstraction called uniform resource identifiers (URIs).
4. **Semantics:** JULEA's semantics is dynamically adaptable according to the applications' I/O requirements.
5. **Stores, Collections and Items:** It is possible to create, remove, open and iterate over all of JULEA's file system objects.

All of the above functionality is available publicly and directly to developers. The two most important features are the ability to specify semantical information and to batch operations. Both approaches give the file system additional information that can be used to optimize accesses. Due to their importance, these two features will be explained in more detail; more information about the other ones can be found in [13].

It is possible for developers and users to specify additional information equivalent to the coarse-grained statement "this is a checkpoint" or the more fine-grained "this operation requires strict consistency semantics". This allows the file system to tune operations for specific applications by itself. Additionally, developers are able to emulate well-established semantics as well as mixing different semantics within one application.

Developers perform all accesses to the file systems via so-called *batches*. Each batch can consist of multiple operations. It is also possible to combine different kinds of operations within one batch. For instance, one batch might create a collection and several items within it, and write data to each of the items. Because the file system has knowledge about all operations within one batch, more elaborate optimizations can be performed.

Traditional POSIX file systems can also try to aggregate multiple operations to improve network utilization. However, this can only be done by caching these operations in the client's main memory for a given amount of time and then performing these optimizations. Because the POSIX interface does not provide enough information to make reliable decisions for these kinds of optimizations, it is necessary to employ heuristics, resulting in suboptimal behavior for border-line cases. Additionally, it is not possible to do this in all cases because it would violate the POSIX semantics. Therefore, users can never be sure when exactly operations are performed in such a system without calling synchronization functions explicitly, which can be very expensive.[1]

To be able to easily overlap calculations and I/O, it is possible to execute batches asynchronously. This support is offered natively by the I/O interface without forcing developers to resort to using background threads or similar techniques. The file system also exports additional information to enable performance optimizations such as aligning data to the file system's stripe size, which is crucial for high performance [2].

2.3 Semantics

JULEA allows many aspects of the file system operations' semantics to be changed at runtime. Several key areas of the semantics have been identified as important to provide opportunities for optimizations: atomicity, concurrency, consistency, ordering, persistency and safety. Even though it is possible to mix the settings for each of these semantics, not all combinations produce reasonable results.

The *atomicity* semantics can be used to specify whether accesses should be executed atomically, that is, whether or not it is possible for clients to see intermediate states of operations. If atomicity is required, some kind of locking has to be performed to prevent other clients from accessing data that is currently being modified. The atomicity semantics is clearly performance-related. Atomic accesses operating on the same data have to be serialized, which implies a performance penalty. If atomicity is not required, all operations can be executed in parallel.

The *concurrency* semantics can be used to specify whether concurrent accesses will take place and, if so, how the access pattern will look like. Depending on the level of concurrency, different algorithms might be appropriate for file system operations such as locking or metadata access. Concurrency semantics are performance-related by allowing simpler and faster centralized algorithms to be used when no concurrent access is happening. For instance, atomicity is only required for overlapping accesses.

The *consistency* semantics can be used to specify if and when clients will see modifications performed by other clients and applies to both metadata and data. This information can be used to enable client-side read caching whenever

---

[1] POSIX's synchronization functions `fsync` and `fdatasync` only allow synchronizing whole files even if this is not necessary.

possible. The consistency semantics is performance-related and can allow caching data and metadata locally.

The *ordering* semantics can be used to specify whether operations within a batch are allowed to be reordered. Because batches can potentially contain a large number of operations, the additional information can be exploited to optimize their execution. The ordering semantics is performance-related as it allows operations to be reordered for more efficient access. It is especially important to group operations of the same type to reduce the amount of network overhead.

The *persistency* semantics can be used to specify if and when data and metadata must be written to persistent storage. This can be used to enable client-side write caching whenever possible. The persistency semantics is performance-related and allows caching modified data and metadata locally. This can be especially advantageous when different levels of storage such as node-local SSDs are available as it allows writing the temporary data to the fast local storage without communicating via the network at all.

The *safety* semantics can be used to specify how safely data and metadata should be handled. It provides guarantees about the state of the data and metadata after the execution of a batch has finished. The safety semantics is performance-related by allowing to adjust the overhead incurred by data safety measures and to optimize network utilization by not waiting for unnecessary replies.

3 Related Work

The current HPC I/O stack has already been identified as problematic regarding future demands due to its complex layering and static architecture [3]. Even though there are a few approaches to provide configurable behavior and semantics in parallel distributed file systems, they are usually limited to single aspects of the file system or too static because they do not allow changes at runtime [17]. JULEA aims to solve these problems using its novel approach.

MosaStore is a versatile storage system that is configurable at application deployment time and thus allows application-specific optimizations [1]. This is similar to JULEA's approach. However, MosaStore provides a storage system bound to specific applications instead of a globally shared one. Additionally, the storage system can not be reconfigured at runtime and keeps the traditional POSIX I/O interface.

CAPFS introduces a new content-addressable file store that allows users to define data consistency semantics at runtime [22]. While providing a client-side plug-in API allows users to implement their own consistency policies, CAPFS is limited to tuning the consistency of file data and keeps the traditional POSIX interface. Additionally, the consistency semantics can only be changed on a per-file basis. JULEA covers a wider range of semantics and features a more fine-grained as well as a more dynamic approach.

Memory ordering and consistency are important factors in parallel programming for shared memory architectures, both for performance and correctness.

CPUs usually reorder memory load and store operations to improve performance [7,8]. Modern concepts such as those supported by C++11 and C11 allow developers to specify different constraints to achieve optimal performance while still maintaining correct execution of their applications [10]. JULEA's ordering semantics provide the same benefits by allowing the developer to provide additional semantical information to optimize execution.

ADIOS offers a novel and developer-friendly I/O interface that allows specifying the I/O configuration in an XML file that can be changed without recompiling the application [11,15]. Version 1.4 of ADIOS has added support for scheduling read operations. Several read operations can be scheduled using the `adios_schedule_read` function and then executed using the `adios_perform_reads` function. Read scheduling is very similar to JULEA's batches as it allows aggregating multiple operations for improved performance. However, JULEA's batches can contain arbitrary operations, making them more versatile.

4   Performance Evaluation

Benchmarks will be used to evaluate different performance aspects of JULEA and Lustre, which strives to support POSIX semantics. In addition to comparing JULEA to the other parallel distributed file system, a number of different semantics will be evaluated. However, due to the sheer amount of different semantics combinations, only those expected to have a significant impact on performance will be analyzed in more detail. JULEA's data performance will be evaluated using different atomicity, concurrency and safety semantics. A prior comparison of the metadata performance has been published in [12].

All evaluations have been conducted on the cluster of the Scientific Computing research group at the University of Hamburg. The benchmarks have been performed using a total of 20 nodes, with 10 nodes running the file system clients and 10 nodes hosting the file system servers. The nodes' hardware and software setup is as follows:

The client nodes each have two Intel Xeon Westmere EP HC X5650 CPUs (2.66 GHz, 12 cores total), 12 GB DDR3/PC1333 ECC RAM, a 250 GB SATA2 Seagate Barracuda 7200.12 HDD and two Intel 82574L Gbit Ethernet NICs. They run Ubuntu 12.04.3 LTS with Linux 3.8.0-33-generic and Lustre 2.5.0 (client); the MPI implementation is provided by OpenMPI 1.6.5.

The server nodes each have one Intel Xeon Sandy Bridge E-1275 CPUs (3.4 GHz, 4 cores total), 16 GB DDR3/PC1333 ECC RAM, three 2 TB SATA2 Western Digital WD20EARS HDDs, one 160 GB SATA2 Intel 320 SSD and two Intel 82579LM/82574L Gbit Ethernet NICs. They run CentOS 6.5 with Linux 2.6.32-358.18.1.el6_lustre.x86_64 and Lustre 2.5.0 (server).

To allow a proper assessment of the results, the following theoretical performance considerations should be kept in mind: The theoretical maximum performance of Gbit Ethernet is 125 MB/s. However, it is usually not possible to reach more than 117 MB/s due to overhead. Consequently, the maximum achievable performance between the clients and servers is approximately 1,170 MB/s.

The average round-trip time between the client and server nodes is 0.228 ms. Ignoring actual processing times, it is therefore possible to send and receive 4,386 requests/s.

The file systems' data performance will be evaluated using a large number of concurrently accessing clients that first write data and then read it back again; the write and read phases are completely separated and barriers ensure that only one type of operation takes place at any given time. To force the clients to read the data from the data servers during the read phase, the clients' cache was dropped after the write phase. The benchmark uses MPI to start multiple processes accessing the file systems in a coordinated fashion. There are two basic modes of operation: Individual files (each process accesses its own file, the individual files are accessed serially) and shared file (all processes access a single shared file concurrently in an interleaved fashion). All accesses use a variable block size and are non-overlapping, that is, no write conflicts occur. The file systems have been set up to provide ten data servers and one metadata server. Each benchmark has been repeated at least three times to calculate the arithmetic mean as well as the standard deviation.

4.1   Lustre

Lustre has been set up using its default options except for the stripe count that has been set to -1 to enable striping over all available object storage targets (OSTs); the stripe size has been set to 1 MiB. While each OST has been provided by one of the servers' HDDs, the meta data target (MDT) has been provided by one of the SSDs. Lustre has been mounted using the client module as a normal POSIX file system with the `flock` option that enables support for file locking. The option should not have any influence on the benchmark results because they do not use file locking.

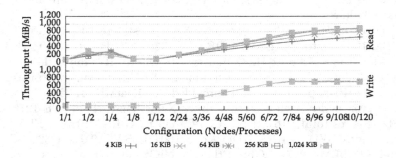

Fig. 3. Lustre: individual files via POSIX

Individual Files. Figure 3 shows Lustre's read and write performance when using individual files via the POSIX interface. Regarding read performance, it is interesting to note that configurations with a single node exhibit different performance characteristics depending on the number of processes. While the configurations with one, eight and twelve processes all achieve a throughput of roughly 100 MiB/s, the configurations with two and four processes deliver 200–300 MiB/s; while this effect has to be related to some data being read from the cache of the operating system, the exact reasons for this are unclear. As explained earlier, the benchmark drops all caches between the read and write phases, therefore, this effect should not occur. The remaining configurations gradually deliver more performance as more nodes are added until reaching their maximum performance with ten nodes. As expected, smaller block sizes result in lower read performance due to additional overhead. However, it is interesting to note that even with a single process and a block size of 4 KiB, Lustre achieves a read performance of roughly 100 MiB/s. As mentioned previously, the Gbit Ethernet network can transfer at most 4,386 requests/s. Taking this into account, Lustre should only be able to read at a maximum of 17 MiB/s. This discrepancy is due to Lustre performing client-side readahead to increase performance. When considering write performance, it can be seen that all block sizes deliver the same performance. This is most probably due to Lustre's use of client-side write caching. Because individual files are used and each file is only accessed by one node, Lustre can utilize caching without sacrificing POSIX compliance.

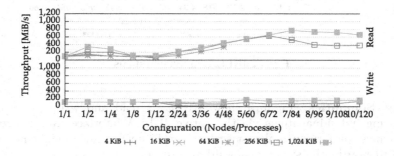

Fig. 4. Lustre: shared file via POSIX

Shared File. Figure 4 shows Lustre's read and write performance when using a single shared file via the POSIX interface. The read performance for the configurations using one node behaves in a similar way to the test case with individual files. For small block sizes, not all results could be collected because Lustre's performance was too low and the jobs exceeded the job scheduler's time limit. For 256 KiB and 1,024 KiB, the performance increases until six and seven nodes, respectively, and afterwards drops with each additional node. This result is surprising because only read operations are performed by all accessing clients, that is, no locking should be required. However, it appears that Lustre still introduces some overhead for these accesses, decreasing overall performance significantly. For the write phase, an interesting effect occurs: While using only a single node, performance is stable for all block sizes. When using more than one accessing nodes, performance drops for all block sizes less than 1,024 KiB. As soon as multiple nodes are involved, Lustre has to send all write operations directly to the data server to achieve POSIX compliance. An additional factor for the low performance could be write locking that needs to be performed due to the concurrently accessing clients.

4.2 JULEA

JULEA has been configured to use a POSIX storage backend on the data servers' system HDDs. Additionally, JULEA was set to use a maximum of six client connections per node because it was observed that the default of twelve caused severe performance problems due to the large amount of TCP connections.

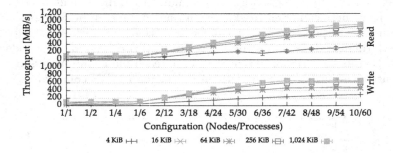

Fig. 5. JULEA: individual items

Default Semantics. Figure 5 shows JULEA's read and write performance when using individual items via the native JULEA interface. Regarding read performance, performance almost scales linearly until seven to eight nodes are used. Afterwards, the speedup slows down, reaching a maximum of more than 900 MiB/s using a block size of 1,024 KiB. As expected, smaller block sizes provide a lower overall performance with the exception of 16 KiB and 64 KiB that are reversed. Regarding write performance, the same effects as in the read case can be observed. Even though the performance does not increase with more than seven clients, it remains at a stable level.

Figure 6 shows JULEA's read and write performance when using a shared item via the native JULEA interface. During the read phase, the performance curve looks almost identical to its counterpart using individual items. While the performance speedup slowed slightly when going from nine to ten nodes using individual items, the shared item case is not affected by this drop. Additionally, the block size of 16 KiB provides a more stable performance curve. During the write phase, the performance curve looks less smooth than when using individual items. For instance, using the largest block size of 1,024 KiB, performance drops when increasing the number of nodes from five to six, only to rise again when using seven nodes. The fact that overall performance is lower than when using

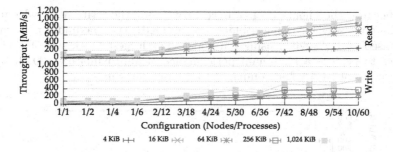

Fig. 6. JULEA: shared item

individual items indicates that the handling of shared files is suboptimal in the Linux kernel. Additional measurements using OrangeFS, different underlying file systems and JULEA's NULL storage backend have shown that these performance inconsistencies are not specific to JULEA, independent of the underlying file system and only occur if the file system is actually accessed using shared files.

To reduce the number of results and exclude the influences of the performance inconsistencies when using a single shared file, the following measurements have only been performed using individual items.

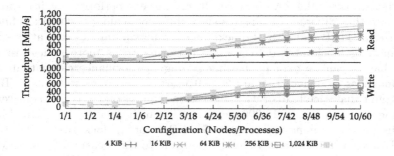

Fig. 7. JULEA: individual items using unsafe safety semantics

Safety Semantics. The following measurements have used the safety semantics to disable write acknowledgments for all write operations.

Figure 7 shows JULEA's read and write performance when using individual items via the native JULEA interface. During the read phase, there are only minor differences in performance in comparison to the default semantics. This is to be expected because the read operations are not handled differently depending on the safety semantics. During the write phase, performance is improved across the board for all block sizes. It is especially interesting to note that even a single process achieves the maximum performance of 110 MiB/s using a block size of

4 KiB because the clients do not have to wait for the write acknowledgments from the data servers. Using a block size of 4 KiB, the maximum performance is increased by 33 % when using ten nodes. The largest block size of 1,024 KiB manages to achieve a maximum performance of approximately 800 MiB/s, an improvement of 23 % when compared to the default semantics.

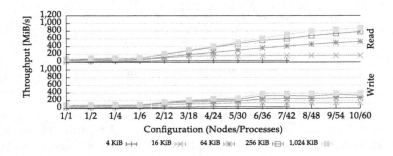

Fig. 8. JULEA: individual items using per-operation atomicity semantics

Atomicity Semantics. The following measurements have used the atomicity semantics to enforce atomic access for each read and write operation. JULEA currently implements atomicity using a centralized per-block locking algorithm.

Figure 8 shows JULEA's read and write performance when using individual items via the native JULEA interface. Regarding read performance, it is interesting to note that different block sizes show different scaling behavior: While the block sizes of 4 KiB and 16 KiB quickly reach a maximum and stay at this level, the remaining block sizes deliver more performance as more nodes are used. This behavior can be explained using a rough performance estimation: MongoDB manages to deliver roughly 20,000 inserts/s and 6,000 removes/s. Taking into account that each read or write operation requires one insert and one remove operation, a maximum of 13,000 operations/s can be performed.[2] This implies a maximum performance of roughly 50 MiB/s for a block size of 4 KiB and 200 MiB/s for a block size of 16 KiB. According to the measurements, 42 MiB/s and 170 MiB/s are reached for block sizes of 4 KiB and 16 KiB, respectively. Because a block size of 64 KiB can already support up to 800 MiB/s according to this approximation, the remaining block sizes' performance scales with the number of nodes. Interestingly, the largest block size of 1,024 KiB almost reaches the same performance as when using the default semantics. For smaller block sizes, the slowdown is more severe, however, resulting in a decrease of almost 30 %. Regarding write performance, the small block sizes manage to deliver almost the same performance as during the read phase. While the block size of 4 KiB reaches a maximum of 40 MiB/s, the block size of 16 KiB is limited to 140 MiB/s. The remaining block sizes perform much worse, however. This is due to the lower write performance that is already present when using the default semantics.

---

[2] This number is only intended to provide a rough estimate. In practice, the number might be lower due to the high discrepancy between insert and remove performance.

4.3 Discussion

The results demonstrate that the current state of parallel distributed file systems is mixed and that performance can be very hard to predict and understand. Even simple access patterns as the ones used for the presented benchmarks do not achieve the maximum performance. This is true for all tested file systems but has different reasons for each of them.

Lustre deals well with a large number of concurrent clients. This is most likely because Lustre can easily use the operating system's file system cache due to being implemented in kernel space. This allows Lustre to aggregate accesses and thus reduce the load on the servers. However, Lustre's performance is abysmal when accessing a single shared file as commonly done in scientific applications: Read performance decreases with more than seven client nodes and write performance does not scale beyond one client node. Consequently, only individual files are efficiently usable because it is not possible to inform Lustre about the application's I/O requirements to mitigate these performance problems.

JULEA's overall performance is held back by problems found within the underlying operating system and file systems. However, its dynamically adaptable semantics allow it to cater to a wide range of I/O requirements:

- Its default semantics enable performance results similar to those of Lustre when using large block sizes. Lustre has advantages for small block sizes due to its client-side caching and readahead functionalities. However, these advantages vanish as soon as shared files are used.
- The safety semantics can be used to reduce the network overhead by not awaiting the data servers' replies. This is similar to Lustre's default behavior when using individual files.
- Atomic operations can be achieved by using the atomicity semantics. While the performance of large read operations is not reduced significantly, write operations suffer a performance penalty of up to 40 %. However, using JULEA's fine-grained semantics, it is possible to use atomic operations only when absolutely necessary.

In contrast to Lustre, JULEA can be adapted to different applications by setting its semantics appropriately. While it is neither possible to improve Lustre's shared file performance due to its POSIX compliance nor to use other file systems such as OrangeFS for workloads requiring overlapping writes, it is possible for JULEA to support and to be tuned for these specific use cases.

5 Conclusion and Future Work

This paper presents a new approach for handling application-specific I/O requirements in HPC. The JULEA framework includes a prototypical implementation of a parallel distributed file system and provides a novel I/O interface featuring dynamically adaptable semantics. It allows applications to specify their I/O requirements using a fine-grained set of semantics. Additionally, batches enable the efficient execution of file system operations.

The results obtained in this paper demonstrate that there is need for I/O interfaces that can adapt to the requirements of applications in order to provide adequate performance for a variety of different use cases. The current circumstances effectively force application developers to adapt their applications to work around limitations found in specific file systems in order to achieve the best possible performance. An indication for this is the wide variety of I/O libraries, such as SIONlib [6], that deal with particular file system constraints. This can significantly increase the development and maintenance overhead because applications have to be optimized for different file systems' semantics instead of being able to optimize the file systems according to their I/O requirements.

The concept introduced by the JULEA framework fills the gap by allowing applications to adapt the file system to their exact I/O requirements instead of the other way around. The available results show that the supplementary semantical information can be used to adapt the file system's behavior in such a way as to optimize performance for specific use cases. Additional results and more in-depth information about JULEA are available in [13].

Even though JULEA provides a convenient testbed to experiment with different semantics and prototype new functionality, it is necessary to provide dynamically adaptable semantics for established I/O interfaces and parallel distributed file systems for widespread adoption of these new features. These interfaces have to be standardized and supported by a sufficiently large subset of file systems to provide consistent functionality across different implementations.

First of all, it is necessary to agree on default semantics suited for modern HPC applications and a common set of parameters that should be configurable. The semantics presented in this paper are meant to provide a good starting point for further evaluation.

5.1 Future Work

As mentioned previously, it is often unreasonable to port applications to new I/O interfaces due to their size and complexity. Thus, to avoid having to rewrite applications to be able to make use of JULEA's novel features, some form of compatibility would be preferable. Because many applications already use high-level I/O libraries such as ADIOS or NetCDF, JULEA could be integrated into applications by providing backends for these I/O libraries. As ADIOS's API design is relatively close to JULEA, a thin backend would be sufficient to enable all ADIOS-aware applications to use JULEA without any further modifications. ADIOS makes use of XML-based configuration files to specify the applications' I/O, which could be easily extended to add more semantical information about the actual data, similar to what has been done in [14].

References

1. Al-Kiswany, S., Gharaibeh, A., Ripeanu, M.: The case for a versatile storage system. SIGOPS Oper. Syst. Rev. **44**(1), 10–14 (2010)

2. Bartz, C.: An in-depth analysis of parallel high level I/O interfaces using HDF5 and NetCDF-4. Master's thesis, University of Hamburg, April 2014
3. Brinkmann, A., Cortes, T., Falter, H., Kunkel, J., Narasimhamurthy, S.: E10 – Exascale IO, May 2014. http://www.eiow.org/home/E10-Architecture.pdf? attredirects=0&d=1. Accessed: April 2015
4. Carns, P.H., Ligon III, W.B., Ross, R.B., Thakur, R.: PVFS: a parallel file system for linux clusters. In: Proceedings of the 4th Annual Linux Showcase and Conference, pp. 317–327. USENIX Association
5. Cluster File Systems Inc.: Lustre: a scalable, high-performance file system, November 2002. http://www.cse.buffalo.edu/faculty/tkosar/cse710/papers/lustre-whitepaper.pdf. Accessed: November 2014
6. Frings, W., Wolf, F., Petkov, V.: Scalable massively parallel I/O to task-local files. In: Proceedings of the Conference on High Performance Computing Networking, Storage and Analysis, SC 2009. ACM, New York (2009). http://doi.acm.org/10.1145/1654059.1654077
7. Gharachorloo, K., Gupta, A., Hennessy, J.: Performance evaluation of memory consistency models for shared-memory multiprocessors. In: Proceedings of the Fourth International Conference on Architectural Support for Programming Languages and Operating Systems, ASPLOS IV, pp. 245–257. ACM, New York (1991). http://doi.acm.org/10.1145/106972.106997
8. Gharachorloo, K., Lenoski, D., Laudon, J., Gibbons, P., Gupta, A., Hennessy, J.: Memory consistency and event ordering in scalable shared-memory multiprocessors. In: Proceedings of the 17th Annual International Symposium on Computer Architecture, ISCA 1990, pp. 15–26. ACM, New York (1990). http://doi.acm.org/10.1145/325164.325102
9. The IEEE and The Open Group: Standard for Information Technology - Portable Operating System Interface (POSIX) Base Specifications, Issue 7. IEEE Std 1003.1, 2013 Edition (incorporates IEEE Std 1003.1-2008, and IEEE Std 1003.1-2008/Cor 1–2013) pp. 1–3906, April 2013
10. ISO/IEC JTC 1/SC 22 - Programming languages, their environments and system software interfaces: ISO/IEC 9899:2011 - Information technology - Programming languages - C, December 2011
11. Klasky, S., Liu, Q., Lofstead, J., Podhorszki, N., Abbasi, H., Chang, C., Cummings, J., Dinakar, D., Docan, C., Ethier, S., Grout, R., Kordenbrock, T., Lin, Z., Ma, X., Oldfield, R., Parashar, M., Romosan, A., Samatova, N., Schwan, K., Shoshani, A., Tian, Y., Wolf, M., Yu, W., Zhang, F., Zheng, F.: ADIOS: powering I/O to extreme scale computing. In: SciDAC 2010 Conference Proceedings, pp. 342–347 (2010). http://computing.ornl.gov/workshops/scidac2010/papers/data_q_liu.pdf
12. Kuhn, M.: A semantics-aware I/O interface for high performance computing. In: Kunkel, J.M., Ludwig, T., Meuer, H.W. (eds.) ISC 2013. LNCS, vol. 7905, pp. 408–421. Springer, Heidelberg (2013)
13. Kuhn, M.: Dynamically adaptable I/O semantics for high performance computing. Ph.D. thesis, University of Hamburg, Germany, November 2014 (to be published)
14. Kunkel, J., Minartz, T., Kuhn, M., Ludwig, T.: Towards an energy-aware scientific I/O interface - stretching the ADIOS interface to foster performance analysis and energy awareness. Comput. Sci. Res. Dev. 27(4), 337–345 (2011)
15. Lofstead, J.F., Klasky, S., Schwan, K., Podhorszki, N., Jin, C.: Flexible IO and integration for scientific codes through the adaptable IO system (ADIOS). In: Proceedings of the 6th International Workshop on Challenges of Large Applications in Distributed Environments, CLADE 2008, pp. 15–24. ACM, New York (2008)

16. Message Passing Interface Forum: MPI: a message-passing interface standard. Version 3.0, September 2012. http://www.mpi-forum.org/docs/mpi-3.0/mpi30-report.pdf. Accessed: November 2014
17. Patil, S., Gibson, G.A., Ganger, G.R., Lopez, J., Polte, M., Tantisiroj, W., Xiao, L.: In search of an API for scalable file systems: under the table or above it? In: Proceedings of the 2009 Conference on Hot Topics in Cloud Computing, HotCloud 2009. USENIX Association, Berkeley (2009)
18. Rew, R., Davis, G.: Data management: NetCDF: an interface for scientific data access. IEEE Comput. Graph. Appl. **10**(4), 76–82 (1990). http://dx.doi.org/10.1109/38.56302
19. The HDF Group: Hierarchical data format version 5, July 2014. http://www.hdfgroup.org/HDF5. Accessed: November 2014
20. The TOP500 Editors: TOP500, June 2014. http://www.top500.org/. Accessed: November 2014
21. Vilayannur, M., Lang, S., Ross, R., Klundt, R., Ward, L.: Extending the POSIX I/O interface: a parallel file system perspective. Technical report ANL/MCS-TM-302, October 2008. http://www.mcs.anl.gov/uploads/cels/papers/TM-302-FINAL.pdf
22. Vilayannur, M., Nath, P., Sivasubramaniam, A.: Providing tunable consistency for a parallel file store. In: Proceedings of the 4th Conference on USENIX Conference on File and Storage Technologies, FAST 2005, vol. 4. USENIX Association, Berkeley (2005)
23. Wikipedia: Festplattenlaufwerk - Geschwindigkeit, November 2014. http://de.wikipedia.org/wiki/Festplattenlaufwerk#Geschwindigkeit. Accessed: November 2014
24. Wikipedia: Mark Kryder - Kryder's Law, November 2014. http://en.wikipedia.org/wiki/Mark_Kryder#Kryder.27s_Law. Accessed: November 2014

Predicting Performance of Non-contiguous I/O with Machine Learning

Julian Kunkel[1]([✉]), Michaela Zimmer[2], and Eugen Betke[2]

[1] DKRZ, Hamburg, Germany
kunkel@dkrz.de
[2] University of Hamburg, Hamburg, Germany

Abstract. Data sieving in ROMIO promises to optimize individual non-contiguous I/O. However, making the right choice and parameterizing its buffer size accordingly are non-trivial tasks, since predicting the resulting performance is difficult. Since many performance factors are not taken into account by data sieving, extracting the optimal performance for a given access pattern and system is often not possible. Additionally, in Lustre, settings such as the stripe size and number of servers are tunable, yet again, identifying rules for the data-centre proves challenging indeed.

In this paper, we (1) discuss limitations of data sieving, (2) apply machine learning techniques to build a performance predictor, and (3) learn and extract best practices for the settings from the data. We used decision trees as these models can capture non-linear behavior, are easy to understand and allow for extraction of the rules used. Even though this initial research is based on decision trees, with sparse training data, the algorithm can predict many cases sufficiently. Compared to a standard setting, the decision trees created are able to improve performance significantly and we can derive expert knowledge by extracting rules from the learned tree. Applying the scheme to a set of experimental data improved the average throughput by 25–50 % of the best parametrization's gain. Additionally, we demonstrate the versatility of this approach by applying it to the porting system of DKRZ's next generation supercomputer and discuss achievable performance gains.

Keywords: MPI · Non-contiguous I/O · Parallel I/O

1 Introduction

With MPI 2, an I/O interface has been standardized which promises to improve performance for parallel applications. Among the supported features, it explicitly supports non-contiguous I/O – one API call accesses multiple file regions, and, with collective I/O, multiple processes can coordinate their file accesses. The standard explicitly allows an implementation to exploit its knowledge about concurrent operations; for example, by scheduling the I/O calls intelligently. Since

We want to express our gratitude to the "Deutsches Zentrum für Luft- und Raumfahrt e.V." as responsible project agency and to the "Bundesministerium für Bildung und Forschung" for the financial support under grant 01 IH 11008 A-C.

© Springer International Publishing Switzerland 2015
J.M. Kunkel and T. Ludwig (Eds.): ISC High Performance 2015, LNCS 9137, pp. 257–273, 2015.
DOI: 10.1007/978-3-319-20119-1_19

there are many factors influencing performance in a supercomputer, extracting the best performance is anything but trivial. The available optimizations offer a selection of parameters to be adapted to target machine and specific workload, and through a wrong choice, performance may be degraded.

It is very difficult for users to estimate how an I/O pattern will perform under a given set of optimization parameters; they therefore typically try various parameters, which resembles a limited brute force approach. While there are some rules of thumb and expert knowledge, e.g. "data sieving helps for small data accesses", they need to be adjusted for each system. DKRZ will install the first phase of its next generation supercomputer HLRE3 this year, providing more than 2 Petaflop/s and 30 Petabyte storage capacity. However, we struggle in the data center to determine good defaults for certain Lustre parameters such as number of servers and stripe size, as they are very specific to system and application. Even the knowledge of specialists often merely helps to direct the exploration of the complex parameter space for data sieving and stripe size. It would be helpful if expert knowledge could be automatically inferred from observations. To alleviate this, in the long run, our research strives to provide a tool that will be aware of system capabilities as well as its performance history, using all to suggest the best parameter set for the task at hand.

Our main contributions are: (1) The evaluation of decision trees to capture and predict non-contiguous performance behavior. (2) The semi-automatic extraction of expert knowledge from the measurements.

This paper is structured as follows: Related work regarding I/O research and machine learning is discussed in Sect. 2. Section 3 presents performance results of experiments with several relevant parameters that are currently missing in data sieving. The overall machine learning approach is introduced in Sect. 4. In Sect. 5, the accuracy of the predictor is investigated and interesting results are shown. We apply the approach to the porting system for DKRZ's next generation system in Sect. 6, to evaluate whether we can extract best practices for this test system; this would permit use of the strategy on the full system as well. Section 7 concludes the paper and discusses future steps.

2   Related Work

Widely used concepts to improve I/O performance are non-blocking I/O, data pre-fetching and write-behind. ROMIO [1], a common MPI-IO implementation, offers collective I/O and data sieving with the promise to speed up performance. *Data sieving* optimizes independent sparse non-contiguous I/O; by accessing larger file regions and discarding unwanted data, it avoids seeks on hard disk drives and improves performance, especially for very small accesses. While holes in the access pattern can just be read and discarded for reads, it is not as easy for writes because they require reading the whole region, modifying changed data and writing it back. Traditional file systems that offer POSIX semantics require locking to avoid conflicts with concurrent writes to an overlapping region. Ching et al. [2] implemented ListIO for PVFS in MPI which supports access to multiple file regions in one request and, thus, does not need such a read-modify-write cycle. Over the last years, there has not been much research into further optimizing non-contiguous I/O.

Optimizing collective I/O has been investigated more deeply. The basic idea of coordinated I/O is that the processes exchange information about accessed file regions; then they compute a schedule assigning responsibility for specific file regions and defining the access order; finally, data is exchanged amongst those processes that ultimately perform the I/O. There are many variations to this basic process: The Two-Phase protocol as discussed by Thakur et al. [1] iterates over communication and I/O phases – in each phase, a maximum amount of data is accessed. Multiphase-I/O [3,4] iteratively increases locality, and Orthrus [5] offers several strategies to optimize either for file or process locality. One difficulty with these approaches is that they require careful analysis and tuning of parameters.

Monitoring and analysis of system state and performance data is important to optimize HPC systems; tools include Vampir [6] and Darshan [7]. While they help in the analysis, they cannot set parameters.

There are several research projects which try to integrate machine learning into the analysis and optimization cycle. One of the first is the work of Madhyastha and Reed [8], comparing classification of I/O access patterns by feed-forward neural networks and by hidden Markov models. Higher level application I/O patterns are inferred and looked up in a table to determine the file system policy to set for the next accesses. The table, however, has to be supplied by an administrator implementing his heuristics. Magpie, a system by Barham et al. [9], traces events under Windows, merging them according to pre-defined schemas specifying event relationships. Their causal chains are reconstructed and clustered into models for the various types of workload observed. Deviations will point to anomalies deserving human attention. Classifying new traces according to these models yields insights into their actual and expected performance, leading to various applications such as capacity planning and on-line latency tuning, as described in [10,11]. Behzad et al. [12] offer a framework that uses genetic algorithms to auto-tune select parameters of a stack consisting of HDF5, MPI and Lustre. But its monolithic view of the system disregards the relations between the layers as well as the users' individual requirements, setting optimizations but once per application run.

All of these systems have in common the need for human intervention to benefit from the results or to apply the solutions to the problems identified. The SIOX framework [13,14] aims to implement a holistic approach covering the full cycle of monitoring, analysis, machine learning of the adequate settings and their automatic enactment.

3   Limits of Non-contiguous I/O

First, we discuss the handling of non-contiguous I/O with data sieving. From the user perspective, the bytes to access are defined by the MPI file view: MPI

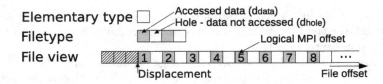

Fig. 1. Example non-contiguous access pattern in which every other elementary data type is accessed.

data types are used to describe the elementary data type (etype) the file consists of (e.g. a structure), and the file type specifies which of those are to be accessed by the current process. A programmer usually accesses data at the granularity of etypes. An offset (the so-called displacement) is added to the beginning of the file to account for e.g. file meta-data. An example file view and mapping of its data to bytes in the file is illustrated in Fig. 1. Here, the etype could be a 4-Byte integer; the file type covers four contiguous regions (first etype is occupied, then a hole, ...) and allows access to every other etype. We will refer to the number of bytes one contiguous region occupies as d_{data}, and to the hole size as d_{hole}. The data sieving algorithm is parameterized by its *state* (*s*: on, off) and a *buffer size* (s_{buffer}) which defines the granularity of data access for reading and writing. It will access data at this size, starting from the bytes needed to be accessed next that are not contained in the current buffer.

3.1 Experiments

To demonstrate the suboptimality and to illustrate the difficulties in parameterizing the current data sieving strategy, we conducted several experiments. The `mpipattern` benchmark has been created to measure performance for arbitrary file views and MPI hints. In the following experiments[1], this benchmark uses a file pattern similar to Fig. 1; the etype is always an integer and we vary d_{data} between 1 KiB and 16 MiB, the data sieving options (*s*, s_{buffer}) and the *fill level*
$$f := \frac{d_{\text{data}}}{d_{\text{data}} + d_{\text{hole}}} = \frac{d_{\text{data}}}{d_{extent}}.$$

The experiments have been conducted on our 20 node cluster: 10 I/O nodes are each equipped with an Intel Xeon E3-1275@3.4 GHz, 16 GByte RAM and one Seagate Barracuda 7200.12. Nodes are interconnected with Gigabit Ethernet and the performance of one HDD is about 100 MiB/s. The I/O nodes run CentOS 6.5 and Lustre 2.5. On one additional compute node, a single `mpipattern` process is run which reports the observed performance. In a production environment, multiple users and applications access the shared storage; this may lead to high fluctuations in observable performance. For a first discussion, this effect is ignored; during the measurement, the whole cluster has been blocked to ensure exclusive access to the I/O servers. The test file is pre-created with 8 GiB of data; between runs, we clear the Linux cache. In the following, we limit our discussion to read calls.

---

[1] Experimental data is taken from Schmidtke's thesis [15].

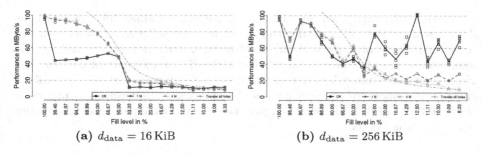

(a) $d_{data} = 16\,\mathrm{KiB}$ **(b)** $d_{data} = 256\,\mathrm{KiB}$

Fig. 2. Independent I/O performance for a variable hole size and two block sizes measured with one client for different data sieving options.

Overall, out of 198 different configurations, the best result is achieved without data sieving in 56 cases, and in 59 and 54 cases with $s_{buffer} = 1\,\mathrm{MiB}$ and $s_{buffer} = 4\,\mathrm{MiB}$, respectively. A 100 MiB buffer never achieved best performance, even for larger datasets and holes. In 29 cases, performance of all settings was similar (relative performance within 95 % of the best). Figure 2a and b show the observed performance for $d_{data} = 16$ and 256 KiB, respectively. The lines in the figures represent the performance with data sieving turned off, or its buffer set to 1 MiB or 4 MiB of data. Additionally, a theoretic line is given: it is based on the maximum network performance (117 MiB/s) and assumes all holes would be read; e.g., for a fill level of 10 %, user data is transferred at 11.7 MiB/s.

For small blocks, data sieving performs better, because it avoids seeks and the system benefits from the Linux read-ahead mechanism. The effects of read-ahead can be seen by comparing performance from fill levels f of 100 % and 98 % ($d_{hole} = 160\,\mathrm{Byte}$). With a low fill level and thus large holes, data sieving actually slows down the operations; the reason is that it actually reads the full buffer size for every required data block even though we only need the first 16 KiB of data. When accessing 256 KiB of data, this strategy also explains the effect starting at $f = 16\,\%$: The 4 MiB buffer is much slower than the 1 MiB buffer. However, a user would expect that larger buffers may increase performance but never decrease it.

Moreover, for the large access granularity, turning data sieving off is beneficial starting with $f = 33\,\%$. For larger accesses, data sieving extracts similar performance in many cases. Several interesting effects can be seen: performance of $f = 98\,\%$ ($d_{hole} = 8\,\mathrm{KiB}$) is slower; with $f = 66\,\%$ ($d_{hole} = 128\,\mathrm{KiB}$), performance converges; and with smaller fill levels, some values attain much better performance. The 128 KiB hole can be explained by Linux read-ahead mechanisms: normally, another 128 KiB block of data is fetched, which is available in any case. We are striping in 1,048,576 Byte blocks; due to the layout, every single 256 KiB access is covered completely by one Lustre object storage target (OST). In these cases, with data sieving, another performance pattern can be observed. Note that for a 1 MiB buffer, each I/O involves one additional OST, all of the requested data of which is discarded.

Presumably, the reason for the zig-zag pattern for small fill levels without data sieving is the OST-centric read-ahead in Lustre. Several patterns lead to sequential access of data on a subset of servers, such as for 25 % and 12.5 %; here, data is read from every (or every other) OST in a sequential fashion. The read_ahead_stats from /proc reveal that per 256 KiB access, about 0.03 and 0.7 cache misses occur for the very good and bad cases, respectively. The osc_read shows about 0.77 to 1.75 operations per access; thus, some patterns trigger more operations than others.

3.2   Performance Factors

There are many factors involved in the performance of non-contiguous I/O that can be classified into the applications' spatial and access pattern, the behavior of file system client and parallel file system, and hardware characteristics. Each individual I/O operation comes with some overhead for the system call and transferring and processing the triggered I/O request within the parallel file system. If data is not cached, the operation is dominated on the server side by the latency of the block storage. Aggregating multiple non-contiguous accesses into one operation alleviates these costs but may transfer irrelevant data from block devices and across the network, and thus benefit depends on the throughput of these components. The file's data distribution (stripe size in Lustre and number of servers) has a big impact on performance, as it should be avoided to involve too many I/O servers with very small requests. Therefore, the alignment of the accessed data on the file system's server is important. An additional factor is the cost for distributed locking needed for writes. The operating system's and file system's pre-fetching mechanisms can transform some read patterns automatically into beneficial sequential access patterns without explicitly requesting large chunks at application level.

The decision whether or not to merge a consecutive operation with the current operation depends on the knowledge of these factors; the best choice may fuse certain blocks and process others individually. As none of these factors are explicitly included in ROMIO's data sieving, and the buffer sizes can only be changed when opening the file, this approach is hard to tune for users and the achieved performance is often suboptimal. Therefore, machine learning may be a suitable technique to analyze the data.

4   Methodology

Every approach to optimization will consist of three basic steps: Identifying the task's fixed parameters, choosing the best set of variable parameters and suggesting or enacting them. While we aim to perform the machine learning with the execution of the application (online), in this study, we measured the performance and investigate the machine learning offline to evaluate the accuracy.

In our use case, the fixed parameters consist of the access pattern, specified by a sequence of (offset, size) tuples (cf. Fig. 1). As this may constitute a sequence of finite but unbounded length, we use a simple first abstraction, computing only the total *size* d_{data} of each data type and its *fill level* f. Further research will target more accurate representations and characteristics of the resulting parameter spaces.

Our variable parameters are the *state* of data sieving (*on, off*) and the *buffer size* s_{buffer} used for it. Our optimization criterion is the performance p, the average (arithmetic mean) throughput achieved under the `mpipattern` benchmark. The data to be used in training and validation was gathered by running the benchmark five times per parameter set, then the performance's arithmetic mean is computed for each configuration. The relevant variable parameters and target labels are stored in a CSV file. The evaluation is conducted by loading the observed performance data into the statistics tool R. We then create the models offline and compare their performance to the best achievable performance. Since the observed performance data volume is small (CSV files of roughly 100 KiB), the time needed for machine learning is negligible in the analysis.

We use standard machine learning techniques to extract knowledge from the data. For our first method to evaluate, we chose Classification And Regression Trees (CART) [16], as implemented in the open source library Shark [17], the statistics tool R and the language python. Our first step is to create a predictor for the performance to be expected from a given set of fixed and variable parameters. This Performance Model (PM) is trained on a number of samples, allowing it to estimate a performance value for any given parameter set (see Fig. 3a). For this model, the CSV file contains: *size, fill level, state, buffer size* and *arithmetic mean performance*. We train the model using a subset of rows in the CSV file (the training set) and predict the performance for the validation set. Since the mean performance of the data is available for the validation set, we can determine the error.

As not all machine learning algorithms are suited to regression, we transformed this task into a classification problem which allows for a full comparison later on. For this, we form classes by quantizing the performance space into intervals, similar to the "shingles" used in the R package `lattice`; parameter sets are classified by mapping them to the interval "class" covering the achieved performance p. For every parameter set thus classified, a representative of the pertinent interval is then chosen as a performance estimate. Since our interval partition is ignorant of the true performance's distribution, we chose the intervals' middle points as representatives to facilitate error bound assertions. Using the median of the values classed within each interval might decrease actual errors as it better approximates clusters within the interval, though. With this set-up, however, uniform intervals are imprecise in the lower ranges, while small relative variations in the higher ranges will mean several classes displacement. We therefore vary interval length with the absolute values they cover: Given a relative error limit ϵ and the maximum performance measured p_{max}, we define $l := \epsilon \cdot p_{\text{max}}$. Between 0 and l, we choose uniform interval lengths $|I_i| := l \cdot 2\epsilon$; above l, we increase them stepwise by $|I_i| := |I_{i-1}| \cdot (1 + 2\epsilon)$. This implies the quantization mean error $err_q := \frac{1}{4n} \sum_{i=0}^{n} (\Delta I_i)$, where ΔI_i is the interval size of the class that belongs to the i-th instance.

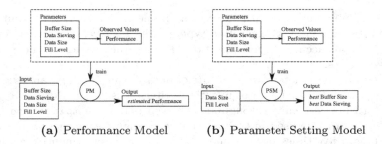

(a) Performance Model   (b) Parameter Setting Model

Fig. 3. PM provides a performance estimate, whereas PSM provides the corresponding "tunable" variable parameters to achieve it.

We imagine an implementation could automatically tune the data sieving parameters online by estimating the performance for all sets of variable parameters and picking the values expected to perform best. This strategy has the advantage that we can validate the prediction accuracy online by comparing estimation with measurement, and disable the predictor if the results differ significantly from the observation.

However, this strategy requires us to assess performance for many different settings. Instead, we chose a complementing strategy to directly predict the variable settings for a given set of fixed parameters; we call this the Parameter Setting Model (PSM) Fig. 3b. Since the performance data is still available to us, we can also quantify the efficiency of this model in our evaluation. Note that in an implementation, the PSM could use the performance prediction of the PM to check its correctness.

5   Evaluation

To assess the quality of the machine learning algorithms, we created simpler models and use them as a baseline: A very naive prediction for a sample would be the arithmetic mean performance. In our experiments, the mean performance is 54.7 MiB/s, which leads to an average error of 28.5 MiB/s. Experimenting with different linear models based on the fixed and variable settings led to a model with a mean error of 12.7 MiB/s.

5.1   Validation

A series of k-fold cross-validation tests (Table 1) shows that on our data set, the CART classifier performs better than the our baseline. Unless noted otherwise, all results cited in this section have been generated with the following parameters: size of training set = size of validation set = 387 instances. Classification parameter: $\epsilon = 0.05$, $p_{max} = 109.554$.

Figure 4a shows the observed and predicted classes when using half the training data. The graph is sorted by the true performance class (black dots) and

Table 1. Prediction errors in MB/s and class errors for training sets under k-fold cross-validation. Values for k = 3..7 lie in between.

k	Performance errors			Class errors		
	min	mean	max	min	mean	max
2	6.74	6.80	6.87	1.46	1.59	1.72
4	5.19	6.25	6.92	0.94	1.34	1.72
8	4.67	5.66	6.77	0.87	1.19	1.62

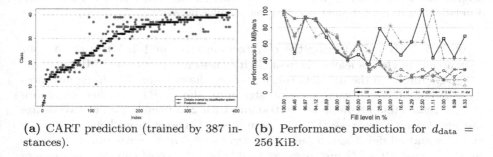

(a) CART prediction (trained by 387 in-stances).

(b) Performance prediction for $d_{\mathrm{data}} = 256\,\mathrm{KiB}$.

Fig. 4. Quality of PM performance prediction.

the red dots show the predicted classes. The actual performance prediction for $d_{\mathrm{data}} = 256\,\mathrm{KiB}$ are presented in Fig. 4b. Often, a predicted performance matches one of the nearby observed values; the reason is that the original data point is not contained in the training set and thus the model learns from nearby values and uses them as approximation. Clearly, the sensitivity of the pattern and thus major performance differences are impossible to predict accurately if instances are missing.

5.2   Investigating Training Set Size

We are working towards a self-optimizing system that stops the optimization process as soon as some convergence criterion is fulfilled, e.g. the learning rate is negligible or the error rate small enough. This bypasses the need for rules or a static formula to calculate an optimal training set size, allowing us to replace learning algorithms and apply this approach to a variety of problems without interdependency with our data acquisition scheme.

Nevertheless, we have investigated the prediction accuracy of PM under various training set sizes, using a variant ("inverse") k-fold cross-validation where one fold is used for training and the remaining $k - 1$ for validation instead of the other way round. The results of the CART classifier are shown in Fig. 5. The 774-instances case validates the overall scheme: The CART classifier was both trained and validated with the whole data set, yielding a prediction mean

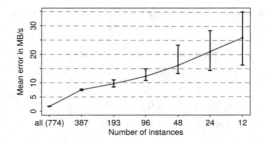

Fig. 5. Mean prediction error of PM by training set size under inverse k-fold cross-validation. Class prediction errors show very similar behavior.

error of $1.7\,\mathrm{MB/s}$. Deducting the quantization error of $1.31\,\mathrm{MB/s}$ due to our assignment to classes leaves the real CART classifier error at $0.39\,\mathrm{MB/s}$.

Beginning with the full data set, we reduce the number of training instances by a factor of $1/2$ in each iteration step until the CART classifier stops producing reasonable predictions. By training with 24 instances, we can recognize the first learning progress: the maximum prediction error drops beneath the raw data's standard deviation. 96 instances were sufficient to outperform the naive approach, and after 387 instances, we could observe a considerable stagnation of the learning rate (cf. Table 1). Moving to random forests [18] yielded very similar results, not justifying the additional computational cost incurred.

The potential benefit of the approach can be assessed by applying the strategy to the experimental data. Assuming the user had parameterized the data sieving for all experiments in the same way, the average performance benefit of choosing the optimal values instead is given in Table 2. As a default, setting data sieving to $1\,\mathrm{MiB}$ would yield the best result, as even optimal parameter settings outperform it by at most $7.6\,\mathrm{MB/s}$. But even here, our CART-driven PSM with training and test set sizes of 387 instances each could improve performance by $1.9\,\mathrm{MB/s}$.

5.3 Decision Rules

By classifying only into three classes (slow, average, fast), the CART classifier applied to the complete data set of mean performance values creates a tree of 221 nodes; the first 4 levels are shown in Fig. 6. The following analysis relies on

Table 2. Average performance improvements that can be achieved with the PSM-learned and best choices for s_{buffer}, compared to one default choice.

Default choice	CART PSM, 387 Inst.	Best choice
Off	$4.2\,\mathrm{MB/s}$	$9.6\,\mathrm{MB/s}$
1 MiB	$1.9\,\mathrm{MB/s}$	$7.6\,\mathrm{MB/s}$
4 MiB	$6.9\,\mathrm{MB/s}$	$12.2\,\mathrm{MB/s}$
100 MiB	$6.9\,\mathrm{MB/s}$	$12.2\,\mathrm{MB/s}$

Fig. 6. First three levels of the CART classifier rules for three classes slow, avg, fast ($[0, 25]$, $(25, 75]$, > 75 MB/s). The dominant label is assigned to the leaf nodes – the probability for each class is provided in brackets.

the fact that the test cases cover the selected parameter space equally. Based on the figure, some rules can be derived: e.g., the left-most path tells us that of non-contiguous accesses with $f < 20\%$ and $d_{\text{data}} = 2$ MiB, 79% will show slow and 20% average behavior. Other rules thus created include: in most cases, sparse access to larger blocks is slow; sequential access to small blocks is fast (due to read-ahead); for $f > 2/3$ and $d_{\text{data}} < 200$ KiB, data sieving is beneficial for almost all accesses; in the case of $f < 2/3$ and 2 MiB $< d_{\text{data}} < 8$ MiB, performance is mostly fast – surprisingly, larger accesses achieve merely average performance. Experts in the field typically know the first rules, but the last two statements are interesting.

6 Learning Best Practices for DKRZ

DKRZ runs a test system to prepare for their next supercomputer that will be installed in Q1 of 2015. We conducted measurements on this porting system to study whether our methodology can be applied to learn appropriate Lustre settings. The test system consists of 20 compute nodes and a Lustre 2.5 file system hosted by one ClusterStor 6000 enclosure (SSU) from Seagate with two OSS servers and 84 HDDs. All nodes are interconnected with FDR-Infiniband.

The following measurements are conducted with our NCT library which is currently in development and offers POSIX-compatible calls for non-contiguous access. Amongst other strategies, it implements the ROMIO algorithm for data sieving, allowing for an analysis similar to the one discussed before: A single process performs reads or writes on a previously created 10 GB file, varying hole size and access granularity. As opposed to the results discussed so far, this evaluation is conducted on the file system shared amongst all users. To gain comparable results, the client cache is cleaned between the runs, and several repetitions are measured. If a value differs more than 20% from the average of all others measured so far for this configuration, an additional run is executed after which this procedure is repeated, resulting in up to 10 measurements for cases with high variation.

Overall, 408 configurations of hole and block size were measured for up to 8 combinations of user controllable settings (one or two Lustre servers, 128 KiB or 2 MiB stripe size, data sieving with 4 MiB or off). 240 of these were run with all 8 settings; of the remainder, 84 more cases each were only evaluated for 128 KiB and 2 MiB stripe sizes, respectively. For validation purposes, the two settings of stripe sizes were also evaluated for one server, which should not make a difference.

Table 3. Frequency in which a setting of the row is better by 20 % (at least 5 MB/s) than the one of a column, out of 240 hole/size configurations.

Data sieving			Off				On			
Server count			1		2		1		2	
Stripe size			128 KiB	2 MiB	128 KiB	2 MiB	128 KiB	2 MiB	128 KiB	2 MiB
Sieving	Server #	Stripe								
Off	1	128 KiB	-	0	0	0	31	31	33	31
		2 MiB	2	-	0	0	31	32	34	32
	2	128 KiB	54	57	-	3	43	43	35	37
		2 MiB	56	59	2	-	39	45	42	37
On	1	128 KiB	114	115	109	93	-	5	8	19
		2 MiB	104	103	90	83	0	-	3	14
	2	128 KiB	112	112	104	107	65	71	-	8
		2 MiB	112	111	104	96	56	69	2	-

First, we look at the frequency at which a particular setting is superior to another. Table 3 shows the number of times the configuration in a row achieves at least 20 % and 5 MB/s better performance than the one in the column. A few unexpected cases are observable: when only one server is used, the variation in stripe sizes should lead to similar performance results. However, e.g. without data sieving, the 2 MiB stripe size is in 2 (out of 240) cases better than the one with 128 KiB which is presumably due to fluctuations on the shared storage resource. Without data sieving, it can be seen that typically one server achieves less performance than two; with data sieving, there are some cases in which one server significantly outperforms two. In the sampled configurations, turning data sieving on is usually superior to turning it off in about 100 cases, the naive I/O is better in about 35 cases. While the configurations are similar to the ones measured on our test cluster, the amount of data accessed is typically small compared to the fast interconnect and storage system, which explains why data sieving dominates the naive approach. With 20 % tolerance, there are a few cases in which the stripe size is relevant; reducing tolerance to 10 %, this number rises to about 50. Nevertheless, we expect that this number will grow much higher on DKRZ's final system than in this preliminary experiment.

6.1   Applying Machine Learning

In the following analysis, used the scikit-learn Python library with its Decision-TreeClassifier (with its entropy criterion) on the CSV file to learn the decision tree and extract knowledge. The triple (sieving, server count, stripe size) of the best possible choice for each configuration is encoded as an integer and learned. Note that we treat all configurations equally – in a real system, each would be weighted based on the probability of observing it, making sure that frequent access patterns will be well optimized.

Looking at some statistics of the achieved performance allows us to quantify the optimization potential: The best observed performances for a single run are up to 800 MB/s and 350 MB/s for read and write operations, respectively. Over the 240 configurations, an average performance of 213 MB/s is observable. The average performance over all configurations, choosing the best setting for each, is 293 MB/s; choosing the worst for each, it is 146 MB/s. Creating a decision tree of depth 1 yields the rule *if (write) select (data sieving=on, servers=2, stripe=128 KiB) else select (data sieving=on, servers=1, stripe=128 KiB)*. Following even this simple rule reduces the gap in average performance compared to the best per-case choice possible to only 16.6 MB/s.

In practice, we will not normally have all settings sampled for a given configuration, resulting in missing values similar to our case with 408 configurations. Using pruned trees with reduced height however, as in this evaluation, rules may still suggest settings that have not been measured so far, and if this recommendation is followed, the sampled portion of the parameter space will grow in the long run. Using all values, the average performance over all measured configurations and settings is 244.7 MB/s. The best setting for each configuration achieves an average performance of 357.7 MB/s, and the worst choice of 179.9 MB/s. Table 4 lists the average performance loss of a given default choice when compared to the best available choices.

Table 4. Tunable settings: expected performance of a user's default choice vs. the per-case optimal setting (absolute in MB/s, relative and performance loss in MB/s compared to the best choice) using arithmetic and harmonic mean. The number of cases in which a setting is the worst or best choice out of all 408 configurations is listed for reference.

Default choice			Best	Worst	Arithmetic mean			Harmonic mean	
Servers	Stripe size	Sieving	Freq.	Freq.	Rel.	Abs.	Loss	Rel.	Abs.
1	128 KiB	Off	20	35	58.4 %	200.1	102.1	9.0 %	0.09
1	2 MiB	Off	45	39	60.7 %	261.5	103.7	9.0 %	0.09
2	128 KiB	Off	87	76	69.8 %	209.5	92.7	8.8 %	0.09
2	2 MiB	Off	81	14	72.1 %	284.2	81.1	8.9 %	0.09
1	128 KiB	On	79	37	64.1 %	245.6	56.7	15.2 %	0.16
1	2 MiB	On	11	75	59.4 %	259.2	106.1	14.4 %	0.15
2	128 KiB	On	80	58	68.7 %	239.6	62.6	16.2 %	0.17
2	2 MiB	On	5	74	62.9 %	258.0	107.3	14.9 %	0.16

When averaging test run performance, two scenarios may apply: Computing centers desire a continually saturated job queue, where the mean achieved over a fixed time is of interest. Users, who typically have a fixed workload to be completed, regard the mean derived from the total time to completion as more important. The first is given by the arithmetic mean, while the harmonic mean yields the second. Another interpretation of the arithmetic columns is

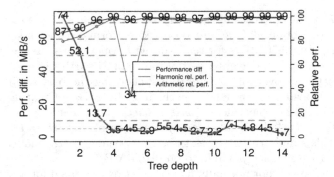

Fig. 7. Performance difference between learned and the best choices, by maximum tree depth, for the DKRZ porting system.

the expected performance when picking a random experiment, while the harmonic performance defines the average throughput expected when executing all experiments with the given setting. The arithmetic mean favors fast execution, the harmonic mean is restricted by slow performance. With one server, 2 MiB stripe size and activated data sieving, for instance, 64.1 % of the best possible performance is expected for any run and the arithmetic mean performance loss compared to the optimal settings is 57 MB/s (achieving 245.6 MB/s). However, when executing all experiments with this setting, only 15.2 % of the best performance is expected resulting in an average harmonic mean performance of only 0.16 MiB/s. This low harmonic mean is due to experiments with large holes and small amounts of data achieving a performance below 1 MB/s. By choosing the optimal tunable settings, the achievable performance can thus be significantly increased, which further underlines the relevance of this early study.

Figure 7 shows the average performance loss between machine learning and the per-case optimum, based on the depth of the tree learned. The figure also includes the relative performance achieved, compared as harmonic and arithmetic means. Even at a very low height, the tree proves very efficient, achieving more than 87 % of the arithmetic mean performance and 79 % of the harmonic[2]. This is much better than all possible fixed defaults (72 % arithm. mean and 15 % harmonic mean performance at best). Therefore, the trees avoid suboptimal choices efficiently. One exception is the tree with a depth of 5: it suggests several slow settings, resulting in a relative harmonic mean performance of 34 %.

A tree of level four (shown as in Fig. 8) achieves good performance (about 3.5 MB/s average gap) at a reasonable size; it can be expected to achieve 99 % of the potential performance (arithmetic and harmonic). The leaves are the choices based on the access pattern. The number of instances in which this choice is

---

[2] Note that for a tree of depth one, 80 choices are made for which no measurement is available; these values are excluded from the calculation of the average performance. For bigger trees, less than a handful of choices are not quantifiable. Therefore, we believe this comparison to be fair.

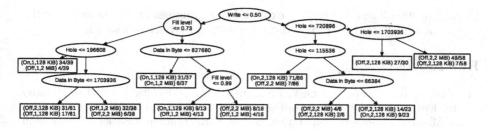

Fig. 8. Decision tree for DKRZ test system with height 4. In the leaf nodes, the settings (Data sieving, server number, stripe size) and number of instances of the best and second best choice are shown.

the best is given in the leaf for convenience, followed by the second best choice. Interestingly, in most cases, both differ only in a single parameter, i.e., either number of servers, data sieving or stripe size. Given an access pattern, this tree allows users (or a library) to select appropriate and efficient settings. Also, using machine learning and extracting rules from such a tree proved far less time consuming and error-prone than studying the measurement results by hand.

7 Conclusions and Future Work

Even constrained to the few parameters governing data sieving, optimizing HPC I/O is anything but trivial. We have discussed the challenges and limitations faced when optimizing non-contiguous access using data sieving, and used Classification and Regression Trees to create a predictor for the I/O performance resulting from a given parameter set. Evaluating this predictor under various training set sizes, we found it a fairly accurate indicator of the performance to be expected. We created another model that will choose the parameter set promising the highest performance, achieving significant improvements over the best default settings and increasing the average I/O performance by several MiB/s. While the decision trees reproduced known heuristics correctly, we also harvested interesting insights from them, yielding best practices for data sieving on our system.

Future work will focus on automatically generating simple rules-of-thumb from the extensive decision trees. Integrating our findings with the SIOX system will allow us to harness this knowledge for optimization as well as for active learning during phases of low utilization. Thus, sparse training data can be supplemented to greatly improve predictor accuracy and overall effectiveness. Since data sieving does not incorporate the important performance factors, observed performance behaves unpredictably in many cases, leading to suboptimal accuracy of the CART when using sparse training data. The parameters discussed in this paper are system dependent, but not affected by the file type and pattern, marking them as candidates for machine learning. We are currently working on an adaptive data sieving algorithm relying on this, and researching more accurate representations and characteristics of the resulting parameter spaces.

Finally, future efforts will further explore ML techniques and their applicability, as well as the effects of selective data acquisition and active learning.

References

1. Thakur, R., Gropp, W., Lusk, E.: Data sieving and collective I/O in ROMIO. In: FRONTIERS 1999: Proceedings of the The 7th Symposium on the Frontiers of Massively Parallel Computation, p. 182. IEEE Computer Society, Washington, DC (1999)
2. Ching, A., Choudhary, A., Coloma, K., Liao, W.K., Ross, R., Gropp, W.: Non-contiguous I/O accesses through MPI-IO. In: Proceedings of the 3rd International Symposium on Cluster Computing and the Grid, CCGRID, p. 104. IEEE Computer Society, Washington, DC (2003)
3. Singh, D.E., Isaila, F., Calderon, A., Garcia, F., Carretero, J.: Multiple-phase collective I/O technique for improving data access locality. In: Proceedings of the 15th Euromicro International Conference on Parallel, Distributed and Network-Based Processing, PDP, pp. 534–542. IEEE Computer Society, Washington, DC (2007)
4. Singh, D.E., Isaila, F., Pichel, J.C., Carretero, J.: A collective I/O implementation based on inspector-executor paradigm. J. Supercomputing **47**(1), 53–75 (2009)
5. Zhang, X., Ou, J., Davis, K., Jiang, S.: Orthrus: a framework for implementing efficient collective I/O in multi-core clusters. In: Kunkel, J.M., Ludwig, T., Meuer, H.W. (eds.) ISC 2014. LNCS, vol. 8488, pp. 348–364. Springer, Heidelberg (2014)
6. Knüpfer, A., Brunst, H., Doleschal, J., Jurenz, M., Lieber, M., Mickler, H., Müller, M.S., Nagel, W.E.: The vampir performance analysis tool-set. In: Resch, M., Keller, R., Himmler, V., Krammer, B., Schulz, A. (eds.) Tools for High Performance Computing, Proceedings of the 2nd International Workshop on Parallel Tools, pp. 139–155. Springer, Heidelberg (2008)
7. Argonne National Laboratory: Darshan. http://www.mcs.anl.gov/project/darshan-hpc-io-characterization-tool
8. Madhyastha, T., Reed, D.: Learning to classify parallel Input/Output access patterns. IEEE Trans. Parallel Distrib. Syst. **13**(8), 802–813 (2002)
9. Barham, P., Donnelly, A., Isaacs, R., Mortier, R.: Using magpie for request extraction and workload modelling. In: Proceedings of the 6th Symposium on Opearting Systems Design and Implementation, vol. 6, pp. 259–272 (2004)
10. Barham, P., Isaacs, R., Mortier, R., Narayanan, D.: Magpie: online modelling and performance-aware systems. In: Proceedings of the 9th Conference on Hot Topics in Operating Systems, vol. 9 (2003)
11. Isaacs, R., Barham, P., Bulpin, J., Mortier, R., Narayanan, D.: Request extraction in magpie: events, schemas and temporal joins. In: Proceedings of the 11th Workshop on ACM SIGOPS European Workshop, EW11. ACM, New York (2004)
12. Behzad, B., Huchette, J., Luu, H.V.T., Aydt, R., Byna, S., Yao, Y., Koziol, Q.: Prabhat: a framework for auto-tuning hdf5 applications. In: Proceedings of the 22nd International Symposium on High-Performance Parallel and Distributed Computing, HPDC 2013, pp. 127–128. ACM, New York (2013)
13. Kunkel, J.M., Zimmer, M., Hübbe, N., Aguilera, A., Mickler, H., Wang, X., Chut, A., Bönisch, T., Lüttgau, J., Michel, R., Weging, J.: The SIOX architecture – coupling automatic monitoring and optimization of parallel I/O. In: Kunkel, J.M., Ludwig, T., Meuer, H.W. (eds.) ISC 2014. LNCS, vol. 8488, pp. 245–260. Springer, Heidelberg (2014)

14. Zimmer, M., Kunkel, J.M., Ludwig, T.: Towards self-optimization in HPC I/O. In: Kunkel, J.M., Ludwig, T., Meuer, H.W. (eds.) ISC 2013. LNCS, vol. 7905, pp. 422–434. Springer, Heidelberg (2013)
15. Schmidtke, D.: Analyse und Optimierung von nicht-zusammenhängende Ein-/Ausgabe in MPI, April 2014
16. Breiman, L., Friedman, J.H., Olshen, R.A., Stone, C.J.: Classification and Regression Trees. Wadsworth & Brooks, Pacific Grove (1984)
17. Igel, C., Heidrich-Meisner, V., Glasmachers, T.: Shark. J. Mach. Learn. Res. **9**, 993–996 (2008)
18. Breiman, L.: Random forests. Mach. Learn. **45**(1), 5–32 (2001)

A Best Practice Analysis of HDF5 and NetCDF-4 Using Lustre

Christopher Bartz[1]([✉]), Konstantinos Chasapis[2], Michael Kuhn[2],
Petra Nerge[2], and Thomas Ludwig[1]

[1] Deutsches Klimarechenzentrum, Bundesstraße 45a, 20146 Hamburg, Germany
bartz@dkrz.de
[2] University of Hamburg, Bundesstraße 45a, 20146 Hamburg, Germany

Abstract. With the constantly increasing number of cores in high performance computing (HPC) systems, applications produce even more data that will eventually have to be stored and accessed in parallel. Applications' I/O in HPC is performed in a layered manner; scientific applications use standardized high-level libraries and data formats like HDF5 and NetCDF-4 to store and manipulate data that is located inside a parallel file system. In this paper, we present a performance analysis of the parallel interfaces of HDF5 and NetCDF-4 using different test configurations in order to provide best practices for choosing the right I/O configuration. Our evaluation follows a breakdown approach where we examine the performance penalties of each layer. The tested configurations include: (*i*) different access patterns, disjoint and interleaved (*ii*) aligned and unaligned accesses (*iii*) collective and independent I/O (*iv*) contiguous and chunked data layout. The main observation is that using interleaved data access in a certain configuration achieves near the maximum performance. Also, we see that NetCDF-4 does not provide the ability to align the access to the Lustre object boundaries. To overcome this we have developed a patch that resolves this issue and improves the performance dramatically.

Keywords: Best practices · HDF5 · NetCDF-4

1 Introduction

Many high performance computing (HPC) applications deal with large volumes of data. A typical example of I/O-intensive applications are simulations from the field of earth system science that generate vast amounts of data as snapshots and model output files. The performance of those applications is highly dependent on the storage system performance. For this reason, they make use of parallel I/O to achieve maximum performance.

Apart from the I/O performance, another important aspect for such applications is efficient data management. To improve this, standardized file formats are used to store and manipulate data so that they can be easily exchanged between institutes and scientists for further processing. Among the commonly

J.M. Kunkel and T. Ludwig (Eds.): ISC High Performance 2015, LNCS 9137, pp. 274–281, 2015.
DOI: 10.1007/978-3-319-20119-1_20

used formats are the Hierarchical Data Format (HDF5) [4] and the Network Common Data Format (NetCDF-4) [10]. They are surrounded by application programming interfaces (APIs), which allow manipulation and retrieval of the data by programs written in various programming languages like C or Fortran.

In this paper we present these common I/O interfaces, evaluate their performance and describe best practices to achieve optimal performance. To conduct our analysis, we used a self-modified version of the I/O Performance Benchmark (IOR) [6] to generate I/O patterns that mimic the I/O routines of real-world applications. We used the parallel distributed file system Lustre [2] due to its prevalence in HPC systems. The main contributions of this paper are: *(i)* an analysis of the complete I/O path of the aforementioned interfaces while using different access patterns and I/O configurations, *(ii)* our proposed performance enhancements for HDF5 and NetCDF-4, and *(iii)* a set of best practices that can be used to achieve peak performance when using HDF5 and NetCDF-4.

The rest of this paper is organized as follows: First, we provide background information in Sect. 2. We discuss the related work in Sect. 3. Our evaluation is presented in Sect. 4. Finally, we summarize our findings in Sect. 5.

2   Background

2.1   Lustre

Lustre [2] is a POSIX-compliant, open-source distributed parallel file system that powers over 60 % of the TOP100 supercomputers [9]. Figure 1 presents its generic architecture. Lustre separates metadata and data handling in Metadata Servers (MDSs) and Object Storage Servers (OSSs), respectively. Lustre's file data storage follows an object-based paradigm: file data is split up into multiple objects called "stripes". The objects are spread and manipulated by the OSSs. The Object Storage Targets (OSTs) and the Metadata Targets (MDTs) hold the actual data and metadata.

2.2   HDF5 and NetCDF-4

The HDF5 and NetCDF-4 APIs provide parallel access to the data. They perform the I/O in a layered manner as illustrated in Fig. 2. The NetCDF-4 API uses

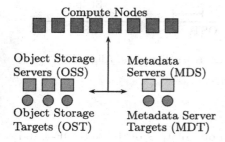

Fig. 1. Lustre architecture

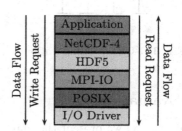

Fig. 2. Layered HPC I/O

HDF5 to store the data. HDF5 uses the I/O implementation of MPI. MPI-IO is built on top of a POSIX-complaint parallel file system. Finally, I/O is performed by the I/O driver.

Both HDF5 and NetCDF-4 formats store data in a self-describing portable way using multi-dimensional arrays. Beyond that, HDF5 and NetCDF-4 distinguish between *contiguous* and *chunked* data storage. Contiguous means that the whole data of a dataset is stored in one contiguous array of bytes apart from the header. Chunked means that the dataset is split into chunks, which are rectangular regions. The chunks are written into independent locations in the file. The locations of the chunks are stored in the header section of the dataset, using a B-tree [1] data structure. B-trees hold the stored data in a sorted way and allow access and manipulation in logarithmic time. They are commonly used in databases and filesystems. Chunking is required if compression of the data is desired.

3 Related Work

Many scientific papers deal with I/O optimization techniques. Dickens et al. in [3] propose that each client communicates with fewer OSTs and disjointly to reduce network and OST contention. They call these patterns x-OST (or all-to-all) depending on the number of OSTs each client is communicating with (see Fig. 3). Modifications to the Two-Phase I/O algorithm used by ROMIO are proposed in [7]. Their modifications aim to *(i)* align the accesses to the file system lock boundaries, *(ii)* reduce network and OSS contention by using I/O aggregators and *(iii)* eliminate interleaved accesses. In [8] it has been argued that a high degree of parallelism leads to high I/O contention at the servers and does not scale with the amount of processors. To overcome this they introduce a system which consists of a set of delegated I/O processes. The authors of [11] show that a large stripe count can degrade the performance because of the increased protocol overhead. In this case, clients must communicate with many OSTs, and have to deal with reduced memory cache locality when the network buffer is multiplexed for many OSTs. A set of optimizations in HDF5 and MPI-IO is presented in [5]. For HDF5, they propose aggregate metadata operations.

Fig. 3. 1-OST communication   **Fig. 4.** Unaligned vs. Aligned

4 Evaluation

In this section we present the main results of our analysis of the NetCDF-4 and HDF5 interfaces concerning parallel I/O access. We include two discrete data access modes: *disjoint* and *interleaved*. Disjoint means that each client accesses a large contiguous region of the data, which leads to interaction between all data servers (all-to-all pattern). In the interleaved access pattern each client accesses a large non-contiguous region (note that we refer to logical and not physical address access). An interleaved access can result in any x-OST pattern.

4.1 Testbed Specifications

We used the following software libraries: HDF5 1.8.11, OpenMPI 1.6.4, Lustre 2.5, NetCDF-4 4.1.3 and IOR 3.0.1. Our system consists of 10 storage servers and 10 client nodes. Each storage server hosts an OSS and an OST. For the sake of simplicity we will refer to OSTs instead of OSSs. The single MDS and MDT are also hosted in one of the data servers. All nodes are connected via a single Gigabit Ethernet with a measured network performance between clients and servers of 1,125 MiB/s.

Each data server node runs CentOS 6.5 and has an Intel Xeon Sandy Bridge E-1275 CPU (3.4 GHz, 4 cores) and 16 GB of RAM. We use a 2 TB SATA2 Western Digital Green HDD for the OST and a 160 GB SATA2 Intel 320 SSD as the MDT. The client nodes consist of two Intel Xeon Westmere EP HC X5650 CPUs (2.66 GHz, 12 cores) and 12 GB of RAM. They use Ubuntu 12.04.3 LTS with Linux 3.8.0-33-generic.

4.2 Experimental Design

In each I/O configuration we perform a write phase followed by a read phase. To ensure the independence of each phase, we restart the system before each write or read and wait for 30 s. In the restart operation we first unmount Lustre from both the clients and servers, then flush the kernel caches and finally remount Lustre. Our plots always show the mean of three different measurements if not stated otherwise.

We use a single IOR process per client node which is sufficient to saturate the network interface. The goal of our experiments is to extract the maximum performance from the system, therefore we use all the client nodes. In each write/read phase we transfer 20 GiB per client node (in total 200 GiB). This exceeds the available memory on the client nodes (see Sect. 4.1) and prevents any artificial client caching effect.

If not stated otherwise, we set the transfer size per read/write call to 1 MiB. We believe that this is a reasonable value, since it matches the chunk size that the Lustre clients use internally to send all their data if possible. Furthermore, the default Lustre stripe size equals 1 MiB. When using chunked I/O, we set the chunk size to 1 MiB, too.

If not specified otherwise, we align the beginning of the data section to the Lustre stripe sizes. This also includes the physical start address of the chunks, when chunked I/O is used. The aligned mechanism is not implemented by the

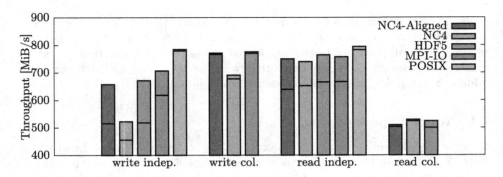

Fig. 5. Disjoint pattern

default NetCDF-4 API. Our evaluation revealed that this results in huge performance penalties thus we have added the respective function call and evaluated the benefit.

4.3 Contiguous Data Layout

Figure 5 shows the results of a test using contiguous and disjoint data layout. The figure does not show the mean but the minimum and maximum obtained throughput, because many results have a high variation when using independent I/O. We believe that the reason lies in the combination of the competition on the OST and the network resources with the lack of synchronization when using independent I/O.

We see that the results are much lower than the practical maximum (1,125 MiB/s). We are sure that this can be explained by the contention on the OSTs and network resources, because the access pattern is an all-to-all OST pattern; each client node is communicating with each OST node.

The results of the analysis of the 1-OST pattern are illustrated in Fig. 6. Writing or reading with POSIX and MPI-IO performs nearly identical, achieving almost the theoretical maximum. The 1-to-1 communication between clients and servers prevents competition on OST and network resources. We observe that HDF5 benefits from independent I/O. On the opposite side, collective I/O adds unnecessary synchronization between the clients when performing a 1-to-1 communication, which slows down the performance.

Contrary to the little overhead of the layering induced by HDF5, the default NetCDF-4 issues unaligned data accesses which performs much worse. This is due to the fact that unaligned accesses leads to communication with more than one OST (see Fig. 4). Implementing the function call to align the data we observe that NetCDF-4 performance improves greatly and performs similar to HDF5. Thus, the lack of alignment in the NetCDF-4 API is a real disadvantage regarding the performance.

Next, we investigate the impact of the transfer size on the performance when using the disjoint pattern. Since the combination of independent I/O with this

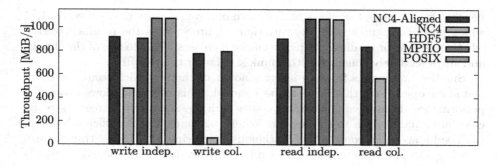

Fig. 6. 1-OST pattern

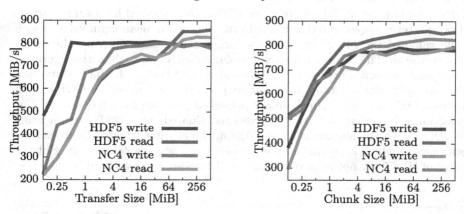

Fig. 7. Varying transfer size   **Fig. 8.** Chunked layout

access pattern results in an inconsistent behavior, we evaluate only the collective I/O configuration. Figure 7 reports the results for both HDF5 and NetCDF-4. We can see that as soon as the transfer size is greater than 0.5 MiB for HDF5 and 4 MiB for NetCDF-4 the write operation reaches the maximum performance which is 800 MiB/s. Furthermore, we see that the read performance increases at a slower pace than the write operation. We believe that this behavior is due to the fact that the write requests can be aggregated and cached by the OSTs, so they can be written out in a efficient way in contrast to the reads that the OSTs have to deliver immediately which can imply seek overhead. However, the seek effect flattens out once the transfer size is larger than 128 MiB.

4.4   Chunked Data Layout

In the following test we analyze the performance when using chunked and disjoint data layout with various chunk sizes. In this configuration the transfer size is fixed to 512 MiB, because our previous tests have indicated that the performance benefits from a large transfer size. Furthermore, we measure only collective I/O which produces figures with low variation. Figure 8 shows the results. Overall, whether writing or reading, the performance increases with the size of the chunks and stays relatively constant with chunk size larger than 4 MiB.

Smaller chunk sizes imply a larger amount of chunks which results in more metadata operations that have to be handled. This overhead slows down the performance dramatically, especially when writing, since the B-tree has to be calculated and written to the header. When the chunk size is sufficiently large, the results are analogous to the contiguous case using 512 MiB as transfer size (see Fig. 7). The reason is that the metadata overhead, mentioned above, is minimized and also the same access pattern is used: Large contiguous regions are accessed by each process.

Figure 9 illustrates the results using HDF5 with chunked layout and various x-OST pattern. We set the chunk size to the maximum meaningful value, which is the value of the block size, because larger chunk sizes decrease the meta-data overhead. The achieved figures are significantly lower than the figures of the disjoint pattern. Furthermore, independent I/O realizes better results than collective I/O. Beyond that, we did also perform tests using NetCDF-4 with various x-OST pattern (figures are not presented here due to lack of space). The performance is similar to HDF5. We also reevaluated the 1-OST pattern using NetCDF-4 with our alignment patch. Again, the alignment patch improved the performance, which is significantly expressed when writing collectively. But the figures of HDF5 are not achieved, which indicates an API overhead in this case.

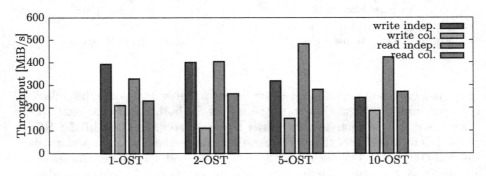

Fig. 9. 1- to 10-OST pattern, HDF5 with chunked I/O

5   Conclusions

In this paper we presented an extensive evaluation of the HDF5 and NetCDF-4 libraries. Our results allow us to provide best practices concerning their usage in order to achieve high throughput. Although our test environment is small in comparison to a large HPC cluster, we believe that our results can be transferred to these systems also.

For HDF5 we see that it performs optimal with contiguous layout and if the 1-OST pattern is used with I/O accesses aligned to the Lustre stripes. Moreover, independent I/O should be used in this case, as the synchronization implied by collective I/O is unnecessary and slows down the performance. Chunked I/O achieves lower performance. However, in some cases it is required (for example, if the use of compression is desired). The best performance with chunking is achieved with the disjoint pattern in combination with large chunk sizes.

Furthermore, collective I/O should be used as we have observed figures with high variation using independent I/O with this access pattern. Finally, we believe that chunking does benefit from large transfer sizes, too. Due to the lack of alignment in the NetCDF-4 API, the disjoint pattern with large transfer sizes is better suited as an interleaved pattern if high performance is desired. Chunked I/O with NetCDF-4 does also perform best with the disjoint pattern.

References

1. Bayer, R., McCreight, E.: Organization and Maintenance of Large Ordered Indexes. Springer, New York (2002)
2. Braam, P.J., Zahir, R.: Lustre: a scalable, high performance file system. Cluster File Systems, Inc. (2002)
3. Dickens, P., Logan, J.: Towards a high performance implementation of MPI-IO on the lustre file system. In: Meersman, R., Tari, Z. (eds.) OTM 2008, Part I. LNCS, vol. 5331, pp. 870–885. Springer, Heidelberg (2008)
4. Group, H., et al.: Hierarchical data format version 5 (2000). Software package, http://www.hdfgroup.org/HDF5
5. Howison, M.: Tuning HDF5 for lustre file systems. In: Workshop on Interfaces and Abstractions for Scientific Data Storage (IASDS 2010), Heraklion, Crete, Greece, 24 September 2010 (2012)
6. IOR: https://github.com/chaos/ior
7. Liao, W.K., Choudhary, A.: Dynamically adapting file domain partitioning methods for collective I/O based on underlying parallel file system locking protocols. In: International Conference for High Performance Computing, Networking, Storage and Analysis, SC 2008, pp. 1–12. IEEE (2008)
8. Nisar, A., Liao, W.K., Choudhary, A.: Scaling parallel I/O performance through I/O delegate and caching system. In: International Conference for High Performance Computing, Networking, Storage and Analysis, SC 2008, pp. 1–12. IEEE (2008)
9. OpenSFS (2014). http://www.opensfs.org/press-releases/lustre-file-system-version-2-5-released/. Accessed December 2014
10. Rew, R., Davis, G., Emmerson, S., Davies, H., Hartnett, E.: The NetCDF users guide-data model, programming interfaces, and format for self-describing, portable data-NetCDF version 4.1. Unidata Program Center (2010)
11. Yu, W., Vetter, J., Canon, R.S., Jiang, S.: Exploiting lustre file joining for effective collective IO. In: Seventh IEEE International Symposium on Cluster Computing and the Grid, CCGRID 2007, pp. 267–274. IEEE (2007)

Striping Layout Aware Data Aggregation for High Performance I/O on a Lustre File System

Yuichi Tsujita$^{(\boxtimes)}$, Atsushi Hori, and Yutaka Ishikawa

RIKEN AICS, Kobe, Hyogo 650-0047, Japan
yuichi.tsujita@riken.jp

Abstract. An MPI-IO library, ROMIO, improves I/O performance for noncontiguous accesses by using its two-phase I/O optimization. When we have multiple MPI processes on each node which has multicore processors, a data aggregation assignment mismatch leads to performance degradation due to network contention. In this paper, we propose an alternative aggregation scheme that manages the striping layout of a Lustre file system to minimize network contention. The optimization has achieved up to about 30 % performance improvements on our 4-node PC cluster system connected via InfiniBand FDR links in performance evaluation by an HPIO benchmark program.

Keywords: MPI-IO · ROMIO · Two-phase I/O · Aggregator · Lustre

1 Introduction

Two-phase I/O optimization of ROMIO [9] repeats read-modify-write sequences for noncontiguous access patterns in collective write operations. The read-modify-write sequence consists of (1) file read, (2) data exchanges among MPI processes, and (3) file write. Two-phase I/O assigns an aggregation task to some or all of the MPI processes, called aggregators, for data collection and file I/O. Various research studies have achieved performance improvements by applying their optimization scheme. However no optimizations currently address network contention problems due to the aggregation task mismatch on a multi-core processor PC cluster system in accessing a Lustre file system [6]. An increase in the number of processes per node increases the number of processes which access a Lustre file system in the same striping round in each node by using the ROMIO. As a result, file I/O throughput is degraded.

In this paper, we propose file striping pattern aware aggregator assignment for performance improvement by minimizing network contention. Performance improvements up to about 30 % has been achieved by a 4-node PC cluster system accessing a Lustre file system. We briefly report the implementation mechanism and performance results of the proposed scheme in the following sections.

© Springer International Publishing Switzerland 2015
J.M. Kunkel and T. Ludwig (Eds.): ISC High Performance 2015, LNCS 9137, pp. 282–290, 2015.
DOI: 10.1007/978-3-319-20119-1_21

2   Two-Phase I/O in Collective Write Operations

Two-phase I/O consists of repetitions of data exchange and file I/O phases to reveal the performance degradation due to noncontiguous accesses. Figure 1 shows a typical two-phase I/O scheme in collective write operations for two processes. When we have data gaps in access patterns, the two-phase I/O proceeds with read-modify-write operations. Here, both MPI processes are assumed to be aggregators, and they read contiguous data including data gaps from their file domains to a temporary buffer named collective buffer. Read data on the buffers are updated by new data to be written after the data exchanges, and are written-back to the target file domain. These operations, numbered from 1 to 3 in Fig. 1, are repeated until the whole target file domain is accessed.

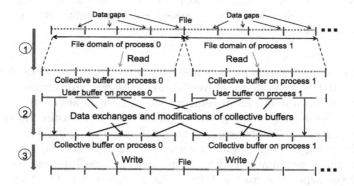

Fig. 1. Two-phase I/O flow in collective write operation for two MPI processes

In a Lustre file system, which is the target file system for our performance improvements, an abstract I/O interface layer of ROMIO named ADIO [8] provides a Lustre driver layer to exploit its performance advantages [1]. In its optimization context, the collective buffer size is aligned to the striping size of a Lustre file system inside the ADIO driver layer.

3   Optimized Aggregator Assignment in Striping Layout Aware Two-Phase I/O

ROMIO assigns one aggregator per node in the default configuration, although optionally we can have multiple aggregators. Figure 2 shows aggregator task assignment layout when we have 4 MPI processes per node by using two nodes to access 2 Object Storage Targets (OSTs) of a Luster file system. The original ROMIO appoints aggregator tasks to the MPI processes in a block manner layout based on its one-dimensional rank list holding MPI ranks. The aggregator layout is independent of the MPI process layout as shown in Fig. 2(a). In this case, network contention occurs in each network link from each PC node because

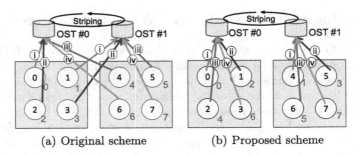

(a) Original scheme   (b) Proposed scheme

Fig. 2. Aggregator assignment layout of ROMIO by (a) original scheme and (b) our proposed scheme for 2 OSTs when we have 4 aggregators per node. The rectangles represent PC nodes, and circles inside rectangles represent MPI processes, where numbers in circles are the MPI rank. Numbers under the circles stand for the assignment order of the aggregators. Arrows from MPI processes represent striping file accesses, where numbers from i to iv of them are striping round.

multiple (or all) aggregators in the same node access different OSTs at the same time in each striping access round by sharing the same interconnect.

For further performance improvements, we propose an alternative aggregator assignment scheme with striping layout awareness on a Luster file system, as shown in Fig. 2(b). We implemented a location-aware grouping scheme for MPI processes by using the host name of each node to generate the striping layout aware aggregator assignment order. In the scheme, two lists, one storing host names and the other one storing MPI ranks, are prepared. The host name list consists of the host name of every node, and the rank list keeps every MPI rank with the same index of the host list. By using the two lists, the proposed scheme carries out host name matching to generate a two-dimensional rank-list, where the outer index stands for a node ID and the inner one corresponds to a process ID in the node. Note that the node ID is numbered from 0 in ascending order. Each element of the original one-dimensional rank list of ROMIO is updated by filling each MPI rank in the two-dimensional list in a outer index (node-ID) major order. As a result, aggregator layout is in a round-robin manner among nodes as shown in Fig. 2(b). Since aggregators in the same striping access round are distributed among nodes and each node has aggregators which access the same OST, we can eliminate the network contention due to shared network link use among aggregators.

The proposed aggregator assignment also has an advantage in minimizing data exchange cost. Figure 3(a), and (b) show the data exchange behavior in the original and our aggregator assignments, respectively. When file I/O is done by using striping accesses for the two OSTs, two aggregators access each target OST at the same time in every striping round. In Fig. 3, the numbers from (i) to (iv), which are depicted by rounded rectangles inside a PC node, represent the striping round order. Prior to the file I/O, every aggregator gathers data from every process including itself. In the original case in Fig. 3(a), the two aggregators

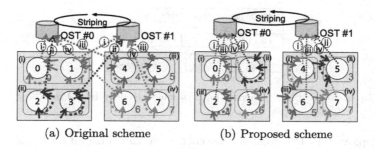

(a) Original scheme   (b) Proposed scheme

Fig. 3. Data exchange behavior in (a) original aggregator assignment scheme and (b) our proposed scheme for 2 OSTs when we have 4 aggregators per node

grouped in a rounded rectangle on the same node collect data simultaneously in each striping round. Thus, they have a total of 8 incoming data transfers (4 incoming data transfers × 2 aggregators per group) through a network link on the same node. Here we only count incoming data transfer through a network link, and exclude incoming data transfers from other processes on the same node.

However, our proposal has 4 incoming data transfers via a network link on each node in each striping round. In this scheme, we can minimize the network contention compared with the original case because the original case shares a network link of each node for 8 incoming data, while our case can separate the same number of incoming data evenly into 2 nodes. This can result in performance gains relative to the original case, and a large improvement is expected when we have more OSTs and PC nodes.

We provided the new aggregator assignment scheme in two data exchange modes to examine its performance impacts in terms of data exchange algorithms; one mode is based on the original implementation, which utilizes pairs of MPI_Isend and MPI_Irecv, followed by MPI_Waitall for data exchange completion check (hereinafter IS_IR), and the other one is an alternative implementation that uses MPI_Alltoallv instead of pairs of MPI_Isend and MPI_Irecv (hereinafter AtoAv).

4   Performance Results

Our proposed scheme was implemented in MVAPICH2 version 2.0rc1 [11]. We used HPIO benchmark [4] on a 4-node PC cluster system with one Intel Xeon E3–1280V2 and 32 GiB memory in each node, connected by Mellanox InfiniBand FDR Host Channel Adapter through an InfiniBand FDR non-intelligent switch, Mellanox SX6005. The collective write operation for noncontiguous access patterns was evaluated on Lustre version 2.6.54 configured with 1 meta data server (MDS) and 2 object storage servers (OSSs) with two OSTs each via Infini-Band FDR links. Every server system consisted of one Intel Xeon E3-1270V3 and 32 GiB memory. It is noted that the 2 OSTs of each OSS were configured by iSCSI storage devices built on RAID 10 storages of a dual Intel Xeon E5-2640V2 Linux server with 64 GiB memory, which was connected to the same InfiniBand switch via an InfiniBand FDR link.

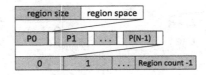

Fig. 4. Noncontiguous access pattern generation by HPIO benchmark

We deployed 4 MPI processes on each node to utilize all CPU cores, and a total of 16 MPI processes were executed on 4 nodes. The HPIO benchmark evaluated collective writes for noncontiguous access patterns by using three parameters; region size, region space, and region count, as shown in Fig. 4. We specified 256 bytes in the data gap (region space) in each 11,744 bytes of data region per process (region size); a data block ((region size + region space) × the number of processes) of about 185 kbytes (= $(11,744 + 256) \times 16$) was formed by the 16 processes. The 16 MPI processes generated 48,000 data blocks and wrote them in a single file of about 8.6 GiB in total in each run. The HPIO benchmark reported mean throughput values through the 12 runs by excluding the highest and lowest performance values.

Figure 5 shows the performance results in the IS_IR case with two kinds of MPI process layouts, bunch and scatter, available in MVAPICH2. This figure shows the results obtained by the original case with one aggregator (ORIG, agg_n=1) and 4 aggregators (ORIG, agg_n=4) per node in addition to the results of our proposed scheme with 4 aggregators per node (RR, agg_n=4) in each process mapping pattern. The original case degraded its performance with an increase in the number of aggregators from 1 to 4 processes per node because of aggregator assignment mismatch. However, our proposed scheme with 4 aggregators per node outperformed the original case with one aggregator by about 25 % because of performance improvements in the file read and data exchanges inside the two-phase I/O. Such two-phase I/O internal behavior is discussed later.

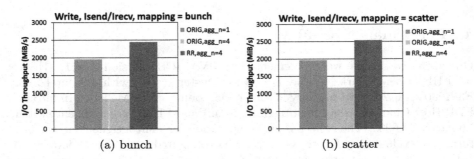

(a) bunch   (b) scatter

Fig. 5. Obtained I/O throughput values in an IS_IR data exchange pattern with two kinds of MPI process layout

Figure 6 shows the performance values obtained in the `AtoAv` case in the same evaluation procedure done for the `IS_IR` case. Our approach denoted as `RR`, `agg_n=4` also outperformed the original layout cases using both 1 and 4 aggregators per node (`ORIG`, `agg_n=1` and `ORIG`, `agg_n=4`, respectively) up to 30 %.

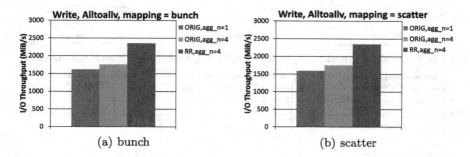

(a) bunch   (b) scatter

Fig. 6. I/O throughput values in an `AtoAv` data exchange pattern with two kinds of MPI process layout

The above performance improvements came from the minimization in time for both data exchanges and file I/O with the help of our striping layout oriented aggregator assignment. Figure 7 shows the internal operation mean times of the two-phase I/O at each MPI process in the `IS_IR` case. We examined three major operations, file read(`read`), data exchange(`exch`), and file write(`write`). Here we measured each operation time at every MPI process independently and showed the mean values of each MPI rank in Fig. 7.

Compared with Fig. 7(a) and (d), where we had one aggregator per node, 4 aggregators per node (Fig. 7(b) and (e)) led to increased operation times, especially in data exchanges. However, our alternative aggregator assignment drastically decreased data exchange times by about 1/4, as shown in Fig. 7(c), and (f). It was considered that the original aggregator assignment shared a network link connected to each node for 48 incoming data (12 incoming data × 4 aggregators per node) through a network link in each node for data exchanges at each striping round in the same way explained in Sect. 3. Our striping layout oriented assignment minimized such network contention with the help of the round-robin layout by reducing the number of incoming data to 1/4 (12 incoming data through a network link in each node). Therefore roughly speaking, our proposal minimized the amount of incoming data per node to 1/4 relative to the original case with 4 aggregators per node. This minimization effect minimized the exchange time.

The same analysis was done for the `AtoAv` data exchange mode, as shown in Fig. 8. Increases in the number of aggregators per node from one (Fig. 8(a) or (d)) to 4 (Fig. 8(b) or (e)) in the original aggregator assignment scheme led to decreases in the data exchange time (`exch`) because of the internal collective communication optimization of MVAPICH2. This minimization led to the

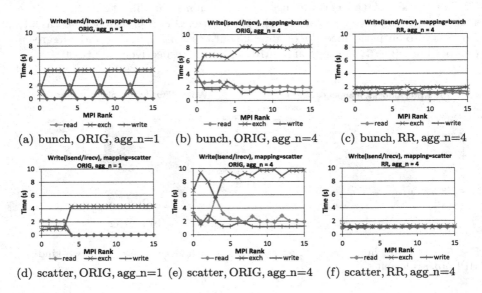

(a) bunch, ORIG, agg_n=1   (b) bunch, ORIG, agg_n=4   (c) bunch, RR, agg_n=4

(d) scatter, ORIG, agg_n=1 (e) scatter, ORIG, agg_n=4 (f) scatter, RR, agg_n=4

Fig. 7. Three major internal operation mean times of collective write with the two-phase I/O using IS_IR data exchanges in 2 MPI process layouts, bunch and scatter

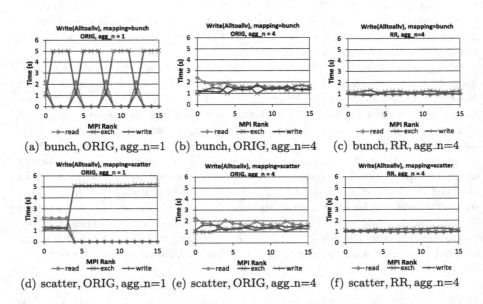

(a) bunch, ORIG, agg_n=1   (b) bunch, ORIG, agg_n=4   (c) bunch, RR, agg_n=4

(d) scatter, ORIG, agg_n=1 (e) scatter, ORIG, agg_n=4 (f) scatter, RR, agg_n=4

Fig. 8. Three major internal operation mean times of collective write with two-phase I/O using using AtoAv data exchanges in 2 MPI process layouts, bunch and scatter

performance improvements observed in Fig. 6. In addition, our affinity-aware aggregator assignment minimized all the internal operation times at almost the same level among MPI ranks. Then we achieved further performance improvements, as shown in Fig. 6.

Overall, the striping layout aware aggregator assignment outperformed other cases in both communication modes, IS_IR and AtoAv. It was found that the striping layout aware aggregator layout minimized the network contention in both data exchanges among MPI processes and data accesses on a target Lustre file system.

5   Related Work

Regarding performance improvement aspects for MPI-IO on a Lustre file system, effective aggregator assignment was also proposed in [2]. This work focuses on affinity-awareness with multiple aggregators per node. In addition, the scheme of that work pays attention to the appointment of aggregation tasks to MPI processes on different CPU sockets. However, it does not consider striping layout awareness in its implementation. On the other hand, our proposal focuses on the affinity of the striping layout in accessing a Lustre file system. Our striping layout aware aggregator assignment can improve I/O performance in any kind of MPI process layout.

Optimization in data aggregation was realized by analyzing the physical data layout on a parallel file system [3] or by using a scientific dataset in structured formats and a parallel file system data distribution [5]. These works are similar to our work regarding file system's data distribution awareness. The work focusing on physical data layouts takes the physical data distribution pattern into account in the redistribution phase among aggregators to improve the I/O performance by eliminating data access contention. The other work focusing on scientific dataset in structured formats and the parallel file system data analyzes the data structure in a high-level user application layer. While our work focuses on optimized aggregator layout by considering affinity-awareness among computing nodes and a target Lustre file system configuration. High-level optimization in the work focusing on scientific datasets may be useful for our implementation if we address to tune application-oriented I/O operations using HDF5 [10] or PnetCDF [7].

6   Summary

We have shown the performance advantages of our striping pattern-aware aggregator assignment scheme as compared with the original ROMIO. Our proposed scheme appointed aggregation tasks to MPI processes in a round-robin manner across PC nodes, where the aggregator layout is suited to the striping layout of a Lustre file system. We deployed the alternative aggregator layout in two data exchange modes; the original data exchange mode using MPI_Isend and MPI_Irecv and the newly implemented mode using MPI_Alltoallv. The proposed scheme outperformed the performance results of the original mode in collective write operations for noncontiguous accesses when using the HPIO benchmark. In the original data exchange mode, our scheme outperformed the original ROMIO by about 25 %, while up to about an 30 % improvement was achieved as compared with the original ROMIO in the newly implemented data exchange mode.

As future work, we will extend the current implementation to cover PC nodes equipped with multiple CPU sockets, where we will have affinity-awareness in the aggregator assignment to achieve higher I/O performance. Further performance improvements in data exchanges with affinity-awareness are also our future work in order to attain higher scalability.

Acknowledgment. Part of this research work was supported by JSPS KAKENHI Grant Number 25330148. The authors would like to thank members of the System Software Research Team at RIKEN AICS for their useful comments.

References

1. Lustre ADIO collective write driver. Technical report, Lustre (September 2008)
2. Cha, K., Maeng, S.: An efficient I/O aggregator assignment scheme for collective I/O considering processor affinity. In: Sheu, J., Wang, C. (eds.) 2011 International Conference on Parallel Processing Workshops, ICPPW 2011, September 13–16 2011, pp. 380–388. IEEE Computer Society, Taipei, Taiwan (2011)
3. Chen, Y., Sun, X.H., Thakur, R., Roth, P.C., Gropp, W.D.: LACIO: a new collective I/O strategy for parallel I/O systems. In: Proceedings of the 25th IEEE International Parallel and Distributed Processing Symposium (IPDPS 2011), pp. 794–804. IEEE Computer Society (2011)
4. Ching, A., Choudhary, A., keng Liao, W., Ward, L., Pundit, N.: Evaluating I/O characteristics and methods for storing structured scientific data. In: Proceedings 20th IEEE International Parallel and Distributed Processing Symposium, p. 49. IEEE Computer Society (2006)
5. Liu, J., Crysler, B., Lu, Y., Chen, Y.: Locality-driven high-level i/o aggregation for processing scientific datasets. In: IEEE International Conference on BigData 2013, pp. 103–111. IEEE (2013)
6. Lustre. http://wiki.lustre.org/index.php/Main_Page
7. Parallel netCDF. http://cucis.ece.northwestern.edu/projects/PnetCDF/
8. Thakur, R., Gropp, W., Lusk, E.: An abstract-device interface for implementing portable parallel-I/O interfaces. In: Proceedings of the Sixth Symposium on the Frontiers of Massively Parallel Computation, pp. 180–187 (1996)
9. Thakur, R., Gropp, W., Lusk, E.: On implementing MPI-IO portably and with high performance. In: Proceedings of the Sixth Workshop on Input/Output in Parallel and Distributed Systems, pp. 23–32 (1999)
10. The National Center for Supercomputing Applications. http://hdf.ncsa.uiuc.edu/HDF5/
11. The Ohio State University: MVAPICH: MPI over InfiniBand, 10GigE/iWARP and RoCE. http://mvapich.cse.ohio-state.edu/index.shtml

Hop: Elastic Consistency for Exascale Data Stores

Latchesar Ionkov$^{(\boxtimes)}$ and Michael Lang

Los Alamos National Laboratory,
Los Alamos, NM 87544, USA
lionkov@lanl.gov

Abstract. Distributed key-value stores are a scalable alternative for relational databases and file systems. Different systems try to provide the right balance between scalability, consistency and reliability for a certain category of applications. Yet many applications don't have a single static set of requirements for all the data they create and use. In order to meet different requirements, the applications end up using multiple data stores, each with its own interface, or suffer the unnecessary performance degradation. This paper describes Hop, our attempt to define an interface that allows specification of different consistency and replication levels, and by allowing the assembly of different implementations of the interface, provides the right balance of consistency, scalability and availability for different parts of application data. We describe the Hop interface and evaluate some of the implementations we created, as well as how they can be combined to provide flexible distributed deployments.

1 Introduction

In recent years many applications try to replace the standard data stores, like relational databases and file systems with distributed key-value stores. The main reason for the change is that the new data stores provide different balance between scalability, reliability and consistency, usually focusing more on the scalability, than reliability and consistency. There is a large variety of storage systems available, each with different functionality, optimizations and guarantees. Most of these systems are designed for particular application or workload, and there is rarely a single system, that fits perfectly for other applications, with slightly different requirements.

Our experience with implementing system services and scientific simulation applications shows that even within a single application, the consistency and performance requirements vary widely across subsets of the data sets, or for the same subsets during different stages of the application execution. For example, a scientific simulation doesn't require strong data consistency within the distributed store while performing a checkpoint (dumping its state to stable storage), performance is more important. Analytic and visualization applications,

LA-UR-13-27636

The rights of this work are transferred to the extent transferable according to title 17 § 105 U.S.C.

J.M. Kunkel and T. Ludwig (Eds.): ISC High Performance 2015, LNCS 9137, pp. 291–306, 2015.
DOI: 10.1007/978-3-319-20119-1_22

on other hand, require the same data set to be in consistent state before they can process it Depending on the way the application partitions the overall work, consistency can be relaxed based on regions of the data sets that are shared by groups of nodes.

Same diverse requirements apply for data replication. In most cases, it is beneficial for the overall performance if the replicas don't share the same physical location (rack, data center, etc.) which usually leads to higher latency and lower performance. In some cases, for instance when the data is temporary and all users are clustered physically, it makes more sense if the replicas are close. For example, there is no reason to keep the list of which nodes within a rack are powered-on replicated outside the rack itself. Power or network failure to the whole rack will make the data unavailable, but as the resources the list describes are unavailable, that loss is irrelevant.

Distributed data stores are currently being evaluated for many exascale tasks where centralized services have reached the limits of scalability. Global services such as namespaces, service registration, provisioning, monitoring, job and resource management, I/O forwarding, fabric management; runtime systems supporting newer distributed programming models all need distributed data services at exascale. In the application space these stores are being evaluated for static and dynamic data tables, such as Equation of State (EOS) for multi physics, and as a general way of dealing with asynchronous access to distributed data structures. Hop is a robust, scalable class of solutions designed for these exascale requirements.

The main goal of the Hop project is to try to define an interface for data access that can be easily used by application and middle-ware developers and implemented by data stores. It should allow data store developers to implement and express various levels of consistency and reliability. The application developers should be able to express the consistency and data replication requirements for particular parts of the data sets and phases of the application. Middle-ware developers should be able to write software that optimizes for particular workloads without sacrificing the requirements defined by the application.

The Hop interface allows users of a data store to define the level of consistency they need while reading the data. The choice varies from "don't care" to "not less recent than" to strong consistency. It allows formation of *consistency domains* where a set of application instances ensure mutual consistency, without paying the performance degradation for strong consistency outside the domain.

Each data entry in Hop is assigned numeric *version* value, which can be used to define the *freshness* of the entry's value. The entry's version is monotonically increasing each time when its value is updated. When retrieving data, the application can specify version value, and will be guaranteed to receive data that is more recent that the specified version. All update operations return the new version value. If an instance that updated some data needs to ensure that another instance will see its updates, it needs to pass its version value to the other instance, which in turn uses that value when reading the entry. There is a special value, `Newest` that forces strong consistency among all instances. Clients can also use future version values as a mechanism to wait until the entry is modified. This feature is useful in cases when it may take some time until updates are propagated across multi-layered systems as well as for implementing publish/subscribe features on top of Hop.

Hop also defines a set of atomic operations on a single data entry, improving the usability of a distributed store without sacrificing the performance. The atomic operations are serialized at the node, responsible for the entry, thus ensuring their correct behavior within the distributed store.

Unlike the commonly used data stores, where clients use a single monolithic service, we envision that Hop will be used similarly to file systems, where each application will use multiple Hop implementations, each providing different functionality, and only some of them used for persistently storing the data to disks. Custom Hop implementations may include caching middle-ware suitable for particular applications, aggregation of data entries, etc.

As part of the project, we developed a number of simple Hop implementations that provide useful functionality and can be used to assemble more complicated configurations that can be used for real-world installations. Our caching service provides support for local and cooperative caching. It also implements a novel concept of consistency domains that allow clients to easily group together and ensure consistency for a subset of the key-value store entries.

The project is novel in that it provides a minimal, easy to implement API, as well as a set of basic building blocks from which to compose larger services based on key-value stores. It allows definition of flexible coherency domains for subsets of the data. Other key contributions are : configurable consistency and replication of individual elements, definition of entries that provide side-effects upon access, support for publish/subscribe over key/value store interface, and a unique aggregation service that redirects based on a simple prefix key.

2   Related Work

Distributed key-value store is an important system service, which serves requests very fast. Memcached [5] is a popular service that stores key/values pairs in RAM and is designed to serve as a caching layer between applications and persistent data stores like databases. Dynamo [2] is a highly available key-value storage implemented by Amazon to provide users with a reliable resource. Cassandra [9] is a distributed storage system developed by Facebook to satisfy the requirements of the Inbox Search problem. It provides SQL-like query language and failure recovery. ZHT [11] is a zero-hop distributed hash table for managing the parallel file system meta-data, and serves as a building block for future distributed system services. Chord [14] is a distributed protocol, which defines how servers communicate with other and how data is distributed among all the servers. As part of the Hop evaluation, we implemented both Chord-like and ZHT-like schemes providing choice to the services so they can select a method that best fits its requirements.

There are systems that use some form of versioning to manage consistency. Project Voldemort [4] is an advanced key-value store that provides multi-version concurrency control for updates. In order to get up-to-date view, the application needs to read data from the majority of the replicas. Similarly to Voldemort, Riak is a data store that uses MVCC and vector clocks to order updates. It also provides tunable consistency at read and write operations by specifying how many replicas must respond to operation.

Comet [6] is a distributed data storage system that allows executable code (handlers) to be attached to the stored entries, making them "active". The handlers may run on specific operations (get, set, etc.), or on timers, at the place where the entry is stored.

COPS [12] tries to improve the eventual consistency, usually used in distributed systems, by presenting a scalable causal consistency with convergent conflict handling.

OceanStore [8] is an infrastructure that can be used to connect data stores across wide-area network and provide provide clients with flexible consistency guarantees. It uses replicas as caching capabilities to provide fail-over and to improve performance. It uses entries' versions to to keep track of the freshness of the data in the replicas and caches. OceanStore also defines algorithms that are used for data placement. The consistency level is defined per session and if client has different consistency requirements for groups of data, it needs to use multiple sessions.

3   Design

The main objective of the project is to define an interface for storing and retrieving data values in distributed systems, while allowing the data users to specify diverse consistency and replication levels for the different types of data they store.

The data store and retrieval requirements for the applications are not uniform, and in many cases they vary even for different data entries within an application. For example, in some cases fast data retrieval is more important than the data freshness. Some of the data is relevant only to the clients in a location (i.e. server rack) and don't need to be replicated outside that location. There are cases when consistency is required for groups of clients while the consistency restrictions across groups can be relaxed.

Generally, a balance is necessary between the number of operations defined in an API and the complexity of the parameters they accept. Small set of operations makes it easier for clients to use it. It also makes the implementation of simple services that support it more straightforward. For complex functionality, though, a small number of operations usually leads to a complex parameter space with too many values with special semantics. In Hop's design we tried to create what we believe is the right balance between the number of operations and parameter idiosyncrasies.

In order to keep the interface simple, Hop defines a single type of keys (string) and a single type of values (byte array). Our evaluation in Sect. 4 shows that these restrictions still allow reasonable level of flexibility.

We intentionally omitted support for partial entry retrieval and update. We believe that large monolithic entries allow applications to encapsulate their data in "file" formats that leave off important metadata information and make it harder for data to be shared across applications. Instead of using a singly entry with all data in it, we encourage developers to adopt more fine-grained approach to data storage. The atomic operation `Replace` provides support for partial data update, which we hope is not going to be abused by the developers.

3.1 Hop Operations

The Hop interface defines 6 operations:

Create. Creates a new entry for a key and sets its initial value.
Remove. Removes an entry associated with a key.
Get. Retrieves the value, associated to a key.
Set. Updates the value, associated with a key.
TestSet. Compares the value of an entry and sets it to a new value if the comparison is true.
Atomic. Performs an atomic operation on an entry.

All Hop operations receive the name (key) of the entry as a parameter. Other approaches, for example assigning a temporary numeric value to an entry (like the file descriptors in the POSIX API) have some advantages, like performing the name look-up and permission checking once at the beginning of a set of operations, smaller message overhead, etc. That approach implies state kept on the servers for each client. In a distributed system, these benefits are smaller than the disadvantages of keeping (and replicating in case of a failure) the state. Many of the key-value stores implicitly create entries, when a value for a key is `set` first. We chose to define an explicit create operation. The main reason is to allow the users to list specific requirements for the entry: how many replicas should be supported, the location of the replicas, etc. Additionally, we prefer to preserve symmetry: an interface with a function that deletes an entry is more complete if it also explicitly creates it.

The interface doesn't define any specific values for the entry's flags, the description what parameters are supported is left for the specific implementations.

In distributed systems, many problems arise when multiple clients concurrently modify an entry's value. Even strong consistency guarantees don't alleviate all the complications. For example, there is no guarantee that incrementing a value is going to produce the correct results. The most common solutions for the problems are support for transactions, or atomic operations. We chose to provide the latter, mostly because distributed transactions are complex to implement, don't scale well and complicate the key/value store interface. Transactions offer many benefits, and we plan to explore them in the future based on the atomic primitives we already defined.

All atomic operations serialize the access to an entry. The value of an entry can't be modified or retrieved while an atomic operation is being processed. The most commonly implemented atomic operation is test-and-set. It compares the value of an entry to a specified value, and if both match, sets it to a new value. Test-and-set returns the value of the entry, as set at the end of the operation. If the two values don't match, the user receives the current entry's value, otherwise the user receives the new value.

In a distributed configuration, where clients and servers might be located on different nodes with high latency network connecting them, test-and-set might be an inefficient method to atomically modify an entry. While a client retrieves the value, modifies it and performs test-and-set, another client may change the entry, forcing the first client to loop multiple times until it succeeds. To improve the latency, we define a set of commonly used operations that are atomically executed by the Hop implementation at the location where the entry is stored. Additional atomic operations can be built on these.

Add. Atomically adds a number to the entry's value.

Sub. Atomically subtracts a number from the entry's value.

BitSet. Atomically sets to 1 one bit in the entry's value that was previously set to 0. Returns the new value as well as the address of the bit that was modified.

BitClear. Atomically sets to 0 one bit in the entry's value that was previously set to 1. Returns the new value as well as the address of the bit that was modified.

Append. Atomically appends the value specified in the operation to the entry's current value.

Remove. Atomically removes from the entry's current value all subarrays that match the value specified in the operation.

Replace. Atomically replaces all subarrays from the entry's current value that match the first value specified in the operation with the second value.

Although the Hop values are arrays of bytes, the arithmetic atomic operations assume the arrays to be big-endian encoding of 8-, 16-, 32-, or 64-bit integers (depending on the size of the array). The Hop implementations can define additional atomic operations.

3.2   Entry Versions

The Hop interface assigns a 64-bit *version* value to each data entry. The version is increased every time the value of the entry is updated. When data is retrieved, in addition to the value, the user receives its current version. The application can specify what version of the value it requires. The Hop service cannot return values associated with versions older than the specified one. They might, however return more recent values. If the value the service is not recent enough, it is expected to wait until the entry reaches the specified version. Caching services may use requests for newer versions as triggers for updating the cached entries. In distributed systems it is possible for requests to arrive in a different order to the servers, therefore versions ensure later requests wait for the earlier ones.

Valid entry version have values between 1 and 2^{63}. The rest of the values can be used to define some special version values that fine-tune the semantics of the data retrieval. The special values that all Hop services are required to support are:

Any. Retrieve any value, no matter how fresh.

Newest. Retrieve the newest value. Instructs all intermediary services to ignore their stored entries and consult the authoritative service that contains the entry.

Wait. Ignore all intermediaries, wait until the entry is modified once, and return the new value. Can be used for implementation of publish/subscribe mechanisms.

Uncommitted. Return values even if they are not yet replicated as required.

All operations that return an entry's value also return its version. Successful operations are required to return a valid version (i.e. between 1 and 2^{31}). If an operation returns 0 for a version, the client is expected to retry the operation (similarly to EAGAIN error code in Unix). In a distributed environment there might be cases when successful completion of the operation is hard, or even impossible to achieve, but returning an error would be the wrong outcome. For example, if an instance in distributed service fails and its responsibilities are assigned to another instance, it is easier to abandon the currently pending operations and ask the clients to retry using the updated configuration.

Instead of keeping only the latest version of an entry, Hop allows the implementations to keep as many older versions as they may see fit. However, Hop would have to be extended to provide any operations for version management.

3.3 Entry Names and Values

Entries' names in Hop are variable-sized UTF-8 encoded strings up to 65535 bytes long. Like most key-value stores, Hop supports a flat namespace. Because Hop doesn't support key enumeration (see Sect. 4.1 though), there is no reason to group keys in hierarchical namespaces. Flat namespaces are also easier to partition in distributed implementations.

An entry's value is an array of bytes, with maximum size of 4 GB. The Hop interface doesn't support partial retrieval of values, and there is no practical reason for bigger values if they are stored and retrieved over the network.

3.4 Entry Side-Effects

Hop implementations can define some, or all of the entries as special entries that have side effects or produce results based on the server or client configurations. One example of that behavior is the #/keys: *regular-expression* entry that will be defined in Sect. 4.1.

4 Implementations and Evaluation

The Hop interface is intentionally kept simple. We envision multiple services implementing it assembled from hop building block services. Real-world installations using a combination of multiple implementations to provide the required levels of consistency, scalability, and reliability. Currently we have created 7 Hop implementations, the more complicated ones using the basic ones as building blocks. In this section we will describe these implementations as examples of how the basic Hop interface can be used and to assemble complex real-world services.

4.1   General Functionality and Guidelines

All of the implementations below provide extra functionality not defined in the basic Hop interface that is useful in building system services.

Local Entries. Entries with names starting with `#/` are considered local and may return different values depending to which node in a distributed system the client connects. Most of these entries are used by the implementation itself to maintain its basic functionality. All our Hop implementations provide `#/id` entry. It is immutable and provides the name of the Hop implementation, as well as additional information about its configuration.

Name Lookup. The basic Hop interface doesn't provide functionality that allows checking the names of existing entries. Our Hop implementations allow name lookup using two special local entries: `#/keys` and `#/keys:` *regexp*. The value of `#/keys` contains the names of all local entries, `#/keys:` *regular-expression* is a special *dynamic* entry that returns all keys that match the specified regular expression. For example, getting the value of `#keys:foo.*bar` will return all keys, with prefix `foo` and suffix `bar`.

The standard rules for Hop versions also apply for the special keys. For example, the user can watch a Hop instance for newly created entries by calling the `Get` operation on `#/keys` with version value `Wait`. The operation will hang until a new entry is created.

If the service has a lot entries, waiting on `#/keys` is impractical, because it will transfer huge amounts of data back to the client. For that reason, we defined another special entry, `#/keynum` that returns the number of keys present in a Hop instance. Waiting on it will also return when an entry is created or removed.

In our future implementations we are planning to use dynamic key names for other purposes, like returning partial values, debugging, etc.

Distributed Implementations. Instead of defining additional protocols, we use the Hop interface and special local entries to implement the communication between the instances in a distributed service. That serves two main purposes: makes the coding of distributed services fast and simple, and tests if the Hop interface is flexible enough for real-world applications. We believe that the inability of using the Hop interface for our own distributed implementations would be an argument for its incompleteness and/or inefficiency.

4.2   Basic Building Blocks

Rmt. The standard Hop interface doesn't define or provide any support for networked deployment of Hop implementations. The simplicity of the standard

Hop interface makes it easier to implement and doesn't tie it to specific network protocol or framework.

Rmt is a package that provides networked client-server support for Hop. It consists of a tightly integrated pair: rmt.srv and rmt.clnt. Rmt.clnt is a Hop implementation that serializes all Hop operations and sends them over a network to rmt.srv. Rmt.srv receives a Hop implementation as a parameter and makes it available over a network connection. When it receives a message, it deserializes it, calls the appropriate Hop operation, serializes the result and sends it back.

Rmt supports TCP and Infiniband Verbs protocols. It allows up to 65536 simultaneous requests for a client-server pair. The requests are multiplexed and the responses are demultiplexed over a single connection.

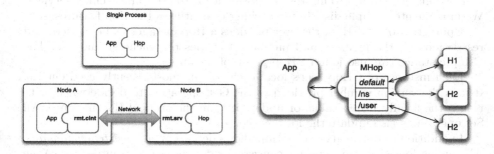

Fig. 1. Example of single-process and remote Hop deployment

Fig. 2. Example of MHop deployment

Figure 1 shows deployment of a Hop interface can be made within a single process, where the Hop implementation and the application are linked together in a single binary, or over the network where rmt.clnt serves as a proxy to the remotely deployed Hop implementation. No changes to the Hop implementation is required in order to make it available over the network.

KHop: Hop Reference Implementation. KHop implements a key-value store in RAM. It is a basic building block that we use in other Hop implementations. KHop implements all required functionality and can be regarded as a reference Hop implementation.

In addition to the default storage in RAM, KHop allows its users to provide per-entry behavior for the entries they create. If the entry objects (created outside the Hop interface operations) implement all or some of the Hop operations, the custom operations are called when required. This functionality allows easy implementation of special entries with dynamic content and/or side effects.

MHop: Hop Aggregation Service. MHop is a proxy implementation that combines the entries from multiple Hop instances into a single namespace. It is somewhat equivalent to the Unix Virtual File System (VFS) for file systems.

MHop allows a Hop instance to be "mounted" to a prefix, passing all operations to keys that start with the prefix to that instance. MHop uses trie structures to minimize the impact of the additional key processing on the performance. Figure 2 shows how MHop can be used to redirect operations to three Hop instances: all operations for keys starting with /ns are redirected to Hop2, the keys starting with /user are redirected to Hop3, all operations for other keys are redirected to the default Hop1 instance.

The purpose of MHop is to provide a centralized access to all available Hop instances and hide the details of their deployment from the applications.

CHop: Distributed Caching Service. One of the main reasons to introduce version numbers in Hop was to allow trading strict consistency for performance. One of the ways to improve performance is to use some caching services. We implemented simple distributed caching that utilizes the Hop features.

Upon creation of CHop, the user provides a Hop instance to be cached, and restrictions on the memory and number of entries the cache should use. The CHop instance can also join a CHop group of instances.

Each instance of CHop keeps local cache of the most recently used entries. It uses the version number provided to the Get operation to decide whether to return the locally stored value, or update it from the original Hop instance. All Set operations also update the local cache.

In addition to the local cache, CHop allows definition of *consistency domains.* All applications that use a specific consistency domain are guaranteed to see the updates that other applications within the domain make, regardless of the version number. There are no guarantees when updates made outside of the consistency domain would be available. Using specific (more recent than the cache or Newest) version while retrieving a value will always retrieve the specified version from the original Hop instance, and ensure that from that moment on, no other application within the consistency domain will receive an older value.

Figure 3 shows an example of a group of six CHop instances, with two consistency domains. The applications using C1 and C3, or C4 and C6 will see consistent views of the entries, provided by the Hop instance, while C2 and C5 may see inconsistencies.

The definition of consistency domains in CHop is implemented by using special prefix #/cache/*domain-name/*. By prepending the prefix while accessing the keys, multiple users of CHop instances can ensure that they will get consistent view of the values. For example, applications A and B can use consistent domain bar to ensure consistent view of key foo by accessing entries with names #/cache/bar/foo. For example, for a resource manager job information(process, memory layout) would be consistent within the nodes of a job but not consistent to jobs on other nodes.

In addition to the consistency domain prefixes, CHop allows the users to create a special Hop instance that hides the prefixes and uses the consistency domain for all entries simplifying implementation.

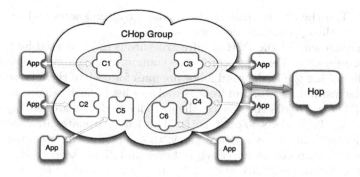

Fig. 3. Example of CHop deployment with 6 instances and 2 consistency domains

4.3   Examples of Using the Building Blocks

The Hop implementations described in this section utilize the basic Hop building blocks to create services that can be used in real deployments.

SHop. SHop builds on KHop by adding special entries that are standard for deployable Hop services. SHop defines the following special entries:

#/id Hop implementation identification.
#/keys Returns all keys in the data store.
#/keys:*regexp* Returns all keys that match the specified regular expression.
#/keynum Returns the number of keys in the data store.

SHop also uses rmt.srv to provide single-instance data store, available over the network.

D2Hop. D2Hop is a distributed Hop implementation that partitions the key space across multiple D2Hop instances, running on different nodes. D2Hop calculates a 32-bit hash value for each key and redirects the operation to the appropriate instance responsible to that value. Each instance is handles a range of hash values. Currently D2Hop supports FNV-1a [3] and Adler-32 hash functions. D2Hop implementation is built on top of the KHop and Rmt building blocks.

Although D2Hop handles most instance failures, it doesn't replicate the entries' data across multiple instances and failures may lead to data loss, this is currently being developed.

The D2Hop instances belong to one of the three categories: leader, followers, or clients. The leader is responsible for keeping track of the followers health and handles joining and leaving the service. Failure of a leader causes failure of the whole service. Followers are responsible for handling the operations for part of the keys' namespace as well as redirecting the operations for the rest of the keys to the appropriate instance. Each follower is connected to all other followers and the leader. The clients are connected to some, or all followers and redirect the operations to the appropriate instance.

The maintenance of the D2Hop infrastructure is implemented by using Hop operations on a special entry #/conf. The content of the entry is a string, with first line describing the leader, and following lines for each of the followers. A line contains the instance network address as well as a list of hash ranges the instance is responsible for. To join the service, the instance performs atomic **Append** with its address to the leader's #/conf entry. The leader updates its configuration and returns the new content of the entry, that includes the new instance and what keys it is responsible for. Each follower and client keep track of version of the configuration they have and constantly tries to retrieve the next version. Once an instance joins or leaves the service, they receive the new configuration and its updated version.

D2Hop can run any Hop implementation as distributed service, its instances simply redirect the calls they receive to the Hop instance, specified on initialization.

Although D2Hop doesn't handle failures, it can be used for deployment where failures are unlikely and serves as a good example how to implement distributed Hop implementations.

ChordHop. ChordHop is a Hop implementation that uses the Chord [14] distributed service for partitioning the key space. It implements Chord's strong stabilization algorithm. CHordHop is built on top of KHop and Rmt.

Similarly to D2Hop, the Chord maintenance protocol is implemented as Hop operations on special entries. Each Chord node defines the following entries:

#/chord/successor: *ID* The value of the entry is the address of the Chord node that is successor of the specified *ID*. The current node might contact other nodes to find out the successor.

#/chord/predecessor Returns the address of the predecessor of the Chord. **TestSet** operation on the entry notifies the node that another node might be its predecessor while returning the old predecessor.

#/chord/finger Returns the current node's finger table. Used for debugging only.

#/chord/ring Returns description of Chord's ring. Used for debugging only.

ChordHop doesn't replicate the entries, so even though Chord stays connected when failures occur, data might be lost. In the future we plan to add replication.

ChordHop clients act similarly to the Chord nodes, maintain correct finger table, etc. But unlike the Chord nodes, they don't join the Chord ring.

5   Results

We evaluated the performance of some of our Hop implementations at small scale and compared one of them to two other key-value stores. All tests were run on a 128-node cluster with Infiniband QDR interconnect. Each node has 16 cores and 32 GB RAM.

To evaluate the performance, we created a simple benchmark that executes random key-value store operation on randomly generated keys and random value sizes. The probability for each type of operation is weighted, giving higher chance of retrieval operations over the ones that create, remove or modify an entry. For the Hop centric tests (Figs. 4 and 6), 55 % of the operations are Get, 35 % are Set, 5 % are Create, 4 % are Remove, 3 % are TestSet, and 3 % are Atomic. For the comparison with other key-value stores (Fig. 5, we removed the atomic operations and had tested with 60 % Get operations, 30 % Set, 5 % Create, and 5 % Remove.

We ran one key-value store server and 16 clients on each node.

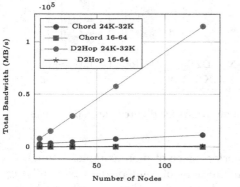

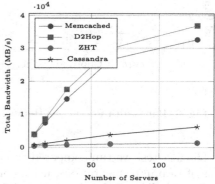

Fig. 4. Performance of D2Hop and Chord for different value sizes

Fig. 5. Performance of Memcached, ZHT, and D2Hop

We run the benchmark for D2Hop and ChordHop implementations, scaling the number of key-value store nodes from 8 to 128. We run the tests for two sizes of the entry values – from 16 to 64 bytes, and from 24 KB to 32 KB. The tests run using the Infiniband Verbs API. Figure 4 shows the results from these tests. As expected, the D2Hop implementation scaled better than Chord due to the additional hops for key look-up required for Chord. Runs with smaller sized entries were latency bound and delivered much worse bandwidth values.

The second test we run compared the D2Hop implementation to some of the other key-value stores that we were able to run on the cluster. We compared our Hop implementation to Memcached [5], Cassandra and ZHT [11]. We used TCP over IB for running this set of tests, because Memcached, Casasandra and ZHT don't support running directly on Infiniband. We used value sizes between 24 KB and 32 KB for these tests. Both Memcached and ZHT were configured to disable data replication. ZHT was set to keep the data in RAM instead of storing it to disk. Cassandra was configured to store its data to ramdisk. We varied the

number of servers handling constant number of clients, running on 128 nodes.
Figure 5 shows the performance of the three key-value stores. Although D2Hop is
not optimized for performance, it slightly outperforms Memcached. Cassandra's
performance suffers because even though it doesn't store its data to real disks, it
performs all operations (like creating commit logs, merging data files, etc.) that
are required for persistence of the data.

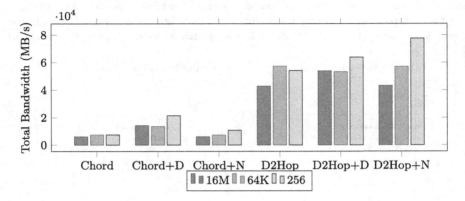

Fig. 6. Bandwidth for various Hop configurations for different key space sizes

The last test we run compared the performance of more complex configurations of Hop implementations, using combinations of some of the basic building
blocks as well as D2Hop and ChordHop. The goal of the tests was to investigate how the utilization of caching with CHop, with and without consistency
domains will affect the overall performance of the key-value store. The tests were
run on 64 nodes, with value sizes between 24 KB and 32 KB. We compared the
performance of running D2Hop and Chord directly (Chord, D2Hop lines) with
running them in combination with CHop with consistency domains (CHord+D,
D2Hop+D) and without consistency domains (Chord+N, D2Hop+N). When
consistency domains are used, we create 8 domains, each with 8 nodes as members. As the efficiency of the cache depends on the key space size, we ran the tests
for three different sizes of the key space –256 keys, 64 K keys and 16 M keys. Half
of the retrieval operations specify **Any** as version (making them candidates for
being served from the CHop cache), while the other half specifies **Newest** ensuring that the operation reaches D2Hop or ChordHop. Figure 6 shows the results
of the tests. For the small number of keys (256), all values can fit in the local
cache, which makes the CHop without consistency domains best performer when
request latency is not very high (as with D2Hop). For larger number of keys,
as well as stores with higher latency (as ChordHop), the cooperative caching of
CHop's consistency domains allow higher cache hit rate within the domain and
result in better performance.

6   Future Work

The most important missing functionality is proper replication for instance failures. Our plan is to implement some of the consensus algorithms (Paxos [10], Raft [13]) as operations on special entries, then build the entry replication on top of them. Similarly to the consistency domains, we are planning to provide support for *replication domains* that provide different replication levels for different sets of entries.

We are also planning to use Hop to implement an instance of Hobbes [1] Global Information Bus and related services. Hobbes is an operating system and runtime (OS/R) framework for extreme-scale systems, funded by the Department of Energy. The Global Information Bus is a software layer that provides mechanisms for sharing status information needed by other components in the OS/R. This include nodes status, locations and availability of various services, performance data, etc.

Another extension of this project we are exploring is using special keys as a way to read and write portions of complex entries. We are planning to create a subset of the DRepl [7] language designed for describing dataset layouts and use it to specify what subsets of the data entries are accessed.

7   Conclusion

The Hop interface allows the implementation and deployment of data store services, middleware and clients with different consistency and reliability requirements. The Hop project provides a set of building blocks as well as some examples on how to use them to create real-world services. The simplicity of the protocol and the support for special entry names allows it to be used as an RPC framework for exascale system services as well as to provide custom representation of data sets.

The services we implemented show that Hop is well fit for various system services implementations and can be used to hide some of the complexity of exascale systems from the user applications.

Acknowledgments. This work was performed at the Ultrascale Systems Research Center in the High Performance Computing Division at Los Alamos National Laboratory, and is supported by the U.S. Department of Energy DE-FC02-06ER25750.

References

1. Brightwell, R., Oldfield, R., Maccabe, A.B., Bernholdt, D.E.: Hobbes: composition and virtualization as the foundations of an extreme-scale OS/R. In: Proceedings of the 3rd International Workshop on Runtime and Operating Systems for Supercomputers, ROSS 2013, pp. 2:1–2:8. ACM, New York (2013). http://doi.acm.org/10.1145/2491661.2481427

2. DeCandia, G., Hastorun, D., Jampani, M., Kakulapati, G., Lakshman, A., Pilchin, A., Sivasubramanian, S., Vosshall, P., Vogels, W.: Dynamo: amazon's highly available key-value store. In: Proceedings of Twenty-First ACM SIGOPS Symposium on Operating Systems Principles, SOSP 2007, pp. 205–220. ACM, New York (2007). http://doi.acm.org/10.1145/1294261.1294281

3. Eastlake, D., Fowler, G., Vo, K.P., Noll, L.: The fnv non-cryptographic hash algorithm (2012)

4. Feinberg, A.: Project voldemort: reliable distributed storage. In: Proceedings of the 10th IEEE International Conference on Data Engineering (2011)

5. Fitzpatrick, B.: Distributed caching with memcached. Linux J. **2004**(124), 5 (2004). http://dl.acm.org/citation.cfm?id=1012889.1012894

6. Geambasu, R., Levy, A.A., Kohno, T., Krishnamurthy, A., Levy, H.M.: Comet: an active distributed key-value store. In: OSDI. pp. 323–336 (2010)

7. Ionkov, L., Lang, M., Maltzahn, C.: Drepl: optimizing access to application data for analysis and visualization. In: 2013 IEEE 29th Symposium on Mass Storage Systems and Technologies (MSST), pp. 1–11 (2013)

8. Kubiatowicz, J., Bindel, D., Chen, Y., Czerwinski, S., Eaton, P., Geels, D., Gummadi, R., Rhea, S., Weatherspoon, H., Weimer, W., et al.: Oceanstore: an architecture for global-scale persistent storage. ACM Sigplan Not. **35**(11), 190–201 (2000)

9. Lakshman, A., Malik, P.: Cassandra: a decentralized structured storage system. SIGOPS Oper. Syst. Rev. **44**, 35–40 (2010). http://doi.acm.org/10.1145/1773912.1773922

10. Lamport, L.: Paxos made simple. ACM Sigact News **32**(4), 18–25 (2001)

11. Li, T., Verma, R., Duan, X., Jin, H., Raicu, I.: Exploring distributed hash tables in highend computing. SIGMETRICS Perform. Eval. Rev. **39**(3), 128–130 (2011). http://doi.acm.org/10.1145/2160803.2160880

12. Lloyd, W., Freedman, M.J., Kaminsky, M., Andersen, D.G.: Don't settle for eventual: scalable causal consistency for wide-area storage with cops. In: Proceedings of the Twenty-Third ACM Symposium on Operating Systems Principles, pp. 401–416. ACM (2011)

13. Ongaro, D., Ousterhout, J.: In search of an understandable consensus algorithm

14. Stoica, I., Morris, R., Karger, D., Kaashoek, M.F., Balakrishnan, H.: Chord: a scalable peer-to-peer lookup service for internet applications. In: ACM SIGCOMM Computer Communication Review, vol. 31, pp. 149–160. ACM (2001)

Energy-Efficient Data Processing Through Data Sparsing with Artifacts

Pablo Graubner[✉], Patrick Heckmann, and Bernd Freisleben

Department of Mathematics and Computer Science, University of Marburg,
Hans-Meerwein-Str. 6, 35032 Marburg, Germany
{graubner,pheckmann,freisleb}@informatik.uni-marburg.de

Abstract. Improving the energy efficiency of software running in a data center is a challenging task. Several application-specific techniques, such as energy-aware heuristics, controlled approximation and energy-conserving I/O, have been proposed to tackle this problem. In this paper, we introduce data sparsing with artifacts, a novel approach to increase the energy efficiency of applications that are robust to input variations, such as speech and image processing. Data sparsing with artifacts is aimed at reducing the processing times and thus the energy efficiency of such applications while preserving the quality of the results by replacing a random subset of the original data with application-specific artifacts. In contrast to previous work, the proposed approach introduces artifacts at the data layer, without application layer modifications and with general purpose hardware. Data sparsing with artifacts has been integrated into a prototypical file system in userspace (FUSE) and the Hadoop Distributed File System (HDFS). Experiments with MapReduce-based face detection, face recognition and speech recognition algorithms show promising energy savings of up to 10% with moderate accuracy losses for different data sparsing rates and artifacts.

1 Introduction

Several companies that deal with vast amounts of user data are currently investigating methods to reduce their costs for energy, infrastructure, cooling and power supply. For example, both the social-network provider Facebook[1] and the instant-messaging provider Snapchat[2] have reported that their users share an average of 350 million photos daily [22]. These companies use highly scalable storage infrastructures that are based on hundreds of thousands of hard disks, storing petabytes of user data. In 2013, Facebook spent 787 million kWh on their data centers, each operating with a Power Usage Effectiveness (PUE) between 1.06 and 1.1[3]. The companies are highly interested in developing more efficient servers, storage and data center infrastructures. For instance, the Facebook engineer Tal [12] has proposed to reduce the hard disk spin speed to a minimum,

---

[1] https://www.facebook.com.
[2] https://www.snapchat.com.
[3] https://www.facebook.com/green/app_439663542812831.

© Springer International Publishing Switzerland 2015
J.M. Kunkel and T. Ludwig (Eds.): ISC High Performance 2015, LNCS 9137, pp. 307–322, 2015.
DOI: 10.1007/978-3-319-20119-1_23

trading lower bandwidth and higher latencies for a reduced energy consumption of the storage infrastructure.

In this paper, we introduce data sparsing with artifacts, a novel approach to increase the energy efficiency of applications that are robust to input variations, such as speech and image processing. Data sparsing with artifacts is aimed at reducing the processing times and energy efficiency of such applications while preserving the quality of the results by replacing a random subset of the original data with application-specific artifacts. Similar to other approaches, data sparsing trades accuracy for energy efficiency. In contrast to previous approaches, data sparsing with artifacts achieves energy savings with general purpose hardware and without application layer modifications. To demonstrate the feasibility of the proposed approach, a prototypical file system in userspace (FUSE) integrating data sparsing with artifacts is presented. Furthermore, an integration into the Hadoop Distributed File System (HDFS) [2] is described. Finally, the approach is evaluated by experimental results. MapReduce-based face recognition and speech recognition algorithms show promising energy savings of up to 10 % with moderate accuracy losses for different data sparsing rates and types.

This paper is organized as follows. Section 2 introduces the concept of data sparsing with artifacts. Section 3 describes the design and the implementation of data sparsing with artifacts in the context of a FUSE file system and HDFS. Section 4 presents experimental results. Section 5 discusses related work. Section 6 concludes the paper and outlines areas for future work.

2   Data Sparsing with Artifacts

Data sparsing with artifacts is inspired by dimensionality reduction methods that are often used in text and image processing, aimed at performing computations in a lower-dimensional subspace while preserving the properties of the higher-dimensional space. These methods are typically based on the theoretical work of Johnson and Lindenstrauss, who state - informally speaking - that any set of points in Euclidean space can be embedded into a lower-dimensional subspace such that all pairwise distances are preserved [10]. In particular, the random projection method [18] piqued many researchers' interest in the past. This dimensionality reduction method uses a random matrix to project points from a higher-dimensional to a lower-dimensional space. It has some interesting properties: The matrix can be constructed in an inexpensive way, since all its vectors are chosen randomly from the higher-dimensional space. Furthermore, the projection matrix can be chosen as a sparse matrix such that all elements are in $\{-1, 0, +1\}$ with probabilities $\{\frac{1}{6}, \frac{2}{3}, \frac{1}{6}\}$ [18]. Empirical results on real-world text and image data have indicated that this method preserves the similarities between data vectors well, even with a moderate number of dimensions [7].

2.1   Data Sparsing

Random projections follow the approach of reducing the amount of data with inexpensive preprocessing based on statistical properties of the problem space.

In a time of vast amounts of data processed in large data centers with high energy consumption, this approach is quite intriguing. Therefore, we propose *data sparsing*: Reducing the execution time and thus energy consumption by processing a sparsed version of the original data. The term *sparsing* is borrowed from the mathematical term of a sparse matrix, a matrix in which most elements are zero. In data sparsing, data blocks are selected in a statistically independent manner and with a standard normal distribution on the basis of an application-dependent *sparse rate* with a given *block size*. It is similar to random sampling, where a sample is selected from a statistical population such that assumptions can be inferred from the sample to the population. However, in contrast to random sampling, data sparsing can not only omit blocks with a given probability, but also introduces a novel concept: Application-specific *artifacts*.

2.2 Artifacts

Artifacts are application-specific data blocks that replace blocks of the original data stream with an application-specific *sparse rate*. In computer science, the term *artifact* usually refers to an *undesired* alternation of data; in particular, compression artifacts stand for a loss in clarity in compressed image or audio files. In data sparsing, an *artifact* is a *desired* alternation of data within a data stream. Its purpose is, informally speaking, to indicate to an application that a given block *should be excluded* from the computation. With this mechanism, the result of the execution can be approximated *without modifying the implementation*.

Thus, instead of sampling the data, i.e., omitting data blocks in order to reduce the amount of data to be processed, *artifacts* are introduced into a data stream. Artifacts are based on the following hypothesis: Applications such as automatic speech recognition or face detection can usually exclude data sections very fast, if a detection within this section is very unlikely. For example, a block of zeros indicating a black rectangle within an image is excluded by a face detection algorithm at an early stage. Therefore, a block of zeros is an appropriate application-specific artifact for a face detection algorithm. On the other hand, a machine learning algorithm trained to detect single-colored shapes would exclude blocks of subsequent black/white colors, but would produce false positives for face detection-specific artifacts. Therefore, our basic hypothesis is: There are application-specific artifacts for each of these applications, and data sparsing with artifacts can decrease the execution time of this kind of applications.

2.3 Energy Efficiency

In general, the energy consumed by a system in the interval $[t_0, t_1]$ is defined as the integral of power consumed in the domain of integration:

$$E(t) := \int_{t_0}^{t_1} P(t)\, \mathrm{d}t. \tag{1}$$

The energy consumed by a system can be reduced by either minimizing the interval $[t_0, t_1]$ (execution time) or $P(t)$ for all $t \in [t_0, t_1]$ (power consumption).

Execution time and power consumption are often conflicting: For example, Chen et al. [9] have examined I/O- vs. performance trade-offs in MapReduce applications. Depending on the compression rate, the use of compression for data transfers via a network is a way to conserve energy. But the compression rate is unknown beforehand, and experiments show that some compressed images increase energy consumption by increasing the use of the CPU.

In contrast, data sparsing with artifacts is applied on the block level, i.e., blocks of data are manipulated without any knowledge about the data or preprocessing the data. We assume that data sparsing with artifacts neither increases power consumption nor decreases an application's execution speed, such that the reduction of execution time directly leads to reduced energy consumption.

On the other hand, active low-power modes, such as CPU dynamic voltage-frequency scaling (DVFS) or spun-down disks, reduce power consumption at moderate performance costs. Barroso et al. [4] stated that typical server hardware is designed to operate most energy-efficiently at the maximum utilization level, and fine-grained active low-power modes can be used to gradually decrease the dynamic power consumption when the utilization level decreases (energy-proportionality) [5]. Conversely, disproportionaotely scaling down CPU voltage and frequency of a server might lead to a reduced energy efficiency. Using data sparsing with artifacts, execution time and thus energy consumption is reduced at moderate accuracy costs. Conceptually, the use of active low-power modes for hard disks, such as spinning down disks according to the sparse rate, would be a complementary method for data sparsing. Unfortunately, typical hard discs only provide inactive low-power modes, i.e., the device is not usable in this mode. On the other hand, DVFS may be applied for additional power savings, according to an application's CPU utilization. In these cases, additional power savings would be application-specific and independent of the data sparsing concept.

More energy savings could be achieved with modified disk controllers that can take advantage of sparsed sectors. However, we did not measure a significant effect of data sparsing on the power consumption of commodity hard disks and solid state drives. This is due to the design of current disks that aim to achieve high throughput by making use of disk buffers and inexpensive read-aheads.

2.4   Applications

In principle, loss-tolerant applications such as image processing, sensor data processing, sound synthesis, as well as applications without unique answers, such as web search or machine leaning can benefit from data sparsing. As stated by Esmaeilzadeh et al. [14], such applications can often tolerate lower precision or accuracy trade-offs. Furthermore, such applications process a growing amount of data: In contrast to former times when the majority of data produced was transactional data, the majority of data today shifts more and more to non-transactional data, produced by all kinds of devices [19]. For example, social network providers like Facebook or Snapchat store petabytes of images and videos. An energy-conserving approach like data sparsing could help to improve the energy efficiency of their data centers. In contrast, applications based on

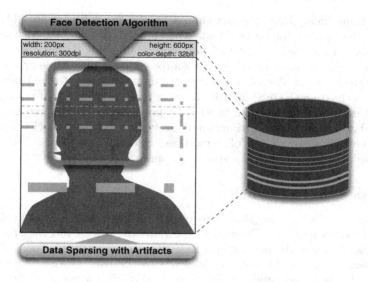

Fig. 1. The principle of sparsed data processing.

transactional data such as log file analysis for accounting and statistics do usually not tolerate modifications of the original data and cannot benefit from data sparsing with artifacts.

3   Data Sparsing in FUSE and HDFS

Data sparsing with artifacts relies on blocks of bytes, i.e., sequences of bytes of a given length. This is due to the fact that the hardware architecture of servers is usually organized into virtual memory pages, hard disk sectors, packet sizes etc. If the *block size* is chosen as a multiple of a virtual memory page, data sparsing with artifacts can make use of page-table mechanisms to sparse the data.

The basic principle of processing sparsed data is depicted in Fig. 1: A program implementing a face detection algorithm is used to process a sparsed version of an image file. The sparse rate and the block size are specified such that the program is still able to process the image file successfully. The image meta-data, which is *sensitive* to data sparsing, is kept unmodified. This is an important assumption: Arbitrary text files may be sparsed without restrictions, but several other types of file contain sections that affect a program's control flow. Introducing an artifact into sensitive sections may result in runtime errors and unexpected program termination. Therefore, as shown in Fig. 1, the raw data block containing the image's dimension and resolution is kept unmodified.

In principle, data sparsing could be implemented within a user program (application layer) or within a special file system (file system layer). In case of Fig. 1, a realization on the application layer would read the original file from persistent storage and sparse it in-memory afterwards. But this design collides with our basic idea: Data sparsing should handle the software as a black box and keep the application unmodified. Therefore, data sparsing with artifacts is implemented on the file system layer. Potentially, this design allows energy savings even for applications where the source code is unavailable or restricted.

Furthermore, we prototypically integrated data sparsing into the Hadoop Distributed File System (HDFS) in order to show the practicability of our approach within a distributed file system. Section 3.1 presents the design and implementation of data sparsing with artifacts in a file system in userspace (FUSE), while Sect. 3.2 describes the design of a modified Hadoop Distributed File System (HDFS) to make use of the data sparsing approach.

3.1 Data Sparsing in FUSE

A data sparsing file system (DSFS) requires a mechanism to mark file blocks as sensitive to data sparsing. Given that the sensitive blocks and the sparse rate have previously been defined when a user program accesses files on a DSFS, a sparsed version of this file can be delivered to the user process. The original data is kept unmodified and can be accessed directly on the local file system. The information about which blocks are sensitive to data sparsing is stored as file system meta-data, such that all file types can be handled equally by this special kind of file system. Write operations to this special kind of file system are simply passed through without modification.

The DSFS developed in the context of our work transparently provides data sparsing with artifacts on the file level. Figure 2 shows the relationship between a

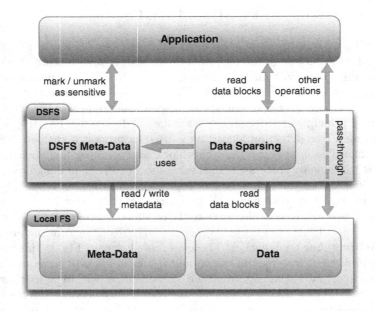

Fig. 2. The design of a Data Sparsing File System (DSFS).

local file system and DSFS. DSFS introduces artifacts during file read access, file write access is passed through to the local file system. Artifacts, sparse rate and the information about sensitive blocks within a file is stored within the DSFS meta-data that is persistently used within the local file system as extended user attributes, each consisting of a key and an associated value.

The concept of extended user attributes is an extension of normal attributes of file system inodes that are supported by a growing number of Unix file systems, such as `ext2`, `ext3` and `ext4`. Our prototypical implementation is implemented as a file system in userspace (`FUSE`) [15], based on the `FUSE`-based open source file system `bindfs` [6]. `bindfs` mirrors already-mounted file system parts to another location, similar to a bind mount (`mount --bind`). However, in contrast to a bind mount, DSFS stores additional meta-data in extended attribute values. File systems like `ext2`, `ext3` and `ext4` store each extended attribute in a single file system block (usually 1 KB, 2 KB or 4 KB). DSFS uses a list of extended user attributes to store the meta-data, to bypass the single block size limit for meta-data that would significantly limit the maximum file size in DSFS. Each of the extended user attributes has a fully qualified name in the form of `user.DSFS_block_n`, where `n` is the number of the meta-data block.

The file system interface is not altered, and operations like `open()`, `close()` or `write()` are unmodified. `ioctl()` is reimplemented to provide read/write access to the DSFS meta-data. A user can mark or unmark data blocks as sensitive, set the sparse rate or specify the artifact. This information is stored with the `setxattr()` command of the underlying file system. The `read()` function relies on the set of sensitive data blocks marked with `ioctl()`, which is retrieved with the `getxattr()` function of the underlying file system.

3.2   Data Sparsing in HDFS

In contrast to a local file system, HDFS provides a non-mountable single virtual file system distributed over many server racks, which is not capable of extended attributes. It provides a separate file system name space. All files are accessed either via the `FSShell` command line interface, or the Java interface.

To introduce data sparsing to HDFS, its data storage needs to be set up on top of a DSFS. Furthermore, the following design changes for HDFS are necessary to support data sparsing: (1) Additional meta-data to mark data blocks as sensitive. (2) A modified block data verification scheme in order to avoid data integrity errors. (3) A modified user interface, i.e., a modified Java interface and commands for the `FSShell` command line interface.

Meta-Data. The key challenge of integrating additional meta-data to mark data blocks is to store it without breaking the high-throughput optimization and the data integrity of the file system. Usually, a single HDFS NameNode is responsible for storing file meta-data such as the number of replicas, the block-ids of the blocks of a single file as well as the whole file system namespace. According to the HDFS architecture, DataNodes are only responsible for reading and writing HDFS blocks. Since HDFS runs on top of a low-level file system, it is a question of granularity on which layer data blocks should be marked as sensitive. However, marking a whole HDFS block as sensitive decreases the amount of sparseable data significantly, since the standard block size of HDFS is 64 MB, and it is even recommended to increase the block size for larger files.

Our design uses the DSFS features to mark sensitive data blocks on a Data-Node. To enable data sparsing for HDFS blocks, new meta-data needs to be introduced into the HDFS data flow. This meta-data is specified by the user *per file*, translated to HDFS meta-data *per HDFS block* by the user client and transferred to the DataNodes, where it is stored persistently using DSFS features.

DataNode Block Verification. Data sparsing is only allowed in DSFS blocks that are not marked as sensitive. Hence, there is still a need for HDFS block verification to ensure data integrity. This feature reflects the fault-tolerance of HDFS, in order to countervail hardware faults of commodity hardware.

HDFS uses a two way integrity check: (1) HDFS verifies checksums on receipt of the block. (2) The HDFS DataNode periodically triggers a checksum-based block integrity test to detect failures due to corrupt hard disk blocks. Both mechanisms are modified with respect to data sparsing during DSFS reads.

User Interface. The information about sensitive blocks is specified manually by the user in a `MetaF` file, which uses a simple `CSV` file format. In this format, the user is able to mark arbitrary ranges of a file stored in HDFS as sensitive by declaring start- and end-offset.

HDFS Block Verification. The periodical block verification method of HDFS, implemented in the class `BlockPoolSliceScanner`, is modified to skip sparsed data blocks during verification. Therefore, the byte stream is partitioned into single blocks that are verified on the block level.

4   Experimental Evaluation

In the following, two use cases for data sparsing with artifacts are evaluated: (i) face detection and recognition and (ii) speech recognition. Data sparsing is performed with a block size of 4 KB and varying sparse rates with different artifacts. 7 different sparse rates are used: 0.5 %, 1 %, 2 %, 5 %, 10 %, 20 % and 50 %. The experiments are conducted in a Hadoop cluster, consisting of 1 NameNode and 2 DataNodes. The cluster size is related to the capacity of the EasyMeter [11] electricity meter that is used for the power and energy measurements. It is connected to a separate Ethernet network via the Multi Utility Communication (MUC) tool and periodically polled at a 5 Hz rate. The servers have an Intel Core i7–4771 with 3.5 GHz, 32 GB RAM and 256 GB SSD and an idle power consumption of 55 W.

4.1   Use Case 1: Face Detection/Recognition

Several social-network or instant-messaging providers need to handle a vast amount of image files. An interesting use case is to detect and to recognize faces within images uploaded by users, in order to provide better services to the users (e.g., suggesting potential friends to the user) or to their advertisers (to improve user-related ads). Therefore, we have implemented a face detection and face recognition use case as a MapReduce application running on top of HDFS with DSFS support. The Hadoop MapReduce framework basically operates on input-, output- and intermediate-data structured using key-value pairs. We use Mapper tasks to process the image with OpenCV [20] or javafaces [16] and Reducer tasks to store detected or recognized images.

For our evaluation of both face detection and face recognition, three types of databases are used: The Yale Face Database [29] (Yale), Caltech Faces [8] (CIT) and a random data set consisting of photos from everystockphoto[4], Flickr[5] and Google image search[6] (Random). In total, over 700 images stored in JPEG format as well as BMP format are used as our test data. A face detector with high detection rates and low execution times as described by Viola and Jones [28] is used, implemented with the Open Source Software OpenCV [20]. For face recognition, the javafaces [16] implementation is used, which is based on eigenfaces [27].

Yale consists of gray-scaled images containing one face per image, 11 individuals in different facial expressions or configurations. It is often used by researchers for face detection and recognition tests. Similarly, CIT contains 27 persons with different lighting/expressions/backgrounds. In contrast to Yale, the location of faces in images is more variable and the images are larger. Random contains a large number of different images with larger file sizes.

Compressed JPEG and uncompressed BMP image files are examined. Since sensitive file headers need to be handled accurately, the first 4KB block is marked as sensitive. Additionally, since JPEG uses a termination marker at the end of a file, the last block is also stored without modification. Table 1 shows the average file size and the percentages of insensitive blocks per file.

Beforehand, an appropriate artifact for these algorithms must be selected. Simply omitting insensitive blocks from image files reduce the quality of the results significantly, because this leads to malformed shapes in an image without any chance of detecting any faces. Good results can be achieved with zero

Table 1. Average file size and average percentage of insensitive blocks.

	Yale	CIT	Random
Avg. file size	159 KB	34 KB	1058 KB
Avg. percentage	95.9 %	70.5 %	99.9 %

---

[4] http://www.everystockphoto.com.
[5] https://www.flickr.com.
[6] https://images.google.com.

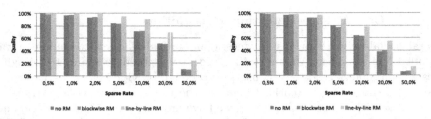

(a) Face detection quality per sparse rate with Yale faces.

(b) Face recognition quality per sparse rate with Yale faces.

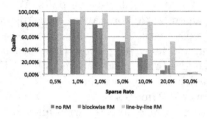
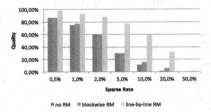

(c) Face detection quality per sparse rate with CIT faces.

(d) Face recognition quality per sparse rate with CIT faces.

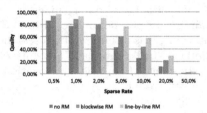
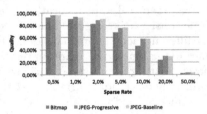

(e) Face detection quality per sparse rate with random images.

(f) Face detection quality per sparse rate with BMP and JPEG-Progressive.

Fig. 3. Face detection and face recognition results.

pages, because the JPEG parser interprets zeros as a termination symbol. Furthermore, the JPEG standard enables the user to insert line-by-line or blockwise restart markers as basic error-correction indicators for the JPEG decoder. Figure 3 shows the experimental results. Quality denotes the number of detected or recognized faces.

90 % Quality. 90 % quality is reached for the Yale data set at sparse rates of up to 2 %; line-by-line restart markers achieve best results with up to 5 %. For CIT, line-by-line markers achieve a quality higher than 90 % for sparse rates of up to 1 %. Furthermore, for Random, only with line-by-line restart markers, 90 % quality can be reached at a 1 % sparse rate.

75 % Quality. 75 % quality is reached for the Yale data set at sparse rates of up to 5 %; line-by-line markers achieve best results with up to 10 %. For CIT, 1 %

(a) Face recognition energy consumption per sparse rate with Yale faces.

(b) Face recognition energy consumption per sparse rate with CIT faces.

(c) Face detection energy consumption per sparse rate with random images.

Fig. 4. Face detection and face recognition energy consumption results.

sparse rate is acceptable, and line-by-line markers achieve a quality higher than 75 % for sparse rates of up to 5 %. Furthermore, for Random, 75 % quality can be reached at 1 % sparse rate without restart markers; with line-by-line restart markers, up to 5 % sparse rate.

Summary. The reason for the drop in quality of the results in CIT and Random without restart markers is that the artifact introduced during data sparsing has a larger negative effect on the JPEG decompression algorithm than predicted. To summarize, the best results are achieved with line-by-line restart markers.

Energy Efficiency. We now investigate the energy consumption for different sparse rates on different data sets. For CIT without restart markers (Fig. 4b), a sparse rate of 50 % cuts the energy consumption in half. Within the range between 0.5 % and 5.0 % sparse rate, where 90 % quality can be achieved, CIT and Random show a slightly reduced energy consumption (CIT: 17 %, Random: 6 %) without restart markers. Unfortunately, although restart markers achieved the best quality, they reduce energy efficiency. Without restart markers, the energy consumption baseline is better in all configurations.

Due to the higher energy consumption of restart markers, at 90 % quality, no energy savings are achieved. For 75 % quality, data sparsing achieves 10 % energy savings for CIT images, and 9 % energy savings for the Random image database.

As Fig. 4a shows, the Yale images are not large enough to have a positive effect on energy consumption. The CIT data set is closer to realistic pictures, and it shows the best results with 1 % sparse rate. Face detection on larger images as in Fig. 4c also shows an increase of energy efficiency within this range.

To summarize, restart markers can increase the quality of the results, but lead to larger energy consumption. Blockwise restart markers introduce a data overhead of 10 %, but do not lead to significantly longer execution times. Nevertheless, for 75 % quality, data sparsing achieves 10 % energy savings for face detection and face recognition on realistic image samples.

4.2 Use Case 2: Speech Recognition

Speech recognition has become a key feature for instant-messaging and mobile application providers. For example, mobile application developers can use cloud-based voice recognition providers like Wit.ai[7] to build voice-controlled applications. Audio files are recorded locally and sent to an analysis backend afterwards[8]. Therefore, a speech recognition use case is evaluated below. For our evaluation, two types of databases are used: An alphanumeric database [23] (AN4), containing 1078 recordings of speakers spelling out personal information (such as name, address, telephone number, birth date) and a PDA speech database [24] (PDA), where the voice was recorded by microphones mounted on a PDA, and different speakers read about 50 sentences, resulting in 836 recodings. The PDA dataset contains Wall Street Journal news text, i.e., natural language with a large vocabulary. In principle, a large vocabulary means less accurate results, i.e., higher expected error rates. All data sets consist of .wav files with 16 bit sample rate.

For recognition, we used Pocketsphinx [25], an open source speech recognition engine that recognizes words with an expected error of 20 %. Pocketsphinx needs a phase of 3 seconds for calibration, which cannot be used for data sparsing. Thus, the file header and the calibration phase are marked as sensitive. As shown in Table 2, this leads to a relatively low percentage of insensitive blocks per file.

Appropriate artifacts for this kind of algorithm are both zero and omitted pages. In case of .wav files, zero pages represent phases of silence, omitted pages interruptions within the recording. As Fig. 5 shows, omitting pages gives slightly better results with respect to the word error rate. With the AN4 database, a 90 % quality (10 % word error rate) can be achieved with 10 % sparse rate in case of omitting pages, and with less than 5 % in case of zero pages. PDA has slightly worse word error rates: 90 % quality can be achieved with only 2 % sparse rate. Furthermore, a 75 % quality (25 % word error rate) can be achieved in AN4 with 20 % sparse rate in case of omitting pages, and with less than 10 % in case of zero pages. PDA can only achieve 75 % quality with less than 10 % sparse rate.

Table 2. Average file size and average percentage of insensitive blocks.

	PDA	AN4
Avg. file size	315 KB	178 KB
Avg. percentage	68,2 %	44,5 %

---

[7] https://wit.ai.
[8] Data sparsing might decrease the energy consumption of micro-controllers as well, due to a reduced transmission energy, but this is beyond the scope of this paper.

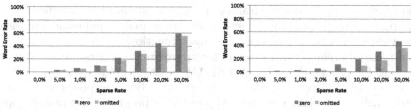

(a) Word error rate per sparse rate with AN4.

(b) Word error rate per sparse rate with PDA.

Fig. 5. Speech recognition results.

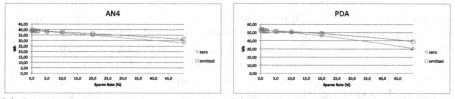

(a) Speech recognition energy consumption per sparse rate with AN4.

(b) Speech recognition energy consumption per sparse rate with PDA.

Fig. 6. Speech recognition energy consumption results.

Energy Efficiency. As indicated by Fig. 6, the energy consumption of both data sets decreases with higher sparse rates. 5 % energy can be saved with 90 % quality, while 8 % energy can be saved with 75 % quality.

5   Related Work

We discuss related work on two relevant topics: Controlled Approximation and Approximate Programming, and Energy-conserving I/O-performance trade-offs.

5.1   Controlled Approximation/Approximate Programming

Several researchers try to find a trade-off between accuracy and energy consumption by using controlled approximation [3] and approximate programming [13]. Code perforation is a technique developed by Agarwal et al. [1] to increase the performance of error resilient applications. The approach basically performs loop approximations for performance improvements. It consists of an extended C/C++ compiler and a corresponding runtime environment, identifying a set of loops that are perforated according to a user defined acceptability metric. Since this works automatically, it is not possible for a programmer to specify loops or parts of the program where code perforation should be omitted. The Green framework developed by Baek and Chilimbi [3] supports energy-conscious programming using controlled approximation, allowing function- and loop-approximation. To use the framework, a programmer has to indicate potential approximation points (e.g., function definitions and loops) using annotations and provide approximate versions of relevant functions.

The focus of architectural support for approximate programming is on voltage scaling for processing units and SRAM, floating point mantissa reduction and reduced DRAM refresh rates, to reduce the dynamic power consumption of CPU, cache and main memory. Approximate programming mainly targets highly utilized systems with high CPU, caches and main memory usage, but the general approach of trading accuracy for energy consumption is applicable to more cases, such as floating-point mantissa reduction [26]. Sampson et al. [21] have proposed EnerJ, an extension of the Java programming language that enables a programmer to explicitly integrate approximation considerations into code. Esmaeilzadeh et al. [13] have introduced architectural support for approximate programming. In recent work, Esmaeilzadeh et al. [14] use artificial neural networks to learn how a region of approximable code behaves and automatically replace the original code with an efficient computation of the learned model.

These approaches target the same classes of applications as data sparsing. In contrast to data sparsing, they rely on specific programming languages, software modifications and custom hardware to increase energy efficiency. Data sparsing introduces artifacts at the data layer, without application layer modifications and with general purpose hardware. Furthermore, approximate programming handles bit flips and floating point mantissa reductions, resulting in a lower precision of computations. However, typical hypervisor and operating system resource management components operate on larger blocks. For example, a typical hard disk block or memory page is 4 KB. Data sparsing utilizes this fact by using memory page sizes as block sizes for artifacts. Furthermore, data sparsing is more than introducing errors into a byte stream, since it uses application-specific artifacts to indicate that a given block should be excluded from the computation.

5.2   Energy-Conserving I/O-Performance Trade-Offs

GreenHDFS developed by Kaushik and Bhandarkar [17] is based on the concept of *hot* and *cold zones*. Rarely accessed files are stored in a *cold zone*, i.e., a set of servers with a low-power hardware design. Regularly accessed files, on the other hand, are stored in a *hot zone*, with higher utilization, performance requirements and power consumption. In contrast to our approach, GreenHDFS is based on system sleep states and low-power hardware at the cost of performance impacts and wake-up penalties. Chen et al. [9] have examined I/O- vs. performance trade-offs in MapReduce. For some applications, the use of compression for data transfers via a network is a way to save energy. Nevertheless, a very low compression ratio of roughly 0.3 is necessary to achieve energy savings. For most data-intensive applications, this condition is not met. For instance, commonly used compression formats like MP3 and JPEG have compression ratios between 0.8 and 0.9 [9].

6   Conclusion

In this paper, data sparsing with artifacts has been introduced, a novel approach aimed at reducing processing times and thus energy efficiency of applications that are robust to input variations while preserving the quality of the results. A proto-typical file system, called DSFS, implementing this approach and its integration into HDFS have been presented. Experimental results have shown promising energy savings of up to 10 % with moderate accuracy losses for different data sparsing rates and types.

Future work will be devoted to provide a theoretical basis and to implement further applications for data sparsing with artifacts. In addition, we will inves-tigate the automatic creation of application-specific artifacts and dynamically adaptable sparse rates for applications. Also, random functions with different probability densities for different placements of artifacts will be considered to improve the quality of the results. Furthermore, the following applications will be considered: Object detection, concept detection, optical character recogni-tion and similarity search in video and image data. We will also compare data sparsing with approaches such as lossy compression. Finally, an interesting ques-tion is how operating system and hardware modifications can be used to further improve the energy efficiency of data sparsing with artifacts.

References

1. Agarwal, A., Rinard, M., Sidiroglou, S., Misailovic, S., Hoffmann, H.: Using Code Perforation to Improve Performance, Reduce Energy Consumption, and Respond to Failures. Technical report, MIT Dspace (2009)
2. Apache Hadoop: Apache Hadoop (2015). http://hadoop.apache.org
3. Baek, W., Chilimbi, T.M.: Green: a framework for supporting energy-conscious programming using controlled approximation. In: Proceedings of the 2010 ACM SIGPLAN Conference on Programming Language Design and Implementation, PLDI 2010, pp. 198–209. ACM (2010)
4. Barroso, L.A., Clidaras, J., Hölzle, U.: The aatacenter as a computer: an intro-duction to the design of warehouse-scale machines. Synth. Lect. Comput. Archit. **8**(3), 1–154 (2013)
5. Barroso, L.A., Hölzle, U.: The case for energy-proportional computing. IEEE Com-put. **40**(12), 33–37 (2007)
6. bindfs: bindfs (2015). http://bindfs.org (2015)
7. Bingham, E., Mannila, H.: Random projection in dimensionality reduction: appli-cations to image and text data. In: Proceedings of the Seventh ACM SIGKDD International Conference on Knowledge Discovery and Data Mining, KDD 2001, pp. 245–250. ACM (2001)
8. Caltech Computational Vision Group: Caltech Faces (2015). http://vision.caltech.edu/Image_Datasets/faces
9. Chen, Y., Ganapathi, A., Katz, R.H.: To compress or not to compress - compute vs. i/o tradeoffs for mapreduce energy efficiency. In: Proceedings of the First ACM SIGCOMM Workshop on Green Networking, pp. 23–28. ACM (2010)

10. Dasgupta, S., Gupta, A.: An elementary proof of a theorem of johnson and linden-strauss. In: Random Structures & Algorithms, vol. 22, pp. 60–65. Wiley Subscription Services (2003)
11. EasyMeter GmbH: EasyMeter Smart Metering Device (2015). http://www.easymeter.com
12. Tal, E.: Saving Data Center Power by Reducing HDD Spin Speed (2015). http://www.opencompute.org/blog/saving-data-center-power-by-reducing-hdd-spin-speed/
13. Esmaeilzadeh, H., Sampson, A., Ceze, L., Burger, D.: Architecture support for disciplined approximate programming. In: 17th International Conference on Architectural Support for Programming Languages and Operating Systems, pp. 301–312. ACM (2012)
14. Esmaeilzadeh, H., Sampson, A., Ceze, L., Burger, D.: Neural acceleration for general-purpose approximate programs. In: Commun. ACM, vol. 58, pp. 105–115. ACM (2014)
15. Filesystem in Userspace: Filesystem in Userspace (FUSE) (2015). http://fuse.sourceforge.net
16. javafaces: javafaces (2015). http://code.google.com/p/javafaces
17. Kaushik, R.T., Bhandarkar, M.: GreenHDFS: Towards an energy-conserving, storage-efficient, hybrid hadoop compute cluster. In: 2010 International Conference on Power Aware Computing and Systems, pp. 1–9. USENIX Association (2010)
18. Li, P., Hastie, T.J., Church, K.W.: Very sparse random projections. In: Proceedings of the 12th ACM SIGKDD International Conference on Knowledge Discovery and Data Mining, pp. 287–296. ACM (2006)
19. Nair, R.: Big Data needs approximate computing: technical perspective. Commun. ACM 58, 104–104 (2014)
20. OpenCV: OpenCV (2015). http://opencv.org
21. Sampson, A., Dietl, W., Fortuna, E., Gnanapragasam, D., Ceze, L., Grossman, D.: EnerJ: approximate data types for safe and general low-power computation. SIGPLAN Not. 46(6), 164–174 (2011)
22. Cooper, S.: Facebook Users are Uploading 350 Million Photos each day (2015). http://www.businessinsider.com/facebook-350-million-photos-each-day-2013-9
23. Sphinx Speech Group, Carnegie Mellon University: CMU Robust Speech Recognition Group: Census Database (2015). http://www.speech.cs.cmu.edu/databases/an4/
24. Sphinx Speech Group, Carnegie Mellon University: CMU Robust Speech Recognition Group: PDA Speech Database (2015). http://www.speech.cs.cmu.edu/databases/pda/
25. Sphinx Speech Group, Carnegie Mellon University: CMU Sphinx Open Source Speech Recognition Toolkit (2015). http://cmusphinx.sourceforge.net
26. Tong, J., Nagle, D., Rutenbar, R.: Reducing power by optimizing the necessary precision/range of floating-point arithmetic. IEEE Trans. Very Large Scale Integr. (VLSI) Syst. 8(3), 273–286 (2000)
27. Turk, M., Pentland, A.: Face recognition using eigenfaces. In: IEEE Conference on Computer Vision and Pattern Recognition, CVPR 1991, pp. 586–591 (1991)
28. Viola, P., Jones, M.: Rapid object detection using a boosted cascade of simple features. In: Proceedings of the 2001 IEEE Computer Society Conference on Computer Vision and Pattern Recognition, vol. 1, pp. 511–518 (2001)
29. Yale University Department of Computer Science: Yale Face Database (2015). http://vision.ucsd.edu/content/yale-face-database

Updating the Energy Model for Future Exascale Systems

Peter M. Kogge[✉]

University of Notre Dame,
Notre Dame, IN 46556, USA
kogge@cse.nd.edu

Abstract. The 2008 DARPA Exascale report had as its goal determining if it were possible to achieve 1000X the computational power of the then-emerging peta-scale systems at a system power of no more than 20 MW. The main conclusion was that there was no such path with technology and architectures as projected at that time. Key to this conclusion were architecturally-tailored models as to how projected advances would translate into system performance. This paper introduces a major update to the "heavyweight" (modern server-class multi-core chips) model, with a detailed discussion on the underlying projections as to technology, chip layout and microarchitecture, and system characteristics. The model is run over the same time period as the 2008 model to verify its accuracy.

Keywords: Exascale · Energy · Technology projection

1 Introduction

The 2008 DARPA Exascale report [17] had as its goal determining if it were possible to achieve 1000X the computational power of the then-emerging peta-scale systems at a system power of no more than 20 MW. The main conclusion was that there was no such path with technology and architectures as projected at that time. Key to this were two projection models as to how future advances could translate into exascale-level system performance, and more importantly what was the power required to achieve that performance. The two models reflected two classes of architectures as they appeared in the TOP500 lists through that time: *heavyweight* systems where the processing was all done on high end server-class conventional processor chips with sophisticated cooling and often separate chips for inter-node networking, and *lightweight* systems where all logic functions were integrated into a single chip and the number of cores and clock rate reduced to the point where relatively simple cooling techniques could be used. The baseline for the heavyweight extrapolations was the 2006 Red Storm system. The lightweight baseline was the IBM BlueGene L system. The models projected how such systems would evolve over time. Since power was a big concern, both at the rack and the system level, special effort was made to estimate both, and then convert the total power and flop rate into a single energy per flop metric. The goal was to find if and when systems would pass below 20 MW for a complete

© Springer International Publishing Switzerland 2015
J.M. Kunkel and T. Ludwig (Eds.): ISC High Performance 2015, LNCS 9137, pp. 323–339, 2015.
DOI: 10.1007/978-3-319-20119-1_24

system. The 2011 update [15] introduced *hybrid* or *heterogeneous* architectures consisting of heavyweight processor chips and separate GPUs.

While the reported characteristics of real systems buttressing the 2008 report has been updated frequently since 2008, using both the "Top10" from the TOP500 [15, 16] and other benchmarks [14, 18, 19], the models themselves have only had relatively minor tweaks to parameters. This paper completely redoes the heavyweight model, with the goal of projecting what is possible under relatively unconstrained future developments. The model's projections start back at the same time as the 2008 model did, so that real-world data from then until now can be compared for model validation. It should be expected that the model will predict systems with better characteristics than we have actually seen in the last 7 years since marketplace factors are not taken into account.

This paper considers only the heavyweight systems; after BlueGene Q there are no planned updates to the lightweight class, and there is insufficient detailed data on the major GPU chips to do as accurate a model as for the other two.

A key point for consideration is the performance metric used here, namely peak flop rate (R_{peak} in TOP500 terms). This is what was used in the Exascale study, and may be reasonable if what we are doing is dense matrix math such as in LINPACK, where efficiencies above 80 % are not uncommon. However, newer benchmarks such as HPCG [8] have early results [1] that imply today's architectures may be at best 1–4 % efficient, and thus making flops less relevant. As these benchmarks mature, the model should be adjusted accordingly.

The following sections discuss this new model in terms of updates to the 2008 model. Section 2 provides background. Section 3 discusses changes in the underlying technology model. Section 4 does the same for the assumed layout and microarchitectures of the processing chips. Section 5 looks at the system-level bounds. Section 6 summarizes the new model. Section 7 concludes.

We note that while extensive data and graphs back up virtually all of the points discussed in the following sections, only selected graphs are shown here. Also for brevity, we refer to [15] for a concise summary of the 2008 assumptions.

2   Background

2.1   Benchmarks, Power, and Energy

The TOP500[1] rankings of sustained performance against dense linear algebra problems have been in existence for over 20 years, with overall power numbers fairly consistently reported after about 2000. After the 2008 Exascale report, the Green500[2] rankings tracked the most energy-efficient systems, in "megaflops per second per watt" (where a flop is a single floating point operation).

A second benchmark involving a graph problem has been tracked since 2010 as the Graph500[3]. In parallel with the Green500, the Green Graph500[4] has been

---

[1]   http://www.top500.org/.

[2]   http://www.Green500.org/.

[3]   http://www.Graph500.org/.

[4]   http://green.Graph500.org/.

gathering data since 2013 on energy efficiency in terms of "megaTEPS per watt" (where 1 TEPS = 1 traversed edge per second).

As useful as these pairs of rankings have been in terms of understanding general trends, in both cases the power numbers have been total system only, for only the one benchmark, and with no breakdown as to where the energy is going. Further, even the total power numbers are not always completely comparable, as different reported numbers are inconsistent in what was measured, such as accounting for associated storage and/or cooling and power conversion.

While both rankings have used "operations per second per watt", the reciprocal "watts per operations per second" is more useful, especially when we replace "watts" by "Joules per second", and cancel out "per second". This leaves "Joules per operation" where a Joule is a basic unit of energy. Thus a "giga operations per second per watt" is the same as 1 "nano Joule (nJ) per operation".

The Exascale study noted that with this metric, if a single operation takes X pico Joules (pJ - where 1 pJ = 10^{-12} Joules), then a machine that can perform 1 exa operations per second (10^{18}) will require X megawatts. The goal for the Exascale study was a 20 MW system that could do 1 exa (fl)ops per second, or 20 pJ per (fl)op. Thus looking for architectures with this 20 pJ characteristic was a key goal. The best of the Green500 is at about 190 pJ per flop for systems much smaller than atop the TOP500, which have energies several times this. The best of the Green Graph500 is at about 17,000 pJ per traversed edge, again with the much faster systems from the Graph500 again several multiples of this.

The key aspect of this measure is that energy is additive; if a benchmark operation like a flop requires on average so many instructions executed, so many cache accesses, so many register file accesses, etc., and we have the energy cost of each individual sub-operation, then the sum is the total energy of the operation, and we can easily compute the relative importance of each sub-operation.

2.2   Moore's Law and Scaling

The original Moore's Law [24] addressed the periodic growth in number of transistors on a chip, and was based on the decrease in the basic **feature size** (linear dimension) of those transistors. This was later extended [23] to include the speed of those transistors, and thus the overall performance of microprocessors. About the same time, a more formal study (now called **Dennard Scaling**) [7] defined parametrically how many different properties of a transistor, and circuits built from such devices, would change as feature size changes. In particular, it predicted a decrease in device capacitance, and in needed supply voltage (denoted V_{dd}), with a consequent increase in possible clock speed, as feature size decreased.

When coupled with an estimate of the power of a circuit as $0.5CfV_{dd}^2$, where C is the aggregate capacitance of the circuit and f the clock rate, Dennard scaling rules have been the backbone of projections of silicon-based systems for years. The annual ITRS roadmap [12] has published the best projections of what is liable to be achievable in the future by industry for years.

A major change in the rate of decrease of V_{dd} around 2004 forced the architectural change from single to multi-core [16].

2.3   Modeling

Virtually all of the most modern CAD packages such as SPICE for chip designs include estimators for power and speed, based on a chosen current technology. Some tools are available that allow projection to future technologies[5]. There are also specific estimators for standard circuit blocks such as SRAM and DRAM [10], backed up by detailed models that allow some forward projections [32].

Moving up, there are chip level architectural models such as Wattch [5] and McPat (especially for multi-core designs) [21], often designed so as to allow estimation using future technologies. There are also modeling tools for emerging technologies such as 3D memory stacks [28]. However, there are few if any multi-node system modeling tools that allow projections into future technologies.

2.4   Exascale

There were actually three Exascale reports, the one on technology and architecture that formed the basis for this paper [17], one on software [3], and one on resiliency [6,9]. After that there were quite a few workshops on algorithms and software for exascale, but at best a few narrow followup studies on exascale energy and architecture [20]. After that there have been multiple projections by acknowledged experts in high performance computing [11,29,31], but very little descriptions of underlying models. For example, [30] projects that future generations of Intel's MIC chip may get within 2-3X of 20 pJ per flop goal. Interestingly, this is only slightly better than the 2008 estimates.

3   Technology Updates

The key technology drivers for the 2008 model were logic feature size, voltage, maximum chip power dissipation, die size, and DRAM chip densities.

Assuming that silicon CMOS will continue as the dominant device technology, key to all the predictions is accurate estimations of how the "feature size" (F) for transistors will change, as this directly drives estimates of such things as die area for cores or capacitance (and thus power) for logic and signaling. The 2008 model assumed the ITRS [12] roadmap available at that time (the 2006 version), with an assumed one year lag from first availability of a new microprocessor to inclusion in systems. Figure 1 includes the trends for both the 2008 model and that from the most recent 2013 roadmap. The most recent version pushes out the smaller feature sizes by perhaps 18 months and lowers the ultimate size. These curves, however, correspond to general industry usage, and foundries such as Intel have done better. Figure 1 also includes red stars representing the feature sizes of actual releases of high end Xeon® chips by Intel [2], and a red line representing the smallest feature sizes of such chips versus time. This line is up to 5 years earlier than either ITRS projection.

---

[5] e.g. PTM http://ptm.asu.edu/.

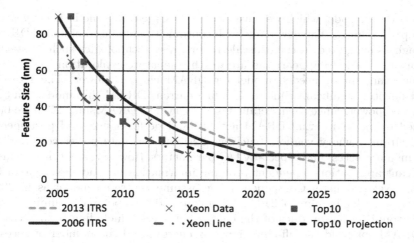

Fig. 1. Trends in silicon feature size.

Also shown are red squares representing the first time systems in the Top10 included such chips. Over the last 10 years they have drawn much closer to the first appearance of a Xeon at the same technology level. The black dashed line is an extrapolation of this trend, ending where the ITRS 2013 does at about 7 nm. This line is what our new model will use. We note that the net effect is about 3 years earlier than the 2008 model for the same feature size (2 years earlier than the 2008 curve, which was 1 year earlier than the assumed systems).

TDP (Thermal Design Power) represents the maximum power that a chip should be allowed to dissipate, typically assuming an air-cooled heat sink. Higher values of TDP allow chips to run faster. The 2006 ITRS numbers forecast up to 200 W per die, whereas the later projections reduced this to around 150. TDPs for actual microprocessors used in Top10 systems over the same period have on average risen from around 80 W to 130 W. In contrast, GPU chips today routinely run above 200 W (as high as 375 W). Since our new model is intended to explore what is possible, not just commercially available, we will assume a linear rise in TDP for exascale-specific microprocessors up to 300 W, starting with the 2006 95 W number. With this model, the values in the 2009–2014 time frame match up reasonably well with real devices. Of course, assuming a continuing rise to 300 W means that cooling must migrate from today's air-cooled to the more elaborate cooling as used in high end GPU accelerator cards, such as closed circuit heat pipes.

Because of cost, most system vendors have used commodity DRAM rather than leading edge as with the microprocessors. Basic cell area between the 2006 and 2013 ITRS is in rough agreement, but the steps for the 2013 projections for commodity DRAM chip capacity are about 3 years later than projected in 2006. This is for economics, as the major vendors have gone to smaller die areas to improve yield and decrease cost. The effect on systems is to reduce the growth in memory per node, which we have already observed over the last few years in the Top10 rankings. The new model will continue to assume commodity DRAM, although as suggested in the exascale report, new technologies such as stacked memory are liable to appear, and are worth a separate exploration.

The other major needed model for DRAM chips is power. The Exascale report devoted significant time to detailing current DRAM chip models and the associated power. Since then, detailed models such as DRAMsim2 [27] have been released to model internal DRAM activity and performance, and part-specific models from memory vendors (such as [22]) can estimate power consumption given memory access and especially I/O parameters. However, all of these require significant application-dependent profiling information beyond the scope of the model developed here. Consequently, we assume the same model as in 2008. We started with a baseline of 210 MW per chip and extrapolated assuming future power would be the product of the energy per access (including both access to the DRAM core and the off-chip signaling energy) and the number of accesses per second, which in turn was assumed to climb linearly with flop rate. Two bounding models were assumed. In one, denoted the *Scaled* model, the inherent energy improved as fast as the flop rate increased, leaving a constant chip power. This is clearly optimistic. In the other, denoted the *Constant* model, total energy per access is fixed, and power is thus proportional to the access rate. This is clearly pessimistic.

One caveat is that it is highly unlikely that the peak access rate of DRAMs as architected to date will ever exceed perhaps 10 times that of the Red Storm parts (today's DDR4 are 3.2 GT/s vs Red Storm's 0.4). This limits the maximum power in the second model, and in either case means that there is a maximum memory bandwidth that will be available per processor, which may not constrain peak performance, but will constrain sustained performance.

4   Layout and Microarchitecture Updates

This section discusses the key characteristics of a single heavyweight microprocessor chip as needed for the new model. The first of these is die area. The 2008 model assumed a constant $220\,mm^2$, while the heavyweight microprocessors in Top10 systems from 1990 until the present have varied from 100 to almost $700\,mm^2$. High end GPU chips today are routinely in the 300 to $500+mm^2$ range. Thus, as with TDP, we will feel free to explore what is possible for an exascale-specific chip by assuming a linear growth in max die size from 300 to $500\,mm^2$.

A second key microarchitectural characteristic is the peak floating point capability of each core, in flops per cycle per core. The original model assumed a bump from 4 flops per cycle to 8 in 2015, and flat thereafter (with the assumption that more flops per cycle than that would be done by chips like GPUs). When we look at the actual data from the Top10 we see the jump to 8 actually first occurred in 2010 (other than for the Earth Simulator's microprocessor [33]) and it has been flat since then. Our new model adopts that.

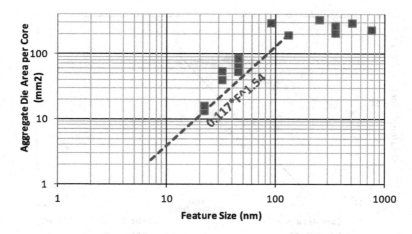

Fig. 2. Core area as die area over core count.

Perhaps the most important parameter is the number of cores per die, which in turn requires a "die area per core". The 2008 model assumed perfect scaling: halving the feature size of a logic block reduces the area of that block by 4. To check on this, Fig. 2 plots data on microprocessor chips that have been used in past Top10 systems. The Y axis is the total area of the die divided by the number of cores. This area includes not just the basic cores but the shared caches, the memory and I/O controllers, inter-core routing, I/O pads, etc.

Around 2004, with the conversion to 90 nm and below, we entered the multi-core region. Before that, the "area per core" had no real trend with feature size, with the growing number of transistors used for improved microarchitecture and bigger caches. After that, we see replication come into play, with an aggregate per core area decreasing with F to the 1.54 power (versus a perfect 2). The difference most probably is the need for circuitry that grows greater than linearly with core count, such as inter-core communication.

A side study used die photos of quad-core Intel Xeons dies to analyze how the die area was used. Figure 3 plots trends in "basic core area" (the true core logic plus just L1) and "area per MB" of cache above L1, all as a function of the feature size. In this data, the area of a core decreased much more slowly than an exponent of 2, or even 1.52, but 0.66. This less than perfect decline is probably due to the growth of microarchitectural features such as bigger unshared caches, more FPUs, bigger TLBs, etc. The area per MB of cache also decreased, but again with an exponent of only 1.2, again which is much less than a perfect scaling of 2. This latter decline is due to the difficulty at smaller feature sizes to decrease SRAM cell areas in a reliable fashion.

An extended study looked at a wider range of Xeon-class microprocessor chips. The growth in total on-chip cache has slowed since 2009, and the amount of cache per core has flattened at about 2.5 MB. This probably reflects the declining effectiveness of caches over that size for typical applications.

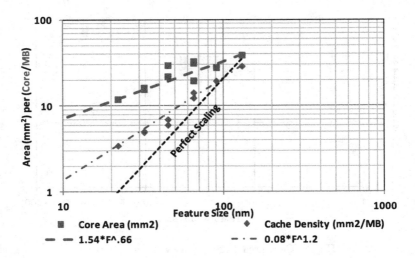

Fig. 3. Side study of quad-core microprocessors.

In terms of the new model, one approach would be to use the derived relationships for shared caches and cores from the above, and develop matching models for all the other functions on a microprocessor die. A second approach would simply use the aggregate formula predicted by Fig. 2 to account for everything. We have chosen the latter here for simplicity.

The next major characteristic is the assumed clock speed of these cores over time. Graphs in [19] summarized how ITRS projections have changed over time. They used as a measurement the intrinsic delay of a 12-inverter chain of high performance transistors (roughly proportional to 1/F). As feature size projections improved, these projections improved yearly until 2004. After that, power issues became more important than raw speed, and a switch in projections was made to assume lower power, but slower, transistors. When it became apparent that even that was overly optimistic, a switch was made to "power-limited" designs. When the clocks for Top10 systems are compared, they line up reasonably well with this last power-limited projection. If we focus just on high-volume Xeon parts as used above, these ITRS clock rates are high by a factor of about 1.55. Given that the Xeon-class parts form the basis for the core energy estimates below, the new model will use the ITRS projections derated by a factor of 0.64.

The 2008 model used the classic CfV_{dd}^2 equation to estimate trends in per core power. We assumed C varied inversely proportional to feature size and V_{dd} varied as predicted by ITRS. The clock rate f was then the maximum value allowed that did not exceed the maximum die dissipation. This failed to account for increases in power for I/O (both the number of signal I/Os and signaling rates increased), and the extra logic for more memory controllers and inter-core routing. Instead, the new model uses an estimate based again on the last decade of microprocessors from the Top10. Figure 4 takes the TDP of the actual

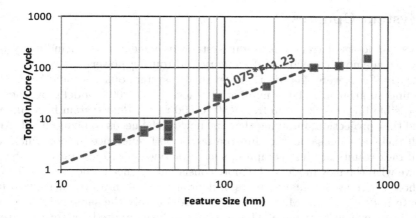

Fig. 4. Per cycle core energy from top10.

microprocessors and divides by the number of cores and the clock rate to give an
energy per cycle for today (22 um) at about 4 nJ, or for a core with up to 8 flops
per cycle, about 500 pJ per flop. The exponent of about 1.23 on feature size in
the trend line makes sense, as we expect about 1 for the decrease in capacitance,
and the remaining 0.23 from remaining small V_{dd} decreases[6]. We note this energy
is still many times larger than the overall energy per flop needed to get to the
original DARPA goal of 20 pJ/flop.

The 2008 baseline Red Storm included a "Seastar" router chip [4] which
accepted packets from the microprocessor and routed them along one of several
links to other nodes. Virtually all heavyweight Top10 systems since then have
incorporated chips like that in their design. (Lightweight systems integrated
these router functions into the main microprocessor chip). The energy of any
one packet routing is approximately constant, meaning that the dynamic power
is proportional to the number of packets routed per second. The 2008 model
assumed a baseline of 55 W for such a chip and then, as with memory, it assumed
two possible bounds. In the Scaled model, the native energy per packet routing
decreased with technology in lock step with the increase in packet frequency
needed to support faster cores. In the Constant model, the energy per packet is
constant, and power is thus proportional to the aggregate packet flow rate. As
with DRAM, there are limits to the maximum routing rate, but there is more
headroom here, with perhaps something approaching a 30X increase over the Red
Storm (56 Gbps vs 3.2 Gbps, plus the potential of doubling the number of lanes).
This is because of a new generation of transceivers (cf. [25]). However, power
dissipation will max out at something approaching the maximum we choose for
the microprocessor die. Also, as with the memory limits, after the bandwidth is
maxed out the sustainable performance of the system will suffer.

---

[6] Prior to 2004, constant field Dennard Scaling had C vary with F and V_{dd} with F^2.
After 2004, V_{dd} has become almost flat, with a much smaller decline with F.

5   System Updates

This section looks at trends in overall system implementation, including system packaging, memory capacity, and memory and routing power.

Clearly if cost were no object, an "exascale" system of sorts could be created by adding an arbitrarily large number of "racks". The 2008 model grew the size of a possible future system up from 150 to 600 racks. Real system have already topped that projection, implying that the new model needs to be modified. Also, not all racks are the same size (up to a factor of 4 difference in footprint), and not all rack counts are just compute, such as service or storage racks.

If we wish the new model to be more consistent, we need a better metric. The one chosen here uses "square meters of floor space" taken up by racks with just compute nodes in them. Most racks are approximately the same height, so this metric is equivalent to volume. This in turn can be computed for Top10 systems by looking at their specific rack characteristics and the maximum number of just compute nodes they contain. Dividing into the number of nodes in the system gives us a count of "compute racks" which is then multiplied by the footprint of one rack. The new model then starts with $100\,m^2$ in 2005, and rises linearly to $1000\,m^2$. This upper bound is a little less than twice the current physically largest system, the K computer [34].

Another metric that was important to the 2008 model was how many processing sockets, and thus compute nodes, could be physically fit within the available rack volume. The 2008 model started with the packaging associated with Red Storm and did some extrapolations from that. With the exception of moving the first step back 2 years, actual data matched well, and is carried forward to the new model. Note that achieving the next step will require a significant advance in cooling, so that today's "heat sink" area is greatly reduced.

The 2008 model projected future peak rack-level power budgets as step-wise growth from that of the Red Storm system. We have compared this against data from the Top10 since then, and found that increased power limits were achieved by real systems much faster than projected. Consequently, the new model assumes the same levels as before but moved earlier in time. The new model also assumes that out of the total power dissipated in a rack only 80 % is available for compute, with the rest for power conditioning, cooling, etc.

The 2008 model postulated that memory capacity would be increased in tandem with the growth in flop rate to match the ratio found in the Red Storm 2006 system (a ratio of 0.31 to 1). This was less than what traditionally had been a "1 byte per flop per second" rule of thumb. Part of this increase was to come from the increase in DRAM chip density and part by increasing the number of chips. As shown in [19], before 2006 this ratio was not uncommon in the Top10, but afterwards it has been dropping by a factor of 0.74 per year, and is now around 0.125 bytes per flop for heavyweight systems, and even lower (0.05 bytes per flop per second) for the GPU-based systems. There are several reasons for this. First, as discussed above, the density of DRAM chips has been growing at a slower rate than foretold in 2008. Second, the number of socket memory channels onto which memory can be attached has increased only from

2 in the Red Storm part to 4 today, as had the number of ranks of DRAM chips per DIMM (also from 2 to 4). Third, there is a limit to the number of DRAM DIMMs that can be attached to any memory channel (typically at most 2 as in Red Storm). Thus, there is perhaps at most a factor of 4 between 2006 and today in the total number of DRAM chips that might be associated with a single socket, with little future increase likely without a dramatic change in memory technology.

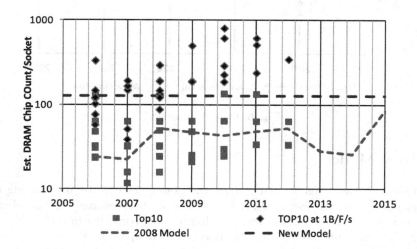

Fig. 5. DRAM chips per socket.

Figure 5 takes the memory per socket for each of the heavyweight Top10 systems and assumes that the DRAM technology used was that available one year prior to the system's introduction. These counts do not include ECC, which should add about 12 % more chips. As can be seen, this count is in a band between about 16 to 128 chips, with no growth over time. Also shown are the same Top10 systems if the memory had been expanded to achieve a 1 byte per flop per second. The DRAM chip count that must be associated with each processor socket rapidly climbs to near 1,000 which, as discussed above, is probably infeasible with current packaging.

Also shown is the chip count projected by the 2008 model. As can be seen, this is in the middle of the actual Top10 points, but as discussed elsewhere this model did not predict as fast a rise in flops per cycle or when new technology would be introduced. The result was an underestimate in performance per socket, and thus less memory to achieve its constant 0.31 bytes/flop per second.

Given these constraints, the new model uses a constant 128 (144 with ECC) DRAM chips of a technology 1 year earlier than the system's introduction, and lets the bytes to flops ratio be whatever it is.

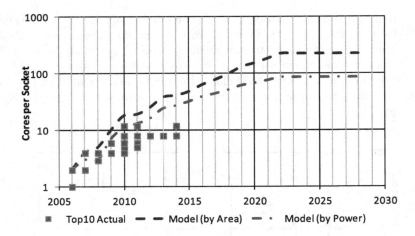

Fig. 6. Cores per socket.

6   New Model

From the prior sections we can project the power per core by multiplying the energy per core by the assumed clock rate. We can then estimate the number of cores per socket in one of two ways: by dividing the core area into the die area, or dividing the core power into the maximum dissipation. Figure 6 diagrams projections for each way as a function of time. As can be seen, the two models seem to bound the real data to date fairly accurately, with most at the power limit. Going forward we assume the power-limited case.

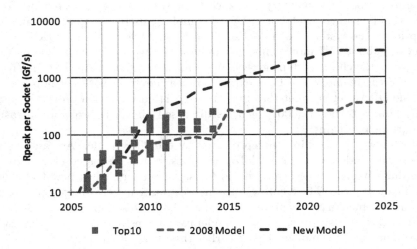

Fig. 7. Peak flops per socket.

Given the number of cores per socket, the clock rate, and the peak flops per cycle, Fig. 7 computes the peak flops per socket. The agreement is rather good. The 2008 model clearly undershot, mainly because it did not predict as fast a rise in flops per cycle, when new technology would be introduced, or the size of the processor dies.

We assume a node consists of a single microprocessor, 144 memory chips, and a single router chip. In calculating power we sum the components from all three, and add an additional 10 % for the on-board voltage regulation and conversion. There is relatively good correspondence to Top10. We note that the constant model suggests that both memory and network bandwidth became power limited around 2009, meaning that if the constant model were correct, then after that point we see a rapidly diminishing memory and network bandwidth to support the growing chip performance.

As discussed earlier, the new model normalized a "rack" to a square meter of floor space. A rack size for many of the Top10 systems is about $0.8\,m^2$, so numbers here will be slightly larger than for a rack today. The number of nodes per this unit area is then bounded as the minimum of two numbers: one based on the packing density and the other in the number of nodes that fit before the peak power for the unit area is reached. Interestingly, the model suggests we crossed from being power to volume-constrained somewhere around 2008 to 2010. This is where the data points in Fig. 7 drops below the blue area/volume bound towards or below the red power/bound line.

Figure 8 diagrams the peak performance of both new models, the 2008 model, and the Top10. To date the new models seem a better fit than the old one.

Figure 9 is perhaps the most important graph from this model, as it shows the decrease in energy per flop over time. The projections from 2006 until now

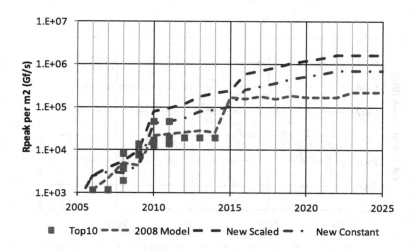

Fig. 8. Rpeak for a square meter.

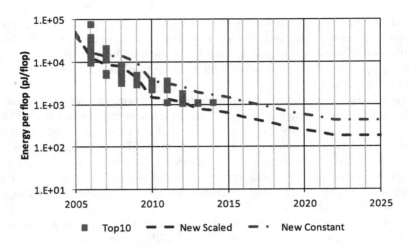

Fig. 9. Energy per flop.

seem fairly good, so if the model holds for the future, the best we will do for heavyweight machines is between 180 and 420 pJ per flop.

To see if a system with a peak exaflop is even feasible, the new model scaled up the total footprint of a multi-rack system as we go out in time, and projected peak performance and memory. Figure 10 implies that if we had been more aggressive we could have had a system with significantly more peak performance than any of the current heavyweights, and going forward, it may be possible to reach an exaflop in about 2020, but it would require about 1200 racks, with a power requirement of about 180 to 425 MW.

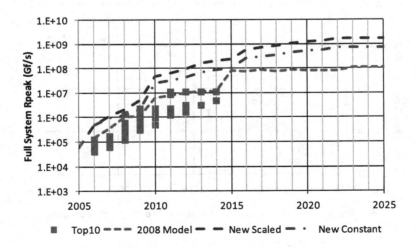

Fig. 10. System performance projections.

7   Conclusions

This paper has redone the overall projection model from the 2008 Exascale report for possible exascale systems using conventional heavyweight processors. These configurations have all been "at any cost", and assumed more of the most advanced technologies than in current systems. The results are better than the 2008 model, both in predictive accuracy and in the potential of reaching a peak of an exaflop, but the cost and power demands are liable to be huge. In addition, it is unclear if we would end up with anything more than a stunt machine, since we very rapidly end up with constrained memory and network bandwidth to go with constrained memory capacity. This may be even worse if performance against more relevant applications require more bandwidth and other resources.

Going forward there are a variety of possibly valuable modifications to this model. First is to fill in missing data from many of the Top10 heavyweight systems, and continue updating from future years TOP500 list. Second is to extend the models to include lightweight and heterogeneous architectures, as both of these may be significantly more efficient architectures, especially in power. The lightweight case is fairly easy, but with no successors to the BlueGene series, this is at best an exercise to coax some vendor to reconsider. Developing the heterogeneous model is more challenging, since data on both architecture and implementation are in significant flux. Newer chips such as the Xeon Phi seem to be cross-overs between all three classes of architectures.

Next, more detailed models for the major components are appropriate, including partitioning between memory, logic, and signaling (both on and off chip). Transceiver power for high speed signaling is key here. In particular, once better models for signaling are incorporated, then other metrics such as bytes per second of bandwidth versus peak flops can also be computed, leading to insight into other possible cliffs as we have seen with the bytes of memory per flop per second. All of these would help extend the model to be relevant to other well-known benchmarks such as Graph500, and newer ones such as HPCG. The effects of "dark silicon" for "wear-leveling" and extra logic for redundancy need to be factored in. Also of real interest going forward are projections based on emerging memory architectures such as 3D stacks [26] or HBM (High Bandwidth Memories) [13]. These will provide significantly more bandwidth, fixing some of the problems discussed above, but with significantly more complex models. These may then lead to alternative architectures other than the three currently discussed, such as some variations of "Processing In/Near Memory".

Acknowledgements. This material is based upon work supported by the Department of Energy, National Nuclear Security Administration, under Award Number(s) DE-NA0002377, as part of the Center for Shock-Wave Processing of Advanced Reactive Materials, University of Notre Dame. It also builds on work performed under the Sandia National Labs XGC project.

References

1. Hpcg: High performance conjugate gradient. https://software.sandia.gov/hpcg/
2. Xeon, February 2015. http://en.wikipedia.org/wiki/Xeon
3. Amarasinghe, S., Campbell, D., Carlson, W., Chien, A., Dally, W., Elnohazy, E., Harrison, R., Harrod, W., Hiller, J., Karp, S., Koelbel, C., Koester, D., Kogge, P., Levesque, J., Reed, D., Schreiber, R., Richards, M., Scarpelli, A., Shalf, J., Snavely, A., Sterling, T.: Exascale software study: Software challenges in extreme scale systems (2009)
4. Brightwell, R., Pedretti, K., Underwood, K.D.: Initial performance evaluation of the cray seastar interconnect. In: Proceedings of the 13th Symposium on High Performance Interconnects, HOTI 2005, pp. 51–57. IEEE Computer Society, Washington, DC (2005)
5. Brooks, D., Tiwari, V., Martonosi, M.: Wattch: A framework for architectural-level power analysis and optimizations. In: Proceedings of the 27th Annual International Symposium on Computer Architecture, ISCA 2000, pp. 83–94. ACM, New York (2000). http://doi.acm.org/10.1145/339647.339657
6. Cappello, F., Geist, A., Gropp, B., Kale, L., Kramer, B., Snir, M.: Toward exascale resilience. Int. J. High Perform. Comput. Appl. **23**(4), 374–388 (2009). http://dx.doi.org/10.1177/1094342009347767
7. Dennard, R., Gaensslen, F., Rideout, V., Bassous, E., LeBlanc, A.: Design of ion-implanted mosfet's with very small physical dimensions. IEEE J. Solid-State Circuits **9**(5), 256–268 (1974)
8. Dongarra, J., Heroux, M.: Toward a new metric for ranking high performance computing systems. Technical report SAND2013-4744, Sandia National Laboratories, June 2013
9. Elnozahy, M., Bianchini, R., El-Ghazawi, T., Fox, A., Godfrey, F., Hoisie, A., McKinley, K., Melhem, R., Plank, J., Ranganathan, P., Simons, J.: System resilience at extreme scale. Technical report, DARPA Technical report (2009)
10. Hewlett Packard: Cacti: An integrated cache and memory access time, cycle time, area, leakage, and dynamic power model. http://www.hpl.hp.com/research/cacti/
11. Hsu, J.: When will we have an exascale supercomputer? In: IEEE Spectrum, vol. 52, pp. 13–15. IEEE, January 2015
12. ITRS: International technology roadmap for semiconductors. http://www.itrs.net/
13. JEDEC: High bandwidth memory (HBM) dram. Technical report, JEDEC Solid State Technology Association, October 2013
14. Kogge, P.: Tracking the effects of technology and architecture on energy through the top 500, green 500, and graph 500. In: 2012 International Conference on Supercomputing, ISC 2012 (2012)
15. Kogge, P., Dysart, T.: Using the top500 to trace and project technology and architecture trends. In: Proceedings of the 2011 ACM/IEEE Conference on Supercomputing, SC 2011 (2011)
16. Kogge, P., Shalf, J.: Exascale computing trends: Adjusting to the new normal for computer architecture. Comput. Sci. Eng. **15**(6), 16–26 (2013)
17. Kogge, P.M., Bergman, K., Borkar, S., Campbell, D., Carlson, W., Dally, W., Denneau, M., Franzon, P., Harrod, W., Hill, K., Hiller, J., Karp, S., Keckler, S., Klein, D., Lucas, R., Richards, M., Scarpelli, A., Scott, S., Snavely, A., Sterling, T., Williams, R.S., Yelick, K.: Exascale computing study: Technology challenges in achieving exascale systems. Technical report. CSE 2008-13, University of Notre Dame, September 2008

18. Kogge, P.M., Resnick, D.R.: Yearly update: Exascale projections for 2013. Technical report SAND2013-9229, University of Notre Dame, Sandia National Laboratories, October 2013
19. Kogge, P.M., Resnick, D.R.: Yearly update: Exascale projections for 2014. Technical report SAND2014-18651, University of Notre Dame, Sandia National Laboratories, 30 September 2014
20. Kogge, P., La Fratta, P., Vance, M.: Facing the exascale energy wall. In: 2010 International Workshop on Innovative Architecture for Future Generation High Performance (IWIA), pp. 51–58, January 2010
21. Li, S., Ahn, J.H., Strong, R.D., Brockman, J.B., Tullsen, D.M., Jouppi, N.P.: Mcpat: An integrated power, area, and timing modeling framework for multicore and manycore architectures. In: Proceedings of the 42nd Annual IEEE/ACM International Symposium on Microarchitecture, MICRO 42, pp. 469–480. ACM, New York (2009). http://doi.acm.org/10.1145/1669112.1669172
22. Micron: Tn-41-01: Calculating memory system power for ddr3. http://www.micron.com/~/media/Documents/Products/Technical%20Note/DRAM/TN4603.pdf
23. Moore, G.: Progress in digital integrated electronics. In: 1975 International Electron Devices Meeting, vol. 21, pp. 11–13 (1975)
24. Moore, G.: Cramming more components onto integrated circuits. Proc. IEEE 86(1), 82–85 (1998)
25. Navid, R., Chen, E.H., Hossain, M., Leibowitz, B., Ren, J., Chou, C.H., Daly, B., Aleksic, M., Su, B., Li, S., Shirasgaonkar, M., Heaton, F., Zerbe, J., Eble, J.: A 40 gb/s serial link transceiver in 28 nm CMOS technology. IEEE J. Solid-State Circ. 50(4), 814–827 (2015)
26. Pawlowski, J.T.: 3D stacked memory architectures for multi-core processors. In: 3D Architectures for Semiconductor Integration and Packaging, San Francisco, CA, USA (2012)
27. Rosenfeld, P., Cooper-Balis, E., Jacob, B.: Dramsim2: A cycle accurate memory system simulator. Comput. Archit. Lett. 10(1), 16–19 (2011)
28. Rosenfeld, P.: Performance exploration of the hybrid memory cube. Ph.D. thesis, University of Maryland, College Park, MD (2014)
29. Simon, H.: no exascale for you! an interview with berkeley lab's horst simon (2013). http://www.top500.org/blog/no-exascale-for-you-an-interview-with-berkeley-labs-horst-simon/
30. Sodani, A.: Race to exascale: Opportunities and challenges, December 2011. http://www.microarch.org/micro44/files/Micro%20Keynote%20Final%20-%20Avinash%20Sodani.pdf
31. Stevens, R.: On the race to exascale (2013). http://www.ci.anl.gov/blog/rick-stevens-race-exascale
32. Thoziyoor, S.: A comprehensive memory modeling tool for design and analysis of future memory hierarchies. Ph.D. thesis, University of Notre Dame, Notre Dame, IN, USA (2008), aAI3442483
33. Yokokawa, M., Habata, S., Kawai, S., Ito, H., Tani, K., Miyoshi, H.: Basic design of the earth simulator. In: Fukuda, A., Joe, K., Polychronopoulos, C.D. (eds.) ISHPC 1999. LNCS, vol. 1615, pp. 269–280. Springer, Heidelberg (1999)
34. Yokokawa, M., Shoji, F., Uno, A., Kurokawa, M., Watanabe, T.: The k computer: Japanese next-generation supercomputer development project. In: Proceedings of the 17th IEEE/ACM International Symposium on Low-power Electronics and Design, ISLPED 2011, pp. 371–372. IEEE Press, Piscataway (2011). http://dl.acm.org/citation.cfm?id=2016802.2016889

High-Order ADER-DG Minimizes Energy- and Time-to-Solution of SeisSol

Alexander Breuer[1]([✉]), Alexander Heinecke[2], Leonhard Rannabauer[1], and Michael Bader[1]

[1] Technische Universität München,
Boltzmannstr. 3, 85748 Garching, Germany
{breuera,bader}@in.tum.de, lrannabauer@mytum.de
[2] Intel Corporation,
2200 Mission College Blvd., Santa Clara, CA 95054, USA
alexander.heinecke@intel.com

Abstract. In this paper we give a comprehensive overview of our node-level optimization of the high-order finite element software SeisSol aiming at minimizing energy- and time-to-solution. SeisSol simulates dynamic rupture and seismic wave propagation at petascale performance in production runs. In this context we analyze the impact that convergence order, CPU clock frequency, vector instruction sets and chip-level parallelism have on the execution time, energy consumption and accuracy of the obtained solution. From a performance perspective, especially on state-of-the-art and future architectures, the shift from a memory- to a compute-bound scheme and the need for double precision arithmetic with increasing orders of convergence is compelling. Our results show that we are able to reduce the computational error by up to five orders of magnitudes when increasing the order of the scheme from 2 to 7, while consuming the same amount of energy.

Keywords: Energy- and time-to-solution · High-order · Vectorization · ADER · Discontinuous galerkin · Finite element method

1 Introduction

In recent years, a lot of research effort has been spent on designing energy-efficient processing units. Microprocessor architectural research rapidly moves into the direction of application-specific accelerators to address dark silicon challenges [25]; e.g. in 2014 an ASIC for deep learning was declared as best paper at MICRO'14 [9] and ASPLOS'14 [8]. In contrast to such developments, general purpose processors (CPUs, coprocessors and GPGPUs) have been enhanced by more and more powerful SIMD units, aiming at increasing the computational throughput at minimal additional energy costs. However, we have to keep in mind that many HPC applications are not bound by floating-point performance [10] on modern chips. Especially CPUs may consume a lot of power when running memory-bound workloads, see Table 1. This transforms algorithms that trade

© Springer International Publishing Switzerland 2015
J.M. Kunkel and T. Ludwig (Eds.): ISC High Performance 2015, LNCS 9137, pp. 340–357, 2015.
DOI: 10.1007/978-3-319-20119-1_25

Table 1. Performance and full-box power consumption when running the STREAM benchmark (triad) and DGEMM (MKL 11.2) on the HSW system. A full utilization of the memory sub-system results into a power draw which does not scale with frequency but also does not stay constant since caches run at higher frequency as well. For DGEMM the power consumption nicely correlates with the achieved performance.

Benchmark	@1.2 GHz		@1.9 GHz	
	Performace	Power	Performace	Power
STREAM - Triad	105 GiB/s	295 W	105 GiB/s	345 W
DGEMM - 60 k × 60 k × 192	610 GFLOPS	250 W	950 GFLOPS	400 W

data movements for computations into a superior alternative. Especially, if the increased amount of compute allows for more accurate results.

For this purpose, we analyze the potential for saving energy by using higher-order finite element methods in the context of seismic simulations. High-order spatial-temporal discretizations are an energy-efficient approach for three reasons. First, they allow for shorter runtimes with respect to accuracy. Second, they lower the pressure on the memory subsystem due to an increased number of local operations. And third, they are able to exploit a core's SIMD capabilities due to increased sizes of the involved matrix operators. We take the Arbitrary high-order accurate DERivative Discontinuous Galerkin (ADER-DG) code *SeisSol* as proxy for our work. SeisSol's back-end requires small sparse and dense matrix multiplication kernels which are selected based on an auto-tuning model to ensure fastest execution times for a given order of convergence and architecture. Having the optimal configuration for the matrix kernels at hand, we analyze important metrics of the overall software such as time-to-solution (in the context of our work the most accurate solution) and most importantly energy-to-solution. Keeping the relation of performance and full-box power consumption for DGEMM and the STREAM benchmark on state-of-the-art hardware – as shown in Table 1 – in mind, we know that for SeisSol's properties a fast compute-bound variant is more energy-efficient than a memory-bound one.

We performed a cross-plattform analysis of SeisSol's performance on several node types and coprocessors found in today's supercomputers with different maturities of the vector instructions sets:

WSM A dual-socket Intel® Xeon® X5690 server, 12 cores @3.46 GHz, 48 GB of DDR3-1333 memory, 128-bit SSE4.2 vector instruction set, 41 GiB/s memory bandwidth, 166 GFLOPS double precision peak performance, idle power consumption of 160 W and DGEMM power consumption of 350 W.

SNB A dual-socket Intel® Xeon® E5-2670 server, 16 cores @2.6 GHz, 128 GB of DDR3-1600 memory, 256-bit AVX vector instruction set, 75 GiB/s memory bandwidth, 333 GFLOPS double precision peak performance, idle power consumption of 100 W and DGEMM power consumption of 280 W.

HSW A dual-socket Intel® Xeon® E5-2699 v3 server, 36 cores @1.9 GHz (guaranteed, P0-frequency is 2.3 GHz), 128 GB of DDR4-1866 memory, 256-bit

AVX2 vector instruction set, 105 GiB/s (cluster-on-die enabled) memory bandwidth, 1.1 TFLOPS double precision peak performance @1.9 GHz, idle power consumption of 75 W and DGEMM power consumption of 400 W.

KNC A Intel® Xeon Phi™ 5110P coprocessor, 60 cores @1.06 GHz, 8 GB of GDDR5 memory, 512-bit MIC vector instruction set, 150 GiB/s memory bandwidth and 1 TFLOPS double precision peak performance, idle power consumption of 100 W and DGEMM power consumption of 225 W.

This cross-platform analysis was carried out on two entirely different benchmark scenarios: (a) a synthetic convergence test in Sect. 4.2 that allows for a comparison of rigorous mathematical error-norms using regularly-refined meshes and (b) the well-established Layer Over Halfspace (LOH.1) benchmark in Sect. 4.3, which operates on a fully unstructured mesh. We also study the effect of using single-precision arithmetic with respect to accuracy and execution time. In order to ensure results that can be easily transferred to a full system perspective, we limit our (detailed) power measurements to full-box numbers rather than RAPL counters [24] for estimating the CPU-only power consumption.

To the best of our knowledge this is the first work that performs a detailed analysis of a higher-order DG code in the stress field of accuracy, execution time and energy-to-solution. Therefore this work should deliver a valuable extension to the fast-growing field of energy awareness in scientific high-performance computing. In [6,14,15] energy-profile changes due to use of vectorization and parallelization are analyzed for several memory- and compute-bound micro-benchmarks on WSM- and SNB-type of architectures. Specifically to large dense linear algebra applications, [1,4,11,12,21] analyze performance with respect to energy consumption for various BLAS and LAPACK routines either using full-box power or processor built-in counters. There is also application-specific work, e.g. in [2,7], where the energy footprint of the weather code COSMO is presented. A similar analysis is performed for N-body algorithms in [20,27]. Additionally, [23,26] present approaches how auto-tuning of applications can help to reduce their energy-footprint.

2   Computational Core

In this section we give a brief introduction into SeisSol's computational core. Please refer to [5,16] for a more detailed description and to [13,18] for a detailed derivation from the underlying system of hyperbolic partial differential equations and for handling of boundary conditions and source terms.

SeisSol solves the elastic wave equations in velocity-stress formulation

$$q_t + Aq_x + Bq_y + Cq_z = 0. \tag{1}$$

$q(\boldsymbol{x}, t) = (u, v, w, \sigma^{xx}, \sigma^{yy}, \sigma^{zz}, \sigma^{xy}, \sigma^{xz}, \sigma^{yz})^T$ is the space-time-dependent vector of elastic quantities. u, v and w are the particle velocities in Cartesian x-, y- and z-direction, σ^{xx}, σ^{yy} and σ^{zz} the normal stresses and σ^{xy}, σ^{xz} and σ^{yz} the shear stress components. $A(\boldsymbol{x})$, $B(\boldsymbol{x})$ and $C(\boldsymbol{x})$ are the three Jacobians including space-dependent material parameters.

SeisSol uses an ADER-DG Finite Element Method for spatial-temporal discretization. For meshing we rely on flexible unstructured tetrahedral meshes. For a given convergence order $\mathcal{O}$ – results for $\mathcal{O} \in \{2, 3, \ldots, 7\}$ are presented in this work – we use $B_{\mathcal{O}}$ basis functions per element discretizing each of the components in the vector of elastic quantities $q(\boldsymbol{x}, t)$ in every tetrahedron. For the considered orders of convergence the number of basis functions are $B_2 = 4$, $B_3 = 10$, $B_4 = 20$, $B_5 = 35$, $B_6 = 56$ and $B_7 = 84$. In total, storing the modes of the basis functions for every elastic quantity results in $B_{\mathcal{O}} \times 9$ degrees of freedom (DOFs) per element. We can split the wave-propagation core into three integration operators performing time-, volume and boundary integration.

ADER. The ADER-time integration derives the time integrated DOFs $\mathcal{T}_k^{n,\Delta t}$ in a tetrahedron k. It integrates the DOFs of an element from time step t^n to the next time step $t^{n+1} = t^n + \Delta t$, where Δt is the time step width:

$$\mathcal{T}_k^{n,\Delta t} := \mathcal{T}_k(Q_k^n, \Delta t) = \sum_{j=0}^{\mathcal{O}-1} \frac{\Delta t^{j+1}}{(j+1)!} \frac{\partial^j}{\partial t^j} Q_k(t^n). \tag{2}$$

With the DOFs at time step t^n as starting point, $\frac{\partial^0}{\partial t^0} Q_k = Q_k^n$, the derivatives $\frac{\partial^j}{\partial t^j} Q_k$ are computed by a recursive scheme:

$$\frac{\partial^{j+1}}{\partial t^{j+1}} Q_k = -\sum_{c=1}^{3} \hat{K}^{\xi_c} \left(\frac{\partial^j}{\partial t^j} Q_k \right) A_{k,c}^\star. \tag{3}$$

$\xi_1 - \xi_2 - \xi_3$ is the reference coordinate system. $\hat{K}^{\xi_c}$ are the three transposed global stiffness matrices (size $B_{\mathcal{O}} \times B_{\mathcal{O}}$) multiplied by the diagonal inverse mass matrix in preprocessing. The star matrices $A_{k,c}^\star$ (size 9×9) summarize the effects of the flux function in reference coordinates and depend on the per-element material parameters.

Volume. The volume kernel discretizes the integration of the time integrated DOFs $\mathcal{T}_k^{n,\Delta t}$ over the volume of the element:

$$\mathcal{V}_k\left(\mathcal{T}_k^{n,\Delta t}\right) = \sum_{c=1}^{3} \tilde{K}^{\xi_c}\left(\mathcal{T}_k^{n,\Delta t}\right) A_{k,c}^\star. \tag{4}$$

$\tilde{K}^{\xi_c}$ are the three non-transposed stiffness matrices (size $B_{\mathcal{O}} \times B_{\mathcal{O}}$) multiplied by the inverse mass matrix in preprocessing. As in the ADER-time integration, $A_{k,c}^\star$ are the three star matrices of size 9×9.

Boundary. As we are using a Discontinuous Galerkin scheme, the numerical solution is allowed to be discontinuous at the interface of two neighboring tetrahedrons k and k_i. This gives rise to General Riemann Problems, which are solved by the boundary integration operator:

$$\mathcal{F}_{k,i}\left(\mathcal{T}_k^{n,\Delta t}, \mathcal{T}_{k_i}^{n,\Delta t}\right) = \hat{F}^{-,i}\left(\mathcal{T}_k^{n,\Delta t}\right) \hat{A}_{k,i}^+ + \hat{F}^{+,i,j_k(i),h_k(i)}\left(\mathcal{T}_{k_i}^{n,\Delta t}\right) \hat{A}_{k,i}^-. \tag{5}$$

In Eq. 5 the per-element-face flux-solver $\hat{A}_{k,i}^{\pm}$ transforms the time integrated DOFs $T_k^{n,\Delta t}$ and $T_{k_i}^{n,\Delta t}$ of tetrahedron k and the i-th a face neighbor k_i to a face-aligned coordinate system, solves the Riemann problem exactly and transform the solution back to reference coordinates. $\hat{F}^{-,i}$ and $\hat{F}^{i,j_k(i),h_k(i)}$ are the 52 global flux matrices [16] (size $B_{\mathcal{O}} \times B_{\mathcal{O}}$) multiplied by the inverse mass matrix in pre-processing.

Explicit Update Scheme. The update scheme from time step t^n to t^{n+1} can be summarized by combining the three integration operators:

$$Q_k^{n+1} = Q_k^n + \mathcal{V}_k - \sum_{i=1}^{4} \mathcal{F}_{k,i}. \tag{6}$$

Time integration (Eq. 2), volume integration (Eq. 4) and the first summand of the boundary integration in Eq. 5 depend on element-local data only. The second summand of the boundary integration in Eq. 5 accounts for the contribution of face neighbor k_i to the boundary integral. Therefore the complete evaluation of the sum in Eq. 6 requires the time integrated DOFs $T_{k_i}^{n,\Delta t}$ of the four face neighbors $k_i, i \in 1 \ldots 4$.

3   Implementation

The recently discussed operations reduce to small dense and sparse matrix multiplications. However, calling a rich math library, which is optimized for large matrix operations, such as Intel MKL, would not result in best performance. We therefore described (in previous work) a code generation approach that takes many specialties of the ADER-DG scheme into account, e.g. zero blocks that are gradually generated during the time integration step [5]. We also pointed out that with more sophisticated vector-instructions sets (longer vectors, support for fused-multiply-add (FMA) operations and fast aligned memory operations) it is beneficial to increase the amount of operations handled as dense [16].

We re-implemented the dense code path of our matrix multiplication code generator from scratch. In contrast to our previous implementation, we now directly generate assembly code (instead of compiler intrinsics) which gives us more control with respect to register allocation. This is important since the biggest change in this re-implementation is the support for arbitrary M, K, LDA, LDB and LDC (BLAS identifiers). Support for leading dimensions allows to mix-and-match the various different shapes in the time and volume kernel and therefore reduce the amount of zero-padding. For best performance we make sure that LDA and LDC are always aligned to the vector-length of the underlying instruction set extension (16 byte for SSE, 32 byte for AVX and AVX2 and 64 byte on MIC). Sufficient alignment avoids load operations to A or store operations to C which suffer from cacheline splits. Furthermore, our optimizations naturally extend to the low-order routines and guarantee high performance in these cases as well.

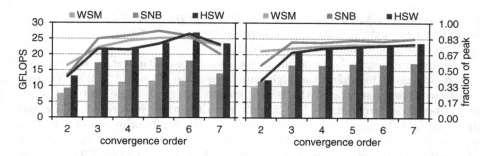

Fig. 1. Double precision GEMM kernel performance for $\mathcal{O}2$ to $\mathcal{O}7$ on WSM, SNB and HSW. DGEMM performance for $B_\mathcal{O} \times 9 \times B_\mathcal{O}$ shapes (left) and $B_\mathcal{O} \times 9 \times 9$ cases (right) is shown. GFLOPS are depicted as bars whereas fraction of peak performance is given by lines. DGEMM operations were repeated for 10,000 times on a hot L1 cache.

As the number of elastic quantities is nine (see Sect. 2), $N = 9$ holds always true and all assembly building blocks are centered around this special case. If needed in future – e.g. for extending our code generation approach to new sets of equations – this limitation can be removed easily. The underlying assembly buildings blocks follow identical ideas as already described in [5,16]. However, in case of generating code for KNC we added more carefully-tuned prefetch instructions. Additionally, the AVX2 FMA-enabled instruction-set extension on HSW allowed us to include a 16×3 building block in addition as the intermediate results no longer need to be kept in registers. Therefore these free registers can be used as accumulators for final results. Furthermore, we added full single precision support for all matrix sizes of interest.

These improvements in the code generation process turn the current version of SeisSol into a code that is naturally optimized for several convergence orders, whereas our previous work [5,16] focused on the $\mathcal{O}6$ case. Whether a certain routine should be executed by a sparse or dense matrix operation is determined up-front by auto-tuning. This step generates an optimal configuration for each combination of target architecture, order of convergence and machine precision. The code generator is publicly available as open source at https://github.com/hfp/libxsmm.

Figure 1 compares the performance for a selection of DGEMM operations used in SeisSol running single-threaded on all different architectures. For SSE, AVX and AVX2 roughly the same efficiency can be reached and this efficiency is comparable to DGEMM performance as being measured when running HPL [17]. Especially the higher-order kernels run up to 30–40 % faster than when calling BLAS libraries. On KNC we observed lower efficiencies (of roughly 70 % of peak performance) which is caused by two facts: a) at least two running threads are needed to fully load a core (therefore we excluded KNC from Fig. 1) and b) $N = 9$ does not allow us to optimally exploit KNC's register file which has 32 entries, out of which we use only 10. In order to leverage the added single precision kernels, slight changes were required in SeisSol as well. We implemented a mixed-precision version of SeisSol: the elastic wave propagation solver runs entirely with single precision arithmetic whereas other parts, such as source term calculations, remain in double precision.

Besides improving the performance of all matrix multiplication routines, we also re-arranged the order of applying updates to an element's DOFs. Whereas before we strictly separated the three different integrators, we switched to an element-centric formulation: first we compute the time integrated DOFs and apply all local updates and second we perform the neighboring part of the flux computation. In low-order runs this change substantially saves bandwidth, for high-order simulations global matrices can be kept in the private L2 caches for the local integration parts.

Additionally, we optimized memory allocation in SeisSol. All global matrix operators are allocated in a single `malloc` operation and a memory manager handles whether a matrix is stored sparse or dense. Furthermore, we split the element-local non-DOF data (star matrices and flux solvers) into two parts, one for the local update and one for the neighboring integral. This ensures more accurate hardware prefetching and shorter access latencies by a NUMA-aware initialization of all data structures. These changes prepare SeisSol for future chips that may offer several memory subsystems, also.

Finally, we want to mention that these improvements of SeisSol's computational back-end result into roughly 15–20 % shorter runtimes while maintaining the same hardware efficiencies. Combining Fig. 1 and Table 1 it becomes obvious that these shorter runtimes directly translate to less consumed energy.

4   Experiments and Results

In the following sections we present a detailed analysis of the modernized SeisSol code incorporating the discussed changes and extensions. This analysis was carried out on two different benchmarks, a synthetic convergence test (in Sect. 4.2) and a standardized verification benchmark (in Sect. 4.3) that utilizes an adaptive unstructured mesh. In both cases we investigate the relationships between order of convergence, clock frequency, vector instruction sets and selected machine precision. However, first we describe our power measurement methodology.

4.1   Power Measurement Setup

As pointed out before, SeisSol is used for high-resolution seismic simulations in large-scale production runs. Since we focus on single-node runs in this work, we need to make sure that the obtained insights can be easily transferred to cluster-sized executions. We therefore decided to measure only full-box power consumptions of standard 2U rack-servers which are a common building block of supercomputers. We did not perform CPU-only measurements through e.g. RAPL performance counters. Additionally, most of our power measurements are taken at full CPU speed, RAPL counter measurements would not gain significant additional information as the CPU runs close to or at their thermal design power

(TDP) limit due to our highly-efficient kernels, cf. Fig. 1. Furthermore, WSM and KNC systems do not offer RAPL counters which would limit comparisons, too.

For the WSM, SNB and HSW systems we used non-intrusive power measurement tools[1] which plug in between the system's power inlet and the wall's power outlet. Both offer a resolution of 1 Hz. This is not a limitation as runs of interest are substantially longer. Furthermore, we disabled the second power supply unit (PSU) (where available) of each server. The Wattsup power data was collected on-the-fly by a second machine (master) to which the device was connected via USB. This master also launched SeisSol over network and saved all relevant application information, such as runtimes and numerical output, for interpreting the power measurements in an application context. On KNC we followed a slightly different procedure. In contrast to [16] we switched from an offload model to native execution in order to prepare SeisSol for future socketable Xeon Phi processors. To exclude various host system overheads, the micsmc utility was used at a sampling rate of 1 Hz to measure full coprocessor power. Limitations and overheads as described in [19] did not show up since we just measured the power for fully-loaded coprocessors. Furthermore, power supply transformation inefficiencies are not included.

4.2   Synthetic Benchmark

Benchmark Description. The synthetic benchmark was introduced for convergence analysis in [13]. It consist of a cubic domain of size $[-50\,\text{m}, 50\,\text{m}]^3$ with constant material parameters. This results in uniform wave speeds throughout the entire domain. Additionally the benchmark uses periodic boundary conditions and assumes smooth initial data leading to waves propagating in diagonal direction. As described in greater detail in [13] after $\sqrt{3} \cdot 100$ seconds of time the propagation of the waves matches exactly the initial data. Thus different error norms of all elastic variables can be computed easily. Together with a simple and controllable mesh refinement this is the motivation for using the synthetic benchmark in this work.

We discretized the cubic domain of the benchmark by a series of regular cubic meshes. Each of the cubes is again subdivided into five tetrahedrons. The result is a total number of $5 \cdot N_{1D}^3$ tetrahedrons, where N_{1D} is the number of cubes per dimension. For temporal discretization we used a time step, that resembles 50 % of the stability limit of Runge-Kutta DG-schemes. Taking into account the CFL condition, wave speeds and in-sphere-diameters, the time step is given explicitly as:

$$\Delta t(\mathcal{O}, N_{1D}) = \frac{50}{(2\mathcal{O} - 1)(\sqrt{3} + 3)N_{1D}}. \tag{7}$$

We performed simulations of the synthetic benchmark for convergence orders $\mathcal{O}2 - \mathcal{O}7$ and increased the number of per-dimension cubes N_{1D} by two in every step: $N_{1D} \in \{4, 6, 8 \ldots\}$.

---

[1] WSM, HSW: Wattsup powermeter (accuracy: $+/- 1.5\,\%$), SNB: MEGWARE clust-safe.

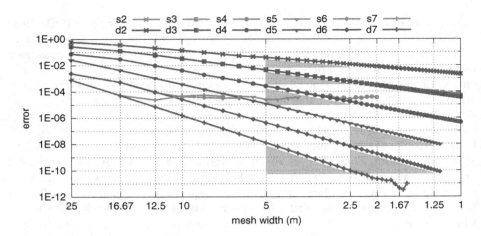

Fig. 2. Convergence of the synthetic benchmark for orders $\mathcal{O}2 - \mathcal{O}7$. Shown is the mesh width $100/N_{1D}$ against the error in the L^∞-norm for the variable σ_{yz}. Orange dashed lines represent single precision, blue solid lines double precision. The slopes of the gray triangles next to the respective curves illustrate the mathematical convergence rate (Color figure online).

In production runs, SeisSol spends almost all of the computational time in the time marching loop – for example 99.56 % for the machine-size production run presented in [16]. Thus for all simulations we measured only the time and energy spent in the time marching loop, neglecting initialization.

Performance. In Fig. 2, we present numerical convergence in the L^∞-norm for the elastic variable σ_{yz} using the synthetic benchmark. All runs were performed on the SNB system using the AVX-instruction set. With respect to convergence alone, the results are representative for all studied architectures because cross-architecture changes of the error-norms (e.g. by FMA instructions) are barely measurable. In extension to the described benchmark setting we performed all runs in double precision and, for the first time, also in single precision with our new unified computational core of SeisSol. For all runs, we observed the high-order convergence expected numerically for increasing mesh sizes. In the single precision runs, we hit the machine precision with an error between 10^{-4} and 10^{-5}, in double precision at 10^{-11}. For clarity we cut off the single precision curves shortly after this stagnation. Before this point the curves of single and double precision of all runs lie on top of each other and thus the quality of the solution is almost identical for single and double precision.

Figure 3 illustrates the L^∞-error of variable σ^{yz} in dependency of the consumed energy for the HSW machine (for all tests in this section the HSW machine is clocked at 1.9 GHz). To ensure reliable power-measurements we increased the original starting point of the study, $N_{1D} = 4$, for every order, such that the simulation consumed at least 50 kJ. In comparison to numerical convergence with respect to mesh width only (Fig. 2), the slope of the curves is smaller. Keeping in mind that the total number of element updates not only depends on the mesh width, but also on the time step width (Eq. (7)) this behavior is expected. Again we observe increasing slopes and a magnitude difference in terms of energy-to-solution for higher orders. For convergence orders $\mathcal{O}2$ and $\mathcal{O}3$, single precision reduces the amount of consumed energy by more than 35 % and 38 %. The theoretically possible 50 % (we measured the same power consumption for single and double precision runs with an error within 3 % on all platforms) are not fully reached, as we align the elements' DOFs to the 32-byte boundary. This, in general, imposes some overheads with longer vectors and switching from double to single precision naturally doubles the vector length.

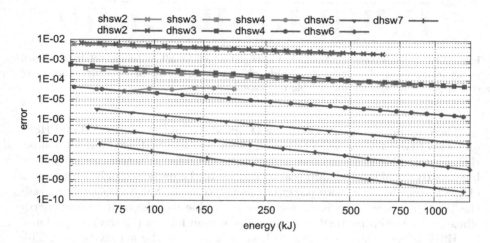

Fig. 3. L^{∞}-error of variable σ^{yz} in dependency of the consumed energy for the HSW machine in single- and double-precision.

Finally, in Fig. 4 we evaluated the measured energy-to-solution curves by linear interpolation in log-log-space at 150 kJ for all architectures (using on-demand frequency for WSM and SNB). For this energy budget we can now easily compare the achieved accuracy depending on convergence order and architecture. Note that we excluded settings beyond convergence and low order settings not fitting into the memory of KNC due to slow convergence. Comparing $\mathcal{O}2$ and $\mathcal{O}7$ on HSW we see an error reduction of five orders of magnitude. For the cross-architecture comparison we select $\mathcal{O}6$. According to Fig. 1 roughly the same efficiency can be reached on all platforms. In this case the error is reduced by a factor of 3.4 when switching from WSM to SNB and 4× when comparing SNB to KNC and HSW. Note that the factors are a combination of architectural improvements and the non-linearity of the high-order convergence.

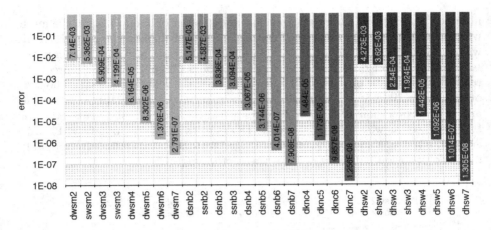

Fig. 4. Error with respect to a 150 kJ energy-budget for all matching settings. Shown is the interpolated L^∞-error of variable σ^{yz} for the different architectures, orders of convergence and single- and double-precision.

These findings align well with the Dennard scaling[2] between SNB and HSW on an iso-frequency and iso-TDP level. From WSM to SNB we even see a superior scaling. This is due to the fact that we use full-box power measurements, but strictly speaking Dennard scaling applies to the processor only. Other parts of the system became more power-efficient, too, such that SNB clearly exceeds the WSM machine. One KNC coprocessor is able to achieve the same energy efficiency as the entire HSW machine. The reason for not (clearly) outperforming HSW is the (already analyzed) lower efficiency of the matrix kernels. This emphasizes that for compute-bound applications the fastest execution is also most likely the most energy-efficient one.

4.3   Layer over Halfspace

Benchmark Description. The Layer Over Halfspace (LOH.1) benchmark is part of the wave propagation model set WP2 of the "SeISmic MOdeling Web INterfacE"[3] (SISMOWINE), a project aiming at the verification of numerical models in seismology.

In this benchmark two different materials are used, one in the upper layer down to 1000 m in depth and one in the halfspace of the remaining domain. Analog to [13] we used an adaptively refined mesh of a computational domain extending $[-15\,km, 15\,km]^2 \times [-17\,km, 0\,km]$ with free-surface boundary conditions on the surface and outflow boundary conditions everywhere else. The mesh

---

[2] Doubling the number of transistors doubles the amount of computations within the same energy budget; number of transistors: WSM: $2 \times 1.17\,B$, SNB: $2 \times 2.26\,B$, HSW: $2 \times 5.57\,B$.

[3] Available at http://www.sismowine.org.

consists of 386,518 elements and is unstructured with faces aligned only to the interface of the two layers and the boundaries. The setup is illustrated in Fig. 5. Elements in the layer are gray, elements in the halfspace are white. The seismic source is located at $(0, 0, -2000)$ and shown in red with a grid for orientation with respect to receiver locations. For verification SISMOWINE offers reference solutions based on the discrete wavenumber method at nine receivers located at the free surface for the first nine seconds in simulated time.

In all runs of the LOH.1 benchmark, we simulated until reaching either the entire nine seconds in simulated time or a minimum of five minutes in computational time. We extended the parameters space as the mesh size is now constant. In contrast to the convergence benchmark in Sect. 4.2, we perform a frequency study within each CPU's supported frequency spectrum. Note, that this was only possible for CPU-based platforms as Xeon Phi does not offer DVFS [19], which can be easily modified by software. Additionally, we study how the consumed power depends on the vector instruction set. We therefore run the LOH.1 benchmark with the SSE, AVX and AVX2 backend on the HSW machine.

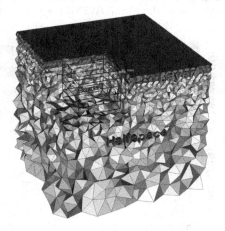

Fig. 5. Setup of the LOH.1 scenario. Shown is a only a part of size $[-2\,\mathrm{km}, 15\,\mathrm{km}]^2 \times [-17\,\mathrm{km}, 0\,\mathrm{km}]$.

Performance. In comparison to the synthetic benchmark of Sect. 4.2 the quality of the solution can not be quantified by simple error-norms due to the complexity of the benchmark. In Fig. 6 we show exemplary a comparison of the particle velocity u at receiver nine $(8{,}647\,\mathrm{m}, \ 5{,}764\,\mathrm{m}, \ 0\,\mathrm{m})$ as given by the reference solution and obtained with SeisSol using convergence orders $\mathcal{O}2$ and $\mathcal{O}7$. Additional we show the envelope misfit [22] of the seismogram in Fig. 7. Visually we reproduce the reference solution and an increasing fit of the high order simulation is clearly visible. A more detailed verification of SeisSol is available at the homepage of the SISMOWINE-project.

Figure 8 depicts the performance when running the LOH.1 benchmark depending on chip frequency and on different machines. We clearly see that low-order runs show nearly no performance improvement with increasing clock frequency. Here we operate close to the memory bandwidth limit. E.g. on HSW the measured average bandwidth is 72 GiB/s (with peaks at 92 GiB/s) and the analytical overall byte/FLOP ratio is 1.3. With Table 1 in mind it is therefore beneficial from an energy perspective to run the memory-bound convergence orders at lowest possible frequency. This is well-aligned with findings presented in [3]. In case of high-order we reach full compute-bound performance with convergence $\mathcal{O}4$ on WSM and SNB and convergence order $\mathcal{O}5$ on HSW. However, on

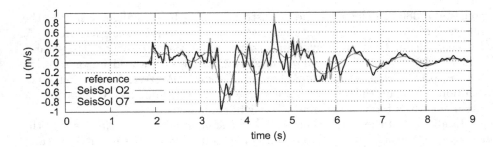

Fig. 6. Comparison of the particle velocity u at receiver nine. Shown is the reference solution of the SISMOWINE project against Seissol using $\mathcal{O}2$ and $\mathcal{O}7$.

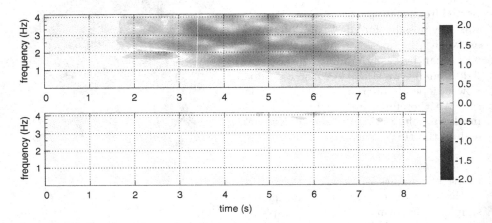

Fig. 7. Comparison of the envelope misfit with respect to the reference solution of the SISMOWINE project. Shown is the misfit for particle velocity u at receiver nine over the simulation time against the frequency for $\mathcal{O}2$ (top) and $\mathcal{O}7$ (bottom).

HSW the performance of $\mathcal{O}4$ is closer to $\mathcal{O}5$ than to $\mathcal{O}3$. Due to 64-byte alignment on KNC best performance is achieved for order $\mathcal{O}6$ since $B_6 = 56$ is divisible by eight (size of a double) and thus no additional zero-padding is required. For these higher-order runs we can also observe the expected frequency dependency in the achieved GFLOPS performance. From a MFLOPS/W perspective, we are able to reproduce the convergence test's excellent results at iso-frequency (1.2 GHz). HSW is delivering 2.6× more performance within the same power budget and having a 2.5× higher transistor count. As a side note we want to highlight that the achieved MFLOPS/W numbers are very close to Green500 entries of similiar clusters, which underlines the high hardware efficiency of SeisSol.

However, maintaining the Dennard scaling is only possible when fully utilizing all functionality and therefore AVX2. Often performing cross-architecture optimizations might appear difficult. Therefore Fig. 9 analyses how the performance

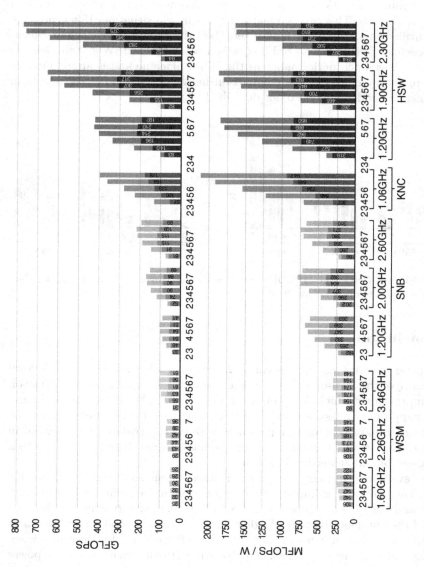

Fig. 8. Non-zero FLOPs (dark colors) in double precision and hardware-level FLOPs (light colors) of the LOH.1 benchmark depending on frequency. Shown are GFLOPS (top) and the MFLOPS per Watt (bottom) over all orders of convergence (Color figure online).

on HSW changes when using older vector instruction sets. We recognize nearly a factor of two between SSE3 and AVX and a difference of up to 1.5 between AVX and AVX2 with respect to performance. Power-wise the factors are 1.6 for SSE3 and AVX and 1.3 between AVX and AVX2. When comparing SSE3 to AVX2, we gain nearly 3× in performance but also have to pay a factor of 2× in power consumption. This can be regarded as a win-win situation. If it is possible to fully utilize the AVX2 instruction set, then the most power-efficient execution is possible. But if only an SSE3 code is available, the HSW system delivers roughly twice as much performance as the WSM machine and is approximately 2.5× more energy efficient. The comparison between SNB and HSW results in similar insights and is therefore not described.

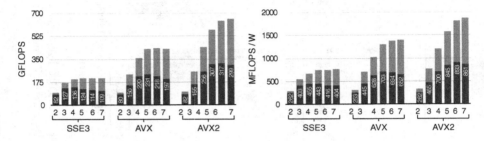

Fig. 9. GFLOPS (left) and MFLOPS per Watt (right) over all convergences orders and instruction sets on HSW @1.9 GHz.

5   Conclusion

In this paper we summarized recent advancements with respect to node-level performance of the high-order finite element seismic simulation software SeisSol. These improvements include Intel Xeon E5 v3 (AVX2), single precision and NUMA support and last but not least a cache-friendly restructuring of the involved operators. Keeping our previous work on the scalability of SeisSol in mind [5,16], we expect that all node-level enhancements directly translate to a faster execution on cluster-level as well.

When evaluating our changes we put a strong focus on energy- and time-to-solution. We analyzed the impact of convergence order, frequency, vector instruction sets and machine precision on the execution time, energy consumption and quality of the obtained solution. We demonstrated that on modern architectures the computational error can be reduced by up to five orders of magnitudes when switching from convergence order $\mathcal{O}2$ to $\mathcal{O}7$, while staying within the same power budget. From a hardware perspective we were able to reproduce Dennard scaling across several generations of CPUs when utilizing the most advanced instruction set in each generation. Recapitulating our frequency scaling experiment we can state the following two aspects from an energy-efficiency point of view. First, memory-bound applications should be executed at the lowest frequency supported by the processor and second, compute-bound application consume minimal energy when running at a medium frequency but at high efficiency. To put it short, the best-optimized and compute-bound high order execution is also the most energy-efficient one from an energy-to-solution perspective.

Acknowledgments. Our project was supported by the Intel Parallel Computing Centre "ExScaMIC - Extreme Scalability on x86/MIC". We gratefully acknowledge the respective support by Intel Corporation.

Optimization Notice: Software and workloads used in performance tests may have been optimized for performance only on Intel microprocessors. Performance tests, such as SYSmark and MobileMark, are measured using specific computer systems, components, software, operations and functions. Any change to any of those factors may cause the results to vary. You should consult other information and performance tests to assist you in fully evaluating your contemplated purchases, including the performance of that product when combined with other products. For more information go to http://www.intel.com/performance. Intel, Xeon, and Intel Xeon Phi are trademarks of Intel Corporation in the U.S. and/or other countries.

References

1. Aliaga, J.I., Barreda, M., Dolz, M.F., Quintana-Orti, E.S.: Are our dense linear Algebra libraries energy-friendly? Comput. Sci. Res. Dev. **30**(2), 187–196 (2015)
2. Anzt, H., Beglarian, A., Chilingaryan, S., Ferrone, A., Heuveline, V., Kopmann, A.: A unified energy footprint for simulation software. Comput. Sci. -Res. Dev. **29**(2), 131–138 (2014)
3. Auweter, A., Bode, A., Brehm, M., Brochard, L., Hammer, N., Huber, H., Panda, R., Thomas, F., Wilde, T.: A case study of energy aware scheduling on supermuc. In: Kunkel, J.M., Ludwig, T., Meuer, H.W. (eds.) ISC 2014. LNCS, vol. 8488, pp. 394–409. Springer, Heidelberg (2014)
4. Bosilca, G., Ltaief, H., Dongarra, J.: Power profiling of cholesky and qr factorizations on distributed memory systems. In: Third International Conference on Energy-Aware High Performance Computing, Hamburg, September 2012
5. Breuer, A., Heinecke, A., Rettenberger, S., Bader, M., Gabriel, A.-A., Pelties, C.: Sustained petascale performance of seismic simulations with seissol on supermuc. In: Kunkel, J.M., Ludwig, T., Meuer, H.W. (eds.) ISC 2014. LNCS, vol. 8488, pp. 1–18. Springer, Heidelberg (2014)
6. Cebrian,J.W., Natvig, L., Meyer, J.C.: Improving energy efficiency through parallelization and vectorization on Intel Core i5 and i7 processors. In: High Performance Computing, Networking Storage and Analysis, SC Companion: 0:675–684 (2012)
7. Charles, J., Sawyer, W., Dolz, M.F., Catalń, S.: Evaluating the performance and energy efficiency of the COSMO-ART model system. Comput. Sci. Res. Dev. **30**(2), 177–186 (2015)
8. Chen, T., Du, Z., Sun, N., Wang, J., Wu, C., Chen, Y., Temam, O.: Diannao: a small-footprint high-throughput accelerator for ubiquitous machine-learning. In: Proceedings of the 19th International Conference on Architectural Support for Programming Languages and Operating Systems, ASPLOS 2014, pp. 269–284. ACM, New York (2014)

9. Chen, Y., Luo, T., Liu, S., Zhang, S., He, L., Wang, J., Li, L., Chen, T., Xu, Z., Sun, N., Temam, O.: Dadiannao: a machine-learning supercomputer. In: ACM/IEEE International Symposium on Microarchitecture (MICRO), December 2014
10. Cheveresan, R., Ramsay, M., Feucht, C., Sharapov, I.: Characteristics of workloads used in high performance and technical computing. In: Proceedings of the 21st Annual International Conference on Supercomputing, ICS 2007, pp. 73–82. ACM, New York (2007)
11. Demmel, J., Gearhart, A.: Instrumenting linear algebra energy consumption via on-chip energy counters. Technical report (2012)
12. Dongarra, J., Ltaief, H., Luszczek, P., Weaver, V.M.: Energy footprint of advanced dense numerical linear algebra using tile algorithms on multicore architecture. In: 2012 Second International Conference on Cloud and Green Computing (CGC), pp. 274–281. IEEE (2012)
13. Dumbser, M., Käser, M.: An arbitrary high-order discontinuous Galerkin method for elastic waves on unstructured meshes - II. The three-dimensional isotropic case. Geophys. J. Int. **167**(1), 319–336 (2006)
14. Hager, G., Treibig, J., Habich, J., Wellein, G.: Exploring performance and power properties of modern multicore chips via simple machine models. CoRR, abs/1208.2908, 2012
15. Hähnel, M., Döbel, B., Völp, M., Härtig, H.: Measuring energy consumption for short code paths using rapl. SIGMETRICS Perform. Eval. Rev. **40**(3), 13–17 (2012)
16. Heinecke, A., Breuer, A., Rettenberger, S., Bader, M., Gabriel, A.-A., Pelties, C., Bode, A., Barth, W., Liao, X-K., Vaidyanathan, K., Smelyanskiy, M., Dubey, P.: Petascale high order dynamic rupture earthquake simulations on heterogeneous supercomputers. In: Proceedings of the International Conference for High Performance Computing, Networking, Storage and Analysis SC14, pp. 3–14. IEEE, New Orleans, November 2014. Gordon Bell Finalist
17. Heinecke, A., Vaidyanathan, K., Smelyanskiy, M., Kobotov, A., Dubtsov, R., Henry, G., Chrysos, G., Shet, A.G., Dubey, P.: Design and implementation of the linpack benchmark for single and multi-node systems based on intel(r) xeon phi(tm) coprocessor. In: 27th IEEE International Symposium on Parallel and Distributed Processing, IPDPS 2013, pp. 126–137. IEEE Computer Society, Cambridge, Boston, USA, 20–24 May 2013
18. Käser, M., Dumbser, M.: An arbitrary high-order discontinuous galerkin method for elasticwaves on unstructured meshesi. the two-dimensional isotropic case withexternal source terms. Geophysical Journal International **166**(2), 855–877 (2006)
19. Lawson, G., Sosonkina, M., Shen, Y.: Energy evaluation for applications with different thread affinities on the intel xeon phi. In: 2014 International Symposium on Computer Architecture and High Performance Computing Workshop (SBAC-PADW), pp. 54–59, October 2014
20. Lawson, G., Sosonkina, M., Shen, Y.: Performance and energy evaluation of comd on intel xeon phi co-processors. In: Proceedings of the 1st International Workshop on Hardware-Software Co-Design for High Performance Computing, Co-HPC 2014, pp. 49–54, IEEE Press, Piscataway, NJ, USA (2014)
21. Ltaief, H., Luszczek, P., Dongarra, J.: Profiling high performance dense linear algebra algorithms on multicore architectures for power and energy efficiency. In: International Conference on Energy-Aware High Performance Computing (EnA-HPC 2011), Hamburg, Germany, September 2011
22. Moczo, P., Kristek, J., Galis, M., Pazak, P., Balazovjech, M.: The finite-difference and finite-element modeling of seismic wave propagation and earthquake motion. Acta phys. slovaca **57**(2), 177–406 (2007)

23. Rahman, S.F.,Guo, J., Yi, Q.: Automated empirical tuning of scientific codes for performance and power consumption. In: Proceedings of the 6th International Conference on High Performance and Embedded Architectures and Compilers, HiPEAC 2011, pp. 107–116. ACM, New York, NY, USA (2011)

24. Rotem, E., Naveh, A., Ananthakrishnan, A., Rajwan, D., Weissmann, E.: Power-management architecture of the intel microarchitecture code-named sandy bridge. Micro, IEEE **32**(2), 20–27 (2012)

25. Taylor, M.B.: Is dark silicon useful?: harnessing the four horsemen of the coming dark silicon apocalypse. In: Proceedings of the 49th Annual Design Automation Conference, DAC 2012, pp. 1131–1136. ACM, New York (2012)

26. Tiwari, A., Laurenzano, M.A., Carrington, L., Snavely, A.: Auto-tuning for energy usage in scientific applications. In: Proceedings of the 2011 International Conference on Parallel Processing - vol. 2, Euro-Par 2011, pp. 178–187. Springer-Verlag, Berlin, Heidelberg (2012)

27. Zecena, I., Burtscher, M., Jin, T., Zong, Z.: Evaluating the performance and energy efficiency of n-body codes on multi-core cpus and gpus. In: 2013 IEEE 32nd International Performance Computing and Communications Conference (IPCCC), pp. 1–8. IEEE (2013)

Modeling the Productivity of HPC Systems on a Computing Center Scale

Sandra Wienke[1,2,3]($\boxtimes$), Hristo Iliev[1,2,3], Dieter an Mey[1,2,3],
and Matthias S. Müller[1,2,3]

[1] IT Center, RWTH Aachen University, 52074 Aachen, Germany
{wienke,iliev,anmey,mueller}@itc.rwth-aachen.de
[2] Chair for High Performance Computing, RWTH Aachen University,
52074 Aachen, Germany
[3] JARA – High-Performance Computing, Schinkelstr. 2, 52062 Aachen, Germany

Abstract. In pursue of exaflop computing, the expenses of HPC centers increase in terms of acquisition, energy, employment, and programming. Thus, a quantifiable metric for productivity as value per cost gets more important to make an informed decision on how to invest available budgets. In this work, we model overall productivity from a computing center's perspective. The productivity model uses as value the number of application runs possible during the lifetime of a given supercomputer. The cost is the total cost of ownership (TCO) of an HPC center including costs for administration and programming effort. For the latter, we include techniques for software cost estimation of large codes taken from the domain of software engineering. As tuning effort increases when more performance is required, we further focus on the impact of the 80-20 rule when it comes to development effort. Here, performance can be expressed with respect to Amdahl's law. Moreover, we include an asymptotic analysis for parameters like number of compute nodes and lifetime. We evaluate our approach on a real-world case: an engineering application in our integrative hosting environment.

Keywords: Productivity · Cost-benefit ratio · Cost efficiency · TCO · Development effort · COCOMO · 80-20 rule · Pareto principle · Computing center · Scalability

1 Introduction

The move towards the exascale era will introduce huge and complex systems, therefore the importance of improving productivity and total cost of ownership (TCO) of computing centers increases. According to the definition of productivity as value per cost, HPC centers are interested in optimizing the spread of their expenses across staff (brainware) and hardware while trying to get the most significant outcome from the scientific simulations running on the cluster. Thus, a tool that supports making informed decisions for the cost-efficient division of the available budget is needed.

© Springer International Publishing Switzerland 2015
J.M. Kunkel and T. Ludwig (Eds.): ISC High Performance 2015, LNCS 9137, pp. 358–375, 2015.
DOI: 10.1007/978-3-319-20119-1_26

Traditional factors that affect productivity are the cluster size, the system types it comprises, its lifetime, its energy consumption, and the performance of the applications exploiting it. However, as future architectures might get more complex to program, it is required to also include costs for developing, parallelizing, and tuning software into the equation. Intuitively, the development effort should be proportional to the number of lines of code (LOCs) to parallelize or optimize, i.e. the kernel code size. Instead, in software engineering, it is suggested that the effort grows exponentially while developing new software. Although it is not proven that exponential growth is also applicable when iteratively parallelizing hotspots in an HPC application, HPC lore suggests that 20 % of the effort is needed to achieve 80 % of the performance and 80 % of effort to achieve the remaining 20 % (80-20 rule). For large-scale applications, achieving high performance is essential, resulting in exponentially increasing effort. Thus, a certain division of investment between hardware and staff not only impacts the number of compute nodes and their lifetime, but also the size or the detail of application optimization and therefore the run time and the value of the application. Finding combinations of these parameters that maximize productivity is needed for cost-efficient computing centers.

In this paper, we show an approach to model productivity at the scale of a computing center. This includes quantifying hardware purchase and maintenance costs and applying a performance model like Amdahl's law to predict the run time of big MPI codes. These large-scale application runs usually deliver more value than single-node executions. Therefore, we also include a weighting factor that represents the quality gained from large-scale runs. We also put into the equation the impact of increasing tuning effort on productivity for complex codes. More detailed, the model supports dependencies on the kernel code size and the speedup and applies rules from software engineering and HPC lore respectively. Further, we include an analysis on the model's asymptotic behavior for large or long-lasting clusters.

In the context of one case study, we show examples of the worth of the productivity metric. Our modeled productivity can be used to answer the question of when to stop tuning a program (here an application from the engineering area). Furthermore, we show that our productivity measure can help to decide how to spend additional money – on brainware or hardware. Third, we investigate the productivity metric over a system's lifetime, which can also indicate when to invest in new technologies. As these results are dependent on many parameters, support for computations with own input values is important. Therefore, we provide an online version of the model called *Aachen HPC Productivity Calculator – aixH(PC)²* [25].

The paper is structured as follows. In Sect. 2, we cover related work. We explain our productivity model that computes the number of application runs per unit of TCO and analyze its asymptotic behavior with respect to the number of compute nodes and system's lifetime in Sect. 3. With the case study in Sect. 4, we illustrate one concrete implementation of our model. Finally, we summarize our findings in Sect. 5.

2 Related Work

The importance of cost-benefit quantification in HPC is increasing. This is also shown by DoE funding a pilot study [13] conducted by IDC in 2013 that investigated the return of investment (ROI) for HPC investments. There, 208 case studies were evaluated with respect to jobs created, revenue, profit or cost savings per invested dollar. The benefit from HPC investment can also be measured in research competitiveness like NSF funding or number of publications [1]. However, the most common approach is the productivity metric that defines the ratio of value over cost and often incorporates the time-to-solution.

Most existing productivity models have been studied between 2002 and 2006 in the context of the DARPA HPCS program [5]. Many focus on the user's perspective and therefore provide simple metrics like relative speedup over relative development effort [28]. Furthermore, they are often applied to compare programming models and can only express relative results. For instance, Zelkowitz et al. [29] derive relative cost per LOC for OpenMP and MPI, whereas Ebcioglue et al. [6] look at C + MPI, UPC, and x10 with the metric time-to-first-correct-parallel-solution. Kennedy et al. [14] model time-to-solution for a problem P by $T(P) = I(P) + r \cdot E(P)$ where I is the implementation time to solve P, E is the average execution time per program run, r is a problem-specific weighting factor that reflects the relative importance of minimizing execution time versus implementation time. Given a reference version P_0, they derive relative power $p_L = I(P_0)/I(P_L)$ and relative efficiency $\epsilon_L = E(P_0)/E(P_L)$ from that. In general, underlying experiments for those studies are usually done with novice parallel programmers in classroom environments [6,28,29], which only allows for small codes, often running on single compute nodes. Further challenges with this kind of experiments are summarized in [21]. Another approach from a user's perspective is taken by McCracken et al. [17], who tries to determine a set of tasks that define the user's workflow and measure the time spent in each task. Our previous work [26] also compared programming models: OpenMP, Intel's Language Extensions for Offload, OpenCL, and OpenACC. For two real-world applications, we investigated performance, programming effort and costs per program run on heterogeneous, single-node computer architectures, i.e. Intel Xeon (regular and Phi) and NVIDIA GPUs.

Here, we extend this approach while focusing on a computing center's perspective and large-scaling codes, where much tuning effort is needed for execution on the whole supercomputer. At the same time, our model is still reducible to a user's view and so in line with the base approaches of [14,28]. We use the number of application runs as value and the TCO of a computing center in the denominator. Only few other works consider TCO as cost factor. Sterling [23] suggests a conceptual framework where productivity over time t is $\Psi_t = \frac{R_t}{C_t \times t}$ with R representing results i.e. complete solutions to a computation problem and C the cost of production over time t (procurement, initial installation, machine operation over time, construction of the application software). However, he does not quantify a real-world example to illustrate his approach. Snir and Bader [22] also include total costs. Their productivity value is expressed by a utility function that can represent the preferences on the outcome. The result is the productivity $\Psi(P, S, T, U) = \frac{U(P,T)}{C(P,S,T)}$ with S the system, P the problem, T the time-to-solution, U the utility function, and C the cost. They do not apply their model to a real-world example either. Kepner [15] takes Sterling's model and combines it with approaches from Kennedy [14], Snir, and Bader [22] to obtain the (SK)^3 synthesis model. He also includes one HPC example use of (SK)^3, but again reduces the model to the user's view of a relative comparison between OpenMP and MPI. In our work, we show the applicability and worth of our model in decision maker's view in an HPC case study. Two other approaches [8,18] also emphasize the view of stakeholders or decision makers.

Additionally, we develop a comprehensive model that does not focus on comparing programming paradigms. Research in software engineering shows that project size, software kind and personnel factors might have stronger impact on effort and software cost than the programming model [16]. We adapt the constructive cost model COCOMO II [2] from software engineering to HPC and link the MPI code size to the tuning effort. Kepner [15] has also thought about this approach and used it in his relative comparison of OpenMP and MPI. Instead, we initialize the model with real (absolute) values. Furthermore, we detail on the kind of software, i.e. HPC applications, whose tuning effort has an impact on performance. While Snir and Bader [22] mention this fact in general, we are the first to our knowledge to model this impact explicitly. We further incorporate a performance model, e.g. Amdahl's law, for large-scale systems. Consequently, our model can be applied to support decisions on expenditure on tuning or system run time. We also include the asymptotic cases of long system lifetime and big number of compute nodes, similar to Snir and Bader [22].

3 Productivity Model from a Computing Center's Perspective

Economically, productivity describes a certain output per unit of input [3], usually a ratio of value and cost. In HPC, finding an applicable definition and quantification of a benefit-to-cost ratio is a challenging task. On the one hand, gathering and quantifying all cost parameters is difficult in computing centers as whole. Here, we started evaluating parameters arising at the RWTH's computing center. On the other hand, the value of HPC is not easily definable as a single number. We investigate the performance of applications or rather the number of application runs over the cluster's lifetime as value. Our focus is to also include common features of large-scale applications. Therefore, we extend our previous TCO formulation [26] with (Amdahl's) scaling law, introduce a weighting factor that describes the quality of large-scale runs compared to small-scale runs, and include programming effort into the equation.

3.1 Productivity Metric

We define productivity as the number of applications runs n_{ex} exploiting the cluster under investigation. The denominator represents the cluster's TCO as

Table 1. One-time and annual costs in € for the use-case application

one-time costs C_{ot}					annual costs C_{pa}							
per node			per node type		per node					per node type		
HW purchase	Building/ infrastruct.	OS/env installation	OS/env. installation	Prog. effort	HW maintenance	Building/ infrastruct.	per watt	OS/env maintenance	Energy	OS/env. maintenance	Compiler/ software	Application maintenance
4,464	0	0	0	9,550	89	36	78	352		0	0	0

$\underbrace{}_{C_A}$ $\underbrace{}_{C_B}$ $\underbrace{}_{C_C}$ $\underbrace{}_{C_D}$

defined in [24]. Both depend on the number of acquired compute nodes n and the system's lifetime in years τ.

$$\text{productivity} = \frac{\text{value}}{\text{cost}} = \frac{n_{ex}(n,\tau)}{\text{TCO}(n,\tau)} \tag{1}$$

The number of application executions n_{ex} is computed by dividing the overall time that the system is available by the application's run time t:

$$n_{ex}(n,\tau) = \frac{\alpha \cdot \tau}{t(n)}. \tag{2}$$

For simplicity, we abstract the actual job mix running on a typical cluster to a single application. Future work will address this issue. The parameter α denotes the system availability rate in percent and has been introduced to account for additional scheduling delays, maintenance periods or unreliability of the system. The TCO value differentiates between one-time costs C_{ot} and annual (operational) costs C_{pa}. We further break down costs depending on the system's lifetime, the number of acquired nodes and their type (e.g. CPUs or GPUs). The latter accommodates e.g. porting an application to a specific type of architecture. Table 1 gives an overview on the different components. If a fixed investment I is given, the computed TCO value is lower than or equal to this budget.

$$I \geq \text{TCO}(n,\tau) = C_{ot}(n) + C_{pa}(n) \cdot \tau = (C_A \cdot n + C_B) + (C_C \cdot n + C_D) \cdot \tau \tag{3}$$

3.2 Parallel Scaling and Run Quality

When modeling MPI applications that include communication across the network, Amdahl's law comes into play. While we incorporate that law into the equation, any other suitable performance model could be used instead. Given Amdahl's law, the run time t is expressed as sum of the serial time t_s and the time t_p spent into parallelizable code:

$$t(n) = t_s + \frac{t_p}{n} = t_1 \cdot (1 - p) + \frac{t_1 \cdot p}{n} \tag{4}$$

where t_1 is the run time of the serial version of the application and p is the percentage of the code that is parallelized. In real life, where serial runs are not always feasible due to run time or memory constraints, t_s and t_p can be obtained by fitting to a set of measured run times from multiple compute nodes. If the absolute productivity is not important, t_1 could simply be set to 1 since it goes linearly into the productivity. Summarizing, productivity evaluates to

$$\text{productivity} = \frac{n_{ex}(n,\tau)}{\text{TCO}(n,\tau)} = \frac{\frac{\alpha \cdot \tau}{t(n)}}{\text{TCO}(n,\tau)} = \frac{\frac{\alpha \cdot \tau}{t_1 \cdot (1-p) + \frac{t_1 \cdot p}{n}}}{\text{TCO}(n,\tau)}. \tag{5}$$

Given Amdahl's law $t(n) \xrightarrow{n \to \infty} t_s$, the application might not efficiently leverage a whole cluster of maybe thousands of nodes. In such case, a threshold n_{scale} representing the maximum number of nodes on which the application scales acceptably can be defined and the n acquired nodes can be divided into multiple partitions of size n_{scale} and a remainder of size n_{rem}:

$$n = \lfloor n/n_{\text{scale}} \rfloor \cdot n_{\text{scale}} + n_{\text{rem}} \text{ with } n_{\text{rem}} = n - \lfloor n/n_{\text{scale}} \rfloor \cdot n_{\text{scale}} \tag{6}$$

$$\Rightarrow \text{productivity} = \frac{\alpha \cdot \tau \cdot \left(\frac{\lfloor n/n_{\text{scale}} \rfloor}{t(n_{\text{scale}})} + \frac{1}{t(n_{\text{rem}})} \right)}{\text{TCO}(n,\tau)}. \tag{7}$$

For non-MPI applications, the formula is still valid. For instance, a single-node application executing a parameter study could have multiple copies working on different parts of the search space and thus $n_{\text{scale}} = 1$ and $t(n) = t_1/n$.

MPI applications usually perform domain decomposition or enable simulations of increased resolution. Therefore, running with up to n_{scale} nodes has a benefit that is not expressed in the number of application runs n_{ex}. To account for this, we introduce a weighting quality factor $q(n)$. It could e.g. have a value of 1 for executions on n_{scale} nodes and then decrease linearly when fewer nodes are used. Of course, $q(n)$ can take a different form depending on the specific case as shown in Subsect. 4.3.

$$\text{productivity} = \frac{\alpha \cdot \tau \cdot \left(q(n_{\text{scale}}) \cdot \frac{\lfloor n/n_{\text{scale}} \rfloor}{t(n_{\text{scale}})} + q(n_{\text{rem}}) \cdot \frac{1}{t(n_{\text{rem}})} \right)}{\text{TCO}(n,\tau)} \tag{8}$$

3.3   Effort Dependence on Code Size and 80-20 Rule

For the parallelization and optimization of an application, the corresponding development effort must also be accounted for in the computation of a real productivity metric since it is a part of the development costs gathered in $\text{TCO}(n,\tau)$. This is especially important for huge codes typically implemented with MPI. Parallelization might be done iteratively by addressing more and more code hotspots or by directly parallelizing the major part of the code. Either way, the size of the application part that is parallelized or tuned impacts the effort needed to accomplish this goal. In software engineering, COCOMO II [2] is popular for estimating the effort with respect to the number of LOCs or function points.

The model assumes exponential effort growth with linear increase of the number of LOCs. An abstraction of this model is given by

$$\text{effort/ work [days]} := w = r \cdot (\text{KLOC})^s \tag{9}$$

where KLOC means thousand LOCs. The parameter r represents the so called effort multipliers. Those describe, for instance, execution time constraints or the capability of the programmer. Ideally, r should be calibrated with data from previously-completed projects within the local institution. The parameter s ranges from 0.91 to 1.226 depending mainly on the growth of interpersonal communication and large-system integration overheads. The nominal value is $s = 1.1$ and for $s > 1$ the so called diseconomy of scale takes place. In software engineering, this estimation model is applied to the development of new software. We believe that most parallel scientific applications start from already existing serial applications and we hypothesize that the effort estimation from COCOMO II can be applied to HPC development with the restriction that the denoted number of LOCs will not be newly developed, but rather describe the parallelizable part of the code. Unfortunately, we do not have a proof of this postulate yet. However, we will investigate this relation in future work.

In the following, we assume that we can apply (9) to our effort estimations. Parameter s is assumed to be 1.16, i.e. low ratings in the scale factors of the COCOMO II model. For r, we can apply a calibration with a given pair of kernel code size LOC_0 and base effort w_0 needed to parallelize or tune this kernel. Effort for further parallelizing more hotspots can then be predicted as:

$$w = \left(\frac{w_0}{\left(\frac{\text{LOC}_0}{1000}\right)^{1.16}} \right) \cdot (\text{KLOC})^{1.16}. \tag{10}$$

Given the increasing effort needed for further parallelization or tuning, its impact on application performance is of peculiar interest. Following the Pareto principle [19], HPC lore states that 20 % of effort will result in 80 % of performance. To gain the remaining 20 % of performance, an effort of further 80 % is needed. The function of this so called 80-20 rule can be modeled by a Pareto distribution:

$$F(w) = \begin{cases} 1 - \left(\frac{m}{w}\right)^h & \text{if } w \geq m \\ 0 & \text{if } w < m \end{cases} \tag{11}$$

where m represents the minimum value of w and h is a positive parameter that represents the ability of a programmer to get a certain performance improvement per day.

In our HPC case, w symbolizes the development effort in person-days and $F(w)$ the percentage of e.g. peak performance. The peak performance of an application on a certain system could be determined e.g. by the roofline model [27] for single nodes or by using the LogP model [4] for clusters. Additionally, HPC experts may assess the percentage of peak performance from experience.

For the application of the 80-20 rule to the effort-performance relation, we must adapt (11). The actual minimum value for the effort is $w = 0$, and no effort results in no performance gain. We therefore shift (11):

$$\text{performance } [\%] = \text{perf}(w) = 1 - \left(\frac{1}{k \cdot w + 1}\right)^h. \tag{12}$$

An example Pareto distribution is shown in Fig. 1. Parameter h can be computed given a reference pair of effort w_0 and the achieved performance perf_0. $k > 0$ accounts for the programmer's background knowledge that effects the amount of effort. By default $k = 1$. If more reference pairs are available, a distribution function that models better the given programmer can be obtained. The value of k could either be computed by inverting the performance equation, or approximated using a least-squares fit.

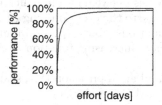

Fig. 1. Example Pareto distribution (80-20 rule) following (12) with $k = 1$

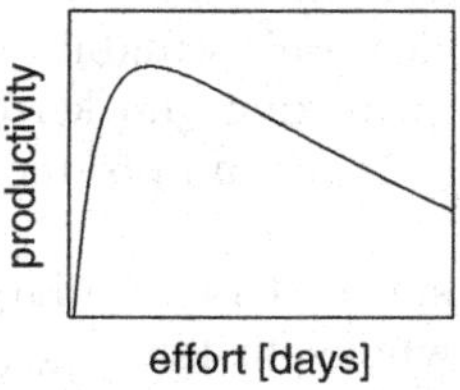

Fig. 2. Example productivity function that contains a maximum due to the impact of effort on performance

The reference performance perf_0 may come as a result of tuning the original kernel. The run time is then $t(n) = t_1 \cdot (1 - p) + t_1 \cdot p/(\text{ksp}_0 \cdot n)$ where ksp_0 is the kernel speedup after the tuning. Finally, the range of values of $\text{perf}(w) \in [0, 1)$ can be mapped from performance percentages to kernel speedups. Using kernel speedup instead of overall speedup is appropriate since the percentage of peak performance can usually be approximated by evaluating the kernel code alone. To get kernel speedups in the range of $[1, \text{ksp}_{\text{max}})$ where $\text{ksp}_{\text{max}} = 1+(\text{ksp}_0-1)/\text{perf}_0$, we apply a simple linear scaling based on the known kernel speedup ksp_0 and performance perf_0. Thus, $\text{ksp}(w)$ predicts the potential speedup of the kernel code after w days of effort invested in tuning it:

$$\text{ksp}(w) = 1 + \left(\frac{\text{ksp}_0 - 1}{\text{perf}_0}\right) \cdot \text{perf}(w). \tag{13}$$

Given the different impact that effort has on both kernel speedup and cost, productivity as function of the effort (with fixed values of n and τ) might have a maximum (see Fig. 2). This maximum estimates the amount of effort that is worth putting into parallelization and tuning. Further effort will result in lower productivity. A threshold for an acceptable productivity has to be set by each institution depending on its own needs, hardware and application configuration.

3.4   Asymptotic Behavior

Computing centers typically operate large cluster systems. In the limit of large but finite number of compute nodes n, acquisition and maintenance costs dominate and then $\text{TCO} \approx (C_A + C_C \cdot \tau) \cdot n$. Consequently, putting more effort affects the total application speedup while the TCO remains the same. A similar case occurs in the limit of very long system lifetime τ. Operational costs then greatly outweigh one-time costs, even when the latter include substantial programming costs, therefore $\text{TCO} \approx C_{pa} \cdot \tau$. Substituting this into (8), the limiting value of the long-term productivity is obtained as:

$$\text{productivity} = \frac{q(n_{scale}) \cdot \frac{\lfloor n/n_{scale} \rfloor}{t(n_{scale})} + q(n_{rem}) \cdot \frac{1}{t(n_{rem})}}{C'_{pa}} \tag{14}$$

where $C'_{pa} = C_{pa}/\alpha$ are the annual costs adjusted with the availability of the system. The numerator (number of program executions per year) is only affected by the application's scalability and by the speedup due to the programming effort put into optimizing the kernel. In both approximations above, programming effort is "for free" and productivity is a monotonically increasing function of the tuning effort.

In the special case of a large number of nodes and an application that scales up to the whole cluster ($n_{scale} = n$), $C_{pa} \approx C_C \cdot n$ and (14) reduces to

$$\text{productivity} = \frac{q(n)}{C'_C} \frac{1}{n \cdot t(n)} \propto q(n) \frac{t_1}{n \cdot t(n)}. \tag{15}$$

The last term could be recognized as the weighted parallel efficiency of the application. Except for embarrassingly parallel problems where the value of the parallel efficiency is always 1, for any application with a non-zero serial part, productivity will monotonically and asymptotically approach zero. With a linearly increasing quality factor, productivity follows the parallel speedup as given by Amdahl's law:

$$\text{productivity} = \frac{1}{n_{scale} \cdot C'_C \cdot t(n)} \propto \frac{t_1}{t(n)}. \tag{16}$$

For some non-scalable applications, $t(n)$ is not a monotonically decreasing function due to the communication and synchronization overhead increasing with the number of compute nodes. Therefore, it could be beneficial to have several concurrent smaller application runs instead of one big run. This also applies to the general case of running non-scalable parallel applications and – in the absence of superlinear scaling effects – the minimum value of n_{scale} after taking into account constraints like project deadlines and memory/storage requirements should be selected.

4   Case Study on Modeling Real-life Acquisitions

In this section, we show the viability of our model with an acquisition done at the IT Center of RWTH Aachen University. As part of its services, the IT

Center offers to the university institutes the possibility to integrate their own compute nodes as part of the RWTH Compute Cluster (integrative hosting). As hardware and software are managed by the same set of tools as the rest of the cluster, administrative costs are minimal.

4.1 Cluster Partition

For the purpose of this study, we used one partition from the integrative hosting acquired in 2010. It consists of 56 Dell PowerEdge compute nodes with two Intel Xeon X5670 processors and 48 GiB of RAM each. A fat-tree QDR InfiniBand network provides the high-speed connectivity. The total of the system costs is 250,000c. The detailed cost decomposition can be found in Table 1. The given one-time and annual costs are real values for our cluster setup [26]. We would like to stress that the following analysis was done after the acquisition was completed and was not used during the procurement. It serves solely to illustrate our model.

4.2 Engineering Application psOpen

One of the important applications running on the partition above is *psOpen* [10] which simulates turbulent flows in the field of combustion technology. It implements a pseudo-spectral Direct Numerical Simulation (DNS) method that solves the discretized Navier-Stokes equations for incompressible fluids in reciprocal (Fourier) space. Part of the calculation is still performed in real space and three-dimensional Fast Fourier Transform (3D-FFT) is used to switch between the two representations. The 3D-FFT kernel takes up to 80 % of the total execution time and is where network communication is involved. The rest of the algorithm performs local point operations only.

Originally, *psOpen* used the open-source library *P3DFFT* [20]. To improve the performance, the application developer made changes to the 3D-FFT routine and fused the filtering step of the pseudo-spectral DNS method with the Fourier transform in 2013. As a result, the amount of data being sent across the network is reduced significantly when compared to the original full 3D-FFT and varying levels of speedup are observed depending on the size of the simulation domain. For the purpose of our analysis, we take the speedup factor of 1.69× achieved for the biggest domain size of 4096^3 points.

In a second optimization phase, the communication pattern of the 3D-FFT routine was analyzed by one of the authors and a comprehensive performance model was derived. The model suggested that a specific domain decomposition should prove more efficient than any other when the application is running on the given cluster partition. Repeated benchmarking showed an overall speedup of 1.82×.

Each optimization phase involved effort equal to one person-month or 17.5 working days based on 210 working days per year [7]. This provides two data points to fit the Pareto distribution. Since there are further actions, e.g. tweaking the MPI runtime parameters, that could possibly bring a small additional speedup, we assume that 98 % of the asymptotically possible speedup was achieved in the second phase, which translates to 95.7 % of the maximum performance. The performance after the first phase is thus 80.5 %. Based on annual TV-L E13 salary for scientific employees of 57,300€ including tax [9], i.e. 272.86€ per day, the cost of the optimization efforts is 9,550€.

Since the 3D-FFT kernel is not the only parallel part of *psOpen*, we employ the following scaling model: $t(n) = t_{io} + t_{pc}(n) + t_{FFT}(n)$. Here, $t_{io} = c_{io} \cdot t_1$ is the serial input-output time, $t_{pc}(n) = c_{pc} \cdot t_1/n$ is the time for local point computations, and $t_{FFT}(n) = c_{FFT} \cdot t_1/(ksp \cdot n)$ is the time it takes to perform the FFT. The following run-time fractions are used below: $c_{io} = 0.02\,\%$, $c_{pc} = 19.98\,\%$, $c_{FFT} = 80.0\,\%$. The size of the kernel portion is about 1 KLOC and the effort in both phases is concentrated on tuning those lines only. For simplicity, we use a constant run quality factor of 1.

4.3   Results

Here we show how our productivity model can be applied to *psOpen* and answer questions such as how much effort should be spent on tuning the code, how much money to spend on brainware vs. hardware, and how long to run the system.

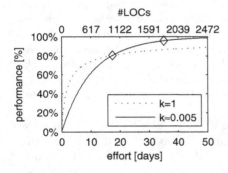
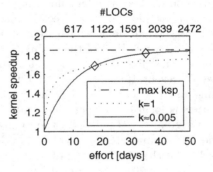

Fig. 3. 80-20 rule w.r.t. % of peak performance applied to *psOpen*. Performance after each tuning phase is shown by diamonds.

Fig. 4. 80-20 rule w.r.t. kernel speedup (see (13)) applied to *psOpen*. Speedup after each tuning phase is shown by diamonds.

How Much Effort to Spend on Tuning? First, we illustrate the impact of increasing tuning effort on the productivity. For the model computations, we set the system's lifetime τ to 5 years. The actual serial run time depends on the type of computation, but since it is simply a multiplier in the productivity equation and it does not change the position of the maximum, we use $t_1 = 1000$. Figure 3 shows the application of the 80-20 rule: gained percentage of peak performance as function of the optimization effort in person-days. The dashed curve represents the Pareto distribution with $k = 1$ and h computed from the values for phase 1 to be 0.56. The solid curve is a plot of (12) with parameters adapted to fit the data points from both phases (indicated by diamond marks): $k \approx 0.0048$ and

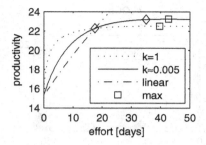

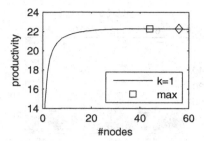

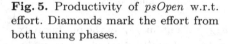

Fig. 5. Productivity of *psOpen* w.r.t. effort. Diamonds mark the effort from both tuning phases.

Fig. 6. Productivity of *psOpen* w.r.t. cluster size given constant quality factor 1. Diamond marks the original system size of 56 nodes.

$h \approx 20.11$. Both curves differ mainly in their initial slope and how quickly they approach the maximum value. The unadapted distribution ($k = 1$) approaches the limiting value very slowly due to $h < 1$. In the following sections, we look at the second (adapted) distribution, if not stated otherwise. Figure 4 shows the effort-performance curves from Fig. 3 scaled to kernel speedup.

The impact of the Pareto distribution on productivity is shown in Fig. 5. While the denominator in the productivity formula, i.e. the TCO, increases roughly linearly with the person-days, the numerator, i.e. the number of application runs, increases log-wise due to the 80-20 rule. The location of the maximum is marked by squares. The tuning effort during phase 1 is located on the positive slope before the maximum. Given the initial distribution with $k = 1$, productivity peaks at 39.6 person-days and a further tuning effort of 22.1 person-days would be optimal with respect to productivity. If we examine the adapted distribution (solid curve), we see that the combined effort from both phases is close to the corresponding maximum at 42.7 person-days. After the maximum, the productivity starts to decrease since further effort does not result in significant performance improvement. Thus, our model can show how long tuning might be worth it with respect to (a threshold on) productivity. For comparison, Fig. 5 also shows the linear increase of performance with effort that could be naively assumed.

Finally, all three figures also show the impact of increased LOCs on effort and thus on productivity. If we assume that double the amount of (kernel) LOCs is parallelized or tuned, then the effort must be increased by a factor $2^{1.16} \approx 2.23$. While this is not an issue in our example case, huge codes might be strongly affected.

How Much to Spend on Brainware vs. Hardware? Our productivity model can also be used to assess whether additional money should be spent on hardware or people. Assume that we were at the end of phase 1 (17.5 days of tuning effort, 80.5 % performance, $k = 1$) and got a productivity of 22.27. To get *more science* out of our program, we have to decide whether to buy an additional

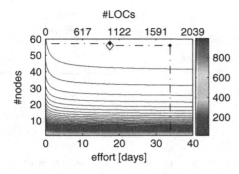
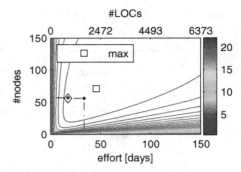

Fig. 7. Contour plot of the impact of no. of nodes and effort on run time of *psOpen*. Diamond marks phase 1 setup. Dots mark additional investment of 4464€.

Fig. 8. Contour plot of the productivity of *psOpen* as function of no. of nodes and effort. Diamond marks phase 1 setup. Dots mark additional investment of 4464€.

compute node at the cost of 4,464€ or to invest the money into further tuning. Spending 4,464€ for tuning would mean approximately one person-month (as $4,464[€]/272.86[€/\text{person-day}] \approx 16.4$ [person-days]).

The first interesting clue is the impact of the node count and the amount of effort on the run time. Figure 7 shows a contour plot of this case, i.e. the intersections of horizontal planes with the 3D run time surface as a function of the number of nodes and the amount of effort. The shape and density of the contour lines suggest that the number of nodes has a stronger impact on the run time than the amount of effort. In contrast, the corresponding contour plot of the productivity function (Fig. 8) suggests that investing more effort is more beneficial than investing in more nodes (as long as the global maximum is not exceeded). Thus, although run time decreases faster with the number of nodes than with the amount of effort, the cost of the nodes increase much faster than the effort cost. Figures 5 and 6 reveal a more detailed view. When buying one additional node, the productivity stays at ~ 22.27. Instead, spending 4,464€ on brainware, the productivity metric increases to 22.5.

Now, we generalize the approach of having a certain fixed investment by setting the TCO to a fixed budget and varying the amount of effort. From that, the number of nodes that can be acquired is determined. The contour plot in Fig. 9 illustrates the distribution of productivity on nodes and person-days for fixed investments up to 750,000€ . Since Amdahl's Law is in place and no weighting factor for large-scale runs was specified, spending 750,000€ into nodes and people does not pay off in terms of productivity. Here, the maximum arises at $\sim 578,000€$ (marked as square) and is located at 45 person-days and 69 nodes when using the adapted effort-performance relation. Thus, investing roughly 12,000€ into tuning effort, i.e. 2 % of the total investment, is the sweet spot. In our case study, larger-scale runs have a benefit over smaller-scale runs. Thus, we use a quality factor (8) of the form $q(n) = (n/n_{\text{scale}})^{1/3}$. The quality of the run is proportional to the simulation resolution and running on more nodes gives access to more system memory and therefore results in better resolution. Now, spending the maximum investment of 750,000€ pays off (Fig. 10). It can also be seen that spending a particular amount of the available budget to people instead of hardware is advantegous.

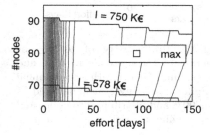 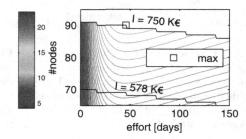

Fig. 9. Contour plot of the productivity of *psOpen* as function of no. of nodes&amount of effort: non-weighted scaling. Investment I is fixed (up to 750 K€) and distributed between brain- & hardware.

Fig. 10. Contour plot of the productivity of *psOpen* as function of no. of nodes & amount of effort: weighted scaling. Investment I is fixed (up to 750 K€) and distributed between brain- & hardware.

How Long to Run an HPC Cluster? The goal of the third analysis is to make an informed decision on where to spend available fixed budgets. In this case, we vary the amount of tuning effort and the system's lifetime. Simultaneously, we want to derive a value for the system lifetime that shows how long the system is beneficial to get employed. For the *psOpen* setup, the productivity levels out at the longest system lifetime possible (see Fig. 11). For a system with non-zero annual costs per node type (C_D in Table 1), the lifetime that results in maximum productivity could be just a couple of years. Figure 12 shows that setting the annual license costs to 5,000€ decreases productivity after 29 years as fewer nodes could be acquired. Bigger clusters with higher software costs could yield optimal system lifetime of approximately 4 or 5 years. If no peak value exists, determining the range of system lifetime values in which productivity rises significantly makes sense. Restrictively, our approach does not take into account that maintenance contracts usually expire after 5 years and that aging system components may break down. Both will impact notably the productivity of long-running clusters and must be addressed in future work. Additionally, this analysis should be carried out every other year to account for the technological advances.

Advances in new technologies also play a role in deciding whether to spend the available budget on a single- or multi-phase installation and – in the multi-phase case – when to buy the different stages. As an example, we want the highest productivity after a certain time period, e.g. governmental funding period,

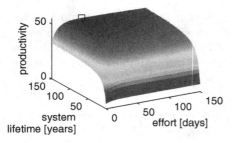
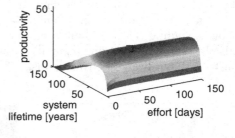

Fig. 11. Productivity of *psOpen* as function of the system's lifetime and the amount of effort. Investment is fixed at 750,000 € and distributed to nodes and people while increasing the lifetime. Global maximum is marked.

Fig. 12. Productivity of *psOpen* as function of the system's lifetime and the amount of effort with added annual compiler costs. Investment is fixed at 750,000 € and distributed to nodes and people while increasing the lifetime.

which is set to 8 years. Figures 13 and 14 show the comparison of a single-phase and two-phase cluster purchase with a total investment of 10 million €. For the two-phase cluster, the investment is split into two chunks of 5 million €, one for each phase. The single-phase cluster is comparable to the first stage of the two-phase cluster, only differing in the amount of investment. The second stage is likely to comprise novel technologies delivering higher performance, bandwidth and energy efficiency. In our example, we assume that the price of the hardware components stays constant while the performance increases. To predict the future performance of the application, we perform a least square fit of base-2 exponential functions to historical data of the InfiniBand network bandwidth [11] and the performance of different generations of similarly-priced Intel Xeon CPUs [12]. The fit yields two characteristic times: $\tau_{\mathrm{CPU}} = 1.61$ years for doubling of the CPU performance and $\tau_{\mathrm{IB}} = 3.57$ years for doubling of the network bandwidth. The execution time on the future system is $t'(n) = t_{\mathrm{io}} + t'_{\mathrm{pc}}(n) \cdot 2^{-\delta/\tau_{\mathrm{CPU}}} + t'_{\mathrm{FFT}}(n) \cdot 2^{-\delta/\tau_{\mathrm{IB}}}$, where δ is the time in years between the start of the first and the second phase. The model assumes that the time for compute-bound point operations is inversely proportional to the CPU performance, while the time for the network-bound FFT kernel is only affected by the increasing network bandwidth. While this is a simple performance model for *psOpen*, which also does not account for the increasing energy efficiency, it still captures the basic trend of the performance increase. Better performance models may improve the worth of the productivity prediction. We should notice, that we effectively model a two-partition system, as many parallel applications – including *psOpen* – are not able to fully utilize clusters with e.g. processors of varying speed. Therefore, we treat the two-phase case as two mostly independent clusters and sum their individual application run counts, which is then divided by the collective TCO in order to obtain the productivity. In Fig. 14, we clearly see that in our case a two-phase cluster acquisition is beneficial over a

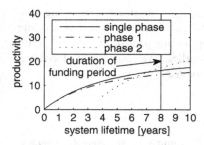

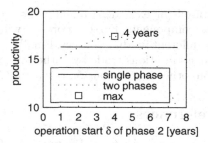

Fig. 13. Productivity comparison of *psOpen* for a single-phase vs. two-phase cluster purchase and as function of years. Overall investment is fixed at 10 M€ (split equally for the two-phase cluster). Funding period is 8 years. Operation start of 2nd phase after 4 years.

Fig. 14. Productivity comparison of *psOpen* for a single-phase vs. two-phase cluster purchase after 8 years. Productivity as function of the year in which the 2nd phase started operating. Overall investment is fixed at 10 M€ (split equally for the two-phase cluster).

single-phase one in most cases. The best time for starting operating the second phase is 4 years after installing the first phase.

5 Conclusion

In this paper, we presented a productivity model with focus on a computing center scale, i.e. running big MPI codes with much tuning effort needed to get good performance. For large-scaling runs, we included a performance model (Amdahl's law) and account for their higher quality using a weighting factor. We linked code size, tuning effort, and performance using an adaptation of COCOMO II and HPC lore's 80-20 rule. Analysis of the asymptotic behavior of large or long-lasting clusters is also incorporated.

In the context of one case study at RWTH Aachen University, we examined the viability and worth of our model by deriving quantitative statements on capital expenditure on tuning time, hardware, and system lifetime. Here, spending a certain portion of the available budget on brainware would pay off. Furthermore, a two-phase cluster acquisition would be beneficial over a single-phase one since the technological advances result in higher productivity. As the productivity results depend on numerous parameters, we also provide an online tool on our web page [25] that could help others make informed decisions on procurement of new HPC systems or upgrading existing ones.

In future, we will improve the predicting power of our productivity metric by further investigating applications of performance, power, and software estimation models. Extensions of the productivity model will also include mixed job executions and an adapted function of system lifetime. The latter will incorporate overlapping development time with system lifetime and the impact of expired (or extended) maintenance contracts and the breakdown of aging system components. Furthermore, we will investigate more use cases such as arguing for different funding sources. Finally, we will support our productivity model and the assumptions made by gathering more case studies. We also ask for feedback from other institutions on our $aixH(PC)^2$ web page.

References

1. Apon, A., Ahalt, S., Dantuluri, V., Gurdgiev, C., Limayem, M., Ngo, L., Stealey, M.: High performance computing instrumentation and research productivity in US universities. J. Inf. Technol. Impact **10**(2), 87–98 (2010)
2. Boehm, B., Abts, C., Brown, A.W., Chulani, S., Clark, B., Horowitz, E., Madachy, R., Reifer, D., Steece, B.: COCOMO II Model Definition Manual, Version 2.1. Technical report, University of Southern California (2000)
3. Chew, W.: No-nonsense guide to measuring productivity. Harvard Bus. Rev. **66**(1), 110–118 (1988)
4. Culler, D.E., Karp, R.M., Patterson, D.A., Sahay, A., Schauser, K.E., Santos, E., Subramonian, R., von Eicken, T.: LogP: Towards a Realistic Model of Parallel Computation. Technical report, Berkeley (1992)
5. Dongarra, J., Graybill, R., Harrod, W., Lucas, R., Lusk, E., Luszczek, P., Mcmahon, J., Snavely, A., Vetter, J., Yelick, K., Alam, S., Campbell, R., Carrington, L., Chen, T.Y., Khalili, O., Meredith, J., Tikir, M.: DARPA's HPCS program: history, models, tools, languages. In: Zelkowitz, M.V. (ed.) Advances in COMPUTERS High Performance Computing, Advances in Computers, vol. 72, pp. 1–100. Elsevier (2008)
6. Ebcioglu, K., Sarkar, V., El-Ghazawi, T., Urbanic, J., Center, P.: An experiment in measuring the productivity of three parallel programming languages. In: Workshop on Productivity and Performance in High-End Computing (P-PHEC), pp. 30–36 (2006)
7. European Commission: Guide to Financial Issues relating to FP7 Indirect Actions (2013)
8. Faulk, S., Gustafson, J., Johnson, P., Porter, A., Tichy, W., Votta, L.: Measuring high performance computing productivity. Int. J. High Perform. Comput. Appl. **18**(4), 459–473 (2004)
9. German Science Foundation (DFG): Personalmittelsätze der DFG für das Jahr (2013)
10. Göbbert, J.H., Gauding, M.: psOpen (2015). http://www.fz-juelich.de/ias/jsc/ EN/Expertise/High-Q-Club/psOpen/_node.html
11. InfiniBand Trade Association (2015). http://www.infinibandta.org/
12. Intel Corporation: Intel Processor ARK (2015). http://ark.intel.com/
13. Joseph, E.C., Conway, S., Dekate, C.: Creating Economic Models Showing the Relationship Between Investments in HPC and the Resulting Financial ROI and Innovation and How It Can Impact a Nation's Competitiveness and Innovation. International Data Corporation (IDC), Technical report (2013)
14. Kennedy, K., Koelbel, C., Schreiber, R.: Defining and measuring the productivity of programming languages. Int. J. High Perform. Comput. Appl. **18**(4), 441–448 (2004)
15. Kepner, J.: High performance computing productivity model synthesis. Int. J. High Perform. Comput. Appl. **18**(4), 505–516 (2004)

16. McConnell, S.: Software Estimation: Demystifying the Black Art. Redmond, Wa. Microsoft Press (2006)
17. McCracken, M., Wolter, N., Snavely, A.: Beyond performance tools: Measuring and modeling productivity in HPC. In: Third International Workshop on Software Engineering for High Performance Computing Applications, SE-HPC 2007, pp. 4–4 (2007)
18. Murphy, D., Nash, T., Lawrence Votta, J., Kepner, J.: A System-wide Productivity Figure of Merit. CT Watch Quarterly 2(4B) (2006)
19. Newman, M.: Power laws, Pareto distributions and Zipf's law. Contemp. Phys. 46(5), 323–351 (2005)
20. Pekurovsky, D.: P3DFFT: a framework for parallel computations of Fourier transforms in three dimensions. SIAM J. Sci. Comput. 34(4), C192–C209 (2012)
21. Sadowski, C., Shewmaker, A.: The Last Mile: Parallel Programming and Usability. In: Proceedings of the FSE/SDP Workshop on Future of Software Engineering Research, FoSER 2010, pp. 309–314. ACM, New York (2010)
22. Snir, M., Bader, D.A.: A framework for measuring supercomputer productivity. Int. J. High Perform. Comput. Appl. 18(4), 417–432 (2004)
23. Sterling, T.: Productivity metrics and models for high performance computing. Int. J. High Perform. Comput. Appl. 18(4), 433–440 (2004)
24. Wang, L., Khan, S.: Review of performance metrics for green data centers: a taxonomy study. J. Supercomputing 63(3), 639–656 (2011)
25. Wienke, S., Iliev, H., Hahnfeld, J., an Mey, D., Müller, M.S.: $aixH(PC)^2$ - Aachen HPC Productivity Calculator (2015). http://www.hpc.rwth-aachen.de/research/tco/
26. Wienke, S., an Mey, D., Müller, M.S.: Accelerators for technical computing: is it worth the pain? A TCO perspective. In: Kunkel, J.M., Ludwig, T., Meuer, H.W. (eds.) ISC 2013. LNCS, vol. 7905, pp. 330–342. Springer, Heidelberg (2013)
27. Williams, S., Waterman, A., Patterson, D.: Roofline: an insightful visual performance model for multicore architectures. Commun. ACM 52(4), 65–76 (2009)
28. Zelkowitz, M., Basili, V., Asgari, S., Hochstein, L., Hollingsworth, J., Nakamura, T.: Measuring productivity on high performance computers. In: IEEE International Symposium on Software Metrics, p. 6 (2005). http://doi.ieeecomputersociety.org/10.1109/METRICS.2005.33
29. Zelkowitz, M., Hollingsworth, J., Basili, V., Asgari, S., Shull, F., Carver, J., Hochstein, L.: Parallel Programmer Productivity: A Case Study of Novice Parallel Programmers. SC Conference 35 (2005). http://dx.doi.org/10.1109/SC.2005.53

Taking Advantage of Node Power Variation in Homogenous HPC Systems to Save Energy

Torsten Wilde[1,2]([✉]), Axel Auweter[1], Hayk Shoukourian[1,2], and Arndt Bode[1,2]

[1] Leibniz Supercomputing Centre of the Bavarian Academy of Science
and Humanity, Garching Bei München, Munich, Germany
[2] Technical University Munich (TUM), Munich, Germany
torsten.wilde@lrz.de

Abstract. Saving energy and, therefore, reducing the Total Cost of Ownership (TCO) for High Performance Computing (HPC) data centers has increasingly generated attention in light of rising energy costs and the technical hurdles imposed when powering multi-MW data centers. The broadest impact on data center energy efficiency can be achieved by techniques that do not require application specific tuning. Improving the Power Usage Effectiveness (PUE), for example, benefits everything that happens in a data center. Less broad but still better than individual application tuning would be to improve the energy efficiency of the HPC system itself. One property of homogeneous HPC systems that hasn't been considered so far is the existence of node power variation.

This paper discusses existing node power variations in two HPC systems. It introduces three energy-saving techniques: node power aware scheduling, node power aware system partitioning, and node ranking based on power variation, which take advantage of this variation, and quantifies possible savings for each technique. It will show that using node power aware system partitioning and node ranking based on power variation will save energy with very minimal effort over the lifetime of the system. All three techniques are also relevant for distributed and cloud environments.

Keywords: HPC · Energy-efficiency · Energy-saving · Data center

1 Introduction

The steady rise in energy consumption of data centers world wide over the last decade [21, 22] and the future 20 MW exascale-challenge in High Performance Computing (HPC) [20] makes saving energy an important consideration for HPC data centers.

Improving data center energy efficiency starts with improved measurement capabilities. Fortunately, the standard measurement capabilities of HPC systems have continuously been improved with the help of the energy efficient HPC community. In Europe the yearly held "European workshop on HPC centre infrastructures" [18] supported by the Partnership for Advanced Computing

© Springer International Publishing Switzerland 2015
J.M. Kunkel and T. Ludwig (Eds.): ISC High Performance 2015, LNCS 9137, pp. 376–393, 2015.
DOI: 10.1007/978-3-319-20119-1_27

in Europe (PRACE [28]) provides an exchange platform for best practices and lessons learned regarding the improvement of HPC data center energy efficiency. The Energy Efficient HPC Working-Group (EEHPCWG) [15] defined a standard measurement methodology [10] for HPC systems and provided HPC system commissioning guidelines [11] that include power and energy measurement requirements. The improved capabilities led to new discoveries and improved energy efficiency. For example, energy aware scheduling [3] would not be possible without detailed power and energy measurements.

During the first in-depth analysis of the EEHPCWG standard measurement methodology [32], variation in overall system power was observed depending on the measured part of the system (1/16, 1/8, full system). This was mainly attributed to the difference of the included subsystems.

Further analysis of HPC systems at Leibniz Supercomputing Centre (LRZ) led to the quantification of node power variability for two homogeneous HPC systems: SuperMUC and CooLMUC.

This paper discusses the findings of the analysis and will propose possible energy savings techniques taking advantage of node power variability.

The rest of the paper is organized as follows. Section 2 will highlight some related areas of energy efficiency research. Section 3 gives an overview of the CooLMUC and SuperMUC HPC systems. Section 4 discusses the discovered node variability in homogenous HPC systems. Section 5 proposes different energy savings techniques based on system node variability. Section 6 quantifies the possible savings using the CooLMUC HPC system. Section 7 discusses future work and Sect. 8 draws the conclusion.

Definitions

The following definitions are used throughout this document:

- Worst nodes - refers to nodes which consume the largest amount of power in the HPC system node power distribution (this implies a ranking of nodes based on power consumption)
- Best nodes - refers to nodes which consume the least amount of power in the HPC system node power distribution (this implies a ranking of nodes based on power consumption)
- EtS - Energy to Solution, the energy consumed by an application to solve a specific problem
- TtS - Time to Solution, the runtime of an application

2   Background

The "4 Pillar Framework for Energy Efficient HPC Data Centers" [39] provides a representation of all parts of a data center that influence its energy efficiency. The four pillars are: Building Infrastructure (Pillar1), HPC System Hardware (Pillar2), HPC System Software (Pillar3), and HPC applications (Pillar4). Typically, optimization performed in Pillar1 will have the broadest scope as optimizations on the building infrastructure will affect the entire center independent from the HPC systems, system software, and applications. Contrary to that, optimizing a single application in Pillar4 will have no effect beyond the energy consumed when running that particular application.

Figure 1 illustrates how the four pillar framework helps classifying the state of the art in energy efficient HPC research. Reducing the system-PUE (sPUE) [38] of an HPC system (Pillar1 and Pillar2) by using the most efficient cooling technology available in the data center (for example, ASHRAE W5 [2] direct liquid cooling) reduces the system overhead for all workloads running on the system. Dynamic Voltage and Frequency Scaling (DVFS) (Pillar2) is used for energy aware scheduling on Supercomputers which can minimize an application's Energy-to-Solution (EtS) [3] (combining information from Pillar 2, 3, and 4). And last but not least, by improving an application performance the energy efficiency of the application is improved (Pillar4).

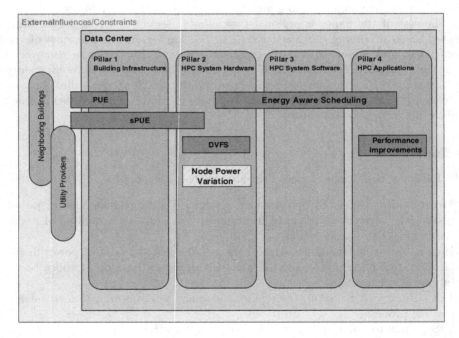

Fig. 1. The four pillar framework for energy efficient HPC data centers and the coverage areas of popular research areas in the field of energy efficient HPC.

The existence of node power variation has been shown previously by Hackenberg et al. [17]. Their analysis of using the SPEC MPI benchmark to quantifying power consumption variations of HPC systems, showed a node power variation of 7 % when idle and 5 % under maximum load for 16 double nodes of an AMD

Opteron cluster. Davis et al. [7] looked into variability of large-scale cluster power models. They stated that inter-node variations in power consumption is one reason that single node power models, when scaled to a large-cluster, show high errors. However, both papers do not consider the use of node power variation for energy savings.

Even though there are a multitude of energy efficient IT system models (for example [31,40]) **node power variation** hasn't been included yet, most probably because previously measuring the variation was difficult if not impossible on large scale systems. However, this paper will show that although the possible savings are small, node power variation is a property of HPC systems that has the potential to improve the system energy efficiency independent of any other energy saving techniques.

3   Test Systems

The data on which this work is based on was collected on two systems operated at the Leibniz Supercomputing Centre of the Bavarian Academy of Sciences and Humanities (LRZ) [23].

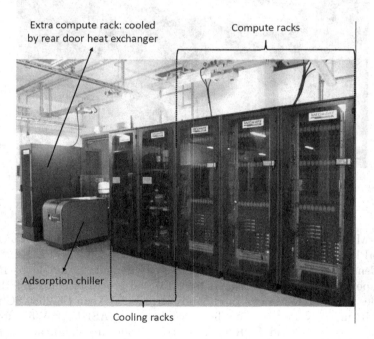

Fig. 2. CooLMUC experimentation HPC cluster at LRZ.

CooLMUC (Fig. 2) was built by MEGWARE and is the first AMD based direct liquid cooled (W5 water) HPC cluster with 178 nodes (8 nodes interactive, 166 nodes batch, and 4 nodes reserved for internal use). A single node

contains two AMD Opteron 6128HE CPUs (MagnyCours) with 8 cores each and
12 MB L3 cache. In their standard setting, the CPUs run at 2 GHz clock frequency. Each node is equipped with 16 GB RAM arranged in eight 2 GB DDR3
modules. The main interconnect network is InfiniBand QDR using a fat tree
topology. In addition, each node has two Gbit Ethernet ports for IPMI and a
service network which is used to boot the diskless nodes and to provide the
root filesystem over NFS. The cluster is completely room neutral, meaning that
there is no requirement for computer room air conditioning (CRAC) units. Power
measurements on CoolMUC are based on smart PDUs which report 1-minute
average power values per node. Sufficiently long benchmark times are used to
minimize the error of the 1-minute readouts.

Fig. 3. SuperMUC super-computer at LRZ.

SuperMUC (Fig. 3) (Nr.14, Top500 List Nov 2014) was built by IBM based
on iDataPlex technology with a peak performance of 3 PetaFLOPS. It is a
Gauss Center for Supercomputing (GCS) system made available to PRACE
users. SuperMUC's thin node islands have 147.456 processor cores in 9216 compute nodes. Each node has two Intel Sandy Bridge-EP Xeon E5-2680 8C processors, 32 GB memory, and is direct liquid cooled using ASHRAE W5 water. The
interconnect is Infiniband FDR10, a fat tree inside an island, and a Pruned
Tree (4:1 blocking factor) between islands. SuperMUC provides multiple levels
of power measurements. For this analysis the "IBM Active Energy Manager" was
used which collects power and energy consumption data at the power supply of
each node.

4   Node Power Variation

A feature of homogenous HPC systems, that wasn't known in detail before the improvement of system power measurement capabilities, is the existence of power variation between nodes when running the same workload.

Figure 4 shows the average node power variation for 174 CooLMUC nodes when running the same single node MPrime benchmark (see also [34]). MPrime was chosen because it is one of the most power consuming benchmarks. In order to account for the specific load pattern, the benchmark was run for over 60 min. As can be observed, there is a difference of 21 W between the node with the least and the node with the highest power consumption (i.e. the worst node consumes 8.75 % more power than the best node).

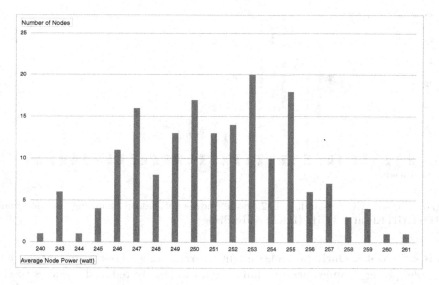

Fig. 4. Histogram of CooLMUC's node power when running single node MPrime at 2.0 GHz (AMD MagnyCours).

A similar variation pattern exists in other HPC systems as well. Figure 5 shows the node power variation of the 516 nodes (512 compute nodes, 4 spare nodes) of island5 of SuperMUC when running the single node FIRESTARTER benchmark on each node at 2.3 GHz (the average of 5 runs was used). FIRESTARTER was developed at TU Dresden, Germany, with the aim to create the highest CPU power consumption possible [16]. It was used instead of MPrime because its constant load pattern allowed a significant reduction of benchmark runtime to 15 min for each run. For island5 of SuperMUC the power difference between the best and worst node is 42 W (18.9 %).

The main contributor to this node power variation is the CPU [13,27]. We suspect this to be due to semiconductor manufacturing tolerances, the same reason for which the finished products are categorized based on their thermal and frequency characteristics, a process called "product binning". It was also observed that the node power variation does not change over the relative short life time of an HPC system even though semiconductors age over time [19]. Yet each node replacement needs to be evaluated and the node power ranking needs to be adjusted. The node power variation will also not change when running different applications since it is a hardware property, good nodes will stay good nodes.

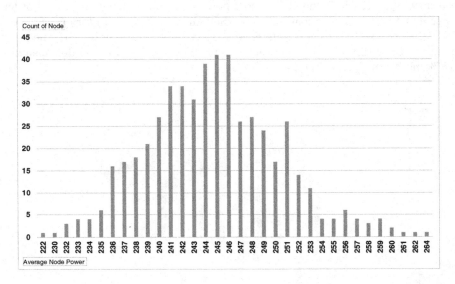

Fig. 5. SuperMUC (island5) 512 node power variation running single node FIRESTARTER at 2.3 GHz (Intel Sandy Bridge).

As a side note: Outlying nodes might warrant some closer examination. For example, power supplies prior to failure tend to supply reduced voltages to the node and, therefore, reduce the nodes power consumption as experienced on CooLMUC. Similarly, a high power consumption paired with a high node temperature could indicate improperly seated heatsinks on systems that use direct liquid cooling as experienced during the PRACE 2nd Implementation Phase project (PRACE 2IP) energy efficient HPC prototyping effort [29].

5   What to do with Node Power Variation

5.1   Node Power Aware Scheduling

Thermal and hot spot aware scheduling [4,36] works well in distributed and cloud computing environments and the same techniques could be used for node power aware scheduling.

Table 1 shows the power and energy consumption of running the High Performance Conjugate Gradient Benchmark (HPCG) [9] on the 10 worst vs. the 10 best nodes of island5. The results show that node variability is not just a factor for stress test workloads but also for applications. At a difference of 26.9 W running on the 10 worst nodes imposes an overhead of 14.4 % in power consumption compared to running on the 10 best nodes.

Table 1. HPCG at 2.3 GHz on 10 best and worst nodes of island5 of SuperMUC (Intel Sandy Bridge)

	EtS (kWh)	average node power (W)	TtS (s)
10 worst nodes	0.658	213.4	1110
10 best nodes	0.575	186.5	1110

To get an idea how larger HPC applications are affected, Table 2 shows the difference when running HPCG on the 256 best or 256 worst nodes of island5. Here the impact of running on the worst nodes is lower (4.3 %) because the node average starts to dominate the distribution. It can also be seen that the application performance is not affected by the selection of nodes. Therefore, power and energy optimization can be used interchangeably.

Table 2. HPCG at 2.3 GHz on 256 best and worst nodes of island5 of SuperMUC (Intel Sandy Bridge)

	EtS (kWh)	average power (W)	TtS (s)
256 worst nodes	15.55	197.7	1106
256 best nodes	15.03	189.6	1115

Obviously, the idea becomes less applicable when considering that in HPC one tries to use all resources 100 % of the time. This means that while one application may run on the best nodes another will run on the worst nodes. The possible gain for an application A and B running on island5 would be the difference between the gain of application A (worst vs best nodes) and the gain of application B (worst vs best nodes) (Fig. 6 and Eq. 1).

$$\text{Saving}_{\text{maxtheoretical}} = |\text{Gain}_A - \text{Gain}_B| = |(P_{A.on.Worst} - P_{A.on.Best}) - (P_{B.on.Worst} - P_{B.on.Best})| \tag{1}$$

For example, by combining HPCG gain (8.1 W per node) with Epoch gain (6.4 W per node) (Table 3), which were both chosen because they reflect real HPC data center workloads, the expected saving is: 1.7 W per node, equaling 870.4 W for the 512 nodes of island5.

This shows that in order to use node power variability for node power aware scheduling one application needs to be less sensitive to the used node set (see Fig. 6 application **B**). Since most of the power consumption comes from the CPU, a combination of CPU bound (high frequency and high power consumption)

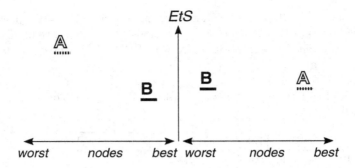

Fig. 6. Node power aware scheduling application A and B.

Table 3. Epoch at 2.3 GHz on 256 best and worst nodes of island5 of SuperMUC (Intel Sandy Bridge)

	EtS (kWh)	average power (W)	TtS (s)
256 worst nodes	9.20	164.2	788
256 best nodes	8.83	157.8	787

applications running on the best nodes with memory/io bound (low frequency and low power consumption) applications running on the worst would be better. In addition, the analysis estimated the maximum theoretical savings, which in comparison to reality where the node allocation would be random, overestimates the possible savings. Therefore, the possible savings might not be substantial enough to account for the additional effort required for the scheduling system to allow for this selection. A more in-depth analysis using application models might be required to really quantify the potential of node power aware scheduling.

5.2 Node Switch-off, Node Power Aware System Partitioning, and Node Ranking Based on Power Variation

The best technique in terms of saving energy is to switch off what is not used. This can have a great impact in distributed and/or virtualized data centers, since in those environments it is possible to consolidate workload to switch off resources. One concrete technique for energy-aware workload placement in cloud computing can be found in [5]. Both All4Green [1] and Fit4Green [12] project deliverables provide many insights into energy saving techniques for distributed data centers. Finally a very comprehensive survey on research related to power and energy-efficient system design and usage can be found in [6]. Unfortunately, the impact of such techniques will be lower in HPC since the goal is to have a 100 % utilization rate of the resources. In addition, one needs to be aware of possible challenges when using node switch-off or sleep mode in very large HPC installations. For example, the sudden removal or addition of possible thousands of nodes can stall the interconnect fabric leading to the termination of jobs. Also,

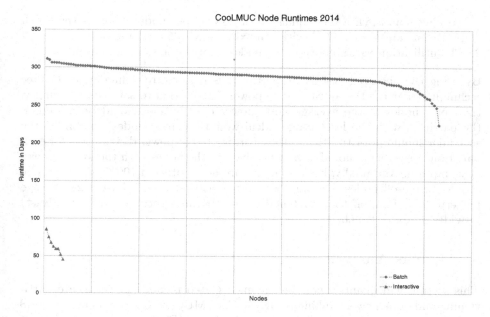

Fig. 7. CooLMUC node utilization in 2014 for batch and interactive partition

Table 4. CooLMUC partition usage for 2014

runtime per node	interactive	batch
min	45.49 days	224.43 days
max	85.62 days	311.19 days
average	63.47 days	289.07 days

the reliable wake-up from sleep-mode of nodes can be affected by the robustness of the software stack, a challenge especially in the early lifetime of the system.

One way to minimize the runtime of the worst nodes in HPC data centers is to exploit usage pattern differences in the HPC system partitions (job queues). CooLMUC for example has two partitions: one batch partition (166 nodes) and one interactive partition (8 nodes). Empty nodes in the batch partition only appear when no small jobs for backfilling are in the queue, or when the system needs to drain nodes in order to start a high priority job with a high node count. The nodes of the interactive partition are mainly used during normal working hours. Figure 7 shows the utilization of each node in the interactive partition and batch partition for the year 2014. Table 4 shows the average, minimum, and maximum utilization for the nodes of each partition for the year 2014.

Two important observations can be made from this data:

1. A significant difference between partitions, depending on their usage pattern, exists. For example, the interactive partition is mainly used during normal

working hours (8 h a day equals 83 days/year per node) whereas the batch partition can be used 24/7 with a maximum of 365 days per node.

2. The utilization varies between the nodes even in the same partition.

By using the observed system properties it is possible to define at least three techniques that use the average node power distribution to save energy. Firstly, the worst nodes of the average node power distribution should be moved to the partition with the least usage (ideal would be spare nodes). Secondly, the scheduler should prioritize the nodes according to the power distribution for each partition. Preference should always be given to the nodes with the lowest power consumption. And finally, because nodes are never utilized 100 % in a year, one should switch-off nodes especially for partitions that do not have a 24/7 usage pattern. Switching off the worst nodes first (because these are used the least) provides an extra benefit.

6   Savings Analysis

This section will quantify possible savings related to node power aware partitioning and node power ranking using the CooLMUC HPC system (174 nodes [8 nodes interactive, 166 nodes batch] are considered). First, the theoretically best and worst system distribution scenarios are compared to get an idea about the maximum possible savings potential. In reality, a system without node power aware partitioning and node ranking based on power variation will have a distribution between the best and worst case scenarios. Therefore, the real-world savings using the actual CooLMUC setup are discussed. PowerDAM [33] was used to collect and analyze power and energy data.

At first, the measured node power distribution (Fig. 4) was normalized using the average power consumption of all nodes during the MPrime benchmark (251.14 W). Given the power consumption of an application on an average node, the normalized power distribution can be used to derive the power consumption of the application when running on good nodes or bad nodes respectively. After that the following system and node statistics were collected:

1. System:
   - average power per node when running jobs on interactive partition
   - runtime of all jobs on the interactive partition
   - average power per node when running job on batch partition
   - runtime of all jobs on the batch partition
2. Nodes:
   - runtime for each node (annual utilization time of each node)
   - average power for each node (average of all power measurements when the node was used by a job during the year)

Table 5 shows the CooLMUC system partitions power and runtime statistics for 2014. The system energy consumption is the sum of the energy consumption of the interactive and batch partitions. The energy consumption of one partition is

Table 5. CooLMUC partitions statistic for 2014

	interactive	batch
average node power (W)	156.20	217.58
runtime (h)	12186.22	1151654.97
energy consumption (kWh)	1903.49	250577.09

the *average yearly node power when running jobs on partition X* multiplied by *partition X runtime*.

Table 6 shows the data for node power aware system partitioning without taking node ranking into consideration. In the worst case, the best nodes are moved into the interactive partition. In the best case, the worst nodes are moved into the interactive partition. Using this technique a maximum theoretical saving of 663.28 kWh per year can be achieved.

Table 6. Best possible savings for CooLMUC using node power aware system partitioning for 2014

	interactive	batch	system
average node power (worst in interactive)	162.26 W	217.17 W	
energy consumption (worst in interactive)	1977.39 kWh	250108.26 kWh	252085.65 kWh
average node power (best in interactive)	152.08 W	217.86 W	
energy consumption (best in interactive)	1853.27 kWh	250895.65 kWh	252748.93 kWh
possible max. savings			663.28 kWh

Table 7 shows the results for power aware system partitioning and node ranking based on power variation. In the worst case the best nodes are moved into the interactive partition and in each partition the nodes are arranged so that the longer the runtime the worse its power consumption. In the best case the worst nodes are moved into the interactive partition and in each partition the nodes are arranged so that the longer the runtime the better its power consumption.

Table 7. Best possible savings for CooLMUC using node power aware system partitioning and node ranking based on power variation for 2014

	interactive	batch	system
energy consumption (worst in interactive)	1962.81 kWh	250059.26 kWh	252022.07 kWh
energy consumption (best in interactive)	1841.05 kWh	251112.44 kWh	252953.49 kWh
possible max. savings			931.42 kWh

Using node ranking based on power variation in each partition saves nearly 50 % more energy than power aware system partitioning alone, increasing the possible theoretical energy savings to 931.42 kWh.

In Reality. CooLMUC consumed 252480.58 kWh in 2014 (Table 5). This leads to a possible savings of 251.77 kWh for 2014 (252480.58 kWh minus 252022.07 kWh (taken from Table 7).

Since each 1 kWh IT power saved will also save cooling costs, the HPC system internal cooling overhead (1.23 for CooLMUC [24]) and sPUE (see Fig. 1) need to be considered. sPUE is defined in [38] as:

$$\text{sPUE} = 1 + \text{Overhead}_{\text{PDCL}} + \sum_{k=1}^{n}(w_k * \frac{1}{\text{COP}_k})$$

$$1 = \sum_{k=1}^{n} w_k$$

Where w_k is the distribution for each heat removal technology k *used in the HPC system and the sum of all w_k is 1 (equaling 100 % heat removal). The data center overhead incurred by cooling the system is represented by $1/COP_k$ which is the power needed to remove 1 W of heat via the heat removal technology* k. *Overhead$_{PDCL}$ is the additional power needed by the data center to provide 1 W of IT power.*

Table 8. LRZ electrical and cooling overhead

	LRZ
PDCL overhead	0.075
Air cooling overhead	0.500
W1 cooling overhead	0.400
W4 cooling overhead	0.050

Using the LRZ data center overhead information from Table 8, and the knowledge that CooLMUC is 100 % cooled using W4, sPUE can be determined:

$$\text{sPUE}_{\text{CooLMUC}} = 1 + 0.075 + 1 * 0.05 = 1.125$$

Using the system internal cooling overhead and sPUE, the final yearly (for 2014) energy savings for CooLMUC would be:

$$\text{Savings}_{\text{CooLMUC}} = 251.77 * 1.23 * 1.125 = 348.39 \text{kWh}$$

If one, in the most simplistic way, scales the CooLMUC (43 kW average system power) result to SuperMUC (2.4 MW average power consumption) then the possible yearly savings would be: 56 times 348.39 kWh = 19509.84 kWh.

7   Future Work

The next step is to apply the proposed techniques in practice. Since CooL-MUC is a prototype system it is available for research activities. The CooLMUC interactive and batch partitions will be changed according to node power aware system partitioning. SLURM, which is the scheduler used on CooLMUC, supports scheduling weights for resources. This might be sufficient to apply node ranking based on power variation. The success of this technique can be verified by checking that the worst nodes have the lowest runtime.

Node power aware scheduling might still be interesting for saving energy but generic models for application power and energy profiles are needed. There is already some work going into understanding the power consumption behavior of nodes in terms of analysing the energy efficiency features of newer processors and quantifying the power and energy costs of computation in terms of data movement, flops, and network communication. Using this information, a more generic estimate of possible power and energy savings using node power aware scheduling needs to be done. A quantification of the impact on scheduling decisions (scheduling complexity increase, scheduling time required, etc.) is required before node power aware scheduling can be judged.

8 Conclusion

This paper made the following contributions to the state of the art in HPC power savings research:

- It showed and quantified the existence of node power variation in current homogenous HPC systems.
- It proposed and evaluated three techniques for saving energy using the node power variation:
  - node power aware scheduling
  - node power aware system partitioning
  - node ranking based on power variation

Node power variation can be used to save energy. The proposed techniques are not limited to HPC data centers and can be used in conjunction with any other energy savings effort. From the three techniques, node power aware system partitioning and node ranking based on power variation are the most practical, requiring very little effort, and will benefit the system over its complete lifetime. In the best theoretical case a combined savings of these two techniques of 0.5 % (using data from Table 7 and multiplying the saving with the system, 1.2, and data center overhead, 1.125) is possible. In reality of course a system will start with a configuration between the worst and best case. The possible savings will vary with the system size, the node power spread (difference between best and worst), and the statistical node power distribution. If a system starts in the middle between the theoretically best and worst distribution, which is a reasonable assumption, then a real world saving of 0.25 % for an HPC system seems possible. In the provided CooLMUC example, a saving of only 0.1 % could be realized.

Even though node power variation might not provide huge energy savings for HPC data centers, it has a high savings potential for data centers with lower resource utilization. As shown in Sect. 5.1, for example, with a 50 % resource utilization rate picking the best nodes saves 4.3 % for the HPC example application. Lower utilization rates will provide even more savings potential. Even though there do not exist many scientific publications analysing the utilization rates of non-HPC data centers (one example is [25] where an average utilization rate of less than 16 % for a week is reported), industry surveys approximate the average utilization rate of most server clusters to be on average 15 % [26,30]. For example, a 2014 white paper by the Natural Resources Defense Council [37] states that current hyper-scale cloud providers (which accounted for only 4 % of the overall data centers power consumption in 2011) can realize average utilization rates of 40 %. And research from Google indicates that typical server clusters (which accounted for 95 % of the overall data centers power consumption in 2011) average anywhere from 10 to 50 percent utilization [37]. The use of virtualized environments improves the average utilization rate but an estimated 20 to 30 percent of servers in large data centers today are idle, obsolete, or unused [35,37].

Although a power saving of around 0.25 % for an HPC data center might not seem like much, it will add up if one considers, for example, the aggregated power consumption of all HPC systems in the November 2014 Green500 list [14] (592.31 MW not including data center cooling infrastructure overhead), or the yearly power consumption of all data centers world wide (38.84 GW for 2013 according to DCD Intelligence [8]).

Acknowledgments. The authors would like to thank Jeanette Wilde (LRZ) for her valuable comments and support.

The work presented here has been carried out within the SIMOPEK project, which has received funding from the German Federal Ministry for Education and Research under grant number 01IH13007A, at the Leibniz Supercomputing Centre (LRZ) with support of the State of Bavaria, Germany, and the Gauss Centre for Supercomputing (GCS).

The EPOCH code used in this research was developed under UK Engineering and Physics Sciences Research Council grants EP/G054940/1, EP/G055165/1 and EP/G056803/1.

References

1. All4Green: http://www.all4green-project.eu/
2. ASHRAE TC 9.9.2011: 2011 thermal guidelines for liquid cooled data processing environments. White paper (2011). www.tc99.ashraetcs.org
3. Auweter, A., et al.: A case study of energy aware scheduling on SuperMUC. In: Kunkel, J.M., Ludwig, T., Meuer, H.W. (eds.) ISC 2014. LNCS, vol. 8488, pp. 394–409. Springer, Heidelberg (2014)
4. Banerjee, A., Mukherjee, T., Varsamopoulos, G., Gupta, S.K.S.: Cooling-aware and thermal-aware workload placement for green hpc data centers. In: GREENCOMP 2010 Proceedings of the International Conference on Green Computing, pp. 245–256. IEEE Computer Society, Washington, DC, USA (2010). http://dx.doi.org/10.1109/GREENCOMP.2010.5598306

5. Beloglazov, A., Abawajy, J., Buyya, R.: Energy-aware resource allocation heuristics for efficient management of data centers for cloud computing. Future Gener. Comput. Syst. **28**(5), 755–768 (2012). http://www.sciencedirect.com/science/article/pii/S0167739X11000689, special Section: Energy efficiency in large-scale distributed systems

6. Beloglazov, A., Buyya, R., Lee, Y.C., Zomaya, A.Y.: A taxonomy and survey of energy-efficient data centers and cloud computing systems. Adv. Comput. **82**, 47–111 (2011). http://dblp.uni-trier.de/db/journals/ac/ac82.html#BeloglazovBLZ11

7. Davis, J.D., Rivoire, S., Goldszmidt, M., Ardestani, E.K.: Accounting for variability in large-scale cluster power models. In: Exascale Evaluation and Research Techniques (2011). http://research.microsoft.com/pubs/146087/EXERT_Variability_CR3.pdf

8. DCD Intelligence: Is the industry getting better at using power? Data Center Dynamics FOCUS 33, January/February 2014 33, 16–17 (2014). http://content.yudu.com/Library/A2nvau/FocusVolume3issue33/resources/index.htm?referrerUrl=

9. Dongarra, J., Heroux, M.A.: Toward a new metric for ranking high performance computing systems. Sandia Report, SAND2013-4744 312 (2013)

10. EEHPCWG: Energy efficient high performance computing power measurement methodology. Tech. rep., Energy Effiicient High Performace Computing Working Group (2013). http://www.green500.org/sites/default/files/eehpcwg/EEHPCWG_PowerMeasurementMethodology.pdf

11. EEHPCWG: Energy efficiency considerations for hpc procurement documents: 2014. Tech. rep., Energy Effiicient High Performace Computing Working Group (2014). http://eehpcwg.lbl.gov/sub-groups/equipment-1/procurement-considerations/procurement-considerations-presentations

12. Fit4Green: http://www.fit4green.eu/

13. Ge, R., Feng, X., Cameron, K.: Modeling and evaluating energy-performance efficiency of parallel processing on multicore based power aware systems. In: IEEE International Symposium on Parallel Distributed Processing, IPDPS 2009, pp. 1–8 (May 2009)

14. Green500 List: http://www.green500.org/

15. Energy Efficient HPC Working Group: http://eehpcwg.lbl.gov/

16. Hackenberg, D., Oldenburg, R., Molka, D., Schone, R.: Introducing firestarter: a processor stress test utility. In: 2013 International Green Computing Conference (IGCC), pp. 1–9 (June 2013)

17. Hackenberg, D., Schöne, R., Molka, D., Müller, M., Knüpfer, A.: Quantifying power consumption variations of HPC systems using spec mpi benchmarks. Comput. Sci. Res. Dev. **25**(3–4), 155–163 (2010). http://dx.doi.org/10.1007/s00450-010-0118-0

18. Workshop on HPC centre infrastructures, E.: http://www-hpc.cea.fr/fr/evenements/Workshop-HPC-2013.htm

19. Keane, J., Kim, C.: An odomoeter for cpus. IEEE Spectr. **48**(5), 28–33 (2011)

20. Kogge, P.: ExaScale computing study: Technology challenges in achieving exascale systems. Univ. of Notre Dame, CSE Dept. Tech. Report TR-2008-13 (September 28, 2008)

21. Koomey, J.G.: Worldwide electricity used in data centers (2008). http://iopscience.iop.org/1748-9326/3/3/034008/pdf/1748-9326_3_3_034008.pdf

22. Koomey, J.G.: Growth in data center electricity use 2005 to 2010 (2011). http://www.twosides.us/content/rspdf_218.pdf

23. Leibniz Supercomputing Centre: http://www.lrz.de
24. Johnsson, L., Netzer, G., Boyer, E., Carpenter, P., Januszewski, R., Koutsou, G., Saastad, O.W., Stylianou, G., Wilde, T.: D9.3.4 Final Report on Prototype Evaluation. PRACE 1IP-WP9 public deliverable, p. 44 (2013). http://www.prace-ri. eu/IMG/pdf/d9.3.4_1ip.pdf
25. Liu, H.: A measurement study of server utilization in public clouds. In: 2011 IEEE Ninth International Conference on Dependable, Autonomic and Secure Computing (DASC), pp. 435–442 (December 2011)
26. Mark Aggar (Microsoft): The IT Energy Efficiency Imperative. White paper (2011)
27. Naffziger, S.: AMD at ISSCC: Bulldozer Innovations Target Energy Efficiency. http://community.amd.com/community/amd-blogs/amd-business/blog/2011/02/ 22/amd-at-isscc-bulldozer-innovations-target-energy-efficiency
28. Partnership for Advanced Computing in Europe: http://www.prace-ri.eu/
29. Partnership for Advanced Computing in Europe: http://www.prace-ri.eu/ prace-2ip/
30. Ravi A. Giri (Staff Engineer, Intel IT) and Anand Vanchi (Solutions Architect, Intel Data Center Group): Increasing Data Center Efficiency with Server Power Measurements. IT@Intel White Paper, p. 7 (2011)
31. Samak, T., Morin, C., Bailey, D.: Energy consumption models and predictions for large-scale systems. In: 2013 IEEE 27th International Parallel and Distributed Processing Symposium Workshops & Ph.D. Forum (IPDPSW), pp. 899–906. IEEE (2013)
32. Scogland, T.R., Steffen, C.P., Wilde, T., Parent, F., Coghlan, S., Bates, N., Feng, W.C., Strohmaier, E.: A power-measurement methodology for large-scale, high-performance computing. In: ICPE 2014 Proceedings of the 5th ACM/SPEC International Conference on Performance Engineering, pp. 149–159. ACM, New York, NY, USA (2014). http://doi.acm.org/10.1145/2568088.2576795
33. Shoukourian, H., Wilde, T., Auweter, A., Bode, A.: Monitoring power data: a first step towards a unified energy efficiency evaluation toolset for HPC data centers. Environ. Model. Softw. **56**, 13–26 (2014). http://www.sciencedirect.com/science/ article/pii/S1364815213002934, thematic issue on Modelling and evaluating the sustainability of smart solutions
34. Shoukourian, H., Wilde, T., Auweter, A., Bode, A.: Predicting the energy and power consumption of strong and weak scaling HPC applications. Supercomput. Front. Innovations **1**(2), 20–41 (2014)
35. Stansberry, M.: Uptime institute annual data center industry survey report and full results (2013). http://www.data-central.org/resource/collection/BC649AE0- 4223-4EDE-92C7-29A659EF0900/uptime-institute-2013-data-center-survey.pdf
36. Wang, L., Khan, S.U., Dayal, J.: Thermal aware workload placement with task-temperature profiles in a data center. J. Supercomput. **61**(3), 780–803 (2012)
37. Whitney, J., Delforge, P.: Scaling up energy efficiency across the Data Center Industry: evaluating Key Drivers and Barriers. Data Center Efficiency Assessment (2014). http://www.nrdc.org/energy/files/data-center-efficiency-assessment-ip.pdf
38. Wilde, T., Auweter, A., Patterson, M., Shoukourian, H., Huber, H., Bode, A., Labrenz, D., Cavazzoni, C.: DWPE, a new data center energy-efficiency metric bridging the gap between infrastructure and workload. In: 2014 International Conference on High Performance Computing Simulation (HPCS), pp. 893–901 (July 2014)

39. Wilde, T., Auweter, A., Shoukourian, H.: The 4 Pillar Framework for energy efficient HPC data centers. In: Computer Science - Research and Development, pp. 1–11 (2013). http://dx.doi.org/10.1007/s00450-013-0244-6
40. Wu, X., Lively, C., Taylor, V., Chang, H.C., Su, C.Y., Cameron, K., Moore, S., Terpstra, D., Weaver, V.: Mummi: multiple metrics modeling infrastructure. In: 2013 14th ACIS International Conference on Software Engineering, Artificial Intelligence, Networking and Parallel/Distributed Computing (SNPD), pp. 289–295 (July 2013)

A Run-Time System for Power-Constrained HPC Applications

Aniruddha Marathe[1]([⊠]), Peter E. Bailey[1], David K. Lowenthal[1],
Barry Rountree[2], Martin Schulz[2], and Bronis R. de Supinski[2]

[1] Department of Computer Science, The University of Arizona, Tucson, USA
{amarathe,pbailey,dkl}@cs.arizona.edu
[2] Lawrence Livermore National Laboratory, Livermore, USA
{rountree,schulzm,bronis}@llnl.gov

Abstract. As the HPC community attempts to reach exascale performance, power will be one of the most critical constrained resources. Achieving practical exascale computing will therefore rely on optimizing performance subject to a power constraint. However, this additional complication should not add to the burden of application developers; optimizing the run-time environment given restricted power will primarily be the job of high-performance system software.

This paper introduces *Conductor*, a run-time system that intelligently distributes available power to nodes and cores to improve performance. The key techniques used are *configuration space exploration* and *adaptive power balancing*. Configuration exploration dynamically selects the optimal thread concurrency level and DVFS state subject to a hardware-enforced power bound. Adaptive power balancing efficiently determines where critical paths are likely to occur so that more power is distributed to those paths. Greater power, in turn, allows increased thread concurrency levels, the DVFS states, or both. We describe these techniques in detail and show that, compared to the state-of-the-art technique of using statically predetermined, per-node power caps, *Conductor* leads to a best-case performance improvement of up to 30 %, and average improvement of 19.1 %.

1 Motivation

The US government, as well as European and Asian agencies, have set a goal to reach exascale computing in less than 10 years. However, if we were to build an exascale machine out of today's hardware, it would consume half of a gigawatt of power [13,21] and effectively require a dedicated power plant. In reality, there is a practical power bound, which is much tighter, and one such bound commonly used by both the research as well as the industrial high-performance computing (HPC) community is 20 MW [2]. It is clear that future HPC systems will have a whole-system power constraint that will filter down to job-level power constraints. The goal at the job-level will be to optimize performance subject to a prescribed power bound.

HPC users have enough to handle with ensuring correctness and maintaining sufficient performance, so the task of enforcing the job level power bound should

© Springer International Publishing Switzerland 2015
J.M. Kunkel and T. Ludwig (Eds.): ISC High Performance 2015, LNCS 9137, pp. 394–408, 2015.
DOI: 10.1007/978-3-319-20119-1_28

be left to HPC system software. More importantly, system software is in an ideal position to dynamically configure applications for the best performance subject to a power constraint. We define a processor's *configuration* as: (1) a value for c, the number of active cores, and (2) the DVFS state. The power constraint states that the total job power consumption must always be no more than the job-level power bound P, and the goal is to minimize application run time. We use Intel's Running Average Power Limit (RAPL) [14], introduced in the SandyBridge microarchitecture, to enforce the power constraint.

This paper describes the *Conductor* run-time system, which efficiently chooses an initial configuration resulting in near-optimal application performance for a given job power bound, then adapts this configuration as necessary during application execution according to changing application behavior and power constraints. The fundamental ideas behind *Conductor* are twofold. First, *Conductor* performs *configuration space exploration*, which dynamically selects the optimal thread concurrency level (DCT) and dynamic voltage frequency state (DVFS) subject to a RAPL-enforced power bound. Second, *Conductor* performs *adaptive power balancing*, which locates non-critical parts of the application (i.e., off the critical path), reduces their power consumption, and uses that excess power to speed up the parts on the critical path.

In *Conductor*, adaptive power balancing itself is done in three stages. First, *Conductor* monitors an application timestep to gauge representative application behavior. Second, *Conductor* continually applies a local, adaptive algorithm to select task configurations to reduce power consumption without increasing task execution time where possible. Third, *Conductor* improves performance by reallocating power at the MPI process level, using a global algorithm that is periodically executed at the end of timesteps. *Conductor* uses RAPL to enforce the chosen power allocation on each MPI process.

Specifically, this paper makes the following contributions.

- We design *Conductor*, the first run-time system that utilizes nonuniform power distribution, RAPL, DVFS, and DCT for optimizing HPC application performance under a power constraint.
- *Conductor* is fully automatic and chooses configurations with no involvement of the application programmer other than marking the end of an application timestep.
- *Conductor* chooses and adapts configurations dynamically based on application characteristics, resulting in efficient execution on a number of applications.

We implement *Conductor* on a large scale cluster at Lawrence Livermore National Laboratory, which has infrastructure for constraining power on a per-processor basis. Our results on up to 64 processors (512 cores) show that over five applications, *Conductor* achieves an average performance improvement of 19.1 % in a range of power limits over the state-of-the-art method, which is statically selected, per-node power caps. Moreover, we observe that *Conductor* achieves best-case performance improvement of 30 % over the static allocation scheme.

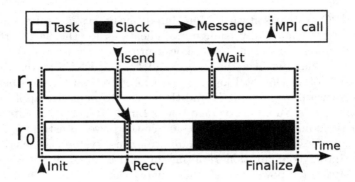

Fig. 1. Execution model on two MPI processes. The process with rank 1 sends a message to the process on rank 0. The process on rank 0 arrives first at MPI_Finalize, inducing slack time.

2 Optimizing Overprovisioned Systems

Traditionally, achieving maximum throughput in HPC clusters has been constrained by the available (fixed) hardware. However, as we move towards exascale, *power*, rather than hardware, will become a limiting factor in achieving optimal performance. With power consumption in a supercomputing cluster becoming critical, the allocation of power to individual jobs must comply to strict power constraints.

Under the given power constraint, which is typically imposed at the facility level, a supercomputing system may run fewer nodes at maximum power or more nodes at a lower power (known as *overprovisioning*). The system-level power constraint translates into job-level power constraints, which motivate the design of techniques to optimize performance under job-level power constraints. The primary objective is to run each job at a configuration that is power-efficient and allocate power to the critical path of the application.

2.1 Execution Model

In order to reason about optimization approaches in overprovisioned systems, we adopt the task based execution model (Fig. 1) that we used in our work on the Adagio run-time system [23]. A *task* is the basic unit of scheduling, comprising total communication and computation that takes place on an MPI process between two consecutive MPI calls. Note that a process must block at a communication call if there is an inbound receive edge and the data has not yet arrived, or if a process arrives late to a collective. This can lead to what we refer to as *slack* time. As an example of the first case, the MPI process with rank 0 arrives before the process with rank 1 at MPI_Finalize in Fig. 1, inducing slack time.

2.2   Assumptions

We use the execution model discussed above to design our optimizing run-time system, which we introduce in the next section. Additionally, we currently focus on applications implemented with the SPMD (Single-Program, Multiple-Data [7]) model and use OpenMP for intra-node parallelism and MPI for inter-node parallelism. We assume that programs use MPI_THREAD_SINGLE, so there are no MPI calls within an OpenMP region. There is nothing that prevents us from conceptually supporting pure MPI programs (i.e., one MPI rank per core), but because our system chooses a given number of cores per processor dynamically, a pure MPI approach would require expensive data redistribution or core over-subscription when the number of cores per processor changes. We assume that an application is composed of several timesteps, and that the programmer identifies the end of a timestep (currently accomplished with inserting MPI_Pcontrol into the application code).

Following the work of Li et al. [18], we also restrict each MPI process (and therefore each OpenMP parallel region), to a single CPU socket/NUMA node, and we assume that we use the same number of active cores for OpenMP regions between consecutive MPI calls. This avoids increasing the number of cache misses due to a change in the number of active cores between two OpenMP regions.

2.3   Challenges

Previous work in the area of power-constrained performance optimization outlines the following challenges in developing a run-time system to adaptively select the best processor configuration for an application. First, the configuration space from which to select the optimal configuration is large, because modern day processors have over a dozen frequency steps and provide 16 or more physical cores. Thus finding the optimal configuration for each processor in a job becomes a large combinatorial problem. Combined with the fact that different configurations can result in vastly different performance [20], the quality of current techniques is unknown. Second, allocating the optimal amount of power to individual processors in a job is complicated by the fact that the critical path may move through multiple processes in a time step. Finally, efficiently monitoring power usage for individual processors allocated to a job and re-allocating power with acceptable overhead is a challenge. *Conductor* addresses all three challenges and provides a novel approach for effective use of large, power-limited systems.

3   *Conductor*: Power-Constrained Runtime Scheduling

Conductor continuously monitors the execution behavior of an application and adjusts its configuration parameters to stay within the job-level power limit while optimizing performance. In particular, we use two knobs in the configuration of an application, on a per-processor basis: the number of active threads in a computation phase and the voltage/frequency setting. For the latter, we use two mechanisms: we use DVFS to control an application's speed and power usage based on observational data (predictive control), while we use RAPL (Runtime Average Power Limit) to set hard power caps for each processor in case our predicted configurations would violate the power constraint (prescriptive control).

The algorithm used in *Conductor* can be split into four steps: initialization, configuration exploration, adaptive reconfiguration, and power reallocation.

3.1 Initialization

During the first timestep of the application, each MPI process is assigned an equal amount of power derived from the job-level power constraint. This is the timestep before *Conductor* starts the configuration exploration step. The process-level power constraint is enforced using RAPL. The execution time and power usage of each application task (i.e., unit of computation between communication events) in the timestep is recorded and stored in a task graph. At the end of the initialization step, the power constraint per process is (temporarily) removed to facilitate the configuration exploration step.

3.2 Configuration Exploration

The next step taken by *Conductor* is to choose the configuration, or combination of thread concurrency level and the DVFS state for each application task. The choice of configuration has a significant impact on program execution time (as much as an 30.9 % difference over our five applications). There are a number of ways to choose the ideal thread concurrency level given a power bound. One way is to profile the code beforehand, which has the distinct disadvantage that it requires at least one extra program execution. Another is to build offline models based on program executions, but the disadvantage is that the model could lack accuracy and generality, especially in the case that a given program differs from the set of programs used to build the model.

In *Conductor*, we take a simpler approach: given n MPI processes executing a given application, we use a small number of application iterations to perform a parallel exploration of the configuration space by selecting a different thread/DVFS configuration on each MPI process. There are k such configurations that we consider, and given n processes, we simply test all of them and choose the best-performing configuration depending on the current process-level power constraint. We retain the set of power-efficient configurations for each task, yielding a per-task power/time Pareto frontier. As mentioned above, we disable the power bound during this step in our current prototype; this can be fixed—at the expense of more overhead—by more carefully executing the configuration exploration.

This clearly adds overhead while we are searching for efficient configurations. In general, it takes $m = \lceil n/k \rceil$ timesteps to finish testing all configurations. Assume an example application with a single task per process in each iteration.

Suppose that during a timestep, the optimal configuration of thread concurrency level and DVFS state takes time t_{opt}, and the process with the slowest configuration on timestep i (during the search phase) takes time t^i_{worst}. Then, the execution time is $T = \sum_{i=1}^{m}(t^i_{worst}) + \sum_{i=m+1}^{n}(t^i_{opt})$, assuming that there are n timesteps in total and m timesteps in the search phase.

Given that high-performance computing applications generally execute many timesteps ($n \gg m$), the overhead in *Conductor*, compared to an oracle that could choose the optimal thread/power configuration a priori, will be generally small because it is amortized over the lifetime of the computation. Because *Conductor* potentially selects the optimal configuration, this overhead can be expressed as $\frac{T}{\sum_{i=1}^{n}(t^i_{opt})}$.

3.3   Adaptive Reconfiguration

The configuration exploration phase makes the assumption that the optimal configuration does not change, which is not true in general. Further, for dynamic applications with load imbalance, this can lead to wasted power during unnecessary wait operations (slack time). To handle both of these issues, we additionally introduce a novel adaptive power-balancing algorithm that changes configurations when appropriate due to application behavior. In addition to application behavior, *Conductor* takes into account the current power constraint, processor DVFS state and thread concurrency level.

***Conductor* Monitoring.** After the thread/DVFS relationships are characterized for each task during the configuration exploration phase, the per-process power constraint is re-enforced using RAPL. *Conductor* monitors application execution during each individual timestep and uses this information to predict the behavior of following, similar tasks. During each timestep, *Conductor* records the elapsed time and power usage for each task in a statically selected configuration. *Conductor* also measures the slack by observing time spent within the MPI library, if any, for each task. This makes the assumption that the significant portion of the time in the MPI library is spent blocking waiting for messages, which works as a useful predictor in the absence of the ability to directly measure slack. This measurement step is borrowed from our previous run-time system, Adagio [23]. It distinguishes tasks based on callstacks and uses a threshold to differentiate slack time from MPI processing time.

Adjusting Task Execution Times. The previous step simply identifies tasks that contain slack. In the following timesteps, *Conductor* adjusts task execution times in such a way that overall execution time will decrease. *Conductor* avoids adding to existing application inter-process communication where possible. Accordingly, *Conductor* handles each task completely locally via the following method.

First, for any task that contains slack, *Conductor* can guarantee that it is *not* on the critical path; by definition, any task that contains slack can be slowed down by some nonzero amount without slowing down overall application execution. Consequently, *Conductor* attempts to fill as much of the slack as possible with computation time without affecting the completion time of the task. For this purpose, *Conductor* leverages both DVFS and thread concurrency levels to fill slack. In other words, *Conductor* will not allow any (non-critical) path through any task with slack to become the critical path. Note that the reason that we adjust DVFS and thread concurrency levels and not the RAPL bound itself is (1) the task granularity is too small to use RAPL, and (2) RAPL does not adjust thread concurrency.

Second, for any task that has no slack, *Conductor* conservatively changes its configuration to the one with next fastest thread/DVFS on the Pareto frontier, which was determined (and saved) as part of the configuration exploration phase. The intuition here is that *Conductor* knows that such a task *may be* critical. Therefore, *Conductor* treats it as a task that should decrease its execution time, because the critical path could potentially decrease. Note that this decision is made locally because the overhead of determining the exact critical path is prohibitive.

3.4   Reallocation of Per-Process Power

While the above step adjusts power consumption using DVFS and thread concurrency selection, the overall power cap per process is as yet unchanged; this

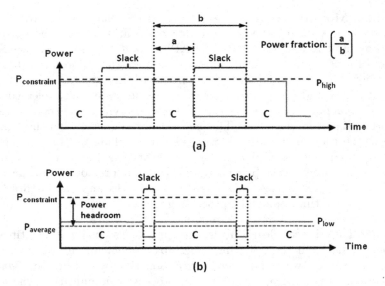

Fig. 2. Opportunity for re-scheduling excess power in an MPI process that runs off the critical path with Adagio. Plot (a) shows near-cap power consumption for computation task (C) at the highest processor DVFS state (highest voltage and frequency). Plot (b) shows lower power consumption for computation task (C) at a lower DVFS/thread concurrency set by Adagio.

cap ensures that the power constraint is not violated. Consequently, even after *Conductor* has adjusted configurations for individual tasks to fill slack, critical tasks may continue to run at or near their process's power constraint, while processes with no critical tasks do not use all of their power allocation. Such a situation may be caused by load imbalance inherent to the application or differences in power efficiency between individual processors [22]. Regardless of the cause, *Conductor* takes advantage of the opportunity to speed up the application by using a global algorithm to reallocate power between processes.

As an example, Fig. 2(a) shows the power consumption profile of an MPI process in an iterative MPI application with repeating computation and communication phases. Since the tasks on this process are off the critical path, there is slack in the communication phase following the computation phase. Figure 2(b) shows that the computation tasks can be slowed down within the slack boundaries using DVFS and thread concurrency selection without affecting the overall execution time.

We define the *power fraction* for a process as the fraction of time between power reallocations that an MPI process spends within a small tolerance of its power constraint. Figure 2(a) shows the fraction of time the process spends operating at power P_{high}, which is essentially at $P_{constraint}$. The process consumes P_{low} power after *Conductor* has slowed down the computation operation as shown in Fig. 2(b). We define the *power headroom* for a processor as the difference between the processor's power constraint and processor's average power consumption. In Fig. 2(b), the power headroom is the difference between $P_{constraint}$ and $P_{average}$.

Conductor gathers power headroom information (which is computed based on *all* tasks) from all processes after a configurable number of timesteps of the application. Using process-level power headroom information, *Conductor* calculates job-level power headroom and reallocates process-level power constraints based on the power fraction. While this technique has the potential disadvantage that the critical path could, for a pathological situation, move through a process that "donates" power to another process, this situation is rare. Moreover, to address it would require power reallocation on task granularity, which is quite complex.

4   Experimental Setup

We performed all experiments on Cab, a 1200-node Xeon E5-2670 cluster at LLNL with an InfiniBand QDR interconnect. Each cab node is composed of two 8-core processors and 32 GB of DRAM.

4.1   Benchmarks and Tools

The codes we use for comparison are CoMD, LULESH 2.0, SP and BT from NAS-MZ, ParaDiS and a synthetic benchmark. These benchmarks were selected because they exhibit performance and scaling behavior typical for a wide range of HPC applications. We note that the most interesting behavior for these benchmarks occurs between 30 and 60 W per processor.

CoMD [1] is a molecular dynamics benchmark. CoMD is unique among our tested benchmarks in that all of its MPI communication is in the form of collectives. As a result, the only tasks that remain for the power-balancing algorithm are to minimize load imbalance by reallocating power between processes at every collective call and to select efficient configurations under processor-level power constraints. We use the input problem size of $20 \times 40 \times 40$ with 100 timesteps.

LULESH 2.0 [17] is a shock hydrodynamics benchmark. In terms of MPI communication, LULESH differs from CoMD in that it relies on a multitude of point-to-point messages between collective calls. This behavior complicates analysis of opportunities to balance power, but we show in Sect. 5.1 that *Conductor* improves performance over state-of-the-art methods for running under a job-level power constraint. We use an input problem size of 32, with 100 timesteps.

ParaDiS [5] is a production dislocation dynamics simulations application that operates on dynamically changing, unbalanced data set sizes across MPI processes. The random nature of data set sizes results in varying computational load, introducing load-imbalance across MPI processes. We use the "Copper" input set provided with ParaDiS with 600 timesteps.

NAS Multi-Zone [27] is an extension of the NAS Parallel Benchmark suite [3]. It involves solving the application benchmarks BT, LU and SP on collections of loosely coupled discretization meshes. In our work, we use Block Tri-diagonal (BT-MZ) and Scalar Penta-diagonal (SP-MZ) algorithms. Both applications use OpenMP for intra-node computation and MPI for inter-node communication. We use a custom class D input size with 500 timesteps.

To quantify how a load-imbalanced application can benefit from power reallocation in *Conductor*, we developed a synthetic benchmark. The synthetic benchmark has two properties. First, it is written in such a way that the best configurations under various power limits use six (out of eight) threads per socket. Second, half of MPI processes execute nearly six times more computation load than the other half, which leads to process-level load imbalance. This synthetic program focuses on the opportunity for *Conductor* to improve performance through power re-allocation for process-level load imbalance.

4.2   Overheads

As we instrument every instance of any potentially blocking MPI call in order to capture slack time and select configurations, our profiler incurs some overhead. The median measurement overhead is $34\,\mu s$ per MPI call and adds less than 0.05 % time to the tested applications. We use 60 configurations that consist of thread concurrency levels of 5 to 8 threads per socket and 15 discrete DVFS states. For SP-MZ, BT-MZ, CoMD and Lulesh, the configuration exploration phase took up to 3 timesteps. For ParaDiS we run the configuration exploration phase locally over each MPI process due to nonuniformity across MPI processes in computation phases. For the configuration exploration phase, we observe an overhead of 1.96 s in the worst case (recall this is amortized over the entire application execution). For the run-time power re-allocation algorithms, all power allocation decisions are coordinated within existing application collective calls, with an average overhead of 566 μs per invocation. For the job sizes tested, we consider this an acceptable trade-off. For larger jobs, a hierarchical power-balancing strategy would be required.

5   Experimental Evaluation

In this section, we compare the performance of *Conductor* to two alternate policies: *Static*, and *Config-Only*. The *Static* algorithm, which is the current state of the art, chooses the largest number of threads possible under the power bound assuming that the frequency is the lowest possible. Then, it increases the frequency as high as possible subject to the power bound. *Config-Only* executes the configuration exploration part of *Conductor* and performs one-time configuration selection for each task, but does *not* execute the adaptive reconfiguration or power reallocation steps.

5.1   Load-Balanced Applications

Figure 3 shows execution times of our three load-balanced applications for each of the three policies. This includes Lulesh on 27 (3^3) MPI processes and BT-MZ

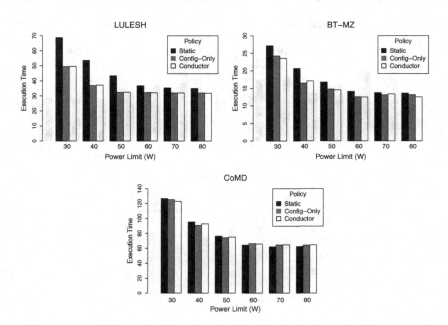

Fig. 3. Comparison of power allocation policies for our three load-balanced applications: Lulesh, BT-MZ, and CoMD. We use 27, 32, and 32 processes, respectively.

and CoMD on 32 processes. The execution times are grouped by process-level power limits on the x-axis ranging 30 W to 80 W in steps of 10 W; each process is confined to a singled processor. We make the following important general observations. First, for lower power limits (30 W and 40 W per processor), *Conductor* performs significantly better than *Static*; the difference is as much as 30.4 % in the case of Lulesh at 27 tasks. The improvement in performance is due to the power-efficient configurations selected by *Conductor* under the MPI process-level power constraint. Second, at higher power limits (60–80 W), the difference between *Static* and *Conductor* remains constant, because the default configuration selected by *Static* and the optimal configuration selected by *Conductor* remain constant. Also, *Conductor* performs almost identically compared to *Config-Only* for the three load-balanced applications. This is because there is virtually no load imbalance. In general, load-balanced applications will execute slightly faster when using *Config-Only* if there is opportunity to select a better configuration over the default configuration chosen by *Static*. This is because both *Config-Only* and *Conductor* choose the same configuration, and *Conductor* does not change the power allocation per MPI process (but does have a slight overhead for monitoring).

5.2   Load-Imbalanced Applications

Figure 4 shows several runs of ParaDiS, SP-MZ, and our synthetic load imbalanced application at 32 (for SP and the synthetic benchmark) and 64 (for

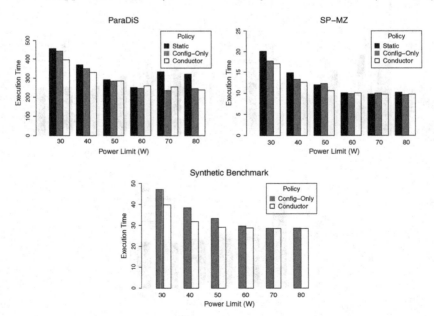

Fig. 4. Comparison of power allocation policies in our three load-imbalanced applications: ParaDis, SP-MZ, and a synthetic microbenchmark. We use 64, 32 and 32 processes, respectively.

ParaDiS) processes under power limits of 30 W to 80 W. For load-imbalanced applications, *Conductor* has each process record power and execution time for all configurations due to potential nonuniformity in the characteristics of computation tasks across MPI processes.

For lower power limits (30 W to 50 W), *Config-Only* benefits from selecting the best configuration for individual computation tasks. However, the benefits of our power re-allocation policy in *Conductor* are more pronounced. The difference in power usage across different MPI processes is up to 15 % and 20 % for process-level power limits of 30 W and 40 W respectively, indicating load-imbalance and potential benefit through power re-allocation.

Compared to *Config-Only*, *Conductor* achieves an improvement of up to 10.4 % (for ParaDiS) and 3.6 % (for SP-MZ) improvement at the power limit of 30 W. For the same power limit, compared to *Static*, *Conductor* achieves an improvement of up to 13.2 % (for ParaDiS) and 14.9 % (for SP-MZ). Compared to *Config-Only*, *Conductor* achieves an improvement of 5.5 % (for ParaDiS) and 5.2 % (for SP-MZ) for a power limit of 40 W.

Compared to *Static*, *Conductor* achieves an improvement of 10.8 % (for ParaDiS) and 15.1 % (for SP-MZ). For a 50-W power limit with ParaDiS, *Conductor* performs similar to *Config-Only* and marginally better than *Static*. However, in case of SP-MZ, *Config-Only* performs marginally worse than *Static* due to non-repeatability in performance at the thread concurrency/DVFS configuration selected at 50 W. At the same time, *Conductor* benefits from load-imbalance and performs better than *Static*.

At higher power limits (60 W to 80 W), *Conductor* generally performs slightly worse than *Config-Only* because the computation tasks consume lower power than the process-level power limit and do not benefit from the power re-allocation scheme. The performance impact of power re-allocation scheme is affected by how accurately it can shuffle power between MPI processes without changing the critical path of the application. We observe that for ParaDiS for power limits of 60 W and 70 W, the power re-allocation scheme alters the critical path of the application before shifting it back during some time steps. As expected, the higher execution times shown by *Static* are due to the choice of sub-optimal configuration of maximum thread concurrency and DVFS state (8 threads per socket and 2.6 GHz on our test system).

For the synthetic program, we show only *Conductor* and *Config-Only*; We leave out the execution times for *Static*, which are inferior to *Config-Only* due to the way we program the synthetic benchmark. For a process-level power limit of 30 W, the computation times in the load-imbalanced synthetic benchmark are 181 ms and 122 ms for *Config-Only* and *Conductor* respectively (*Conductor* is 32 % faster). The corresponding change in frequency was from 1.2 GHz to 1.8 GHz. This improvement in computation time results in an overall execution time improvement of 25 % with *Conductor*. For the power limit of 40 W, the corresponding execution times for computation tasks are 123 ms and 86 ms (30 % faster with *Conductor*), and the corresponding change in frequency was from 1.9 GHz to 2.6 GHz. For higher power limits (60 W to 80 W), the difference between the two policies diminishes as power is not a limiting factor on any process, regardless of the load imbalance.

6 Related Work

The closest work to *Conductor* is our own on Adagio [23] and Jitter [16]. In fact, *Conductor* can be thought of as fusing modified versions of Adagio and Jitter together.

Adagio saves energy in HPC programs with a negligible increase in execution time. *Conductor* differs from Adagio in three important ways. First, *Conductor* optimizes performance under a power bound, which is a completely different goal. Second, *Conductor* determines an efficient thread/frequency configuration, while Adagio assumed single-threaded programs. Third, while *Conductor* and Adagio both decrease frequency of tasks that block (and are therefore off of the critical path), *Conductor* (but not Adagio) simultaneously chooses a faster thread/frequency configuration of tasks that may be on the critical path.

Conductor differs from Jitter in two ways. First, *Conductor* shifts power to improve performance, while Jitter lowers frequency to save energy. Second, *Conductor* measures power and makes some power decisions at the task level, while Jitter *solely* operates at timestep granularity.

There is other work in optimizing performance under a power bound, especially on overprovisioned HPC clusters. This includes an empirical study on the effect of different configurations [20] and choosing configurations via interpolation [26]. In addition, Isci et al. optimized performance under a power bound on a single multicore node [15], and Bailey et al. did the same for a CPU+GPU node [4]. There has also been work on scheduling algorithms to improve performance under a power bound [8,9,25]. Finally, there has been work on overprovisioning for commercial applications in a datacenter, where the goal is increased throughput [10], as well as in improving performance under power constraints in virtualized clusters in datacenters [19].

Other related work is focused on saving power/energy under a time bound in HPC. There has been work using linear programming to find near-optimal energy savings with zero time increase [24]. Other run-time approaches to save energy include those that trade off power/energy saving for (hopefully minimized) performance degradation [6,11,12,18].

7 Conclusion

Current run-time systems are leaving performance on the table and wasting power, and these problems will only become more costly with future generations of supercomputers. *Conductor* effectively allocates power to the parts of the application that primarily impact application performance. In our experiments, we found that selecting the optimal configuration and adaptively re-allocating power to the critical path can result in up to a 30 % performance improvement compared to the state-of-the-art algorithm for the same power constraint. In theory, our system can adapt to the job-level power constraint, which may vary during application execution time because of external factors, and adaptively select application configuration and power allocation. Our results also highlight that incorporating OpenMP (or other configurable node-level parallelism) in addition to MPI goes a long way toward the goal of flexible power and performance management.

Acknowledgements. Part of this work was performed under the auspices of the U.S. Department of Energy by Lawrence Livermore National Laboratory under contract DE-AC52-07NA27344 (LLNL-CONF-667408).

References

1. CoMD (2013). https://github.com/exmatex/CoMD
2. Ashby, S., Beckman, P., Chen, J., Colella, P., Collins, B., Crawford, D., Dongarra, J., Kothe, D., Lusk, R., Messina, P., Mezzacappa, T., Moin, P., Norman, M., Rosner, R., Sarkar, V., Siegel, A., Streitz, F., White, A., Wright, M.: The opportunities and challenges of exascale computing (2010)
3. Bailey, D., Barszcz, E., Barton, J., Browning, D., Carter, R., Dagum, L., Fatoohi, R., Frederickson, P., Lasinski, T., Schreiber, R., et al.: The NAS parallel benchmarks summary and preliminary results. In: Supercomputing, pp. 158–165 (1991)
4. Bailey, P.E., Lowenthal, D.K., Ravi, V., Rountree, B., Schulz, M., de Supinski, B.R.: Adaptive configuration selection for power-constrained heterogeneous systems. In: ICPP (2014)
5. Bulatov, V., Cai, W., Fier, J., Hiratani, M., Hommes, G., Pierce, T., Tang, M., Rhee, M., Yates, K., Arsenlis, T.: Scalable line dynamics in ParaDiS. In: Supercomputing (2004)
6. Cameron, K.W., Feng, X., Ge, R.: Performance-constrained distributed DVS scheduling for scientific applications on power-aware clusters. In: Supercomputing (2005)
7. Darema, F., George, D.A., Norton, V.A., Pfister, G.F.: A single-program-multiple-data computational model for EPEX/FORTRAN. Parallel Comput. **7**(1), 11–24 (1988)
8. Etinski, M., Corbalan, J., Labarta, J., Valero, M.: Optimizing job performance under a given power constraint in HPC centers. In: IGCC (2010)
9. Etinski, M., Corbalan, J., Labarta, J., Valero, M.: Linear programming based parallel job scheduling for power constrained systems. In: HPCS (2011)
10. Femal, M.E., Freeh, V.W.: Safe overprovisioning: using power limits to increase aggregate throughput. In: Falsafi, B., VijayKumar, T.N. (eds.) PACS 2004. LNCS, vol. 3471, pp. 150–164. Springer, Heidelberg (2005)
11. Ge, R., Feng, X., Feng, W., Cameron, K.W.: CPU Miser: a performance-directed, run-time system for power-aware clusters. In: ICPP (2007)
12. Hsu, C.-H., Feng, W.-C.: A power-aware run-time system for high-performance computing. In: Supercomputing, November 2005
13. InsideHPC. Power consumption is the exascale gorilla in the room. http://insidehpc.com/2010/12/10/power-consumption-is-the-exascale-gorilla-in-the-room/

14. Intel. Intel-64 and IA-32 Architectures Software Developer's Manual, Volumes 3A and 3B: System Programming Guide, December 2011
15. Isci, C., Buyuktosunoglu, A., Cher, C., Bose, P., Martonosi, M.: An analysis of efficient multi-core global power management policies: maximizing performance for a given power budget. In: IEEE/ACM International Symposium on Microarchitecture, pp. 347–358 (2006)
16. Kappiah, N., Freeh, V.W., Lowenthal, D.K.: Just in time dynamic voltage scaling: exploiting inter-node slack to save energy in MPI programs. In: Supercomputing, November 2005
17. Karlin, I., Keasler, J., Neely, R.: Lulesh 2.0 updates and changes. Technical report LLNL-TR-641973, August 2013
18. Li, D., de Supinski, B., Schulz, M., Cameron, K., Nikolopoulos, D.: Hybrid MPI/OpenMP power-aware computing. In: IPDPS (2010)
19. Nathuji, R., Schwan, K., Somani, A., Joshi, Y.: VPM tokens: virtual machine-aware power budgeting in datacenters. Cluster Comput. 12(2), 189–203 (2009)
20. Patki, T., Lowenthal, D.K., Rountree, B., Schulz, M., de Supinski, B.R.: Exploring hardware overprovisioning in power-constrained, high performance computing. In: ICS (2013)
21. Pawlowski, S.S.: Exascale science: the next frontier in high performance computing. In: International Conference on Supercomputing, June 2010
22. Rountree, B., Ahn, D.H., de Supinski, B.R., Lowenthal, D.K., Schulz, M.: Beyond DVFS: a first look at performance under a hardware-enforced power bound. In: HPPAC (2012)
23. Rountree, B., Lowenthal, D.K., de Supinski, B., Schulz, M., Freeh, V.W.: Adagio: making DVS practical for complex HPC applications. In: ICS (2009)
24. Rountree, B., Lowenthal, D.K., Funk, S., Freeh, V.W., de Supinski, B., Schulz, M.: Bounding energy consumption in large-scale MPI programs. In: Supercomputing, November 2007
25. Sarood, O., Langer, A., Gupta, A., Kale, L.: Maximizing throughput of overprovisioned HPC data centers under a strict power budget. In: Supercomputing (2014)
26. Sarood, O., Langer, A., Kalé, L., Rountree, B., De Supinski, B.: Optimizing power allocation to CPU and memory subsystems in overprovisioned HPC systems. In: CLUSTER (2013)
27. van der Wijngaart, R.F., Haopiang, J.: NAS parallel multi-zone benchmarks (2003)

A Machine Learning Approach for a Scalable, Energy-Efficient Utility-Based Cache Partitioning

Isa Ahmet Guney, Abdullah Yildiz, Ismail Ugur Bayindir,
Kemal Cagri Serdaroglu, Utku Bayik, and Gurhan Kucuk[✉]

Department of Computer Engineering, Yeditepe University, Istanbul, Turkey
{iguney,ayildiz,ubayindir,kserdaroglu,
utkubayik,gkucuk}@cse.yeditepe.edu.tr
http://cse.yeditepe.edu.tr

Abstract. In multi- and many-core processors, a shared Last Level Cache (LLC) is utilized to alleviate the performance problems resulting from long latency memory instructions. However, an unmanaged LLC may become quite useless when the running threads have conflicting interests. In one extreme, a thread can make benefit from every portion of the cache whereas, in the other end, another thread may just want to thrash the whole LLC. Recently, a variety of way-partitioning mechanisms are introduced to improve cache performance. Today, almost all of the studies utilize the Utility-based Cache Partitioning (UCP) algorithm as their allocation policy. However, the UCP look-ahead algorithm, although it provides a better utility measure than its greedy counterpart, requires a very complex hardware circuitry and dissipates a considerable amount of energy at the end of each decision period. In this study, we propose an offline supervised machine learning algorithm that replaces the UCP look-ahead circuitry with a circuitry requiring almost negligible hardware and energy cost. Depending on the cache and processor configuration, our thorough analysis and simulation results show that the proposed mechanism reduces up to 5 % of the overall transistor count and 5 % of the overall processor energy without introducing any performance penalty.

Keywords: Last level cache · Way-partitioning · Utility-based cache partitioning · Machine learning

1 Introduction

In a typical multi-core processor setup, a shared Last Level Cache (LLC) is usually needed as a last resort for hiding the latency of the main memory. In these processors, each running thread assumes that it has the full control over the cache. Obviously, when the multi-core processor allows full LLC accesses from each thread, the required control circuitry for the cache becomes very simple. However, this naive approach does not perform very well, when the only major concern is the improved processor throughput.

© Springer International Publishing Switzerland 2015
J.M. Kunkel and T. Ludwig (Eds.): ISC High Performance 2015, LNCS 9137, pp. 409–421, 2015.
DOI: 10.1007/978-3-319-20119-1_29

The actual source of performance drop can be explained with the variability of the run-time behavior of each running thread. First, a thread may go into various program phases at different time periods. For example, it can start with a memory-intensive phase, which initializes all the data structures it would like to use. Then, the thread may step into a computation-intensive phase, which might not require any memory instruction. After that, the thread may jump into a cache thrashing phase, which generates heavy memory traffic with no address locality. This temporal change in behavior of each thread shows that the LLC may be treated differently by each running thread at different times. Secondly, in a multi-core processor, there might be multiple threads, which run simultaneously. The behavior of each thread is also affected by the program phases of the other running threads. For instance, when a thread jumps into a memory-intensive phase and the other running threads go into computation-intensive phases, the working set of the first thread may fit into the LLC. In such a case, the thread may perform at its peak performance. However, in another run, when the memory-intensive phases of the simultaneously running threads overlap, the working set of the first thread may no longer fit into the LLC resulting in a noticeable performance drop. This type of variability in thread behavior on neighboring cores shows that the LLC may be treated differently by each running thread with different workloads.

To manage the LLC in a more-efficient way by dedicating portions of it to simultaneously running threads, various cache partitioning mechanisms are recently proposed [1–6]. A partitioning mechanism consists of a sequence of steps: (1) an allocation algorithm, (2) a victim selection policy, and, finally, (3) a size enforcement mechanism. In the initial step, the allocation algorithm decides how much of the cache is beneficial to each thread for satisfying an overall target metric. This target metric is usually chosen to be the processor throughput, such as the Instructions Per Cycle (IPC). However, recently, other metrics, such as fairness and power, are also becoming popular, as well. The well-known Utility-based Cache Partitioning (UCP) algorithm completes this step by calculating a utility metric for each running thread [1]. This utility metric can be calculated by the help of extra cache structures, known as the Auxiliary Tag Directories (ATD). In the end, the thread with the best utility score receives the largest portion of the LLC.

The allocation algorithms of the UCP mechanism are heavily adopted by other partitioning mechanisms such as PIPP, Vantage and Futility Scaling [2,5,6]. These methods usually ignore the second step and mainly focus on the third step of the LLC partitioning, the size enforcement mechanism. In the original UCP study, the size enforcement mechanism is known to be quite strict. When, the allocation algorithm decides that m ways of an N-way cache must be given to a thread, those m ways are immediately dedicated to that thread and no other thread can claim new cache lines from those cache ways, afterwards. However, there is no clue given on how those m ways are selected among N cache ways in the original UCP paper. The second step of the partitioning algorithm should decide on the portion of the cache that is to be taken from a thread and given to another one. This can be a very complicated task, especially when the number of receiver-threads and/or giver-threads is more than one. Besides, certain questions should be addressed by the victim selection policy, such as which cache ways are to be abandoned when a thread is to loose cache partitions? or which cache ways are to be allocated to achieve better performance when a thread is to receive cache partitions?. In pseudo partitioning mechanisms, such as PIPP and Vantage, a target size cannot be immediately allocated to a thread, and the time that is required to reach to a target partition size may be considerably long when the difference between the current partition size and the target size is large. This slow-pace size adaptation schemes might have a detrimental effect on the overall cache performance, since the target size is almost always missed in an environment in which the behaviors of the running threads are quickly and continuously changing.

In this study, we propose a new allocation policy that is based on an offline supervised machine learning approach. Specifically, we take the highly complex look-ahead allocation algorithm of the UCP, and turn it into a series of simpler hardware functions. The resulting mechanism has four main advantages. First, we show that the resulting circuitry is much less complex than the original look-ahead hardware, and it requires a smaller number of transistors. Second, our simulation results show that energy dissipation of the proposed mechanism is much lower. Third, the time complexity of our algorithm is just $O(1)$ whereas the time complexity of the original algorithm is $O(N^2)$. Thus, we named our proposed algorithm as the *look-up* mechanism, since the original look-ahead algorithm is really turned into a series of simple look-up functions, which might be evaluated at a single step. Finally, fourth, we show that the proposed look-up allocation mechanism performs no worse than the original look-ahead mechanism, on the average. Here, we must also state that, just like in the original UCP paper, we only focus on a multicore processor with single-threaded cores. As a result, hereafter, we use the terms *thread* and *core*, interchangeably.

The paper is organized as follows. In Sect. 2, we describe the current state of the art on the UCP mechanism, and give the details of the look-ahead algorithm. This section also gives an extra motivation for our proposed design. The third section focuses on a machine learning-based technique, the look-up algorithm, which tries faithfully mimicking the behavior of the original look-ahead algorithm. In Sect. 4, we elaborate our experimental methodology, and provide the results of our tests comparing our proposed mechanism with the original algorithm in terms of processor performance, energy and complexity. Finally, in Sect. 5, we conclude our study.

2 The Current State of the Art: Original UCP Look-Ahead Algorithm

The original partitioning algorithm, which is shown in Algorithm 1, is known as the UCP look-ahead allocation algorithm [1]. Its name implies that it looks further in terms of cache partitions and is wiser than a simple greedy approach. The input of the algorithm comes from the ATDs that enable the control logic to count the number of cache misses for each thread when the number of allocated cache ways are changed. The *utility* metric of a thread is measured by the number of cache ways, which the thread really makes any benefit of. At each round, the algorithm calculates the maximum marginal utility for each thread, and, then, selects the thread with the maximum of individual maximum marginal utility values. The marginal utility is the change in number of cache misses when the number of ways allocated to a thread is increased. For instance, if a thread currently owns m cache ways, and when we allocate n more cache ways if the number of cache misses is reduced by r, the marginal utility for this instance becomes simply r/n. To calculate the marginal utility on hardware, we only need the cache hit counts for each way in the ATD structure of each thread.

Algorithm 1. The original look-ahead algorithm

1: allocations[i] ← 1, for each thread i
2: balance ← (Number of cache ways - Number of threads)
3: **while** balance is not zero **do**
4:      **for** i in threads **do**
5:          maxmu ← -1
6:          blocksRequired[i] ← 0, for each thread i
7:          **for** j=1 to balance **do**
8:              mu ← 0
9:              **for** w=allocations[i] to allocations[i]+j **do**
10:                 **for** s=0 to MAXDSS **do**
11:                     mu ← mu + ATD[i][s][w]
12:                 **end for**
13:             **end for**
14:             mu ← mu / j
15:             **if** mu <maxmu **then**
16:                 maxmu ← mu
17:                 blocksRequired[i] ← j
18:             **end if**
19:         **end for**
20:     **end for**
21:     winner is thread with maximum value of maxmu
22:     allocations[winner] ← allocations[winner] + blocksRequired[winner]
23:     balance ← balance - blocksRequired[winner]
24: **end while**

The worst case time complexity of the algorithm is $O(N^2)$, since there are two nested loops within the algorithm: (1) The outer loop that continues until *balance* becomes zero, and (2) The inner j loop that iterates through the remaining *balance* number of cache ways. Here, we assume that the most inner s loop, which calculates the sum of hit counts of each way, is totally avoided by storing cumulative hit values in small vectors of N elements per ADT before running the look-ahead algorithm, where N is the associativity of the cache.

The hardware complexity of the look-ahead mechanism might be enormous when the allocation decisions are instantly needed. However, there is always enough time slack for this type of a process, assuming that this task is not in the critical path of the processor. In this study, we assume that there are enough 32-bit adders and T 32-bit dividers to calculate a single iteration of the Look-ahead algorithm for T threads. Considering the ATD structure described in the original study, and assuming that the sum of hit counts for $MAXDSS$ number of sets are read from a precalculated table, the number of adders required for a single iteration of the algorithm simply becomes $T \times (W \times (W + 1)) / 2$, where T denotes the number of threads and W is the number of cache ways.

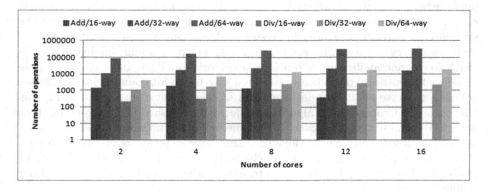

Fig. 1. The number of arithmetic operations required for each run of the original UCP look-ahead algorithm

Finally, we also studied the number of addition and division operations required for different processor and cache configurations. As shown in Fig. 1, these numbers are quite high even for a two-core processor with an eight-way set-associative LLC configuration. Note that, in the bar chart, we discarded some configurations, which do not make any sense, such as a 16-core processor with a 16-way set-associative LLC. This figure further motivates our study, and it also demonstrates that the look-ahead algorithm has an inherent complexity issues originated from its nature. There are alternative implementation methods with less number of addition and division operations, as well. For instance, we can apply a memoization technique in hardware by keeping an SRAM structure, which holds all the precalculated values of all hit counter combinations, instead of recalculating them by reusing the adders and dividers. However, in such a case the design complexity shifts to the SRAM structure. The power and latency cost of calculating the result of an addition operation by the use of an adder circuitry would be comparable, if not lower than, to the look up, retrieval and routing cost of the same data from an SRAM structure. What we aim in this study is to get rid off the complex hardware required by the look-ahead mechanism and still be able to perform as well as the original algorithm.

3 The Look-Up Algorithm: A Complexity-Effective, Power-Efficient Look-Ahead Variant

Application of machine learning techniques to the area of computer architecture research is not new. Choi et al. investigate learning-based simultaneous multithreading (SMT) resource distribution techniques [7]. In that notable work, the authors first study the limits of the SMT resource distribution by applying an ideal off-line exhaustive search technique. Next, they propose a runtime learning mechanism that varies the resource share of the multiple threads towards the direction that improves the overall processor throughput. In another study, Bitirgen et al. propose an Artificial Neural Network (ANN) hardware that learns each thread's performance response to different resource distributions on a multicore processor [8]. The authors claim that their approach makes it possible to anticipate the system-level performance impact of resource allocation decision at runtime. In this study, we carry out a similar approach. First, we apply an off-line learning approach to extract coefficients of our look-up algorithm. Then, at runtime, we plug those coefficients and periodically collected way-based hit counters into hardware counters to make allocation decisions on LLC cache ways. As a result, for a specific cache configuration, our algorithm requires a look-ahead UCP-based analysis prior to its deployment. However, at runtime, we do not need further offline analyses. This analysis can be even done on a simulator. All that is needed is to set a vector of precalculated theta values, which are obtained at the end of this offline phase. In this section, we would like to focus on the detailed description of our offline learning phase.

The gradient descent is an algorithm, which is used for minimizing functions in the context of supervised machine learning. Given a function defined by a set of parameters, the gradient descent algorithm starts with an initial set of parameter values and iteratively minimizes a defined function. We have applied gradient descent to minimize our squared error cost function J in our linear regression method. Equation 1 shows how gradient descent updates each coefficient Θ_i on each iteration. In our setup, we set the total number of iterations to 10000. In Eq. 1, α represents the learning rate, which controls the size of each step we take downhill in the search space to reach a local minima.

$$\Theta_i = \Theta_i - \alpha \frac{\partial}{\partial \Theta_i} J(\Theta_i) \tag{1}$$

In our linear regression model, we used the training data gathered from the look-ahead algorithm. This data consist of cache hit counters obtained from the ATD structures interpreted as explanatory variables and allocation decisions of the look-ahead algorithm as dependent variables. In our offline learning experiments, we found that only first four cache hit counters of an ADT is representative enough for training purposes, and we carried out our tests by integrating those four hit counters to our offline learning phase. At the end of the learning phase, we extract T different functions for T threads by applying T different regression models based on our training data. Note that, the proposed look-up algorithm, which is given in Algorithm 2, has a time complexity of O(1) since the number of operations is fixed, and that number does not change as the associativity of the cache increases.

Algorithm 2. The proposed look-up algoritm

1: totalScore ← 0
2: total ← 0
3: input ← number of hits obtained from ADT
4: size ← the number of inputs - 1
5: theta ← set of coefficients obtained from offline learning
6: numWays ← number of cache ways
7: numThreads ← number of threads
8: **for** i in threads **do**
9:     score[i] ← input[0] * theta[i][0] + ... + input[size] * theta[i][size]
10:    **if** score[i] <0 **then**
11:        score[i] ← 0
12:    **else**
13:        totalScore ← totalScore + score[i]
14:    **end if**
15: **end for**
16: **if** totalScore = 0 **then**
17:    **for** i in threads **do**
18:        allocations[i] ← numWays / numThreads
19:    **end for**
20: **else**
21:    **for** i = 0 to numThreads -2 **do**
22:        rate ← score[i] / totalScore
23:        allocations[i] ← 1 + round(rate * (numWays - numThreads))
24:        total ← total + allocations[i]
25:    **end for**
26:    allocations[numThreads-1] ← numWays - total
27: **end if**

After careful observation of the results, we found that the number of ways allocated to threads are not linearly correlated with the number of hits obtained from the ATD structures, as we already expected. Actually, number of hits each thread receives in their corresponding ATDs range over a wide scale, and it would be very naive to expect definite answers from any type of learning algorithm in such situations. However, we observed that the relation among cache hits from different ATDs is somewhat correlated with the resulting allocations. With these findings, we designed a mechanism which distributes ways to threads based on the weighted average of calculated scores. Specifically, our control mechanism computes the score of each thread using the formula in Eq. 2 at runtime. Each thread uses its own set of coefficients (Θ) determined by our offline learning phase. Meanwhile, all threads share the same input set (x) provided by the set of ATD structures.

$$score = \Theta_0 + \sum_{i=1}^{n} \Theta_i x_i \qquad (2)$$

Due to the existence of negative values among coefficients, in some cases the score of a thread can become negative, which may cause our mechanism to allocate a negative number of ways to a thread. To avoid such inconsistency problems, the score of a thread is reset to zero when it becomes negative.

The functions obtained from the regression analysis do not always smoothly map the number of ways that are actually allocated by the original look-ahead algorithm. To ensure fairness among threads(with respect to their scores) and all ways are allocated to threads, number of ways allocated to each thread is computed using the weighted average of scores, as shown in Eq. 3. Our mechanism guarantees that each thread receives at least one cache way and the last thread receives the remaining cache ways (not shown in the equation).

$$ways_j = 1 + Round(\frac{score_j}{total\_score} * (num\_ways - num\_threads)) \qquad (3)$$

4   Tests and Results

We use MacSim [9] for evaluating our proposed mechanism. Details of the processor configuration are kept similar to that of the original UCP study, and given in Table 1. All parameters except number of cores and the associativity of the LLC cache are kept constant. For creating workloads, we use random combinations of 14 spec2006 benchmarks (astar, bzip2, hmmer, omnetpp, soplex, sjeng, mcf, namd, libquantum, milc, href264, povray, gcc, and lbm) [10]. Fifty workloads are simulated for the 2-core and the 4-core configurations, whereas twenty workloads are simulated for the 8-core configuration. All workloads are simulated for 50 million cycles, starting from the SimPoint locations [11].

We start by elaborating the hardware complexity reduction that we can achieve with our proposed approach. For the evaluations of our proposed approach and the comparisons with the look-ahead algorithm, arithmetical circuits for both algorithms are designed in Verilog HDL at RTL level and then the evaluations are made on Synopsys Design Compiler by using Cadence 45-nm Generic Process Design Kit (GPDK) without any explicit or particular optimization.

Table 1. Processor configuration

Core	8-way, 256-entry ROB, out-of-order execution
	1-thread per core
L1 Cache	32 KB I-Cache and 16 Kb D-Cache;
	64 byte line size and 3 cycle access latency
L2 Cache	64 byte line size, 1024 sets
	15 cycle access latency

Table 2. Comparison between two methods with respect to transistor counts (t.c.) and arithmetic operations per partitioning

# of cores	# of ways	t.c. for addition		t.c. for division		t.c. for multiplication	
		look-ahead	look-up	look-ahead	look-up	look-ahead	look-up
2	16	382.1 K	433 K	711.6 K	51 K	0	406.7 K
	32	1.6 M		2.2 M			
	64	6.4 M		5.4 M			
4	16	764.2 K	917 K	6.8 M	101.7 K		1.6 M
	32	3.2 M		9.9 M			
	64	12.8 M		16.2 M			
8	16	1.5 M	2 M	19 M	203.3 K		6.5 M
	32	6.3 M		25.1 M			
	64	25.7 M		37.7 M			

Furthermore, all the arithmetical circuits for both algorithms (look-ahead and look-up) are designed with 32-bit I/O size and transistor counts are derived from the equivalent NAND gate count of the circuits and the respective technology library characteristics.

The Table 2 shows the overall breakdown in transistor counts of the two rival approach for various machine configurations. For the 2-core configuration with a 16-way LLC, the look-up algorithm has 19 % less number of transistors compared to the look-ahead algorithm. Here, we show that our algorithm is scalable, since we do not utilize any extra hardware for the 32-way and 64-way cache configurations. As a result, our transistor count savings become 77 % for the 32-way and 92 % for the 64-way LLC configurations. When we move to the 4-core configuration, the savings become much more clear. For the 16-way, 32-way and 64-way LLC configurations, the savings are 65 %, 80 % and 91 %,respectively. Finally, for the 8-core configurations, we achieve similar savings for the same three LLC configurations, 58 %, 72 % and 86 %, respectively.

In its extreme case, with an 8-core, 64-way LLC configuration, the original mechanism requires almost 64M transistors. If we consider a processor core that consists of 1 billion transistors, that means the UCP lookahead circuitry covers more than 6 % of the overall die area. These results show that the scalability of the original mechanism is quite limited whereas our proposed mechanism always requires less than 1 % of the overall die area in all configurations.

Next, we focus on the energy comparison of the two approaches. Figure 2 shows the energy dissipation of the look-ahead and the proposed look-up mechanisms compared to the energy dissipation of a Register File (RF). To calculate the energy dissipation on the RF, first we used the CACTI tool [12] to collect single read and write energy of an SRAM structure in the size of a Register File. Then, by the help of the processor simulator, we obtained average number of read and write accesses to this structure, in the clock cycle granularity. Finally, we multiplied energy and access numbers to calculate the average energy dissipation of the RF structure in a single clock cycle. For calculating the energy dissipation of the look-ahead and the look-up algorithms, we collected energy figures from the already published papers for a single CMOS adder, a multiplier and a division circuitry [13–15]. We scaled all energy numbers to 45 nm process technology, and, then, we multiplied those numbers with the number of operations required for each algorithm. Figure 2 presents energy results for two different UCP periods, 5M and 3M clock cycles. Here, we show that the look-ahead algorithm is not scalable for large machine configurations with large LLC associativities. Especially, when the UCP period is stretched to 3M cycles, the look-ahead algorithm starts dissipating as much as the half of the RF energy, in 8-core and 64-way LLC configuration.

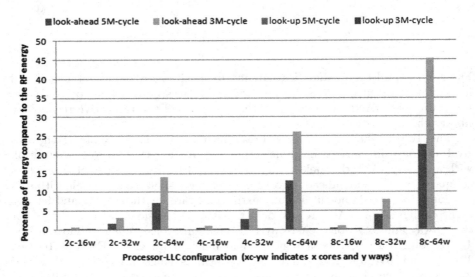

Fig. 2. Energy dissipation of the look-ahead and look-up mechanism compared to the energy dissipation of a single Register File in 5M- and 3M-cycle of UCP periods

In one of the milestone papers by D.Folegnani and A.Gonzalez, the percentage of energy dissipation of a RF is evaluated to be approximately 12 % of the overall energy dissipation [16]. These results shows that, in the extreme case, the original mechanism dissipates as much as 5 % of the overall processor energy. On the contrary, the look-up algorithm dissipates at most 0.06 % of the overall RF energy, across all configurations, and it is scalable to manycore architectures, as well.

Figure 3 shows the performance of the look-up algorithm in all 50 workloads tested for the 2-core configuration. The results are normalized to the performance of the look-ahead algorithm, and workloads are sorted from the worst performing to the best performing for each legend separately. On the average, for the 8-way and 16-way LLC configurations, our look-up algorithm performs 0.41 % better and 0.12 % worse than the look-ahead algorithm, respectively. Similarly, Fig. 4 shows the performance of the look-up algorithm in all 50 workloads tested for the 4-core configuration. On the average, for the 16-way and 32-way LLC

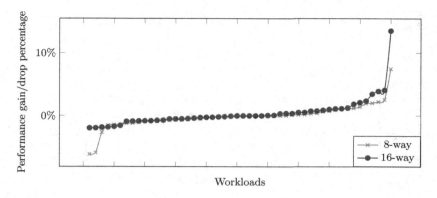

Fig. 3. S-curve model of the look-up algorithm for the 2-core configuration

configurations, our look-up algorithm performs 0.20 % and 0.09 % better than the look-ahead algorithm, respectively. However, in the 64-way configuration, the look-up performs slightly worse (0.27 %), on the average across all simulated workloads. Finally, Fig. 5 shows the performance results for the 8-core 32-way and 64-way LLC configurations, respectively. Here, our proposed look-up algorithm performs 0.20 % worse (for the 32-way LLC) and 1.07 % worse (for the 64-way LLC) than the look-ahead algorithm, on the average. 8-core results show that when the scale of the multicore processor increases, the learning algorithm that is based on a first-order optimization algorithm starts to fail. However, compared to the scale of energy and complexity reduction in such a large processor configuration, we believe that these performance results are still within acceptable limits. These results show that, although, our look-up algorithm is not perfect while tracking down every allocation of the original algorithm, similar performance figures still can be achieved, on the average.

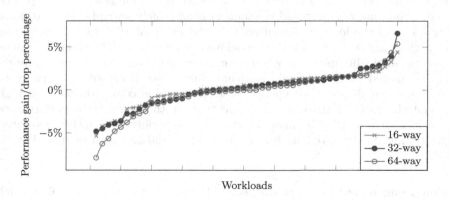

Fig. 4. S-curve model of the look-up algorithm for the 4-core configuration

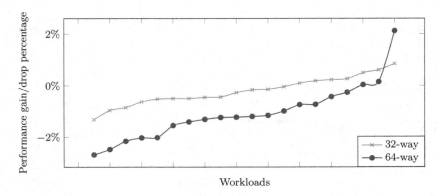

Fig. 5. S-curve model of the look-up algorithm for the 8-core configuration

5   Conclusion

The cache partitioning is an interesting research area for multicore processors, especially when there is a last level cache structure shared by the running cores. The utility-based cache partitioning (UCP) is one of the most popular way-partitioning mechanisms, in the literature. It proposes a way allocation algorithm, known as the *look-ahead*, to assign cache ways to running threads according to their cache utilization. However, the look-ahead algorithm requires a rather complex hardware especially when the number of cores and cache ways are large. Additionally, its power constraints and large time complexity affect its scalability. In this study, we propose the look-up algorithm, which is devised from an offline supervised machine learning approach with time complexity of $O(1)$. Specifically, the proposed algorithm aims to mimic the behavior of the UCP look-ahead algorithm by applying the runtime collected cache statistics on hardware functions that are generated by the offline learning step. The results show that our proposed mechanism is extremely scalable. The hardware complexity of the look-up algorithm is in the range of 19 % to 92 % less than the original algorithm for a various machine configurations. The transistor count reduction might be up to 5 % when we consider a billion-transistor core. Moreover, compared to the original algorithm, our proposed algorithm saves up to 5 % of the overall processor energy for large machine configurations and high associativity LLCs. Finally, we also show that, on the average, the performance of the look-up algorithm is almost identical to the performance of the look-ahead algorithm, in all simulated machine configurations and across all simulated workloads.

Acknowledgement. This work is supported by the Scientific and Technical Research Council of Turkey (TUBITAK) for *Wise-Cache* Project under Grant No: 114E119.

References

1. Qureshi, M.K., Patt, Y.N.: Utility-based cache partitioning: a low-overhead, high-performance, runtime mechanism to partition shared caches. In: Proceedings of the 39th Annual IEEE/ACM International Symposium on Microarchitecture, pp. 423–432. IEEE Computer Society, Washington, DC (2006)
2. Xie, Y., Loh, G.H.: PIPP: promotion/insertion pseudo-partitioning of multi-core shared caches. In: SIGARCH Computer Architecture News, pp. 174–183. ACM, New York (2009)
3. Qureshi, M.K., Jaleel, A., Patt, Y.N., Steely, S.C., Emer, J.: Adaptive insertion policies for high performance caching. In: Proceedings of the 34th Annual International Symposium on Computer Architecture, pp. 381–391. ACM, New York (2007)
4. Jaleel, A., Hasenplaugh, W., Qureshi, M., Sebot, J., Steely, Jr., S., Emer, J.: Adaptive insertion policies for managing shared caches. In: Proceedings of the 17th International Conference on Parallel Architectures and Compilation Techniques, pp. 208–219. ACM, New York (2008)
5. Sanchez, D., Kozyrakis, C.: Vantage: scalable and efficient fine-grain cache partitioning. In: SIGARCH Computer Architecture News, pp. 57–68. ACM, New York (2011)
6. Wang, R., Chen, L.: Futility scaling: high-associativity cache partitioning. In: 47th IEEE/ACM International Symposium on Microarchitecture (MICRO) (2014)
7. Choi, S., Yeung, D.: Learning-based SMT processor resource distribution via hill-climbing. In: SIGARCH Computer Architecture News, pp. 239–251. ACM, New York (2006)
8. Bitirgen, R., Ipek, E., Martinez, J.F.: Coordinated management of multiple interacting resources in chip multiprocessors: a machine learning approach. In: Proceedings of the 41st Annual IEEE/ACM International Symposium on Microarchitecture (MICRO 41), pp. 318–329. IEEE, Computer Society, Washington DC (2008)
9. Macsim simulator. http://code.google.eom/p/macsim/
10. Henning, J.: SPEC CPU2006 benchmark descriptions. ACM SIGARCH Comput. Archit. News **34**(4), 1–17 (2006)
11. Hamerly, G., Perelman, E., Lau, J., Calder, B.: SimPoint 3.0: faster and more flexible program phase analysis. J. Instr. Level Parallelism **7**, 1–28 (2005)
12. Muralimanohar, N., Balasubramonian, R., Jouppi, N.: Optimizing NUCA organizations and wiring alternatives for large caches with CACTI 6.0. In: Proceedings of the 40th Annual IEEE/ACM International Symposium on Microarchitecture (MICRO 40), pp. 3–14. IEEE Computer Society, Washington, DC (2007)
13. Tran, A.T., Baas, B.M.: Design of an energy-efficient 32-bit adder operating at sub-threshold voltages in 45-nm CMOS. In: Third International Conference on Communications and Electronics (ICCE), pp. 87–91 (2010)
14. Mehmood, N., Hansson, M., Alvandpour, A.: An energy-efficient 32-bit multiplier architecture in 90-nm CMOS. In: IEEE 24th Norchip Conference, pp. 35–38 (2006)
15. Pham, T.N., Swartzlander, E.E.: Design of Radix 4 SRT dividers for single precision DSP in deep submicron CMOS technology. In: IEEE International Symposium on Signal Processing and Information Technology, pp. 236–241 (2006)
16. Folegnani, D., Gonzalez, A.: Energy-effective issue logic. In: IEEE International Symposium on Computer Architecture, pp. 230–239 (2001)

A Case Study - Cost of Preemption for Urgent Computing on SuperMUC

Siew Hoon Leong[1,2]($\boxtimes$) and Dieter Kranzlmüller[1,2]

[1] Leibniz Supercomputing Centre, Garching Near Munich, Germany
siew-hoon.leong@lrz.de, h.leong@campus.lmu.de
[2] Ludwig-Maximilians-Universität München, Munich, Germany

Abstract. Urgent computing requires computations to commence in short order and complete within a stipulated deadline so as to support mitigation activities in preparation, response and recovery from an event that requires immediate attention. As such, acquiring computation resources swiftly is crucial. Preemptive scheduling, terminating an existing job(s) to make way for an urgent job, is one of the most common approach considered. However, public resource providers are typically faced with policy restrictions that forbid them from allowing preemption. The interruption of existing jobs is believed to have a significant consequence, i.e. cost, to the users and resource providers. This case study on a public HPC resource, SuperMUC, hosted at Leibniz Supercomputing Centre aims to study the cost of preemption. Two cost models, least cost and least disruptive, will be used. With this, we want to demonstrate that the cost of preemption is in fact much lower in comparison to the loss mitigation that can be achieved by allowing an urgent computation. The ultimate aim is to provide evidence to convince policy makers on the feasibility and benefits of supporting urgent computing on public resources.

Keywords: Urgent computing · Cost · Preemption · HPC · SuperMUC

1 Introduction

Public high performance computing (HPC) infrastructure is an untapped source of computation resources that urgent computing can leverage on. This is particularly the case in Germany where there are three national HPC centres, together known as the Gauss Centre for Supercomputing (GCS). Each of these national HPC centres offers petaflops of peak performance that can compute most if not all urgent computing use cases swiftly, i.e. within the stipulated deadline, and potentially mitigate the loss that are typically in the range of millions to billions.

In spite of the many advantages of public HPC resources, they are not commonly being leveraged upon for urgent computing [7]. Since urgent events typically occur unexpectedly and require computation resources in short order, the existing mode of operation is unable to support it. The usual advance reservation strategy,

© Springer International Publishing Switzerland 2015
J.M. Kunkel and T. Ludwig (Eds.): ISC High Performance 2015, LNCS 9137, pp. 422–433, 2015.
DOI: 10.1007/978-3-319-20119-1_30

which requires knowing how much and when the resources are required in advance, is unable to cater to the unexpectedness and in short order characteristics.

Preemptive scheduling, a common strategy in real-time computing, is arguably the most effective method to get resources on public HPC resources swiftly when an urgent event occurs unexpectedly. However, this requires a change in the mode of operation, i.e. policy change, since existing users will be affected. A cost study of preemption on an existing HPC resource, SuperMUC, hosted at Leibniz Supercomputing Centre (LRZ), one of the three national HPC centres in GCS, is thus conducted. The aim is to show that the cost of preemption is in fact insignificant when compared to the loss of an urgent event. Two cost approaches, the least cost (LC) and least disruptive (LD), are used to demonstrate the cost of preemption. The LC approach is chosen to illustrate the stand, i.e. minimum cost, of policy makers while the LD approach is selected to reflect the resource provider' concerns, i.e. disrupting minimum jobs and users.

This paper is organised as follows. In Sect. 2, related work in preemption is shared. Technical information on SuperMUC and how it compares to similar on-demand resources from Amazon are discussed in Sect. 3. The cost of preemption is elaborated in Sect. 4. Section 5 illustrates the two cost approaches, LC and LD. The result is shared in Sect. 6. Finally the conclusion and future work are discussed in Sect. 7.

2 Related Work

Preemption is not a new concept. It is a technique that is utilised by the kernels of most modern computers to support multitasking. Naturally, it is also not something new in the HPC world. It is a common tool utilised by system administrators to drain a machine for maintenances and/or to make way for an advance reservation. Widely used batch schedulers, e.g. LoadLeveler and Slurm, support preemption either implicitly or explicitly. LoadLeveler[1] supports two types of preemption, system-initiated and user-initiated via job classes, while Slurm[2] manages preemption via the job's partition priority or its quality of service (QoS). Generally, batch schedulers only provide accounting data in terms of number of cores/nodes used and final wallclock time of completed, both successful and failed, jobs. Actual accounting information in terms of core-hours are usually computed with additional scripts or programs with post-processing. As such, the cost of preemption, which requires a snapshot of an instance in time of a machine, cannot be directly or easily inferred.

SPRUCE (Special Priority and Urgent Computing Environment) science gateway project [2] was the first known framework to successfully enable urgent computing on public HPC resources within TeraGrid, predecessor project of Extreme Science and Engineering Discovery Environment (XSEDE)[3]. Within SPRUCE,

---

[1] http://www-01.ibm.com/support/knowledgecenter/SSFJTW_5.1.0/com.ibm.cluster.loadl.v5r1.load100.doc/am2ug_preemptgang.htm.

[2] http://slurm.schedmd.com/preempt.html.

[3] https://www.xsede.org/.

there was only limited resources that supported preemption [14] and only on specially reserved smaller segments of the resources. The less intrusive elevated-priority, next-to-run, etc. strategies were more widely adopted. The criteria used for preemption included elapsed time for the existing job, number of nodes and jobs per user [9, p. 14]. By 2012, it was reported that there was no longer any HPC resources in SPRUCE that supported preemption [3, p. 1680]. Cloud resources, Computing as a Service, became the seemly more popular recommendation within SPRUCE, particularly if preemption was required. However, the limited parallel support (8 cores) within the provided cloud resource was insufficient for the storm surge researchers [3] and consequently a dedicated HPC machine was purchased to continue their urgent computations.

Preemptive scheduling is already a well-known strategy in real-time system, in particular hard real-time system, a computing paradigm with strong similarities to urgent computing. Most work [1,11] revolves around task level preemption, communication, etc., and are frequently focus on one (uni-) processor. Preemption cost is usually not a concern since it is a justified strategy when compared to the cost that may be incurred if a hard deadline is not met. The main goal of this paper is to show that preemption is also a justified strategy in urgent computing on HPC resources for similar reasons as in real-time computing.

3 SuperMUC

SuperMUC[4] is an IBM high performance computer hosted at LRZ in Germany and is made up of four segments from two phases of updates. It utilises an array of Intel processors, Westermere-EX, Sandy Bridge-EP, Ivy-Bridge and Phi, and Haswell. The segment that will be used in this case study is the "thin node islands" that are composed of Intel Sandy Bridge-EP Intel Xeon E5-2680 8 C processors. This segment has a peak performance of 3.185 PFlop/s by utilising 9216 nodes, i.e. 147,456 cores, with 2 GByte of memory per core and has LoadLeveler as a batch scheduler.

The cost of a core per hour on the thin node island on SuperMUC is estimated (rounded up) to be 0.016 EUR, i.e. 0.256 EUR per node per hour. This estimation is calculated using the average annual funding for the system, its system software, direct system personnel, electricity, cooling system and mandatory independent commercial software, i.e. compilers, debuggers, etc. The total core-hours SuperMUC can offer per year is approximated from the usage statistic collected in 2014. This estimated cost does not include the building cost, non-system support personnel, extra commercial software, e.g. MATLAB, etc.

3.1 Comparing SuperMUC to On-demand Resources

To illustrate the economical value of utilising a public resource such as SuperMUC, this cost is compared in Table 1[5] to a similar on-demand resource,

---

[4] http://www.lrz.de/services/compute/supermuc/systemdescription.

[5] http://aws.amazon.com/ec2/pricing/.

Table 1. Cost of SuperMUC and AWS

Site	Type	Cores or vCPU	Processor type	Processor frequency (GHz)	Memory (GB)	Storage (GB)	Cost per hour
LRZ	SuperMUC thin island	16	Intel Xeon E5-2680 8C	2.7	32	100 (NAS) + 1000 (GPFS)	0.256 EUR
AWS	m3.2xlarge	8	Intel Xeon E5-2670 v2	2.6	30	160 (SSD)	0.665 USD ($\approx$0.585 EUR)
AWS	c4.4xlarge	16	Intel Xeon E5-2680 v2	2.8	30	- (EBS)	1.032 USD ($\approx$0.909 EUR)

i.e. Sandy Bridge processors, offers by Amazon Web Services (AWS)[6], which is hosted in the region EU (Frankfurt) in January 2015.

The information collected from AWS is known to be correct and up-to-date on 23 January 2015. Since the cost offered by AWS is based on USD, the cost is converted to EUR using the exchange rate of 1 USD to 0.88 EUR. This is the rounded live exchange rate provided by XE.com[7] on 23 January 2015.

The per node-hour cost at LRZ is comparatively cheaper than that offered by AWS since LRZ is a public resource provider and is thus not expecting a profit. However AWS resources have the advantage of being available on demand and thus swiftly without any additional and in particular manual interference from AWS. It also has the flexibility and ease of setting up and configuring the resource as a user/use case requires.

Table 2. SuperMUC and AWS EC2 C3 cluster

Site	Type	Nominal frequency	Peak performance	Cores	Memory
LRZ	SuperMUC thin island (Intel Xeon E5-2680 8C)	2.7 GHz	3.185 PFlop/s	147,156	288 TB
AWS	Amazon EC2 C3 Instance Cluster (Intel Xeon E5-2680v2)	2.8 GHz	593.51 TFlop/s	26,496	0.105984 TB

Table 2 compares SuperMUC and the HPC machine AWS made in November 2014 for the Top500 list[8]. In spite of the many advantages of on-demand resources, when HPC resources are required, public HPC resources like SuperMUC are simply computationally more powerful, i.e. significantly bigger number of cores, faster network, bigger and faster storage. As such, public HPC resources are a highly valuable class of resources for urgent computing.

---

[6] http://aws.amazon.com/ec2/instance-types.
[7] http://www.xe.com/.
[8] http://top500.org/system/178321.

4   Cost of Preemption

In urgent computing, the cost of an urgent computation (C_c) should be less than the cost incurred from an urgent event (C_e) for a computation to be considered as worthwhile. However, this is only true in the ideal situation where the actual cost of the event is zero as a result of a perfect mitigation decision. A more appropriate representation of the computation and event cost is shown in (1) [8] where α is to be derived e.g. from previous events of similar nature.

$$C_c \leq (1 - \alpha)C_e \quad (0 \leq \alpha \leq 1) \tag{1}$$

4.1   Public Resource

Public resources are an important class of resources that urgent computing can utilise. The cost of urgent computation on such resources can be represented as follows:

$$C_c = C_p + C_u + C_{qos} \tag{2}$$

C_p, C_u and C_{qos} refer to the cost of preemption, urgent job and loss in quality of service (QoS) respectively. For a particular urgent event, the cost of an urgent job (C_u) on a specific HPC resource is fixed. C_u is illustrated in (3) where n is the number of cores/nodes used, t is the wallclock time used (typically round up to next hour) and C_n is the computation cost of each core/node.

$$C_u = n \cdot t \cdot C_n \tag{3}$$

The cost of preemption and loss of QoS are dynamic and are dependent on the running state of the targeted resource. C_p can be represented as shown in (4) and is strongly dependent on the jobs that will be preempted. Thus the decision on which jobs to preempt can strongly influence C_p. n_i and t_i refer to the number of cores/nodes used and the current wallclock time used by job i respectively. C_p is thus a sum of the cost of these preempted jobs. C_p can be simply seen as the direct cost of preemption.

$$C_p = (\sum n_i \cdot t_i)C_n \tag{4}$$

C_{qos} is the indirect cost of preemption and is a more difficult cost to measure and quantify. This is particularly so for public resources like SuperMUC where computation resources are given to scientist for free based on their scientific relevance. Generally, if more jobs and thus users are disrupted, the higher the perceived incurred indirect cost. Naturally other factors, e.g. time left until job is completed, possibility to resume job instead of a complete restart, number of jobs per user being preempted, frequency of preemption, when the preempted jobs are restarted, will also influence the perceived loss of quality of service.

5   Approaches

In order to study the cost of preemption, two approaches, the LC and the LD, were used. The LC approach aims to minimise the direct cost of preemption, C_p. The LD approach's goal is to minimise the number of affected jobs (or users), i.e. C_{qos}, while keeping the affected number of preempted cores and/or cost as low as possible. These two approaches allow more flexibility over which jobs should be preempted and thus more insight into the cost of preemption when compared to the preemption support within LoadLeveler. Both approaches were realised with Apache Spark[9].

5.1   Least Cost (LC) Approach

The LC approach aims to minimise the direct cost of preempting running jobs to make way for the urgent job(s). To reduce the direct cost, the "cheapest" jobs are preempted. The "cheapness" of a job is dependent on the elapsed wallclock time and the number of nodes used and can also be illustrated by Eq. (3).

The least cost algorithm applied is as follows:

$$C_p(n_o) = min(CJ(n_o), LEJ(n_o)) \qquad (5)$$

where

- n_o is the number of nodes that have to be preempted
- $C_p(n_o)$ is the direct cost of preempting n_o or more nodes
- $CJ(n_o)$ is the sum of the cost of preempting the cheapest running jobs to free n_o or more nodes
- $LEJ(n_o)$ is the sum of the cost of preempting the least wallclock elapsed jobs to free n_o or more nodes
- $min(.., ..)$ selects the minimum preemption cost

The LC approach will minimise the cost of preemption by preempting the cheapest (Fig. 1a) or least elapsed wallclock time (Fig. 1b) jobs, thus favouring the preemption of smaller or newly submitted jobs respectively. If more nodes are removed than required, the list will be filtered using with Knapsack algorithm [12] where the most expensive redundant job combination will be removed from the preemption list. If more nodes are still preempted in LEJ, the Knapsack algorithm (minimisation) is additionally used to find possible job/job combination with a lower cost within the wallclock range that is smaller and equal to the last job selected for preemption.

5.2   Least Disruptive (LD) Approach

The LD approach as shown in Fig. 2 aims to minimise the number of jobs preempted, thus the number of users affected. A job that utilises a bigger number of nodes than n_o will be preempted as compared to e.g. preempting two smaller cheaper jobs to free n_o nodes. If no jobs using $\geq n_o$ can be found, the least number of jobs to get n_o or more nodes are selected.

---

[9] https://spark.apache.org/.

```
function Cheapest_Job
  input Integer  n_o
  //Jobs are sorted on cost in ascending order
  //Iterate through the sorted job list
  while n < n_o
      Add job j_i with n_i nodes to preempt_list
      n+ = n_i
  end
  if n > n_o
    KnapSack_Algo to find the most expensive
    job combination.
    Remove the job combination found from
    preempt_list(n)
    n- = n_i
  end
  if n > n_o
    KnapSack_Algo to find cheapest job
    combination within same wallclock range
    //use this set if cost is lower
  end
end
```

(a) $CJ(n_o)$

```
function Least_Elapsed_Job
  input Integer  n_o
  //Jobs are sorted on wallclock elapsed time
  in ascending order
  //Iterate through the sorted job list
  while n < n_o
      Add job j_i with n_i nodes to preempt_list
      n+ = n_i
  end
  if n > n_o
    Knapsack_Algo to find the most expensive
    job combination to remove.
    Remove the job combination found from
    preempt_list(n)
    n- = n_i
  end
end
```

(b) $LEJ(n_o)$

Fig. 1. Least cost algorithm

```
function least_disruptive
  input Integer n_o
  //Jobs ares sorted based on nodes in descending order and cost in ascending order
  Case 1: n_i == n_o
    Find job j_i with the lowest cost Where n_i == n_o
        Add job j_i to preempt_list
        n = n_i
  Case 2: n_i > n_o
    Find job j_i with the smallest job size n_i Where n_i > n_o
    And the lowest cost among jobs of the same size
        Add job j_i to preempt_list
        n = n_i
  Case 3: SUM(n_i) >= n_o
    Find jobs j_i Where SUM(n_i) > n_o
    if SUM(n_i) == n_o
        Add jobs j_i to preempt_list
        n = n_o
    else //SUM(n_i) > n_o
        //Iterate through the job list
        n = 0
        while n < n_o
            if n_i <= n_o - n
                Add job j_i to preempt_list
                n+ = n_i
            else
                Continue to iterate through the list to Find for the smallest n_i
                Where n_i > n_o - n And cost is the lowest among jobs of the same size
                    Add job j_i to preempt_list
                    n+ = n_i
            end
        end
    end
  end
end
```

Fig. 2. Least disruptive algorithm

6   Result

The LC and LD algorithms were applied on SuperMUC, while it was on full load, in late December 2014 and early January 2015 at random times to reflect the unexpectedness of urgent events. The cost of preemption, C_p, is collected for 16, 32, 64, 128, 256, 512, 1024, 2048 compute nodes. Only nodes that are in the same job class as the required compute nodes can be considered for the preemption. Samples were taken within minutes, hours and days, to capture the dynamic nature, i.e. a constant stream of new jobs, in the queue for smaller jobs and the more invariant behaviour in the queue for larger jobs. Since there is no QoS penalty at this moment for preempting jobs on SuperMUC, C_{qos} is assumed to be zero for simplicity. In principle, C_{qos} can be inferred from the number of trouble tickets, i.e. complaints, received as a result of the preemptive activities.

Figure 3 shows the preemption cost, number of jobs and nodes preempted when 2048 nodes are required for urgent computing over the case study period. The preemption cost can vary significantly and is strongly dependent on when the preemption should take place, i.e. the status of the running jobs on the machine and the profile of jobs running on the machine. Typically the same set of jobs is running for 48 h and thus the cost will only increase during this period of time independent of the approach. Comparing the LC approach to the LD approach, the preemption cost is frequently only half or less. As a result, the number of affected jobs is more than double, implying more affected users. The LC approach also resulted in more nodes to be preempted than required since cheaper jobs are selected as opposed to jobs with the "right size".

The average preemption cost, number of jobs and nodes preempted for different number of compute nodes are summarised in Fig. 4, where results is collected at the same timestamps as shown in Fig. 3. Similar conclusions can be drawn from the average numbers. In general, the cost of preemption and the number of jobs preempted are inversely related. The LD approach adopts a more conservation strategy, i.e. minimise the number of jobs affected, to preemption at the expense of cost.

Table 3 shows the estimated cost of four severe but different disasters that occurred in the last decade. Typically, it will take a number of years before the full extent of the cost can be collected. These disasters cost in the range of ten to hundred of billions of EUR. In comparison, the cost of preemption, which is in the range of ten of thousands of EUR appears like a pittance. Naturally, the cost of an urgent computation includes more than just cost of the preemption as shown in Eq. 2. Assuming 2048 nodes are required for a period of 48 h, the maximum allowed walltime limit without additional arrangement, for an urgent computation, the computation cost, C_u, can be computed using Eq. 3 and is approximately 25165 EUR. Using the worst case preemption cost, 23599 EUR, as shown in Fig. 3, the total computation cost, C_p, is expected to be around 48764 EUR. This is still insignificant when compared to a costly disaster. Finally, based on Eq. 1, urgent computation will be worthwhile if the result is expected to be useful for mitigation activities that can reduce the incurred cost by α.

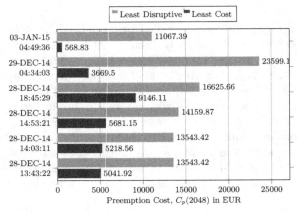

(a) Preemption Cost

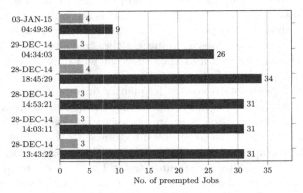

(b) Preempted Jobs

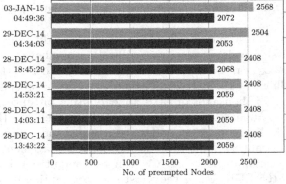

(c) Preempted Nodes

Fig. 3. Preemption cost, preempted jobs and nodes for 2048 nodes

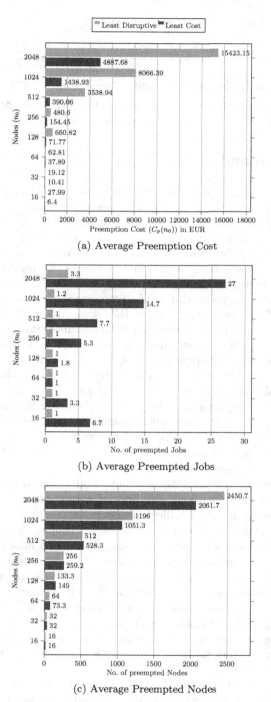

Fig. 4. Average preemption cost, preempted jobs and nodes

Table 3. Cost of some disasters in recent years

Disasters	Year	Country	Estimated loss (EUR)
Flood [6]	2013	Germany	15 billion
Tōhoku Earthquake/Tsunami [10,13]	2011	Japan	273 billion
Deepwater Horizon Oil Spill [4]	2010	Gulf of Mexico	53–88 billion
Hurricane Katrina [5]	2005	United States	88 billion

7   Conclusion and Future Work

Public resources, in particular HPC resources, can potentially be leveraged on to solve most if not all urgent computing use cases. Unfortunately, the existing policies are too restrictive to support this class of computing. Preemption, a common strategy, in urgent computing is not supported due to policy restrictions. The impact of preemption on other users is believed to be significant, i.e. costly. A case study was thus carried out on one of the public HPC resources, SuperMUC, to investigate the cost.

To simulate the unpredictability of urgent events, the case study was carried out at random times while SuperMUC was on full load. Eight different numbers of compute nodes were considered for preemption. Their corresponding preemption cost, number of compute nodes preempted and number of jobs preempted were collected. Two preemption approach, LC and LD, were used. The LC approach aims to minimise the preemption cost while the LD approach's goal is to minimise the number of preempted jobs. These approaches attempt to illustrate to the perspectives of the policy makers and the resource providers. A production version of the preemption algorithm will have to merge the LC and LD approaches and include also the perspectives of other stack-holders, i.e. the urgent and non-urgent users, where other criteria, e.g. nodes proximity and time until completion, has to be considered.

The computation cost for 2048 compute nodes, the maximum number of nodes that can be used without any special arrangement, is then compared to the cost of some of the deadliest disasters in recent decade. The cost of an urgent computation is in the range of ten of thousands of EUR while the cost of the deadliest disasters are in the range of ten to hundreds of billions of EUR. The cost of computation with preemption is insignificant in comparison. Naturally, not all cost of a disaster can be mitigated with urgent computations. In the case of disasters that cost billions of EUR, if an urgent computation can mitigate 0.001 % of the incurred cost, it is more than worthwhile to support urgent computing and preemption. An urgent computation(s) is thus justified if its cost including preemption is less than or equal to the expected reduction in severity of the event from mitigation activities planned using the results of the urgent computation(s).

More work is still required in the field of urgent computing, in particular on HPC infrastructures. Future work includes improving the preemption algorithms for production purposes, estimating/predicting the computation time of an urgent computation code for efficient scheduling and how it corresponds to the stipulated deadline. The ultimate goal is an urgent computing framework that can easily enable urgent computing use cases on generic resources.

Acknowledgments. The author would like to thank Anthes, Heller, DRG group, etc. at Leibniz Supercomputing Centre for their valuable motivations, suggestions, feedbacks and support. A big thanks to Brehm for sharing the cost information on SuperMUC.

References

1. Baruah, S., Mok, A., Rosier, L.: Preemptively scheduling hard-real-time sporadic tasks on one processor. In: Proceedings of the 11th RTSS, pp. 182–190, December 1990
2. Beckman, P., Nadella, S., Trebon, N., Beschastnikh, I.: SPRUCE: a system for supporting urgent high-performance computing. In: Gaffney, P.W., Pool, J.C.T. (eds.) Grid-Based Problem Solving Environments. IFIP, vol. 239, pp. 295–311. Springer, Boston (2007)
3. Blanton, B., McGee, J., et al.: Urgent computing of storm surge for North Carolina's coast. In: ICCS. Procedia Computer Science, vol. 9, pp. 1677–1686. Elsevier (2012)
4. Cohen, M.: A taxonomy of oil spill costs - what are the likely costs of the deepwater horizon spill? Technical report, Resources for the Future (2010)
5. Dolfman, M., Wasser, S., Bergman, B.: The effects of Hurricane Katrina on the New Orleans economy. Technical report, Bureau of Labor Statistics of the U.S. Department of Labor (2007)
6. Gennies, S., Funk, A., et al.: Hochwasser-Bilanz 2013 Wie schlimm war die Flut wirklich? June 2013. http://www.tagesspiegel.de/politik/hochwasser-bilanz-2013-wie-schlimm-war-die-flut-wirklich/8416770.html
7. Leong, S.H., Frank, A., Kranzlmüller, D.: Leveraging e-infrastructures for urgent computing. In: ICCS. Procedia Computer Science, vol. 18, pp. 2177–2186. Elsevier (2013)
8. Leong, S.H., Kranzlmüller, D.: Towards a general definition of urgent computing. To be published in Proceedings of ICCS 2015
9. Marru, S., Gannon, D., et al.: LEAD cyberinfrastructure to track real-time storms using SPRUCE urgent computing. CTWatch Q. 4(1), 5–16 (2008)
10. Nanto, D., Cooper, W., Donnelly, J.: Japans 2011 earthquake and tsunami- economic effects and implications for the United States. Technical report, Congressional Research Service(2011)
11. Scaife, N., Caspi, P.: Integrating model-based design and preemptive scheduling in mixed time- and event-triggered systems. In: Proceedings of the 16th Real-Time Systems, ECRTS, pp. 119–126, June 2004
12. Trick, M.A.: A dynamic programming approach for consistency and propagation for knapsack constraints. In: Annals of Operations Research, pp. 113–124 (2001)
13. Ujikane, K.: Japan Forecasts Earthquake Damage May Swell to $309 Billion, March 2011. http://www.bloomberg.com/news/articles/2011-03-23/japan-sees-quake-damage-up-to-309-billion-almost-four-katrinas
14. Yoshimoto, K.K., Choi, D.J., et al.: Implementations of urgent computing on production HPC systems. In: ICCS. Procedia Computer Science, vol. 9, pp. 1687–1693. Elsevier (2012)

Designing Non-blocking Personalized Collectives with Near Perfect Overlap for RDMA-Enabled Clusters

Hari Subramoni[1][(✉)], Ammar Ahmad Awan[1], Khaled Hamidouche[1],
Dmitry Pekurovsky[2], Akshay Venkatesh[1], Sourav Chakraborty[1],
Karen Tomko[3], and Dhabaleswar K. Panda[1]

[1] Department of Computer Science and Engineering,
The Ohio State University, Columbus, OH, USA
{subramoni.1,awan.10,hamidouche.2,venkatesh.19,
chakraborty.52,panda.2}@osu.edu
[2] San Diego Supercomputer Center, San Diego, California
dmitry@sdsc.edu
[3] Ohio Supercomputer Center, Columbus, OH, USA
ktomko@osc.edu

Abstract. Several techniques have been proposed in the past for designing non-blocking collective operations on high-performance clusters. While some of them required a dedicated process/thread or periodic probing to progress the collective others needed specialized hardware solutions. The former technique, while applicable to any generic HPC cluster, had the drawback of stealing CPU cycles away from the compute task. The latter gave near perfect overlap but increased the total cost of the HPC installation due to need for specialized hardware and also had other drawbacks that limited its applicability. On the other hand, the Remote Direct Memory Access technology and high performance networks have been pushing the envelope of HPC performance to multi-petaflop levels. However, no scholarly work exists that explores the impact such RDMA technology can bring to the design of non-blocking collective primitives. In this paper, we take up this challenge and propose efficient designs of personalized non-blocking collective operations on top of the basic RDMA primitives. Our experimental evaluation shows that our proposed designs are able to deliver near perfect overlap of computation and communication for personalized collective operations on modern HPC systems at scale. At the microbenchmark level, the proposed RDMA-Aware collectives deliver improvements in latency of up to 89 times for MPI_Igatherv, 3.71 times for MPI_Ialltoall and, 3.23 times for MPI_Iscatter over the state-of-the-art designs. We also observe an improvement of up to 19 % for the P3DFFT kernel at 8,192 cores on the Stampede supercomputing system at TACC.

Keywords: Non-blocking collectives · Remote Direct Memory Access · HPC · InfiniBand

This research is supported in part by National Science Foundation grants #CCF-1213084, #CNS-1419123, and #IIS-1447804.

J.M. Kunkel and T. Ludwig (Eds.): ISC High Performance 2015, LNCS 9137, pp. 434–453, 2015.
DOI: 10.1007/978-3-319-20119-1_31

1   Introduction and Motivation

Supercomputing systems have grown in size and scale over the last decade. Two key drivers fueling the growth of supercomputers are the current trends in multi-/many-core architectures and the availability of commodity, RDMA-enabled, and high-performance interconnects such as InfiniBand [9] (IB). Such HPC systems are allowing scientists and engineers to tackle grand challenges in various scientific domains. Users of HPC systems rely on parallel programming models to parallelize their applications and obtain performance improvements.

Message Passing Interface (MPI) [26] is a very popular parallel programming model for developing parallel scientific applications. The MPI Standard [27] offers primitives for various point-to-point, collective, and synchronization operations. Collective operations defined in the MPI standard offer a very convenient abstraction to implement group communication operations. Owing to their ease of use and performance portability, collective operations are widely used across various scientific domains. Collective operations can broadly be classified as personalized and non-personalized depending on the kind of data transmitted by one process to its peers. A personalized colelctive operations is one where each process sends distinct data to many other processes. Consequently, personalized collective operations transfer more volume of data and hence put a heavier load on the communication subsystem when comapred to the non-personalized ones. Until recently, the MPI Standard defined all collective operations to be blocking, i.e., the application processes had to wait in the MPI library, until their role in the collective operation is complete. This affects the overall performance and scalability of parallel applications. To address these limitations, the MPI community has introduced Non-Blocking Collectives (NBC) in the current MPI Standard, MPI-3. A high performance implementation of a non-blocking interface for collective operations would ideally be expected to deliver near-perfect communication/computation overlap, together with acceptable communication latency. Furthermore, applications also need to be re-designed to take advantage of this feature and to overlap expensive collective communication operations with independent calculations.

Although the concept of NBC seems simple and the benefits obvious, there are several caveats that need to be addressed before end applications begin to see the benefits offered by this novel programming interface. Given the dominant nature of the MPI programming model in the scientific computation domain, it is likely that the key driver for the acceptance of this interface by the application community will be the real benefits offered by intelligent MPI designs and implementations of NBC.

Simplistic designs of NBC that require applications to progress the communication explicitly through CPU intervention, e.g., calling MPI_Test [6], offset much of the benefit of non-blocking communication by stealing CPU cycles away from the computation. Further, estimating the optimal number of MPI_Test / MPI_Probe / MPI_Iprobe calls required is hard for application developers. Similarly, if each MPI process launches a separate thread within the library for communication progress, the application performance can be affected by interrupt processing, thread scheduling and other similar factors [3]. While functional partitioning approaches [5, 14, 29, 35] that dedicate one compute core for communication alleviate this to some extent, they still take one compute core away from the application resulting in potential sub-par computation performance. It is also critical for a non-blocking collective interface to ensure performance portability. In this context, network vendors are offering advanced hardware features to enable asynchronous communication progress for collective operations. Mellanox has introduced network offload features in their ConnectX-2 [23], ConnectX-3 [24] and Connect-IB [25] adapters. Using this feature, generic lists of communication tasks can be offloaded to the network interface [21]. Such an interface eliminates the need for the host processor to explicitly progress the communication. It also provides a low-level mechanism that can be leveraged to design non-blocking collective communication algorithms. However, as discussed in [12, 13], there are several performance and scalability limitations in the current generation hardware that may limit the adoption of these features on mainstream supercomputing systems. Similar hardware-based offload collectives are also possible with the Portals interface [32].

As described above and in [7, 8], the overlap potential is limited by the wasted CPU cycles in progressing the communication rather than performing useful computation. Except for designs using core-direct feature [12, 13, 21] available only with Mellanox OFED, the current implementations and designs of NBC operations require CPU cycles to progress the communication. Many researchers have been trying to maximize the potential of overlap by finding the appropriate numbers of MPI_Test / MPI_Probe / MPI_Iprobe calls. On the other hand, the Remote Direct Memory Access (RDMA) technology powered high performance interconnects have become the de-facto choice to design HPC systems. Prior work by researchers in the field [2, 37] has shown that it is possible to design efficient collective communication operations using the basic RDMA primitives offered by high performance interconnects like IB. However, there exists no scholarly work that explores whether one can use such primitives to design efficient non-blocking collective operations with near perfect overlap of communication and computation and good communication latency.

2   Contributions

In this paper, we take up this challenge and design high performance non-blocking personalized collective operations that offer near perfect overlap of computation and communication and good communication latency for RDMA enabled HPC interconnects like IB. In particular, we focus on primitives offering All-to-all, All-to-one and One-to-all communication patterns namely MPI_Ialltoall, MPI_Igather / MPI_Igatherv and MPI_Iscatter / MPI_Iscatterv. The overlap optimality of our approach comes from reducing the number of MPI_Test / MPI_Probe / MPI_Iprobe calls to Zero. To summarize, this paper makes the following important contributions:

- Propose a generic approach to design non-blocking collectives with near-perfect overlap for RDMA-based networks
- Design RDMA-Aware non-blocking collectives for three personalized communication patterns - All-to-all, All-to-one and One-to-all
- Enhance the OSU microbenchmarks by adding NBC benchmarks to measure overlap, init time and wait time. Add option to the proposed OSU NBC microbenchmarks to insert MPI_Iprobe calls equally during computation
- Perform a careful analysis of the benefits of our approaches with the proposed OSU NBC microbenchmarks and P3DFFT application kernel at a large scale

Our experimental evaluation shows that our proposed designs are able to deliver near perfect overlap of computation and communication for personalized collective operations on modern HPC systems at scale. At the microbenchmark level, the proposed RDMA-Aware collectives deliver improvements in latency of up to 89 times for MPI_Igatherv, 3.71 times for MPI_Ialltoall, and 3.23 times for MPI_Iscatter over the state-of-the-art designs. We also observe an improvement of up to 19 % for the P3DFFT kernel at 8,192 cores on Stampede [39].

3   Background

In this section, we provide the necessary background information for this paper.

3.1   InfiniBand

InfiniBand [9] is a popular switched interconnect standard being used by more than 44 % of the Top500 Supercomputing systems [40]. The InfiniBand FDR adapter from Mellanox can deliver up to 56 Gb/s bandwidth, and communication latency of less than 1 micro-second. InfiniBand supports memory communication semantics through Remote Direct Memory Access (RDMA) operations, such as RDMA-Write and RDMA-Read. RDMA operations are one-sided and do not require software involvement at the target. The remote host does not have to issue any work request for the data transfer. The memory regions that are used for the RDMA operations are required to be registered with the InfiniBand network interface through the *ibv_reg_mr* operation, which returns a memory handle, *ibv_mr*, that contains the virtual address and the RDMA key information. Processes that wish to communicate via the RDMA operations need to exchange ibv_mr objects before issuing the network operations on the corresponding memory buffers.

3.2   MPI Collective Operations

The current MPI Standard, MPI-3 [27] defines support for non-blocking collective operations. The latest open-source versions of the MPICH2 [11] and MVA-PICH2 [17] software libraries offer basic host-based support for non-blocking collectives.

3.3 InfiniBand Hardware-Multicast Based Collectives

One of the notable features provided by InfiniBand is the ability to send a message to a *multicast address* and have it delivered to multiple processes on different nodes. Compared to performing multiple point-to-point operations, hardware-multicast can achieve reduced network load by allowing the switches to duplicate the message as well as significantly lower latency by reducing the number of operations performed at the host [18]. MVAPICH2 has support for efficient collectives based on hardware-multicast capabilities [15,22]. Figure 1 shows the performance of hardware-multicast based MPI_Bcast and MPI_Scatter on Stampede [39].

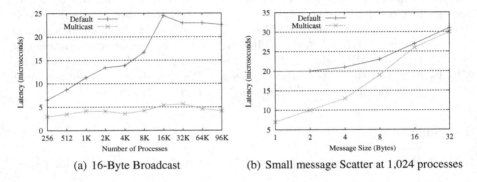

(a) 16-Byte Broadcast   (b) Small message Scatter at 1,024 processes

Fig. 1. Scalability and performance of hardware-multicast based collectives

3.4 P3DFFT

Many applications in areas including Direct Numerical Simulations of Turbulence, and astrophysics rely on highly scalable 3D FFTs [1,34]. The Parallel Three-Dimensional Fast Fourier Transforms (P3DFFT) library [31] from the San Diego Supercomputer Center (SDSC) is a portable, high performance, open source implementation based on the MPI programming model. It leverages the fast serial FFT implementations of either IBM's ESSL or FFTW. P3DFFT uses a 2D, or pencil, decomposition and overcomes an important limitation to scalability inherent in FFT libraries by increasing the degree of parallelism up to N^2, where N is the linear size of the data grid. It has been used in various Direct Numerical Simulation (DNS) turbulence applications [1]. The original version of the P3DFFT kernel relies on blocking MPI_Alltoallv / MPI_Alltoall operations on the row and column communicators. Typically, the processor grids are chosen to fit the row communicator within a compute node, while each of the column communicators include one process per compute node. Previously, we redesigned this kernel to take advantage of network-offload-based MPI_Ialltoallv operation to achieve latency hiding [13]. We use this version of P3DFFT with support for overlapping computation with communication for our experiments in this paper.

4   Problem Space for Designing Non-blocking Collectives

In this section we consider the different state-of-the-art approaches in the literature for designing non-blocking collective operations. We compare different solutions using the following metrics: communication latency, computation/communication overlap, network scalability, and need for a dedicated core to progress communication.

LibNBC: The initial support for NBC was introduced in LibNBC. The default support for NBC in MPICH and MVAPICH2 extends this design. This approach requires applications to call MPI_Test / MPI_Probe / MPI_Iprobe to progress NBC [6]. However, as noted in Sect. 1, it is not easy to determine the right frequency and the exact number of MPI_Test / MPI_Probe / MPI_Iprobe calls that have to be performed to achieve communication/computation overlap. Further, this approach also steals compute cycles away from the application resulting in non-optimal overlap of computation and communication. Another approach relies on each MPI process spawning its own asynchronous progress-thread. In such a design, the MPI process and its progress-thread share the same address space, and the progress thread can directly execute the collective operation on behalf of the MPI processes. While this method does not require the application developer to "guess" the correct number of MPI_Test / MPI_Probe / MPI_Iprobe calls required to achieve communication/computation overlap, it requires sufficient number of idle CPU cores on each node, to ensure that the MPI processes and their progress threads do not contend for the same set of resources [3]. This leads to inefficient utilization of the available CPU cycles and is not a practical solution on modern multi-core systems. We demonstrate this design alternative in Fig. 2(a).

InfiniBand CORE-Direct: While the CORE-Direct interface potentially offers near-perfect overlap and can lead to application-level benefits, the current version of the interface has several limitations [13]. Owing to the lack of hardware-level tag-matching, MPI libraries need to create separate Queue-Pairs (QPs) and Completion-Queues (CQs) for each communicator, which leads to scalability issues. Additionally, the communication performance of this interface has been demonstrated to be worse than the basic InfiniBand verbs-layer, and this can adversely affect small message non-blocking collectives [12]. Further, the feature being available only on Mellanox hardware limits the portability of the designs to other RDMA based networks.

Functional Partitioning (FP) Approaches: Several approaches that advocate the use of one dedicated processor core to progress the communication phases of NBC have been proposed in the literature [5,14,29,35]. While these schemes have significantly less overhead to progress communication when compared to the asynchronous progress-thread mentioned above, they still take one compute core away from the application resulting in sub-par computation performance. However, on systems where there are several less powerful CPU cores available, functional partitioning may be a viable approach as the CPU resources consumed will be low. This alternative is depicted in Fig. 2(b).

Proposed Approach: In our work, we propose to use the basic RDMA mechanisms defined by high performance interconnects such as InfiniBand, iWARP, and RoCE to design scalable NBC designs that deliver good communication latency and near perfect overlap of computation and communication. Our approach, depicted in Fig. 2(c), does not require any changes to the application code, does not require dedicated cores to progress communication (and hence has minimal overhead regardless of the types of cores on the system), and has better portability and network scalability than existing hardware based approaches such as CORE-Direct.

Table 1 summarizes the strengths and weaknesses of various approaches and highlights the merits of our proposed framework for designing MPI-3 non-blocking collective operations in a high-performance and scalable manner.

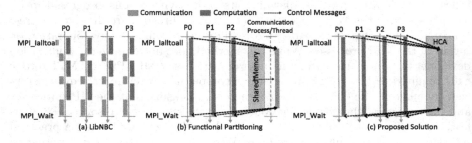

Fig. 2. Design alternatives for non-blocking collectives

Table 1. Overall design-space for MPI-3 non-blocking collectives

Metric	LibNBC	CORE-Direct	FP	Proposed Approach
Communication Latency	Good	Fair	Good	Good
Computation / Communication Overlap	Poor	Good	Good	Good
Network Scalability	Good	Poor	Good	Good
Availability of Cores for Compute	Poor	Good	Fair	Good

5   Design of RDMA-Aware Non-blocking Personalized Collectives

In this section, we discuss our proposed designs for implementing high-performance, scalable, and personalized MPI-3 non-blocking collectives. We develop our designs to meet the following major characteristics: (1) maximize computation / communication overlap, (2) eliminate the need for MPI_Test /

MPI_Probe / MPI_Iprobe calls to progress communication and (3) achieve good communication latency and network scalability.

Although the current collective designs in high performance MPI libraries like MVAPICH2 are already using RDMA, the data transfer is still based on underlying two-sided point-to-point communication semantics that require CPU intervention to progress control messages and completion. Thus, we need operations that rely on direct RDMA / one-sided semantics to avoid the requirement for CPU intervention to progress communication. Further, to achieve good communication latency, it is better to design collectives directly on top of low level RDMA operations (or RDMA-Aware) than on top of underlying point-to-point operations. The main challenges in designing high performance and scalable RDMA-Aware NBC are: (1) efficiently exchanging the tuple of $< remote\_memory\_address, remote\_rkey >$ required to perform RDMA operations (RDMA-Write and RDMA-Read) between processes (as described in Sect. 3.1), (2) exchanging data using appropriate RDMA primitives over the network to remote peers, and (3) notifying the remote peer of the completion of the data transfer.

In the following sections, we elaborate on how we address these challenges to design efficient RDMA-Aware non-blocking collective algorithms to perform All-to-all, All-to-one, and One-to-all communication patterns.

5.1   Design of Non-blocking RDMA-Aware All-to-all

There are several algorithms available to implement the All-to-all collective operation in the literature. However, most researchers agree that for large message sizes and large system sizes, one needs some sort of a pairwise exchange algorithm where all processes talk directly to each other without any intermediate process routing the messages on their behalf. Such a communication pattern is extremely amenable to designing using basic RDMA operations as there are no intermediate steps in the communication that require intervention either from a process/thread or a hardware collective offload engine like Core-Direct.

On entering the collective operation, each process first registers the send / receive buffers passed by the application with the IB HCA to obtain the "remote_rkey". Although registering buffers with the IB HCA is a costly operation, the "IB memory registration cache" [28] mechanism in MVAPICH2 allows us to hide the cost of registration by caching the registered entries for future use. Each process also allocates and registers (with the IB HCA) a temporary buffer to check for completion of data transfers from remote processes. A small message (24 byte) MPI_Allgather is then performed between all processes taking part in the All-to-all operation to collect the tuple of $< remote\_memory\_address, remote\_rkey >$ from all processes required to perform RDMA operations and notify them of its completion. On completion of the Allgather, each process schedules data transfer and completion notification operations for each peer on a remote node by posting RDMA-Read or RDMA-Write operations to the IB HCA. For peers residing on the same physical node as the processes, we choose the shared memory communication channel [20] for small messages (<3 KB) and the loopback communication channel through the IB HCA for large messages (>32 KB). Although, shared memory channel offers a higher performance route for intra-node communication from the point of view of latency, we choose the loopback channel through the IB HCA due its ability to overlap the communication with computation operation. Once the RDMA operations have been posted to the IB HCA, the process is free to exit the MPI library and perform its computation without having to progress the collective operation. Since the IB HCA is taking care of progressing the collective communication, this design will meet the first and second design criteria we outlined above.

Caching Mechanism to Avoid MPI_Allgather: Although the overhead introduced by the Allgather operation is small, we introduce a caching mechanism to store the tuple of $< remote\_memory\_address, remote\_rkey >$ from all processes in order to avoid invoking the Allgather operation in each iteration of the All-to-all. After registering the send / receive buffers passed by the application with the IB HCA, the processes participating in the All-to-all will compare the current address / remote_key with the cached address / remote_key. Due to the "IB memory registration cache" in MVAPICH2, it is highly likely that if the addresses of the send / receive buffer passed by the application remains unchanged, the remote_key will also be the same. After the local comparison phase, all the processes involved in the All-to-all will perform an MPI_Allreduce operation (with an operator of MPI_LAND) to see if all processes had a "cache hit". If so, then they skip the MPI_Allgather operation. If the result of the MPI_Allreduce was a "cache miss", then the processes go ahead and perform the MPI_Allgather. As an MPI_Allreduce operation (which transfers constant amount of data and completes in Log(N_Nodes) number of steps) is significantly less expensive and more scalable than an Allgather, we expect to have good performance benefits with this caching approach thus achieving the third design criteria identified earlier. Note that the MPI_Allgather that is being performed as part of the All-to-all operation only exchanges very small messages (24 bytes) and will only take a small fraction of the time compared to the All-to-all (< 0.1 %) at large scales.

RDMA_Write vs RDMA_Read: We evaluated the performance of the All-to-all operation using both the RDMA_Write and RDMA_Read primitives that IB offers. We saw that the performance being offered by the RDMA_Write primitive has higher than the RDMA_Read primitive. We believe that this is due to the limitation on the number of back-to-back RDMA_Read operations that can be posted to the IB HCA. Hence we choose the RDMA_Write primitive to implement the All-to-all collective operation.

Temporary Memory Overhead: The overhead in terms of memory introduced by our RDMA-Aware scheme is negligible. We will only consume about 3.0 MB of memory per process for an All-to-all involving 131,072 (128 K) processes. This can quite easily be offset by tuning the number and size of the intra-node shared-memory rendezvous buffers that the MPI library allocates [19]. As our

RDMA-Aware design uses IB based loopback communication even for intra-node transfers such tuning will have no effect on the communication performance either. Note that our approach will not use any additional internal communication buffers in the MPI library for transferring Request To Send (RTS) / Clear To Send (CTS) packets that are part of high performance rendezvous based communication protocols for large messages [38]. This will result in additional memory savings when compared to the default non RDMA-Aware All-to-all algorithm.

5.2   Design of Non-blocking RDMA-Aware All-to-one and One-to-all

There are several algorithms available to implement the All-to-one and One-to-all collective operation in the literature. The result of extensive performance tuning done for collective operations in the MVAPICH2 MPI library on different generations of interconnects and processors indicates that the "direct" algorithm, where all processes send / receive data directly to the "root" of the All-to-one / One-to-all operation, leads to the best performance on most modern HPC processors (like Westmere / SandyBridge / IvyBridge) and interconnects (like IB-QDR-32 Gbps / IB-FDR-56 Gbps). As with the pairwise All-to-all exchange, this communication pattern is also very amenable to designing using basic RDMA operations as there are no intermediate steps in the communication that require intervention either from a process/thread or a hardware collective offload engine like Core-Direct.

On entering the collective operation, the processes register either the send or the receive buffer passed by the application with the IB HCA to obtain the "remote_rkey". In case of All-to-one, the root will register the receive buffer while the non-root processes will register the send buffer. For One-to-all on the other hand, the root will register the send buffer while the non-root processes will register the receive buffer. Once the root has registered the buffers, it will use a Broadcast operation of 12 bytes to inform the non-root processes of its $< remote\_memory\_address, remote\_rkey >$ tuple. We use the hardware multicast based MPI_Bcast in MVAPICH2 (described in Sect. 3.3) to implement this broadcast to achieve good scalability and performance. Once the non-root processes have the $< remote\_memory\_address, remote\_rkey >$ tuple from the root, they go ahead and initiate the RDMA operations for transferring the data and posting completion notification to the root. In the data transfer phase, the non-root processes will use the RDMA-Write operation for the All-to-one collective pattern and the RDMA-Read operation for the One-to-all collective pattern. We choose different RDMA primitives for these collectives to reduce the load on the IB HCA at the root of the collective. We use the RDMA-Write primitive for the completion notification for both collective patterns as it is just a one byte transfer.

Optimization to Avoid Memory Registration for Small Messages: InfiniBand supports transferring small messages as "INLINE" transfers without having to pre-register it with the IB HCA [9]. We use this feature as an optimization for designing small message All-to-one collectives. If the message size is less that "INLINE_THRESHOLD", the non-root processes will skip registering the send buffer with the IB HCA and directly post the RDMA-Write operation. We expect this to improve the latency of small message transfers.

Extensions for "v" variants: The "v" variants of the All-to-one (MPI_Igatherv) and One-to-all (MPI_Iscatterv) collectives need additional enhancements to the design to account for the potential variable sized data transfers that the non-root processes can initiate to the root. To this end, we add an additional 4 byte based blocking One-to-all collective (MPI_Scatter) operation. We use the hardware multicast based MPI_Scatter in MVAPICH2 (described in Sect. 3.3) to implement this One-to-all operation to achieve good scalability and performance. The root will use this operation to inform its peers about the displacements at which they need to read or write the data.

5.3   Extending OSU Micro-Benchmarks for Non-blocking Collectives

To evaluate our RDMA-Aware design, we have introduced non-blocking collective benchmarks to our OSU Micro-Benchmarks (OMB) suite [30]. In order to implement these new benchmarks, we extend our current blocking collective benchmarks by replacing the blocking calls with corresponding non-blocking ones. Since, the non-blocking calls can be polled (tested) for completion, we are using the MPI_Wait call to wait for completion of the collective. The purpose of non-blocking collectives is to provide an opportunity for the application programmers to do useful computation while the communication proceeds in the background. This is usually referred to as the overlap. To calculate the overlap of communication and computation, we first measure the communication time using the initialization call to a collective e.g., MPI_Ibcast() immediately followed by an MPI_Wait.

The current collective benchmarks in OMB display only average, minimum, and maximum latency. This is not meaningful for a non-blocking benchmark so we have added some new fields to the display. We display the overall latency (the total time taken when computation is overlapped with communication), the communication and the computation time, and the overlap percentage. In addition, we are also timing the initialization overhead (displayed as Coll.Init) and the wait time (displayed as MPI.Wait). The popular Intel MPI Benchmarks Suite (IMB) [10] displays the percentage overlap, overall, computation, and communication latency for the IMB-NBC. However, IMB does not display the initialization overhead and the time spent in the wait call (as they are not timing these operations individually). Several other bechmarks have been proposed to measure the overlap of computation and communication. NBCBench [4] was proposed with the LibNBC which measures overlap of NBC operations in the LibNBC library. Sandia MPI Micro-Benchmark Suite (SMB) [36] and Communication Offload MPI-based Benchmark (COMB) [16] also provide the facility to measure overlap. SMB uses a host-processor overhead method and measures availability of the host for computation during a non-blocking MPI send or receive operation. COMB proposed two benchmarking methods for measuring the overlap. The first one is a simple polling method while the second one is called post-work-wait method. Both methods use two phases to calculate availability as ration of time(work without messaging) to time(work plus MPI calls while messaging). For this paper, we have calculated the percentage overlap based on the formula in Fig. 3.

$$overlap \; = max(0, 100 - \left\{ \frac{overall \; time \; - \; compute \; time}{communication \; time} * 100 \right\});$$

Fig. 3. Formula to calculate overlap of communication and computation

The computation time is calculated by timing a dummy compute function that multiplies a 2D array allocated through malloc(). We have used a cache unfriendly access and malloc() on purpose to avoid any optimizations done by the compiler. We have also added support in the OMB suite to use MPI_Iprobe() calls inside our dummy computation function. This will allow us to simulate the behavior that most applications will use to progress communication while doing the overlapped computation. Although this support is added at the benchmark level, it may also provide a ballpark figure for the number of probe calls that real applications can also use. The probe calls are evenly distributed between actual compute function calls.

6   Experimental Results

In this section, we describe the experimental setup used to conduct our experiments. An in-depth analysis of the results is also provided to correlate design motivations and observed behavior. All results reported here are averages of multiple (five) runs to discard the effect of system noise. Note that while all the experiments presented here are based on Mellanox IB based systems, the techniques and designs are equally applicable to other interconnects that support the RDMA technology such as iWARP [33]. We do not present these results due to the lack of access to such large scale systems.

6.1   Experimental Setup

We used the TACC Stampede [39] system for all our experiments. Each node on Stampede is equipped with with Intel SandyBridge series of processors, using Xeon dual eight-core sockets, operating at 2.70 GHz with 32 GB RAM. Each node is equipped with MT4099 FDR ConnectX HCAs (56 Gbps data rate) with PCI-Ex Gen2 interfaces. The operating system used is CentOS release 6.3, with kernel version 2.6.32-279.el6 and OpenFabrics version 1.5.4.1.

6.2   Microbenchmark Level Evaluation

We start the evaluation of the proposed design with the extended version of OMB introduced in Sect. 5.3. Using both latency and overlap as metrics, we evaluate the performance of the three different communication patterns of personalized collective operations; All-to-one, One-to-all and All-to-all as well as their V-version respectively. The comparison is performed up to 2,048 cores for All-to-one and One-to-all and up to 4,096 cores for All-to-all among these four different schemes:

- Default - The default scheme with only the non-blocking collective followed by the wait operation.
- RDMA-Aware - The proposed RDMA-Aware scheme.
- Default-Iprobe - The default scheme with the proposed NBC benchmarks calling MPI_Iprobe 1,000 times at equal intervals between the non-blocking collective and the wait. We ran the proposed benchmarks with three different values for the number of MPI_Iprobe calls (1,000, 10,000 and 50,000) and identified that we get maximum overlap with 1,000 calls itself. So we use this value for all our experiments.
- Default-Thread - The default scheme with one MPICH async thread progressing communication in the background for each process.

Performance of All-to-one Operation. Figure 4(a) and (b) show latency and overlap comparison respectively of non-blocking MPI_Igather operation for 2,048 processes. In the short message region, the cost of broadcasting the tuple consisting of rkey and the receive buffer address has a near-constant overhead for the *RDMA-Aware* scheme while the baseline *Default* scheme does not incur these costs (Fig. 4(a)). At larger message sizes, however, the cost of registration adds to initialization overheads and more importantly the latency of *RDMA-Aware* scheme grows super-linearly as bandwidth limitations and HCA contention weigh in and possibly results in network serialization. Scheme *Default-Thread* closely matches the latency of the *Default* scheme because of the large number of MPI_Iprobe calls which progress outstanding data transfers. Despite this, the *RDMA-Aware* scheme yields good overlap in the short message range and near-perfect overlap in the large message range compared to other schemes (Fig. 4(b)). The short message region yields below 100 % overlap because of the broadcast overhead, but in comparison this overhead is negligible for the larger message range which is the primary target region for non-blocking collectives. The trends of both latency and overlap metrics are in favor of the *RDMA-Aware* scheme for MPI_Igatherv operation as shown in Fig. 5(a) and (b). As we can observe in Fig. 5(a), the *RDMA-Aware* scheme is able to deliver improvements in latency of up to 89 times compared to the state-of-the-art for small to medium message sizes. In the short message range the *Default* scheme uses MPI_Issend operation for scalability reasons (so that the root process is not overwhelmed with messages from the non-root processes). However, this leads to poor latency and overlap. The performance of *Default-Thread* was significantly worse compared to the other approaches for MPI_Igatherv. Hence, we do not show them in Fig. 5.

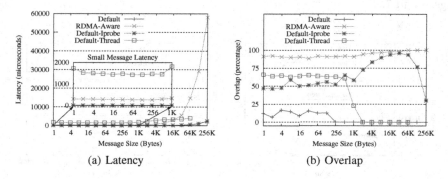

(a) Latency   (b) Overlap

Fig. 4. Performance of MPI_Igather with different NBC designs at 2,048 processes

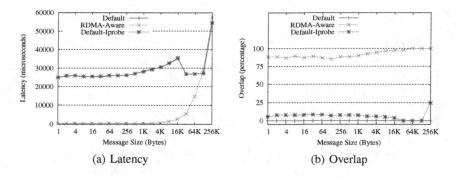

(a) Latency   (b) Overlap

Fig. 5. Performance of MPI_Igatherv with different NBC designs at 2,048 processes

Performance of One-to-all Operation. The One-to-all operation, being the inverse of the All-to-one operation, exhibits favorable trends of good latency and near-perfect overlap but for one difference — The latency of the MPI_Iscatter operation does not show super-linear growth at 16 KB range possibly due to the *read* nature of underlying network operation which does not alter the contents of the root of the One-to-all operation. As Fig. 6(a) depicts, our proposed *RDMA-Aware* scheme is able to deliver up to 3.23 times improvement in communication latency when compared to the state-of-the-art for MPI_Iscatter in the medium to large message range. The benefits observed increase as the message size increases with the peak benefit seen at a message size of 256 KB. There is, however, a small degradation in the overlap achieved with for 2,048 processes in the 16 KB range which can be attributed to tuning effects. For the MPI_Iscatterv collective, the proposed *RDMA-Aware* scheme is able to deliver performance and overlap similar to the state-of-the-art schemes as depicted in Fig. 7. Note that the performance of *Default-Thread* was significantly worse compared to the other approaches for MPI_Iscatter and MPI_Iscatterv. Hence, we do not show them in Figs. 6 and 7.

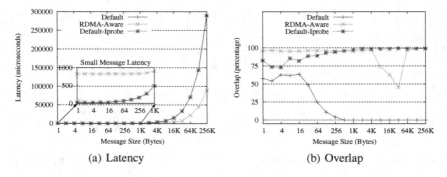

(a) Latency   (b) Overlap

Fig. 6. Performance of MPI_Iscatter with different NBC designs at 2,048 processes

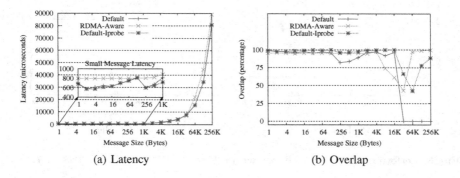

(a) Latency   (b) Overlap

Fig. 7. Performance of MPI_Iscatterv with different NBC designs at 2,048 processes

Performance of All-to-all Operation. Figure 8 shows the latency and overlap performance of the non-blocking All-to-all operation for 512 and 4,096 processes. For this operation, the *RDMA-Aware* scheme yields the best latency compared to the rest of the schemes as well nearly 100 % overlap in the medium and large message range. The allgather operation issued decouples control message exchange and data transfer operations and this yields good overlap and latency. As shown in Fig. 8(c), the latency of the *RDMA-Aware* non-blocking All-to-all is up to 3.71 times lesser than the *Default* scheme at a message size of 32 KB. However, as message size increases, the performance of the two schemes converge as network bandwidth becomes the chief bottleneck.

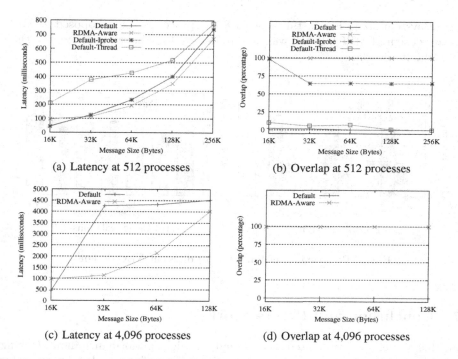

(a) Latency at 512 processes

(b) Overlap at 512 processes

(c) Latency at 4,096 processes

(d) Overlap at 4,096 processes

Fig. 8. Performance of MPI_Ialltoall with different NBC designs at 512 and 4,096 processes

6.3 Evaluation with Application Kernels : P3DFFT

In this section, we study the characteristics of our proposed solution with the P3DFFT Kernel with support for overlapping computation and communication described in Sect. 3.4. Note that we have used the "-DUSE_EVEN" build option to make P3DFFT use MPI_Ialltoall instead of MPI_Ialltoallv.

We perform weak scaling experiments where the problem size increases with the size of the job. In all experiments the problem size was chosen so as to keep the percentage of memory consumed by the P3DFFT kernel at about 75 % to 80 % of available system memory. Figure 9 shows the performance of P3DFFT for different NBC designs. We do not consider the *Default-Iprobe* design here due to the fact that it requires re-design of the P3DFFT kernel. We observe that our proposed design can lead to significant improvements in the execution time of the P3DFFT kernel in all cases. As we can see, *RDMA-Aware* performs the best for all system sizes. *Default-Thread*, on the other hand, performs the worst. We believe this is due to MPICH async threads stealing compute cycles away from the main application thread. Based on this observation, we eliminate *Default-Thread* from further runs at larger scales. In Fig. 9(b), we compare the performance of *Default* and *RDMA-Aware* at large scales. As with Fig. 9(a), we see that our proposed *RDMA-Aware* approach performs better than "Default" for all system sizes. For instance, with 8,192 processes, our proposed *RDMA-Aware* design of MPI_Ialltoall was able to deliver 19 % better performance than the default version.

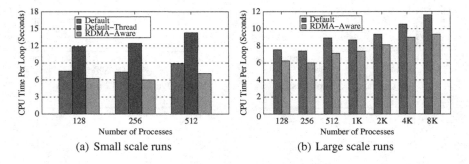

(a) Small scale runs   (b) Large scale runs

Fig. 9. Performance of P3DFFT for different NBC designs

7   Conclusion and Future Work

In this paper, we presented the design of high performance non-blocking personalized collective operations that offer near-perfect overlap of computation and communication and good communication latency for RDMA enabled HPC interconnects like IB. We proposed a generic approach to design non-blocking collectives with near-perfect overlap for RDMA-based networks and designed RDMA-Aware non-blocking collectives for three personalized communication patterns - All-to-all, All-to-one and One-to-all. We enhanced the OSU microbenchmarks by adding NBC benchmarks to measure overlap, init time and wait time. We also added an option to the proposed OSU NBC microbenchmarks to insert MPI_Iprobe calls equally during computation. We also performed a careful analysis of the benefits of our approaches with the proposed OSU NBC microbenchmarks and P3DFFT application kernel at a large scale. Our experimental evaluation showed that our proposed designs are able to deliver near-perfect overlap of computation and communication for personalized collective operations on modern HPC systems at scale. At the microbenchmark level, the proposed RDMA-Aware collectives delivered improvements in latency of up to 89 times for MPI_Igatherv, 3.71 times for MPI_Ialltoall and, 3.23 times for MPI_Iscatter over the state-of-the-art designs. We also observed an improvement of up to 19 % for the P3DFFT kernel at 8,192 cores on the Stampede supercomputing system at TACC.

In future, we plan to evaluate P3DFFT, PSDNS, as well as other kernels and applications that use personalized collectives at larger scales and on other RDMA-enabled networks. Further, we aim to study the applicability of such RDMA-Aware techniques to designing other non-personalized collective communication operations such as Reduce, Allreduce and Broadcast. We also plan to publicly release the RDMA-Aware design for NBC and the OSU NBC microbenchmarks with future releases of the MVAPICH2 MPI library.

References

1. Donzis, D., Yeung, P.K., Pekurovsky, D.: Turbulence simulations on $O(10^4)$ processors. In: TeraGrid, June 2008
2. Gupta, R., Balaji, P., Panda, D.K., Nieplocha, J.: Efficient collective operations using remote memory operations on VIA-based clusters. In: 2003 Proceedings of the International Parallel and Distributed Processing Symposium, p. 9, April 2003
3. Hoefler, T., Lumsdaine, A.: Message progression in parallel computing - to thread or not to thread?. In: Cluster (2008)
4. Hoefler, T., Schneider, T., Lumsdaine, A.: Accurately measuring collective operations at massive scale. In Proceedings of the 22nd IEEE International Parallel & Distributed Processing Symposium, PMEO 2008 Workshop, April 2008
5. Hoefler, T., Siebert, C., Lumsdaine, A.: Group operation assembly language - a flexible way to express collective communication. In: ICPP-2009 - The 38th International Conference on Parallel Processing. IEEE, September 2009
6. Hoefler, T., Squyres, J.M., Rehm, W., Lumsdaine, A.: A case for non-blocking collective operations. In: Min, G., Di Martino, B., Yang, L.T., Guo, M., Rünger, G. (eds.) ISPA Workshops 2006. LNCS, vol. 4331, pp. 155–164. Springer, Heidelberg (2006)
7. Hoefler, T., Gottschling, P., Lumsdaine, A., Rehm, W.: Optimizing a conjugate gradient solver with non-blocking collective operations. Parallel Comput. **33**(9), 624–633 (2007)
8. Hoefler, T., Lumsdaine, A., Rehm, W.: Implementation and performance analysis of non-blocking collective operations for MPI. In: 2007 Proceedings of the 2007 ACM/IEEE Conference on Supercomputing, SC 2007, pp. 1–10. IEEE (2007)
9. InfiniBand Trade Association. http://www.infinibandta.com
10. Intel MPI Benchmarks (IMB). https://software.intel.com/en-us/articles/intel-mpi-benchmarks
11. Liu, J., Jiang, W., Wyckoff, P., Panda, D.K., Ashton, D., Buntinas, D., Gropp, B.,Tooney, B.: High Performance Implementation of MPICH2 over InfiniBand with RDMA Support. In: IPDPS (2004)
12. Kandalla, K., Yang, U., Keasler, J., Kolev, T., Moody, A., Subramoni, H., Tomko, K., Vienne, J., Panda, D.K.: Designing non-blocking allreduce with collective offload on infiniband clusters: a case study with conjugate gradient solvers. In: IEEE International Symposium on Parallel and Distributed Processing (IPDPS) (2012)
13. Kandalla, K., Subramoni, H., Tomko, K., Pekurovsky, D., Sur, S., Panda, D.K.: High-performance and scalable non-blocking all-to-all with collective offload on InfiniBand clusters: a study with parallel 3D FFT. Comput. Sci. **26**, 237–246 (2011)
14. Kandalla, K.C., Subramoni, H., Tomko, K., Pekurovsky, D., Panda, D.K.: A novel functional partitioning approach to design high-performance MPI-3 non-blocking alltoallv collective on multi-core systems. In: 42nd International Conference on Parallel Processing, ICPP 2013, Lyon, France, 1–4 October 2013, pp. 611–620 (2013)

15. Kini, S.P., Liu, J., Wu, J., Wyckoff, P., Panda, D.K.: Fast and scalable barrier using rdma and multicast mechanisms for infiniband-based clusters. In: Dongarra, J., Laforenza, D., Orlando, S. (eds.) EuroPVM/MPI 2003. LNCS, vol. 2840, pp. 369–378. Springer, Heidelberg (2003)
16. Lawry, W., Wilson, C., Maccabe, A.B., Brightwell, R.: COMB: a portable benchmark suite for assessing MPI overlap. In: IEEE Cluster, pp. 23–26 (2002)
17. Liu, J., Jiang, W., Wyckoff, P., Panda, D.K., Ashton, D., Buntinas, D., Gropp, W., Toonen, B.: Design and implementation of MPICH2 over InfiniBand with RDMA support. In: Proceedings of Int'l Parallel and Distributed Processing Symposium (IPDPS 2004), April 2004
18. Liu, J., Mamidala, A., Panda, D.K.: Fast and scalable MPI-level broadcast using InfiniBand's hardware multicast support. In: Proceedings of Int'l Parallel and Distributed Processing Symposium (IPDPS 04), April 2004
19. Luo, M., Wang, H., Vienne, J., Panda, D.K.: Redesigning MPI shared memory communication for large multi-core architecture. computer science - research and development, pp. 1–10. doi:10.1007/s00450-012-0210-8
20. Luo, M., Wang, H., Vienne, J., Panda, D.K.: Redesigning MPI shared memory communication for large multi-core architecture. Comput. Sci. 28(2–3), 137–146 (2013)
21. Venkata, M., Graham, R., Ladd, J., Shamis, P., Rabinovitz, I., Vasily, F., Shainer, G.: ConnectX-2 CORE-direct enabled asynchronous broadcast collective communications. In: Proceedings of the 25th IEEE International Parallel and Distributed Processing Symposium, Workshops (2011)
22. Mamidala, A., Liu, J., Panda, D.K.: Efficient barrier and allreduce on IBA clusters using hardware multicast and adaptive algorithms. In: IEEE Cluster Computing (2004)
23. ConnectX-2 VPI with CORE-Direct Technology. http://www.mellanox.com/page/products_dyn?product_family=61&mtag=connectx_2_vpi
24. Programmable ConnectX-3 Pro Adapter Card Dual-Port Adapter with VPI. http://www.mellanox.com/page/products_dyn?product_family=202&mtag=programmable_connectx_3_pro_vpi_card
25. Connect-IB Single/Dual-Port InfiniBand Host Channel Adapter Cards. http://www.mellanox.com/page/products_dyn?product_family=142
26. Message Passing Interface Forum. MPI: A Message-Passing Interface Standard, March 1994
27. MPI-3 Standard Document. http://www.mpi-forum.org/docs/mpi-3.0/mpi30-report.pdf
28. Network-Based Computing Laboratory. MVAPICH: MPI over InfiniBand, 10GigE/iWARP and RoCE. http://mvapich.cse.ohio-state.edu/
29. Nomura, A., Ishikawa, Y.: Design of kernel-level asynchronous collective communication. In: Keller, R., Gabriel, E., Resch, M., Dongarra, J. (eds.) EuroMPI 2010. LNCS, vol. 6305, pp. 92–101. Springer, Heidelberg (2010)
30. OSU Micro-benchmarks. http://mvapich.cse.ohio-state.edu/benchmarks/
31. Pekurovsky, D.: P3DFFT: a framework for parallel computations of fourier transforms in three dimensions. SIAM J. Sci. Comput. 34(4), C192–C209 (2012)
32. Portals Network Programming Interface. http://www.cs.sandia.gov/Portals/
33. Romanow, A., Bailey, S.: An overview of RDMA over IP. In: Proceedings of International Workshop on Protocols for Long-Distance Networks (PFLDnet2003) (2003)
34. Laizet, S., Lamballais, E., Vassilicos, J.C.: A numerical strategy to combine high-order schemes, complex geometry and parallel computing for high resolution dns of fractal generated turbulence. Comput. Fluids 39, 471–484 (2010)

35. Schneider, T., Eckelmann, S., Hoefler, T., Rehm, W.: Kernel-based offload of collective operations – implementation, evaluation and lessons learned. In: Jeannot, E., Namyst, R., Roman, J. (eds.) Euro-Par 2011, Part II. LNCS, vol. 6853, pp. 264–275. Springer, Heidelberg (2011)
36. Sandia MPI Micro-Benchmark Suite (SMB). http://www.cs.sandia.gov/smb/index.html
37. Sur, S., Bondhugula, U.K.R., Mamidala, A.R., Jin, H.-W., Panda, D.K.: High performance RDMA based all-to-all broadcast for infiniband clusters. In: Bader, D.A., Parashar, M., Sridhar, V., Prasanna, V.K. (eds.) HiPC 2005. LNCS, vol. 3769, pp. 148–157. Springer, Heidelberg (2005)
38. Sur, S., Jin, H.-W., Chai, L., Panda, D.K.: RDMA read based rendezvous protocol for MPI over InfiniBand: design alternatives and benefits. In: Proceedings of the Eleventh ACM SIGPLAN Symposium on Principles and Practice of Parallel Programming, PPoPP 2006, pp. 32–39. ACM, New York, NY, USA (2006)
39. Texas Advanced Computing Center. Stampede Supercomputer. http://www.tacc.utexas.edu/
40. TOP 500 Supercomputer Sites. http://www.top500.org

Design Methodology for Optimizing Optical Interconnection Networks in High Performance Systems

Sébastien Rumley[1(✉)], Madeleine Glick[2], Simon D. Hammond[3],
Arun Rodrigues[3], and Keren Bergman[1]

[1] Lightwave Research Laboratory, Columbia University, New York, USA
{rumley,bergman}@ee.columbia.edu
[2] College of Optical Science, University of Arizona, Tucson, USA
mglick@optics.arizona.edu
[3] Sandia National Laboratories, Albuquerque, USA
{sdhammo,afrodri}@sandia.gov

Abstract. Modern high performance computers connect hundreds of thousands of endpoints and employ thousands of switches. This allows for a great deal of freedom in the design of the network topology. At the same time, due to the sheer numbers and complexity involved, it becomes more challenging to easily distinguish between promising and improper designs. With ever increasing line rates and advances in optical interconnects, there is a need for renewed design methodologies that comprehensively capture the requirements and expose trade-offs expeditiously in this complex design space. We introduce a systematic approach, based on Generalized Moore Graphs, allowing one to quickly gauge the ideal level of connectivity required for a given number of end-points and traffic hypothesis, and to collect insight on the role of the switch radix in the topology cost. Based on this approach, we present a methodology for the identification of Pareto-optimal topologies. We apply our method to a practical case with 25,000 nodes and present the results.

Keywords: Topology · Network · HPC · Interconnect

1 Introduction

As aggregated computing power approaches the Exascale mark, and more importantly, as parallelism reaches unprecedented levels, modern interconnects need to provide ever growing bandwidths and connectivity. For rack-to-rack links, and in the near future, for all types of connections, this trend is likely to lead to the increased use of photonic networks. This transition provides an opportunity to re-examine interconnect design methodologies. Photonic systems differ in many aspects from conventional electrical ones. Depending on which optical technology is used, and how it is used, a particular design can be well suited or on the contrary fairly ill-adapted.

In this work, we examine the selection of the interconnect topology using two criteria: the switch radix, and the number of links. There is considerable research into increasing the port count of different flavors of optical switches [1, 2]. It would be

© Springer International Publishing Switzerland 2015
J.M. Kunkel and T. Ludwig (Eds.): ISC High Performance 2015, LNCS 9137, pp. 454–471, 2015.
DOI: 10.1007/978-3-319-20119-1_32

helpful to system designers and component researchers to have a clearer view of the goals and trade offs. The situation is the same at the link level. There is considerable progress in components and also work on power efficient and/or power proportional systems. We aim to establish a methodology that can clearly expose the benefits and shortcomings of various topologies along these axes.

A great variety of topology descriptions are available in existing literature. Multi-dimensional tori and hierarchical structures (fat-trees) have been the dominant supercomputer interconnects for many years (mid 1980 s to mid 2000 s) [3]. Tori fundamentally replicate the same structure as many of the simulations they support (2D or 3D stencils) [4]. They offer bandwidth in a very specific manner, which can be very efficient if the supporting code follows the same structure [5]. On the other hand, fat-trees can be constructed as virtual crossbars offering general purpose connectivity [6, 7]. Connectivity patterns, have, however, recently received renewed attention and these toroidal or hierarchical architectures have been progressively superseded by more complex schemes. This can be partly explained by the advent of two trends. On one hand, there is a growing imbalance between the energy costs of computation and communication. Tighter transistor integration allows computing circuits to be more efficient, but contributes little in decreasing bit displacement costs [8]. Networks are thus growing contributors to overall energy consumption - and subsequently dissipation, which is also a serious concern. On the other hand, increased expectations in terms of aggregated computing power, coupled with the progressive saturation of both CPU and chip computing power, leads to a general inflation of the interconnect size [9]. As underlined in several studies (e.g. [10]) as well as in what follows, the cost of traditional tori and fat-trees becomes discouraging at very large scale and under arbitrary traffic. More scalable alternatives, in particular, Flattened Butterfly [3], Dragonfly [11], Jelly-fish [12] and Slim-fly [13] have thus been proposed.

All these studies, however, address the question "what is the ideal topology?" by promoting a recipe to assemble a topology and by comparing it to other instances. In this paper, we dig deeper and propose an analytical approach to evaluate the fundamental connectivity requirements. Unless a radical breakthrough is achieved, larger interconnects will continue to be required, they will represent an increasing part of the operational costs, and they will integrate an increasing proportion of photonics. The motivation is thus to more clearly define metrics, requirements and options to gauge suitability of design options. Our proposed methodology, by allowing a rapid evaluation of the switch radix/capacity requirement, addresses these needs. It is also general enough to be applied in multiple contexts, even photonic-free ones.

Our approach is based on a capacity-flow analysis, and uses Generalized Moore Graphs. These graphs minimize the average routing distance. As such, they can be used as an optimal bound in terms of connectivity, as developed in Sect. 3. In Sect. 4, we further develop our approach in order to support a broader range of input cases. In particular, we integrate in our formulation a variable concentration factor, which represents the number of nodes or servers that share an entry switch. Varying this factor allows us to explore the fundamental cost/performance/hardware requirements trade-offs that exists in terms of topologies, for various global interconnect sizes. We use these results to derive conclusions on fundamental future needs in terms of the switch radix. In Sect. 5, we evaluate several classical topologies against the bound, and show that Flattened Butterflies, despite their relative simplicity, achieve good performance. Since routing in these networks can be made very simple, they are still of interest for future large scale machines. Finally we sketch future research directions where our approach could be of further use, or further developed, and draw final conclusions in Sects. 6 and 7.

2 Related Work

Most classical means to interconnect multiple Processing Elements (PE) have been investigated in the 1970 s—1980 s. Preparata et al. proposed the Cube-Connected-Cycles network architecture [14], Bhuyan et al. summarized the properties of Hypercube networks [15] previously proposed by Pease [16] and Leiserson described the Fat-Tree concept [6]. Dally investigated the performance of n-dimensional tori [17]. These analyses targeting parallel computing were preceded by those realizing efficient automated switches for telephone networks [18]. The fundamental performance and cost metrics that apply to connection networks (average traffic delay, average traffic density, total connection cost, connections per node, reliability) are analyzed in the most "obvious" types of interconnection by Wittie [19].

Most of these references are over 20 years old. Since then, the computing power of supercomputers has generally doubled every year on average in two eras. Until the early 2000 s, most of this increase was covered by the increase of the single CPU power (either through higher clocking or increased instruction level parallelism). The increase in terms of CPU (or core, as multi-core appeared) parallelism, although continuous, was less strong. Consequently, over this period, interconnect node count increased only modestly and results obtained in the literature cited above were sufficient to meet demand.

At the turn of the millennium, however, the scaling limitation of a single processor [9] became apparent. This triggered renewed interest in interconnection structures, in particular in those supported by high radix switches [20]. These switches, instead of providing only 8 to 24 bi-directional ports, pushed the port count to 64 [21] by 2006, and to more than 100 by today [22]. With such high port counts, more highly connected and compact topologies become feasible. The Flattened Butterfly [3], Dragonfly [11], and more recently, Slim-fly [13] architectures all enter in this new generation of topologies.

There are various reasons that might promote one topology over another. Some structures make routing decisions (Flattened Butterfly [3], Tori [17]), traffic-balancing (Dragonfly [11]) or incremental deployment (Exchanged Crossed Cube [23], Jellyfish [12]) easier. As the interconnect size grows, however, the economic argument becomes dominant, favoring designs involving as few resources as possible.

The aim of efficient resource utilization naturally leads one to a graph theoretic approach. The relation to the Moore Graph and Moore bound is mentioned by Von Conta [24], who also analyzes the structure of Tori and proposes other graphs (and methods to create them) to approach the Moore bound. The suitability of some Cayley graphs for designing interconnection networks is underlined by Akers and Krishnamurthy [25]. Hsieh and Hsiao showed k-valent Cayley graphs are maximally fault tolerant [26].

McKay, Miller and Siran propose a method (exploited to create the Slim-fly architecture) to construct non-Cayley graphs of unlimited sizes, all of diameter two (shortened as MMS) [27]. Most of these MMS graphs are the largest diameter 2 graphs known so far. A table of the largest graphs (of any diameter <10) is provided in Reference [28].

The usage of optimal graphs as the Petersen or the Hoffman-Singleton graph has also been proposed [29]. Random search methods have been exploited to identify large graphs of small diameter [30, 31]. Random addition of links to rings [32] or simply random wiring of switches [12] has also been investigated. The optimal properties of the Generalized Moore Graph for comparison purposes have been previously exploited in the context of Metropolitan Network planning [33].

Topologies are generally compared and considered in the literature under maximal all-to-all traffic, as a proxy for worst conditions. In practice, observed utilization pattern almost always clearly differ from all-to-all, as illustrated by Vetter et al. [34] or Kandula et al. [35]. A significant effort is also invested to improve the matching between (actual or future) parallel codes requirements and topology capabilities, in particular through large-scale simulation [36, 37].

3 Identifying Ideal Connectivities

We start by defining terms and notations, and by clarifying the framework of this study. The decision problem can be summarized as follows: how does one connect N processing elements (PE) such that each PE pair can communicate (even minimally). We assume that each PE has a single bidirectional link with the outside world. We also assume that every link has a given, constant capacity, for example 10 Gb/s. In our calculations, all capacity and traffic measures are normalized to this reference capacity. Consequently, there is no need to retain its absolute value, and a PE can be assumed to have a communication capacity of 1 unit (u), in both directions. We also neglect how links are implemented. In practice links may be composed of multiple parallel lanes or even cables. We finally assume that PEs are attached to a single switch through a unique, bidirectional link of $1u$.

We denote r the number of ports available in each switch, i.e. the switch radix. All switches are assumed equivalent and capable of achieving 100 % throughput as long as flows are (on the medium term) well balanced among the input and outputs. Unless r is larger than the number of PEs N, each switch is connected to at least one other switch to ensure global connectivity among all PEs. Two switches can be connected by more than one link in order to support a sustained traffic flow larger than $1u$.

We further assume that PEs are distributed as equally as possible among the switches, and hence that we have $S = \lceil N/C \rceil$ switches, where C is the concentration factor. With this assumption, we focus our study on direct interconnection networks as opposed to indirect ones. This assumption also allows us to consider all switches as equivalent [25].

We are interested in determining how many links must be placed between each switch pair. In raw optimization terms, this means finding $S(S-1)$ positive integer values, which become an unmanageable problem, especially if S is equal or larger than one thousand as it is the case in recent supercomputers.

We start by investigating how many switch pairs should be connected, or, stated slightly differently, how highly connected should the topology be. We define the connectivity of a topology, noted R, as the average number of direct neighbors a switch has, excluding the PEs. This is equivalent to the average vertex degree in graph theory. R can be as large as $S-1$, in which case the topology is a full-mesh. If the topology forms a ring, $R = 2$. Topologies with a connectivity $R < 2$ are possible but are not fault tolerant, a quality that we expect from HPC interconnects. Establishing how highly connected should the topology be means therefore finding the appropriate value of R between 2 and $S-1$.

R determines the global capacity of the topology. Hence, without further assumption about the way given PE pairs communicate, and since all switches are equivalently connected to PE, there is no first order reason to concentrate more connections around a particular switch or between a particular switch pair. If n links have to be installed between two switches to adequately support the traffic, n links will also be required between any of the connected pairs. This allows us to observe that, under this assumption, the total number of links is $nSR/2$ and the total installed capacity is nSR.[1]

Considering the traffic demand, the amount of data that is injected into the interconnect, and the instants at which that data is injected is affected by multiple factors: node or server computing power and architecture, type of software executed, implementation of the software, or even input-data currently processed by the software. Quantifying the requirements is therefore a difficult task. To obtain an idea of the design requirements one generally defines a challenging scenario, as the maximal uniform traffic case: each of the PEs of the system uses its maximum networking capacities to distribute messages equally among all other PEs, i.e. each PEs sends a flow of $1/(N-1)\ u$ to each other PE. Under this traffic assumption, and that one PE is connected to each switch, i.e. $C = 1$, we can formulate the total traffic flow as

$$N(N-1) \cdot \frac{1}{N-1} \cdot \Delta = N\Delta$$

which is the product of the number of flows, the flow magnitude and the average routing distance (in hops), Δ. Hence, the more hops a message has to travel, the more time it occupies links and switches. Note that the knowledge of the average distance is sufficient as long as all flows have the same magnitude.

We have shown that in a regular topology with S switches, each associated with 1 PE ($S = N$ as $C = 1$) and under maximum uniform traffic, the total traffic is $N\Delta$. On other hand, the capacity obtained maintaining symmetry is $nSR = nNR$. In order to have the topology at least asymptotically supporting the traffic, the inequality $N\Delta \le nNR$ must hold.

To evaluate the connectivity R, and to this aim, express Δ as a function of R, we assume that the topology will be organized such that distances between switches are

---

[1] Each switch is connected on average to R others with n links, thus nSR ports are occupied in total. As each link connects two ports, the number of links is $nSR/2$. Since each link is assumed bidirectional, it represents two units of capacity so the total capacity is nSR.

kept short. We can expect the final topology, whatever its R being, to be closely related to an ideal one of same size that minimizes the average distance Δ. In the best case, this ideal topology is a Generalized Moore Graph (GMG - described in the Appendix) and the average distance $\Delta_{GMG}(R)$ between a switch and its $S-1$ neighbors (and thus between any node pair) can be written as

$$\Delta_{GMG}(R) = \frac{R + 2R(R-1) + 3R(R-1)^2 + \ldots + (D-1)R(R-1)^{D-2} + Dx}{S-1} \quad (1)$$

where $x = S - 1 - R - R(R-1) - R(R-1)^2 - \ldots - R(R-1)^{D-2}$ is the number of neighbors at a maximum distance D, and R is the maximum degree in the topology (D is also the diameter).

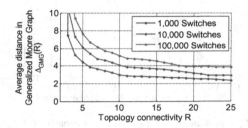

Fig. 1. Evolution of the average distance in a Generalized Moore Graph.

With Δ expressed as a function of R, we rewrite the inequality as $\Delta_{GMG}(R) \le nR$. We simplify further by showing that n can be assumed to be equal to one. As we are interested in minimizing the topology costs, which we assume highly correlated with the number links, we also want to minimize the product nR. As shown in Fig. 1, the average distance $\Delta_{GMG}(R)$ decreases with larger values R, and with it the total traffic. In contrast, changing n has no influence on the traffic. We can exploit this fact. Taking the case $n = 2$ and $R = 4$, thus $nR = 8$. By rebalancing the factors using $n' = 1$ and $R' = 8$, the product is unchanged. On the contrary, the traffic side of the equation may be smaller but will never be larger. Therefore, under the assumptions listed so far, choosing $n = 1$ never leads to less economical topologies.

Finally, this allows us to state that the smallest integer value R for which the inequality $\Delta_{GMG}(R) \le R$ holds, R_{opt}, is the connectivity of the most economical topology that supports N PEs, each connected to a switch and exchanging maximum uniform traffic.

There is no evident closed-form expression for R_{opt}. However, as shown in Fig. 2a, R_{opt} grows relatively slowly with $N = S$, it is therefore easy to find R_{opt} by calculating $\Delta_{GMG}(R)$ for increasing values of R. This approach allows one to also identify the diameter of the most economical GMG, D_{opt} (Fig. 2b). Note that D_{opt} is not monotonically increasing. When considering topologies of increasing sizes, at some points the larger size justifies a larger connectivity. As this increment of R allows more switches to be present at closer distances, it generally allows one to "remove" a level in the hierarchy, causing a drop in D_{opt}.

The evaluation of R_{opt} also allows us to analyze the capacity requirements of the most economical GMG topologies, which is given by $CAP_{opt} = NR_{opt}$, and plotted in Fig. 2c. Notably, the total amount of resources increases supra linearly with the number of PEs, even in the optimal case: larger topologies thus induce a "complexity" penalty.

The values above are based on the conjecture that a GMG topology with N vertices and maximal degree R_{opt} exists. As in practice very few such graphs have been proven to exist, and even fewer have been constructed, these values must be considered as indicators and not as absolute goals. In Sect. 5 real topologies are compared to the GMG "bound" graph.

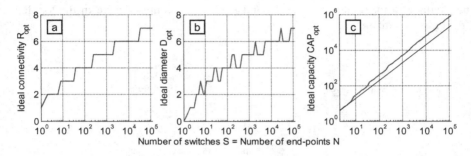

Fig. 2. Connectivity R_{opt} (a), diameter D_{opt} (b) and total capacity CAP_{opt} (c) of the ideal GMG topologies of increasing sizes with concentration factor $C = 1$ (one end-point per switch, $S = N$). A strictly linear progression is drawn in (c) for reference.

4   Generalization to Other Concentrations and Traffic Patterns

As described so far, our approach indicates the ideal level of connectivity required to obtain a balanced topology under two assumptions: (1) there is only one PE per switch and, (2) the traffic is uniformly distributed among sources and destinations and injected at maximum rate. In this section we show how our approach can be extended to higher concentrations, and to other traffic assumptions.

Having a concentration factor $C > 1$ modifies the distances between PEs. Supposing a GMG shaped interconnect, PE has now $(C-1)$ PEs at topological distance[2] 0, CR at distance 1, $CR(R-1)$ at distance 2 etc. The minimum average topological distance between PEs must be rewritten as follows:

$$\Delta_{GMG}(C,R) = \frac{CR + 2CR(R-1) + 3CR(R-1)^2 + \ldots + C(D-1)R(R-1)^{D-2} + CDx}{N-1} \quad (2)$$

---

[2] Topological distance refers to the number of hops achieved over the topology itself and excludes access and egress hops. A topological distance of 0 reflects the situation where messages are immediately forwarded to their final destination after hitting the first switch.

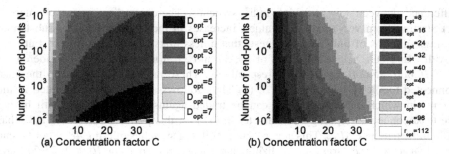

Fig. 3. Dependence of the ideal diameter D_{opt} (a) and of the ideal practical radix r_{opt} (b) on the number of end-points N and the concentration factor C, when considering Generalized Moore Graph topologies.

The total traffic is $N\Delta_{GMG}(C,R)$ and the resulting capacity is now nNR/C. For the same reasons described above, minimum capacity is guaranteed when $n = 1$ which leaves us with the following inequality: $\Delta_{GMG}(C,R) \leq R/C$.

Larger concentrations lead to a reduced number of switches, thus to more compact topologies with smaller average topological distance. This in turn reduces the total traffic rate, which eventually translates into weaker requirements in terms of total capacities. Note also that $N(C-1)$ PE pairs have topological distance 0. If the concentration C is equal to N, there is a single switch in the topology so no inter switch links are required at all. One the other hand, large concentrations require the existence of switches with a large number of ports r, as r has to be greater or equal to $C + R$.

R_{opt}, D_{opt} and CAP_{opt} have been evaluated for several values of N up to 100,000, and different concentrations. Figure 3 shows the evolution of D_{opt} (a) and of the required switch radix $r_{opt} = C + R_{opt}$ (b) across this parameter space. To ease the rendering of the figure, and since real switches often have these number of ports, resulting r_{opt} values are rounded up to multiples of 8 up to 48, and to multiples of 16 above 48. Figure 3 shows that if higher concentrations require higher requirements in terms of radix, they also limit the diameter of the topology. As the diameter represents the longest shortest-path in the topology, it is a proxy for the largest zero-load latency. If one desires to maintain this diameter to 2 [13], while achieving ideal connectivity, concentrations larger than 2, 14 and 29 are required for $N = 100, 10,000$ and $100,000$ respectively.

By superimposing the data of Fig. 3a and b, one obtains the Pareto front of the largest topologies with the smallest switch radix, for different diameters, as plotted in Fig. 4a. To maintain a diameter 2 for $N \geq 100,000$ nodes, 96 ports are required. This requirement falls to 32 ports if diameter 3 is acceptable.

If both diameter and radix are crucial indicators of the performance and the technological requirement, they do not fully reflect the cost of the topology, in particular the operational cost (mainly energy) which can be expected to be proportional to the number of links. Figure 4b offers this perspective for three values of N and different concentrations. A fundamental trade-off exists between minimizing the switch radix and the number of links. The final choice of the concentration hence depends on cost difference between low and high radix switches. There are three zones of interest. (1) Starting from very small r_{opt} values, increases in the first translates to substantial savings in terms of links. This suggests that unless links can be kept low cost at both CAPEX and OPEX levels, radixes of *16, 24* and *32* at least should be considered for $N \geq 10,000, 25,000$ and *100,000* respectively. These radixes correspond to the least connected topology with diameter *3*. (2) Then follows a trade-off zone (tinted in the figure) in which capacity savings can be traded against larger radixes, until hitting the least connected topology of diameter *2*. (3) Past this point, an increased radix has little influence on CAP_{tot}. This suggests that building switches offering *48, 64* or *96* can be taken as a good target for realizing interconnects supporting *10,000, 25,000* and *100,000* PEs respectively. Under the assumptions considered, larger values will reduce the average distance and therefore the required capacities, but not in the same proportion.

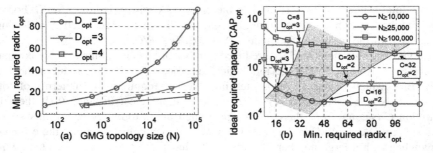

Fig. 4. (a) Evolution of the minimum practical radix r_{opt} required to interconnect N end-points for a given maximum diameter. Ensuring $D_{opt} = 2$ induce high radixes requirements as N scales. Accepting larger diameters allows to decrease the absolute radix needs. (b) Concentration factors can be utilized to obtain different optimal capacity/radix trade-offs. Resulting topologies diversely populate the capacity/required radix Pareto front. Topologies with $D_{opt} = 3$ (tinted zone) appears as interesting trade-offs.

The approach presented here can also be used to analyze interconnect requirements under different traffic assumptions. Traffic predictions can be linearly reduced by assuming that each PE emits uniform traffic at a fraction of its maximum capacity. If this fraction is noted z, the inequality becomes $z\Delta_{GMG}(C,R) \leq R/C$. One can also examine more subtle traffic scenarios in which traffic flows between closely or remotely located PEs are imbalanced. Instead of estimating the traffic injected by a PE through the average distance, one can suppose that each PEs send a fraction p_i of its traffic to the other PEs located at distance i. The traffic sent by each PE thus become $p_1 + 2p_2 + \ldots + (D-1)p_{D-1} + Dp_D$ with the conditions that $0 \leq \sum_i p_i \leq 1$ and that each p_i is positive. If $p_1 = \frac{CR}{N-1}, p_2 = \frac{CR(R-1)}{N-1}, \ldots p_D = \frac{Cx}{N-1}$, i.e. that $(1/N-1)$ of the traffic is sent to the CR PEs located at distance 1, to the $CR(R-1)$ ones located at distance 2, etc., the traffic is uniform at maximal rate again. Another combination of interest is the one where $p_0...p_{D-1} = 0$ and $p_D = 1$. This situation assumes that every PE sends at maximum rate messages to its most distant peers exclusively. It is therefore the worst-case scenario in terms of total traffic magnitude (adversarial traffic scenario).

Figure 5a and b show how these alternative traffic assumptions modify the optimal diameter value for various N and C. For uniform traffic at 50 % load and $N = 25,000$, diameter 2 topologies are equilibrated capacity wise for concentrations of 30 at least. In presence of adversarial traffic, this number falls to 19.

Figure 5c compares the switch radix/installed capacity trade-offs across the three traffic cases (50 % and 100 % uniform, adversarial) for $N \geq 100,000$, which is in general the maximum scale desired for Exascale computers. As pointed out in several studies [3, 13], switches with port counts in this range are currently available, with line rates of several tens of Gb/s. However, Exascale HPC systems will require much larger line rates, in the range of the Tb/s [9]. In this context, the requirement of 100 port switches will become a challenge. As shown in Fig. 5c, dimensioning the topology for 50 % of the maximum injection rate drastically diminishes the radix requirements. If high radix switches cannot be developed for line rates of 1 Tb/s or greater, then smaller radix ones supporting even higher rates may provide an alternative.

In this context, transparent optical switches may be an option. MEMS based switches with more than three hundred ports are already available, however, they suffer from low switching speed. Integrated optics-based ultra-fast switches [2], in contrast, are fundamentally capable of sub-nanosecond switching times. Recent results indicate that 32x32 optical switches based on silicon photonics ring resonators, supporting 20x10 Gb/s parallel (WDM) signals, are feasible without recourse to intermediate amplification [1].

More generally, the analysis provided here indicates that realizing a 32-port switch capable of 1 Tb/s line rate (32 Tb/s total bandwidth) is a reasonable minimum target for realizing an Exascale-class interconnect.

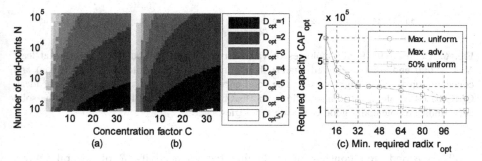

Fig. 5. Impact of the traffic assumption on the ideal diameter D_{opt} for various N and C (a) with $z = 0.5$ (50 % uniform traffic) (b) for worse-case traffic. (c) Capacity/radix trade-off of GMG topologies supporting $N = 100,000$ end-points using various concentration factors and different traffic assumptions

5   Identifying Topologies Close to the Bound

As indicated above, all R_{opt}, CAP_{opt}, D_{opt} or r_{opt} values provided so far have been calculated on the premise that GMGs of any size and degree can be constructed. In reality, most of these GMG topologies either not yet been identified, or have been proven not to exist. In this section we therefore identify a host of topologies whose wiring is known, with adequate connectivity, and compare them to the ideal GMG ones. At the same time, we show how the knowledge of R_{opt} eases this identification process.

In order to find good candidate topologies to interconnect at least *25,000* PEs, able to support maximum uniform traffic, we start with an evaluation of R_{opt} for a range of realistic concentrations (typically 1 to 40), and plot these values against the number of switches corresponding to each concentration, i.e. $\lceil 25,000/C \rceil$. These values form the black line on Fig. 6.

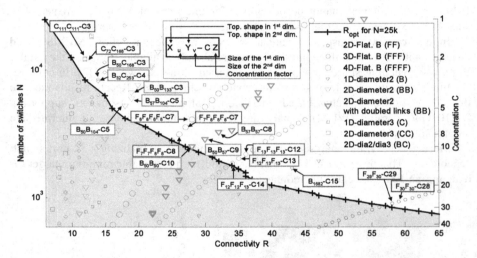

Fig. 6. Connectivity R of topologies of various types and sizes (but all supporting at least $N = 25,000$ end-points) reported against their number of these switches S (left y-axis) and concentration factor C (right y-axis). The solid curve represents the connectivity R_{opt} of ideal, GMG based topologies, and also delimits the feasibility region. Dots located close to the solid curve indicate potentially good candidate topologies.

The second step consists of evaluating the connectivity R of several known topologies such as Flattened Butterflies of different dimensions. We consider the 3D-Flattened Butterfly (3D-FB) as an example: switches are arranged in a 3-dimensional lattice. If concentration $C = 1$ is employed, this 3D lattice should be at least of size $29 \times 29 \times 30 = 25,230$. Therefore, each switch is connected to $R_{3D\text{-}FB,C=1} = 28 + 28 + 29 = 85$ other switches. If $C = 13$, the lattice is $12 \times 13 \times 13 = 2,038$ ($2,038 \times 13 = 26,494$) and switches have a connectivity $R_{3D\text{-}FB,C=13} = 11 + 12 + 12 = 35$. Hence, to each topology type (e.g. 3D-Flattened Butterfly) and concentration C there corresponds a connectivity value (for a given N). This connectivity evaluation is shown in Fig. 6 - for 2D, 3D and 4D-Flattened Butterflies [3] (denoted as FF, FFF and FFFF), for the largest known graphs of diameter 2 and limited degree (denoted as B) including ones exploited by Slim-fly [13], the largest ones of diameter 3 and limited degree (C), and for a 2-dimensional combination[3] of these largest known graphs (BB, BC and CC). We also included the connectivity of BB topologies whose links have been doubled to obtain a higher connectivity. Toroidal interconnects have not been included in Fig. 6 in an effort to not overload the image. If included, they would appear as vertical lines: for example, a 5D-torus has a constant connectivity $R = 10$ for any number of switches. If the links of this 5D-torus are doubled, the connectivity becomes $R = 20$.

All points located at the left of the R_{opt} curve can be excluded: they show a too weak connectivity which will oblige one to interconnect switches with more than one link ($n > 1$). In contrast, practical topologies located close to the optimality curve, but to the right of it, i.e. the ones whose connectivity is slightly higher than the strict required minimum, are of great interest. Obviously, as "real" topologies, one can expect them to show a higher average distance than "virtual" GMG of similar size, but their higher connectivity might be sufficient to compensate this distance penalty.

Finally we further analyze the topologies of greatest interest (those indicated with boxes in Fig. 6 plus several tori) by (1) constructing each topology (2) routing individual flows (using shortest-path routing only) over the topology, (3) looking for the most congested connection between two switches, (4) rounding up this congestion value and multiplying it by the number of edges in the topology (for multi-dimensional topologies, we do that for each dimension separately). By this method we obtain the capacity required in practice to secure a complete absorption of the traffic. This also allows us to determine the minimum required switch radix (rounded to multiples of 8 and 16 as previously). These values are represented on Fig. 7.

Starting from the right side of the graph, the $F_{29}F_{30}$-C29 fails to approach the bound. The dimension of size 29 is not connected enough which obliges us to double its links to ensure sufficient capacity. This is a general problem with Flattened Butterflies. They are in theory capable of any connectivity R, but unless the lattice is equally sized in all dimensions, this total connectivity is not adequately balanced across the dimensions. In contrast, $F_{30}F_{30}$-C28 closely approximates the bound, but requires a large radix of 96. The Slim-fly topology B_{1682}-C15 is the next Pareto dominant datapoint. Similarly to the 2D–FB, it is a diameter two topology, but due to its close to optimal wiring, it requires smaller radix than the 2D-FB. It lies ahead of the bound, however. As visible on Fig. 6, there are relatively few known large graphs of diameter 2 (among them the MMS ones exploited by Slim-fly) which obliged us to consider a topology of higher connectivity than strictly required (43 instead of 35). This explains the distance to the bound. The $F_{13}F_{13}F_{13}$–C12 is also Pareto dominant, followed by the $B_{57}B_{57}$–C8. Although the base graph B_{57} is the largest one found so far for degree 8, by

---

[3] In the Flattened Butterfly topology, all vertices sharing a dimension in the lattice as interconnected (Full-Mesh). In a torus, all these vertices are connected along a ring. In our 2-dimensional construction, vertices sharing a dimension are interconnected by following the structure of the largest known graph for a given diameter and maximum degree.

using it in two dimensions *and* by doubling its edge we diluted its close to optimum properties. Still, it appears as a Pareto dominant topology. The 4D Flattened Butterfly can be realized with the same radix of 40, and for a slight increase in the capacity requirements. As routing and workload mapping is probably made easier with this topology than with the $B_{57}B_{57}$ one, it might also be considered, although not strictly part of the Pareto front. After the 4D–FB, the next Pareto dominant topology is the $B_{50}B_{133}$-C3 but as it lie far from the bound, it shows little value unless large radixes cannot be utilized. More generally, the Pareto front created by Pareto dominant topologies progressively diverges from the bound. This reveals a need for topologies close to the GMG bound, of diameter 3 and larger, and of diverse sizes. These topologies are also harder to emulate with symmetric constructions as the Flattened Butterfly or tori.

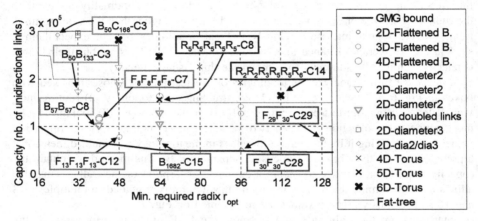

Fig. 7. Capacity/radix trade-off of practical topologies supporting at least 25,000 PEs.

Two additional datapoints have been highlighted on Fig. 7. They reflect topologies used in current dominant Supercomputers. $R_5R_5R_5R_5R_5$-C8 is a 5D-torus as the one available in Sequoia, while $R_2R_2R_3R_5R_5R_6$-C14 mimics the Tofu interconnect [38] (6D-torus) of the K computer. $R_5R_5R_5R_5R_5$-C8 is the best 5D-torus for N = 25,000 maximal and uniform traffic. It dominates all other combinations of sizes and concentrations leading to realistic radixes. Still, its average distance Δ (just above 6) is more than three times larger than $\Delta_{GMG}(C = 21, R = 42) = 1.963$ which would also require a radix of 64. This directly translate to greater than 3 times the capacity requirements (156,250, where the bound indicates 50,022). Other tori, including the best Tofu-like 6D-torus, lie even further from the bound, and no 3D-tori appears in the ranges of Fig. 7. This demonstrates that tori are fairly ill-suited to traffic conditions similar to uniform traffic at large scales. However, as mentioned in the introduction, tori can compensate this hindrance by providing bandwidth in a very structured way, a feature that is generally vastly exploited by workloads.

Although not directly related to our approach, fat-trees with no over-subscription (i.e. full-bisectional bandwidth) can also be characterized by a number of links and radix, and therefore be represented in Fig. 7. For all radixes, a fat-tree involves at least twice as many links than the bound. They are clearly outperformed by the Pareto optimal topologies, expect for small radixes. However, as pointed out above, other close to ideal topologies of larger diameter (not investigated here) might exist and outperform the fat-tree for smaller radixes, too.

6 Discussion and Future Directions

The methodology described here does not cover all facets of the topology selection process. The hypothesis that all links are equivalent, and that traffic is uniformly or arbitrarily distributed, excludes the Dragonfly topology which precisely assumes imbalanced traffic flows. All aspects related to embedding the topology onto back-planes and inter-rack/cabinet cables is also neglected although this may play an important role in the process of choosing one topology over another. The goal of this study is, however, not to provide a final choice of a topology but rather to define a framework allowing us to explore the main trade-offs and minimal requirements. More exhaustive comparisons will be realized in future publications. Still, Fig. 7, covering Tori, Fat-trees, Flattened Butterflies and Slim-flies of various sizes and shape, provide a rather inclusive set of "realistic" topologies that populate current Supercomputers.

No traffic simulations have been conducted on the practical topologies compared in the previous Section. However, if such simulations would be driven with uniform traffic, they would mainly confirm that no surge in latency occurs for loads <1, as all topologies are precisely dimensioned for this aim. In contrast, simulating real workloads in large-scale architectures equipped with the different Pareto optimal topologies would be of high-interest. In particular, we would expect such experiments to confirm the statement that limited diameters are highly desirable. Our future plans include realizing such experiments.

Our approach also allows us to derive further insights on practical topologies. In results not shown here we have found that it allows one to identify how improper wiring, connectivity that is too large or too small, and an unfavorable number of end-points each contribute to making a particular topology sub-optimal.

7 Conclusion

In this study, we concentrate on the relationship between traffic, capacities (i.e. number of links) and switch radixes, and do not deal with other aspects such as maintenance, organization in racks, incremental deployment, load balancing, etc. Surprisingly, even in this reduced scope, there is no clearly dominant recipe for building a topology. We conclude that the choice of the topology should not be made too early in the design process, and not on the sole assumption that one topology or another has been proved optimal in a given context. A final choice among Pareto dominant data points of Fig. 7 (i.e. 5–10 options) can be made after comparison under real traffic with large scale simulators, or based on a detailed economical analysis once the costs of links and switches are known.

Results also show that if 2D-Flattened Butterflies and Slim-flies, both of diameter 2, land close to the bound, approaching the bound with larger diameters, corresponding to tighter radix availabilities, appears trickier. Provided that wide radixes might be hard to adapt to larger line-rates, there is a need for topologies of diameter 3 and 4, not necessarily of largest size, but showing close to optimal average routing distance. Similar topologies of diameter 2 would offer a good complement to the Slim-fly set which appears too scattered to adequately support the whole range of system sizes.

This study also shows that tori appear sensibly dominated by other topologies, although they account for a vast portion of modern Supercomputer interconnects. This suggests that for now workload structures can be mapped reasonably well over their hardware equivalent. However, with the advent of asynchronous parallel programming method, or adaptive workload balancing, traffic profiles may loose their structure. In this case, topologies as close to a GMG as possible seems the most logical choice.

Acknowledgement. This work has been realized in the context of Department of Energy (DoE) ASCR project "Data Movement Dominates". It has been partly supported by the U.S. Department of Energy (DoE) National Nuclear Security Administration (NNSA) Advanced Simulation and Computing (ASC) program through contract PO1426332 with Sandia National Laboratories. Sandia National Laboratories is a multi-program laboratory managed and operated by Sandia Corporation, a wholly owned subsidiary of Lockheed Martin Corporation, for the U.S. Department of Energy's National Nuclear Security Administration under contract DE-AC04-94AL85000.

Appendix

A Generalized Moore Graph can be described as follows. Consider a vertex, V, in any graph of degree R (i.e. whose vertices have never more than R incident links). V cannot have *more* than R direct neighbors. It also cannot have *more* than $R(R-1)$ neighbors at

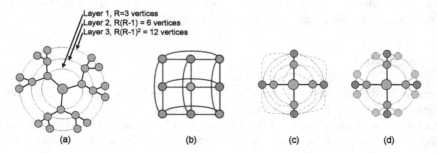

Fig. 8. (a) Maximal expansion possibilities for connectivity/degree $R = 3$ and three layers. Generalized Moore Graphs follow this structure, except that the last layer does not have to be totally filled (b) Example of Generalized Moore Graph (a 3x3 torus) (c) The 3x3 torus reorganized to show the layers (d) A representation of unfilled slots in the last layer

distance 2 (each of its neighbors have R neighbors but V does not count as it is one of them), and generally cannot have *more* than $R(R-1)^{D-1}$ neighbors at distance D. A GMG is a graph which maximally uses this expansion possibilities offered by the degree R: in a GMG graph, each vertex has *exactly* R direct neighbors, *exactly* $R(R-1)^{i-1}$ neighbors at distance i ($i = 2..D-1$), and all the remaining vertices are at distance D. Figure 8 exemplifies the GMG concept. Because inner layers are maximally filled, there is no way to get a vertex closer without interchanging it with another vertex. This means that no distance between two vertices can be reduced, thus that the average distance in the graph is minimized.

References

1. Nikolova, D., Rumley, S., Calhoun, D., Li, Q., Hendry, R., Samadi, P., Bergman, K.: Scaling silicon photonic switch fabrics for data center interconnection networks. Opt. Express **23**(2), 1159–1175 (2015)
2. Lee, B.G., Dupuis, N., Pepeljugoski, P., Schares, L., Budd, R., Bickford, J.R., Schow, C.L.: Silicon photonic switch fabrics in computer communications systems. IEEE Journal of Lightwave Technology (in press)
3. Kim, J., Dally, W.J., Abts, D.: Flattened butterfly: a cost-efficient topology for high-radix networks. In: Proceedings of the International Symposium on Computer Architecture (ISCA), pp. 126–137 (2007)
4. Bhatelé, A., Kalé, L.V.: Benefits of topology aware mapping for mesh interconnects. Parallel Program. Lett. **18**(4), 549–566 (2008)
5. Dally, W.J.: Principles and Practices of Interconnection Networks. Morgan Kaufmann, San Francisco (2004)
6. Leiserson, C.E.: Fat-trees: universal networks for hardware-efficient supercomputing. IEEE Trans. Comput. **C-43**(10), 892–901 (1985)
7. Sano, K.: Interconnection Network: Design Space Exploration of Networks for Supercomputers. Sustained Simulation Performance, Springer, 151–161, 2015
8. Borkar, S.: Role of interconnects in the future of computing. IEEE J. Lightwave Technol. (JLT) **31**(24), 3927–3933 (2013)
9. Rumley, S., et al.: Silicon photonics for exascale systems. IEEE J. Lightwave Technol. (JLT) **33**(3), 547–562 (2015)
10. Bradonjic, M., Saniee, I., Widjaja, I.: Scaling of capacity and reliability in data center networks. In: Proceedings of the SIGMETRICS (2014)
11. Faanes, G., et al.: Cray cascade: a scalable HPC system based on a Dragonfly network. In: Proceedings of the International Conference on High Performance Computing, Networking Storage and Analysis (SC 2012) (2012)
12. Singla, A., Hong, C.-Y., Popa, L., Godfrey, P.B.: Jellyfish: networking data centers randomly. In: Proceedings of the USENIX Symposium on Networked Systems Design and Implementation (NSDI 2012) 2012
13. Besta, M., Hoefler, T.: Slim fly: a cost effective low-diameter network topology. In: Proceedings of the International Conference on High Performance Computing, Networking Storage and Analysis (SC 2014) (2014)
14. Preparata, F.P., Vuillemin, J.: The cube-connected cycles: a versatile network for parallel computation. Commun. ACM **24**(5), 300–309 (1981)

15. Bhuyan, L.N., Agrawal, D.P.: Generalized hypercube and hyperbus structures for a computer network. IEEE Trans. Comput. **C-33**(4), 323–333 (1984)
16. Pease, M.C.: The indirect binary n-Cube microprocessor array. IEEE Trans. Comput. **C-26** (5), 478–482 (1977)
17. Dally, W.J.: Performance analysis of k-ary n-cube interconnection networks. IEEE Trans. Comput. **39**(6), 775–785 (1990)
18. Benes, V.E.: Optical rearrangeable multistage connecting networks. Bell Syst. Tech. J. **43** (4), 1641–1656 (1964)
19. Wittie, L.D.: Communication structures for large networks of microcomputers. IEEE Trans. Comput. **C-30**(4), 264–273 (1981)
20. Kim, J., Dally, W.J., Towles, B., Gupta, A.K.: Microarchitecture of a high radix router. In: Proceedings of the International Symposium on Computer Architecture (ISCA), pp. 420–431 (2005)
21. Scott, S., Abts, D., Kim, J., Dally, W.J.: The blackwidow high-radix clos network. In: Proceedings of the International Symposium on Computer Architecture (ISCA), pp. 16–28 (2006)
22. Barriuso, R., Knies, A.: 108-Port InfiniBand FDR SwitchX Switch Platform Hardware User Manual (2014)
23. Li, K., Mu, Y., Li, K., Min, G.: Exchanged crossed cube: a novel interconnection network for parallel computation. IEEE Trans. Parallel Distrib. Syst. (TPDS) **24**(11), 2211–2219 (2013)
24. Von Conta, C.: Torus and other networks as communication networks with up to some hundred points. IEEE Trans. Comput. **32**(7), 657–666 (1983)
25. Akers, S.B., Krishnamurthy, B.: A group-theoretic model for symmetric interconnection networks. IEEE Trans. Comput. **38**(4), 555–566 (1989)
26. Hsieh, S.-Y., Hsiao, T.-T.: The k-valent graph: a new family of cayley graphs for interconnection networks. In: Proceedings of the International Conference on Parallel Processing (ICPP) (2004)
27. McKay, B.D., Miller, M., Sirán, J.: A note on large graphs on diameter two and given maximum degree. J. Comb. **61**, 1–63 (1998)
28. Miller, M., Sirán, J.: Moore graphs and beyond: a survey of the degree/diameter problem. Electronic Journal of Combinatorics, Dynamic Survey D 14 (2005)
29. Boa, W.-T., et al.: A high-performance and cost-efficient interconnection network for high-density servers. J. Comput. Sci. Technol. **23**(2), 281–292 (2014)
30. Samples, M.: Large networks with small diameter. In: Möhring, R.H. (ed.) WG 1997. LNCS, vol. 1335, pp. 288–302. Springer, Heidelberg (1997)
31. Loz, E., Sirán, J.: New record graphs in the degree-diameter problem. Autralasian J. Comb. **41**, 63–80 (2008)
32. Koibuchi, M., Matsutani, H., Amano, H., Hsu, D.F., Casanova, H.: A case for random shortcut topologies for HPC interconnects. In: Proceedings of the International Symposium on Computer Architecture (ISCA), pp. 177–188 (2012)
33. Guan, K.C., Chan, V.W.S.: Cost-efficient fiber connection topology design for metropolitan area WDM networks. IEEE/OSA J. Opt. Commun. Netw. **1**(1), 158–175 (2009)
34. Vetter, J., et al.: Quantifying architectural requirements of contemporary extreme-scale scientific applications. In: High Performance Computing Systems. Performance Modeling, Benchmarking and Simulation, Springer LNCS (2014)
35. Kandula, S., Sengupta, S., Greenberg, A., Patel, P., Chaiken, R.: The nature of data center traffic: measurements and analysis. In: Proceedings of the ACM Conference on Internet Measurement (IMC), pp. 202–208 (2009)

36. Hendry, G.: The role of optical links in HPC system interconnects. In: Proceedings of the IEEE Optical Interconnects Conference (2013)
37. Hammond, S., et al.: Towards a standard architectural simulation framework. In: Proceedings of the Workshop on Modeling & Simulation of Exascale Systems & Applications (2013)
38. Ajima, Y., Inoue, T., Hiramoto, S., Shimizu, T.: Tofu: interconnect for the K computer. Fujistu Sci. Tech. J. **48**(3), 280–285 (2012)

Quantifying Communication in Graph Analytics

Andreea Anghel[✉], German Rodriguez, Bogdan Prisacari,
Cyriel Minkenberg, and Gero Dittmann

IBM Research — Zurich, Zurich, Switzerland
{aan,rod,bpr,sil,ged}@zurich.ibm.com

Abstract. Data analytics require complex processing, often taking the shape of parallel graph-based workloads. In ensuring a high level of efficiency for these applications, understanding where the bottlenecks lie is key, particularly understanding to which extent their performance is computation or communication-bound. In this work, we analyze a reference workload in graph-based analytics, the Graph 500 benchmark. We conduct a wide array of tests on a high-performance computing system, the MareNostrum III supercomputer, using a custom high-precision profiling methodology. We show that the application performance is communication-bound, with up to 80 % of the execution time being spent enabling communication. We equally show that, with the increase in scale and concurrency that is expected in future big data systems and applications, the importance of communication increases. Finally, we characterize this representative data-analytics workload and show that the dominating data exchange is uniform all-to-all communication, opening avenues for workload and network optimization.

Keywords: Workload characterization · Graph 500 · Profiling · Uniform all-to-all · Graph analytics

1 Introduction

Today's systems generate large volumes of data that need to be transferred, stored, but most of all processed to gain insights. As an example, over the last years, social networks have experienced an exponential growth up to as much as one billion active users with an average of more than one hundred connections each [8]. The complex processing involved in the exploitation of these large data sets requires the use of distributed workloads executed on massively parallel systems. To guarantee a high level of performance for these workloads, it is essential to identify what their bottlenecks are, particularly whether their execution is computation or communication-dominated. In the latter case, optimization is especially of interest, as data motion is expected to become the dominant power consumption component in future HPC systems [15]. One solution to address this challenge is the development of mechanisms that better orchestrate the data motion through the system [10]. However, to implement such mechanisms it is necessary to first understand the application communication patterns.

© Springer International Publishing Switzerland 2015
J.M. Kunkel and T. Ludwig (Eds.): ISC High Performance 2015, LNCS 9137, pp. 472–487, 2015.
DOI: 10.1007/978-3-319-20119-1_33

In the context of data analytics workloads, one particularly relevant class of applications is graph-based analytics. Indeed, the large sets of data generated by social networks and business analytics are often modeled as graphs that need to be processed on large-scale distributed systems using scalable parallel algorithms. A representative of this class is the Graph 500 benchmark suite [20], which has been introduced to guide the design of systems envisioned to support data-intensive applications. The benchmark is designed to assess the performance of supercomputing systems by solving a well-defined graph problem, i.e., the breadth-first search (BFS) graph traversal.

In this paper, we use the MareNostrum III supercomputer [2] to conduct a thorough communication characterization of the most scalable reference MPI implementation of Graph 500. We analyze the data exchange across processes and the variability of the communication-to-computation ratio with the problem size (scale, edge factor) and number of processes. To the best of our knowledge, this is the first study that shows the actual communication pattern of the benchmark, offering preliminary guidance for future application or network design optimization efforts. To improve the precision of our results, we introduce an alternative tracing methodology enabling us to minimize the tracing overhead and adjust communication time for data dependencies.

The remainder of this paper is organized as follows. We start with providing background information about the Graph 500 benchmark and its MPI-simple implementation (Sect. 2). In Sect. 3 we present a selection of related work. We continue in Sect. 4 with a brief description of the computing system and tools we used in the benchmarking process, as well as with a description of the parameters we used for the Graph 500 experiments. In Sect. 5 we present characterization results representative of out-of-the-box utilization of standard profiling tools. Section 6 introduces the custom application characterization methodology for communication profiling and presents the experimental results. We proceed in Sect. 7 with describing the experimental results obtained for the communication patterns study. Finally, we summarize and discuss the main take-aways of this paper in Sects. 8 and 9.

2   Background on Graph 500

Graph 500 is a large-scale benchmark for data-intensive applications. The problem size is given by the *scale* and the *edge factor* parameters of the input graph. If scale is equal to V then the number of vertices equals 2^V and if the edge factor is equal to E then the graph has $2^V \cdot E$ edges. The benchmark implements two main kernels: graph generation and BFS. First, the benchmark generates a list of edges and constructs an undirected graph. The graph construction phase uses the Kronecker graph generator which is similar to the graph generation algorithm presented in [11]. 64 graph nodes are randomly selected and, for each node, the BFS tree with that node as root is computed. The BFS step is validated to ensure that the generated trees are correct. The output of the benchmark is the time necessary to perform the BFS and the number of traversed edges per second (TEPS). In this paper, we focus on the analysis of the BFS kernel as in a graph analytics setting the graph itself would already exist.

Graph 500 provides four implementations of the BFS algorithm: simple, replicated-csr, replicated-csc and one-sided. All four implementations use a level-synchronized BFS algorithm, that is, all the vertices at a given level in the BFS tree are all processed before any vertex in a lower level of the tree is processed [7]. For the remainder of the paper we will focus on the MPI-simple implementation, which, despite its name, is actually the most scalable among all the reference MPI implementations [24].

The MPI-simple version of Graph 500 implements the BFS algorithm as follows. Each MPI process uses two queues: a current queue (*CurrentQueue*) and a next queue (*NextQueue*). *CurrentQueue* hosts all the vertices that have to be visited at the current level. *NextQueue* hosts all the vertices that will need to be visited at the next level. At the end of a level, the two queues are swapped. In addition, each MPI process uses two arrays: *Predecessors* (list of parents) and *Visited* (to track if a vertex has already been visited or not). If an MPI process A needs to visit a vertex that is assigned to another MPI process B, then process A will send a message to process B (via the MPI Isend function), requesting that process B visit that specific vertex. The information passed via this MPI message will include the vertex to be visited, as well as the predecessor in A that triggered the visit. For optimization, multiple such requests can be aggregated in messages of a certain size. This *coalescing* size is a tunable parameter. In this study we use the default value of 4 KB.

3   Related Work

The work presented in this paper lies at the intersection of two research topics: (A) Graph 500 related characterization and (B) communication profiling tools.

3.1   Graph 500 Analysis and Characterization

Previous Graph 500-related research efforts, such as [12,21,24], have implemented optimized versions of the benchmark, tested them on large-scale computing systems and reported their optimization techniques and performance results. In this paper, we do not propose yet another optimized implementation of the benchmark, but we rather focus on an in-depth workload characterization of the most scalable MPI reference implementation of the benchmark.

In the characterization space, Jose et al. [16] report their findings on profiling the execution of the MPI-simple implementation version of Graph 500—tested with 128 processes and a problem scale of 26 and edge factor of 16—using unified MPI+PGAS communication runtime over InfiniBand[TM]. Excluding the synchronization cycles spent in the MPI *all-reduce* calls, a total amount of 60 % of the total BFS time is predicted to represent communication. However, the runtime breakdown of one single problem size may not be sufficient to understand how the communication varies across different problem sizes and/or number of processes.

Suzumura et al. [23] perform a performance evaluation study of Graph 500 on a distributed-memory supercomputer for different types of implementations, including MPI-simple. The study reports profiling results for computation, communication and stall times. Even though the execution breakdowns are shown only for the replicated-based implementations (*replicated-csr* and *replicated-csc*), the authors expect the MPI-simple implementation to have similar performance characteristics as *replicated-csc*. The results show that communication and stall times account for less than 50 % of the total execution time, even when increasing the number of nodes from 1 to 64.

In this paper, we analyze the breakdown of the execution time of the MPI-simple implementation, but across multiple scale, edge factor and number of processes values. This allows us to identify trends in the execution breakdown of the benchmark. We show that the communication time might be underestimated and that communication represents in some cases more than 70 % of the total execution time. In contrast to the cited related work, we also perform an in-depth analysis of the MPI-simple communication patterns across threads (Sect. 7).

3.2 Profiling Tools for Parallel Applications

Crovella et al. [14] propose a methodology for measuring and modeling sources of overhead in parallel Fortran applications. The sources identified are load imbalance, insufficient parallelism, synchronization loss (defined as processor cycles spent acquiring a lock or waiting for a barrier), resource contention or communication loss. We propose a way to achieve a similar breakdown by distinguishing within the communication loss between time spent at the destination waiting for data to be sent by the source (which we call data dependency loss) and time spent waiting for data already in flight (actual communication loss). Furthermore, we propose an alternative methodology for quantifying these losses and use it to perform measurements for the Graph 500 benchmark.

A first step towards extracting characterization information from a parallel application is the use of profiling tools. The information provided by these tools is useful to break down the execution time of the application into time spent in communication and computation. For MPI applications, a typical way to do so is by interposing instrumentation functions between the MPI library functions and the MPI calls of the application. Such profiling tools will intercept application calls, particularly those involving communication: sends, receives, collective operations. This allows keeping a trace, generally in memory with regular flushes to disk, of the communication activity of the application. Some tools are able to provide more detail, such as performance counters before and after each profiled call, more information about the protocols and/or parameters with which the communication took place, or the user function from which the communication primitive was called, etc. Moreover, these tools are able to profile with more or less overhead, or dynamically, re-compiling the application not being necessary. Regardless of these particularities that differentiate the performance of one tool over another, the operating principle of all these tools is essentially the same. Some examples of profiling tools are: Vampir [17], Tau [22], the HPC

Toolkit [13], or Extrae [3], among many others. For this work we will use Extrae, but we could have used any other tool, as we did not require any special feature or modification of the code of Extrae.

4   Preliminaries on Characterization

Our objective is to understand the application performance bottlenecks by profiling its execution. Thus, we have instrumented the Graph 500 MPI-simple implementation and used the Extrae tool to monitor, with minimal changes to the code, the time the application spent in: (i) in MPI asynchronous point-to-point communication calls (calls to MPI Irecv, MPI Isend); (ii) in polling MPI Test calls; (iii) in MPI all-reduce calls; and (iv) outside of MPI functions.

We executed the instrumented code on 4 to 64 nodes with a total of 16 to 256 concurrent processes, on the MareNostrum III supercomputer and obtained a set of preliminary results, presented in Sect. 5. By performing a more detailed data-dependency analysis, we obtained a second set of more detailed results, shown in Sect. 6. Using the Paraver and Paramedir analysis tools [18] on the resulting execution traces, we were able to (i) quantify the proportion of the overall completion time that was spent waiting for communication to complete, performing computation or waiting due to data dependencies, as well as (ii) identify the application's data exchange pattern.

4.1   Benchmarking Platform

To benchmark Graph 500 we used a large-scale supercomputing cluster, MareNostrum III [2], currently ranked 57th in the November 2014 Top 500 list [6]. The cluster consists of more than 3,056 compute nodes and 48,896 cores. Each compute node has two Intel SandyBridge-EP E5-26701600 20 M processors, each with 8 cores running at 2.6 GHz, and is equipped with 32 GB of memory (DDR3-1600). Nodes are interconnected using an InfiniBand^{TM} FDR-10 network.

4.2   Graph 500 Configuration

We downloaded the Graph 500 reference code [4] and compiled it on the supercomputing cluster using the Intel compiler version 13.0.1 and the Intel MPI 4.1.1 default version. The only modification we have made to the reference code was to insert events that mark the beginning and the end of each BFS (after the collection of the time statistics). In terms of problem size, we ran the benchmark for scales as small as 16 and as large as 26, while the edge factors used range between 16 and 256 in successive powers of 2. We used a number of concurrent processes ranging from 32 to 256.

4.3   Tracing and Analysis Tools

To extract the MPI traces of the Graph 500 benchmark we use a light-weight tracing tool, *Extrae*, formerly known as *mpitrace*, developed at the Barcelona Supercomputing Center. The traces have been further processed using two additional tools: a GUI-based trace analyzer called *Paraver*, and *Paramedir*, a command-line analysis tool based on Paraver. The two tools can filter the trace data and visualize time-lines, compute statistics, generate traffic matrices, i.e., spatial traffic distributions, etc.

The tracing library *Extrae* is implemented as an *interposition* library that intercepts the MPI library calls. The tool stores the minimum amount of information needed to, in a later (off-line) phase, match all the communication partners and generate a single trace file that comprises all the communication activity, including parameters of MPI calls. The library also provides an API allowing custom emission of user events. We employ this capability, in particular by using *Extrae*'s API to mark the entry and exit to the relevant code segments of the Graph 500 benchmark. As we are measuring application completion time, it is important to quantify the overhead of the tracing tool. In all our experiments, the impact of tracing on the application runtime did not exceed 15 %.

5   Standard Application Characterization

As an initial approach, we used Extrae to profile all MPI calls that the Graph 500 simple implementation makes. This does not require changing the code of the benchmark in any way. However, in the course of a complete run of the benchmark, there is an initial graph construction phase, after which multiple BFS computation steps (which are the ones we are interested in analyzing), alternate with validation steps (necessary only for solution verification and estimation of the number of traversed edges per second). As such, for convenience, we did minimal changes to the code to signal to the tracing tool the beginning and end of actual BFS tree computations, by means of emitting custom events. Only two events were needed, each requiring a single API call.

Using this straightforward approach, we were able to determine that during the execution of the benchmark, the application is performing one of four types of activities: (1) asynchronous point-to-point communication (MPI Isend or MPI Irecv); (2) polling of pending asynchronous messages (MPI Test); (3) calls to MPI all-reduce; (4) computation, quantified as the time spent outside of any MPI calls.

5.1   Experimental Results

The results obtained using standard characterization are outlined in Fig. 1. The figure shows the percentual breakdown of the application execution into each of the activities enumerated above. The three sub-figures present the impact on this breakdown of three main application parameters: the scale and the edge factor (which determine the problem size) and the number of concurrent processes

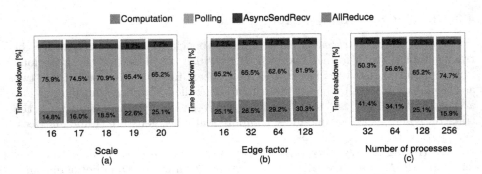

Fig. 1. Standard instrumentation. Single BFS execution time percentual breakdown for varying graph scales under a constant edge factor (16) and 128 concurrent processes (a), for varying edge factors under constant graph scale (20) and 128 concurrent processes (b), and for varying number of concurrent processes under constant graph scale (20) and edge factor (16) (c).

executing the application. Several insights can be extracted from these results. First, the majority of the execution time of the application is spent in either computation or waiting for data to arrive from other processes (polling). In general, polling time dominates, accounting for more than 50 % of the time in all scenarios and for more than 60 % of the time in typical scenarios (where a reasonably high number of concurrent processes are employed). Second, there are a few clear trends of breakdown evolution with the three application parameters, namely: (i) as the scale increases, computation becomes more important, (ii) as the edge factor increases, computation becomes more important, and (iii) increasing the number of concurrent processes significantly decreases the importance of computation. Overall, in a scenario where increasingly larger problems would be solved by means of increasingly more computational resources, the problem will remain highly communication-bound.

6   Custom Application Characterization

In an application which uses synchronous communication, waiting for data from another process is typically performed via a single blocking call (either a blocking receive or a wait), which is logged in a communication trace very efficiently. In contrast, in an application using asynchronous communication, waiting for data takes the form of polling, that is, MPI test calls that query the communication infrastructure multiple times unsuccessfully before ultimately receiving a confirmation of data being available. Logging every failed test in the communication trace can lead to it becoming extremely large as well as inducing a high tracing overhead (and thus a warped view of the application). However, particularly in the case of a communication-bound application, it is precisely the failed tests that convey the time spent waiting for data.

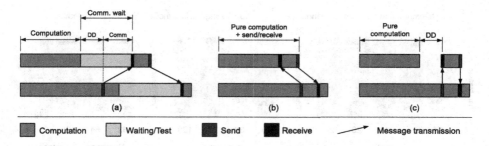

Fig. 2. Three types of traces for a minimal application with two concurrent processes. (a) shows a standard trace, (b) shows the trace where the communication is emulated from locally stored data, and (c) shows the trace were communication is emulated from locally stored data but the temporal data dependencies (DD) between MPI Isends and their corresponding MPI Irecvs are enforced.

To address this issue, we imagined the following thought experiment. Let us assume that failed tests are not logged in the trace, and instead time spent performing them appears as being outside of any communication event. This means that what now appears to be computation time in the trace is a mix of actual computation and polling. Should we be able to execute the application on the same system but ensuring ideal (zero-latency, infinite-throughput) communication, then whatever the completion time of this ideal run is, that would exclusively be the actual computation. To achieve this ideal setup, we replaced the standard MPI calls with custom calls that wrap the former and additionally have the capability to *record* traffic and *replay* it at ideal speed (i.e., incurring node-side delays such as memory copies, but not incurring any network-side delay). This allowed us to identify the time spent performing exclusively non-communication related computation (Fig. 2 (a) and (b)). The advantage of such an approach is not only that the trace itself is much more efficiently stored and collected, but more importantly, the actual computation is measured without any tracing overhead, and thus estimated much more precisely.

However, with this record-replay approach, removing polling time that is falsely registered as computation was not possible while at the same time maintaining the data dependencies between concurrent processes. Indeed, when executing a parallel workload, a process can be caught in a sequence of polling phases in two main circumstances:

1. the next steps the process has to execute depend on data in flight that takes a certain amount of time to arrive due to imperfections or simply inherent limitations of the underlying communication system;
2. the next steps the process has to execute depend on data that has not yet been sent by the corresponding source process (labeled as DD in Fig. 2).

While the former circumstance is related to communication, the latter stems from application inherent data-dependencies between concurrent processes.

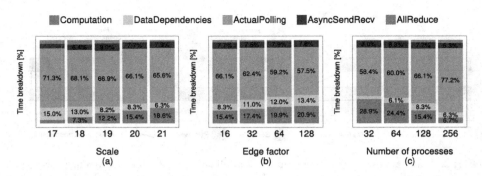

Fig. 3. Custom instrumentation. Single BFS execution time percentual breakdown for varying graph scales under a constant edge factor (16) and 128 concurrent processes (a), for varying edge factors under constant graph scale (20) and 128 concurrent processes (b), and for varying number of concurrent processes under constant graph scale (20) and edge factor (16) (c).

To be able to quantify the actual communication time, we therefore need to partition the waiting time into the two categories above. For every message exchanged, the trace comprises both the source and the destination processes. As such, it provides all the necessary dependency information to achieve this partitioning. However, in order to be able to order the dependencies properly in time, we used another tool, called Dimemas [9], which is capable of ingesting traces captured with Extrae, replay them maintaining the semantic data dependencies and additionally model the inter-process communication for arbitrary levels of bandwidth, latency and network congestion. Using this tool, we were able to determine the application runtime in the absence of communication delays (Fig. 2(c)). This runtime, coupled to the ideal runtime above and the real runtime, the latter two measured on the real system, are sufficient to allow us to identify with high accuracy the time the application spends in each of the following five types of activities: (1) asynchronous point-to-point communication; (2) calls to MPI all-reduce; (3) actual (as opposed to apparent) communication related polling; (4) inherent data dependency related polling; (5) actual computation.

6.1   Experimental Results

Using this custom methodology, we re-ran the experiments presented in the previous section and obtained the results illustrated in Fig. 3. First, as expected, the results show that a significant amount of what appeared to be computation time was actually overhead due to tracing (particularly due to the inclusion of the failed tests). While relative to the entire application execution, this overhead was moderate ($< 15\,\%$), as it was accounted for practically entirely in the computation part of the trace, it made up a significant portion of that part. Indeed, while

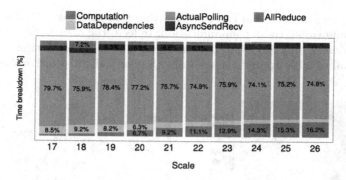

Fig. 4. Custom instrumentation. Single BFS execution time percentual breakdown for varying graph scales under a constant edge factor (16) and 256 concurrent processes.

the previously identified trends are still present, actual computation is in fact approximately 40 % smaller than what the standard instrumentation estimated.

Second, data dependencies make up a non-negligible part of the execution time, which now the custom characterization correctly identifies. In terms of trends, data dependencies seem to become percentually less important with the increase of the scale and more important with the increase of the edge factor. Also, as the degree of parallelism increases, their importance relative to the time spent computing increases significantly.

With the custom methodology and the resulting smaller traces, we are also able to handle larger problem sizes and degrees of parallelism. Figure 4 shows the results obtained for scales as large as 26 and 256 concurrent processes (the edge factor was set to the standard benchmark value of 16). We can see that the previously identified trends hold, with communication remaining by far the dominating component, accounting for more than 80 % of the total execution time (more than 75 % of which is spent waiting for data).

7   Communication Patterns

So far, we have shown that communication delays constitute an overwhelming part of the application runtime. Thus, optimizing the data exchange is key to improving the performance of graph-based analytics applications. Understanding the characteristics of the data exchanges is crucial to developing efficient systems and networks that enable these optimizations. Fortunately, the tracing and analysis tools we have at our disposal have a high enough granularity to allow data motion characterization. Indeed, from the communication traces, we were able to determine the amount of data that each (source, destination) task pair exchange, in time. The resulting traffic-matrix heatmap for a representative scenario (scale 20, edge factor 64 and 64 concurrent processes) for the entire duration of a single BFS is shown in Fig. 5(a). Figure 5(b) shows the distribution of the amounts of data exchanged across all individual (source, destination) pairs.

From both illustrations, one can see that the data exchange pattern strongly resembles uniform all-to-all communication. Indeed, the distribution has a standard deviation of only 8.6 % around the mean and is almost entirely contained in an interval of 20 % around the mean, with a very slight positive skew.

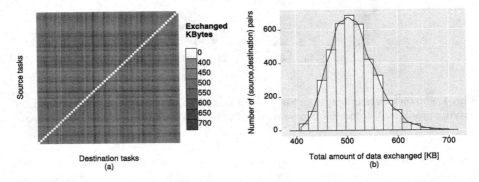

Fig. 5. Representative single BFS computation for scale 20, edge factor 64 and 64 concurrent processes. (a) illustrates the traffic matrix between the processes and suggests that data exchanges are approximately uniformly distributed between all possible (source, destination) pairs. (b) shows the actual distribution of (source, destination) pairs communication volumes across possible data amounts. The volumes are distributed approximately Gaussian around a mean of 512 KB with a standard deviation of only 8.6 % and a slight positive skew.

While these results suggest a uniform all-to-all traffic pattern, they are not sufficient to reach such a conclusion. A given (source, destination) pair could indeed exchange over the execution time of the program as many bytes as any other pair. However, the performance of the exchange and the communication pattern itself can vary strongly depending on how this global amount of data is aggregated into messages. Exchanging the 512 KB in numerous small messages or a few very large messages will lead to very different traffic signatures. To shed light on this aspect, we continue the characterization by extracting a similar heatmap (Fig. 6(a)) and distribution across communicating pairs (Fig. 6(b)) for the average message size. This analysis shows that the variability in the case of the message size is even smaller than in the case of the aggregated amount of data exchanged. Indeed, across communicating pairs, the standard deviation is only 0.7 % around a mean of 3.75 KB per message. It should be noted that message size is a direct function of the (configurable) coalescing size parameter. For this study, we did not change the default 4 KB value. Choosing a different value for this parameter might have performance implications, but (for a reasonable range) it will not impact the conclusions of the data motion characterization.

Finally, even under low variability distributions of both aggregate communication volume and message size, a third aspect must also be taken into consideration when characterizing a potentially uniform all-to-all communication

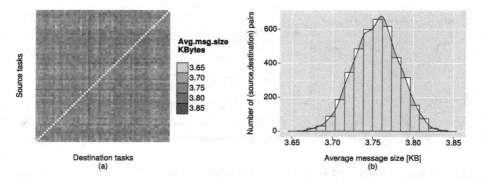

Fig. 6. Representative single BFS computation for scale 20, edge factor 64 and 64 concurrent processes. (a) illustrates the distribution of the size of the exchanged messages across every possible pair of communicating tasks. The distribution is highly regular, with an average message size 3.75 KB and an extremely small variability (standard deviation is 0.7 %), as illustrated in detail by the histogram in (b).

pattern, and that aspect is the distribution of the data exchange in time. To perform this analysis, we divide the entire runtime of the BFS into 20 intervals (each interval corresponding to 5 % of the BFS execution time) For each interval, we perform the same two analyses that we performed before for the entire run, i.e., we compute the total and per-message communication volume and represent each resulting per-interval distribution by its mean and standard deviation. In addition, we also look at the number of active communicator pairs per time interval. The results are shown in Fig. 7.

Figure 7(a) illustrates the percentage of active communicating pairs per time window. During 80 % of the execution time, all pairs are in active communication. Figure 7(b) shows the data volume exchanged per communicating pair per time window. During 80 % of the execution time, the amount of data per time window exchanged by an arbitrary communicating pair is similar to that of any other communicating pair (the standard deviation is lower than 20 % in the majority of cases). Finally, the distribution of the size of the messages exchanged is even more regular, as illustrated in Fig. 7(c). During 65 % of the time, there is no variability, i.e., every source is sending exclusively 4 KB messages, while during an additional 15 % of the time the variability is very low (the standard deviation is lower than 20 %). The remaining four windows (highlighted in red) manifest larger deviations from what would be expected from a uniform all-to-all exchange—only a subset of (source, destination) pairs communicate, and across that subset there are large variations in both the amount of data exchanged and the size of the messages used. However, we would argue that these intervals are not necessarily indicative of periods when a different communication pattern is taking place, but rather signs that imperfections/limitations of the communication infrastructure or load imbalance issues cause a limited subset of messages to experience long end-to-end latencies. Such tail effects can subsequently impact the application globally, leading to increased completion time and low network utilization.

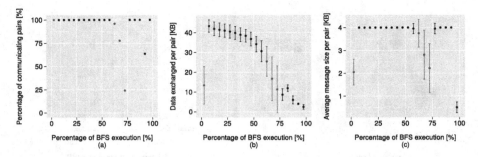

Fig. 7. Interval analysis of the communication pattern of a single BFS (scale 20, edge factor 64, 64 processes). The X axis represents the execution of the BFS in percentages. For every 5 % of the execution time, we isolate the messages that are sent in that time window. For every time window: (a) shows the fraction of all (source, destination) pairs that communicate in that interval; (b) illustrates the mean and standard deviation of the amount of data exchanged in the interval across (source, destination) pairs; (c) shows the mean and standard deviation of the average message size exchanged in the interval across (source, destination) pairs. For 80 % of the intervals, the communication has the characteristics of a uniform all-to-all exchange.

In summary, these results suggest that system or network designs and optimizations targeting high-performance uniform all-to-all traffic have a high potential of positively impacting the communication performance of data analytics applications, and, consequently, the overall high performance of these communication-bound workloads.

8   Discussion

The main take-away from this work is that graph analytics workloads for which the Graph 500 benchmark is representative are communication dominated. Indeed, we have shown that the vast majority (more than 75 %) of the execution time is spent in polling operations that represent waiting periods for messages in flight. This means that improvements in the messaging infrastructure (such as network bandwidth and latency or workload specific routing or process to node allocation) will translate directly into a proportional decrease of what we identified as polling. In turn, the application itself will benefit greatly.

In performing this characterization, we also addressed several issues that a tracing tool will encounter when profiling applications using asynchronous communication. These include minimizing the tracing overhead, reducing the trace size by avoiding the storing of failed MPI test events and perhaps most importantly by pinpointing polling time due to data dependencies. Indeed, to make sure that we do not erroneously account in the communication time inherent synchronization waiting periods between applications (time spent in one process waiting for a message that another process has not yet sent), we carefully isolated this portion of execution time in the form of a data dependency time.

While for the purposes of this study we made use of the Extrae tracing tool, the conclusions are not characteristic of Extrae alone, but rather of the entire class of tracing/profiling tools, e.g., Vampir [17], Tau [22], the HPC Toolkit [13].

Concerning the choice of the Graph 500 benchmark as representative for the graph analytics space, we are aware that other frameworks and implementations exist. Some of the notable examples are Giraph [1] and Graphlab [19]. Giraph is an iterative graph processing framework built on top of Apache Hadoop. It is written mostly in Java and uses sockets for communication. GraphLab is a distributed framework that allows easy implementation of asynchronous, dynamic and graph-parallel algorithms, built on top of an RPC library. We have nonetheless, for the purposes of this paper, limited our analysis to Graph 500, because our current tools are implemented on top of MPI and as such are incompatible with the other two frameworks. As future work, we are looking into adapting the same methodology for TCP socket communication as well as extending it beyond the data analytics space by applying it to other relevant HPC benchmarks, e.g., SPEC MPI2007 [5].

Last but not least, within the Graph 500 benchmark, several implementations are supplied, but we have chosen to focus on the MPI-simple implementation. This is because, while the other implementations are expected to behave better than the *simple* approach in a small-scale environment with few nodes, they do not (as shown for example by Ueno et al. [25]) scale to the system sizes that are now usual in practice in datacenter and HPC systems.

9 Conclusions

The goal of this work was to perform an in-depth characterization and data motion analysis of a representative application in the graph-based analytics space. To this end, we chose to analyze the Graph 500 benchmark suite, which is widely considered a key application in assessing the performance of supercomputing systems on data-intensive applications. In particular, we focused on the most scalable implementation of the reference benchmark, namely the MPI-simple code.

Initial attempts of characterization using standard profiling exposed several limitations, mainly a high spatial and temporal overhead and a lack of support for data dependencies. Using a custom approach, we addressed these issues and were able to target larger problem sizes and degrees of parallelism (up to scale 26 and 256 concurrent processes), while improving the accuracy of the characterization. We were able to quantify the time spent in enabling communication as making up to 80 % of the total execution time of each BFS iteration, clearly indicating the main performance bottleneck of this application. Furthermore, we quantified how the characterization changes with the problem size and the number of concurrent processes. Most importantly we identified that communication becomes less dominant with the increase of the *scale*, but significantly more dominant as more computational resources (concurrent processes) are assigned to the application. Moreover, we managed to separately quantify waiting times due to data dependencies and show that they can become important for the high levels of parallelism characteristic of HPC systems. Last but not least, analyzing the spatial and temporal distribution of the data exchange, we identified that the dominating communication pattern of the benchmark is uniform all-to-all, opening avenues for further workload-specific data motion optimization of the Graph 500 benchmark.

Acknowledgments. This work is partially conducted in the context of the joint ASTRON and IBM DOME project and is funded by the Netherlands Organisation for Scientific Research (NWO), the Dutch Ministry of EL&I, and the Province of Drenthe. We would like to thank the Barcelona Supercomputing Center for providing support and access to the MareNostrum III supercomputing cluster.

References

1. Apache Giraph. http://giraph.apache.org/
2. Barcelona Supercomputing Center (BSC) Marenostrum supercomputer. http://www.bsc.es/marenostrum-support-services/mn3
3. Extrae instrumentation package. http://www.bsc.es/computer-sciences/extrae
4. Graph 500 benchmark. http://www.graph500.org/
5. SPEC MPI2007. https://www.spec.org/mpi/
6. Top 500 list, November 2014. http://www.top500.org/list/2014/11/. Accessed 10 February 2015
7. Agarwal, V., Petrini, F., Pasetto, D., Bader, D.A.: Scalable graph exploration on multicore processors. In: Proceedings of the 2010 ACM/IEEE International Conference for High Performance Computing, Networking, Storage and Analysis, SC 2010, pp. 1–11. IEEE Computer Society, Washington, DC (2010). http://dx.doi.org/10.1109/SC.2010.46
8. Bader, D., Riedy, J., Meyerhenke, H.: Applications and challenges in large-scale graph analysis. In: HPC Graph Analytics Workshop (2013)
9. Badia, R.M., Labarta, J., Gimenez, J., Escale, F.: DIMEMAS: predicting MPI applications behavior in grid environments. In: Workshop on Grid Applications and Programming Tools (GGF8), vol. 86, pp. 52–62 (2003)
10. Borkar, S., Chien, A.: The future of microprocessors. Commun. ACM **54**(5), 67–77 (2011)
11. Chakrabarti, D., Zhan, Y., Faloutsos, C.: R-MAT: A recursive model for graph mining. SIAM (2004)
12. Checconi, F., Petrini, F.: Massive data analytics: the graph 500 on IBM blue gene/Q. IBM J. Res. Dev. **57**(1/2), 10 (2013)
13. Chung, I.H., Walkup, R.E., Wen, H.F., Yu, H.: MPI performance analysis tools on blue gene/L. In: Proceedings of the 2006 ACM/IEEE Conference on Supercomputing, SC 2006. ACM, New York (2006). http://doi.acm.org/10.1145/1188455.1188583
14. Crovella, M.E., LeBlanc, T.J.: Parallel performance prediction using lost cycles analysis. In: Proceedings of the 1994 ACM/IEEE Conference on Supercomputing, Supercomputing 1994, pp. 600–609. IEEE Computer Society Press, Los Alamitos (1994)

15. Dally, B.: Power, programmability, and granularity: the challenges of exascale computing. In: IEEE Parallel & Distributed Processing Symposium, pp. 878–878 (2011)
16. Jose, J., Potluri, S., Tomko, K., Panda, D.K.: Designing scalable graph500 benchmark with hybrid MPI+OpenSHMEM programming models. In: Kunkel, J.M., Ludwig, T., Meuer, H.W. (eds.) ISC 2013. LNCS, vol. 7905, pp. 109–124. Springer, Heidelberg (2013). http://dx.doi.org/10.1007/978-3-642-38750-0_9
17. Knpfer, A., et al.: The vampir performance analysis tool-set. In: Resch, M., Keller, R., Himmler, V., Krammer, B., Schulz, A. (eds.) Tools for High Performance Computing, pp. 139–155. Springer, Heidelberg (2008). http://dx.doi.org/10.1007/978-3-540-68564-7_9
18. Labarta, J., Girona, S., Pillet, V., Cortes, T., Gregoris, L.: DiP: a parallel program. In: Fraigniaud, P., Mignotte, A., Robert, Y., Bougé, L. (eds.) Euro-Par 1996. LNCS, vol. 1124, pp. 665–674. Springer, London (1996)
19. Low, Y., Bickson, D., Gonzalez, J., Guestrin, C., Kyrola, A., Hellerstein, J.M.: Distributed graphlab: a framework for machine learning and data mining in the cloud. Proc. VLDB Endow. 5(8), 716–727 (2012). http://dx.doi.org/10.14778/2212351.2212354
20. Murphy, R.C., Wheeler, K., Barrett, B., Ang, J.: Introducing the Graph 500. Cray Users Group (CUG) (2010)
21. Satish, N., Kim, C., Chhugani, J., Dubey, P.: Large-scale energy-efficient graph traversal: a path to efficient data-intensive supercomputing. In: Proceedings of the International Conference on High Performance Computing, Networking, Storage and Analysis, SC 2012, pp. 14:1–14:11 (2012)
22. Shende, S.S., Malony, A.D.: The Tau parallel performance system. Int. J. High Perform. Comput. Appl. 20(2), 287–311 (2006). http://dx.doi.org/10.1177/109434 2006064482
23. Suzumura, T., Ueno, K., Sato, H., Fujisawa, K., Matsuoka, S.: Performance characteristics of Graph500 on large-scale distributed environment. In: Proceedings of the 2011 IEEE International Symposium on Workload Characterization, IISWC 2011, pp. 149–158 (2011)
24. Ueno, K., Suzumura, T.: 2D partitioning based graph search for the Graph500 benchmark. In: Proceedings of the 2012 IEEE 26th International Parallel and Distributed Processing Symposium Workshops & PhD Forum, IPDPSW 2012, pp. 1925–1931 (2012)
25. Ueno, K., Suzumura, T.: Highly scalable graph search for the graph500 benchmark. In: Proceedings of the 21st International Symposium on High-Performance Parallel and Distributed Computing, HPDC 2012, pp. 149–160. ACM, New York (2012). http://doi.acm.org/10.1145/2287076.2287104

Formal Metrics for Large-Scale Parallel Performance

Kenneth Moreland$^{(\boxtimes)}$ and Ron Oldfield

Sandia National Laboratories, Albuquerque, NM 87185, USA
{kmorel,raoldfi}@sandia.gov

Abstract. Performance measurement of parallel algorithms is well studied and well understood. However, a flaw in traditional performance metrics is that they rely on comparisons to serial performance with the same input. This comparison is convenient for theoretical complexity analysis but impossible to perform in large-scale empirical studies with data sizes far too large to run on a single serial computer. Consequently, scaling studies currently rely on ad hoc methods that, although effective, have no grounded mathematical models. In this position paper we advocate using a rate-based model that has a concrete meaning relative to speedup and efficiency and that can be used to unify strong and weak scaling studies.

1   Introduction

Empirical scaling studies are an important component in the analysis of parallel algorithms and systems. A scaling study tests the performance of a parallel algorithm using different numbers of processing elements and usually over different amounts of data. A good scaling study shows how effectively additional processing elements are used by the algorithm and through trends provides evidence of behavior at future larger scales.

The practice of measuring scaling relies on the well studied models for the theory of parallel performance. However, current theoretic models rely on comparisons with algorithm behavior on a single, serial processing element. Empirically measuring serial behavior for sufficiently large parallel problems is impractical.

1.1   Performance Analysis Theory

The following is a brief overview of parallel algorithm performance.

The *speedup* of a parallel algorithm is defined as

$$S(n,p) = \frac{T^*(n)}{T(n,p)} \tag{1}$$

where $T(n,p)$ is the time it takes to run the parallel algorithm on p processing elements with an input of size n, and $T^*(n)$ the time for the best serial algorithm on the same input. The best possible serial algorithm may be different than the parallel algorithm although using the same algorithm is also common practice.

© Springer International Publishing Switzerland 2015
J.M. Kunkel and T. Ludwig (Eds.): ISC High Performance 2015, LNCS 9137, pp. 488–496, 2015.
DOI: 10.1007/978-3-319-20119-1_34

In theory the best possible speedup achievable is $S(n,p) = p$ [5] (although superlinear measurements can occur in practice [8]). Thus, we measure the *efficiency* as the ratio of the observed speedup to the ideal speedup.

$$E(n,p) = \frac{S(n,p)}{p} = \frac{T^*(n)}{p\,T(n,p)} \qquad (2)$$

Amdahl [1] famously observes the limits of scaling any parallel algorithm based on the fraction f of inherently serial computation that exists in any algorithm. The equation derived from this observation is known as *Amdahl's law*.

$$S(n,p) \leq \frac{1}{f + (1-f)/p} \qquad (3)$$

Gustafson [7] observes that the serial fraction tends to go down for larger data sizes in parallel algorithms, which justifies the use of parallel computing for large problems. The *Gustafson-Barsis law* reformulates speedup in terms of the parallel execution rather than the serial execution.

$$S(n,p) \leq p + (1-p) \cdot s(n,p) \qquad (4)$$

where $s(n,p)$ is the fraction of time in the parallel execution performing sequential operations. This law shows that speedup can be increased indefinitely as long as the serial fraction drops commensurately with the processing element increase, which can often be done by increasing the problem size. Grama et al. [6] introduce an *isoefficiency* relation that determines how much a problem needs to grow to maintain a desired level of efficiency. Given a desired efficiency E_d, the following inequality must hold.

$$T(n,1) \geq \frac{E_d}{1 - E_d} T_o(n,p) \qquad (5)$$

where $T_o(n,p)$ is the total overhead (redundant, idle, and extra computation plus communication) for running the algorithm on p processing elements for data of size n.

Performance analysis theory is reviewed in much more detail in many parallel computing textbooks such as Quinn's [14].

1.2   Limitations of Performance Analysis

Although our definition for speedup and its derived quantities work well for theoretical complexity analysis, they all rely in some way on knowing the serial performance. With large-scale simulations today reaching orders of billions to trillions of elements [2,3,9,15], directly measuring serial performance is often impossible. The Gustafson-Barsis law needs only the serial fraction, but estimates for serial fraction such as the *Karp-Flatt* metric [12] require knowing the serial performance anyway.

Because of this issue, most studies attempt to assess scalability with a pair of trends named strong scalability and weak scalability [11]. *Strong scaling* demonstrates an algorithm's behavior by measuring its run time on a particular data set for various numbers of processing elements. Perfect strong scaling has a running time proportional to $1/p$. As we shall see in examples later, it is difficult to compare the quality of plotted curves to this perfect hyperbolic on both linear and log scales.

Per Amdahl's law, there are inevitable limits to strong scaling. In contrast *weak scaling* varies the problem size proportionally with the number of processing elements. It may not always be possible to keep the problem size proportional to the job size, which makes weak scaling more difficult. The metrics advocated in this paper simplify studying scalability by removing the dependence between problem size and number of processing elements. We encourage using them to sample the 2D parameter space of problem size and number of processing elements as widely as possible for a broader view of the scalability.

Some studies use an ad hoc version of speedup or efficiency that replaces the immeasurable $T^*(n)$ with some arbitrarily chosen measurement, usually the time run on the smallest number of processing elements. The problem with this approach is that the absolute meaning of "speedup" and "efficiency" changes between experiments in a study. Furthermore, the metric cannot be used in weak scaling because the problem size is not held constant.

Finally, some studies use rate in terms of the size of input computed per unit time rather than absolute run time to assess scalability [11]. Rate is formally defined as

$$R(n,p) = \frac{n}{T(n,p)} \tag{6}$$

Some analysts have discovered that rate, being essentially a reciprocal of time, provides a much better visual analysis of scaling, and it is an essential mechanism advocated in this position paper.

This paper establishes a more pragmatic definition and efficiency that can be easily measured empirically. Furthermore, we demonstrate how rate can be used as a proxy for speedup and can unify strong and weak scaling to provide a more complete analysis. These metrics are demonstrated using real performance data.

2   Deriving Efficiency from Cost Analysis

In this section we will use *cost*, a metric that is simple to measure, to define efficiency in lieu of the immeasurable speedup. Cost is intuitively the number of processing elements used multiplied by the amount of time they are used.

$$C(n,p) = p\, T(n,p) \tag{7}$$

Cost is sometimes used in theoretical algorithm analysis [10] and is often used for HPC allocations, which are typically measured in core-hours.

Clearly the most efficient algorithm will be the one that costs the least to run. Although we expect the cost to go up with the problem size, a perfectly scaled algorithm on a fixed input size will cost the same regardless of how many processors are used. That is, adding processors reduces the time proportionally. Given a strong scaling study on a problem of a particular size, we can identify the best (minimal) cost, $C^*(n)$, that uses p^* processing elements. With this best cost we can redefine efficiency as the ratio of this best cost to the actual cost.

$$E(n, p) = \frac{C^*(n)}{C(n, p)} \qquad (8)$$

If we make the typical assumptions that the minimal cost is when the serial algorithm is run $(C^*(n) = T^*(n))$, then we observe that Eq. 8 simplifies to Eq. 2, making this definition of efficiency equivalent but broader than the traditional definition. And unlike the traditional definition of efficiency, determining efficiency from cost is straightforward at large scales.

3   Strong and Weak Scaling with Cost per Unit

Our previous definition of efficiency (Eq. 8) works well for strong scaling where the data size is constant but cannot be compared across different data sizes for weak scaling. To describe efficiency under weak scaling we define the new metric *cost per unit*, C_u. Cost per unit is the amortized computational cost for one unit of data.

$$C_u(n, p) = \frac{C(n, p)}{n} = \frac{p\, T(n, p)}{n} = \frac{p}{R(n, p)} \qquad (9)$$

The important feature of cost per unit is that under perfect scaling the cost per unit is constant under any number of processing elements *or* data sizes. Thus, given multiple strong scaling studies over data of different sizes, we can find the best cost per unit, C_u^*, that uses p^* processing elements operating on data of size n^*. The best cost per unit is generally the minimum. We are not considering, however, outlier experiments where data sizes are not representative of practical runs. For example, it is well known that a sufficiently small data size could fit in the cache of a sufficiently large parallel job [8]. An experiment of this nature would report a much lower cost per unit but would be of little relevance to the scale of problems run in practice and therefore should be disqualified from ideal.

With this best cost per unit we can adjust the efficiency to be comparable across all possible configurations.

$$E(n, p) = \frac{C_u^*}{C_u(n, p)} \qquad (10)$$

This this definition of efficiency allows us to combine strong and weak scaling studies into one unified analysis.

4   Rate as a Proxy for Speedup

Both efficiency and speedup are good metrics for parallel performance analysis. However, many analysts prefer using speedup, particularly for visual (chart) analysis. This is because good scaling shows an upward sloping speedup as jobs get larger whereas even a good scaling algorithm will show a gradual drop-off from a perfect efficiency of 1.

Although there is no way to compute the speedup at large scales, we can show that rate (Eq. 6) is a valid proxy for speedup. If we substitute rate for time in Eq. 1, we get the following.

$$S(n,p) = \frac{T^*(n)}{T(n,p)} = \frac{T^*(n)}{n} R(n,p) \tag{11}$$

We can observe that for a given problem size (i.e. n held constant) the speedup is proportional to the rate. This means that the rate curve will have the exact same shape as the speedup curve, and visually they will be identical with the appropriate scaling of the ordinate axis.

For a proper parallel performance analysis we need to compare our measured metrics with the ideal metrics. These ideal values are implicit in the definition of efficiency ($E_{\text{ideal}}(n,p) = 1$) and speedup ($S_{\text{ideal}}(n,p) = p$). The ideal rate can be derived from Eq. 10 by substituting the cost per unit with the rate (Eq. 9) and solving for rate when the efficiency is the optimal value of 1.

$$R_{\text{ideal}}(n,p) = \frac{p}{C_u^*} \tag{12}$$

Note that the curve for $R_{\text{ideal}}(n,p)$ is independent of n, which means we can use the same ideal rate for both strong and weak scaling analysis and can compare these rates with each other.

5   Examples

In the previous sections we provide mathematical derivations to show how to use rate as a proxy for speedup and to use cost per unit to find the efficiency and ideal rate across all scales. In this section we demonstrate using these metrics on real measured data. We can observe that the metrics of rate and efficiency make it easier to visually identify the behavior and trends at different scales of processing elements.

5.1   Gordon Bell Finalist

Our first data set comes from a study by Habib et al. [9], which is one of the 2013 Gordon Bell finalists. We choose this source because in addition to showing impressive scaling, the authors make many measurements across many scales and report the results completely enough to extract the information and continue analysis. In particular, we look at the performance data for scaling the full HACC code on Titan (Sect. 4.3.2 in the original paper).

Figure 1 on the left shows the performance data from the strong and weak scaling studies using a traditional time plot. The curves for the data are very similar for what we would expect for perfect scaling: a hyperbolic curve for strong scaling and a horizontal line for weak scaling. Habib et al. also provide an ad hoc metric of time over data size to unify the curve shape of the two plots, which is also replicated in Fig. 1 on the right. Again, both curves appear close to perfect.

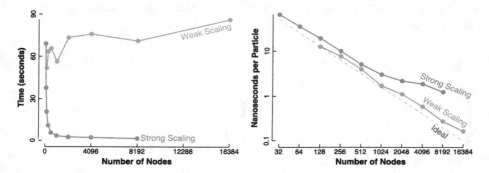

Fig. 1. Data from the Habib et al. [9] Gordon Bell finalist. The left chart shows the data using a traditional time metric. The right chart replicates the presentation of Fig. 3 in the original paper using an ad hoc metric and a log-log scale. Both charts present the data in a way to suggest near perfect scaling for both scaling studies.

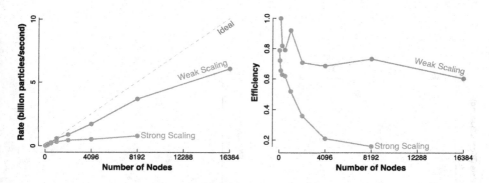

Fig. 2. Data from the Habib et al. [9] Gordon Bell finalist using the rate (left) and efficiency (right) metrics advocated in this paper. These plots give a more realistic and visually measurable representation of scaling than the charts in Fig. 1.

Figure 2 shows the same data using the rate and efficiency metrics advocated in this paper. The weak scaling is shown to diverge from ideal by a measurable fraction, which is to be expected when scaling over 3 orders of magnitude. The strong scaling study is shown to diverge very far from ideal, which is not at all apparent in the original charts.

5.2   Imperfect Scaling

Our second data set comes from a study by Oldfield et al. [13]. In this study a visualization algorithm has a high communication overhead and therefore has a known limit on its scalability. The study shows how transferring data between parallel jobs of different sizes can sometimes be faster than combining both in one large job.

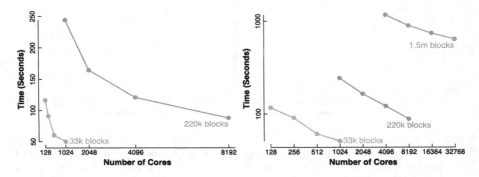

Fig. 3. Data from the Oldfield et al. [13] simulation-visualization integration study where the visualization (shown here) has a high communication overhead. These plots use the traditional method of showing the trend of run time using linear and log-log scaling.

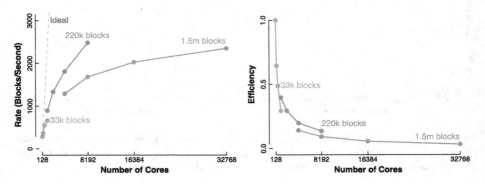

Fig. 4. Data from Oldfield et al. [13] using rate (left) and efficiency (right) to reveal that the communication overhead has a severe impact on the overall scalability.

A traditional plot of the time of the visualization component shown in Fig. 3 gives curves that suggest good scaling performance. However, when we show the same data using the rate and efficiency metrics, shown in Fig. 4, we can clearly see the effect the communication overhead has on the scalability of the algorithm. Without such a presentation, erroneous interpretation of the performance is sure to occur.

6   Discussion

In this paper we discuss limitations of traditional parallel performance analysis and problems with the current metrics often used. We provide derivations of rate as a proxy for speedup, ideal rate, and efficiency and demonstrate with real data how these provide accurate visual representations of scalability. As scientists, we should demand this high level of transparency and honesty in performance analysis.

With these observations, we provide the following recommendations for the visual display of parallel performance.

- Do not rely on running time for performance analysis. Instead use rate, efficiency, or both.
- Avoid using log-log scaling on plot axes, which hides major inefficiencies. If necessary, repeat linear plots at different scales.
- Rather than performing separate weak and strong scaling studies, incorporate them in one. Perform several strong scaling studies at different scales of data size. Then find an overall minimal practical cost per unit and plot all the measurements together as demonstrated in the figures in this paper.

As architectures continue to advance, many are beginning to advocate measuring electrical power instead of or in addition to speed [4]. As future work we advocate using a cost model for this as well. It would be interesting to derive efficiency in terms of optimal watt-hours per data unit (although rate may lose meaning).

The use of rate or efficiency to measure parallel performance is not itself a new technique. After all, the ubiquitous "FLOPS" measurement is itself a rate, and measurements given in data unit per time unit can be found throughout the literature. However, other metrics of varying effectiveness are also found in published material with little or no justification for the choice. The decision for scaling metrics should not be arbitrary; it can have enormous impact on the viability of the analysis. Our intention is to show that the metric visualized does matter, to provide a best practices for measuring scalability, and to explain why these metrics work better than others.

Acknowledgment. This material is based in part upon work supported by the U.S. Department of Energy, Office of Science, Office of Advanced Scientific Computing Research, Scientific Discovery through Advanced Computing (SciDAC) program under Award Number 12-015215.

Sandia National Laboratories is a multi-program laboratory managed and operated by Sandia Corporation, a wholly owned subsidiary of Lockheed Martin Corporation, for the U.S. Department of Energy's National Nuclear Security Administration under contract DE-AC04-94AL85000.   SAND 2015-2890 C

References

1. Amdahl, G.M.: Validity of the single processor approach to achieving large scale computing capabilities. In: Proceedings of the AFIPS 1967, pp. 483–485, April 1967. doi:10.1145/1465482.1465560
2. Bernaschi, M., Bisson, M., Fatica, M., Melchionna, S.: 20 Petaflops simulation of proteins suspensions in crowding conditions. In: Proceedings of the SC 2013, November 2013. doi:10.1145/2503210.2504563
3. Bussmann, M., et al.: Radiative signatures of the relativistic Kelvin-Helmholtz instability. In: Proceedings of the SC 2013, November 2013. doi:10.1145/2503210.2504564
4. Cameron, K.W., Ge, R.: Generalizing Amdahl's law for power and energy. IEEE Comput. **45**(3), 75–77 (2012). doi:10.1109/MC.2012.92
5. Faber, V., Lubeck, O.M., White Jr., A.B.: Superlinear speedup of an efficient sequential algorithm is not possible. Parallel Comput. **3**(3), 259–260 (1986). doi:10.1016/0167-8191(86)90024-4
6. Grama, A.Y., Gupta, A., Kuma, V.: Isoefficiency: measuring the scalability of parallel algorithms and architectures. IEEE Parallel Distrib. Technol.: Syst. Appl. **1**(3), 12–21 (1993). doi:10.1109/88.242438
7. Gustafson, J.L.: Reevaluating Amdahl's law. Commun. ACM **31**(5), 532–533 (1988). doi:10.1145/42411.42415
8. Gustafson, J.L.: Fixed time, tiered memory, and superlinear speedup. In: Proceedings of the Fifth Distributed Memory Computing Conference, pp. 1255–1260 April 1990. doi:10.1109/DMCC.1990.556383
9. Habib, S., et al.: HACC: Extreme scaling and performance across diverse architectures. In: Proceedings of the SC 2013, November 2013. doi:10.1145/2503210.2504566
10. JáJá, J.: An Introduction to Parallel Algorithms. Addison Wesley, Boston (1992). ISBN 0-201-54856-9
11. Kaminsky, A.: Big CPU, Big Data: Solving the World's Toughest Computational Problems with Parallel Computing. Unpublished manuscript (2015), retrieved from http://www.cs.rit.edu/ark/bcbd
12. Karp, A.H., Flatt, H.P.: Measuring parallel processor performance. Commun. ACM **33**(5), 539–543 (1990). doi:10.1145/78607.78614
13. Oldfield, R.A., Moreland, K., Fabian, N., Rogers, D.: Evaluation of methods to integrate analysis into a large-scale shock physics code. In: Proceedings of the ICS 2014, pp. 83–92. June 2014. doi:10.1145/2597652.2597668
14. Quinn, M.J.: Parallel Programming in C with MPI and OpenMP. McGraw-Hill, New York (2004). ISBN 978-0-07-282256-4
15. Rossinelli, D., et al.: 11 PFLOP/s simulations of cloud cavitation collapse. In: Proceedings of the SC 2013, November 2013. doi:10.1145/2503210.2504565

Hunting Down Load Imbalance:
A Moving Target

Christoph Pospiech[✉]

Lenovo Deutschland GmbH, Stuttgart, Germany
cpospiech@lenovo.com

Abstract. Load imbalance is known to be a major bottleneck to scalability, particularly when aiming for large parallel partitions. Apart from re-balancing the distribution of the input data, several cures have been proposed. Pretty much all of them assume that the load imbalance is coming from a fixed source. This paper presents an investigation for the climate modelling version CCLM of the weather forecast code COSMO [4]. An adapted MPI trace library is used to collect information about the load imbalance thus introducing a load imbalance measure. Using the visualization software OpenDX [6], this information is correlated to geography and weather forecast results. The resulting pictures show that the locations of high computational load move in space and time. They appear to be correlated to some weather phenomena. In principle this correlation is known for many years [8], but now it has been made visible.

Keywords: Parallel computing · Load imbalance · Scalability · Weather forecast model

1 Introduction

Load imbalance is defined in [2, p. 3] as "processor cycles spent idling while unfinished parallel work exists." As parallel speed up results from distributing a work load onto several processors and idling processors don't contribute to the solution, any load imbalance will necessarily prolong the time to solution. To pin down the exact nature of this prolongation, we use a mathematical formalization to reveal a close similarity to Gustavsons formulation [5, p. 532] of Amdahls law [1]. The similarity is particularly close for the special case of a "spiked load imbalance".

The "spiked load imbalance" might be an instructive example, but the source for the load imbalance is very localized and stationary. Switching to a "real life" example of the climate modelling version CCLM of the weather forecast code COSMO [4], we can demonstrate that the sources for load imbalance are moving around. Using the visualization software OpenDX [6], this information is correlated to geography and weather forecast results. This is done by color coding wind speed arrows red or blue depending on the amount of load imbalance. The resulting pictures show that the locations of the red wind speed arrows move in space and time. They are not only gone by the wind, but seem to follow areas of rain or snow fall.

© Springer International Publishing Switzerland 2015
J.M. Kunkel and T. Ludwig (Eds.): ISC High Performance 2015, LNCS 9137, pp. 497–505, 2015.
DOI: 10.1007/978-3-319-20119-1_35

2   General Load Imbalance Considerations

2.1   Definitions

We have a parallel application based on finite grids or finite elements in mind, but are abstracting from that by defining (atomic) work load entities $W = \{0, 1, \ldots, n - 1\}$. Each entity has an associated time t_i, $i \in W$. Similarly we abstract from processors, (SMT) threads or places in a partitioned global address space (PGAS) by defining $N > 0$ parallel entities $P = \{0, 1, \ldots, N - 1\}$.

The Workload W is parallelized by defining a map $f : W \to P$. The inverse image $W_j := f^{-1}(j)$ for any $j \in f(W)$ denotes the work load entities handled by the parallel entity $j \in P$. This defines a split of W into pairwise disjoint subsets W_j. The work load entities in W_j are executed serially by the same parallel entity. Hence the time for executing the work entities in W_j is T_j defined as

$$T_j(f) := \sum_{i \in W_j} t_i$$

All these W_j are executed in parallel. Hence the total elapsed time $T(f)$ for map f can be defined as

$$T(f) := \max_{j \in f(W)} T_j(f) = \max_{j \in f(W)} \sum_{i \in W_j} t_i$$

We are interested in the scalability, i.e. how $T(f_N)$ changes with f_N, if we increase the size N of P.

2.2   Special Cases

As a special case, we have the serial execution, characterized by the map $f_0 : W \to \{0\}$. In this case we have the following.

$$T_0 := T(f_0) = \max_{j \in \{0\}} T_j(f_0) = \sum_{i \in W} t_i$$

Another less trivial special case can be called "spiked load imbalance". It is described by the following assumptions.

– There are only two different time values $t_0 > t_1$. Without loss of generality, the index 0 is chosen for t_0.

$$t_i := \begin{cases} t_0, & \text{if } i = 0; \\ t_1, & \text{if } i > 0. \end{cases}$$

– The items in W are distributed equally to the processors,

$$\text{card}(W_j) = \begin{cases} m + 1, & \text{if } 0 \le j < r; \\ m, & \text{if } j \ge r. \end{cases},$$

where $m = \lfloor N/n \rfloor \in \mathbb{N}$ is the integer division of n by N ($\lfloor \ \rfloor$ indicating the floor of a real number) and r is the remainder of this division.

By construction the maximum $T(f_N)$ of execution times $T_j(f_N)$ is attained at the parallel entity that hosts the "spike". Computing the speed up by dividing $T(f_0)$ by $T(f_N)$ we can recover something close to Gustavsons formulation [5, p. 532] of Amdahls law [1]. We only have to associate t_0 to the serial time s in Gustavsons paper, $t_1 * (n-1)$ to the parallel time p.

$$\frac{T(f_0)}{T(f_N)} = \frac{t_0 + (n-1) * t_1}{t_0 + \lfloor n/N \rfloor * t_1} \xrightarrow[N \to \infty]{} \frac{t_0 + (n-1) * t_1}{t_0}$$

The only difference comes from integer division $\lfloor n/N \rfloor$. We can even retain the result for the asymptotic limit $N \to \infty$, that the total time for the "spiked load imbalance" case approaches the serial time t_0 and hence the speed up converges to the reciprocal of the "serial fraction" t_0/T_0.

2.3 Maximal Speedup

Eventually, this asymptotic result can be extended to the general case, i.e. to parallelization of an arbitrary workload W by general maps $f_N : W \to P$, where N is the cardinality of P.

Theorem 1. *Let* $W = \{0, 1, \ldots, n-1\}$ *a set of work entities with associated times* t_i, $i \in W$. *Let* T_0 *denote the sum and* t_0 *be the maximum of all* t_i.

$$T_0 = \sum_{i \in W} t_i , \qquad t_0 = \max_{i \in W} t_i$$

Then the maximum speedup over all P *and possible maps* $f : W \to P$ *is given by the following formula.*

$$\max_{f : W \to P} \frac{T_0}{T(f)} = \frac{T_0}{t_0}$$

For the proof we need the following lemma.

Lemma 1. *Let* W, T_0 *and* t_0 *as above. If* f_m *is a map attaining the minimum*

$$\min_{f : W \to P} T(f) = T(f_m),$$

$m \in f_m(W)$ *a parallel entity and* $W_m = f_m^{-1}(m)$ *the corresponding inverse image of* f_m *attaining the maximum as follows*

$$T(f_m) = \max_{j \in f_m(W)} \sum_{i \in W_j} t_i = \sum_{i \in W_m} t_i,$$

then at least one W_m *thus defined has cardinality 1.*

Proof. Suppose, all of the W_m thus defined have at least two elements. Then we can get a speed up by splitting all these work loads and assigning them to new parallel entities as needed - contradicting the assumption that f_m is a map attaining the minimum.

Proof (of Theorem 1). As we keep W and subsequently T_0 constant for all maps f, we only have to proof that

$$\min_{f:W \to P} T(f) = t_0.$$

We can restrict ourselves to the case where P has finite cardinality less or equal to the cardinality of W. Employing more parallel entities than there is work to do cannot be minimal. Therefore the minimum exists and must be attained by a map f_m. Applying Lemma 1, we find a $W_m = \{k\}$ of cardinality 1 such that $T(f_m) = t_k$. If $t_k \neq t_0$, then $t_k < t_0$ by definition of t_0. Additionally, we find the index 0 in a set $0 \in W_0 \neq W_m$ because $W_m = \{k\}$. But then we have the following inequality.

$$\sum_{i \in W_m} t_i = t_k < t_0 \leq \sum_{i \in W_0} t_i$$

contradicting the definition that W_m should be the set where the maximum is attained. Hence $t_k = t_0$, which proves the assertion.

3   Investigating CCLM Load Imbalance

3.1   CCLM Parallelization Schema

The climate modelling version CCLM of the weather forecast code COSMO [4] runs a dynamic core and a physical model on rotated geographical coordinates and a generalized terrain following height coordinates. The parallelization is done by domain decomposition along horizontal coordinates. In more detail, each MPI rank is allotted a rectangular subdomain and the README_5.0.htm file, distributed with the COSMO_RAPS 5.0 distribution, indicates placement of MPI ranks in a two-dimensional processor grid. In Fig. 1 the MPI rank for an 8×4 processor grid is shown as an opaque colored step function, placed on top of the computational domain.

For each time step, this could be rephrased in the above abstract notation. The (atomic) work load entities would be defined by the work executed for a single horizontal grid point. The parallelization would map rectangular subsets of these to the same MPI rank. If we knew the time for each horizontal grid point, we could think of plotting the time rather than the MPI rank in Fig. 1. This would show a "time mountain", and guided by Theorem 1 we would focus on the highest hill top t_0, as this is limiting the maximum speedup.

Currently the parallelization of CCLM is MPI only and it is exhibiting load imbalance. The question arises whether a hybrid parallelization would do better. If we keep the work load entities as before (i.e. parallelize horizontal loops only) and only change the mapping to the parallel entities by adding threads to the MPI ranks, Theorem 1 indicates that this doesn't change the upper limit for speed up. Of course we have to be careful with a verdict like that, as Theorem 1 is based on a performance model that neither includes communication time nor cache or memory effects. But at least height of the hill top t_0 is a fact, that can't be easily argued away.

Fig. 1. MPI rank representation by height and color for an 8×4 processor grid (Color figure online)

Even if a parallelization strategy - yet to be found - further divides the current atomic workloads, we still have to take into account that OpenMP is a shared memory parallelization and the mapping of workloads to parallel entities has to respect node boundaries. The current preferred placement of MPI ranks to nodes tries to minimize nearest neighbour communication across node boundaries by placing a rectangular sub-domain of the processor grid onto each node. As a consequence, the horizontal grid points on the same node are also exhibiting geographic proximity. If we are to hope for some load balancing with the new parallelization strategy, we have to find valleys in the "time mountain" geographically close to the hill top t_0. Otherwise we don't find horizontal grid points with free cycles that can take over the work load for the horizontal grid point under hill top t_0.

Alternatively, we might deliberately take a performance hit by changing the mapping of MPI ranks to nodes, bringing distant "time valleys" onto the same node as the hill top. But then he have to know the location of these "time valleys" in advance.

To shed some light on this question, the following graphic visualization maps computation time data to geographic location and weather phenomena. It is based on data from a run with $450 * 438$ horizontal grid points, 40 vertical layers and a $16 * 32$ processor grid.

3.2 Importing NetCDF Data

CCLM writes binary data in NetCDF4 format. Per Fortran namelist parameter the frequency of output can be specified. In the CCLM case under consideration,

NetCDF data are written every 3 forecast hours. Additionally, there is an extra NetCDF file written at the start of the model run that contains "constant" data (in the sense that they don't change during the forecast). The data import module of OpenDX [6] version 4.4.4 can read NetCDF4 out of the box. The terrain following coordinates [4, p. 31] allow to extract a topographic map from the NetCDF4 file of constant data. The tutorial [3] explains in detail how this can be accomplished. Adding wind speeds as arrows and isobares is pretty straight forward.

The NetCDF data also contain fields labeled "QR" (mass fraction of rain in air) and "QS" (mass fraction of snow in air). Unlike NetCDF field "QV" (specific humidity), "QR" and "QS" show water content that is already condensated. "QR" and "QS" are added to form mass fraction of precipitation in air. In Figs. 2 and 3, areas of high mass fraction of precipitation in air are indicated as opaque, turquoise colored clouds.

3.3   Load Imbalance Data

Load imbalance data come from a different source and are not automatically available for the grid as used in Fig. 2. Load imbalance is defined in [2, p. 3] as "processor cycles spent idling while unfinished parallel work exists." Naturally, these idling processor cycles pile up at a synchronization point such as a MPI_Barrier or any other global blocking collective MPI communication. Both, by CCLM namelist settings and some additional MPI instrumentation, extra calls to MPI_Barrier are added to the code and timers around these barriers are used to harvest and measure the idling cycles. Actually, the complement of the sum of idling cycles and communication time, is taken. This is the computation time, which better fits to our previous reasoning about a "time mountain". In order to align these data to the temporal resolution of 3 forecast hours (as outlined in Subsect. 3.2), we only consider harvested data in the forecast time interval 20 forecast minutes prior to the output time until output time. The value of 20 forecast minutes was pretty much chosen *ad libitum*. Further research should test whether the results change if this value is varied.

By the above construction, for each output period, the values for communication time are given per MPI rank, not per geographical grid point. These values are integrated into the geographical grid for the weather data by using a step function as shown in Fig. 1. By construction this step function has a constant computation time value for each horizontal grid point that is mapped to the same MPI rank. This is kind of a "discretized" representation of our "time mountain".

3.4   Relating Load Imbalance to Weather Phenomena

We are now adding these load imbalance data by coloring the wind speed arrows. This means that "red" arrows indicate areas with high computation time that cause the other MPI ranks to wait at MPI_Barriers. Blue arrows, however, indicate a lightweight compute load.

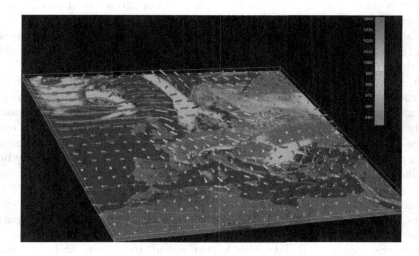

Fig. 2. Weather and load imbalance 1.1.2000, 03 h (Color figure online)

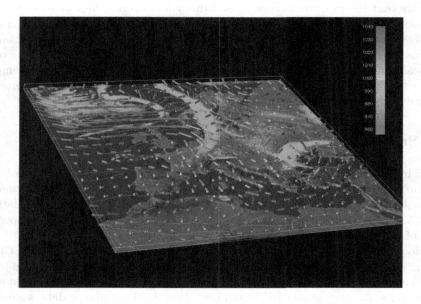

Fig. 3. Weather and load imbalance 1.1.2000, 12 h (Color figure online)

Looking at Figs. 2 and 3, the red and blue arrows appear in different places. It appears that "red" arrows only occur in (or close) to areas of precipitation. That would mean that they are not stationary but move along with the rain or show sheets. Particularly when creating more of those images and connecting them to a short video [7], we can clearly see this movement of red arrows along with the precipitation fronts.

In retrospect this might not be as surprising as it first seems. Weather forecast codes frequently use a fixed domain decomposition along horizontal grid points. As stated in [8, p. 112], "because atmospheric processes occur nonuniformly within the computational domain, e.g., active thunderstorms may occur within only a few subdomains of the decomposed domain, the load imbalance across processors can be significant." If atmospheric processes have already been identified as source for load imbalance, these load imbalances will move along in time.

This already ends all hopes for an explicit static schema to combine "time valleys" with "time mountains" as they can't be located in advance. Anticipating the future location may be as complicated as forecasting the weather itself.

A second look at this data reveals that not all red arrows fit to the above observation. While the precipitation front crossing Norway and Sweden West to East carries the red arrows along nicely, there are some "outplaced" red arrows in Fig. 3 north of the Black Sea. It is not clear whether this is an artificial effect coming from the step function implementation as explained in Subsect. 3.3.

Turning to the question whether we can do local dynamic load balancing, it appears that the rain front crossing Scandinavia is offering blue arrows close to a peaked area of red arrows. Here the prerequisites identified in Subsect. 3.1 are satisfied. North of the Black Sea, however, we rather see a flat "time mountain" top, as the red arrows are flanked by amber and yellow arrows. Here the success of local dynamical load balancing might be limited. Even this singular example shows that the stakes for local dynamic load balancing may vary with the precise nature of the atmospheric processes that cause the load imbalance.

4   Summary

Load imbalance is known to be a major bottleneck to scalability, but it is hard to find a cure. We used a mathematical formalization to describe and formally define load imbalance. This revealed a close similarity to Gustavsons formulation [5, p. 532] of Amdahls law [1]. This similarity was particularly close for the special case of a "spiked load imbalance".

However, a "real life" example such as the climate modelling version CCLM of the weather forecast code COSMO [4] showed a much more complicated load imbalance behavior than a simple stationary spike. Both, by CCLM namelist settings and some additional MPI instrumentation, load imbalance data were collected per MPI rank and forecast interval of 3 h. Using the visualization software OpenDX [6], this information is correlated to geography and weather forecast results. The graphic representation indicated that sources for load imbalance are not stationary but move along with the rain or snow sheets. This excludes some common strategies against load imbalance while limiting the hopes for others.

References

1. Amdahl, G.M.: Validity of the single processor approach to achieving large scale computing capabilities. In: Proceedings of the Spring Joint Computer Conference, 18–20 April 1967, pp. 483–485. ACM (1967)
2. Crovella, M.E., LeBlanc, T.J.: Parallel performance prediction using lost cycles analysis. In: Proceedings of the 1994 ACM/IEEE Conference on Supercomputing, pp. 600–609. IEEE Computer Society Press (1994)
3. Dalhousie University, Department of Oceanography: Data explorer tutorials (1995). http://www.phys.ocean.dal.ca/docs/DX_tutorial.html. Accessed 13 February 2015
4. Doms, G.: A description of the nonhydrostatic regional cosmo model. part 1: Dynamics and numerics. DWD, Offenbach, Germany (2011). http://www.cosmo-model. org/content/model/documentation/core/cosmoDyncsNumcs.pdf. Accessed 13 February 2015
5. John, L.: Reevaluating Amdahl's law. Commun. ACM **31**(5), 532–533 (1988)
6. IBM OpenDX. Open visualization data explorer (2002). http://www.opendx.org/. Accessed 13 February 2015
7. Pospiech, C.: Hunting down load imbalance: a moving target (2015). https://youtu. be/wPIplbq8fDA. Accessed 05 April 2015
8. Xue, M., Droegemeier, K., Weber, D.: Numerical prediction of high-impact local weather: a driver for petascale computing. In: Petascale Computing: Algorithms and Applications, pp. 103–124 (2007)

Orchestrating Docker Containers in the HPC Environment

Joshua Higgins$^{(\boxtimes)}$, Violeta Holmes, and Colin Venters

The University of Huddersfield, Queensgate, Huddersfield, UK
{joshua.higgins,v.holmes,c.venters}@hud.ac.uk

Abstract. Linux container technology has more than proved itself useful in cloud computing as a lightweight alternative to virtualisation,
whilst still offering good enough resource isolation. Docker is emerging as a popular runtime for managing Linux containers, providing both
management tools and a simple file format. Research into the performance of containers compared to traditional Virtual Machines and bare
metal shows that containers can achieve near native speeds in processing,
memory and network throughput. A technology born in the cloud, it is
making inroads into scientific computing both as a format for sharing
experimental applications and as a paradigm for cloud based execution.
However, it has unexplored uses in traditional cluster and grid computing. It provides a run time environment in which there is an opportunity
for typical cluster and parallel applications to execute at native speeds,
whilst being bundled with their own specific (or legacy) library versions
and support software. This offers a solution to the Achilles heel of cluster
and grid computing that requires the user to hold intimate knowledge
of the local software infrastructure. Using Docker brings us a step closer
to more effective job and resource management within the cluster by
providing both a common definition format and a repeatable execution
environment. In this paper we present the results of our work in deploy-
ing Docker containers in the cluster environment and an evaluation of
its suitability as a runtime for high performance parallel execution. Our
findings suggest that containers can be used to tailor the run time environment for an MPI application without compromising performance, and
would provide better Quality of Service for users of scientific computing.

Keywords: Linux containers · Docker · Cluster · Grids · Run time
environment

1 Introduction

Cloud computing has been driven by the Virtual Machine (VM). They are widely
deployed to achieve performance and resource isolation for workloads by constraining the amount of virtual memory and processor cores available to a guest
system. This allows resource sharing on a massive scale; VMs can be provisioned
with any software environment and kept separate from other guests on the same
physical server [18].

© Springer International Publishing Switzerland 2015
J.M. Kunkel and T. Ludwig (Eds.): ISC High Performance 2015, LNCS 9137, pp. 506–513, 2015.
DOI: 10.1007/978-3-319-20119-1_36

Linux container technology is classed as an operating system virtualisation method. It allows the creation of separate userspace instances in which the same kernel is shared. This provides functionality similar to a VM but with a lighter footprint. The Docker project provides a management tool and its own library for communicating with containment features in the OS kernel [2].

Resource isolation takes a back seat in HPC systems which generally execute a user's job within the same OS environment that runs directly on the hardware to gain the best performance. This poses a problem for application portability, especially in grid systems where a remote resource may lack the libraries or support software required by a job. This undermines efforts by middleware vendors to unify resources and provide a common format for accessing heterogeneous systems [8]. In this respect some features of the cloud are desirable in cluster computing.

Docker containers offer an opportunity to create cloud-like flexibility in the cluster without incurring the performance limitations of a VM. This paper investigates the performance gains that can be achieved using Docker containers for executing parallel applications when compared to the KVM hypervisor [5] in a typical scientific cluster computing environment. We also propose a method of executing an MPI job encapsulated in a Docker container through the cluster resource manager.

In the sections of this paper, a short review of Docker containers versus Virtual Machines will be conducted. The current work will be then discussed. Section 4 describes the proposed Docker in the HPC cluster solution. The results from the deployment of this implementation will be evaluated and future work identified.

2 Docker vs KVM

2.1 Architecture

KVM is a popular hypervisor for Linux that introduces virtualisation support into the Linux kernel. The hypervisor provides an illusion to the guest OS that it is managing it's own hardware resources [15]. A request from the guest must be translated into a request to the underlying physical hardware; a process in modern hypervisors that is highly optimised and transparent to the guest. This allows the hypervisor to host a VM without modifications to the OS that has been chosen.

Docker containers do not require a layer of translation. On Linux, they are implemented using 'cgroups'; a feature in the Linux kernel that allows the resources (such as CPU, memory and network) consumed by a process to be constrained [14]. The processes can then be isolated from each other using kernel 'namespaces' [13]. This fundamental difference requires that the guest system processes are executed by the host kernel, restricting containers on a Linux host to only other Linux flavours. However, it means that an executable within the container system essentially runs with no additional overhead compared to an executable in the host OS. A container is not required to perform any system initialisation - its process tree could contain just the program being run and any other programs or services that it depends on.

2.2 Performance

A benchmark by IBM Research demonstrates that the performance of a Docker container equals or exceeds KVM performance in CPU, memory and network benchmarks [12]. The results show that both methods do not introduce a measurable overhead for CPU and memory performance. However the Linpack performance inside KVM is shown to be very poor; the hypervisor abstracts the hardware and processor topology which does not allow tuning and optimisation to take place.

They also suggest that the preferential scaling topology for Docker containers is by processor socket. By not allowing a container to span cores distributed over multiple processor sockets, it avoids expensive inter-processor bus communication. This is in line with the philosophy already ingrained in cluster computing applications in which a process per core is executed on compute nodes. However, the effect may not be appreciable in distributed memory applications where the bandwidth of the network interconnect may be many orders of magnitude slower.

2.3 Storage

A Virtual Machine is traditionally accompanied by a disk image which holds the OS and run time applications. To create or modify this disk image would require the user to hold the knowledge of installing the OS, or systems management experience. The resulting image file may span several gigabytes. This places a large burden on storage and may be inconvenient to transfer between systems.

The Docker project introduces a concept of a 'Dockerfile' which allows the userspace of a container to be described as a list of directives in a text file that construct the real image [3]. Each directive produces a layer of the final system image, which are combined at run time using a copy-on-write method to appear to the container as a single unified image. This allows multiple containers to share common image layers, potentially reducing the amount of data required to transfer between systems. The Dockerfile itself is significantly easier to customise and can be easily version controlled or shared.

3   Current Work

The flexibility of the cloud allows one to create multiple clusters where each individual virtual cluster can have it's own customised software environment. This draws parallels with the development of the now defunct OSCAR-V middleware [17] and Dynamic Virtual Clustering [11] concepts, which are able to provision a virtual cluster based on the requirements of a job at the time of submission. These systems still incur the overhead of running a VM as the job execution environment and inherit the associated performance limitations.

The Agave API is a gateway platform that provides services typically found in grid systems tailored for scientific users. It has a strong focus on web standards and boasts support for running applications packaged in Docker containers in a cloud [10]. However, Agave orchestrates a single container per job, which limits the scope for running parallel applications [9].

HTCondor is a middleware for high-throughput computing that has support for running jobs in parallel on dedicated machines, using 'universes' to distinguish between different execution paradigms. HTCondor itself already supports 'cgroups' to constrain the resources available to a job on Linux hosts and a universe is under development to provide support for the container format [16]. HTCondor has powerful resource discovery features but is the usefulness of a container in not needing to know?

4   Docker in the HPC Cluster

To implement existing container and VM solutions in HPC systems requires modifications to the software stack of the local HPC resources. The HPC systems would already have resource management and job scheduling in place. The methodology should follow the concept of containers, that is to abstract the application from the software stack of the resource. Modifying core components of this stack to support containers introduces a portability problem. Any standard resource manager provides all the information required to orchestrate a Docker container within a resource.

A resource manager such as Torque uses a script that is the core of the job execution and is responsible for configuring the environment and passing the required information to a process starter, such as 'mpirun'. We use both the MPICH [6] and OpenMPI [7] launchers regularly in our systems, which support SSH to enable remote process execution.

4.1   Choosing a Container Model

Since we concluded that running a container has no appreciable overhead over running a normal executable, we propose two different container models for parallel execution. A single container could be started to mimic the worker node, as shown in Fig. 1, which would hold all the processes assigned to that node.

Secondly, a container per process could also be orchestrated as shown in Fig. 2. Whilst it is unlikely that processes within the same job would require different run time environments, this presents an interesting opportunity for resource usage accounting and can offer real time adjustment of the resource constraints per process through 'cgroups'. It can also enforce a process to be mapped to a specific processor core if this functionality is missing from the process launcher.

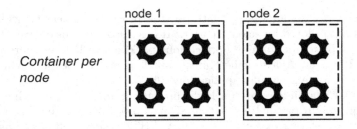

Fig. 1. A container per node that holds all respective processes

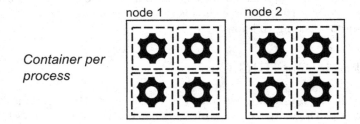

Fig. 2. A container per process is orchestrated on each node

4.2   Container Model Implementation

The resource manager will not be aware of any containers, so the script that is central to the job execution will be used to prepare the nodes and start the containers, before the process launcher starts the parallel job. An overview of this process is described in Fig. 3. We cannot assume that the user is able to SSH to the worker nodes to run the container preparation commands. In this case the bootstrap script can also be invoked through the process launcher first and then the process launcher is called a second time to invoke the parallel job. The overview of the script process supports both container models.

When the process launcher is called, the environment has been modified in two ways: the container will randomise it's SSH port and expose it on the same interface as the host. The SSH configuration is temporarily changed so that the process launcher will use this port instead of the default, thereby launching the process within the container and not on the node. However, if the process launcher forks the process on the rank 0 node instead of using SSH, the process will run outside the container. To avoid this condition, the script will write a unique hostname alias for each node into the SSH configuration that maps to the container on that node. These are substituted into the list of nodes provided by the resource manager before being passed to the process launcher.

5   Deployment of Container Model on HPC Cluster

Eridani is the general purpose, 136 core cluster within the QueensGate Grid at the University of Huddersfield. Like the other clusters within this campus grid, it

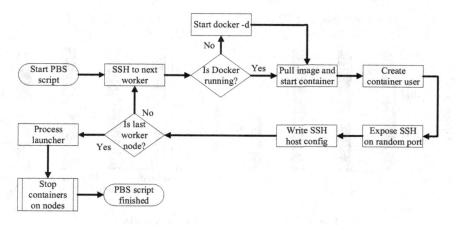

Fig. 3. Overview of script process

uses the Torque resource manager running on CentOS 6.5 and accepts jobs in a PBS script format. The Intel-optimised parallel LINPACK version 11.2.1.009 [4] benchmark was used to measure the performance of 2 nodes with 4 cores each.

In order to validate the claim in [12] that for the non-optimised use case there is no appreciable difference in the CPU execution performance between a Docker container and a VM, the same benchmark was run using the reference BLAS version 3.5.0 library without architecture specific optimisations [1].

The containers were orchestrated in both container per-core and container per-node models, using the implementation described in the previous section. The VMs were created to consume all available cores on the host and appropriate memory to fit the LINPACK problem size.

5.1 Results

Figure 4 shows the experimental results using both the Intel-optimised parallel LINPACK and generic BLAS library comparing native, Docker container models and KVM performance. The results have been obtained from 10 runs of each configuration. The peak performance observed per configuration is shown.

5.2 Evaluation

The LINPACK experimental results echo those obtained by previous research [12], showing that the performance of Docker containers has no appreciable difference compared to running natively, whilst the VM achieves approximately half the peak performance of the container. However, this work differs significantly in that the parallel LINPACK uses a distributed memory model, not shared memory, utilising a network interconnect for message passing to achieve data sharing between processes.

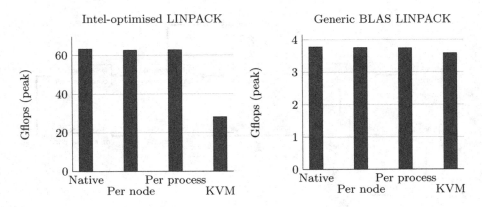

Fig. 4. LINPACK benchmarking results

Without optimisation for the processor architecture, the performance of a VM and container are mostly comparable. However, the overall peak performance is considerably lower for this application. This suggests that the Docker container is therefore a more appropriate execution method for high performance parallel applications where we are likely to employ these types of optimisation.

There is no difference in performance between the two container orchestration models proposed. This is expected given that a process within the container is essentially a process running in the host kernel with 'cgroup' limitations.

6 Summary

One of the requirements of grid computing is to run a job transparently to the user on any resource they desire without requiring knowledge of the local software configuration. Based on our research and experimental results conducted, it is evident that Docker containers can facilitate this by abstracting the software environment of the local HPC resource without compromising performance. This improves Quality of Service for our users by

- Allowing parallel jobs to run on traditional PBS clusters with arbitrary run time environments.
- Reducing the entry level of customising the run time environment to that of the average user.
- Running jobs on resources within the grid that was previously not possible due to software configuration.

7 Future Work

The container per process model offers many advantages by allowing us to apply 'cgroup' constraints to each process in a HPC job. This would allow resource management to be improved based on job requirements as more fine grained control can be achieved for network and disk I/O usage in addition to CPU time [14]. It also provides scope for optimising the power consumption of a job as limits can be changed in real time without restarting the process.

In our future work we will perform benchmarking to appreciate the impact of Docker's NAT networking on message passing. We will also investigate orchestration of Docker containers that contain parallel applications in the cloud environment as opposed to traditional cluster computing.

Acknowledgments. The experimental results for this work could not have been obtained without the resources and support provided by the QueensGate Grid (QGG) at The University of Huddersfield.

References

1. Blas (basic linear algebra subprograms). http://www.netlib.org/blas/
2. Docker. https://www.docker.com/
3. Dockerfile reference - docker documentation, Version 1.4. https://docs.docker.com/reference/builder/
4. Intel math kernel library linpack download. https://software.intel.com/en-us/articles/intel-math-kernel-library-linpack-download
5. Kernel based virtual machine. http://www.linux-kvm.org/
6. MPICH high performance portable MPI. http://www.mpich.org/
7. Open MPI: Open source high performance computing. http://www.open-mpi.org/
8. Charlie, C.: Standards for grid computing: global grid forum. J. Grid Comput. **1**(1), 3–7 (2003)
9. Dooley, R.: Agave docker quickstart (2014). https://bitbucket.org/deardooley/agave-docker-support/
10. Dooley, R., Vaughn, M., Stanzione, D., Terry, S., Skidmore, E.: Software-as-a-service: the iplant foundation API. In: 5th IEEE Workshop on Many-Task Computing on Grids and Supercomputers, November 2012
11. Emeneker, W., Stanzione, D.: Dynamic virtual clustering. In: 2007 IEEE International Conference on Cluster Computing, pp. 84–90, September 2007
12. Felter, W., Ferreira, A., Rajamony, R., Rubio, J.: An updated performance comparison of virtual machines and linux containers. Technology **28**, 32 (2014)
13. Kerrisk, M.: Namespaces in operation, part 1: namespaces overview (2014). http://lwn.net/Articles/531114/. Accessed 7 February 2015
14. Menage, P.: Cgroups. https://www.kernel.org/doc/Documentation/cgroups/cgroups.txt. Accessed 7 February 2015
15. Smith, J., Nair, R.: Virtual Machines: Versatile Platforms for Systems and Processes. Morgan Kaufmann, San Francisco (2005)
16. Tannenbaum, T.: Htcondor and hep partnership and activities (2014). Presented at the HEPiX Fall 2014 Workshop. University of Nebraska, Lincoln, 13–17 October 2014
17. Vallee, G., Naughton, T., Scott, S.L.: System management software for virtual environments. In: Proceedings of the 4th International Conference on Computing Frontiers, pp. 153–160. ACM (2007)
18. Weiss, A.: Computing in the clouds. netWorker **11**(4), 16–25 (2007)

Performance and Scaling of WRF on Three Different Parallel Supercomputers

Zaphiris Christidis[✉]

Lenovo, Morrisville, USA
zchristidis@lenovo.com

Abstract. A WRF weather model configuration with high I/O frequency was tested on three IBM supercomputers for up to 6144 cores. Scalability, overall performance, and I/O throughput was examined for a 12-h forecast with hourly I/O intervals. The three parallel systems tested were the (a) POWER 775 cluster (p7-IH, IBM POWER7, HFI interconnect), (b) the POWER 460 cluster (Pure-flex IBM POWER7, Dual QDR Infiniband interconnect) and (c) the iDataPlex cluster (dx360M4 Intel Sandybridge, FDR14 interconnect). MPI traces were obtained on all systems for runs with 128, 256, 512, 1024, 1536, 2048, 3072, 4096 and 6144 cores. I/O quilting was employed, and the number of MPI tasks (including task grids), OpenMP threads and I/O quilting tasks was kept Identical across all three systems. The effects of computation, communication, I/O throughput, load imbalance and simultaneous multithreading (SMT), was examined across all three systems and for all core counts. It was found that all systems performed similarly, despite significant differences in interconnect, processor, I/O subsystems and software/compiler technologies.

Keywords: WRF · idataplex · Pureflex · Power 775 · 460 · I/O · Performance

1 Introduction

Supercomputer systems at Major Operational Numerical Weather Prediction (NWP) Centers have the primary goal to reliably ingest massive amounts of weather observation data from all over the world, run large weather forecasts on the collected data using Regional and Global weather forecasting models and then release the generated forecast products to the field by the same time every day. The secondary goal is to support a research and development effort that will further scientific advances in Numerical Weather Forecast models. The best methods to do this are computationally intensive and are limited by the power of available computer systems. Thus the value of supercomputers in NWP Centers is measured in their overall utilization, decreased system downtime, and efficiency in the delivery of their forecasting products which is as important as performance and speed when millions of dollars are being spent towards their purchase.

The computer systems installed in NWP Centers must be powerful enough to handle the computationally expensive and complex models used to generate the forecasting products. As such, they must be capable of solving a single large problem very fast. Solving large numbers of small problems in parallel on a capacity

© Springer International Publishing Switzerland 2015
J.M. Kunkel and T. Ludwig (Eds.): ISC High Performance 2015, LNCS 9137, pp. 514–528, 2015.
DOI: 10.1007/978-3-319-20119-1_37

maximizing system is not sufficient. The cost of delivering computational performance as capability is usually higher than the cost of delivering a capacity optimized system. Therefore, the capability requirements drive the total cost of the system. In addition, the algorithms used to simulate the atmosphere and the algorithms used to ingest and assimilate the data required for the weather models, are computationally demanding. Accuracy of the simulation is determined by the available computer power and available data processing capability. Improved accuracy has reduced weather and climate risk to life and property and further improvements will continue to reduce these risks. NWP Centers need increased processing capability as soon as it is available to achieve these reductions. Additional processing power allows more accurate weather forecasts, severe weather risk assessments, storm track and intensity forecasting, and many other benefits.

Another portion of an NWP Center workload includes data assimilation and analysis projects to better describe past states of the atmosphere. This portion of the work can strain capacity resources more than capability. All of these tasks require very high speed I/O for large amounts of data and extremely high data storage capacities in order to save and analyze the past atmosphere states. I/O requirements (transaction rate, bandwidth, and capacities) will scale near linearly with computational capabilities and the future supercomputer system must satisfy all three I/O requirements, which are driven by the increasing power of the simulation algorithms, (more and larger forecasts and simulation outputs), and by rapid increases in data available for use by these algorithms.

It is quite important for NWP Centers to evaluate the overall performance of various supercomputers in order to examine how well they can serve activities that are critical to their mission. In this paper, the performance of three supercomputers is examined while benchmarking a very popular capability weather application, known as the Weather Research and Forecasting model, WRF [1, 2].

1.1   Motivation

WRF is used today by a community of over 5,000 meteorologists conducting weather and climate studies, and it runs operationally on a variety of supercomputer platforms. Arnold et al. [16], Morton et al. [17] and Kerbyson et al. [18] have studied the performance of WRF on a variety of computer architectures, while Porter and Ashworth [19], investigated the performance of WRF on CRAY systems. The WRF benchmark site at NCAR [3], is the only source of information on the performance of standardized WRF test cases (2.5 km and 12 km CONUS) among various supercomputers. However, this site has not been updated since 2010. In addition, the site does not offer information on I/O workloads and communication characteristics for the CONUS test cases. The lack of a direct comparison of identical WRF configurations with typical I/O on several supercomputer systems was used as motivation for this study. It was initiated by a request issued by the China Meteorological Administration (CMA), where an operational WRF test case was distributed to computer vendors for benchmarking. As such, the CMA WRF was tested on the following parallel computer systems.

2   Tested Parallel Systems

2.1   The IBM 775 POWER Parallel System (p775)

IBM announced the p775 system in 2011 [5], as an extremely dense supercomputer node that boasts 256 POWER7 processor cores in just 2U of rack space. The p775 is the sixth generation of very high density compute nodes based on the POWER processor. The p775 uses 8–core 3.836 GHz POWER7 processors packed four apiece into Quad Chip Modules (QCM). Each core supports Simultaneous Multithreading (SMT), which can enable up to four instruction threads to run simultaneously per core. The system can support up to 256 processor cores in a slim 2U rack drawer. Each 2U drawer (CEC) contains eight QCMs so that each node has 256 cores. These QCMs are interconnected via copper switching technology. A maximum of twelve of these node drawers can be housed in custom water cooled rack along with optional 4U disk enclosures. The system is logically configured into octant nodes with each octant containing thirty two (32) processor cores. Thus, each drawer contains 8 Octant nodes. IBM has used parallel optics on the p775 system, driven by the so-called torrent chip. The tested system was outfitted with the interconnection fabric known as HFI (Host Fabric Interface). Four node drawers (32 node octants) were interconnected with HFI L-links, comprising a so called Super-node, while Super-nodes were interconnected with HFI D-links. A total of 192 diskless octant nodes were used for computations, with an additional four octant nodes acting as Generalized Parallel File system (GPFS [8]) servers. A total of 3 disk enclosures were used for I/O. Each node of this cluster contained 128 GB of memory, and the standard IBM AIX software stack (AIX 7.1, XLF14, VAC 12, GPFS, IBM Parallel Environment (PE), LoadLeveler, MPI profile and Mathematical Acceleration Subsystem Libraries - MASS [11]).

2.2   The IBM 460 POWER Parallel System (p460)

IBM announced the p460 [6] in 2012, a supercomputer node that boasts 32 POWER7 processor cores in just 2U of rack space. This compute node runs in IBM Flex System Enterprise Chassis units to provide a high-density, high-performance compute node environment. The p460 is a full wide, four socket node that uses four Dual Chip Modules (DCM). Each DCM consists of eight POWER7 cores operating at 3.55 GHz. DCMs are interconnected via copper switching technology. Each DCM has 4 MB L3 cache per core and an integrated memory controller with four memory channels. Each core supports SMT4, which enables four instruction threads to run simultaneously per core, just like in system p775. The tested system consisted of 224 total compute nodes. Each standard computer rack holds a total of 28 nodes and it can be either air or water cooled via rear door heat exchangers. Individual nodes were interconnected with a dual QDR Infiniband network. The I/O subsystem of this cluster consisted of 8 p740 POWER 7 nodes operating as GPFS servers. A total of 8 DSC3700 storage devices were directly attached to the GPFS servers via four dual-port fiber channel adaptors, such that each DSC3700 was connected to two p740 in a dual ring configuration. Each p460 node of this cluster contained 128 GB of memory, and the standard IBM AIX software stack.

2.3   The IBM iDataPlex Parallel System (dx360M4)

The IBM iDataPlex dx360M4 system [7] is a parallel supercomputer that is based on the Intel processor technology and it is designed to optimize density and performance within typical data center infrastructures. Each compute rack of the system can contain up to 84 individual nodes, with each node consisting of 2-socket 8-core Intel E5 2560 Sandy-bridge processors operating at 2.6 GHz. Thus each rack can host up to 1344 cores. The Intel cores consist of 32 KB data and instruction Level 1 caches, and 256 KB Level 2 data caches, much like the POWER 7 cores in the p775 and p460 systems. However, each Sandy-bridge processor had 20 MB L3 cache that is shared among the 8 cores within the processor. Each node of the system had 32 GB of physical memory, one hard disk drive and one Infiniband Mellanox connect X – FDR adapter. A total of 6912 compute nodes were interconnected with a Mellanox IB4X FDR full-bisection Fat-Tree Infiniband network, while the system contained 10 Intel 3650 M4 storage nodes serving GPFS through 20 DSC3700 storage devices. The system was outfitted with the RHEL6.2 Operating system, including the Intel Studio with the FORTRAN 13 and C/C++ 11 compilers. In addition, the system included GPFS, the IBM PE, with the Platform LSF batch queuing system.

Table 1 contains a summary of all three tested systems with their components.

Table 1. Tested systems with their hardware and software configurations.

System	p775	p460	dx360M4
Total cores used	6144	6144	6144
Total compute nodes	192	192	384
Total cores per node	32	32	16
Core frequency (GHz)	3.84	3.55	2.60
L1 cache/core (KB)	32	32	32
L2 cache/core (KB)	256	256	256
L3 cache/core (MB)	4	4	2.5
Memory (GB/core)	4	4	2
Core vector capability	VSX	VSX	AVX
Interconnect fabric	HFI	QDR Infiniband	FDR Infiniband
Operating system	AIX 7.1	AIX 7.1	RHEL 6.2
Compilers	XLF14, VAC12	XLF14, VAC12	IFORT13, IC11
Storage nodes (GPFS)	4 NSD	10 NSD	10 NSD
Parallel environment	IBM PE	IBM PE	IBM PE
Queueing system	LoadLeveler	LoadLeveler	LSF
Libraries	MPI trace, MASS	MPI trace, MASS	MPI trace

3   The WRF Mesoscale Model

The Weather Research and Forecasting (WRF) Model is a next-generation Mesoscale numerical weather prediction system designed to serve both operational forecasting and atmospheric research needs. It features multiple dynamical cores, a 3-dimensional variation (3DVAR) data assimilation system, and a software architecture allowing for computational parallelism and system extensibility. WRF is suitable for a broad spectrum of applications across scales ranging from meters to thousands of kilometers. The effort to develop WRF has been a collaborative partnership, principally among the National Center for Atmospheric Research (NCAR), the National Oceanic and Atmospheric Administration (the National Centers for Environmental Prediction (NCEP) and the Forecast Systems Laboratory (FSL), the Air Force Weather Agency (AFWA), the Naval Research Laboratory, Oklahoma University, and the Federal Aviation Administration (FAA). WRF allows researchers the ability to conduct simulations reflecting either real data or idealized configurations. WRF provides operational forecasting a model that is flexible and efficient computationally, while offering the advances in physics, numerics, and data assimilation contributed by the research community.

3.1   WRF Benchmark Test Case

For this study, the WRF version 3.2 was used, installed and compiled on all tested systems. The objective of this study was to examine the scalability of a large domain WRF test case with frequent I/O for up to 6,144 cores [4]. This is a typical weather workload on capacity oriented parallel systems. Thus, the WRF configuration consisted of a 5 km horizontal grid with 2200 grid points in the east west direction and 1600 grid points in the north south direction. A total of 28 vertical layers were configured for this test, the time step was set to 6 s, while WRF was set to perform a 12-h forecast, with output frequency every forecast hour. Boundary conditions were ingested every three hours.

3.2   WRF Compilation

WRF was compiled to execute in mixed mode parallelism (MPI + OpenMP) on all systems. Large file support was enabled during compilation as each output step was close to 7.5 GB of storage. The objective was to compile WRF with the most aggressive compiler options on all systems, in order to maximize performance. As such the code was compiled on the POWER systems to account for the VSX SIMD vector units [10]. It was found that the XL FORTRAN compiler option to enable VSX (-qsimd) was not effective towards overall performance gains, and thus not included. On the other hand, enablement of the Intel vector AVX was beneficial towards performance on the Intel E5-2670 cores, despite the fact they do not support compound multiply and add instructions, like the IBM POWER7 cores. The VSX units on the POWER7 processors are enabled when intrinsic mathematical functions (log, exp, pow, etc.) are evaluated via the use of the scalar MASS libraries.

Table 2, shows the compiler options used on all 3 systems.

Compiling on the POWER7 system with the most aggressive optimization flags (-O3 -qhot), forces the compiler to automatically insert intrinsic functions in a vector form whenever possible (within simple do-loop constructs).

Table 2. Compiler options and libraries used on all systems.

System	p775	p460	dx360M4
FCOPTIM	-O3 –qhot –qarch = pwr7 –qtune = pwr7		-O3 –xAVX -fp-model fast = 2 –ip
FCBASEOPTS	-qsmp = omp –qcache = auto –qfloat = rsqrt		-ip -fno-alias -w -ftz -no-prec-div -no-prec-sqrt -align all –openmp
Libraries	netcdf, pnetcdf, massp7_simd, mpihpm		netcdf, pnetcdf, mpitrace

3.3 WRF Load Imbalances

When executing WRF on parallel systems, computational performance depends largely on the workload imbalance among participating MPI tasks. Workload imbalances can be attributed to:

- Communication imbalances among participating MPI tasks.
  - MPI tasks at the boundaries of a computational domain communicate less data.
  - I/O is performed by a single MPI task (task 0) or by the designated I/O or quilting tasks. In the case of I/O write operations by the quilting tasks, computation and I/O can be overlapped, except when the compute tasks have to send their I/O data to the quilting tasks. Parallel I/O read operations with pnetcdf can scale up to a certain degree, as I/O contention can occur.
- Computational imbalances among participating MPI tasks.
  - Areas covered by land, have more complex physical processes associated with them as opposed to ocean areas, hence requiring more processing time towards their computation. In ocean areas, planetary boundary layer processes are much simpler, since sea surface temperatures do not change during simple runs.
  - Storm movement within the computational grid, requires more complex microphysics for the computations of the non-convective precipitation in the grid areas covered by specific MPI tasks. As such, convective precipitation in certain areas of the computational grid has a detrimental effect towards the balance of the computations among participating MPI tasks.
  - Uneven grid distribution among participating MPI tasks is one of the major reasons for computational imbalances in WRF, as its parallel implementation does not allow for a dynamic workload distribution scheme. In many cases, the grid cannot be distributed as evenly as possible among participating tasks. Hence some tasks will have less workload, and most likely they will need to wait longer, in order to receive necessary data from MPI tasks that have more workload. When the workload is distributed among a large number of MPI tasks, the chance of a workload imbalance becomes smaller. The designated method for performing computations in this case, is to enable OpenMP threads in order to carry the workload within each node dynamically. In turn, MPI can

be used across nodes in order to exchange necessary data with other nodes for parallel computational consistency.

3.4   WRF Tunable Parameters

The WRF namelist input file contains several tunable parameters that can affect both performance and accuracy. It was decided not to alter any of the parameters that affect accuracy of the generated forecast results on all systems. In addition, it was decided to fix the namelist.input parameters that affect performance to the ones that yield the best possible performance on the POWER systems.

WRF I/O: WRF performed a 12-h forecast and outputted a 7.5 GB file for each forecast hour.. In order to handle this I/O requirement, I/O quilting via dedicated I/O tasks was enabled by increasing the parameter nio_tasks_per_group in the namelist.input for the namelist_quilt block. It is noted that the I/O write operations take place asynchronously by the quilting tasks, while the computing tasks perform computations. The message in the rsl.out.0000 file (Timing for Writing wrfout) does not represent the actual I/O time, but the time it takes for the compute tasks to perform the point-to-point MPI operations by sending their data to the I/O tasks participating in the computation. It is also noted that the read operations are performed synchronously by MPI task 0. In this case, while MPI task 0 reads the initial and boundary data, the remainder compute tasks have to wait for the read to occur until the necessary data is broadcasted by MPI task 0. Since this WRF test case involved a high amount of I/O for the initial data ingest (6.5 GB) as well as the boundary data (2.0 GB each) it was decided to introduce the parallel version of Netcdf (pnetcdf [12, 13]) in order to read the initial and boundary data. It was found that quilting for the write operations was quite efficient, so there was no need to introduce pnetcdf for the writing to the disk subsystem. The only drawback in this approach was the writing of the last output file, before the termination of the WRF execution. Since the compute tasks exited the computation at the end of the integration, the quilting tasks had to perform the last I/O step synchronously.

WRF namelist.input: nproc_x, nproc_y, numtiles. It was necessary to test WRF for a proper choice of the parameters nproc_x, nproc_y and numtiles, present in the &domains block of the namelist.input file, in order to achieve the best performance for all scaling runs. This particular choice for the above parameters was non-trivial at first, and all possible combinations for participating MPI tasks and OpenMP threads were tested, to achieve optimum performance. The parameters nproc_x and nproc_y essentially "shrink" the original domain (patch) to smaller sub-domains that reside within the MPI tasks (Fig. 1).

It was observed that significant performance improvements can be obtained with a proper choice of the above parameters on the IBM POWER7 p775 and p460 systems. This can be attributed to better cache utilization, as smaller contiguous arrays (computational sub-domains) fit more efficiently in local caches, and consequently they are computed faster, especially in the cases of "thin" decompositions (nproc_x < nproc_y) which promote computations with minimal stride (minimal cache misses). In addition, loading north-south MPI communication buffers is done out

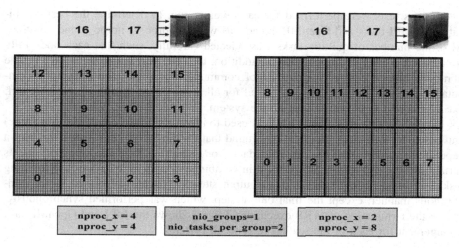

Fig. 1. Possible MPI task partitioning for WRF with 16 MPI and 2 I/O tasks

of stride, so the thinner the decomposition, the smaller the out-of-stride vector copies from the application to the communication buffers. As a result cache misses could be minimized. The third reason which seems to increase performance in thin decomposition configurations could be the application of vector MASS library calls by the compiler, when the options $-O3$ $-qhot$ are selected during compilation. Performance of MASS vector is essential when computing large vectors. Thus, when the x-direction is decomposed across many MPI tasks, MASS vector calls are performed with a few elements only, hurting computational efficiency. Figure 1 depicts two possible decompositions among 16 computational and 2 I/O tasks (total of 18 MPI tasks), controlled by the choice of nproc_x and nproc_y, as well as nio_tasks_ per_group.

It is possible that a choice of nproc_x, nproc_y might lead to uneven workload imbalance and at the same time yield the best performance. Thus it was important to conduct several tests with various nproc_x and nproc_y, in order to obtain the maximum performance for a given number of MPI tasks, without worrying that the particular task partitioning would exhibit less than optimal workload balance.

3.5   WRF Runtime Environment

During test runs, it was found that the p775 and p460 systems exhibited better computational throughput for low core counts when using SMT. Thus runs with up to 2048 cores on the p775 and 512 cores on the p460 were performed with SMT. In both scenarios, one extra OpenMP thread was allocated for each MPI task within compute nodes, such that the total MPI and OpenMP threads per node was equal to 64. For scaling runs beyond 2048 (p775) and 512 (p460) cores, it was found that 32 computational tasks per node was sufficient. No such behavior was exhibited on the dx360M4 system, where Hyper-threading was detrimental to overall performance for all scaling runs. For high core counts, and to exploit better scalability, fewer MPI tasks were assigned on each node for all systems, with 2 or 4 OpenMP threads to each MPI task.

Various tests were performed for each scaling run, to determine the best combination of MPI tasks and OpenMP threads, as well as nproc_x, nproc_y and numtiles. Also, the number of quilting tasks was selected carefully, such that each node fully contributed in I/O or computations. In addition, the code was linked to an MPI profile library in order to assess the amount of communication performed during the computations. LoadLeveler scripts were used for all scaling runs, and the executable wrf. exe was bound to physical cores on the system.

Parallel Netcdf (read option 11) was used to ingest the initial conditions (one time) and boundary data (four times). It was found that for the core counts tested, this was a superior method to read the provided data. For outputting the meteorological results serial Netcdf (read option 2) was used in combination with at least four I/O (quilting tasks) for each scaling run. Thus all output steps (13) were performed in an asynchronous manner, except the final output step, which was performed synchronously, before the termination of WRF execution. Table 3 shows the MPI and OpenMP task arrangement for each of the scaling runs on all systems.

Table 3. Runtime parameters chosen for each scaling run.

Number of cores	MPI tasks	nproc_x × nproc_y	nio_groups × nio_tasks_per_group	OpenMP threads			numtiles
				p775	p460	dx360M4	
128	124	4 × 31	1 × 4	2	2	1	4
256	252	6 × 42	1 × 4	2	2	1	4
512	504	8 × 63	1 × 8	2	2	1	4
1024	506	11 × 46	1 × 6	4	2	2	4
1536	760	19 × 40	1 × 8	4	2	2	4
2048	1020	20 × 51	1 × 4	4	2	2	4
3072	760	19 × 40	1 × 8	4	4	4	4
4096	1020	17 × 60	1 × 4	4	4	4	4
6144	1530	18 × 85	1 × 6	4	4	4	4

4   WRF Scaling Runs

Scaling WRF runs were produced for 128, 256, 512, 1024, 1536, 2048, 3072, 4096, and 6144 cores and various components, such as computation, communication and I/O were isolated for analysis to better understand its scalability characteristics.

In order to perform identical comparisons on all tested systems, it was decided to fix all the input parameters in the namelist.input file. It is realized that the particular choices of the nproc_x, nproc_y parameters favored the p775 and p460 systems due to cache effects arising from the choice of "thin" decompositions. Table 4 reports the total elapsed time for 6144 cores (18 × 85 MPI task arrangement) on the p775, p640 and dx360M4 systems. The last column includes the elapsed time on the dx360M4 system for a 30 × 51 task arrangement, which is the best result on 6144 core runs among all systems.

WRF internal timers report elapsed times for each compute and I/O time step. The elapsed times for read or write operations are accumulated into the time step following the I/O operation. The elapsed time to read the initial conditions is not summed over the

Table 4. 6144-core Elapsed times for p775 p460 and dx360M4 systems

System	p775	p460	dx360M4	dx360M4
nproc_x × nproc_y	18 × 85	18 × 85	18 × 85	30 × 51
Elapsed time (s)	830.7	874.1	807.2	759.4

computational time steps. Finally, the elapsed time due to the last I/O step is derived from the total elapsed time, minus the sum of all computational time steps (which include I/O) plus the first I/O step to ingest the initial conditions. This is a conservative estimate, since the total elapsed time includes loading of the executable, reading of namelist.input file, initialization of parallel tasks, termination of parallel tasks and vacation of the executable from the queue. In order to have a better understanding of the WRF runtime parameters on the tested systems, further analysis was performed with the aid of the included MPI profiling libraries.

1. The total runtime without I/O was extracted by summing the elapsed times of the computational steps, removing the elapsed times due to the 12 asynchronous I/O steps and the last synchronous I/O write step, and the reading of the boundary conditions from the 4 boundary data ingests.
2. Communication was defined as the minimum communication measured among all the MPI tasks involved.
3. Load imbalance was defined as the difference of the median and the minimum communication time among all MPI tasks.
4. Total computation in item 1 above, was broken into pure computation plus communication (item 2) plus Load imbalance (item 3).
5. Total I/O was computed as the time it takes to read the initial and boundary data plus the time to write the 12 asynchronous and the last synchronous write step.

Figures 2, 3 and 4 display the total elapsed times with all the above components on the p775, p460 and dx360M4 systems respectively.

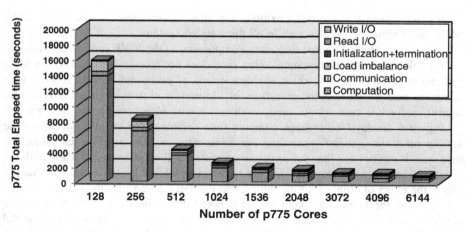

Fig. 2. Runtime components of WRF on the p775 system.

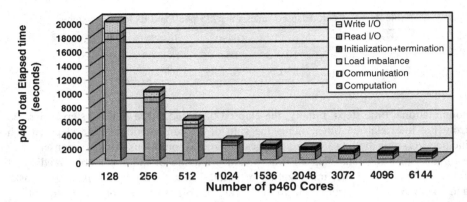

Fig. 3. Runtime components of WRF on the p460 system.

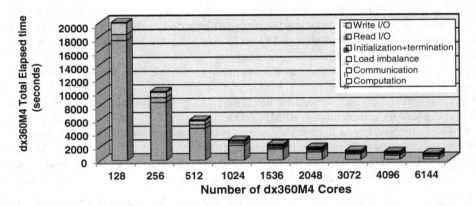

Fig. 4. Runtime components of WRF on the dx360M4 system.

It can be seen that the p775 exhibits superior performance for low core counts, while the computation scales well in all three tested systems.

Figure 5 displays the most important components of the WRF runs on all systems.

It is observed that the communication time does not change significantly for large core counts on all systems, which is characteristic of grid-point weather models with dominant near-neighbor communication. In addition, load imbalance while relatively significant for low core counts, tends to diminish with high core counts, as expected.

Figure 6 displays the average compute time per time step on all systems for the scaling runs, the average write time per write step, and the average read time per time step. It can be seen that the computation scales well on all systems, while both the average read and write per time step are rather insignificant for the entire run, mainly due to the effect of quilting for the writes, and parallel `netcdf` for the read operations for ingesting the boundary conditions. It is noted that write I/O operations are more efficient when SMT is not employed. In addition, read I/O operations with the parallel `netcdf` library are shown to rise when more cores are used, which can be attributed to

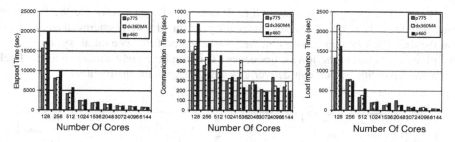

Fig. 5. Total computation, communication and Load imbalance times on all tested systems

declining parallel I/O scalability. In addition, the 3072-core run was conducted with 8 quilting tasks and hence demonstrates efficient write I/O rates per each write time step. Other runs were conducted with the best possible combination of compute and I/O tasks, with focus to maximize overall performance for a given number of cores.

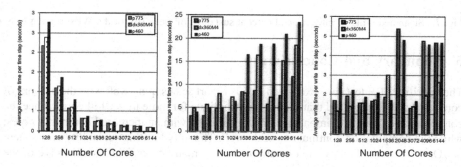

Fig. 6. Average times per time steps for computation, read and write operations on all systems.

GFLOP rates were obtained for all scaling runs on the p775 system, by instrumenting each run with the hardware performance monitor (HPM) of POWER7 [14]. The GFLOP rates with 128 cores show that WRF has achieved a 10 % performance off peak. Peak performance is derived from the core frequency (3.84 GHz) times the maximum floating point operations per cycle (8) times the total cores used (128). Thus the peak performance of four nodes (128 cores) is 3932 GFLOPs. Similarly, the 6144 core run (peak performance 188744 GFLOPs) yielded 8140 GFLOPs, which is 4.3 % off peak. The POWER7 processor incorporates special purpose registers for the HPM which are initialized and get accumulated during each run with relevant floating point operations. Hence, sustained GFLOP rates are computed as:

```
p775 GFLOPS =(10⁻⁹/p775_runtime)*(Accumulated flops from HPM)
```

The sustained GFLOP rates for the p460 and dx360M4 systems are approximated as:

```
p460    GFLOPS = p775 GFLOPS * (p775_runtime / p460_runtime)
dx360M4 GFLOPS = p775 GFLOPS * (p775_runtime / dx360M4_runtime)
```

Figure 7a displays the sustained GFLOP rates for all systems for the WRF scaling runs, while Fig. 7b displays the percentage off-peak on all tested systems. It can be seen that the dx360M4 system delivers the best sustained performance on all systems, even though its cores run at the lowest frequency. This can be clearly attributed to the Intel compiler capability, which can deliver efficient AVX vector instructions.

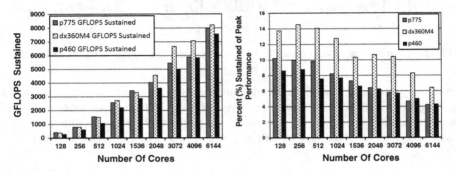

Fig. 7. Sustained GFLOP rates (a) and percent sustained off peak (b) for the WRF scaling runs.

5 Summary and Conclusions

The specific WRF test case examined in this report scales quite well with the amount of cores tested. It is expected that scaling will continue for more than 6144 cores, since the communication and load imbalance effects diminish with an increased number of cores, while the computation continues to scale well. The only limiting scalability component is I/O, for both read and write operations and for many cores. This is indicative of the increasing I/O rates as the number of cores increases.

The code sustained close to 14 % off peak on 8 dx360M4 nodes, and about to 6 % off peak with 384 nodes, despite the fact this particular test case performed heavy I/O, outputting thirteen 7.5-GB files for every integration hour, while reading compatible in size initial data and boundary conditions.

The Intel FORTRAN compiler was quite effective in producing efficient AVX vector instructions on the E5-2670 Intel Sandy-bridge cores, which along with the single-precision nature of the WRF code were the top reasons for the highest sustained performance among all tested systems. The vector units on the POWER systems (VSX) did not deliver additional performance when WRF was compiled with appropriate SIMD options, and hence were not used. The compiler generated vector MASS calls for the intrinsic functions on the POWER systems were quite effective and contributed with up to 15 % in additional performance with 128 cores.

The proper choice of the runtime parameters nproc_x and nproc_y were critical towards better performance on the p775 and p460 systems when thin rectangular decompositions were selected (nproc_x > nproc_y). In contrast, performance on the dx360M4 system was favored under square task decompositions. The runtime choice of the parameter numtiles did not affect performance on the p775 and p460 systems, while it had a positive effect in the dx360M4 system when it was set to twice the number of OpenMP threads.

SMT was beneficial to the systems with POWER processors, especially to the p775, due to the cores having twice as many channels to memory as compared to the p460 processors. Hyper-threading did not have a positive performance effect on the dx360M4 system, and hence was not employed.

The interconnect fabric of all three systems performed effectively, mainly due to the near-neighbor communication characteristics in the MPI implementation of WRF, which did not stress extensively the communication subsystems on all tested supercomputers.

Acknowledgements. The author wishes to acknowledge the China Meteorological Administration and Ms. Wei Min, for configuring WRF and preparing the Initial and boundary conditions for the runs. Acknowledgement is extended to Mr. James Abeles of IBM for performing the WRF scaling runs on the iDataPlex dx360M4 system.

References

1. Weather Research and Forecasting (WRF) model. http://www.wrf-model.org
2. Skamarock, W.C., Klemp, J.B., Dudhia, J., Gill, D.O., Barker, D.M., Duda, M., Huang, X.-Y., Wang, W., Powers, J.G.: A Description of the Advanced Research WRFVersion 3, NCAR Technical Note (2008)
3. WRF V3 Parallel Benchmark Page. http://www.mmm.ucar.edu/wrf/WG2/benchv3/
4. Michalakes, J., Hacker, J., Loft, R., McCracken, M.O., Snavely, A., Wright, N.J., Spelce, T., Gorda, B., Walkup, R.: WRF nature run. J. Physics: Conf. Series **125**(1), 012022 (2008). SciDAC 2008, 13–17 July 2008, Washington, USA, 2008
5. The IBM p775 System. http://www.redbooks.ibm.com/redbooks/pdfs/sg248003.pdf
6. The IBM p460 System. http://www.redbooks.ibm.com/redbooks/pdfs/sg247989.pdf
7. The IBM dx360M4 iDataPlex. http://www.redbooks.ibm.com/redbooks/pdfs/sg247629.pdf
8. The IBM GPFS. http://www.redbooks.ibm.com/redbooks/pdfs/sg247844.pdf
9. Langkamp, T., Bohner, J.: Influence of the compiler on multi-CPU performance of WRFv3. Geosci. Model Dev. **4**, 611–623 (2011)
10. https://publib.boulder.ibm.com/infocenter/clresctr/vxrx/index.jsp?topic=%2Fcom.ibm. cluster.essl.v5r2.essl100.doc%2Fam5gr_servsx.htm
11. http://www-01.ibm.com/support/docview.wss?rs=2021&uid=swg27005374
12. NetCDF. http://www.unidata.ucar.edu/software/netcdf/
13. Jianwei L., Liao, W.-K., Choudhary, A., Ross, R., Thakur, R., Gropp, W., Latham, R., Siegel, A., Gallagher, B., Zingale, M.: Parallel netCDF: a scientific high-performance I/O interface. In: Proceedings of the 15th Supercomputing Conference, Phoenix, AZ, November 2003
14. https://www.power.org/wp-content/uploads/2012/09/POWER7_PMU_Detailed_Event_ Description.pdf
15. Hoisie, A., Johnson, G., Kerbyson, D.J., Lang, M., Pakin, S.: A performance comparison through benchmarking and modeling of three leading supercomputers: blue Gene/L, red storm, and purple. In: Proceedings of IEEE/ACM Supercomputing (SC 2006), Tampa, FL (2006)

16. Arnold, D., Morton, D., Schicker, I., Jorba, O., Harrison, K., Zabloudil, J., Newby, G., Seibert, P.: WRF benchmark for regional applications. In: WRF User's Workshop (2011)
17. Morton, D., Nudson, O., Stephenson, C.: Benchmarking and evaluation of the weather research and forecasting (WRF) model on the Cray XT5. In: Proceedings of CUG (2009)
18. Kerbyson, D.J., Barker, K.J., Davis, K.: Analysis of the weather research and forecasting (WRF) model on large-scale systems. In: Proceedings of the Conference on Parallel Computing. Advances in Parallel Computing, vol. 15. IOS Press (2008). ISSN 0927-5452, ISBN 978-1-58603-796-3
19. Porter, A.R., Ashworth, M.: Configuring and optimizing the weather research and forecast model on the CRAY XT. In: 2010 Cray User Group Proceedings

Author Index

Printed in the United States
By Bookmasters